Data Breach Disclosure Laws

A State-by-State Perspective

3rd Edition

Philip Alexander, CHFI, CISSP-ISSMP

ASPATORE

Project Manager, Caitlin Keiper; edited by Melanie Zimmerman; proofread by Michelle Levigne

For additional copies or customer service inquiries, please e-mail west.customer.service@thomson.com.

ISBN 978-0-314-28207-1

Mat #41294181

ASPATORE

Aspatore Books, a Thomson Reuters business, exclusively publishes C-Level executives and partners from the world's most respected companies and law firms. Each publication provides professionals of all levels with proven business and legal intelligence from industry insiders—direct and unfiltered insight from those who know it best. Aspatore Books is committed to publishing an innovative line of business and legal titles that lay forth principles and offer insights that can have a direct financial impact on the reader's business objectives.

CONTENTS

Acknowledgements

I want to acknowledge two men who have had a tremendous impact on my life. The first is my father, Dr. Manfred Alexander. From my dad I learned to value education as well as an "old school" work ethic. My father was one of the smartest people I have ever met. He also possessed a quiet strength I will always strive to obtain in myself. The other man was my father's best friend, Maxwell Pfeifer. Uncle Max and my dad were best friends for over fifty years, going back to when they were young boys. Since my dad's passing back in 1988, Uncle Max has been like a father to me. A prominent New York attorney, he always has the time to take my phone calls and give me the fatherly advice I have come to appreciate more and more over the years. Thank you, Uncle Max. I'm sure the SVS is smiling upon both of us.

I also want to thank my wife, Cency, and our two sons, Freddy and Danny, for their understanding. They put up with my long hours in front of the computer working on this book over many months. I can't emphasize enough how important having a supportive family is.

Preface

We are in the midst of an information explosion, and we have been for some time now. Not that long ago, the Internet was in its infancy. Today, Internet cafés and wireless "hot spots" are everywhere. Wireless networks are in most major cities across the United States. You almost cannot drive down a major commercial or residential neighborhood without being surrounded by wireless networks. In fact, "war drivers" do just that. They drive around looking for unprotected wireless networks. Some do it just to gain free Internet access, while others are trying to steal a company's data.

It is not just that computers are able to hold huge amounts of data. It is the nature of the data itself. Today our medical information, financial records, spending habits, and other kinds of personally identifiable information are being stored on computers in companies located throughout the country and abroad.

When you combine the ability to electronically store data with the sheer volume of information floating around, some unfortunate outcomes were inevitable. For one, not all companies will be responsible stewards of the data we, the consumer, entrust to them. Companies are in the business of making a profit. That is certainly not a prophetic thought, as it has been the cornerstone of the free market for many centuries. So, companies will expend their limited resources in activities that go directly toward the bottom line. Non-profit organizations, while by definition not as focused on profit, still concentrate their efforts on the services they provide. For example, a public hospital will focus on providing medical care for its patients, and rightfully so. Neither non-profit nor for-profit companies will have as their primary focus the security of sensitive personal data they have about all of us.

With regards to the electronic storage and transmission of data, our capabilities have grown faster than our knowledge. Today the term is administrative assistant, and twenty years ago, they were called secretaries. Back when computers in the private sector were brand new, it was not uncommon for small to medium-sized companies to make their secretaries their computer administrators. Then as computer networks grew in complexity, there came the realization of the need for trained people to maintain them. Several major software and hardware suppliers began offering courses and certifications to train people to use their products. An example would be Microsoft and their Microsoft Certified Systems Engineer, or MCSE, program. The companies are offering these training programs, for they know there is a direct correlation between selling their products and having peopled trained to support them. The advent of computers and networks in the workplace was soon followed by the Internet. The Internet has led to an explosion of data never before seen by man. So in years prior, being a "techie" was the hottest job in computers. When the Internet boomed onto the stage, the hottest computer job became the "webbie." Through it all, there was something missing in the stampede to build faster computers, higher-capacity networks, and a more functional Internet. What was missing was securing the personal data that was now traveling the "information superhighway." It is a classic example of our reach exceeding our grasp.

I mention the old practice of the administrative assistant/server administrator to illustrate the phenomena that exists today in the field of data security. The profession of electronic data security is as new today as that of computer engineer was in the early to mid-1980s. That being the case, many computer engineers are actually adding to data insecurity. As computer networks grow in size, the focus is to get the servers into production fast. Large networks make the effective administration of access rights more difficult. This has led to giving people more access than is necessary, because it is easier than performing the due diligence necessary to only give them the access they need to get their work done. Least privileged access is a cornerstone to comprehensive data security. Giving the average end user administrative rights to a computer is dangerous for two reasons. Administrative privileges give the end user a greater ability to really foul up their system, sometimes to a point beyond a computer engineer's ability to fix it. Secondly, if a hacker gains access to a computer, they often inherit the rights of the user. So, if the end user has administrative rights, so will the hacker. Lastly, end users with administrator rights often download unsafe software or open unknown attachments they receive in e-mails. These activities can introduce viruses, Trojans, and other forms of malware in a company's network. I have often used a term called "lazy engineering" to describe the practice of giving users, or even support personnel, administrative rights. It is easier than finding out precisely what level of access they need.

Another attack vector used by hackers is the many security flaws found in most applications being used today. Today's computers are so powerful that it is not unusual for a software program to contain hundreds of thousands or even millions of lines of code. That presents the risk of inadvertently placing any number of security vulnerabilities spread throughout that huge code base. Software developers are focused on writing their applications fast and getting them into production quickly. Many companies are sending their software development projects offshore to countries like India for the cheap labor. One only needs to take notice of the fact that software suppliers are constantly advising the public to install the latest patch to fix security holes in their software. The focus of this book is not in-depth review of the various vulnerabilities found in application source code today. However, as this is so critical in protecting a company's electronic data, I invite my readers to go to www.vulncat.fortifysoftware.com. The website provides a good overview of a wide range of exploits found in propriety software that is being used today.

The private sector, on the whole, has not been very responsible stewards of the sensitive data entrusted to them, either. It is axiomatic that when the private sector fails to police itself, government will step in and enact laws to elicit the desired behaviors. The privacy of personal data stored electronically is no different. There were numerous cases of people's private, personal information being stolen. Identity theft is so prevalent today that some companies now offer insurance to help protect people. However, insurance merely spreads the risk among policyholders, while real protection comes from actually securing the data. Unfortunately, our technical ability to transmit and store private data is growing faster than our knowledge on how to secure it.

The requirements of complying with one state's data privacy laws could very well find you in violation of another state's laws. With that in mind, the primary focus of this book is to look at the different data privacy laws with regards to their disclosure requirements in the event of a data breach.

For companies with a multi-state presence, it is important to be familiar with these different requirements. A multi-state presence includes Internet-based companies, and not just those with a brick-and-mortar footprint in numerous states. Many believe that merely encrypting sensitive data is the answer. In fact, many state privacy laws see the encryption of data as the equivalent to securing the data. Several of them will specifically offer an exemption to their disclosure requirements if the information that was lost or stolen was encrypted. The hard truth is that encrypting data is not the equivalent of securing data. A comprehensive, defensive, in-depth approach to data security is required to offer the highest level of protection. One of the most common attack vectors used today will circumvent encryption. This is because encryption works off the premise of protecting data's confidentiality from unauthorized access. However, if a hacker "fools" a system into believing it is an authorized user, the encryption will no longer afford any real protection. There are several ways a hacker can gain access to a system. So, an important aspect in protecting sensitive data is to utilize effective authentication and authorization measures. A low-tech way to gain access to a company's computer systems is called "social engineering," or tricking somebody into giving you information that will ultimately let the hacker break into their company's computer network.

In addition to encryption, you should look for another recurring theme in many of the laws of the various states. Companies that outsource sensitive personal information to third parties still own the liability in the event of a data breach. I have often called that outsourcing the work while still "in-sourcing" the liability. Some states' disclosure laws apply only to the private sector, specifically exempting state agencies. Some allow an exemption from the disclosure requirement if, upon an investigation, it is decided that no harm will come because of the data breach. I found this very interesting, or perhaps I should say troubling. I ask myself, how can any investigator know what the intent is of those who stole the data? Even if it was just for the "challenge," how can you know the person will not post the data on the Internet to collect their hard-earned bragging rights? It would be my hope that any business would base their conclusion that misuse is unlikely on compensating logical controls, rather than trying to divine the intent of the hacker. There is a wide degree of variance when it comes to estimating the cost to a company in having to disclose that they have suffered a security breach. Some of the costs will depend on what business you are in. They can include things such as the actual cost of the disclosure, credit protection for the effected consumers, bad press, and loss of consumer confidence. If you are a bank, the last two items can be the most damaging. I have seen estimates of over $200 per customer record. So, if the data breach included a million customer records, we are talking a sizable amount of money. There is a clear conflict of interest to allow a company to conduct their own investigation to determine whether they need to disclose the breach. The penalties for failing to report a data breach when such a disclosure is required vary from very small fines to those in the tens of thousands of dollars, and some carry jail time. Only time will tell if the corporate veil will protect individual decision-makers from serving actual time behind bars.

Data privacy concerns are not limited to the financial and health care sectors. Almost every major business today collects data about its customers. Department stores offer credit cards, grocery chains offer frequent shopper cards, bookstores have frequent reader club cards, not to mention the amount of personal information your tax preparer has about you. So, from a business standpoint, who should be concerned about data privacy laws? The answer is any company that has personally identifiable information about its customers.

With the new awareness for the need for data security has come some industry standards for conducting reviews of a company's data security posture. There is the Statement on Auditing Standards (SAS) 70 Type II review and a Financial Institute Shared Assessment Program (FISAP) review. While these reviews are of value, they generally focus on data security policies from more of an audit standpoint, which is not the end-all to protecting data. There is a vast difference in skill sets between an auditor and a computer security engineer. To obtain a more accurate measure of your company's data security posture, a review of the actual controls from those with the requisite technical skills is invaluable.

In addition to laws specific to the disclosure requirements in the event of a data breach, the various states also have passed laws with regards to things such as the proper disposal of data, specific requirement surrounding Social Security numbers, and even how many digits of a credit card account number can be printed on a receipt. As with the disclosure laws, being compliant with the requirements of one state can put you out of compliance with the requirements of another state.

Most of the laws are very new, having been passed in only the past few years. Many of them are also quite vague, which is usually by design, and can actually be interpreted as being positive. I say this because it puts the specifics of data protection in the hands of those with the technical expertise. Governmental auditors will provide their opinions that serve as a guide for companies in developing a comprehensive data security program. What I cannot emphasize enough is that knowledge is power. Seek out the best and brightest in the field in the areas of compliance, policy, as well as computer security. When I attend data security seminars across the United States, I have been fortunate enough to meet some very talented people in their respective fields.

In many instances, I have taken the actual disclosure laws right from the government website of the respective states. In those instances, the text is **bolded**. I did this to differentiate that from cases where I provide my own synopsis of a particular law.

Third Edition Update

I first published *Data Breach Disclosure Laws: A State-by-State Perspective* back in March 2007. At that time, thirty-five states plus the District of Columbia had enacted their own data breach disclosure laws. Fast forward to 2012, and now forty-six states have enacted their own data breach disclosure laws. A number of states have also updated their existing laws, mainly around the areas of breach notification.

Chapter 1: Alabama

The state of Alabama is one of only four states that have yet to enact a data breach disclosure law. The other states are Kentucky, New Mexico, and South Dakota.

This brings up an interesting question. How should a company handle a disclosure in the event of a data breach that includes residents of states that have such laws as well as those that do not?

If your company is located in Texas, their data breach disclosure law applies to all persons, and not just to residents of the state. Beyond that, I would caution companies against making selective disclosures, in the event of a security breach involving data about customers that reside in numerous states. The potential public relations fallout could be more damaging than the breach itself. Remember, in the Internet age, we live in a 24/7 news cycle. News travels fast, both good and bad.

It is an understandably difficult decision, as there are serious repercussions involved. The exact timing of a disclosure, how notifications are made, especially if there is an active police investigation going on. Some states even require specific details to be included in a disclosure in the event of a breach. While this book can help serve as a guide, it goes without saying that you will need to seek competent legal assistance when faced with these types of decisions.

If you want to minimize the odds of having a data breach in the first place, the best course of action is to have a mature and robust data security program. That would entail having a team of professionals with skill sets that cross multiple areas. They would include: compliance, audit, cryptography, vendor management, risk assessment, access controls, networking/firewalls, and more. A mistake that I see all too often is companies relying on people who are a *Jack of all trades*, rather than investing in true professionals that are subject matter experts in their respective fields. As the old saying goes, when the kitchen is on fire, it is too late to think about investing in a fire extinguisher.

So, now that we have established that being prepared is the best course of action, let us arm ourselves with information about the data breach disclosure laws from the various states.

Chapter 2: Alaska

House Bill 31

"An Act relating to breaches of security involving personal information, credit report and credit score security freezes, consumer credit monitoring, credit accuracy, protection of social security numbers, care of records, disposal of records, identity theft, furnishing consumer credit header information, credit cards, and debit cards, and to the jurisdiction of the office of administrative hearings; amending Rule 60, Alaska Rules of Civil Procedure; and providing for an effective date."

BE IT ENACTED BY THE LEGISLATURE OF THE STATE OF ALASKA:

* Section 1. AS 40.21.110 is amended to read:

Sec. 40.21.110. Care of records. Except for public records lawfully in the possession of a person other than the state, public records of existing or defunct agencies of the state, territorial, and Russian governments in Alaska are the property of the state and shall be created, maintained, preserved, stored, transferred, destroyed or disposed of, and otherwise managed in accordance with the provisions of this chapter <u>and AS 45.48.500 - 45.48.530</u>. Records shall be delivered by outgoing officials and employees to their successors, and may not be removed, destroyed or disposed of, except as provided in this chapter <u>and AS 45.48.500 - 45.48.530</u>.

* Sec. 2. AS 44.64.030(a) is amended by adding a new paragraph to read: (35) AS 45.48.080(c) (breach of security involving personal information)

* Sec. 3. AS 45 is amended by adding a new chapter to read:

Chapter 48. Personal Information Protection Act.

Article 1. Breach of Security Involving Personal Information.

Sec. 45.48.010. Disclosure of breach of security. (a) If a person owns or uses personal information that includes personal information on a state resident, and a breach of the security of the information system containing the personal information occurs, the person shall, after discovering or being notified of the breach, disclose the breach to each state resident whose personal information was subject to the breach.

(b) An information collector shall make the disclosure required by (a) of this section in the most expeditious time possible and without unreasonable delay, except as provided in AS 45.48.020 and as necessary to determine the scope of the breach and restore the reasonable integrity of the information system.

Sec. 45.48.020. Allowable delay in notification. An information collector may delay disclosing the breach under AS 45.48.010 if an appropriate law enforcement agency determines that disclosing the breach will interfere with a criminal investigation. However, the information collector shall disclose the breach to the state resident in the most expeditious time possible and without unreasonable delay after the law enforcement agency informs the information collector in writing that disclosure of the will no longer interfere with the investigation

Sec. 45.48.030. Methods of notice. An information collector shall make the disclosure required by AS 45.48.010

(1) by a written document sent to the most recent address the information collector has for the state resident;

(2) by electronic means if making the disclosure by the electronic means is consistent with the provisions regarding electronic records and signatures required for notices legally required to be in writing under 15 U.S.C. 7001 et seq. (Electronic Signatures in Global and National Commerce Act); or

(3) if the information collector demonstrates that the cost of providing notice would exceed $250,000, that the affected class of state residents to be notified exceeds 50,000, or that the information collector does not have sufficient contact information to provide notice, by

(A) electronic mail if the information collector has an electronic mail address for the state resident;

(B) conspicuously posting the disclosure on the Internet website of the information collector if the information collector maintains an Internet site; and

(C) providing a notice to major statewide media.

Sec. 45.48.040. Notification of certain other agencies.

(a) If an information collector is required by AS 45.48.010 to notify more than 1,000 state residents of a breach, the information collector shall also notify without unreasonable delay all consumer reporting agencies that compile and maintain files on consumers on a nationwide basis and provide the agencies with the timing, distribution, and content of the notices.

(b) This section may not be construed to require the information collector to provide the consumer reporting agencies identified under (a) of this section with the names or other personal information of the state residents whose personal information was subject to the breach.

(c) This section does not apply to an information collector who is subject to 15 U.S.C. 6801 - 6827 (Gramm-Leach-Bliley Financial Modernization Act).

(d) In this section, "consumer reporting agency that compiles and maintains files on consumers on a nationwide basis" has the meaning given in 15 U.S.C. 1681a(p).

Sec. 45.48.050. Exception for employees and agents. In AS 45.48.010 - 45.48.090, the good faith acquisition of personal information by an employee or agent of an information collector for a legitimate purpose of the information collector is not a breach of the security of the information system if the employee or agent does not use the personal information for a purpose unrelated to a legitimate purpose of the information collector and does not make further unauthorized disclosure of the personal information.

Sec. 45.48.060. Waivers. A waiver of AS 45.48.010 - 45.48.090 is void and unenforceable.

Sec. 45.48.070. Treatment of certain breaches. (a) If a breach of the security of the information system containing personal information on a state resident that is maintained by an information recipient occurs, the information recipient is not required to comply with AS 45.48.010 - 45.48.030. However, immediately after the information recipient discovers the breach, the information recipient shall notify the information distributor who owns the personal information or who licensed the use of the personal information to the information recipient about the breach and cooperate with the information distributor as necessary to allow the information distributor to comply with (b) of this section. In this subsection, "cooperate" means sharing with the information distributor information relevant to the breach, except for confidential business information or trade secrets.

(b) If an information recipient notifies an information distributor of a breach under (a) of this section, the information distributor shall comply with AS 45.48.010 - 45.48.030 as if the breach occurred to the information system maintained by the information distributor.

Sec. 45.48.080. Violations.

(a) If an information collector who is a governmental agency violates AS 45.48.010 - 45.48.090 with regard to the personal information of a state resident, the information collector (1) is liable to the state for a civil penalty of up to $500 for each state resident who was not notified under AS 45.48.010 - 45.48.090, but the total civil penalty may not exceed $50,000; and

(2) may be enjoined from further violations. (b) If an information collector who is not a governmental agency violates AS 45.48.010 - 45.48.090 with regard to the personal information of a state resident, the violation is an unfair or deceptive act or practice under AS 45.50.471 - 45.50.561. However, the information collector is not subject to the civil penalties imposed under AS 45.50.551 but is liable to the state for a civil penalty of up to $500 for each state resident who was not notified under AS 45.48.010 - 45.48.090, except that the total civil penalty may not exceed $50,000.

(c) The Department of Administration may enforce (a) of this section against a governmental agency. The procedure for review of an order or action of the department under this subsection is the same as the procedure provided by AS 44.62 (Administrative Procedure Act), except that the office of administrative hearings (AS 44.64.010) shall conduct the hearings in contested cases and the decision may be appealed under AS 44.64.030(c).

(d) In this section, "governmental agency" means a state or local governmental agency, except for an agency of the judicial branch. Sec. 45.48.090. Definitions. In AS 45.48.010 - 45.48.090, (1) "breach of the security" means unauthorized acquisition, or reasonable belief of unauthorized acquisition, of personal information that compromises the security, confidentiality, or integrity of the personal information maintained by the information collector; in this paragraph, "acquisition" includes acquisition by (A) photocopying, facsimile, or other paper-based method;

(B) a device, including a computer, that can read, write, or store information that is represented in numerical form; or

(C) a method not identified by (A) or (B) of this paragraph;

(2) "information collector" means a person who owns or uses personal information in any form if the personal information includes personal information on a state resident; (3) "information distributor" means a person who is an information collector and who owns or licenses personal information to an information recipient; (4) "information recipient" means a person who is an information collector but who does not own or have the right to license to another information collector the personal information received by the person from an information distributor;

(5) "personal information" means information in any form on an individual that is not encrypted or redacted, or is encrypted and the encryption key has been accessed or acquired, and that consists of a combination of (A) an individual's name, address, or telephone number; in this subparagraph, "individual's name" means a combination of an individual's (i) first name or first initial; and (ii) last name; and (B) one or more of the following information elements: (i) the individual's social security number; (ii) the individual's driver's license number or state identification card number; (iii) the individual's account number, credit card account number, or debit card account number; (iv) account passwords or personal identification numbers or other access codes.

Article 2. Credit Report and Credit Score Security Freeze.

Sec. 45.48.100. Security freeze authorized. A consumer may prohibit a consumer credit reporting agency from releasing all or a part of the consumer's credit report or credit score without the express authorization of the consumer by placing a security freeze on the consumer's credit report.

Sec. 45.48.110. Placement of security freeze. (a) To place a security freeze, a consumer shall make the request to the consumer credit reporting agency

(1) by certified mail to the address designated by the consumer credit reporting agency to receive security freeze requests; or

(2) as allowed by (b) of this section. (b) A consumer may make a request under (a) of this section by telephone or by fax, the Internet, or other electronic media if the consumer credit reporting agency has developed procedures for using the telephone or an electronic medium to receive and process the request in an expedited manner. (c) A consumer credit reporting agency shall place a security freeze within five business days after receiving a request under (a) or (b) of this section and proper identification from the consumer.

Sec. 45.48.120. Confirmation of security freeze.

(a) Within 10 business days after a consumer makes the request under AS 45.48.110, a consumer credit reporting agency shall send a written confirmation of the placement of the security freeze to the consumer.

(b) At the same time that the consumer credit reporting agency sends a confirmation under (a) of this section, the consumer credit reporting agency shall provide the consumer with a unique personal identification number, password, or similar device to be used by the consumer when the consumer authorizes the release of the consumer's credit report or credit score under AS 45.48.130.

Sec. 45.48.130. Access and actions during security freeze.

(a) While a security freeze is in place, a consumer credit reporting agency shall allow a third party access to a consumer's credit report or credit score if the consumer requests that the consumer credit reporting agency allow the access.

(b) To make a request under (a) of this section, the consumer shall contact the consumer credit reporting agency by certified mail to the address designated by the consumer credit reporting agency to receive security freeze requests or as allowed by

(c) of this section, authorize the consumer credit reporting agency to allow the access, and provide the consumer credit reporting agency with

(1) proper identification to verify the consumer's identity; (2) the unique personal identification number, password, or similar device provided under AS 45.48.120(b); and (3) the proper information necessary to identify the third party to whom the consumer credit reporting agency may allow the access or the time period during which the consumer credit reporting agency may allow the access to third parties who request the access. (c) In addition to certified mail, a consumer may make a request under (a) of this section by telephone or by fax, the Internet, or other electronic media if the consumer credit reporting agency has developed procedures for using the telephone or an electronic medium to receive and process the request in an expedited manner.

(d) A consumer credit reporting agency that receives a request from a consumer under (b) or (c) of this section shall comply with the request immediately after receiving the request by telephone or by an electronic medium or within three business days after receiving the request by certified mail.

(e) If a security freeze is in place, a consumer credit reporting agency may not release the credit report or credit score to a third party without the prior express authorization of the consumer.

(f) If a security freeze is in place on a consumer's credit report and credit score and if a third party applies to a consumer credit reporting agency to provide the third party with access to the consumer's credit report or credit score, the consumer credit reporting agency and, except as provided for insurers under (g) of this section, the third party may treat the third party's application as incomplete unless the consumer authorizes the access under (a) of this section.

(g) If an insurer requests access to a consumer report on which a security freeze is in place, unless the consumer authorizes access under (a) of this section, the insurer may, notwithstanding AS 21.36.460, (1) treat the consumer's application as incomplete; (2) decline the consumer's application if the consumer does not lift the security freeze for the insurer after a request by the insurer or the insurer's agent; (3) treat the consumer as if the consumer has a neutral credit rating; (4) exclude the use of credit information as a factor and use only underwriting criteria; or (5) treat the consumer in a manner that is otherwise approved by the division of insurance.

(h) If a security freeze is in place, a consumer credit reporting agency may not change the consumer's official information in the credit report without sending a written statement of the change to the consumer within 30 days after the change is made. A consumer credit reporting agency is not required to send a written statement if the consumer credit reporting agency makes a technical change in the consumer's official information. If a consumer credit reporting agency makes a change, other than a technical change, in a consumer's address, the consumer credit reporting agency shall send the written statement to the consumer at both the new address and the former address. In this subsection, (1) "official information" means name, birth date, social security number, and address; (2) "technical change" means changing spelling, transposing numbers or letters, abbreviating a word, or spelling out an abbreviation.

(i) This section is not intended to prevent a consumer credit reporting agency from advising a third party that requests access to a consumer's credit report or credit score that a security freeze is in effect.

(j) The procedures used by a consumer credit reporting agency for implementing the provisions of this section may include the use of telephone, facsimile, or electronic means if making the disclosure by the electronic means is consistent with the provisions regarding electronic records and signatures required for notices legally required to be in writing under 15 U.S.C. 7001 et seq. (Electronic

Signatures in Global and National Commerce Act), Internet, electronic mail, or another electronic method.

Sec. 45.48.140. Removal of security freeze.

(a) Except as provided by AS 45.48.130, a consumer credit reporting agency may not remove a security freeze unless(1) the consumer requests that the consumer credit reporting agency remove the security freeze under (b) of this section; or (2) the consumer made a material misrepresentation of fact to the consumer credit reporting agency when the consumer requested the security freeze under AS 45.48.110; if a consumer credit reporting agency intends to remove a security freeze on a consumer's credit report under this paragraph, the consumer credit reporting agency shall notify the consumer in writing before removing the security freeze.

(b) A consumer credit reporting agency shall remove a security freeze immediately after receiving a request for removal from the consumer who requested the security freeze.

(c) To make a request under (b) of this section, the consumer shall contact the consumer credit reporting agency by certified mail or as allowed by (d) of this section, authorize the consumer credit reporting agency to remove the security freeze, and provide the consumer credit reporting agency with (1) proper identification to verify the consumer's identity; and (2) the unique personal identification number, password, or similar device provided under AS 45.48.120(b).

(d) In addition to certified mail, a consumer may make a request under (b) of this section by telephone or by fax, the Internet, or other electronic media if the consumer credit reporting agency has developed procedures for using the telephone or an electronic medium to receive and process the request in an expedited manner.
Sec. 45.48.150. Prohibition. When dealing with a third party, a consumer credit reporting agency may not suggest, state, or imply

that a consumer's security freeze reflects a negative credit score, history, report, or rating.

Sec. 45.48.160. Charges.

(a) Except as provided by (b) of this section, a consumer credit reporting agency may not charge a consumer to place or remove a security freeze, to provide access under AS 45.48.130, or to take any other action, including the issuance of a personal identification number, password, or similar device under AS 45.48.120, that is related to the placement of, removal of, or allowing access to a credit report or credit score on which a security freeze has been placed.

(b) If a consumer fails to retain a personal identification number, password, or similar device issued under AS 45.48.120, a consumer credit reporting agency may charge the consumer up to $5 for each time after the first time that the consumer credit reporting agency issues the consumer another personal identification number, password, or similar device because the consumer failed to retain the personal identification number, password, or similar device.

Sec. 45.48.170. Notice of rights. When a consumer credit reporting agency is required to give a consumer a summary of rights under 15 U.S.C. 1681g (Fair Credit Reporting Act), a consumer credit reporting agency shall also give the consumer the following notice:

Consumers Have the Right to Obtain a Security Freeze

You may obtain a security freeze on your credit report and credit score at no charge to protect your privacy and ensure that credit is not granted in your name without your knowledge. You have a right to place a "security freeze" on your credit report and credit score under state law (AS 45.48.100 - 45.48.290). The security freeze will prohibit a consumer credit reporting agency from releasing your credit score and any information in your credit report without your express authorization or approval. The security freeze is designed to prevent credit, loans, and other services from being approved in your name without your consent. However, you should be aware that using a security freeze to take control over who gets access to the personal and financial information in your credit report and credit score may delay, interfere with, or prohibit the timely approval of any subsequent request or application you make regarding a new loan, credit, a mortgage, a governmental service, a governmental payment, rental housing, employment, an investment, a license, a cellular telephone, a utility, a digital signature, an Internet credit card transaction, an extension of credit at point of sale, and other items and services. When you place a security freeze on your credit report and credit score, within 10 business days you will be provided a personal identification number, password, or similar device to use if you choose to remove the freeze on your credit report and credit score or to temporarily authorize the release of your credit report and credit score to a specific third party or specific third parties or for a specific period of time after the freeze is in place. To provide that authorization, you must contact the consumer credit reporting agency and provide all of the following:

(1) proper identification to verify your identity;

(2) the personal identification number, password, or similar device provided by the consumer credit reporting agency;

(3) proper information necessary to identify the third party or third parties who are authorized to receive the credit report and credit score or the specific period of time for which the credit report and credit score are to be available to third parties. A consumer credit reporting agency that receives your request to temporarily lift a freeze on a credit report and credit score is required to comply with the request immediately after receiving your request if you make the request by telephone, or an electronic method if the agency provides an electronic method, or within three business days after receiving your request if you make the request by certified mail. A security freeze does not apply to circumstances where you have an

existing account relationship and a copy of your credit report and credit score are requested by your existing creditor or its agents or affiliates for certain types of account review, collection, fraud control, or similar activities. If you are actively seeking credit, you should understand that the procedures involved in lifting a security freeze may slow your own applications for credit. You should plan ahead and lift a freeze, either completely if you are shopping around, or specifically for a certain creditor, days before applying for new credit. You have a right to bring a civil action against someone who violates your rights under these laws on security freezes. The action can be brought against a consumer credit reporting agency.

Sec. 45.48.180. Notification after violation. If a consumer credit reporting agency violates a security freeze by releasing a consumer's credit report or credit score, the consumer credit reporting agency shall notify the consumer within five business days after the release, and the information in the notice must include an identification of the information released and of the third party who received the information.

Sec. 45.48.190. Violations and penalties.

(a) A consumer who suffers damages as a result of a person's violation of AS 45.48.100 - 45.48.290 may bring an action in court against the person and recover, in the case of a violation where the person acted (1) negligently, actual damages, including loss of wages, and, when applicable, damages for pain and suffering; (2) knowingly, (A) damages as described in (1) of this subsection; (B) punitive damages that are not less than $100 nor more than $5,000 for each violation as the court determines to be appropriate; and (C) other relief that the court determines to be appropriate.

(b) A consumer may bring an action in court against a person for a violation or threatened violation of AS 45.48.100 - 45.48.290 for injunctive relief, whether or not the consumer seeks another remedy under this section.

(c) Notwithstanding (a)(2) of this section, a person who knowingly violates AS 45.48.100 - 45.48.290 is liable in a class action for an amount that the court allows. When determining the amount of an award in a class action under this subsection, the court shall consider, among the relevant factors, the amount of any actual damages awarded, the frequency of the violations, the resources of the violator, and the number of consumers adversely affected.

(d) In this section, "knowingly" has the meaning given in AS 11.81.900.

Sec. 45.48.200. Exemptions. The provisions of AS 45.48.100 - 45.48.290 do not apply to the use of a credit report by (1) a person, the person's subsidiary, affiliate, or agent, or the person's assignee with whom a consumer has or, before the assignment, had an account, contract, or debtor-creditor relationship if the purpose of the use is to review the consumer's account or to collect a financial obligation owing on the account, contract, or debt; (2) a subsidiary, an affiliate, an agent, an assignee, or a prospective assignee of a person to whom access has been granted under AS 45.48.130 if the purpose of the use is to facilitate the extension of credit or another permissible use; (3) a person acting under a court order, warrant, or subpoena; (4) an agency of a state or municipality that administers a program for establishing and enforcing child support obligations; (5) the Department of Health and Social Services, its agents, or its assigns when investigating fraud; (6) the Department of Revenue, its agents, or its assigns when investigating or collecting delinquent taxes or unpaid court orders or when implementing its other statutory responsibilities; (7) a person if the purpose of the use is prescreening allowed under U.S.C. 1681b(c) (Fair Credit Reporting Act); (8) a person administering a credit file monitoring subscription service to which the consumer has subscribed; (9) a person providing a consumer with a copy of the consumer's credit report or credit score at the consumer's request; (10) a consumer credit reporting agency if the data base or file of the consumer credit reporting agency consists entirely of information concerning and used solely for one or more of the following purposes:

(A) criminal record information;

(B) personal loss history information;

(C) fraud prevention or detection;

(D) tenant screening; or

(E) employment screening; or

(11) a person who acts only as a reseller of consumer information by assembling and merging information contained in the data bases of consumer credit reporting agencies and does not maintain a permanent data base of consumer information from which new consumer credit reports are produced. Sec. 45.48.290. Definitions. In AS 45.48.100 - 45.48.290, (1) "account review" means activities related to account maintenance, account monitoring, credit line increases, and account upgrades and enhancements; (2) "consumer" means an individual who is the subject of a credit report or credit score; (3) "consumer credit reporting agency" has the meaning given in AS 45.48.990, but does not include a person who issues reports

(A) on incidents of fraud or authorizations for the purpose of approving or processing negotiable instruments, electronic funds transfers, or similar methods of payments; or

(B) regarding account closures because of fraud, substantial overdrafts, automated teller machine abuse, or similar negative information regarding a consumer to inquiring banks or other financial institutions for use only in reviewing consumer requests for deposit accounts at the inquiring banks or financial institutions; (4) "security freeze" means a prohibition against a consumer credit reporting agency from releasing all or a part of a consumer's credit report or credit score without the express authorization of the consumer; (5) "third party" means a person who is not

(A) the consumer who is the subject of the consumer's credit report or credit score; or

(B) the consumer credit reporting agency that is holding the consumer's credit report or credit score.

Article 3. Consumer Credit Monitoring; Credit Accuracy.

Sec. 45.48.300. Required disclosure. A consumer credit reporting agency shall, if a consumer makes the request and the request is not covered by the free disclosure provision of 15 U.S.C. 1681j(a) - (d) (Fair Credit Reporting Act), clearly and accurately disclose to the consumer the information described under AS 45.48.310.

Sec. 45.48.310. Information to be disclosed. (a) The following information must be disclosed under AS 45.48.300: (1) all information in the consumer's file when the consumer makes the request, except that this paragraph may not be construed to require a consumer credit reporting agency to disclose information concerning credit scores, risk scores, or other predictors that are governed by 15 U.S.C. 1681g; (2) the sources of the information described in (1) of this subsection; (3) an identification of each person, including each end user identified under 15 U.S.C. 1681e, who procured a report on the consumer (A) for employment purposes during the two-year period that precedes the date when the consumer's request is made; or (B) for a purpose other than employment purposes during the one-year period that precedes the date when the consumer's request is made; (4) the dates, original payees, and amounts of any checks that (A) provide the basis for an adverse characterization of the consumer; and (B) are included in the file when the disclosure is made or can be inferred from the file; (5) a record of all inquiries that were received by the consumer credit reporting agency during the one-year period that precedes the request and that identify the consumer in connection with a credit or insurance transaction that was not initiated by the consumer; and (6) a statement that the consumer may request and obtain a credit score if the consumer requests the credit file and not the credit score. (b) The information to be disclosed under (a)(3) of this section must include (1) the name of the person or, if applicable, the full trade name under which the person conducts business; and (2) the address and telephone number of the person if requested by the consumer. (c) A consumer credit reporting agency is not required to disclose the information described in (a)(3) of this section if (1) the end user is an agency of the United States government and procures the consumer's credit report from the consumer credit reporting agency to determine the eligibility of the consumer to receive access or continued access to classified information; in this paragraph, "classified information" has the meaning given in U.S.C. 1681b; and (2) the individual who is in charge of the end user makes a written finding as prescribed under 15 U.S.C. 1681b(b)(4)(A). Sec. 45.48.320. Cost of disclosure. (a) A consumer credit reporting agency may impose a reasonable charge on a consumer for making a disclosure under AS 45.48.300. The charge may not exceed (1) $2 for each of the first 12 requests from the consumer in a calendar year; (2) $8 for each request beyond the 12 requests covered by (1) of this subsection in a calendar year. (b) The consumer credit reporting agency shall disclose the charge to the consumer before making the disclosure under AS 45.48.300.

Sec. 45.48.330. Form of disclosure.

(a) A consumer may make a request under AS 45.48.300 in writing, in person, by telephone if the consumer has made a written request for the disclosure, by electronic means if the consumer credit reporting agency offers electronic access for any other purpose, or by any other reasonable means that is available from the consumer credit reporting agency.

(b) To make a request in person under (a) of this section, the consumer shall, after reasonable notice to the consumer credit reporting agency, appear during normal business hours at the consumer credit reporting agency's place of business where the consumer credit reporting agency normally provides disclosures under AS 45.48.300.

Sec. 45.48.340. Timing of disclosure. A consumer credit reporting agency shall provide a consumer with the disclosure under AS 45.48.300 within (1) 24 hours after the date on which the request is made if the disclosure is made by electronic means under AS 45.48.330(a); or (2) five days after the date on which the request is made if the disclosure is made in writing, in person, by telephone, or by any other reasonable means that is available from the consumer credit reporting agency, except by electronic means.
Sec. 45.48.350. Credit accuracy.

(a) A person who does business in the state by distributing information about an individual's credit history, score, or ranking shall, when notified that the information that the person is distributing is inaccurate, immediately stop distributing the information until the accuracy of the information can be verified or the inaccuracies in the information corrected.

(b) If a person who does business in the state by distributing information about an individual's credit history, score, or ranking releases information about an individual that is inaccurate, the person shall, as quickly as possible after discovering that inaccurate information is being distributed,

(1) repair, to the extent possible, the damage to the individual caused by the release of the inaccurate information; and (2) pay fair and reasonable compensation to the individual for the damage caused to the individual by the release of the inaccurate information.

(c) If a person fails to comply with (b) of this section, an individual may bring an action in court to compel the person to comply with (b) of this section.

(d) In this section, "does business in the state" means engages in activities that provide at least the minimum contacts required by substantive due process for the state to exercise jurisdiction over the person who is engaging in the activities.

Article 4. Protection of Social Security Number.

Sec. 45.48.400. Use of social security number. A person may not

(1) intentionally communicate or otherwise make available to the general public an individual's social security number; (2) print an individual's social security number on a card required for the individual to access products or services provided by the person; (3) require an individual to transmit the individual's social security number over the Internet unless the Internet connection is secure or the social security number is encrypted; (4) require an individual to use the individual's social security number to access an Internet site unless a password, a unique personal identification number, or another authentication device is also required to access the site; or (5) print an individual's social security number on material that is mailed to the individual unless

(A) local, state, or federal law, including a regulation adopted under AS 45.48.470, expressly authorizes placement of the social security number on the material; or

(B) the social security number is included on an application or other form, including a document sent as a part of an application process or an enrollment process, sent by mail to establish, amend, or terminate an account, a contract, or a policy, or to confirm the accuracy of the social security number; however, a social security number allowed to be mailed under this subparagraph may not be printed, in whole or in part, on a postcard or other mailer that does not require an envelope, or in a manner that makes the social security number visible on the envelope or without the envelope's being opened.

Sec. 45.48.410. Request and collection.

(a) A person who does business in the state, including the business of government, may not request or collect an individual's social security number. This subsection does not prohibit a person from asking for another form of identification from the individual.

(b) The prohibition in (a) of this section does not apply (1) if the person is expressly authorized by local, state, or federal law, including a regulation adopted under AS 45.48.470, to demand proof of the individual's social security number, to collect the individual's social security number, or to submit the individual's social security number to the local, state, or federal government; (2) to a financial institution that is regulated by 15 U.S.C. 6801 - 6827 (Gramm-Leach-Bliley Financial Modernization Act) if the financial institution requests or collects the individual's social security number to facilitate a transaction of the individual; (3) to a communication to or from a consumer reporting agency; in this paragraph, "consumer reporting agency" has the meaning given in 15 U.S.C. 1681a (Fair Credit Reporting Act); or (4) if the request or collection is for a background check on the individual, law enforcement purposes, or the individual's employment, including employment benefits.

Sec. 45.48.420. Sale, lease, loan, trade, or rental.

(a) A person may not sell, lease, loan, trade, or rent an individual's social security number to a third party.

(b) The prohibition in (a) of this section does not apply if the sale, lease, loan, trade, or rental is (1) expressly authorized by local, state, or federal law, including a regulation adopted under AS 45.48.470; (2) part of a report prepared by a consumer credit reporting agency in response to a request by a person and the person submits the social security number as part of the request to the consumer credit reporting agency for the preparation of the report.

Sec. 45.48.430. Disclosure.

(a) A person doing business, including the business of government, may not disclose an individual's social security number to a third party.

(b) The prohibition in (a) of this section does not apply if (1) the disclosure is expressly authorized by local, state, or federal land; including a regulation adopted under AS 45.48.470; (2) the third party is a financial institution that is regulated by U.S.C. 6801 - 6827 (Gramm-Leach-Bliley Financial Modernization Act), and the disclosure is to facilitate a transaction of the individual; (3) the disclosure is part of a report prepared by a consumer credit reporting agency in response to a request by a person and the person submits the social security number as part of the request to the consumer credit reporting agency for the preparation of the report; or (4) the disclosure is for a background check on the individual, law enforcement purposes, or the individual's employment, including employment benefits.

Sec. 45.48.440. Interagency disclosure. Notwithstanding the other provisions of AS 45.48.400 - 45.48.480, a state or local governmental agency may disclose an individual's social security number to another state or local governmental agency or to an agency of the federal government if the disclosure is required in order for the agency to carry out the agency's duties and responsibilities.

Sec. 45.48.450. Exception for employees, agents, and independent contractors.

(a) Notwithstanding the other provisions of AS 45.48.400 - 45.48.480, a person may disclose an individual's social security number to an employee or agent of the person for a legitimate purpose established by and as directed by the person, but the employee or agent may not use the social security number for another purpose or make an unauthorized disclosure of the individual's personal information. (b) Notwithstanding the other provisions of AS 45.48.400 - 45.48.480, and except as provided for an agent under (a) of this section, a person may disclose an individual's social security number to an independent contractor of the person to facilitate the purpose or transaction for which the individual initially provided the social security number to the person, but the independent contractor may not use the social security number for another purpose or make an unauthorized disclosure of the individual's personal information.

Sec. 45.48.460. Employment-related exception. The provisions of AS 45.48.400 - 45.48.480 may not be construed to restrict a person's use or exchange of an individual's social security number (1) in the course of the administration of a claim, benefit, or procedure related to the individual's employment by the person, including the individual's termination from employment, retirement from employment, and injury suffered during the course of employment; or (2) to check on an unemployment insurance claim of the individual.

Sec. 45.48.470. Agency regulations. If regulations are necessary in order for a state agency to carry out the state agency's duties and responsibilities, a state agency may adopt regulations under AS 44.62 (Administrative Procedure Act) to establish when the state agency or a person regulated by the state agency may (1) print an individual's social security number on material that is mailed to the individual; (2) demand proof from an individual of the individual's social security number, collect from an individual the individual's social security number, or submit an individual's social security number to a local, state, or federal agency; (3) ask an individual to provide the state agency with the individual's social security number; (4) disclose an individual's social security number to a third party; (5) sell, lease, loan, trade, or rent an individual's social security number to a third party.

Sec. 45.48.480. Penalties.

(a) A person who knowingly violates AS 45.48.400 - 45.48.430 is liable to the state for a civil penalty not to exceed $3,000.

(b) An individual may bring a civil action in court against a person who knowingly violates AS 45.48.400 - 45.48.430 and may recover actual damages or $5,000, whichever amount is greater, and court costs and attorney fees allowed by the rules of court.

(c) A person who knowingly violates AS 45.48.400 - 45.48.430 is guilty of a class A misdemeanor.

(d) In this section, "knowingly" has the meaning given in AS 11.81.900.

Article 5. Disposal of Records. Sec. 45.48.500. Disposal of records.

(a) When disposing of records that contain personal information, a business and a governmental agency shall take all reasonable measures necessary to protect against unauthorized access to or use of the records.

(b) Notwithstanding (a) of this section, if a business or governmental agency has otherwise complied with the provisions of AS 45.48.500 - 45.48.590 in the selection of a third party engaged in the business of record destruction, the business or governmental agency is not liable for the disposal of records under AS 45.48.500 - 45.48.590 after the business or governmental agency has relinquished control of the records to the third party for the destruction of the records.

(c) A business or governmental agency is not liable for the disposal of records under AS 45.48.500 - 45.48.590 after the business or governmental agency has relinquished control of the records to the individual to whom the records pertain.

Sec. 45.48.510. Measures to protect access. The measures that may be taken to comply with AS 45.48.500 include (1) implementing and monitoring compliance with policies and procedures that require the burning, pulverizing, or shredding of paper documents containing personal information so that the personal information cannot practicably be read or reconstructed; (2) implementing and monitoring compliance with policies and procedures that require the destruction or erasure of electronic media and other nonpaper media containing personal information so that the personal information cannot practicably be read or reconstructed; (3) after due diligence, entering into a written contract with a third party engaged in the business of record destruction to dispose of records containing personal information in a manner consistent with AS 45.48.500 - 45.48.590. Sec. 45.48.520. Due diligence. In AS 45.48.510(3), due diligence ordinarily includes performing one or more of the following: (1) reviewing an independent audit of the third party's operations and its compliance with AS 45.48.500 - 45.48.590; (2) obtaining information about the third party from several references or other reliable sources and requiring that the third party be certified by a recognized trade association or similar organization with a reputation for high standards of quality review; or (3) reviewing and evaluating the third party's information security policies and procedures, or taking other appropriate measures to determine the competency and integrity of the third party.

Sec. 45.48.530. Policy and procedures. A business or governmental agency shall adopt written policies and procedures that relate to the adequate destruction and proper disposal of records containing personal information and that are consistent with AS 45.48.500 - 45.48.590. Sec. 45.48.540. Exemptions.

(a) A business or a governmental agency is not required to comply with AS 45.48.500 - 45.48.530 if federal law requires that the business or governmental agency act in a way that does not comply with AS 45.48.500 - 45.48.530.

(b) A business is not required to comply with AS 45.48.500 - 45.48.530 if (1) the business is subject to and in compliance with 15 U.S.C. 6801 - 6827 (Gramm-Leach-Bliley Financial Modernization Act); or (2) the manner of the disposal of the records of the business is subject to 15 U.S.C. 1681w (Fair Credit Reporting Act) and the business is complying with 15 U.S.C. 1861w.

Sec. 45.48.550. Civil penalty.

(a) An individual, a business, or a governmental agency that knowingly violates AS 45.48.500 - 45.48.590 is liable to the state for a civil penalty not to exceed $3,000.

(b) In this section, "knowingly" has the meaning given in AS 11.81.900.

Sec. 45.48.560. Court action. An individual who is damaged by a violation of AS 45.48.500 - 45.48.590 may bring a civil action in court to enjoin further violations and to recover damages for the violation and court costs and attorney fees allowed by the rules of court.

Sec. 45.48.590. Definitions. In AS 45.48.500 - 45.48.590, (1) "business" means a person who conducts business in the state or a person who conducts business and maintains or otherwise possesses personal information on state residents; in this paragraph,

(A) "conducts business" includes engaging in activities as a financial institution organized, chartered, or holding a license or authorization certificate under the laws of this state, another state, the United States, or another country;

(B) "possesses" includes possession for the purpose of destruction;

(2) "dispose" means (A) the discarding or abandonment of records containing personal information; (B) the sale, donation, discarding, or transfer of (i) any medium, including computer equipment or computer media, that contains records of personal information; (ii) nonpaper media, other than that identified under (i) of this subparagraph, on which records of personal information are stored; and (iii) equipment for nonpaper storage of information;

(3) "governmental agency" means a state or local governmental agency, except for an agency of the judicial branch; (4) "personal information" means information that identifies, relates to, describes, or is capable of being associated with a particular individual, and includes a name, signature, social security number, fingerprint, photograph, computerized image, physical characteristic, physical description, address, telephone number, passport number, driver's license, state identification number, date

of birth, medical information, bank account number, credit card number, debit card number, and financial information;

(5) "records" means material on which information that is written, drawn, spoken, visual, or electromagnetic is recorded or preserved, regardless of physical form or characteristics, but does not include publicly available directories containing names, addresses, telephone numbers, or other information an individual has voluntarily consented to have publicly disseminated or listed.

Article 6. Factual Declaration of Innocence after Identity Theft; Right to File Police Report Regarding Identity Theft.

Sec. 45.48.600. Factual declaration of innocence after identity theft.

(a) A victim of identity theft may petition the superior court for a determination that the victim is factually innocent of a crime if

(1) the perpetrator of the identity theft was arrested for, cited for, or convicted of the crime using the victim's identity; (2) a criminal complaint was filed against the perpetrator of the identity theft; (3) the victim's identity was mistakenly associated with a record of a conviction for a crime.

(b) In addition to a petition by a victim under (a) of this section, the department may petition the superior court for a determination under (a) of this section, or the superior court may, on its own motion, make a determination under (a) of this section.

Sec. 45.48.610. Basis for determination. A determination of factual innocence under AS 45.48.600 may be heard and made on declarations, affidavits, police reports, or other material, relevant, and reliable information submitted by the parties or ordered to be made a part of the record by the court.

Sec. 45.48.620. Criteria for determination; court order.

(a) A court shall determine that a victim is factually innocent of a crime if the court finds that the petition or motion brought under AS 45.48.600 is meritorious and that (1) there is not a reasonable cause to believe that the victim of the identity theft committed the crime for which the perpetrator of the identity theft was arrested, cited, or convicted, or was subject to a criminal complaint in the victim's name; or (2) the victim's identity was mistakenly associated with a record of a conviction of a crime.

(b) If a court finds under this section that the victim is factually innocent of a crime, the court shall issue an order indicating this determination of factual innocence and shall provide the victim with a copy of the order.

Sec. 45.48.630. Orders regarding records. After a court issues an order under AS 45.48.620, the court may order the name and associated personal information of the victim of identity theft that is contained in the files, indexes, and other records of the court that are accessible by the public deleted, sealed, or labeled to show that the name and personal information of the victim of identity theft is incorrect.

Sec. 45.48.640. Vacation of determination. A court that has issued an order under AS 45.48.620 may, at any time, vacate the order if the petition, or any information submitted in support of the petition, is found to contain a material misrepresentation or fraudulent material.

Sec. 45.48.650. Court form. The supreme court of the state may develop a form to be used for the order under AS 45.48.620.

Sec. 45.48.660. Data base. The department may establish and maintain a database of individuals who have been victims of identity theft and who have received an order under AS 45.48.620. The department shall provide a victim or the victim's authorized representative access to a data base established under this section to establish that the individual has been a victim of identity theft.

Access to the a data base established under this section is limited to criminal justice agencies, victims of identity theft, and individuals and agencies authorized by the victims.

Sec. 45.48.670. Toll-free telephone number. The department may establish and maintain a toll-free telephone number to provide access to information in a database established under AS 45.48.660. Sec. 45.48.680. Right to file police report regarding identity theft.

(a) Even if the local law enforcement agency does not have jurisdiction over the theft of an individual's identity, if an individual who has learned or reasonably suspects the individual has been the victim of identity theft contacts, for the purpose of filing a complaint, a local law enforcement agency that has jurisdiction over the individual's actual place of residence, the local law enforcement agency shall make a report of the matter and provide the individual with a copy of the report. The local law enforcement agency may refer the matter to a law enforcement agency in a different jurisdiction.

(b) This section is not intended to interfere with the discretion of a local law enforcement agency to allocate its resources to the investigation of crime. A local law enforcement agency is not required to count a complaint filed under (a) of this section as an open case for purposes that include compiling statistics on its open cases.

Sec. 45.48.690. Definitions. In AS 45.48.600 - 45.48.690,

(1) "crime" has the meaning given in AS 11.81.900;

(2) "department" means the Department of Law;

(3) "identity theft" means the theft of the identity of an individual;

(4) "perpetrator" means the person who perpetrated the theft of an individual's identity;

(5) "victim" means an individual who is the victim of identity theft.
Article 7. Consumer Credit Header Information.

Sec. 45.48.700. Consumer credit header information.

(a) A consumer credit reporting agency may not furnish by a written, an oral, or another method of communication a consumer's credit header information to a person unless (1) the person has a permissible purpose under 15 U.S.C. 1681b (Fair Credit Protection Act) to obtain the consumer's credit report; or (2) the disclosure is part of a report prepared by the consumer credit reporting agency in response to a request by a person and the person submits the social security number as part of the request to the consumer credit reporting agency for the preparation of the report.

(b) In this section, "credit header information" means the social security number of a consumer, or a derivative of the social security number, the maiden name of the mother of the consumer, the birth date of the consumer, and other personally identifiable information of a consumer that is derived from nonpublic personal information, except the name, address, and telephone number of the consumer listed in a residential telephone directory available in the locality of the consumer.

Article 8. Truncation of Card Information.

Sec. 45.48.750. Truncation of card information.

(a) A person who accepts credit cards or debit cards for the transaction of business may not print more than the last five digits of the card number or the expiration date on any receipt provided to the cardholder at the point of the sale or transaction.

(b) This section applies only to receipts that are electronically printed and does not apply to transactions in which the sole means of recording a credit card or debit card account number is by handwriting or by an imprint or copy of the card.

(c) An individual may bring a civil action in court against a person who knowingly violates this section and may recover actual damages or $5,000, whichever is greater, and court costs and attorney fees allowed by the rules of court.

(d) A person who knowingly violates this section is liable to the state for a civil penalty not to exceed $3,000.

(e) A person who knowingly violates this section is guilty of a class A misdemeanor.

(f) In this section, (1) “credit” means the right granted by a creditor to a debtor to defer payment of debt, to incur debts and defer payment of the debt, or to purchase property or services and defer payment of the purchase; in this paragraph, “creditor” means a person who regularly extends, renews, or continues credit, a person who regularly arranges for the extension, renewal, or continuation of credit, or an assignee of an original creditor who participates in the decision to extend, renew, or continue credit; (2) “credit card” means a card, plate, coupon book, or other credit device existing for the purpose of obtaining money, property, labor, or services on credit; (3) “debit card” means a card issued by a financial institution to a consumer for use in initiating an electronic fund transfer from the account of the consumer at the financial institution for the purpose of transferring money between accounts or obtaining money, property, labor, or services; (4) “knowingly” has the meaning given in AS 11.81.900.

Article 9. General Provisions. Sec. 45.48.990. Definitions.

In this chapter, unless the context indicates otherwise, (1) “consumer” means an individual; (2) “consumer credit reporting agency” means a person who, for monetary fees, dues, or on a cooperative nonprofit basis, regularly engages in whole or in part in the practice of assembling or evaluating consumer credit information or other information on consumers for the purpose of furnishing credit reports to third parties; (3) “credit report” means a written, oral, or other communication of information by a consumer credit reporting agency bearing on a consumer's credit worthiness, credit standing, credit capacity, character, general reputation, personal characteristics, or mode of living if the communication is used or expected to be used or collected in whole or in part to serve as a factor in establishing the consumer's eligibility for (A) credit or insurance to be used primarily for personal, family, or household purposes; (B) employment purposes; or (C) any other permissible purpose authorized under section 15 U.S.C. 1681b; (4) "information system" means any information system, including a system consisting of digital data bases and a system consisting of pieces of paper; (5) "person" has the meaning given in AS 01.10.060 and includes a state or local governmental agency, except for an agency of the judicial branch; (6) "state resident" means an individual who satisfies the residency requirements under AS 01.10.055.

Sec. 45.48.995. Short title. This chapter may be cited as the Alaska Personal Information Protection Act.

* Sec. 4. AS 45.50.471(b) is amended by adding a new paragraph to read: an information collector, other than a governmental agency, violating AS 45.48.010 - 45.48.090 (breach of security involving personal information); in this paragraph, (A) "governmental agency" has the meaning given in AS 45.48.080; (B) "information collector" has the meaning given in AS 45.48.090.

* Sec. 5. The uncodified law of the State of Alaska is amended by adding a new section to read:

INDIRECT COURT RULE AMENDMENT. AS 45.48.640, enacted by sec. 3 of this Act, has the effect of changing Rule 60(b), Alaska Rules of Civil Procedure, by allowing a court to vacate an order on its own motion and at any time and by establishing a specific criterion for vacating the order under AS 45.48.640.

* Sec. 6. AS 45.48.470, enacted by sec. 3 of this Act, takes effect immediately under 12 AS 01.10.070(c).

Chapter 3: Arizona

In Arizona Senate Bill 1338, look for the term unredacted in addition to the encryption reference as exemptions to the disclosure requirements. There is a term in data privacy that says mitigate or eliminate. To mitigate a data risk would mean to put the necessary protections in place to safeguard the data. To eliminate the risk would mean to not use sensitive data in the first place. For example, some companies are now assigning each of their customers a unique identifier that only has meaning to their systems. This is safer than using an individual's Social Security number as an identifier. You will note that Arizona House Bill 2429 puts restrictions on how Social Security numbers may be used.

Notification for Compromised Personal Information, Senate Bill S.B. 1338, requires a business or governmental entity conducting business in Arizona to notify state residents of a breach of their security system when personal information of the individuals has been compromised.

A. When a person that conducts business in this state (Arizona) and that owns or licenses unencrypted computerized data that includes personal information becomes aware of an incident of unauthorized acquisition and access to unencrypted or unredacted computerized data that includes an individual's personal information, the person shall conduct a reasonable investigation to promptly determine if there has been a breach of the security system. If the investigation results in a determination that there has been a breach in the security system, the person shall notify the individuals affected. The notice shall be made in the most expedient manner possible and without unreasonable delay subject to the needs of law enforcement as provided in subsection C of this section and any measures necessary to determine the nature and scope of the breach, to identify the individuals affected or to restore the reasonable integrity of the data system.

B. A person that maintains unencrypted computerized data that includes personal information that the person does not own shall notify and cooperate with the owner or the licensee of the information of any breach of the security of the system following

discovery of the breach without unreasonable delay. Cooperation shall include sharing information relevant to the breach of the security of the system with the owner or licensee. The personal that owns or licenses the computerized data shall provide notice to the individual pursuant to this section. The person that maintained the data under an agreement with the owner or licensee is not required to provide notice to the individual pursuant to this section unless the agreement stipulates otherwise.

C. The notification required by subsection A of this section may be delayed if a law enforcement agency advises the person that the notification will impede a criminal investigation. The person shall make the notification after the law enforcement agency determines that it will not compromise the investigation.

D. The disclosure required by subsection A of this sectional shall be provided by one of the following methods:

1. Written notice

2. Electronic notice if the person's primary method of communication with the individual is by electronic means or is consistent with the provisions regarding electronic records and signatures set forth in the electronic signatures in Global and Nation Commerce Act (P.L. 106-229; 114 STAT. 464; 15 UNITED STATES CODE SECTION 7001).

3. Telephonic notice

4. Substitute notice if the person demonstrates that the cost of providing notice pursuant to paragraph 1, 2 or 3 of this subsection would exceed $50,000 or that the affected class of individuals to be notified exceeds 100,000 persons, or the person does not have sufficient contact information. Substitute notice shall consist of ALL of the following:

(a) Electronic mail (e-mail) notice if the person has e-mail addresses for the individuals subject to the notice.

(b) Conspicuous posting of the notice on the website of the person if the person maintains one.

(c) Notification to major statewide media.

E. A person who maintains the person's own notification procedures as part of an information security policy for the treatment of personal information and is otherwise consistent with the requirements of this section shall be deemed to be in compliance with the notifications requirements of this section if the person notifies subject individuals in accordance with the person's policies if a breach of the security systems occurs.

F. A person that complies with the notification requirements or security breach procedures pursuant to the rules, regulation, procedures, guidance or guidelines established by the person's primary or functional federal regulator is deemed to be in compliance with this section.

G. A person is not required to disclose a breach of the security of the system if the person or a law enforcement agency, after a reasonable investigation, determines that a breach of the security of the system has not occurred or is not reasonable likely to occur.

H. This section may only be enforced by the Attorney General. The Attorney General may bring an action to obtain actual damages for a willful and knowing violation of this section and a civil penalty not to exceed $10,000 per breach of the security of the system or series of breaches of a similar nature that are discovered in a single investigation.

I. The state legislature determines that security system breach notification is a matter of statewide concern. The power to regulate security breach notification is preempted by this state and this section shall supersede and preempt all municipal and county laws, charters, ordinances and rules relating to issues regulated by this chapter.

J. This section does not apply to either of the following:

1. A person subject to Title V of the Gramm Leach Bliley Act of 1999 (P.L. 106-102; 113 STAT. 1338; 15 UNITED STATES CODE SECTIONS 6801 through 6809).

2. Covered entities as defined under regulations implementing The Health Insurance Portability and Accountability Act, , 45 Code of Federal Regulations section 160.103 (1996).

K. A law enforcement agency, a prosecution agency and a court shall create and maintain an information security policy that includes notification procedures for a breach of the security system of the law enforcement agency, the prosecuting agency or the court.

L. For the purposes of this section:

1. “Breach”, “breach of the security of the system”, “security breach” means an unauthorized acquisition of and access to unencrypted or unredacted computerized data that materially compromises the security or confidentiality of personal information maintained by a person as part of a database of personal information regarding multiple individuals and that causes or is reasonable likely to cause substantial economic loss to an individual. Good faith acquisition of personal information by an employee or agent of the person for the purposes of the person is not a breach of the security system if the personal information is not used for a purposed unrelated to the person or subject to further willful unauthorized disclosure.

2. “Court” means the Supreme Court, Court of Appeals, Superior Court, courts inferior to the Superior Court and Justice Courts.

3. "Encrypted" means use of an algorithmic process to transform data into a form in which the data is rendered unreadable or unusable without use of a confidential process or key.

4. "Individual" means a person that is a resident of this state (Arizona) as determined by a principal mailing address in this state as reflected in the records of the person conducting business in this state at the time of the breach.

5. "Law enforcement agency" means the Department of Public Safety, county sheriff departments or municipal police departments.

6. "Person" means a nature person, corporation, business trust, estate, trust, partnership, association, joint venture, government, governmental subdivision or agency or any other legal or commercial entity. Person does not include a law enforcement agency, a prosecution agency or a court.

7. "Personal information":

(a) Means an individual's first name or first initial AND last name in combination with any one or more of the following data elements, when the data element is not encrypted, redacted or secured by any other method rendering the element unreadable or unusable:

(i) The individual's Social Security number

(ii) The individual's number on a driver license issued pursuant to Section 28-3166 or number on a non-operating identification license issued pursuant to Section 28-3165.

(iii) The individual's financial account number OR credit or debit card number in combination with any required security code, access code or password that would permit access to the individual's financial account.

(b) Does not include publicly available information that is lawfully made available to the general public from federal, state or local government records or widely distributed media.

8. "Prosecution agency" means the Attorney General, any county attorney, or any municipal prosecutor.

9. "Redact" means alter or truncate data such that no more than the last four (4) digits of a Social Security number, driver license number, non-operating identification license number, financial account number or credit or debit card number is accessible as part of the personal information.

Sec. 2. Effective date

This act is effective from and after December 31, 2006.

Sec. 3. Conditional repeal; notice

A. Title 44, chapter 32, Arizona Revised Statutes, as added by this act, is repealed one year after the effective date of the federal personal data privacy and security act.

B. The attorney general shall notify in writing the director of the Arizona legislative council of this date.

Restricted use of Social Security numbers - House Bill 2429, states that beginning on January 1, 2005 a person or entity may not do the following:

1) Communicate an individual's Social Security number and make it available to the general public.

2) Print an individual's Social Security number on any card required for the individual to receive products or services provided by the person or entity.

3) Require an individual's Social Security number over the Internet unless the connection is secure or the Social Security number is encrypted.

4) Require the transmission of an individual's Social Security number to access an Internet website, unless a password or unique identification is also required to access the Internet site.

5) Print an individual's Social Security number on any materials that are mailed to the individual, unless state or federal law requires the Social Security number to be on the document.

Requires insurers, health care service organizations, hospital, medical, dental or optometric service corporations to comply with provisions of this act for all new contracts issued on or after January 1, 2005. Specifies that contract agreements already in existence must comply upon the renewal of the policies or no later than January 1, 2006. Specifies that a person or entity using an individual's Social Security number in a manner inconsistent with this legislation, prior to July 1, 2004, may continue using that individual's Social Security number if the use of the Social Security number is continuous. States that the entity must provide the individual with an annual written disclosure of the individual's right to stop the use of the Social Security number. States that upon request of the individual, the entity must stop using the Social Security number within 30 days and may not charge a fee for implementing the request. Specifies that the legislation does not prevent the collection or release of a Social Security number for internal verification or administrative purposes. Clarifies that the use of Social Security numbers by an agency of this state or by a county, city, town or other political subdivision are exempt from the confidentiality provisions. Clarifies that documents or records that are required to be open to the public pursuant to the constitution, laws of this state or by court order are exempt from the confidentiality provisions. Clarifies that it does not prevent the mailing of documents that include Social Security numbers sent as an application or enrollment process or to establish, amend or terminate an account, contract or policy or to verify a Social Security number. Clarifies that, upon enactment, the state and political subdivisions of this state shall not use Social Security numbers on state issued or political subdivision issued forms of identification. Makes conforming changes to the effective date. Clarifies that the bill does not limit public access to documents or public records that are recorded or required to be open to the public. Stipulates that this article does not apply to the use of Social Security numbers by an agency of this state or by a county, city, town or other political subdivision of this state. It specifies that these entities must comply with provisions of the act prohibiting the printing of an individual's Social Security number on any card required for the receipt of products or services, or printing the Social Security number on materials that are mailed unless state or federal law requires the Social Security number. States that this article does not apply to documents or records that are recorded or required to be open to the public by the constitution, laws, or by court rule. Defines "individual" as a resident of this state.

Consumer protection: rules: confidentiality: unlawful practice – House Bill 2132, provides that an electric utility cannot release customer-specific information without prior written consent from the customer, with the following exceptions:

A. For the purposes of law enforcement
B. In order to conduct account collection activities
C. To provide safe and reliable service to the customer
D. Excludes public agencies from obtaining customer specific information.

The Arizona Corporation Commission has acted to adopt rules allowing regulated utilities to share customer information under specific circumstances Arizona Administrative Code R-14-203(a)(2) *HB 2132*

Relating to consumer reporting agencies - House Bill 2233, prohibits the sale of information obtained by insurance inquiry, with the following exceptions:

A. A consumer reporting agency shall not provide or sell data or lists that include any information that in whole or in part was submitted in conjunction with an insurance inquiry about a consumer's credit information or a request for a credit report or insurance score.

B. Subsection A does not apply to data or lists that the consumer reporting agency supplies to the insurance producer from whom the information was received, the insurer on whose behalf the producer acted or the insurer's affiliates or holding companies.

C. This section shall not restrict an insurer from being able to obtain history or a motor vehicle report.

Information obtained or disseminated by state and local governments – House Bill 2024, states that a governmental agency shall develop and establish commercially reasonable procedures to ensure the entity identifying information or personal identifying information that is collected or obtained by the governmental agency is secure and cannot be access, viewed or acquired unless authorized by law.

Taking identity of another person or entity – House Bill 2484,

A. A person commits taking the identity of another person or entity if the person knowingly takes, purchases, manufactures, records, possesses or uses any personal identifying information or entity identifying information of another person or entity, including a real or fictitious person or entity, without the consent of that other person or entity, with the intent to obtain or use the other person's or entity's identity for any unlawful purpose or to cause loss to a person or entity whether or not the person or entity actually suffers any economic loss as a result of the offense.

B. On the request of a person or entity, a peace officer in any jurisdiction in which an element of the offense is committed, a result of the offense occurs or the person or entity whose identity is taken resides or is located shall take a report. The peace officer may provide a copy of the report to any other law enforcement agency that is located in a jurisdiction in which a violation of this section occurred.

C. If a defendant is alleged to have committed multiple violations of this section within the same county, the prosecutor may file a complaint charging all of the violations and any related charges under other sections that have not been previously filed in any precinct in which a violation is alleged to have occurred. If a defendant is alleged to have committed multiple violations of this section within the state, the prosecutor may file a complaint charging all of the violations and any related charges under other sections that have not been previously filed in any county in which a violation is alleged to have occurred.

D. This section does not apply to a violation of section 4-241 by a person who is under twenty-one years of age.

E. If a defendant is convicted of a violation of this section and the court sentences the defendant to a term of probation, the court shall order that as an initial condition of probation the defendant be imprisoned in the county jail for a period of not less than sixty days. This jail term of incarceration shall not be deferred, deleted or otherwise suspended. If a person is sentenced to serve a period of incarceration in the state department of corrections and the period of incarceration will be followed immediately by a term of probation, the court may waive the jail term of incarceration prescribed by this subsection.

F. Taking the identity of another person or entity is a class 4 felony. Sec. 2. Section 13-2009, Arizona Revised Statutes, is amended to read:

13-2009. Aggravated taking identity of another person or entity; classification

A. A person commits aggravated taking the identity of another person or entity if the person knowingly takes, purchases, manufactures, records, possesses or uses any personal identifying information or entity identifying information of either:

1. Five or more other persons or entities, including real or fictitious persons or entities, without the consent of the other persons or entities, with the intent to obtain or use the other persons' or entities' identities for any unlawful purpose or to cause loss to the persons or entities whether or not the persons or entities actually suffer any economic loss.

2. Another person or entity, including a real or fictitious person or entity, without the consent of that other person or entity, with the intent to obtain or use the other person's or entity's identity for any unlawful purpose and causes another person or entity to suffer an economic loss of three thousand dollars or more.

B. In an action for aggravated taking the identity of another person or entity under subsection A, paragraph 1 of this section, proof of possession out of the regular course of business of the personal identifying information or entity identifying information of five or more other persons or entities may give rise to an inference that the personal identifying information or entity identifying information of the five or more other persons or entities was possessed for an unlawful purpose.

C. This section does not apply to a violation of section 4-241 by a person who is under twenty-one years of age.

D. If a defendant is convicted of a violation of this section and the court sentences the defendant to a term of probation, the court shall order that as an initial condition of probation the defendant be imprisoned in the county jail for a period of not less than one hundred eighty days. This jail term of incarceration shall not be deferred, deleted or otherwise suspended. If a person is sentenced to serve a period of incarceration in the state department of corrections and the period of incarceration will be followed immediately by a term of probation, the court may waive the jail term of incarceration prescribed by this subsection.

E. Aggravated taking the identity of another person or entity is a class 3 felony.

Sec. 3. Section 13-2010, Arizona Revised Statutes, is amended to read:

13-2010. Trafficking in the identity of another person or entity; classification

A. A person commits trafficking in the identity of another person or entity if the person knowingly sells, transfers or transmits any personal identifying information or entity identifying information of another person or entity, including a real or fictitious person or entity, without the consent of the other person or entity for any unlawful purpose or to cause loss to the person or entity whether or not the other person or entity actually suffers any economic loss.

B. This section does not apply to a violation of section 4-241 by a person who is under twenty-one years of age.

C. If a defendant is convicted of a violation of this section and the court sentences the defendant to a term of probation, the court shall order that as an initial condition of probation the defendant be imprisoned in the county jail for a period of not less than two hundred forty days. This jail term of incarceration shall not be deferred, deleted or otherwise suspended. If a person is sentenced to serve a period of incarceration in the state department of corrections and the period of incarceration will be followed immediately by a term of probation, the court may waive the jail term of incarceration prescribed by this subsection.

D. Trafficking in the identity of another person or entity is a class 2 felony.

Sec. 4. Title 44, Arizona Revised Statutes, is amended by adding chapter 32, to read:

CHAPTER 32. RECORD DISCARD AND DISPOSAL

ARTICLE 1. DISCARD AND DISPOSAL OF PERSONAL IDENTIFYING INFORMATION RECORDS

44-7501. Discarding and disposing of records containing personal identifying information; civil penalty; costs; affirmative defenses; enforcement; definition

A. An entity shall not KNOWINGLY discard or dispose of records or documents without redacting the information or destroying the records or documents if the records or documents contain an individual's first and last name or first initial and last name in combination with a corresponding complete:

1. Social Security number
2. Credit card, charge card or debit card number.
3. Retirement account number.
4. Savings, checking or securities entitlement account number.
5. Driver license number or non-operating identification license number.

B. An entity shall Take actions that the entity reasonably believes will ensure that no unauthorized person will have access to the information listed in subsection a contained in the records or documents for the period between the record's or document's discard or disposal and the record's destruction.

C. This section may be enforced by either of the following:

1. A county attorney in the county in which the records or documents were wrongfully discarded or disposed. If a violation occurs by the same entity in multiple counties and the attorney general does not enforce this section pursuant to paragraph 2 of this

subsection, a county attorney in a county in which records or documents were not properly discarded or disposed of, after filing a notice of intent to enforce this section, may send a copy of the notice to the county attorney in each county in which records or documents were not properly discarded or disposed of and may request that the actions be consolidated.

2. The attorney general if the wrongful discard or disposal occurs in multiple counties or if the county attorney in the county in which the record or document was wrongfully discarded or disposed consents to enforcement by the attorney general.

D. A civil penalty shall be imposed for each violation of subsection A arising out of one incident. The civil penalty shall not exceed:

1. Five hundred dollars for a first violation.
2. One thousand dollars for a second violation.
3. Five thousand dollars for a third or subsequent violation.

E. An entity that maintains and complies with the entity's own procedures for the destruction or disposal of records or documents containing the information listed in subsection A that is consistent with the requirements of this section shall be deemed to be in compliance with the destruction or disposal requirements of this section.

F. This section does not apply to any of the following:

1. An entity subject to title V of the Gramm Leach Bliley Act of 1999 (P.L. 106-102; 113 Stat. 1338; 15 United States Code sections 6801 through 6809).

2. Covered entities as defined under regulations implementing the health insurance portability and accountability act, 45 Code of Federal Regulations section 160.103 (1996).

3. An entity subject to the federal fair credit reporting act, 15 United States Code section 1681X.

G. For the purposes of this section, "Entity" includes a corporation, foreign corporation, not for profit corporation, profit and not for profit unincorporated association, nonprofit corporation, sole proprietorship, close corporation, corporation sole or limited liability company, a professional corporation, association or limited liability company, a business trust, estate, partnership, registered limited liability partnership, trust or joint venture, government, governmental subdivision or agency or any other legal or commercial entity."

House Bill 2470

This bill imposes a $100 civil penalty on a person or entity that violates the Social Security number confidentiality restrictions. It also specifies that the penalty applies to the restriction of putting a Social Security number on any card required for the individual to receive products or services provided by the person/entity. The bill also goes on to state that the penalty applies to those who knowingly or intentionally violate the restriction, and directs that the penalty apply to each violation. The bill further requires that monies received from civil penalties be deposited into the state General Fund.

House Bill 2382

This bill prohibits all agencies except the Arizona Department of Revenue and state, county, city, town, and political subdivision law enforcement agencies from using an individual's Social Security number in full. Those entities may utilize the full number except where otherwise prohibited. It allows state, county, city, town, and political subdivision agencies to use the last four numbers of an individual's Social Security number. It does allow an Arizona state agency to transmit an individual's Social Security number in full over the Internet in the administration of employee payroll, employee benefits, or workers compensation. The bill also allows the industrial commission to transmit an individual's Social Security number in full in the transmission of workers compensation claims to the interested parties by mail. The bill does prohibit government agencies from transmitting material that contains an individual's Social Security number and bank, savings and loan association, or credit union account numbers, except in the application, amendment, termination, or confirmation of the account or Social Security number.

Senate Bill 1219

This bill makes a heading change to Title 44, Chapter 9, Article 17, from confidentiality of Social Security numbers to confidentiality of personal identifying information. The bill stipulates that recorded documents and records that are made available on a public website must not contain more than five of an individual's Social Security numbers. It prohibits the documents/records from containing the following personal identifying information: (1) credit, charge, or debit card numbers, (2) retirement account numbers, and (3) savings, checking, or securities entitlement account numbers. The bill permits only the attorney general, county attorney, or both individuals to file a legal action for a violation of the provisions of this bill. The bill contains a provision to assess a $500 civil penalty for violations of the provisions. It does make an exception for the person or entity that transmits the document for recording purposes only. The bill does exempt a county agency from civil liability for any action relating to recorded information.

Senate Bill 1617

This bill relates to Financial Information Privacy Act.

Section 1. Title 6, Arizona Revised Statutes, is amended by adding chapter 16, to read:

CHAPTER 16

FINANCIAL INFORMATION PRIVACY ACT

ARTICLE 1. GENERAL PROVISIONS

6-1601. Definitions

In this chapter, unless the context otherwise requires:

1. "Account verification service" means any person that, for monetary fees or dues or on a cooperative nonprofit basis, regularly engages, in whole or in part, in the practice of either:

(a) Assembling information on the frequency and location of depository account openings or attempted openings by a customer or forced closings by a depository institution of accounts of a customer.

(b) Authenticating or validating social security numbers or addresses for the purpose of reporting to third parties for use in fraud prevention.

2. "Affiliate" or "affiliated company" means any company that controls, is controlled by or is under common control with another company as that term is used in 15 United States Code section 1681a(d).

3. "Credit reporting agency" means any person that, for monetary fees or dues or on a cooperative nonprofit basis, regularly engages in whole or in part in the practice of assembling or evaluating consumer credit information or other information on consumers for the purpose of reporting to third parties on the credit rating or creditworthiness of any consumer.

4. "Customer" means any person that deposits, borrows or invests with a financial institution, including a surety or a guarantor on a loan.

5. "Financial institution" means any institution, the business of which is engaging in financial activities as described in 12 United States Code section 1843(k), that does business in this state.

6. "Mercantile agency" means any person that, for monetary fees or dues or on a cooperative nonprofit basis, regularly engages in whole or in part in the practice of assembling or evaluating business credit information or other information on businesses for the purpose of reporting to third parties on the credit rating or creditworthiness of any business.

7. "Nonaffiliated party" means any person that is not an affiliate of the financial institution.

8. "Personal financial information" means information that is not widely available to the general public and that is an original or copy of information derived from any of the following:

(a) A document that grants signature authority over a deposit or share account.

(b) A statement, ledger card or other record of a deposit or share account that shows transactions in or with respect to that deposit or account.

(c) A check, clear draft or money order that is drawn on a financial institution or issued and payable by or through a financial institution.

(d) Any item, other than an institutional or periodic charge, that is made under an agreement between a financial institution and another person's deposit or share account.

(e) Any information that relates to a loan account or an application for a loan.

(f) Evidence of a transaction conducted by electronic or telephonic means.

6-1602. Personal financial information protected; opt in consent

A. Except as provided in section 6-1603, a financial institution shall not sell, share, transfer or otherwise disclose personal financial information to or with any nonaffiliated party without the explicit prior consent of the customer to whom the nonpublic personal information relates. This may be called "opt in" consent.

B. Any person that receives personal financial information from a financial institution shall not disclose this information to any other person, unless the disclosure would be lawful if made directly to the other person by the financial institution.

C. The superintendent shall direct the size, typesize and wording of an opt in consent form.

6-1603. Exceptions to disclosure prohibition

The prohibitions prescribed in section 6-1602 do not apply to:

1. The disclosure of information to the customer after verification of the customer's identity.

2. Disclosure explicitly authorized by the customer and limited to the scope and purpose authorized.

3. The disclosure of information to agencies of this state or any political subdivision of this state that is authorized by state law.

4. The disclosure of information pursuant to a lawful subpoena or court order.

5. The preparation, examination, handling or maintenance of financial records by any officer, employee or agent of a financial institution that has custody of the records.

6. The examination of financial records by a certified public accountant while engaged by the financial institution to perform an independent audit.

7. The disclosure of information to a collection agency or its employees or agents or to any person engaged by the financial institution to assist in recovering an amount owed to the financial institution, if the disclosure is made in the furtherance of recovering that amount.

8. The examination of financial records by, or the disclosure of financial records to, any officer, employee or agent of a regulatory agency for use only in the exercise of that person's duties as an officer, employee or agent.

9. The publication of information derived from financial records if the information cannot be identified to any particular customer, deposit or account.

10. The making of reports, disclosures or returns required by federal or state law.

11. The disclosure of any information permitted to be disclosed under the laws governing dishonor of negotiable instruments.

12. The exchange in the regular course of business of credit information between a financial institution and a credit reporting agency. The exchange shall be in compliance with the federal fair credit reporting act (15 United States Code sections 1681 through 1681x).

13. The exchange in the regular course of business of information between a financial institution and an account verification service. The exchange shall be in compliance with the federal fair credit reporting act (15 United States Code sections 1681 through 1681x).

14. The exchange in the regular course of business of information between a financial institution and a mercantile agency. The exchange shall be in compliance with the federal fair credit reporting act (15 United States Code sections 1681 through 1681x).

15. The exchange of loan information that specifically affects a sale, foreclosure or loan closing. The exchange shall be for the purpose of accomplishing the sale, foreclosure or loan closing.

16. Disclosure of suspected criminal activities to civil or criminal law enforcement authorities for use in the exercise of the authority's duties or the sharing of information within an industry network.

17. Disclosure in accordance with rules adopted by the superintendent to carry out the clear intent of this section.

6-1604. Enforcement

A. A person that negligently discloses or shares personal financial information in violation of this chapter shall be liable, irrespective of the amount of damages suffered by the customer as a result of that violation, for a civil penalty of not more than two thousand five hundred dollars per violation. However, if the disclosure or sharing results in the release of personal financial information of more than one individual, the total civil penalty awarded pursuant to this subsection shall not exceed five hundred thousand dollars.

B. A person that knowingly and willfully obtains, discloses, shares or uses nonpublic personal information in violation of this chapter shall be liable for a civil penalty of not more than two thousand five hundred dollars per individual violation, irrespective of the amount of damages suffered by the customer as a result of that violation.

C. If a violation of this chapter results in the taking the identify of another person or entity pursuant to section 13-2008 or the aggravated taking the identity of another person or entity pursuant to section 13-2009, the civil penalties set forth in this section shall be doubled.

D. The superintendent shall adopt rules necessary to enforce this section.

Sec. 2. Short title

Title 6, chapter 16, Arizona Revised Statutes, as added by this act, may be cited as the "Financial Information Privacy Act."

Sec. 3. Severability

If a provision of this act or its application to any person or circumstance is held invalid, the invalidity does not affect other provisions or applications of the act that can be given effect without the invalid provision or application, and to this end the provisions of this act are severable.

Sec. 4. Retroactivity

This act is effective retroactively to from and after June 30, 2007.

Chapter 4: Arkansas

The disclosure requirements of Arkansas Senate Bill 1167 make an exemption for data that was either encrypted or redacted. You will also note that Senate Bill 1167 has specific requirements for the destruction of sensitive data on printed paper. As a veteran myself, I was pleased to see that Arkansas House Bill 1345 specifically protects those who have served our country.

The Personal Information Privacy Act, Senate Bill S.B. 1167, provides notice to consumers of the disclosure of their personal information. It is the intent of the General Assembly to ensure that sensitive personal information about Arkansas residents is protected. To that end, the purpose of this subchapter is to encourage individuals, businesses, and state agencies that acquire, own, or license personal information about the citizens of the state of Arkansas to provide reasonable security for the information. It defines a breach of the security of the system to mean unauthorized acquisition of computerized data that compromises the security, confidentiality, or integrity of personal information maintained by a person or business. The legislation defines a business to include sole proprietorships, partnerships, corporations, and associations, however organized and whether or not they operate for a profit.

With regards to the nature of the data covered by this particular legislation, the following definitions are offered.

'Medical information' means any individually identifiable information, in electronic or physical form, regarding the individual's medical history or medical treatment or diagnosis by a health care professional.

'Personal information' means an individual's first name or first initial and his or her last name, in combination with any one (1) or more of the following data elements, when either the name or the data element is not encrypted or redacted;

1. **Social Security number,**
2. **driver's license number or**
3. **Arkansas identification card, account number, credit card number, or debit card number in combination with any required security code, access code, or password that would permit access to an individual's financial account, and medical information.**

The law goes on to state that a person or business shall take all reasonable steps to destroy or arrange for destruction of a customer's records within its custody or control containing personal information that is no longer to be retained by the person or business by shredding, erasing, or otherwise modifying the personal information in the records to make it unreadable or undecipherable through any means. A person or business that acquires, owns, or licenses personal information about an Arkansas resident shall implement and maintain reasonable security procedures and practices appropriate to the nature of the information to protect the personal information from unauthorized access, destruction, use, modification, or disclosure.

The law does have a disclosure component. It states that any person or business that acquires, owns, or licenses computerized data that includes personal information shall disclose any breach of the security of the system following discovery or notification of the breach of the security of the system to any resident of Arkansas whose unencrypted personal information was, or is reasonably believed to have been, acquired by an unauthorized person. The law stipulates that the disclosure shall be made in the most expedient time and manner possible and without unreasonable delay, consistent with the legitimate needs of law enforcement or any measures necessary to determine the scope of the breach and restore the reasonable integrity of the data system. The disclosure may be delayed if a law enforcement agency determines that the notification will impede a criminal investigation. It does require disclosure after the law enforcement agency determines it will not compromise the investigation.

A gift for you

Enjoy your gift.

Any person or business that maintains computerized data that includes personal information the person or business does not own shall notify the owner or licensee of any breach of security of the system immediately following discovery if the personal information was, or is reasonably believed to have been, acquired by an unauthorized person. In short, this means if you send personally identifiable data to a third party for some sort of processing or storage, and they have a data breach, they notify you, and you have to notify your customers.

The disclosure may be in the form of a written notice or an e-mail. The law does allow for substitute notice if the person or business can demonstrate that the cost of providing notice would exceed $250,000, the effected class of persons to be notified is greater than 500,000, or the person or business does not have sufficient contact information. Substitute disclosure notice shall consist of all of the following: e-mail notice when the person or business has an e-mail address for the subject persons, conspicuous posting of the notice on the website of the person or business if they have a website, and notification by a statewide media.

The law does provide for exemption stating that it does not apply to a person or business that is regulated by a state or federal law that provides greater protection to personal information and at least as thorough disclosure requirements of the security breach of personal information than that provided by this law. Arkansas Ark. Code Ann. §4-110-101 *et seq*. Violations of this act are punishable by the attorney general under the provision of Sections 4-88-101 through 4-88-115.

An act to protect veterans from identity theft, House Bill 1345, makes military service discharge records stored with the country record confidential.

Section 1. Arkansas Code §14-2-102, regarding records of military discharges, is amended to add additional subsections to read as follows:

(c)(1) A military service discharge record or DD Form 214 for a veteran discharged from service less than seventy (70) years

the current date and filed with the county recorder shall be confidential and may be viewed or reproduced only by:

(A) The veteran;

(B) The veteran's spouse or child;

(C) A person with a signed and notarized authorization from the veteran;

(D) A county or state veterans' service officer that is assisting the veteran or the veteran's family with a veteran's benefit application; or

(E) A person authorized by the court to view or copy the military service discharge record or DD Form 214 upon presentation of a court order.

(2) The county recorder shall record the names and addresses of all persons viewing or copying a military service discharge record or Form DD 214 under this subsection (c).

(3) No fee shall be charged for reproduction cost under this subsection (c).

(d)(1) A military service discharge record for a veteran discharged from service more than seventy (70) years from the current date and filed with the county recorder shall be public record.

(2) No fee shall be charged for reproduction cost under this subsection (d).

(e) The county recorder may maintain a record book that contains any of the following information about veterans for public record:

(A) Name;
(B) Rank;

(C) Unit of military service;
(D) Dates of military service;
(E) Medals conferred upon the veteran; and
(F) Awards conferred upon the veteran.

Section 2. Arkansas Code §25-19-105(b), regarding documents exempted from the Arkansas Freedom of Information Act, is amended to add an additional subdivision to read as follows:

(15) Military service discharge records or DD Form 214 for veterans discharged from service less than seventy (70) years from the current date and filed with the county recorder as provided under §14-2-102.

Website privacy policies, House Bill 2495, requires state and local governments and state agencies to incorporate machine-readable privacy polices into their website, and for other purposes, no later than July 1, 2004. The law goes on to say that the privacy statements shall include:

(A) A description of the data the unit of government or agency collects on its website and how the data will be used by the unit of government or agency;

(B) The type of data and the purposes for which data is shared with other entities;

(C) Whether the unit of government's or agency's data collecting and sharing practices are mandatory, or allow a browser to opt in or opt out of those practices; and

(D) An explanation that certain information collected by the governmental unit or agency is subject to disclosure under the Arkansas Freedom of Information Act of 1967, §25-19-105 et seq.; and a link to, or instructions for, locating the website's policy reference file, which shall identify the uniform resource locator for the website's policy statements and shall indicate those portions of the website and the website's cookies that are covered by

statement; and a link to the website's human-readable privacy policy.

House Bill 1106

This bill creates the Student Identity Protection Act and prohibits the use of a student's Social Security number as a student identification number.

SECTION 1. Arkansas Code §6-18-208 is amended to add an additional subsection to read as follows: (d)(1) Beginning with the 2005-2006 school year, no school or school district shall: (A) Use, display, release, or print a student's Social Security number or any part of the number on any report, identification card, identification badge, or any document that will be made available or released to the public, a student, or a student's parent or guardian without the express written consent of the student's parent, if the student is a minor, or the student, if the student is eighteen (18) years of age or older; or (B) Make a student's Social Security number available by reading the magnetic strip or other encoded information on the student's identification card.(2) This section shall not apply to educational records that are transferred to or between the Department of Education, other public schools or school districts, or other governmental agencies as allowed or required by federal law, state law, or State Board of Education rule.

House Bill 1117

This bill amends the petition form for an order of protection to eliminate any requirements for disclosure of Social Security numbers.

House Bill 2706

This bill amends Arkansas laws concerning the use of Social Security numbers in pleadings, motions, and decrees. It is now no longer required to provide the Social Security number of either the plaintiff or the defendant in such proceedings.

Senate Bill 335

SECTION 1. Arkansas Code Title 4, Chapter 86, Subchapter 1 is amended to add an additional section to read as follows: 4-86-107. Prohibiting the misappropriation of Social Security numbers.

(a) As used in this section:

(1) "Person" means an individual, corporation, partnership, organization, or any other entity; and

(2) "Publicly post" or "publicly display" means to intentionally communicate or otherwise make available to the general public.

(b) Except as provided in subsection (c) of this section, a person may not do any of the following:

(1) Publicly post or publicly display in any manner an individual's Social Security number;

(2) Print an individual's Social Security number on any card required for the individual to access products or services provided by the person or entity;

(3) Print an individual's Social Security number on a postcard or other mailer not requiring an envelope or in a manner in which the Social Security number is visible on the envelope or without the envelope being opened; or

(4) Require an individual to transmit his or her Social Security number over the Internet unless the connection is secure or the Social Security number is encrypted.

(c) This section does not prevent the collection, use, or release of a Social Security number as required or explicitly authorized by federal or state law, or pursuant to state or federal court rules.

(d) This section does not apply to an entity providing an electronic communications service to the public that is used by another person to violate this section unless the entity conspires with another person to violate this section or intentionally aids and abets another person in the violation of this section.

(e) This section shall not be asserted as a means to avoid compliance with an otherwise valid request for records pursuant to the Freedom of Information Act, §25-19-101 et seq.

(f) The Attorney General may:

(1) Bring suit against any person for violating the provisions of this section;

(2) Collect civil penalties of up to two hundred fifty dollars ($250) per violation along with attorney's fees and costs incurred in the investigation and prosecution of the matter; and

(3) Seek appropriate injunctive relief.

(g) This section shall become effective on January 1, 2007, and apply to acts occurring on or after January 1, 2007.

H.B. 2477

This bill enhances the protection of personal information. It requires notice to a consumer of an unauthorized breach of the consumer's personal information within the past five years.

Chapter 5: California

California Senate Bill 1386 is one of the nation's most frequently referenced data privacy laws. Many of the subsequent laws adopted by other states are patterned at least in part by this law. It is the first law I list in this chapter. However, before I go into the specifics of the legislation, I wanted to provide a brief synopsis of the implication of this law.

While the law is limited to the "personal data of California residents," few businesses have the ability or desire to protect customer data from one geographic region over another. It would also be very hard to tell customers in other states that you did not protect their data to the same level as those who lived in California. So there are a few policy areas to consider for compliance with this bill.

Data Encryption Policies

Perhaps the simplest way to deal with the bill's requirements is to have a policy of encrypting customer data while it is stored, since encrypted data does not require disclosure. However, this policy will likely not cover you unless you also have policies to encrypt data in transit as well.

Data Classification Policies

Your policies should clearly indicate the level of protection required for various information types. In this case, personal customer information would be highly sensitive data that requires a higher level of protection. Does your organization have data classification policies? If so, do they specifically mention these types of customer data? Many companies are wrestling with the task of trying to encrypt all of the data on their systems. This law does not require that, and being able to identify sensitive information as described by this and other like pieces of legislation will help determine what data does and does not need to be encrypted to be compliant.

Incident Response Policies and Procedures

Obviously, an organization should have existing incident response policies, including specifications about what forensic data should be saved and in what way. The incident response policies should include a minimum required timeframe for forensic or other analysis to help determine your organization's "reasonable" notification time. Overall, it is better to have your own documented procedures than to allow a courtroom to determine what "reasonable" was. Detailed logs and computer forensics will also help you determine what data may in fact have been compromised. A breach of a system does not necessarily mean all the data contained on it was stolen.

Incident Disclosure Policies

The best case scenario is to have specific incident disclosure policies that address the bill's requirements. These policies would include discussion of the types of breaches, the data potentially lost in the breaches, and the proper people and channels responsible for notification of outside agencies.

Personal Information: Privacy Senate Bill 1386

Existing law regulates the maintenance and dissemination of personal information by state agencies, as defined, and requires each agency to keep an accurate account of disclosures made pursuant to specified provisions. Existing law also requires a business, as defined, to take all reasonable steps to destroy a customer's records that contain personal information when the business will no longer retain those records. Existing law provides civil remedies for violations of these provisions. This bill, operative July 1, 2003, would require a state agency, or a person or business that conducts business in California, that owns or licenses computerized data that includes personal information, as defined, to disclose in specified ways any breach of the security of the data, as defined, to any resident of California whose unencrypted personal information was, or is reasonably believed to have been, acquired by an unauthorized person. The bill would permit the notifications required by its provisions to be delayed if a law enforcement agency determines it would impede a criminal investigation. The bill would require an agency, person, or business that maintains computerized data that includes personal information owned by another to notify the owner or licensee of the information of any breach of security of the data, as specified. The bill would state the intent of the legislature to preempt all local regulation of the subject matter of the bill. This bill would also make a statement of legislative findings and declarations regarding privacy and financial security.

THE PEOPLE OF THE STATE OF CALIFORNIA DO ENACT AS FOLLOWS:

SECTION 1. (a) The privacy and financial security of individuals is increasingly at risk due to the ever more widespread collection of personal information by both the private and public sector. (b) Credit card transactions, magazine subscriptions, telephone numbers, real estate records, automobile registrations, consumer surveys, warranty registrations, credit reports, and Internet websites are all sources of personal information and form the source material for identity thieves. (c) Identity theft is one of the fastest growing crimes committed in California. Criminals who steal personal information such as Social Security numbers use the information to open credit card accounts, write bad checks, buy cars, and commit other financial crimes with other people's identities. The Los Angeles County Sheriff's Department reports that the 1,932 identity theft cases it received in the year 2000 represented a 108 percent increase over the previous year's caseload. (d) Identity theft is costly to the marketplace and to consumers. (e) According to the Attorney General, victims of identity theft must act quickly to minimize the damage; therefore expeditious notification of possible misuse of a person's personal information is imperative. SEC. 2. Section 1798.29 is added to the Civil Code, to read: 1798.29. (a) Any agency that owns or licenses computerized data that includes personal information shall disclose any breach of the security of the system following discovery or notification of the breach in the security of the data to any resident of California whose unencrypted personal

information was, or is reasonably believed to have been, acquired by an unauthorized person. The disclosure shall be made in the most expedient time possible and without unreasonable delay, consistent with the legitimate needs of law enforcement, as provided in subdivision (c), or any measures necessary to determine the scope of the breach and restore the reasonable integrity of the data system. (b) Any agency that maintains computerized data that includes personal information that the agency does not own shall notify the owner or licensee of the information of any breach of the security of the data immediately following discovery, if the personal information was, or is reasonably believed to have been, acquired by an unauthorized person. (c) The notification required by this section may be delayed if a law enforcement agency determines that the notification will impede a criminal investigation. The notification required by this section shall be made after the law enforcement agency determines that it will not compromise the investigation. (d) For purposes of this section, "breach of the security of the system" means unauthorized acquisition of computerized data that compromises the security, confidentiality, or integrity of personal information maintained by the agency. Good faith acquisition of personal information by an employee or agent of the agency for the purposes of the agency is not a breach of the security of the system, provided that the personal information is not used or subject to further unauthorized disclosure. (e) For purposes of this section, "personal information" means an individual's first name or first initial and last name in combination with any one or more of the following data elements, when either the name or the data elements are not encrypted:

(1) Social Security number.

(2) Driver's license number or California Identification Card number.

(3) Account number, credit or debit card number, in combination with any required security code, access code, or password that would permit access to an individual's financial account. (f) For

purposes of this section, "personal information" does not include publicly available information that is lawfully made available to the general public from federal, state, or local government records.

(g) For purposes of this section, "notice" may be provided by one of the following methods:

(1) Written notice.

(2) Electronic notice, if the notice provided is consistent with the provisions regarding electronic records and signatures set forth in Section 7001 of Title 15 of the United States Code.

(3) Substitute notice, if the agency demonstrates that the cost of providing notice would exceed two hundred fifty thousand dollars ($250,000), or that the affected class of subject persons to be notified exceeds 500,000, or the agency does not have sufficient contact information. Substitute notice shall consist of all of the following:

(A) E-mail notice when the agency has an e-mail address for the subject persons.

(B) Conspicuous posting of the notice on the agency's website page, if the agency maintains one.

(C) Notification to major statewide media. (h) Notwithstanding subdivision (g), an agency that maintains its own notification procedures as part of an information security policy for the treatment of personal information and is otherwise consistent with the timing requirements of this part shall be deemed to be in compliance with the notification requirements of this section if it notifies subject persons in accordance with its policies in the event of a breach of security of the system. SEC. 3. Section 1798.82 of the Civil Code is amended and renumbered to read: (a) Any customer injured by a violation of this title may institute a civil action to recover damages, (b) Any business that violates, proposes to violate, or has violated this title may be enjoined. (c) The rights and remedies available under this section are cumulative to each other and to any other rights and remedies available under law. SEC. 4. Section 1798.82 is added to the Civil Code, to read: 1798.82.

(a) Any person or business that conducts business in California, and that owns or licenses computerized data that includes personal information, shall disclose any breach of the security of the system following discovery or notification of the breach in the security of the data to any resident of California whose unencrypted personal information was, or is reasonably believed to have been, acquired by an unauthorized person. The disclosure shall be made in the most expedient time possible and without unreasonable delay, consistent with the legitimate needs of law enforcement, as provided in subdivision (c), or any measures necessary to determine the scope of the breach and restore the reasonable integrity of the data system. (b) Any person or business that maintains computerized data that includes personal information that the person or business does not own shall notify the owner or licensee of the information of any breach of the security of the data immediately following discovery, if the personal information was, or is reasonably believed to have been, acquired by an unauthorized person. (c) The notification required by this section may be delayed if a law enforcement agency determines that the notification will impede a criminal investigation. The notification required by this section shall be made after the law enforcement agency determines that it will not compromise the investigation. (d) For purposes of this section, "breach of the security of the system" means unauthorized acquisition of computerized data that compromises the security, confidentiality, or integrity of personal information maintained by the person or business. Good faith acquisition of personal information by an employee or agent of the person or business for the purposes of the person or business is not a breach of the security of the system, provided that the personal information is not used or subject to further unauthorized disclosure. (e) For purposes of this section, "personal information" means an individual's first name or first initial and last name in combination with any one or more of the following data elements, when either the name or the data elements are not encrypted:

(1) Social Security number.

(2) Driver's license number or California Identification Card number.

(3) Account number, credit or debit card number, in combination with any required security code, access code, or password that would permit access to an individual's financial account. (f) For purposes of this section, "personal information" does not include publicly available information that is lawfully made available to the general public from federal, state, or local government records.

(g) For purposes of this section, "notice" may be provided by one of the following methods:

(1) Written notice.

(2) Electronic notice, if the notice provided is consistent with the provisions regarding electronic records and signatures set forth in Section 7001 of Title 15 of the United States Code.

(3) Substitute notice, if the person or business demonstrates that the cost of providing notice would exceed two hundred fifty thousand dollars ($250,000), or that the affected class of subject persons to be notified exceeds 500,000, or the person or business does not have sufficient contact information. Substitute notice shall consist of all of the following:

(A) E-mail notice when the person or business has an e-mail address for the subject persons.

(B) Conspicuous posting of the notice on the website page of the person or business, if the person or business maintains one.

(C) Notification to major statewide media. (h) Notwithstanding subdivision (g), a person or business that maintains its own notification procedures as part of an information security policy for the treatment of personal information and is otherwise consistent with the timing requirements of this part, shall be deemed to be in compliance with the notification requirements of this section if the person or business notifies subject persons in accordance with its policies in the event of a breach of security of the system.

SEC. 5. This act shall become operative on July 1, 2003.

SEC. 6. This act deals with subject matter that is of statewide concern, and it is the intent of the Legislature that this act supersede and preempt all rules, regulations, codes, statutes, or ordinances or all cities, counties, cities and counties, municipalities, and other local agencies regarding the matters expressly set forth in this act.

California SB 24

In August 2011, California passed Senate Bill 24, as an update to its 2003 data breach disclosure law SB 1386. Notable differences in SB 24 require that organizations that experience a data breach provide more details about the nature of the incident to the breach victims.

The law requires that the breach notification:

- Be written in plain language;
- Include the name as well as the contact information of the agency that suffered the breach;
- Provide a list of the personal information reasonable believed to have been included in the breach;
- State the date of the breach, the estimate date, or date range, when the breach occurred;
- Specify whether the notification was delayed as a result of a law enforcement investigation;
- Offer a general description of the incident;

- Provide toll-free telephone numbers and addresses of the major credit reporting agencies, if the breach exposed a Social Security number, a driver's license, or California identification card number;
- Outline steps individuals may take to protect themselves.

The text of SB 24 is below.

SB 24, Simitian. Personal information: privacy.

Existing law requires any agency, and any person or business conducting business in California, that owns or licenses computerized data that includes personal information, as defined, to disclose in specified ways, any breach of the security of the system or data, as defined, following discovery or notification of the security breach, to any California resident whose unencrypted personal information was, or is reasonably believed to have been, acquired by an unauthorized person.

This bill would require any agency, person, or business that is required to issue a security breach notification pursuant to existing law to fulfill certain additional requirements pertaining to the security breach notification, as specified. The bill would also require any agency, person, or business that is required to issue a security breach notification to more than 500 California residents pursuant to existing law to electronically submit a single sample copy of that security breach notification to the Attorney General, as specified.

This bill would provide that a covered entity under the federal Health Insurance Portability and Accountability Act of 1996 is deemed to have complied with these provisions, if it has complied with existing federal law, as specified. The bill would also incorporate additional changes made by the Governor's Reorganization Plan No. 1 of 2009.

THE PEOPLE OF THE STATE OF CALIFORNIA DO ENACT AS FOLLOWS:

SECTION 1. Section 1798.29 of the Civil Code is amended to read: 1798.29.

(a) Any agency that owns or licenses computerized data that includes personal information shall disclose any breach of the security of the system following discovery or notification of the breach in the security of the data to any resident of California whose unencrypted personal information was, or is reasonably believed to have been, acquired by an unauthorized person. The disclosure shall be made in the most expedient time possible and without unreasonable delay, consistent with the legitimate needs of law enforcement, as provided in subdivision (c), or any measures necessary to determine the scope of the breach and restore the reasonable integrity of the data system.

(b) Any agency that maintains computerized data that includes personal information that the agency does not own shall notify the owner or licensee of the information of any breach of the security of the data immediately following discovery, if the personal information was, or is reasonably believed to have been, acquired by an unauthorized person.

(c) The notification required by this section may be delayed if a law enforcement agency determines that the notification will impede a criminal investigation. The notification required by this section shall be made after the law enforcement agency determines that it will not compromise the investigation.

d) Any agency that is required to issue a security breach notification pursuant to this section shall meet all of the following requirements:

(1) The security breach notification shall be written in plain language.

(2) The security breach notification shall include, at a minimum, the following information:

(A) The name and contact information of the reporting agency subject to this section.

(B) A list of the types of personal information that were or are reasonably believed to have been the subject of a breach.

(C) If the information is possible to determine at the time the notice is provided, then any of the following:

(i) the date of the breach,

(ii) the estimated date of the breach, or

(iii) the date range within which the breach occurred. The notification shall also include the date of the notice.

(D) Whether the notification was delayed as a result of a law enforcement investigation, if that information is possible to determine at the time the notice is provided.

(E) A general description of the breach incident, if that information is possible to determine at the time the notice is provided.

(F) The toll-free telephone numbers and addresses of the major credit reporting agencies, if the breach exposed a social security number or a driver's license or California identification card number.

(3) At the discretion of the agency, the security breach notification may also include any of the following:

(A) Information about what the agency has done to protect individuals whose information has been breached.

(B) Advice on steps that the person whose information has been breached may take to protect himself or herself.

(C) Any agency that is required to issue a security breach notification pursuant to this section to more than 500 California residents as a result of a single breach of the security system shall electronically submit a single sample copy of that security breach notification, excluding any personally identifiable information, to the Attorney General. A single sample copy of a security breach notification shall not be deemed to be within subdivision (f) of Section 6254 of the Government Code.

(D) For purposes of this section, "breach of the security of the system" means unauthorized acquisition of computerized data that compromises the security, confidentiality, or integrity of personal information maintained by the agency. Good faith acquisition of personal information by an employee or agent of the agency for the purposes of the agency is not a breach of the security of the system, provided that the personal information is not used or subject to further unauthorized disclosure.

(E) For purposes of this section, "personal information" means an individual's first name or first initial and last name in combination with any one or more of the following data elements, when either the name or the data elements are not encrypted:

(1) Social security number.

(2) Driver's license number or California Identification Card number.

(3) Account number, credit or debit card number, in combination with any required security code, access code, or password that would permit access to an individual's financial account.

(4) Medical information.

(5) Health insurance information.

(H)

(1) For purposes of this section, "personal information" does not include publicly available information that is lawfully made available to the general public from federal, state, or local government records.

(2) For purposes of this section, "medical information" means any information regarding an individual's medical history, mental or physical condition, or medical treatment or diagnosis by a health care professional.

(3) For purposes of this section, "health insurance information" means an individual's health insurance policy number or subscriber

identification number, any unique identifier used by a health insurer to identify the individual, or any information in an individual's application and claims history, including any appeals records.

(i) For purposes of this section, "notice" may be provided by one of the following methods:

(1) Written notice.

(2) Electronic notice, if the notice provided is consistent with the provisions regarding electronic records and signatures set forth in Section 7001 of Title 15 of the United States Code.

(3) Substitute notice, if the agency demonstrates that the cost of providing notice would exceed two hundred fifty thousand dollars ($250,000), or that the affected class of subject persons to be notified exceeds 500,000, or the agency does not have sufficient contact information. Substitute notice shall consist of all of the following:

(A) E-mail notice when the agency has an e-mail address for the subject persons.

(B) Conspicuous posting of the notice on the agency's Internet website page, if the agency maintains one.

(C) Notification to major statewide media and the Office of Information Security within the California Technology Agency.

(j) Notwithstanding subdivision (i), an agency that maintains its own notification procedures as part of an information security policy for the treatment of personal information and is otherwise consistent with the timing requirements of this part shall be deemed to be in compliance with the notification requirements of this section if it notifies subject persons in accordance with its policies in the event of a breach of security of the system.

SEC. 2. Section 1798.82 of the Civil Code is amended to read:

1798.82. (a) Any person or business that conducts business in California, and that owns or licenses computerized data that includes personal information, shall disclose any breach of the security of the system following discovery or notification of the breach in the security of the data to any resident of California whose unencrypted personal information was, or is reasonably believed to have been, acquired by an unauthorized person. The disclosure shall be made in the most expedient time possible and without unreasonable delay, consistent with the legitimate needs of law enforcement, as provided in subdivision (c), or any measures necessary to determine the scope of the breach and restore the reasonable integrity of the data system.

(b) Any person or business that maintains computerized data that includes personal information that the person or business does not own shall notify the owner or licensee of the information of any breach of the security of the data immediately following discovery, if the personal information was, or is reasonably believed to have been, acquired by an unauthorized person.

(c) The notification required by this section may be delayed if a law enforcement agency determines that the notification will impede a criminal investigation. The notification required by this section shall be made after the law enforcement agency determines that it will not compromise the investigation.

(d) Any person or business that is required to issue a security breach notification pursuant to this section shall meet all of the following requirements:

(1) The security breach notification shall be written in plain language.

(2) The security breach notification shall include, at a minimum, the following information:

(A) The name and contact information of the reporting person or business subject to this section.

(B) A list of the types of personal information that were or are reasonably believed to have been the subject of a breach.

(C) If the information is possible to determine at the time the notice is provided, then any of the following:

(i) the date of the breach,

(ii) the estimated date of the breach, or

(iii) the date range within which the breach occurred. The notification shall also include the date of the notice.

(D) Whether notification was delayed as a result of a law enforcement investigation, if that information is possible to determine at the time the notice is provided.

(E) A general description of the breach incident, if that information is possible to determine at the time the notice is provided.

(F) The toll-free telephone numbers and addresses of the major credit reporting agencies if the breach exposed a social security number or a driver's license or California identification card number.

(3) At the discretion of the person or business, the security breach notification may also include any of the following:

(A) Information about what the person or business has done to protect individuals whose information has been breached.

(B) Advice on steps that the person whose information has been breached may take to protect himself or herself.

(e) A covered entity under the federal Health Insurance Portability and Accountability Act of 1996 (42 U.S.C. Sec. 1320d et seq.) will be deemed to have complied with the notice requirements in subdivision (d) if it has complied completely with Section 13402(f)of the federal Health Information Technology for Economic and Clinical Health Act (Public Law 111-5). However, nothing in this subdivision shall be construed to exempt a covered entity from any other provision of this section.

(f) Any person or business that is required to issue a security breach notification pursuant to this section to more than 500 California residents as a result of a single breach of the security system shall electronically submit a single sample copy of that security breach notification, excluding any personally identifiable information, to the Attorney General. A single sample copy of a security breach notification shall not be deemed to be within subdivision (f) of Section 6254 of the Government Code.

(g) For purposes of this section, "breach of the security of the system" means unauthorized acquisition of computerized data that compromises the security, confidentiality, or integrity of personal information maintained by the person or business. Good faith acquisition of personal information by an employee or agent of the person or business for the purposes of the person or business is not a breach of the security of the system, provided that the personal information is not used or subject to further unauthorized disclosure.

(h) For purposes of this section, "personal information" means an individual's first name or first initial and last name in combination with any one or more of the following data elements, when either the name or the data elements are not encrypted:

(1) Social security number.

(2) Driver's license number or California Identification Card number.

(3) Account number, credit or debit card number, in combination with any required security code, access code, or password that would permit access to an individual's financial account.

(4) Medical information.

(5) Health insurance information.

(i) (1) For purposes of this section, "personal information" does not include publicly available information that is lawfully made available to the general public from federal, state, or local government records.

(2) For purposes of this section, "medical information" means any information regarding an individual's medical history, mental or physical condition, or medical treatment or diagnosis by a health care professional.

(3) For purposes of this section, "health insurance information" means an individual's health insurance policy number or subscriber identification number, any unique identifier used by a health insurer to identify the individual, or any information in an individual's application and claims history, including any appeals records.

(j) For purposes of this section, "notice" may be provided by one of the following methods:

(1) Written notice.

(2) Electronic notice, if the notice provided is consistent with the provisions regarding electronic records and signatures set forth in Section 7001 of Title 15 of the United States Code.

(3) Substitute notice, if the person or business demonstrates that the cost of providing notice would exceed two hundred fifty thousand dollars ($250,000), or that the affected class of subject persons to be notified exceeds 500,000, or the person or business does not have sufficient contact information. Substitute notice shall consist of all of the following:

(A) E-mail notice when the person or business has an e-mail address for the subject persons.

(B) Conspicuous posting of the notice on the Internet website page of the person or business, if the person or business maintains one.

(C) Notification to major statewide media and the Office of Privacy Protection within the State and Consumer Services Agency.

(k) Notwithstanding subdivision (j), a person or business that maintains its own notification procedures as part of an information security policy for the treatment of personal information and is otherwise consistent with the timing requirements of this part, shall

be deemed to be in compliance with the notification requirements of this section if the person or business notifies subject persons in accordance with its policies in the event of a breach of security of the system.

Social Security Number Displayed During Mailing—Assembly Bill (A.B.) 763

This bill prohibits a Social Security number that is otherwise permitted to be mailed from being printed, in whole or in part, on a postcard or other mailer or visible on the envelope or without the envelope having been opened.

Information Security–Assembly Bill (A.B.) 1950

This has as its stated purpose to "encourage businesses that own or license personal information about Californians to provide reasonable security" for that information. The law requires any business, whether for profit or not, that owns or licenses personal information about a California resident to "implement and maintain reasonable security procedures and practices appropriate to the nature of the information." Further, businesses that disclose personal information to a non-affiliated third party must require by contract that the third party also "implement and maintain reasonable security procedures and practices appropriate to the nature of the information." Vendor information security concerns are normally addressed by representations and warranties, side agreements, due diligence, and/or other assurances and measures. The law provides virtually no guidance as to what procedures will be sufficient to satisfy the reasonableness standard, does not articulate what security procedures must be demanded from non-affiliated third parties, and is silent as to how security procedures and agreements must be documented.

Anti-Spam Cause of Action–Senate Bill 1457

California also created a state cause of action for sending commercial e-mail advertisements that are false or misleading. Because S.B 1457 limits itself to "false or misleading" e-mail, it is not preempted by the federal Controlling the Assault of Non-Solicited Pornography and Marketing Act of 2003 (CAN-SPAM Act), 15 U.S.C. §7707(b)(1). (The federal law expressly disclaims preemption of state laws that regulate "falsity or deception in any portion of a commercial electronic mail message.") Specifically, S.B. 1457 provides damages where an e-mail has a falsified, misleading, or forged header, uses a third party's domain name without permission, or contains a misleading subject line. The bill does not define "misleading," but it provides damages of up to $1,000 for each such e-mail received. S.B. 1457 also provides for reduced damages where the defendant has "established and implemented, with due care, practices and procedures reasonably designed" to prevent misleading e-mails.

Anti-Spyware Legislation: Consumer Protection against Computer Spyware Act, 1436

This act is designed to "protect California consumers from the use of spyware and malware." While the statute does not define either term, it forbids any person or entity from downloading software that causes a variety of problems, from the relatively innocuous action of changing a computer's Internet home page, to far more serious actions such as disabling anti-virus software, keystroke memorization, or stealing personal information from the computer. The statute requires "actual knowledge" or willful action on the part of the person or entity that is causing the spyware or malware to be installed. S.B. 1436 does not specifically provide a private right of action for those victimized by spyware or malware.

Social Security Number Display–Senate Bill 1618

This bill states that beginning on January 1, 2008, employers will no longer be permitted to display any more than the last four digits of an employee's Social Security number on the employee's paycheck.

Security Breach Disclosure–California Civil Code §1798.82

In the first law to impose liability for failing to disclose a breach of a corporate security system, California mandated disclosure of security breaches. Section 1798.82 requires that any time a California resident's unencrypted personal information was, or is reasonably believed to have been, acquired by an unauthorized third party, the relevant company must notify the individual of the breach. Businesses may inform the California consumer of the breach by mail, or if a business does not have a mailing address, notification can also be accomplished by e-mail or a conspicuous posting on a company website.

Online Privacy–California's Online Privacy Protection Act of 2003—Assembly Bill 68 Cal. Bus. & Prof. Code §§22575-22579

California law requires that operators of commercial websites that collect California consumers' personally identifiable information post a privacy policy on their website. As of July 1, 2004, the privacy policy must be conspicuously posted on the website, and California law mandates that the website operator adhere to its own policy. An operator is in violation for failure to post a policy within thirty days of being notified of non-compliance, or if the operator either knowingly and willfully or negligently and materially fails to comply with the provisions of its policy. The privacy policy must identify the categories of information collected, identify those third parties with whom the site operator shares the information, and notify the consumer of any process by which that individual can request changes to his or her information. Finally, the website operator must inform consumers of the effective date of the policy and explain how the consumer will be informed of any changes to the policy.

Disclosure of Consumer Information to Third Parties—"Shine the Light" Law–Senate Bill 27

This bill, which went into effect in California on January 1, 2005, requires a business with twenty or more employees that discloses a California consumer's personal information to third parties (including affiliates) for the purpose of direct marketing to provide the consumer with a means by which that consumer can learn, at no cost to the consumer, the parties to which the business discloses personal information for direct marketing purposes during the previous calendar year.

The provisions of S.B. 27 that relate to affiliates may be preempted by the federal Fair Credit Reporting Act, 15 U.S.C. §§1681-1681x (FCRA). As is discussed in the summary of S.B. below, the scope of the FCRA's preemption is still unclear. Additionally, there may be another provision of the FCRA, not litigated in the S.B. context, that preempts S.B. 27 with respect to its requirements concerning affiliate sharing. Within the definition of S.B. 27, this includes a consumer's name, address, telephone number, e-mail address, date of birth, height, weight, race, religion, occupation, political party affiliation, medical information, information about the consumer's children, types of products the consumer has purchased, Social Security number, bank account numbers, credit card numbers, and the payment history on the consumer's accounts. Under S.B. 27, businesses are permitted to receive inquiries from consumers by telephone, fax, or e-mail. Within thirty days of receiving a request, a business must, either in writing or by e-mail, inform the consumer regarding what types of information have been shared with third parties and the names and addresses of all the third parties that received personal information during the last calendar year for direct marketing purposes. In many instances, if a consumer requests the information through an alternate means, such as calling the wrong phone number or sending a request to the wrong address, the business must respond within a reasonable time, not to exceed 150 days. S.B. 27 allows an alternate means of compliance for those businesses that have already adopted and disclosed to the public a policy that requires opt-in consent for sharing information for direct marketing purposes, or provides an opportunity for the consumer to opt out. The business may simply inform the consumer of his or her right to prevent disclosure and then provide the consumer with a cost-free means to exercise that right.

Sharing of Financial Information–California Financial Information Privacy Act–Senate Bill: 1

This went into effect on July 1, 2004. It regulates the sharing of "non-public personal information" by financial institutions. S.B. 1 requires financial institutions to obtain the consumer's "opt-in" before sharing non-public personal information with third parties, although there are numerous exceptions to the opt-in requirement. S.B. 1 also requires that financial institutions that wish to share such information with an affiliate must:

(a) provide the California consumer notice that their information will be shared and

(b) provide the consumer with the ability to opt-out of that information sharing.

Unlike the federal Fair Credit Reporting Act (FCRA), S.B. 1 does not limit the opt-out for purposes of affiliate sharing to "consumer report" information, i.e., information relating to certain consumer characteristics that is collected, used, or expected to be used in connection with an eligibility determination for credit, insurance, employment, or other statutorily described matters. It is still an open question whether S.B. 1's affiliate sharing provisions are preempted by FCRA and its subsequent amendment by the Fair and Accurate Credit Transactions Act of 2003 (FACT Act).

The United States District Court for the Eastern District of California recently addressed the question of pre-emption in *American Bankers Association* v. *Lockyer*, available on California's Department of Financial Institution's website (http://www.dfi.ca.gov/SB1/063004decision.pdf). The American Bankers Association, the Financial Services Roundtable, and the Consumers Bankers Association brought the action seeking to prevent enforcement of the affiliate sharing provisions of S.B. 1. To the surprise of many practitioners, the District Court determined that FCRA does not preempt the affiliate sharing provisions of S.B. 1. Instead, the District Court determined that, although the plain language of FCRA suggests otherwise, Congress did not intend to preempt those laws that did not specifically address the sharing of actual consumer reports. The opinion was quickly appealed on an expedited basis to the Ninth Circuit. The case was argued before a three-judge panel of Judges Alex Kozinski, Betty Binns Fletcher, and Jay S. Bybee on December 6, 2004. There are reasonable arguments in favor of reversing the District Court's opinion and an

opinion from the Ninth Circuit is expected some time in the early part of 2005. However, the provisions of S.B. 1 that govern information sharing with third parties clearly are not preempted. At the federal level, information sharing by a financial institution with a nonaffiliated third party is governed by the Gramm-Leach-Bliley Act. Unlike FCRA, the Gramm-Leach-Bliley Act expressly disclaims preemption of state laws that provide stronger limitations on third-party sharing than those provided by Gramm-Leach-Bliley. Thus, financial institutions that choose to share information about California consumers with third parties should obtain opt-in consent under S.B. 1, regardless of how the "affiliate" preemption appeal is decided.

The state of California also has a rather long list of laws pertaining to issues such as identity theft, the secure handling of sensitive information, as well as penalties for non-compliance. A synopsis of some of the most recent ones are below.

Crime Defined

Use of personal information for unlawful purposes is a misdemeanor/felony "wobbler." Requires notation of court record if an imposter is convicted in the victim's name. California Penal Code §530.5

Credit Report Can Be Corrected with a Police Report

If the victim submits a police report to a credit bureau listing the fraudulent accounts, the credit bureau must promptly block the information about those accounts and inform the credit grantors that the information has been removed. California Civil Code §1785.16(k)

Security Alert

States that a credit bureau must place a security alert within five business days of receipt of the alert from the consumer. California Civil Code §1785.11.1. Effective January 1, 2004, civil penalty of $2,500 plus attorneys' fees for failure to place the alert. California Civil Code §1785.11.1(k), SB 602

Any person who uses a credit report in connection with credit approval may not extend credit or complete a purchase, lease, or rental of goods or services, after notice of a security alert without taking reasonable steps to verify the consumer's identity, to ensure that the application is not the result of identity theft. If the consumer has specified a phone number in the security alert, the consumer should be contacted at that number. California Civil Code §1785.11.1, SB 25, effective July 1, 2004

Security Freeze

Credit bureau must enable consumer to establish a "freeze," prohibiting the credit bureau from giving a report to anyone without the consumer's consent. California Civil Code §§1785.11.2 (effective January 1, 2003). Effective January 1, 2004, a credit reporting agency cannot charge more than $10 to place or remove the freeze, or $12 to temporarily lift the freeze. California Civil Code §1785.11.2(m), SB 602

Monthly Free Credit Reports for Identity Theft Victims

An identity theft victim who provides the credit bureau with a copy of a police report is entitled to twelve free credit reports, one per month, in the twelve months from the date of the police report. California Civil Code §1785.15.3, effective July 1, 2003

Duty to Cooperate with Identity Theft Victims

Banks, credit unions, savings associations, trust companies, mobile radio services, utilities, and as of January 1, 2004, mail forwarding services and office or desk rental services, must provide on request of law enforcement or of an identity theft victim copies of applications, checks, account statements, and records of transactions initiated by an imposter. California Penal Code §530.8, AB 1772, On January 1, 2004, this duty is expanded to include the addition of a new user of an existing account, renewal of accounts, and other changes to existing accounts. California Penal Code §530.8, SB 602, SB 684

Credit Reporting Agency Must Match Information

Where a prospective user of a consumer report is a retail seller and intends to issue credit in person to a consumer who applied in person, credit reporting agency must match at least three categories of information. California Civil Code §1785.14(a)(1)

Creditor Must Verify a Change of Address on a Mailed Solicitation

In cases where credit is to be extended by mail pursuant to a mailed solicitation, requirement to mail the extension of credit to the same address as the solicitation unless the creditor verifies any address change by contacting the consumer. California Civil Code §1785.14(a)(3)

User of a Credit Report Must Verify That There Was No Identity Theft Where Address Is Mismatched

Establishes a requirement for the users of credit reports to verify requested extension of credit is not an instance of identity theft, where the address on the application does not match the address on the credit report. Civil Code §1785.20.3 06

Address Verification by Creditor

Credit issuer must verify address if both of the following occur: an application for credit shows a different address than the one on the pre-approved offer, and a request for an additional credit card comes within ten days of a request for a change of address. California Civil Code §1747.06

Truncation of Credit Card Number on Transaction Slip

No more than the last five digits of a credit card number may be printed on electronic receipts. California Civil Code §1747.09. Effective January 1, 2004

Author's Note: This is a perfect example of how some states only allow the last four digits of a credit card number to be printed on electronic receipts, while others allow five. For businesses with a multi-state presence, I would recommend using four. In addition to helping with compliance, it also negates the need to support two systems.

Contact Information Must Be Included in Credit Report

Credit report must contain names, addresses, and if provided, phone numbers for customer service, of those who furnished information from the credit report. California Civil Code §1785.10(c)

No Forwarding of Instant Loan Checks

Requirement that "instant loan checks" be mailed in envelope that does not indicate a negotiable instrument is enclosed and that is marked "do not forward."

California Financial Code §22342

Credit reporting agency must get certification of identification from retailer.

Credit reporting agency does not meet requirement to take reasonable steps to verify the identity of user of a credit report where the prospective user of a consumer report is a retail seller and intends to issue credit in person to a consumer who applied in person, unless the retail seller certifies in writing to the credit reporting agency that the seller instructs employees to inspect photo identification at the time of application. California Civil Code §1785.14(a)(2)

Right to Sue to Clear Your Name

Grants the right of identity theft victims to bring action or assert defense against anyone claiming a right to money or property in connection with a transaction procured through identity theft. California Civil Code §1798.93

Criminal Statute of Limitations

The statute of limitations begins to run when the crime is discovered. California Penal Code §803, AB 1105, effective January 1, 2004

Penalties for Trafficking in Personal Information

Every person who, with the intent to defraud, acquires, transfers, or retains possession of personal identifying information of another person, is guilty of a crime punishable by up to $1,000 and one year in county jail. California Penal Code §530.5

Local police department must take a victim's police report.

States that local police departments must take a police report even if crime is committed elsewhere. California Penal Code §530.6

Clearing Up Criminal Identity Theft

Judicial process for clearing your name - California Penal Code §530.6(b)

Data base of criminal identity theft victims - California Penal Code §530.7

California Attorney General ID Theft Hotline: (888) 880-0240

Established a streamlined process for showing identity error in criminal cases. California Penal Code §§853.5, 853.6, Vehicle Code §§40303, 40305, 40305.5, 40500, 40504, SB 752, effective January 1, 2004

Debt Collection

Creditor cannot sell a debt to a debt collector once the individual has reported to the credit bureau that the debt resulted from fraud. California Civil Code §1785.16.2

A victim of identity theft may seek an injunction against a creditor or debt collector who pursues payment from the victim of a debt incurred by a thief. California Civil Code §§1798.92-97

States that a debt collector must stop temporarily collecting a debt after written certification by the consumer that an identity thief incurred the debt. Collection may resume only if the collector makes a good faith determination that the information provided does not establish that the consumer does not owe the debt. California Civil Code §1788.18, AB 1294, effective January 1, 2004

Destruction of Customer Records: The "Shredding" Law

Businesses are required to take reasonable steps to destroy records containing personal information upon disposal of the records by shredding, erasing, or modifying the information to make it unreasonable. California Civil Code §§1798.80-82

Hacker Law: Disclosure of Computer Security Breaches

Requires business and government agencies to notify individuals when unencrypted personal information in the categories of Social Security number, driver's license number, account number, or credit or debit card number has been accessed in a computer security breach. California Civil Code §1798.29

Confidentiality of Social Security Numbers

California Civil Code §1798.85, phased in from July 2002 to July 2005. Timeline changed by SB 25

Individuals and commercial entities, and under a phase-in from January 1, 2004 to January 1, 2007, certain government entities, including public colleges and universities, <u>may not:</u>

1) **Publicly display or post SSNs**
2) **Print Social Security numbers on ID cards or badges**

3) **Require people to transmit Social Security numbers over the Internet unless the connection is secure or the number is encrypted**
4) **Require people to use the Social Security number to logon to the Internet without a password**
5) **Print Social Security numbers on mailed documents, unless required by state or federal law**
6) **Embed or encode a Social Security number on a card or document where it cannot otherwise be printed. This includes chips, magnetic technology and bar coding**
7) **Mail SSN where number visible without opening envelope California Civil Code §1798.85(a), AB 763, effective January 1, 2004.**

In addition, a Social Security Number which is part of a family court proceeding must be placed in a confidential portion of the court file. California Family Code §2024.5, SB 660, effective January 1, 2004.

Financial Privacy

Prohibits financial institutions from sharing or selling personally identifiable non-public information without obtaining a consumer's consent. The bill (SB1) requires affirmative consent for sharing with an unaffiliated third party, the opportunity to opt out of information sharing with a financial institution's affiliates that are in a different line of business. California Financial Code §§4050-4060, effective July 1, 2004

Credit Card Consumer May Not Be Required to Pay by Check

Prohibition on recording credit card number where consumer pays by negotiable instrument (check). California Civil Code §1725

Personal Info May Not Be Required to Use Credit Card

Person accepting credit card may not record personal information. California Civil Code §1748.8

Notice That Warranty Card Is Unnecessary

Requirement that "warranty" cards clearly and conspicuously disclose that the card is a product registration card and failure to complete and return the card does not affect warranty rights. Effective January 1, 2004. California Civil Code §1793.1

Swiping of Driver's Licenses

Restricts certain uses and retention of data encoded on driver's licenses. California Civil Code §1798.90.1, SB 602, effective January 1, 2004

Marketing Disclosure

A business that discloses a consumer's personal information to a third party for direct marketing purposes must give the customer, upon request, the recipients of that information and a description of the categories of the information disclosed. Financial institutions may be exempt. California Civil Code §1798.83, SB 27, effective January 1, 2005

Assembly Bill 782

This bill establishes procedures for keeping the location or identifying information about the assets and liabilities of the parties in a dissolution matter sealed. Requires a related Judicial Council form to be revised no later than July 1, 2005, in accordance with those procedures and would make other related changes. It repeals a provision that allows Social Security numbers to be kept in a confidential portion of the court files. The bill also authorizes a petitioner or respondent to redact Social Security numbers from pleadings, attachments, documents, or other material filed with the court, except as specified.

Senate Bill 1618

This bill requires an employer to furnish each employee with an accurate, itemized statement at the time of payment showing the last four digits of the employee's Social Security number.

Senate Bill 101

This bill clarifies existing law to require that an employer, by January 1, 2008, include on the itemized statement provided to an employee the last four digits of the employee's Social Security number or an existing employee identification number other than a Social Security number. Further clarifies existing law to require, by January 1, 2008, that the state, or any city, county, city and county, district, or any other governmental entity, if it furnishes its employees with a check, draft, or voucher paying the employee's wages, to use no more than the last four digits of the employee's Social Security number or to use an existing employee identification number other than the Social Security number on an itemized statement to accompany the check, draft, or voucher.

Senate Bill 158

This bill eliminates the requirement of the Social Security number from a person to designate power of attorney under the Uniform Statutory Form Power of Attorney Act.

Assembly Bill 372

This bill makes technical, non-substantive changes to provisions of existing law that allows an injured customer to institute a civil action to recover damages or for injunctive relief relating to existing law that requires businesses to destroy customer records, to implement and maintain reasonable security procedures and practices to protect personal information from unauthorized access, destruction, use, modification, or disclosure, and to make sure that third parties getting such information maintain procedures.

Assembly Bill 429

This bill prohibits an innkeeper from disseminating the personal information of a guest, as defined, to any third party, with specified exceptions.

Senate Bill 364

Existing California law requires any agency that owns or licenses computerized data that includes personal information, as defined, to disclose in specified ways, any breach of the security of the data, as defined, to any California state resident whose unencrypted personal information was, or is reasonably believed to have been, acquired by an unauthorized person. Existing state law allows an agency to provide that disclosure by substitute notice, as specified, if the agency demonstrates that the cost of disclosure would exceed $250,000, or that the affected class exceeds 500,000 persons, or that the agency does not have sufficient contact information. In addition to the other substitute notice provisions, this bill allows for substitute notice if the agency demonstrates that the cost of disclosure would exceed $100,000. The bill also repeals a duplicative provision of law.

Chapter 6: Colorado

Colorado's disclosure law, House Bill 1119, requires that an investigation be performed once it has been determined that there has been a breach. If upon that investigation it is believed that the stolen data has not been, and likely will not be, misused, then disclosure is not required. Now, an investigation to determine what data was lost and how the system(s) were breached is just good practice. It is the aspect of trying to determine that stolen data will not be misused and hence exempt the company from disclosure that I have my concerns with.

Notification of Security Breach–House Bill 1119

This bill requires an individual or a commercial entity that conducts business in Colorado and that owns or licenses computerized data that includes personal information to notify customers who are residents of Colorado of any breach of the security of the system following the discovery of a breach in the security of personal information of the Colorado resident whose unencrypted personal information was, or is reasonably believed to have been, acquired by an unauthorized person. Requires notice to be made in good faith, in the most expedient time possible, and without unreasonable delay, consistent with the legitimate needs of law enforcement and with any measures necessary to determine the scope of the breach and to restore the reasonable integrity of the computerized data system. Requires the notification to be either written or electronic unless the cost of the notice exceeds $250,000, the affected class exceeds 250,000 people, or there is insufficient contact information, in which case conspicuous Internet posting and notification to statewide media suffices. Allows the attorney general to file suit to enforce the act.

NOTE: This bill has been prepared for the signature of the appropriate legislative officers and the Governor. To determine whether the Governor has signed the bill or taken other action on it, please consult the legislative status sheet, the legislative history, or the Session Laws.

Be it enacted by the General Assembly of the State of Colorado:

SECTION 1. Part 7 of article 1 of title 6, Colorado Revised Statutes, is amended BY THE ADDITION OF A NEW SECTION to read:

6-1-716. Notification of security breach. (1) Definitions. AS USED IN THIS SECTION UNLESS THE CONTEXT OTHERWISE REQUIRES :(a) "BREACH OF THE SECURITY OF THE SYSTEM "MEANS THE UNAUTHORIZED ACQUISITION OF UNENCRYPTED COMPUTERIZED DATA THAT COMPROMISES THE SECURITY CONFIDENTIALITY, OR INTEGRITY OF PERSONAL INFORMATION MAINTAINED BY AN INDIVIDUAL OR A COMMERCIAL ENTITY GOOD FAITH ACQUISITION OF PERSONAL INFORMATION BY AN EMPLOYEE OR AGENT OF AN INDIVIDUAL OR COMMERCIAL ENTITY FOR THE PURPOSES OF THE INDIVIDUAL OR COMMERCIAL ENTITY IS NOT A BREACH OF THE SECURITY OF THE SYSTEM IF THE PERSONAL INFORMATION IS NOT USED FOR OR IS NOT SUBJECT TO FURTHER UNAUTHORIZED DISCLOSURE.

(b) "COMMERCIAL ENTITY" MEANS ANY PRIVATE LEGAL ENTITY, WHETHER FOR-PROFIT OR NOT-FOR -PROFIT.

(c) "NOTICE" MEANS:

(I) WRITTEN NOTICE TO THE POSTAL ADDRESS LISTED IN THE RECORDS OF THE INDIVIDUAL OR COMMERCIAL ENTITY;

(II) TELEPHONIC NOTICE;

(III) ELECTRONIC NOTICE, IFA PRIMARY MEANS OF COMMUNICATION BY THE INDIVIDUAL OR COMMERCIAL ENTITY WITH A COLORADO RESIDENT IS BY ELECTRONIC MEANS OR THE NOTICE PROVIDED IS CONSISTENT WITH THE PROVISIONS REGARDING

ELECTRONIC RECORDS AND SIGNATURES SET FORTH IN 15 U.S.C. SEC 7001 ET SEQ.; OR

(IV) SUBSTITUTE NOTICE, IF THE INDIVIDUAL OR THE COMMERCIAL ENTITY REQUIRED TO PROVIDE NOTICE DEMONSTRATES THAT THE COST OF PROVIDING NOTICE WILL EXCEED TWO HUNDRED FIFTY THOUSAND DOLLARS, THE AFFECTED CLASS OF PERSONS TO BE NOTIFIED EXCEEDS TWO HUNDRED FIFTY THOUSAND COLORADO RESIDENTS, OR THE INDIVIDUAL OR THE COMMERCIAL ENTITY DOES NOT HAVE SUFFICIENT CONTACT INFORMATION TO PROVIDE NOTICE SUBSTITUTE NOTICE CONSISTS OF ALL OF THE FOLLOWING:

(A) E-MAIL NOTICE IF THE INDIVIDUAL OR THE COMMERCIAL ENTITY HAS E-MAIL ADDRESSES FOR THE MEMBERS OF THE AFFECTED CLASS OF COLORADO RESIDENTS;

(B) CONSPICUOUS POSTING OF THE NOTICE ON THE WEBSITE PAGE OF THE INDIVIDUAL OR THE COMMERCIAL ENTITY IF THE INDIVIDUAL OR THE COMMERCIAL ENTITY MAINTAINS ONE; AND

(C) NOTIFICATION TO MAJOR STATEWIDE MEDIA.

(d) (I) "PERSONAL INFORMATION "MEANS A COLORADO RESIDENT'S FIRST NAME OR FIRST INITIAL AND LAST NAME IN COMBINATION WITH ANY ONE OR MORE OF THE FOLLOWING DATA ELEMENTS THAT RELATE TO THE RESIDENT, WHEN THE DATA ELEMENTS ARE NOT ENCRYPTED, REDACTED, OR SECURED BY ANY OTHER METHOD RENDERING THE NAME OR THE ELEMENT UNREADABLE OR UNUSABLE:

(A) SOCIAL SECURITY NUMBER;

(B) DRIVER'S LICENSE NUMBER OR IDENTIFICATION CARD NUMBER;

(C) ACCOUNT NUMBER OR CREDIT OR DEBIT CARD NUMBER, IN COMBINATION WITH ANY REQUIRED SECURITY CODE, ACCESS CODE, OR PASSWORD THAT WOULD PERMIT ACCESS TO A RESIDENT'S FINANCIAL ACCOUNT.

(II) "PERSONAL INFORMATION" DOES NOT INCLUDE PUBLICLY AVAILABLE INFORMATION THAT IS LAWFULLY MADE AVAILABLE TO THE GENERAL PUBLIC FROM FEDERAL, STATE , OR LOCAL GOVERNMENT RECORDS OR WIDELY DISTRIBUTED MEDIA.

(2) Disclosure of breach.

(a) AN INDIVIDUAL OR A COMMERCIAL ENTITY THAT CONDUCTS BUSINESS IN COLORADO AND THAT OWNS OR LICENSES COMPUTERIZED DATA THAT INCLUDES PERSONAL INFORMATION ABOUT A RESIDENT OF COLORADO SHALL, WHEN IT BECOMES AWARE OF A BREACH OF THE SECURITY OF THE SYSTEM, CONDUCT IN GOOD FAITH A PROMPT INVESTIGATION TO DETERMINE THE LIKELIHOOD THAT PERSONAL INFORMATION HAS BEEN OR WILL BE MISUSED THE INDIVIDUAL OR THE COMMERCIAL ENTITY SHALL GIVE NOTICE AS SOON AS POSSIBLE TO THE AFFECTED COLORADO RESIDENT UNLESS THE INVESTIGATION DETERMINES THAT THE MISUSE OF INFORMATION ABOUT A COLORADO RESIDENT HAS NOT OCCURRED AND IS NOT REASONABLY LIKELY TO OCCUR. NOTICE SHALL BE MADE IN THE MOST EXPEDIENT TIME POSSIBLE AND WITHOUT UNREASONABLE DELAY, CONSISTENT WITH THE LEGITIMATE NEEDS OF LAW ENFORCEMENT AND CONSISTENT WITH ANY MEASURES NECESSARY TO DETERMINE THE SCOPE OF

THE BREACH AND TO RESTORE THE REASONABLE INTEGRITY OF THE COMPUTERIZED DATA SYSTEM

(b) AN INDIVIDUAL OR A COMMERCIAL ENTITY THAT MAINTAINS COMPUTERIZED DATA THAT INCLUDES PERSONAL INFORMATION THAT THE INDIVIDUAL OR THE COMMERCIAL ENTITY DOES NOT OWN OR LICENSE SHALL GIVE NOTICE TO AND COOPERATE WITH THE OWNER OR LICENSEE OF THE INFORMATION OF ANY BREACH OF THE SECURITY OF THE SYSTEM IMMEDIATELY FOLLOWING DISCOVERY OF A BREACH, IF MISUSE OF PERSONAL INFORMATION ABOUT A COLORADO RESIDENT OCCURRED OR IS LIKELY TO OCCUR. COOPERATION INCLUDES SHARING WITH THE OWNER OR LICENSEE INFORMATION RELEVANT TO THE BREACH; EXCEPT THAT SUCH COOPERATION SHALL NOT BE DEEMED TO REQUIRE THE DISCLOSURE OF CONFIDENTIAL BUSINESS INFORMATION OR TRADE SECRETS.

(c) NOTICE REQUIRED BY THIS SECTION MAY BE DELAYED IF A LAW ENFORCEMENT AGENCY DETERMINES THAT THE NOTICE WILL IMPEDE A CRIMINAL INVESTIGATION AND THE LAW ENFORCEMENT AGENCY HAS NOTIFIED THE INDIVIDUAL OR COMMERCIAL ENTITY THAT CONDUCTS BUSINESS IN COLORADO NOT TO SEND NOTICE REQUIRED BY THIS SECTION. NOTICE REQUIRED BY THIS SECTION SHALL BE MADE IN GOOD FAITH, WITHOUT UNREASONABLE DELAY, AND AS SOON AS POSSIBLE AFTER THE LAW ENFORCEMENT AGENCY DETERMINES THAT NOTIFICATION WILL NO LONGER IMPEDE THE INVESTIGATION AND HAS NOTIFIED THE INDIVIDUAL OR COMMERCIAL ENTITY THAT CONDUCTS BUSINESS IN COLORADO THAT IT IS APPROPRIATE TO SEND THE NOTICE REQUIRED BY THIS SECTION.

(d) IF AN INDIVIDUAL OR COMMERCIAL ENTITY IS REQUIRED TO NOTIFY MORE THAN ONE THOUSAND COLORADO RESIDENTS OF A BREACH OF THE SECURITY OF THE SYSTEM PURSUANT TO THIS SECTION, THE INDIVIDUAL OR COMMERCIAL ENTITY SHALL ALSO NOTIFY, WITHOUT UNREASONABLE DELAY, ALL CONSUMER REPORTING AGENCIES THAT COMPILE AND MAINTAIN FILES ON CONSUMERS ON A NATIONWIDE BASIS, AS DEFINED BY 15 U.S.C. SEC. 1618a (p), OF THE ANTICIPATED DATE OF THE NOTIFICATION TO THE RESIDENTS AND THE APPROXIMATE NUMBER OF RESIDENTS WHO ARE TO BE NOTIFIED. NOTHING IN THIS PARAGRAPH

(d) SHALL BE CONSTRUED TO REQUIRE THE INDIVIDUAL OR COMMERCIAL ENTITY TO PROVIDE TO THE CONSUMER REPORTING AGENCY THE NAMES OR OTHER PERSONAL INFORMATION OF BREACH NOTICE RECIPIENTS. THIS PARAGRAPH

(d) SHALL NOT APPLY TO A PERSON WHO IS SUBJECT TO TITLE V OF THE FEDERAL "GRAMM-LEACH-BLILEY ACT", 15 U.S.C. SEC. 6801ET SEQ.

(3) Procedures deemed in compliance with notice requirements.

(a) UNDER THIS SECTION, AN INDIVIDUAL OR A COMMERCIAL ENTITY THAT MAINTAINS ITS OWN NOTIFICATION PROCEDURES AS PART OF AN INFORMATION SECURITY POLICY FOR THE TREATMENT OF PERSONAL INFORMATION AND WHOSE PROCEDURES ARE OTHERWISE CONSISTENT WITH THE TIMING REQUIREMENTS OF THIS SECTION SHALL BE DEEMED TO BE IN COMPLIANCE WITH THE NOTICE REQUIREMENTS OF THIS SECTION IF THE INDIVIDUAL OR THE COMMERCIAL ENTITY NOTIFIES AFFECTED COLORADO CUSTOMERS IN ACCORDANCE WITH ITS

POLICIES IN THE EVENT OF A BREACH OF SECURITY OF THE SYSTEM

(b) AN INDIVIDUAL OR A COMMERCIAL ENTITY THAT IS REGULATED BY STATE OR FEDERAL LAW AND THAT MAINTAINS PROCEDURES FOR A BREACH OF THE SECURITY OF THE SYSTEM PURSUANT TO THE LAWS, RULES, REGULATIONS, GUIDANCES, OR GUIDELINES ESTABLISHED BY ITS PRIMARY OR FUNCTIONAL STATE OR FEDERAL REGULATOR IS DEEMED TO BE IN COMPLIANCE WITH THIS SECTION

(4) Violations. THE ATTORNEY GENERAL MAY BRING AN ACTION IN LAW OR EQUITY TO ADDRESS VIOLATIONS OF THIS SECTION AND FOR OTHER RELIEF THAT MAY BE APPROPRIATE TO ENSURE COMPLIANCE WITH THIS SECTION OR TO RECOVER DIRECT ECONOMIC DAMAGES RESULTING FROM A VIOLATION, OR BOTH. THE PROVISIONS OF THIS SECTION ARE NOT EXCLUSIVE AND DO NOT RELIEVE AN INDIVIDUAL OR A COMMERCIAL ENTITY SUBJECT TO THIS SECTION FROM COMPLIANCE WITH ALL OTHER APPLICABLE PROVISIONS OF LAW.

SECTION 2. Effective date - applicability. This act shall take effect September 1, 2006, and shall apply to breaches of the security of the system, as defined in section 6-1-716 (1) (a), Colorado Revised Statutes, occurring on or after said date.

House Bill 1169

This bill requires the Colorado State Court administrator to convene a committee of interested parties, including representatives of the news media, family law attorneys, and the courts, to make recommendations concerning access to divorce records. Directs the committee to consider issues related to identity theft, protecting children, transparency in government, and open access to public information. Requires the state court administrator to report any committee recommendations to the legislative council no later than December 1, 2006.

Consumer and Commercial Transactions, House Bill 1272

This bill prohibits a person from recording a Social Security number or credit card number when accepting a check. Exempts checks written to provide payment on a credit card account or student loan. Clarifies that a person may ask for a credit card when cashing a check, but may not record more than the type and issuer of the card.

4-3-506. Recording Credit Card or Social Security Numbers Prohibited

When payment is made by check or other negotiable instrument, a personal shall not record or require the maker of the check to record a credit card number or Social Security number given as identification of proof of creditworthiness.

Concerning Public Employee Retirement Plans-Senate Bill 107

This bill requires specified personal financial information of participants and benefit recipients of the state deferred compensation plan and the public officials' and employees' defined contribution plan to be kept confidential. Approved April 1, 2004.

Subsequent sections of S.B. 107 read as follows:

24-52-106. Confidentiality of personal financial information. ALL INFORMATION CONTAINED IN RECORDS OF PARTICIPANTS, FORMER PARTICIPANTS, INACTIVE PARTICIPANTS, AND BENEFIT RECIPIENTS AND THEIR DEPENDENTS THAT SPECIFICALLY IDENTIFIES ANY FINANCIAL INFORMATION OF SUCH PERSONS SHALL BE KEPT CONFIDENTIAL BY THE COMMITTEE.

24-52-207. Confidentiality of personal financial information. ALL INFORMATION CONTAINED IN RECORDS OF PARTICIPANTS, FORMER PARTICIPANTS, INACTIVE PARTICIPANTS, AND BENEFIT RECIPIENTS AND THEIR DEPENDENTS THAT SPECIFICALLY IDENTIFIES ANY FINANCIAL INFORMATION OF SUCH PERSONS SHALL BE KEPT CONFIDENTIAL BY THE COMMITTEE.

House Bill 263

This bill states that unless required by federal law or mandated as a condition of the state receiving federal funds, prohibits the Division of Wildlife in the Department of Natural Resources from requiring submission of a license applicant's Social Security number.

House Bill 1311

This bill prohibits the display of a person's Social Security number on a license, pass, or certificate, issued by a public entity, unless it is necessary to further the purpose of the pass or required by state or federal law. It proscribes a public entity from requesting a person's Social Security number over the phone, via the Internet, or by mail unless it is required by federal law or is essential to the public entity's service. Requires public and private entities to develop a policy for disposal of documents containing personal identifying information. Considers a public entity that is compliant with the state archives act to have met its policy development obligation. Exempts trash haulers from having to verify that documents have been destroyed or properly disposed. Allows an insured to require that an insurance company not display the insured's Social Security number on the insured's insurance identification card or proof of insurance card. Requires the insurer to reissue the card without the Social Security number, if the insured makes the request. Prohibits an insurance company, after January 1, 2006, from issuing an insurance identification card or proof of insurance card displaying the insured's Social Security number. Makes it a Class 1 misdemeanor to possess another's personal identifying information with the intent to use the information, or to aid or permit another to use the information, to unlawfully gain a benefit or to injure or defraud another.

Senate Bill 62

This bill requires a school district to submit the name, date of birth, and Social Security number of each non-licensed person employed by the district from the human resource electronic data communications and reporting system to the Colorado Department of Education. Directs the department to create and maintain a database of the information. At the beginning of each semester, compels the school district to notify the department when a non-licensed employee no longer works for the school district. Directs the department to purge the database at least annually. Directs the department, beginning November 15, 2004, and by August 30 each year thereafter, to provide a list of the current employees of each school district to the Colorado Bureau of Investigation.

House Bill 1156

This bill prohibits any person or entity from:

1. Publicly posting or displaying in any manner an individual's Social Security number
2. Printing an individual's Social Security number on a card required for the individual to access products or services provided by the person or entity
3. Requiring an individual to transmit his or her Social Security number over the Internet, unless the connection is secure or the Social Security number is encrypted
4. Requiring an individual to use his or her Social Security number to access an Internet website, unless a password or unique personal identification number or other authentication device is also required to access the Internet website
5. Printing an individual's Social Security number on any materials that are mailed to the individual, unless state or federal law requires, permits, or authorizes the Social Security number to be on the document to be mailed.

Lists exceptions, including uses required, permitted, or authorized by state or federal law. Allows a preexisting, non-conforming use of a Social Security number to continue if all of the following conditions are met: the use of the Social Security number is continuous, and the person or entity provides the individual with an annual disclosure that informs the individual that he or she has the right to stop the non-conforming use of his or her Social Security number. Requires the person or entity to implement a written request by an individual to stop the non-conforming use within thirty days after the receipt of the request. Prohibits the person or entity from denying services to an individual because the individual makes such a written request. Includes a Social Security number in financial data that may not be inspected as part of a public record, unless disclosure is required, permitted, or authorized by state or federal law.

House Bill 1267

This bill removes the requirement that a child support obligor's Social Security number appear on child support notices.

Chapter 7: Connecticut

Connecticut's disclosure law, Senate Bill 650, has a provision requiring the consumer credit bureaus, such as Experian, TransUnion, and Equifax, to offer security freezes. This is an effective tool to combat identity theft. Notice is not required if the breached entity determines in consultation with federal, state, and local law enforcement agencies that the breach will not likely result in harm to the individuals.

An Act Requiring Consumer Credit Bureaus to Offer Security Freezes–Senate Bill 650

This bill requires notice of security breach by persons who conduct business in the state and have a breach of the security of unencrypted computerized data, electronic media, or electronic files containing personal information.

Be it enacted by the Senate and House of Representatives in General Assembly convened:

Section 1. (NEW) (*Effective January 1, 2006*) As used in this section and section 2 of this act:

(1) "Consumer" means any person who is utilizing or seeking credit for personal, family or household purposes;

(2) "Credit rating agency" means credit rating agency, as defined in section 36a-695 of the general statutes;

(3) "Credit report" means credit report, as defined in section 36a-695 of the general statutes;

(4) "Creditor" means creditor, as defined in section 36a-695 of the general statutes; and

(5) "Security freeze" means a notice placed in a consumer's credit report, at the request of the consumer, that prohibits the credit

rating agency from releasing the consumer's credit report or any information from it without the express authorization of the consumer.

Sec. 2. (NEW) (*Effective January 1, 2006*) (a) Any consumer may submit a written request, by certified mail or such other secure method as authorized by a credit rating agency, to a credit rating agency to place a security freeze on such consumer's credit report. Such credit rating agency shall place a security freeze on a consumer's credit report not later than five business days after receipt of such request. Not later than ten business days after placing a security freeze on a consumer's credit report, such credit rating agency shall send a written confirmation of such security freeze to such consumer that provides the consumer with a unique personal identification number or password to be used by the consumer when providing authorization for the release of such consumer's report to a third party or for a period of time.

(b) In the event such consumer wishes to authorize the disclosure of such consumer's credit report to a third party, or for a period of time, while such security freeze is in effect, such consumer shall contact such credit rating agency and provide: (1) Proper identification, (2) the unique personal identification number or password described in subsection (a) of this section, and (3) proper information regarding the third party who is to receive the credit report or the time period for which the credit report shall be available. Any credit rating agency that receives a request from a consumer pursuant to this section shall lift such security freeze not later than three business days after receipt of such request.

(c) Except for the temporary lifting of a security freeze as provided in subsection (b) of this section, any security freeze authorized pursuant to the provisions of this section shall remain in effect until such time as such consumer requests such security freeze to be removed. A credit rating agency shall remove such security freeze not later than three business days after receipt of such request provided such consumer provides proper identification to such credit rating agency and the unique personal identification number or password described in subsection (a) of this section at the time of such request for removal of the security freeze.

(d) Any credit rating agency may develop procedures to receive and process such request from a consumer to temporarily lift or remove a security freeze on a credit report pursuant to subsection (b) of this section. Such procedures, at a minimum, shall include, but not be limited to, the ability of a consumer to send such temporary lift or removal request by electronic mail, letter or facsimile.

(e) In the event that a third party requests access to a consumer's credit report that has such a security freeze in place and such third party request is made in connection with an application for credit or any other use and such consumer has not authorized the disclosure of such consumer's credit report to such third party, such third party may deem such credit application as incomplete.

(f) Any credit rating agency may refuse to implement or may remove such security freeze if such agency believes, in good faith, that: (1) The request for a security freeze was made as part of a fraud that the consumer participated in, had knowledge of, or that can be demonstrated by circumstantial evidence, or (2) the consumer credit report was frozen due to a material misrepresentation of fact by the consumer. In the event any such credit rating agency refuses to implement or remove a security freeze pursuant to this subsection, such credit rating agency shall promptly notify such consumer in writing of such refusal not later than five business days after such refusal or, in the case of a removal of a security freeze, prior to removing the freeze on the consumer's credit report.

(g) Nothing in this section shall be construed to prohibit disclosure of a consumer's credit report to: (1) A person, or the person's subsidiary, affiliate, agent or assignee with which the consumer has or, prior to assignment, had an account, contract or debtor-creditor relationship for the purpose of reviewing the account or collecting the financial obligation owing for the account, contract or debt; (2) a subsidiary, affiliate, agent, assignee or prospective assignee of a person to whom access has been granted under subsection (b) of this section for the purpose of facilitating the extension of credit or other permissible use; (3) any person acting pursuant to a court order, warrant or subpoena; (4) any person for the purpose of using such credit information to prescreen as provided by the federal Fair Credit Reporting Act; (5) any person for the sole purpose of providing a credit file monitoring subscription service to which the consumer has subscribed; (6) a credit rating agency for the sole purpose of providing a consumer with a copy of his or her credit report upon the consumer's request; or (7) a federal, state or local governmental entity, including a law enforcement agency, or court, or their agents or assignees pursuant to their statutory or regulatory duties. For purposes of this subsection, "reviewing the account" includes activities related to account maintenance, monitoring, credit line increases and account upgrades and enhancements.

(h) The following persons shall not be required to place a security freeze on a consumer's credit report, provided such persons shall be subject to any security freeze placed on a credit report by another credit rating agency: (1) A check services or fraud prevention services company that reports on incidents of fraud or issues authorizations for the purpose of approving or processing negotiable instruments, electronic fund transfers or similar methods of payment; (2) a deposit account information service company that issues reports regarding account closures due to fraud, substantial overdrafts, automated teller machine abuse, or similar information regarding a consumer to inquiring banks or other financial institutions for use only in reviewing a consumer request for a deposit account at the inquiring bank or financial institution; or (3) a credit rating agency that: (A) Acts only to resell credit information by assembling and merging information contained in a database of one or more credit reporting agencies; and (B) does not maintain a permanent database of credit information from which new credit reports are produced.

(i) A credit rating agency may charge a fee of not more than ten dollars to a consumer for each security freeze, removal of such freeze or temporary lift of such freeze for a period of time, and a fee of not more than twelve dollars for a temporary lift of such freeze for a specific party.

(j) An insurer, as defined in section 38a-1 of the general statutes, may deny an application for insurance if an applicant has placed a security freeze on such applicant's credit report and fails to authorize the disclosure of such applicant's credit report to such insurer pursuant to the provisions of subsection (b) of this section.

Sec. 3. (NEW) *(Effective January 1, 2006)* (a) For purposes of this section, "breach of security" means unauthorized access to or acquisition of electronic files, media, databases or computerized data containing personal information when access to the personal information has not been secured by encryption or by any other method or technology that renders the personal information unreadable or unusable; "personal information" means an individual's first name or first initial and last name in combination with any one, or more, of the following data: (1) Social Security number; (2) driver's license number or state identification card number; or (3) account number, credit or debit card number, in combination with any required security code, access code or password that would permit access to an individual's financial account. "Personal information" does not include publicly available information that is lawfully made available to the general public from federal, state or local government records or widely distributed media.

(b) Any person who conducts business in this state, and who, in the ordinary course of such person's business, owns, licenses or maintains computerized data that includes personal information, shall disclose any breach of security following the discovery of the breach to any resident of this state whose personal information was, or is reasonably believed to have been, accessed by an unauthorized person through such breach of security. Such disclosure shall be made without unreasonable delay, subject to the provisions of subsection (c) of this section and the completion of an investigation by such person to determine the nature and scope of the incident, to identify the individuals affected, or to restore the reasonable integrity of the data system. Such notification shall not be required if, after an appropriate investigation and consultation with relevant federal, state and local agencies responsible for law enforcement, the person reasonably determines that the breach will not likely result in harm to the individuals whose personal information has been acquired and accessed.

(c) Any person that maintains computerized data that includes personal information that the person does not own shall notify the owner or licensee of the information of any breach of the security of the data immediately following its discovery, if the personal information was, or is reasonably believed to have been accessed by an unauthorized person.

(d) Any notification required by this section shall be delayed for a reasonable period of time if a law enforcement agency determines that the notification will impede a criminal investigation and such law enforcement agency has made a request that the notification be delayed. Any such delayed notification shall be made after such law enforcement agency determines that notification will not compromise the criminal investigation and so notifies the person of such determination.

(e) Any notice required by the provisions of this section may be provided by one of the following methods: (1) Written notice; (2) telephone notice; (3) electronic notice, provided such notice is consistent with the provisions regarding electronic records and signatures set forth in 15 USC 7001; (4) substitute notice, provided such person demonstrates that the cost of providing notice in accordance with subdivision (1), (2) or (3) of this subsection would exceed two hundred fifty thousand dollars, that the affected class of subject persons to be notified exceeds five hundred thousand persons or the person does not have sufficient contact information.

Substitute notice shall consist of the following: (A) Electronic mail notice when the person, business or agency has an electronic mail address for the affected persons; (B) conspicuous posting of the notice on the website of the person, business or agency if the person maintains one; and (C) notification to major state-wide media, including newspapers, radio and television.

(f) Any person that maintains its own security breach procedures as part of an information security policy for the treatment of personal information and otherwise complies with the timing requirements of this section, shall be deemed to be in compliance with the security breach notification requirements of this section, provided such person notifies subject persons in accordance with such person's policies in the event of a breach of security. Any person that maintains such a security breach procedure pursuant to the rules, regulations, procedures or guidelines established by the primary or functional regulator, as defined in 15 USC 6809(4), shall be deemed to be in compliance with the security breach notification requirements of this section, provided such person notifies subject persons in accordance with the policies or the rules, regulations, procedures or guidelines established by the primary or functional regulator in the event of a breach of security of the system.

(g) Failure to comply with the requirements of this section shall constitute an unfair trade practice for purposes of section 42-110b of the general statutes and shall be enforced by the Attorney General.

An act concerning the confidentiality of insurance department information - Senate Bill 836

Requires the Insurance commissioner to maintain certain information as confidential relating to

1. investigations,
2. personal, financial or medical information,
3. information that would harm the reputation of any person or would affect the safety or soundness of any person whose

activities are subject to the regulation of the commissioner and disclosure would not be in the public interest.

An act concerning nondisclosure of private tenant information in a sale of public housing to a private entity – Substitute House Bill 6184

Be it enacted by the Senate and House of Representatives in General Assembly convened:

Section 1. (NEW) (*Effective from passage*)

1. No entity purchasing a housing project or a portion of a housing project from a housing authority shall disclose to the public the Social Security number or a bank account number of a tenant of said project that is contained in the tenant's lease agreement.

2. No housing authority may disclose to any private person, except a purchaser of a housing project owned by the authority, the Social Security number or bank account number of any tenant of said project without the permission of such tenant.

3. Any person who violates any provision of this section shall be fined not more than two hundred dollars.

An act preventing bank fraud and identity theft – Substitute House Bill 6831

No provision of sections 36a-41 to 36a-45, inclusive, shall be construed to prohibit:

(1) The preparation, examination, handling or maintenance of any financial records by any officer, employee or agent of a financial institution having custody of such records or the examination of such records by a certified public accountant engaged by the financial institution to perform an independent audit;

(2) the examination of any financial records by, or the furnishing of financial records by a financial institution to any official, employee or agent of a supervisory agency solely for use in the exercise of the duties of such official, employee or agent;

(3) the publication of data furnished from financial records relating to customers where such data does not contain information identifying any particular customer or account;

(4) the making of reports or returns required under the Internal Revenue Code of 1986, or any subsequent corresponding internal revenue code of the United States, as from time to time amended;

(5) disclosure of information permitted under the Uniform Commercial Code concerning the dishonor of any negotiable instrument;

(6) the exchange, in the regular course of business, of credit information between a financial institution and other financial institutions or commercial enterprises, directly or through a consumer reporting agency;

(7) disclosures to appropriate officials of federal, state or local governments upon suspected violations of the criminal law;

(8) disclosures pursuant to a search warrant issued by a judge of the Superior Court or a judge trial referee under the provisions of section 54-33a;

(9) disclosures concerning lawyers' clients' funds accounts made to the state-wide grievance committee pursuant to any rule adopted by the judges of the Superior Court;

(10) disclosures to the purported payee or to any purported holder of a check, draft, money order or other item, whether or not such check, draft, money order or other item has been accepted by such payee or holder as payment, or to any financial institution

purportedly involved in the collection process of a check, draft, money order or other item whether such check, draft, money order or other item would be paid if presented at the time of such disclosure;

(11) any disclosure made in connection with a financial institution's attempts to preserve its rights or determine its liabilities with regard to any funds transfer or any check, draft, money order or other item drawn by or upon it or handled by it for collection or otherwise;

(12) disclosures to the purported payee or to any purported holder of a check, draft, money order or other item, whether or not such check, draft, money order or other item has been accepted by such payee or holder as payment, or to any financial institution purportedly involved in the collection process of a check, draft, money order or other item whether such check, draft, money order or other item would be paid if presented at the time of such disclosure;

(13) any other disclosure required under applicable state or federal law or authorized to be made to any regulatory or law enforcement agency under applicable state or federal law;

(14) disclosures made to a broker-dealer or investment advisor that is engaged in a contractual networking arrangement with the financial institution making the disclosure, provided, it is clearly and conspicuously disclosed to the customer that the information may be communicated among such entities and the customer is given a reasonable opportunity, before the time that the information is initially communicated, to direct that such information not be communicated among such entities;

(15) disclosures made to a customer service representative who is employed by, or otherwise acts as an agent for, both the financial institution and a broker-dealer, or both the financial institution and

an investment advisor, where such broker-dealer or investment advisor is engaged in a contractual networking arrangement; [and]

(16) disclosures to other employees or agents of a broker-dealer or investment advisor engaged in a contractual networking arrangement in order to comply, or verify compliance, with applicable laws governing the activities of the financial institution, broker-dealer or investment advisor;

(17) any disclosure of information to an information network for fraud prevention accessed by financial institutions and law enforcement authorities for the exclusive purpose of detecting or protecting against actual or potential fraud or unauthorized transactions; and

(18) disclosures made to a victim of identity theft pursuant to the federal Fair Credit Reporting Act, 15 USC 1681g.

For purposes of this section, the phrase "contractual networking arrangement" means a contractual arrangement between a financial institution and a broker-dealer registered in this state or an investment advisor registered in this state or that has filed a notice of exemption pursuant to subsection (e) of section 36b-6, where the broker-dealer or investment advisor offers securities related services to the customers of the financial institution.

An Act Concerning Electronic Mail Message Phishing–Substitute Senate Bill 566 Public Act 06-50

This act states that no person shall, by means of an Internet web page, electronic mail message, or otherwise using the Internet, solicit, request, or take any action to induce another person to provide identifying information by representing that the person, either directly or by implication, is an online Internet business, without the authority or approval of such online Internet business.

House Bill 5184

This bill concerns the non-disclosure of private tenant information in a sale of public housing to a private entity, including the tenant's Social Security number and bank account number.

Chapter 8: Delaware

Like many states, Delaware has a law that requires disclosure to be made if the personal information of any of its residents is acquired, or reasonably believed to have been acquired, by unauthorized personnel. The law also makes an exception to the disclosure requirement if the data was encrypted. In the synopsis of the bill as provided by the official website for the state of Delaware, the law specifically makes reference to the California law. For many states, California Senate Bill 1386 was the model their data privacy laws were patterned after.

An Act to Amend Title 6 of the Delaware Code Relating to Computer Security Breaches–House Bill 116

This bill will help ensure that personal information about Delaware residents is protected by encouraging data brokers to provide reasonable security for personal information.

This bill borrows from a similar California statute that requires companies to notify residents in the event of a security breach involving personal financial data. California is the only state so far with such a law. Pennsylvania is considering a computer security breach law.

This bill requires an individual or a commercial entity that conducts business in Delaware and that owns or licenses computerized data that includes personal information to notify a resident of Delaware of any breach of the security of the system immediately following the discovery of a breach in the security of personal information of the Delaware resident whose unencrypted personal information was, or is reasonably believed to have been, acquired by an unauthorized person. Notification must be made in good faith, in the most expedient time possible, and without unreasonable delay, consistent with the legitimate needs of law enforcement and with any measures necessary to determine the scope of the breach and to restore the reasonable integrity of the computerized data system.

Alternative notification procedures are provided in §12B-103. In a civil action to recover damages (for example, losses due to identity theft), the award is triple the amount of actual damages plus reasonable attorney fees.

A violation of this Act falls under the enforcement duties and powers of the Consumer Protection Division of the Department of Justice, which may bring an action in law or equity to address violations of the Act and other appropriate relief. The provisions of this Act do not nullify or impair any common law or statutory right that a person may have in regard to violations under the Act.

"Section 1. Amend Title 6 of the Delaware Code by adding thereto a new chapter to read:

§12B-101. Definitions.

For purposes of this chapter:

(1) 'breach of the security of the system' means the unauthorized acquisition of unencrypted computerized data that compromises the security, confidentiality, or integrity of personal information maintained by an individual or a commercial entity. Good faith acquisition of personal information by an employee or agent of an individual or a commercial entity for the purposes of the individual or the commercial entity is not a breach of the security of the system, provided that the personal information is not used or subject to further unauthorized disclosure;

(2) 'commercial entity' includes corporations, business trusts, estates, trusts, partnerships, limited partnerships, limited liability partnerships, limited liability companies, associations, organizations, joint ventures, governments, governmental subdivisions, agencies, or instrumentalities, or any other legal entity, whether for profit or not-for-profit;

(3) 'personal information' means a Delaware resident's first name or first initial and last name in combination with any one or more of the following data elements that relate to the resident, when either the name or the data elements are not encrypted:

(i) Social Security number;

(ii) driver's license number or Delaware Identification Card number; or

(iii) account number, or credit or debit card number, in combination with any required security code, access code, or password that would permit access to a resident's financial account.

The term 'personal information' does not include publicly available information that is lawfully made available to the general public from federal, State, or local government records;

(4) 'notice' means:

(i) written notice;

(ii) telephonic notice, but only if actual telephonic notice is given directly to the affected Delaware resident. Leaving a voice mail message or leaving a message with a third party does not constitute 'notice' under this chapter;

(iii) electronic notice, if the notice provided is consistent with the provisions regarding electronic records and signatures set forth in §7001 of Title 15 of the United States Code; or

(iv) substitute notice, if the individual or the commercial entity required to provide notice demonstrates that the cost of providing notice will exceed $250,000, or that the affected class of Delaware residents to be notified exceeds 500,000 residents, or that the individual or the commercial entity does not have sufficient contact information to provide notice. Substitute notice consists of all of the following:

a. e-mail notice if the individual or the commercial entity has e-mail addresses for the members of the affected class of Delaware residents; and

b. conspicuous posting of the notice on the website page of the individual or the commercial entity if the individual or the commercial entity maintains one; and

c. notice to major statewide media.

§12B-102. Disclosure of breach of security of computerized personal information by an individual or a commercial entity.

(a) An individual or a commercial entity that conducts business in Delaware and that owns or licenses computerized data that includes personal information about a resident of Delaware shall, when it becomes aware of a breach of the security of the system, conduct in good faith a reasonable and prompt investigation to determine the likelihood that personal information has been or will be misused. If the investigation determines that the misuse of information about a Delaware resident has occurred or is reasonably likely to occur, the individual or the commercial entity shall give notice as soon as possible to the affected Delaware resident. Notice must be made in the most expedient time possible and without unreasonable delay, consistent with the legitimate needs of law enforcement and consistent with any measures necessary to determine the scope of the breach and to restore the reasonable integrity of the computerized data system.

(b) An individual or a commercial entity that maintains computerized data that includes personal information that the individual or the commercial entity does not own or license shall give notice to and cooperate with the owner or licensee of the information of any breach of the security of the system immediately

following discovery of a breach, if misuse of personal information about a Delaware resident occurred or is reasonably likely to occur. Cooperation includes sharing with the owner or licensee information relevant to the breach.

(c) Notice required by this chapter may be delayed if a law enforcement agency determines that the notice will impede a criminal investigation. Notice required by this chapter must be made in good faith, without unreasonable delay and as soon as possible after the law enforcement agency determines that notification will no longer impede the investigation.

(d) An individual or a commercial entity that is required to give notice of a breach in the security of personal information pursuant to this chapter shall also promptly provide written notification of the nature and circumstances of the breach to the Consumer Protection Division of the Department of Justice.

§12B-103. Procedures deemed in compliance with notice requirements.

Pursuant to the enforcement duties and powers of the Consumer Protection Division of the Department of Justice under 29 Del. C. §2517, the Attorney General may bring an action in law or equity to address violations of this chapter and for other relief that may be appropriate to ensure proper compliance with this chapter or to recover damages, or both. The provisions of this chapter are not exclusive and do not relieve an individual or a commercial entity subject to this chapter from compliance with all other applicable provisions of law."

An Act to Amend Titles 11 and 29 of the Delaware Code Relating to Credit and Debit Card Receipts-Senate Bill 11

This act requires electronically printed receipts to contain no more than five digits of the account number. Credit and debit card takers in business before January 1, 2004, have until January 1, 2005, to comply. It applies immediately to all those who begin to accept credit or debit cards on or after January 1, 2004. The penalty is an unclassified misdemeanor (up to thirty days and up to a $575 fine), and the Consumer Protection Unit of the Attorney General's Office is given the authority to bring actions to enforce this act.

House Bill 265

This bill ensures that Social Security numbers provided by hunting, fishing, and trapping license holders would not be released to the public. Senate Bill No. 9, passed by the 142nd General Assembly and signed into law by the governor, mandated that license holders disclose their Social Security number in compliance with federal legislation associated with child support laws that deny licenses to persons delinquent in support payments.

Senate Bill 138

This bill forbids health insurers from using Social Security numbers as identification numbers on their health insurance cards.

Senate Bill 160

This bill brings the State of Delaware Code into compliance with the Intelligence Reform and Terrorism Prevention Act of 2004 by prohibiting an individual's Social Security number from being displayed on the driver's license or identification card document in either printed form or electronically recorded in the bar code.

Chapter 9: Florida

Like many laws, Florida has a law that requires disclosure if personally identifiable information is accessed by an unauthorized individual, its House Bill 481. Similar to the laws of the other states, it provides an exception if the data was encrypted. The law also provides an exception to the disclosure requirement if, upon meeting certain investigatory guidelines, it can be reasonably determined that the breach will not likely result in hardship to the individuals whose personal information has been acquired and accessed.

Unlawful Use of Personal Identification Information: House Bill 481

This bill includes other information within the definition of the term "personal identification information"; defines the term "counterfeit or fictitious personal identification information"; revises criminal penalties relating to the offense of fraudulently using, or possessing with intent to fraudulently use, personal identification information; provides minimum mandatory terms of imprisonment; creates the offenses of willfully and fraudulently using, or possessing with intent to fraudulently use, personal identification information concerning a deceased individual; provides criminal penalties; provides for minimum mandatory terms of imprisonment; creates the offense of willfully and fraudulently creating or using, or possessing with intent to fraudulently use, counterfeit or fictitious personal identification information; provides criminal penalties; provides for reclassification of offenses; provides for reduction or suspension of sentences; requires business persons maintaining computerized data that includes personal information to provide notice of breaches of system security; provides for administrative fines; authorizes delays of such disclosures; provides for alternative notice methods; provides definitions; specifies conditions of compliance for persons maintaining alternative notification procedures; specifies conditions under which notification is not required; provides an administrative fine for failing to document failures to comply; provides requirements for such documentation and maintenance of documentation; authorizes the Department of

Legal Affairs to institute proceedings to assess and collect fines; requires notification of consumer reporting agencies of breaches of system security.

For the purposes of this bill, the term 'personal information' means an

- Individual's first name, first initial and last, or any middle name and last name, in combination with any one or more of the following data elements when the data elements are not encrypted:

    - Social Security number
    - Driver's license number or Florida Identification Card number
    - Account number, credit card number, or debit card number, in combination with

        - Any required security code
        - Access code – or
        - Password

      that would permit access to an individual's financial account.

For the purposes of this bill, notice may be provided by one of the following methods:

- Written notice;
- Electronic notice, if the notice provided is consistent with the provisions regards electronic records and signatures set for in 15 U.S.C. s. 7001; or
- Substitute notice, if the person demonstrates that the cost of providing notice would exceed $250,000, the affected class of subject persons to be notified exceeds 500,000, or the person does not have sufficient contact information. Substitute notice shall consist of all of the following:

- Electronic mail or email notice when the person has an electronic or email address for the subject persons.
- Conspicuous posting of the notice on the web page of the person, if the person maintains a web page.
- Notification to major statewide media.

There is an exception to the disclosure requirement under the following circumstances.

(10) (a): Notwithstanding subsection (2), notification is not required if, after an appropriate investigation and after consultation with relevant federal, state, and local agencies responsible for law enforcement, the person reasonably determines that the breach has not and will not likely result in hard to the individuals whose personal information has been acquired and access. Such determination must be documented in writing and the documentation must be maintained for 5 years.

Any person that is required to document a failure to notify affected persons who fail to document the failure as required in this subsection or who, if documentation was created, fails to maintain the documentation for the full 5 years as required in this subsection is liable for an administrative fine in the amount up to $50,000 for such failure.

The administrative sanctions outline above shall not apply in the case of personal information in the custody of any governmental agency or subdivision, unless that governmental agency or subdivision has entered into a contract with a contactor or third-party administrator to provide governmental services. In such case the contractor or third-party administrator shall be a person to whom the administrative sanction outline above would apply, although such contractor or third-party administrator found in violation of the documentation and maintenance of documentation requirements in this subsection would not have an action for contribution or set-off available against employing agency or subdivision.

An act relating to a review under the Open Government Sunset Review Act; Senate Bill No. 512 amending s. 119.0712, F.S.,

Relating to an exemption from public records requirements for personal identifying information, contained in certain records held by the Department of Health which relate to an individual's personal health or eligibility for health services; excluding bank account numbers and debit, charge, and credit card numbers contained in such records from the exemption; saving the exemption from repeal under the Open Government Sunset Review Act; deleting provisions that provide for the repeal of the exemption; providing an effective date.

Be It Enacted by the Legislature of the State of Florida: Section 1. Subsection (1) of section 119.0712, Florida Statutes, is amended to read: 119.0712 Executive branch agency-specific exemptions from inspection or copying of public records.—

(1) DEPARTMENT OF HEALTH.

All personal identifying information; contained in records relating to an individual's personal health or eligibility for health-related services held by the Department of Health are confidential and exempt from s. 119.07(1) and s. 24(a), Art. I of the State Constitution, except as otherwise provided in this subsection. Information made confidential and exempt by this subsection shall be disclosed:

(a) With the express written consent of the individual or the individual's legally authorized representative.

(b) In a medical emergency, but only to the extent necessary to protect the health or life of the individual.

(c) By court order upon a showing of good cause.

(d) To a health research entity, if the entity seeks the records or data pursuant to a research protocol approved by the department, maintains the records or data in accordance with the approved protocol, and enters into a purchase and data-use agreement with the department, the fee provisions of which are consistent with s. 119.07(4). The department may deny a request for records or data if the protocol provides for intrusive follow-back contacts, has not been approved by a human studies institutional review board, does not plan for the destruction of confidential records after the research is concluded, is administratively burdensome, or does not have scientific merit. The agreement must restrict the release of any information that would permit the identification of persons, limit the use of records or data to the approved research protocol, and prohibit any other use of the

An act relating to a public records exemption for the Florida Kidcare program – House Bill 1031

Expands exemption for identifying information of applicants to Florida Kidcare program to provide that any information identifying program applicant or enrollee held by Agency for Health Care Administration, Children and Family Department, Health Department, and Florida Healthy Kids Corporation is confidential and exempt; provides for disclosure of such information to governmental entities under certain circumstances.

An act relating to a public records exemption for the Florida Kidcare program; amending s. 409.821, F.S.; expanding the exemption for identifying information of applicants to the Florida Kidcare program to provide that any information identifying a program applicant or enrollee held by the Agency for Health Care Administration, the Department of Children and Family Services, the Department of Health, and the Florida Healthy Kids Corporation is confidential and exempt; providing for disclosure of such information to governmental entities under certain circumstances; providing a penalty for unlawful disclosure of such information; adding clarifying language; making editorial changes;

providing for retroactive application; removing the October 2, 2003, repeal of the exemption scheduled pursuant to the Open Government Sunset Review Act of 1995; providing for future review and repeal of the exemption; providing a statement of public necessity; providing an effective date. Be It Enacted by the Legislature of the State of Florida: Section 1. Notwithstanding the October 2, 2003, repeal of said section scheduled pursuant to the Open Government Sunset Review Act of 1995 section 409.821, Florida Statutes, is amended to read:

409.821 Florida Kidcare program public records exemption Sections 409.810-409.820; confidential information.—Notwithstanding any other law to the contrary, any information identifying a Florida Kidcare program applicant or enrollee, as defined in s. 409.811, held by the Agency for Health Care Administration, the Department of Children and Family Services, the Department of Health, or the Florida Healthy Kids Corporation contained in an application for determination of eligibility for the Florida Kidcare program which identifies applicants, including medical information and family financial information, and any information obtained through quality assurance activities and patient satisfaction surveys which identifies program participants, obtained by the Florida Kidcare program under ss. 409.810-409.820, is confidential and is exempt from s. 119.07(1) and s. 24(a), Art. I of the State Constitution. Such information may be disclosed to another governmental entity only if disclosure is necessary for the entity to perform its duties and responsibilities under the Florida Kidcare program. The receiving governmental entity must maintain the confidential and exempt status of such information. Furthermore, such information may not be released to any person Except as otherwise provided by law, program staff or staff or agents affiliated with the program may not release, without the written consent of the program applicant or the parent or guardian of the applicant, to any state or federal agency, to any private business or person, or to any other entity, any confidential information received under ss. 409.810-409.820. This exemption applies to any information identifying a Florida Kidcare program applicant or enrollee held by the Agency for Health Care

Administration, the Department of Children and Family Services, the Department of Health, or the Florida Healthy Kids Corporation before, on, or after the effective date of this exemption. A violation of this section is a misdemeanor of the second degree, punishable as provided in s. 775.082 or s. 775.083 Section 2. Section 409.821, Florida Statutes, is subject to the Open Government Sunset Review Act of 1995 in accordance with s. 119.15, Florida Statutes, and shall stand repealed on October 2, 2008, unless reviewed and saved from repeal through reenactment by the Legislature.

Section 3. The Legislature finds that it is a public necessity that any information identifying a Florida Kidcare program applicant or enrollee, irrespective of whether such information is located in an application or other record, be held confidential and exempt in order to protect sensitive personal, financial, and medical information. If the exemption were not expanded to include such identifying information contained in other records in addition to the application, the purpose of the exemption would be defeated. Applicant and enrollee identifying information would be available pursuant to a public records request via other records, thereby causing an unwarranted invasion into the life and privacy of the program applicants and enrollees. In addition, expanding the public records exemption to include the identifying information of a program applicant or enrollee contained in other records in addition to the application is necessary in order for the Agency for Health Care Administration, the Department of Children and Family Services, the Department of Health, and the Florida Healthy Kids Corporation to effectively and efficiently administer the Florida Kidcare program. If such identifying information contained in other records were not granted the same protection afforded the identifying information contained in the application, the administration of the Florida Kidcare program would be significantly impaired because applicants would be less inclined to apply to the program due to the fact that such identifying information would be made available to the public, which would cause an unwarranted invasion into the life and privacy of program applicants and enrollees, hereby significantly decreasing the

number of program enrollees. Finally, it is a public necessity that such identifying information be held confidential and exempt in order to comply with federal law. The current exemption only applies to such information contained in an application for the Florida Kidcare program. The expansion of the exemption to include identifying information contained in any other records in addition to the application ensures compliance with federal law. In addition to the applicant, the identifying information of a program enrollee should also be held confidential and exempt. The expansion of the exemption is a public necessity in order for Florida to adhere to federal law requiring that certain program applicant and enrollee identifying information be protected from public disclosure.

Senate Bill 2082

This bill provides for the confidentiality of personal identifying information, including Social Security numbers, contained in records for US attorneys, assistant US attorneys, judges of the US Courts of Appeal, US district judges, US magistrate judges, and their spouses and children.

Senate Bill 2082

This bill provides an exemption from public records requirements for the names, home addresses, telephone numbers, Social Security numbers, and photographs of children who participate in government-sponsored recreation programs or camps, the names and locations of the schools attended by such children, and the names, home addresses, telephone numbers, and Social Security numbers of the parents or guardians of such children. It provides for future review and repeal of the exemption.

House Bill 1591

This bill exempts a voter's Social Security number and signature from the public records laws.

Senate Bill 1024

This bill removes the October 2, 2005, repeal of information regarding an active investigation or office review of certified capital company scheduled under Oil, Gas and Salt Resources Act. It also eliminates the exemption from public records requirements for Social Security numbers of any customers of certified capital company, complainants, or persons associated with said company or qualified business.

Senate Bill 1320

This bill provides an exemption from public records requirements for personal identifying information of specified personnel of the Department of Juvenile Justice, spouses and children of such personnel, and the names and locations of schools and daycare facilities attended by children of such personnel. It provides for review and repeal.

House Bill 687

This bill exempts an individual's name, address, birth date, Social Security number, phone number, and license numbers contained in records maintained by the Division of Licensing of the Department of Agriculture and Consumer Services of individuals who have applied for or received a license to carry a concealed weapon or firearm from the public record. Disclosure of information is possible under certain circumstances.

House Bill 1563

This bill revises the date until which confidential and exempt Social Security number or exempt complete bank account, debit, charge, or credit card numbers included in court files may be included as part of court records available for public inspection and copying unless redaction is requested. It requires county recorder to use his or her best efforts to redact all said information from electronic copies of official records.

Senate Bill 662

This bill provides limited public records exemption for personal identifying information of current or former human resource, labor relations, or employee relations directors, assistant directors, managers, or assistant managers of any local government agency or water management district with specified duties and spouses and children of such personnel.

Senate Bill 664

This bill provides for limited public records exemption for personal identifying information of current and former code enforcement officers and spouses and children of such officers. It removes scheduled repeal of exemption under Oil, Gas and Salt Resources Act.

Chapter 10: Georgia

Georgia's Senate Bill 230, specific to the disclosure requirements if personal information is compromised, grants an exception if the data was encrypted or redacted. Redaction of sensitive information is again mentioned in Georgia's House Bill 213, specific to what information may be printed on a receipt.

Senate Bill 230

This bill relates to selling and other trade practices, so as to provide definitions. It requires investigative consumer reporting agencies to give notice to consumers of certain security breaches.

To amend Chapter 1 of Title 10 of the Official Code of Georgia Annotated, relating to selling and other trade practices, so as to provide legislative findings; to provide definitions; to require information brokers to give notice to consumers of certain security breaches; to provide for related matters; to provide an effective date; to repeal conflicting laws; and for other purposes.

SECTION 1.

Chapter 1 of Title 10 of the Official Code of Georgia Annotated, relating to selling and other trade practices, is amended by adding a new Article 34 to read as follows:

"ARTICLE 3410-1-910.

The General Assembly finds and declares as follows:

(1) The privacy and financial security of individuals is increasingly at risk due to the ever more widespread collection of personal information by both the private and public sectors;

(2) Credit card transactions, magazine subscriptions, real estate records, automobile registrations, consumer surveys, warranty

registrations, credit reports, and Internet websites are all sources of personal information and form the source material for identity thieves;

(3) Identity theft is one of the fastest growing crimes committed in this state. Criminals who steal personal information such as Social Security numbers use the information to open credit card accounts, write bad checks, buy cars, purchase property, and commit other financial crimes with other people′s identities;

(4) Implementation of technology security plans and security software as part of an information security policy may provide protection to consumers and the general public from identity thieves;

(5) Information brokers should clearly define the standards for authorized users of its data so that a breach by an unauthorized user is easily identifiable;

(6) Identity theft is costly to the marketplace and to consumers; and

(7) Victims of identity theft must act quickly to minimize the damage; therefore, expeditious notification of unauthorized acquisition and possible misuse of a person′s personal information is imperative.

10-1-911.

As used in this article, the term:

(1) 'Breach of the security of the system' means unauthorized acquisition of an individual′s computerized data that compromises the security, confidentiality, or integrity of personal information of such individual maintained by an information broker. Good faith acquisition of personal information by an employee or agent of an information broker for the purposes of such information broker is not a breach of the security of the system, provided that the

personal information is not used or subject to further unauthorized disclosure.

(2) 'Information broker' means any person or entity who, for monetary fees or dues, engages in whole or in part in the business of collecting, assembling, evaluating, compiling, reporting, transmitting, transferring, or communicating information concerning individuals for the primary purpose of furnishing personal information to nonaffiliated third parties, but does not include any governmental agency whose records are maintained primarily for traffic safety, law enforcement, or licensing purposes.

(3) 'Notice' means:

(A) Written notice;

(B) Electronic notice, if the notice provided is consistent with the provisions regarding electronic records and signatures set forth in Section 7001 of Title 15 of the United States Code; or

(C) Substitute notice, if the information broker demonstrates that the cost of providing notice would exceed $250,000.00, that the affected class of individuals to be notified exceeds 500,000, or that the information broker does not have sufficient contact information to provide written or electronic notice to such individuals. Substitute notice shall consist of all of the following:

(i) E-mail notice, if the information broker has an e-mail address for the individuals to be notified;

(ii) Conspicuous posting of the notice on the information broker's website page, if the information broker maintains one; and

(iii) Notification to major state-wide media.

Notwithstanding any provision of this paragraph to the contrary, an information broker that maintains its own notification procedures as part of an information security policy for the treatment of personal information and is otherwise consistent with the timing requirements of this article shall be deemed to be in compliance with the notification requirements of this article if it notifies the individuals who are the subjects of the notice in accordance with its policies in the event of a breach of the security of the system.

(4) 'Person' means any individual, partnership, corporation, limited liability company, trust, estate, cooperative, association, or other entity. The term 'person' as used in this article shall not be construed to require duplicative reporting by any individual, corporation, trust, estate, cooperative, association, or other entity involved in the same transaction.

(5) 'Personal information' means an individual's first name or first initial and last name in combination with any one or more of the following data elements, when either the name or the data elements are not encrypted or redacted:

(A) Social Security number;

(B) Driver´s license number or state identification card number;

(C) Account number, credit card number, or debit card number, if circumstances exist wherein such a number could be used without additional identifying information, access codes, or passwords;

(D) Account passwords or personal identification numbers or other access codes; or

(E) Any of the items contained in subparagraphs (A) through (D) of this paragraph when not in connection with the individual´s first name or first initial and last name, if the information compromised would be sufficient to perform or attempt to perform identity theft against the person whose information was compromised.

The term 'personal information' does not include publicly available information that is lawfully made available to the general public from federal, state, or local government records.

10-1-912.

(a) Any information broker that maintains computerized data that includes personal information of individuals shall give notice of any breach of the security of the system following discovery or notification of the breach in the security of the data to any resident of this state whose unencrypted personal information was, or is reasonably believed to have been, acquired by an unauthorized person. The notice shall be made in the most expedient time possible and without unreasonable delay, consistent with the legitimate needs of law enforcement, as provided in subsection (c) of this Code section, or with any measures necessary to determine the scope of the breach and restore the reasonable integrity, security, and confidentiality of the data system.

(b) Any person or business that maintains computerized data on behalf of an information broker that includes personal information of individuals that the person or business does not own shall notify the information broker of any breach of the security of the data immediately following discovery, if the personal information was, or is reasonably believed to have been, acquired by an unauthorized person.

(c) The notification required by this Code section may be delayed if a law enforcement agency determines that the notification will compromise a criminal investigation. The notification required by this Code section shall be made after the law enforcement agency determines that it will not compromise the investigation.

(d) In the event that an information broker discovers circumstances requiring notification pursuant to this Code section of more than 10,000 residents of this state at one time, the information broker shall also notify, without unreasonable delay, all consumer

reporting agencies that compile and maintain files on consumers on a nation-wide basis, as defined by 15 U.S.C. Section 1681a, of the timing, distribution, and content of the notices."

Restricting Information That May Be Printed on Receipts–House Bill 213

This bill relates to business administration, making changes to certain definitions. It provides for restrictions on information that may be printed on receipts for certain payment card transactions, and clarifies the administrator's duties and powers and procedure related to enforcement of this chapter. The bill also provides for civil and criminal penalties and provides for related matters.

House Bill 1437

This bill provides that public disclosure shall not be required for records that would reveal the home address or telephone number, Social Security number, or insurance or medical information of employees of the Georgia State Department of Revenue.

House Bill 437

This bill relates to exceptions from the requirements of public disclosure, so as to exempt disclosure of certain personal information, including Social Security number, of public employees.

House Bill 1253

This bill provides that Social Security numbers shall not be used on driver's licenses.

Senate Bill 588

Prohibits the use or display of Social Security numbers except in specific circumstances.

To amend Part 2 of Article 15 of Chapter 1 of Title 10 of the Official Code of Georgia Annotated, relating to fair business practices, so as to prohibit the use or display of Social Security numbers except in specified circumstances; to provide for related matters; to provide for an effective date; to repeal conflicting laws; and for other purposes.

BE IT ENACTED BY THE GENERAL ASSEMBLY OF GEORGIA:

SECTION 1.

Part 2 of Article 15 of Chapter 1 of Title 10 of the Official Code of Georgia Annotated, relating to fair business practices, is amended by inserting a new Code Section 10-1-393.8, immediately following Code Section 10-1-393.7, relating to solicitations during final illness, to read as follows:

"10-1-393.8.

(a) Except as otherwise provided in this Code section, a person, firm, or corporation shall not:

(1) Publicly post or publicly display in any manner an individual's Social Security number. As used in this Code section, 'publicly post' or 'publicly display' means to intentionally communicate or otherwise make available to the general public;

(2) Require an individual to transmit his or her Social Security number over the Internet, unless the connection is secure or the Social Security number is encrypted; or

(3) Require an individual to use his or her Social Security number to access an Internet website, unless a password or unique personal identification number or other authentication device is also required to access the Internet website.

(b) This Code section shall not apply to:

(1) The collection, release, or use of an individual's Social Security number as required by state or federal law;

(2) The inclusion of an individual's Social Security number in an application, form, or document sent by mail, electronically transmitted, or transmitted by facsimile:

(A) As part of an application or enrollment process;

(B) To establish, amend, or terminate an account, contract, or policy; or

(C) To confirm the accuracy of the individual's Social Security number;

(3) The use of an individual's Social Security number for internal verification or administrative purposes; or

(4) An interactive computer service provider's or a telecommunications provider's transmission or routing of, or intermediate temporary storage or caching of, an individual's Social Security number.

(c) This Code section shall not impose a duty on an interactive computer service provider or a telecommunications provider actively to monitor its service or to affirmatively seek evidence of the transmission of Social Security numbers on its service.

(d) Notwithstanding the provisions of this Code section, the clerks of superior court of this state and the Georgia Superior Court Clerks' Cooperative Authority shall be held harmless for filing, publicly posting, or publicly displaying any document containing an individual's Social Security number that the clerk is otherwise required by law to file, publicly post, or publicly display for public inspection."

Chapter 11: Hawaii

Senate Bill 2290

This bill requires any business doing business in Hawaii, as well as any government agency that owns, licenses, collects, or maintains personal information of Hawaii residents, to notify affected persons that a security breach has occurred following the discovery or receipt of notification of the breach. The bill contains provisions for a civil penalty up to $2,500 for each violation against any business in violation, a private cause of action, and an award of reasonable attorneys' fees to the prevailing party. It requires government agencies in Hawaii to submit a detailed written report to the legislature within twenty days after discovering the security breach at the government agency, unless the report will impede a criminal investigation.

Identity Theft Prevention: Senate Bill 2290

SECTION 1. The privacy and financial security of individuals is increasingly at risk due to the widespread collection of personal information by the private sector and government agencies. Numerous sources include personal information that forms the source material for identity thieves. Identity theft is one of the fastest growing crimes committed throughout the United States, including Hawaii. Criminals who steal personal information, such as Social Security numbers, use the information to open credit card accounts, write bad checks, buy cars, and commit other financial crimes with other people's identities. The purpose of this Act is to alleviate the growing plague of identity theft by requiring businesses and government agencies that maintain records containing resident individuals' personal information to notify an individual whenever the individual's personal information has been compromised by unauthorized disclosure.

SECTION 2. The Hawaii Revised Statutes is amended by adding to title 26 a new chapter to be appropriately designated and to read as follows:

"CHAPTER NOTIFICATION OF SECURITY BREACHES

§-1 Definitions. As used in this chapter, unless the context otherwise requires: "Business" means a sole proprietorship, partnership, corporation, association, or other group, however organized, and whether or not organized to operate at a profit. The term includes a financial institution organized, chartered, or holding a license or authorization certificate under the laws of the State, any other state, the United States, or any other country, or the parent or the subsidiary of any such financial institution. The term also includes an entity whose business is records destruction. "Encryption" means the use of an algorithmic process to transform data into a form in which the data is rendered unreadable or unusable without the use of a confidential process or key. "Government agency" means any department, division, board, commission, public corporation, or other agency or instrumentality of the State or of any county. "Personal information" means an individual's first name or first initial and last name in combination with any one or more of the following data elements, when either the name or the data elements are not encrypted:

(1) Social Security number;

(2) Driver's license number or Hawaii identification card number; or

(3) Account number, credit or debit card number, access code, or password that would permit access to an individual's financial account. "Personal information" does not include publicly available information that is lawfully made available to the general public from federal, state, or local government records.

"Records" means any material on which written, drawn, spoken, visual, or electromagnetic information is recorded or preserved, regardless of physical form or characteristics. "Redacted" means the rendering of data so that it is unreadable or is truncated so that no more than the last four digits of the identification number are accessible as part of the data. "Security breach" means an incident of unauthorized access to and acquisition of unencrypted or unredacted records or data containing personal information where illegal use of the personal information has occurred, or is reasonably likely to occur and that creates a risk of harm to a person. Any incident of unauthorized access to and acquisition of encrypted records or data containing personal information along with the confidential process or key constitutes a security breach. Good faith acquisition of personal information by an employee or agent of the business for a legitimate purpose is not a security breach; provided that the personal information is not used for a purpose other than a lawful purpose of the business and is not subject to further unauthorized disclosure.

§-2 Notice of security breach. (a) Any business that owns or licenses personal information of residents of Hawaii, any business that conducts business in Hawaii that owns or licenses personal information in any form (whether computerized, paper, or otherwise), or any government agency that collects personal information for specific government purposes shall provide notice to the affected person that there has been a security breach following discovery or notification of the breach. The disclosure notification shall be made without unreasonable delay, consistent with the legitimate needs of law enforcement as provided in subsection (c)of this section, and consistent with any measures necessary to determine sufficient contact information, determine the scope of the breach, and restore the reasonable integrity, security, and confidentiality of the data system. (b) Any business located in Hawaii or any business that conducts business in Hawaii that maintains or possesses records or data containing personal information of residents of Hawaii that the business does not own or license, or any government agency that maintains or possesses records or data containing personal information of residents of Hawaii shall notify the owner or licensee of the information of any security breach immediately following discovery of the breach, consistent with the legitimate needs of law enforcement as provided in subsection (c). (c) The notice required by this section shall be delayed if a law enforcement agency informs the business or government agency that notification may impede a criminal investigation or jeopardize national security and requests a delay; provided that such request is made in writing, or the business or government agency documents the request contemporaneously in writing, including the name of the law enforcement officer making the request and the officer's law enforcement agency engaged in the investigation. The notice required by this section shall be provided without unreasonable delay after the law enforcement agency communicates to the business or government agency its determination that notice will no longer impede the investigation or jeopardize national security. (d) The notice shall be clear and conspicuous. The notice shall include a description of the following:

(1) The incident in general terms;

(2) The type of personal information that was subject to the unauthorized access and acquisition;

(3) The general acts of the business or government agency to protect the personal information from further unauthorized access;

(4) A telephone number that the person may call for further information and assistance, if one exists; and

(5) Advice that directs the person to remain vigilant by reviewing account statements and monitoring free credit reports.

(e) For purposes of this section, notice to affected persons may be provided by one of the following methods:

(1) Written notice to the last available address the business or government agency has on record;

(2) Electronic mail notice, for those persons for whom a business or government agency has a valid electronic mail address and who

have agreed to receive communications electronically if the notice provided is consistent with the provisions regarding electronic records and signatures for notices legally required to be in writing set forth in 15 U.S.C. Section 7001;

(3) Telephonic notice, provided that contact is made directly with the affected persons; and

(4) Substitute notice, if the business or government agency demonstrates that the cost of providing notice would exceed $100,000 or that the affected class of subject persons to be notified exceeds two hundred thousand, or if the business or government agency does not have sufficient contact information or consent to satisfy paragraph (1), (2), or (3), for only those affected persons without sufficient contact information or consent, or if the business or government agency is unable to identify particular affected persons, for only those unidentifiable affected persons. Substitute notice shall consist of all the following:

(A) Electronic mail notice when the business or government agency has an electronic mail address for the subject persons;

(B) Conspicuous posting of the notice on the website page of the business or government agency, if one is maintained; and

(C) Notification to major statewide media.

(f) In the event a business provides notice to more than one thousand persons at one time pursuant to this section, the business shall notify in writing, without unreasonable delay, the State of Hawaii's office of consumer protection and all consumer reporting agencies that compile and maintain files on consumers on a nationwide basis, as defined in 15 U.S.C. Section 1681a(p), of the timing, distribution, and content of the notice.

(g) The following businesses shall be deemed to be in compliance with this section:

(1) A financial institution that is subject to the Federal Interagency Guidance on Response Programs for Unauthorized Access to Consumer Information and Customer Notice published in the Federal Register on March 29, 2005 by the Board of Governors of the Federal Reserve System, the Federal Deposit Insurance Corporation, the Office of the Comptroller of the Currency, and the Office of Thrift Supervision, or subject to 12 C.F.R. Part 748, and any revisions, additions, or substitutions relating to said interagency guidance; and

(2) Any health plan or healthcare provider that is subject to and in compliance with the standards for privacy or individually identifiable health information and the security standards for the protection of electronic health information of the Health Insurance Portability and Accountability Act of 1996.

(h) Any waiver of the provisions of this section is contrary to public policy and is void and unenforceable.

§-3 Penalties; civil action. (a) Any business that violates any provision of this chapter shall be subject to penalties of not more than $2,500 for each violation. The attorney general or the executive director of the office of consumer protection may bring an action pursuant to this section. No such action may be brought against a government agency. (b) In addition to any penalty provided for in subsection (a), any business that violates any provision of this chapter shall be liable to the injured party in an amount equal to the sum of any actual damages sustained by the injured party as a result of the violation. The court in any action brought under this section may award reasonable attorneys' fees to the prevailing party. No such action may be brought against a government agency.

(c) The penalties provided in this section shall be cumulative to the remedies or penalties available under all other laws of this State.

§-4 Reporting requirements. A government agency shall submit a written report to the legislature within twenty days after discovery of a security breach at the government agency that details information relating to the nature of the breach, the number of individuals affected by the breach, a copy of the notice of security breach that was issued, the number of individuals to whom the notice was sent, whether the notice was delayed due to law enforcement considerations, and any procedures that have been implemented to prevent the breach from reoccurring. In the event that a law enforcement agency informs the government agency that notification may impede a criminal investigation or jeopardize national security, the report to the legislature may be delayed until twenty days after the law enforcement agency has determined that notice will no longer impede the investigation or jeopardize national security."

SECTION 3. This Act shall take effect on January 1, 2007.

Identity Theft; Personal Records: H.B. 2674

SECTION 1. The 2004 Annual Report of the Federal Trade Commission (FTC) reports that identity theft is the number one consumer complaint, accounting for forty-two per cent of all complaints filed with the FTC in 2003. In 2003, Hawaii ranked twenty-fifth among the states in the number of identity theft victims, with almost fifty-two victims per one hundred thousand population. As many as six hundred forty-nine Hawaii consumers reported complaints about identity theft to the FTC. However, the true number of Hawaii victims may be far more than reported because many victims do not report claims to the FTC.

Hawaii consumers primarily complained about credit or charge card fraud, bank fraud, and phone or utilities fraud. Examples of credit or charge card and bank fraud included establishing new accounts or accessing existing accounts with the victim's identity. Bank fraud also included theft through electronic fund transfers. Utilities fraud typically involved establishing new accounts, such as wireless telephone accounts, with the victim's identity. Hawaii consumers also complained about forged government documents, such as driver's licenses, Social Security cards, tax returns, and loans obtained with the victim's identity.

Nearly one third of the victims lived in Honolulu. Most of the remaining victims lived in Kaneohe, Kailua, Mililani, Wahiawa, and Waipahu. About seventy-five per cent of the Hawaii victims are between eighteen to forty-nine years of age.

The legislature finds that identity theft is a serious problem for consumers. The legislature finds that one important step toward protecting consumers from identity theft is by protecting against the use and disclosure of Social Security numbers. The Social Security number is a unique identifier that is used in conjunction with other personal information for many purposes, including obtaining credit or loans, opening financial accounts, and even enrolling in school.

The purpose of this Act is to:

(1) Ensure that Social Security numbers are exempt from disclosure in documents that are otherwise public records; and

(2) Prohibit retail merchant club card issuers from requesting personal identifiers, such as Social Security numbers, driver's license numbers, and birth dates except in limited circumstances and restricting their use of consumer information.

SECTION 2. The Hawaii Revised Statutes is amended by adding a new chapter to be appropriately designated and to read as follows:

"Chapter RETAIL MERCHANT CLUB CARDS

§-1 Definitions. For purposes of this chapter:

"Cardholder" means any consumer to whom a retail merchant club card is issued, and may include all persons holding the club card under the same account.

"Cardholder information" means the cardholder's name, mailing address, electronic mail address, and any unique membership identifiers assigned by the club card issuer to the cardholder for purposes of targeting marketing activities.

"Club card" means any card or device used for the purpose of obtaining access to purchase retail products through membership, for price discounts, or to receive other no-cost benefits provided by the retail merchant. A "club card" is not a credit card, charge card, or check cashing card.

"Club card issuer" means a retail merchant that provides club cards to consumers, and includes a contract information services provider of the retail merchant.

"Marketing purposes" means the categorization of cardholders based on the cardholder's shopping patterns, spending history, or behavioral characteristics derived from account activity that is provided to an unaffiliated third party for consideration.

"Personal information" means information associated with an actual person that is a name, an address, a telephone number, an electronic mail address, a driver's license number, a Social Security number, an employer, a place of employment, information related to employment, an employee identification number, a mother's maiden name, an identifying number of a depository account, a bank account number, a password used for accessing information, a taxpayer identification number, health insurance identification number, date of birth, a personal identification number (PIN), a government passport number, credit card number, or any other name, number, or code that is used to access personal financial information about the actual person.

"Retail merchant" means any retailer that sells food, products, or merchandise.

"Unaffiliated third party" means a business that is not under the corporate control or common ownership of the club card issuer or is not a contract information services provider of the retail merchant.

§-2 Retail merchant club cards; requirements. (a) No club card issuer shall request in a club card application, or require as a condition of obtaining a club card, that the applicant provide any personal information except name, address, and telephone number. If the club card issuer requires a unique identifier to confirm the identity of the applicant, the club card issuer may ask for the last four digits of the applicant's Social Security number.

(b) No club card issuer may sell or share a cardholder's name, address, telephone number, or any personal information to any unaffiliated third party except as permitted in this subsection. A club card issuer may share cardholder information for marketing purposes if the club card issuer complies with all the following:

(1) The club card issuer charges an annual fee for the club card and requires the cardholder to renew the club card annually;

(2) The club card issuer allows only cardholders to make purchases and not members of the general public;

(3) The club card issuer provides a written statement to the cardholder upon payment of the annual fee that notifies the cardholder that:

(A) The cardholder information may be shared with other businesses for purposes of marketing information;

(B) Payment of the annual fee means the cardholder has agreed to allow the club card issuer to share cardholder information; and

(C) The cardholder may choose to opt-out from the sharing of cardholder information; and

(4) The club card issuer obtains a written confidentiality agreement from the unaffiliated third party that the shared information will not be transferred to any other entity.

(c) The restrictions of subsection (a) shall not apply when the club card application form is used for the dual purpose of club card membership and establishing privileges for check cashing, check verification, or as a credit application; provided that no club card issuer shall require as a condition of obtaining a club card that the cardholder obtain the club card as an identification card for purposes of check cashing or credit.

(d) Nothing in this section prohibits a club card issuer from including on its club card application form a credit application to a designated credit card company and transmitting the credit application to the credit card company, provided that:

(1) The credit application form is separately identified as an option on the club card application form; and

(2) The credit application clearly discloses that the cardholder is applying for credit with the designated credit card company."

SECTION 3. Section 92F-12, Hawaii Revised Statutes, is amended by amending subsection (a) to read as follows:

"(a) Any other law to the contrary notwithstanding, each agency shall make available for public inspection and duplication during regular business hours:

(1) Rules of procedure, substantive rules of general applicability, statements of general policy, and interpretations of general applicability adopted by the agency;

(2) Final opinions, including concurring and dissenting opinions, as well as orders made in the adjudication of cases;

(3) Government purchasing information, including all bid results, except to the extent prohibited by section 92F-13;

(4) Pardons and commutations, as well as directory information concerning an individual's presence at any correctional facility;

(5) Land ownership, transfer, and lien records, including real property tax information and leases of state land;

(6) Results of environmental tests;

(7) Minutes of all agency meetings required by law to be public;

(8) Name, address, and occupation of any person borrowing funds from a state or county loan program, and the amount, purpose, and current status of the loan;

(9) Certified payroll records on public works contracts[;] except that Social Security numbers of individuals shall not be disclosed;

(10) Regarding contract hires and consultants employed by agencies:

The contract itself, the amount of compensation[,];

The duration of the contract[,]; and

The objectives of the contract;

(11) Building permit information within the control of the agency;

(12) Water service consumption data maintained by the boards of water supply;

(13) Rosters of persons holding licenses or permits granted by an agency that may include name, business address, type of license held, and status of the license;

(14) The name, compensation (but only the salary range for employees covered by or included in chapter 76, and sections 302A-602 to 302A-640, and 302A-701, or bargaining unit (8)), job title, business address, business telephone number, job description, education and training background, previous work experience, dates of first and last employment, position number, type of appointment, service computation date, occupational group or class code, bargaining unit code, employing agency name and code, department, division, branch, office, section, unit, and island of employment, of present or former officers or employees of the agency; provided that this paragraph shall not require the creation of a roster of employees; and provided further that this paragraph shall not apply to information regarding present or former employees involved in an undercover capacity in a law enforcement agency;

(15) Information collected and maintained for the purpose of making information available to the general public; and

(16) Information contained in or compiled from a transcript, minutes, report, or summary of a proceeding open to the public."

SECTION 4. Section 92F-14, Hawaii Revised Statutes, is amended by amending subsection (b) to read as follows:

"(b) The following are examples of information in which the individual has a significant privacy interest:

(1) Information relating to medical, psychiatric, or psychological history, diagnosis, condition, treatment, or evaluation, other than directory information while an individual is present at such facility;

(2) Information identifiable as part of an investigation into a possible violation of criminal law, except to the extent that disclosure is necessary to prosecute the violation or to continue the investigation;

(3) Information relating to eligibility for social services or welfare benefits or to the determination of benefit levels;

(4) Information in an agency's personnel file, or applications, nominations, recommendations, or proposals for public employment or appointment to a governmental position, except:

(A) Information disclosed under section 92F-12(a)(14); and

(B) The following information related to employment misconduct that results in an employee's suspension or discharge:

(i) The name of the employee;

(ii) The nature of the employment related misconduct;

(iii) The agency's summary of the allegations of misconduct;

(iv) Findings of fact and conclusions of law; and

(v) The disciplinary action taken by the agency;

when the following has occurred: the highest non-judicial grievance adjustment procedure timely invoked by the employee or the employee's representative has concluded; a written decision sustaining the suspension or discharge has been issued after this procedure; and thirty calendar days have elapsed following the issuance of the decision; provided that this subparagraph shall not apply to a county police department officer except in a case which results in the discharge of the officer;

(5) Information relating to an individual's nongovernmental employment history except as necessary to demonstrate compliance with requirements for a particular government position;

(6) Information describing an individual's finances, income, assets, liabilities, net worth, bank balances, financial history or activities, or creditworthiness;

(7) Information compiled as part of an inquiry into an individual's fitness to be granted or to retain a license, except:

(A) The record of any proceeding resulting in the discipline of a licensee and the grounds for discipline;

(B) Information on the current place of employment and required insurance coverages of licensees; and

(C) The record of complaints including all dispositions;

(8) Information comprising a personal recommendation or evaluation; and

(9) Social Security numbers."

Relating to Identity Theft–House Bill 2674

This bill exempts the disclosure of Social Security numbers from government payroll records that are public information. It restricts retail merchant card issuers from requesting personal information except for credit purposes and from sharing cardholder information.

Senate Bill 1042

This bill allows only the last four digits of a registered voter's Social Security number on nomination papers filed on behalf of a candidate.

Senate Bill 2293

This bill prohibits businesses, subject to limited exceptions, from disclosing an individual's Social Security number to the general public. The bill also prohibits them from printing the Social Security number on an identification card or in mailings to customers, requiring the transmission of a Social Security number to third parties, and selling or otherwise disclosing the Social Security number to third parties without written consent.

Senate Bill 662

This bill allows government agencies to withhold personal information contained in final opinions or orders made in the adjudication of cases where the disclosure of the information would be an unwarranted invasion of personal privacy. The bill excludes Social Security number information of an individual under contract with the government from disclosure.

Senate Bill 1042

This bill allows only the last four digits of a registered voter's Social Security number on nomination papers filed on behalf of a candidate.

Senate Bill 662

This bill allows government agencies to withhold personal information contained in final opinions or orders made in the adjudication of cases where the disclosure of the information would be an unwarranted invasion of personal privacy. It excludes Social Security number information of an individual under contract with the government from disclosure.

Senate Bill 2293

This bill prohibits businesses, subject to limited exceptions, from disclosing an individual's Social Security number to the general public, printing the Social Security number on an identification card or in mailings to customers, requiring the transmission of a Social Security number to third parties, and selling or otherwise disclosing the Social Security number to third parties without written consent.

Senate Bill 9

This bill requires both public as well as private entities responsible for the inadvertent or unauthorized disclosure of personal financial information to pay for access to credit reports for at least one year.

House Bill 246

BE IT ENACTED BY THE LEGISLATURE OF THE STATE OF HAWAII:

SECTION 1. Chapter 487, Hawaii Revised Statutes, is amended by adding a new section to be appropriately designated and to read as follows:

§487- Inadvertent, unauthorized disclosure of personal financial information by public or private entities; duty to notify and pay for credit monitoring reports.

(a) Any public or private entity responsible for the inadvertent, unauthorized disclosure of personal financial information that may result in a crime being committed under section 708-839.6, 708-839.7, or 708-839.8 shall be liable for the costs of providing each person whose personal financial information was disclosed with, at a minimum, a one year subscription to a credit reporting agency's services.

(b) Within three calendar days of a public or private entity's discovery of the inadvertent, unauthorized disclosure of personal financial information, the public or private entity responsible for the inadvertent, unauthorized disclosure of personal financial information shall provide the executive director of the office of consumer protection and each person whose personal financial information was inadvertently disclosed without the person's authorization with notice of the disclosure, the requirements imposed upon the responsible entity, and the credit monitoring and

reporting options that will be available to the person pursuant to this section.

(c) Within seven calendar days of a public or private entity's discovery of the inadvertent, unauthorized disclosure of personal financial information, the public or private entity responsible for the inadvertent, unauthorized disclosure of personal financial information shall provide each person with a choice of not less than two credit reporting agencies from which the person may select. The person, if the person so chooses, shall select a credit reporting agency and the credit monitoring and reporting services the person requires and shall inform the responsible public or private entity of the person's selection. If a person elects not to subscribe to any credit monitoring and reporting services offered by a credit reporting agency, the person shall notify the responsible public or private entity in writing of the person's choice to not subscribe to any credit monitoring or reporting services. The public or private entity responsible for the inadvertent, unauthorized disclosure of the person's personal financial information shall keep a record of each person's credit monitoring and reporting services selection, or election to not subscribe to such services, for at least three years after the receipt by the public or private entity of a person's selection or election under this subsection.

(d) The responsible public or private entity shall enroll the person into the credit monitoring and reporting plan of the person's choice within seven calendar days of receipt of a person's selection made under subsection (c) and shall pay all costs associated with the one year subscription of the services of the selected credit reporting agency.

(e) For the purposes of this section:

"Credit reporting agency" means a nationwide consumer reporting agency, such as Equifax, Experian, or TransUnion, or any successor entity thereof, that provides consumer credit monitoring and reporting services.

"Inadvertent, unauthorized disclosure" or "disclosure" means any compromising of sensitive, personal, or financial information that could result in a person being a victim of identity theft under section 708-839.6, 708-839.7, or 708-839.8. The term does not include any willful or wanton act by a public or private entity or employee or agent thereof that could or does result in a crime being committed under section 708-839.6, 708-839.7, or 708-839.8.

"Personal financial information" means any sensitive, personal, or financial information that, if inappropriately disclosed or obtained, could result in a person being a victim of identity theft under section 708-839.6, 708-839.7, or 708-839.8.

"Public or private entity", in the case of a public entity, has the same meaning as "government entity" as that term is defined in section 663-10.5. In the case of a private entity, the term includes a sole proprietorship, corporation, limited liability company, association, partnership, joint stock company, joint venture, mutual fund, trust, joint tenancy, or other similar form of business organization or other legal entity, whether organized for-profit or not-for-profit.

(f) The executive director of the office of consumer protection may adopt rules in accordance with chapter 91 to effectuate this section."

SECTION 2. New statutory material is underscored.

SECTION 3. This Act shall take effect upon its approval.

Chapter 12: Idaho

Like many other states, Idaho's disclosure law does not require disclosure if, upon investigation of the breach, it can be determined that the data has not, and likely will not be, misused. As I have before, I recommend proceeding with caution here. If it were to get out that a company chose not to disclose based on their own internal investigation, the fallout could be more costly than the disclosure itself.

Relating to Personal and Financial Information on Computerized Databases–Senate Bill 1374

This bill adds to existing law to provide for disclosure of breach of security of computerized personal information by an agency, individual, or a commercial entity, to provide procedures deemed in compliance with security breach requirements, and to provide penalties for violations.

SECTION 1. That Part 1, Chapter 51, Title 28, Idaho Code, be, and the same is hereby amended by the addition thereto of <u>NEW SECTIONS</u>, to be known and designated as Sections 28-51-104, 28-51-105, 28-51-106 and 28-51-107, Idaho Code, and to read as follows:

28-51-104. DEFINITIONS. For purposes of sections 28-51-104 through 28-51-107, Idaho Code:

(1) "Agency" means any "public agency" as defined in section 9-337, Idaho Code.

(2) "Breach of the security of the system" means the illegal acquisition of unencrypted computerized data that materially compromises the security, confidentiality, or integrity of personal information for one or more persons maintained by an agency, individual or a commercial entity. Good faith acquisition of personal information by an employee or agent of an agency, individual or a commercial entity for the purposes of the agency, individual or the commercial entity is not a breach of the security of

the system, provided that the personal information is not used or subject to further unauthorized disclosure.

(3) "Commercial entity" includes corporation, business trust, estate, trust, partnership, limited partnership, limited liability partnership, limited liability company, association, organization, joint venture and any other legal entity, whether for profit or not-for-profit.

(4) "Notice" means:

(a) Written notice to the most recent address the agency, individual commercial entity has in its records;

(b) Telephonic notice;

(c) Electronic notice, if the notice provided is consistent with the pro- visions regarding electronic records and signatures set forth in 15 U.S.C. section 7001; or

(d) Substitute notice, if the agency, individual or the commercial entity required to provide notice demonstrates that the cost of providing notice will exceed twenty-five thousand dollars ($25,000), or that the number of Idaho residents to be notified exceeds fifty thousand (50,000), or that the agency, individual or the commercial entity does not have sufficient contact information to provide notice. Substitute notice consists of all of the following:

(i) E-mail notice if the agency, individual or the commercial entity has e-mail addresses for the affected Idaho residents; and

(ii) Conspicuous posting of the notice on the website page of the agency, individual or the commercial entity if the agency, individual or the commercial entity maintains one; and

(iii) Notice to major statewide media.

"Personal information" means an Idaho resident's first name or first initial and last name in combination with any one (1) or more of the following data elements that relate to the resident, when either the name or the data elements are not encrypted:

(a) Social Security number;

(b) Driver's license number or Idaho identification card number; or

(c) Account number, or credit or debit card number, in combination with any required security code, access code, or password that would permit access to a resident's financial account.

The term "personal information" does not include publicly available information that is lawfully made available to the general public from federal, state, or local government records or widely distributed media.

(6) "Primary regulator" of a commercial entity or individual licensed or chartered by the United States is that commercial entity's or individual's primary federal regulator, the primary regulator of a commercial entity or individual licensed by the department of finance is the department of finance, the primary regulator of a commercial entity or individual licensed by the department of insurance is the department of insurance and, for all agencies and all other commercial entities or individuals, the primary regulator is the attorney general.

28-51-105. DISCLOSURE OF BREACH OF SECURITY OF COMPUTERIZED PERSONAL INFORMATION BY AN AGENCY, INDIVIDUAL OR A COMMERCIAL ENTITY.

(1) An agency, individual or a commercial entity that conducts business in Idaho and that owns or licenses computerized data that includes personal information about a resident of Idaho shall, when it becomes aware of a breach of the security of the system, conduct in good faith a reasonable and prompt investigation to determine

the likelihood that personal information has been or will be misused. If the investigation determines that the misuse of information about an Idaho resident has occurred or is reasonably likely to occur, the agency, individual or the commercial entity shall give notice as soon as possible to the affected Idaho resident. Notice must be made in the most expedient time possible and without unreasonable delay, consistent with the legitimate needs of law enforcement and consistent with any measures necessary to determine the scope of the breach, to identify the individuals affected, and to restore the reasonable integrity of the computerized data system.

(2) An agency, individual or a commercial entity that maintains computerized data that includes personal information that the agency, individual or the commercial entity does not own or license shall give notice to and cooperate with the owner or licensee of the information of any breach of the security of the system immediately following discovery of a breach, if misuse of personal information about an Idaho resident occurred or is reasonably likely to occur. Cooperation includes sharing with the owner or licensee information relevant to the breach.

(3) Notice required by this section may be delayed if a law enforcement agency advises the agency, individual or commercial entity that the notice will impede a criminal investigation. Notice required by this section must be made in good faith, without unreasonable delay and as soon as possible after the law enforcement agency advises the agency, individual or commercial entity that notification will no longer impede the investigation.

28-51-106. PROCEDURES DEEMED IN COMPLIANCE WITH SECURITY BREACH REQUIREMENTS.

(1) An agency, individual or a commercial entity that maintains its own notice procedures as part of an information security policy for the treatment of personal information, and whose procedures are otherwise consistent with the timing requirements of section 28-51-

105, Idaho Code, is deemed to be in compliance with the notice requirements of section 28-51-105, Idaho Code, if the agency, individual or the commercial entity notifies affected Idaho residents in accordance with its policies in the event of a breach of security of the system.

(2) An individual or a commercial entity that is regulated by state or federal law and that maintains procedures for a breach of the security of the system pursuant to the laws, rules, regulations, guidances, or guidelines established by its primary or functional state or federal regulator is deemed to be in compliance with section 28-51-105, Idaho Code, if the individual or the commercial entity complies with the maintained procedures when a breach of the security of the system occurs.

28-51-107. VIOLATIONS. In any case in which an agency's, commercial entity's or individual's primary regulator has reason to believe that an agency, individual or commercial entity subject to that primary regulator's jurisdiction under section 28-51-104(6), Idaho Code, has violated section 28-51-105, Idaho Code, by failing to give notice in accordance with that section, the primary regulator may bring a civil action to enforce compliance with that section and enjoin that agency, individual or commercial entity from further violations. Any agency, individual or commercial entity that intentionally fails to give notice in accordance with section 28-51-105, Idaho Code, shall be subject to a fine of not more than twenty-five thousand dollars ($25,000) per breach of the security of the system.

House Bill 134

The bill amends existing law to provide restrictions on the information printed on receipts for payment card transactions by prohibiting the printing of more than the last five digits of the account number, and to provide penalties. This does not apply in situations where the sole means of recording a payment card's account number is by handwriting or by an imprint of copy of the payment card. A merchant who violates this section shall be subject to a civil penalty of not more than $250 for the first violation and $1,000 for a second and subsequent violation.

Senate Bill 1259

This bill amends existing law and requires that members' account numbers rather than Social Security numbers be specified in approved domestic retirement orders. It also deletes the requirement that Social Security numbers be provided for alternate payees in domestic retirement orders, and requires that Social Security numbers of alternate payees be provided to the Public Employee Retirement System Board prior to the approval of domestic retirement orders.

Chapter 13: Illinois

Where some other states exempt their government agencies from the disclosure requirements in the event of a data breach, Illinois does not. In fact, not only is there no such exemption, Illinois Senate Bill 1799 specifically covers the state's Department of Revenue with regards to disclosure requirements.

Personal Information Protection Act–House Bill 1633

This bill creates the Personal Information Protection Act. It provides that any data collector that owns or uses personal information in any form, whether computerized, paper, or otherwise, that includes personal information concerning an Illinois resident shall notify the resident that there has been a breach of the security of the system data following discovery or notification of the breach, without regard for whether the data has been accessed by an unauthorized third party for legal or illegal purposes. It provides that the notification required pursuant to the act may be delayed if a law enforcement agency determines that the notification may impede a criminal investigation. It amends the Consumer Fraud and Deceptive Business Practices Act. It provides that a violation of the Personal Information Protection Act is a violation of the Consumer Fraud and Deceptive Business Practices Act.

Section 5. Definitions. In this Act:

"Data Collector" may include, but is not limited to, government agencies, public and private universities, privately and publicly held corporations, financial institutions, retail operators, and any other entity that, for any purpose, handles, collects, disseminates, or otherwise deals with nonpublic personal information.

"Breach of the security of the system data" means unauthorized acquisition of computerized data that compromises the security, confidentiality, or integrity of personal information maintained by the data collector.

"Breach of the security of the system data" does not include good faith acquisition of personal information by an employee or agent of the data collector for a legitimate purpose of the data collector, provided that the personal information is not used for a purpose unrelated to the data collector's business or subject to further unauthorized disclosure.

"Personal information" means an individual's first name or first initial and last name in combination with any one or more of the following data elements, when either the name or the data elements are not encrypted or redacted:

(1) Social Security number.

(2) Driver's license number or State identification card number.

(3) Account number or credit or debit card number, or an account number or credit card number in combination with any required security code, access code, or password that would permit access to an individual's financial account.

"Personal information" does not include publicly available information that is lawfully made available to the general public from federal, State, or local government records.

Section 10. Notice of Breach.

(a) Any data collector that owns or licenses personal information concerning an Illinois resident shall notify the resident that there has been a breach of the security of the system data following discovery or notification of the breach. The disclosure notification shall be made in the most expedient time possible and without unreasonable delay, consistent with any measures necessary to determine the scope of the breach and restore the reasonable integrity, security, and confidentiality of the data system.

(b) Any data collector that maintains computerized data that includes personal information that the data collector does not own or license shall notify the owner or licensee of the information of any breach of the security of the data immediately following discovery, if the personal information was, or is reasonably believed to have been, acquired by an unauthorized person.

(c) For purposes of this Section, notice to consumers may be provided by one of the following methods:

(1) written notice;

(2) electronic notice, if the notice provided is consistent with the provisions regarding electronic records and signatures for notices legally required to be in writing as set forth in Section 7001 of Title 15 of the United States Code; or

(3) substitute notice, if the data collector demonstrates that the cost of providing notice would exceed $250,000 or that the affected class of subject persons to be notified exceeds 500,000, or the data collector does not have sufficient contact information. Substitute notice shall consist of all of the following:

(i) email notice if the data collector has an email address for the subject persons;

(ii) conspicuous posting of the notice on the data collector's website page if the data collector maintains one; and

(iii) notification to major statewide media.

(d) Notwithstanding subsection (c), a data collector that maintains its own notification procedures as part of an information security policy for the treatment of personal information and is otherwise consistent with the timing requirements of this Act, shall be deemed in compliance with notification requirements of this Section if the data collector notifies subject persons in accordance

with its policies in the event of a breach of the security of the system data.

Section 15. Waiver. Any waiver of the provisions of this Act is contrary to public policy and is void and unenforceable.

Section 20. Violation. A violation of this Act constitutes an unlawful practice under the Consumer Fraud and Deceptive Business Practices Act.

Credit Card and Debit Card Account Disclosure Act–House Bill 259

This bill provides that a person or entity that provides anything of value upon presentation of a credit card or debit card may not print or otherwise reproduce on the cardholder's receipt either of the following: any part of the credit card or debit card account number, other than the last five digits or characters, or the expiration date of the credit card or debit card. Provides that the prohibition does not apply where the person to whom the credit card or debit card is presented cannot record credit card or debit card numbers except in writing or by imprint. Provides that the prohibition does not apply to electronic benefits transfers under the federal Food Stamp Program. Provides that a person who violates the prohibition is liable to the issuer or the cardholder for any actual damages resulting from the use of the cardholder's credit card or debit card without his or her permission and for costs and attorneys' fees. Provides that the act becomes operative on January 1, 2005, with respect to any credit card or debit card transaction receipt device that is in use prior to January 1, 2004, and becomes operative on January 1, 2004 with respect to any such device first put to use on or after January 1, 2004.

House Bill 761

This bill amends the School Code, various acts relating to the governance of the public universities in Illinois, and the Public Community College Act. It also prohibits a school district, university, or community college from providing a student's name, address, telephone number, Social Security number, e-mail address, or other personal identifying information to a business organization or financial institution that issues credit or debit cards, unless the student is twenty-one years of age or older.

The Children's Privacy Protection and Parental Empowerment Act–Senate Bill 404

This bill provides that a child is a person under the age of sixteen (instead of eighteen). It defines "parent" as a parent, step-parent, or legal guardian, deletes provisions prohibiting the processing of personal information concerning a child by prisoners or convicted sex offenders or distributing or exchanging a child's personal information that one has reason to believe will be used to harm or abuse the child. The bill changes the requirements for information brokers to broker or facilitate the sale of personal information concerning children and provides that the consent of a parent to the sale or purchase of information concerning a child is presumed unless the parent withdraws consent. Amends the School Code. Provides that the state Board of Education shall prepare and disseminate information concerning the Children's Privacy Protection and Parental Empowerment Act and post a notice of rights under the act on its website.

House Bill 4449

The bill amends the Personal Information Protection Act, providing that the notice of the breach of the security of the system data shall be provided at no charge. The bill provides for notice requirements for state agencies that have a breach of security of the system data or written material. Provides that any state agency that collects personal data and has had a breach of security of the system data or written material shall submit an annual report to the General Assembly listing the breaches and outlining any corrective measures that have been taken to prevent future breaches of the security of the system data or written material. Provides that, in addition to the annual report, any state agency that collects personal data and has had a breach of security shall submit a report to the General Assembly within five business days of the discovery or notification of the breach. The bill also provides that, if a state agency is required to notify more than 1,000 persons of a breach of security, the state agency shall also notify, without unreasonable delay, all consumer reporting agencies that compile and maintain files on consumers on a nationwide basis of the timing, distribution, and content of the notices. Provides that any state agency that collects personal data that is no longer needed or stored at the agency shall dispose of the personal data or written material it has collected in such a manner as to ensure the security and confidentiality of the material.

House Bill 4712

This bill amends the Consumer Fraud and Deceptive Business Practices Act, making it an unlawful practice to publicly post or display an individual's Social Security number or print an individual's Social Security number on any card required to access products or services. The bill states that you cannot require an individual to transmit his or her Social Security number over the Internet, or require an individual to use his or her Social Security number to access an Internet website, or print an individual's Social Security number on materials that are mailed to the individual, subject to various exceptions. The bill also provides that the new provisions do not apply to the collection, use, or release of a Social Security number by the state, a subdivision of the state, or an individual in the employ of the state or a subdivision of the state in connection with his or her official duties. The bill also provides that a person or entity that provides an insurance card must print on the card an identification number unique to the holder of the card in the format prescribed by the Uniform Prescription Drug Information Card Act.

House Bill 5165

This bill creates the Social Security Number Protection Task Force Act and establishes the Social Security Number Protection Task Force to examine the procedures used by Illinois to protect an individual against the unauthorized disclosure of his or her Social Security number when the state requires the individual to provide his or her Social Security number to an officer or agency of the state.

Senate Bill 2545

This bill amends the Consumer Fraud and Deceptive Business Practices Act. The bill provides that a person or entity may not print an individual's Social Security number on an insurance card that is used to establish the eligibility of an individual or his or her dependents to receive health, dental, optical, or accident insurance benefits, prescription drug benefits, or benefits under a managed care plan or a plan provided by a health maintenance organization, a health services plan corporation, or a similar entity. The bill also provides that existing insurance cards with an individual's Social Security number must be replaced with one that is compliant with this bill.

House Bill 128

This bill amends the Social Security Number Protection Task Force Act, providing for the appointment of an additional member to the Task Force to represent the Illinois courts and the Department of Aging. It requires the Task Force to present its findings to the General Assembly no later than March 1, 2006.

House Bill 173

This bill amends the Income Withholding for Support Act, providing that the court, at its discretion, may withhold the Social Security numbers of the child or children from being disclosed in the income withholding notice.

House Bill 188

This bill amends the Prevailing Wage Act, and provides that the contractor and each subcontractor must submit monthly, in person, by mail, or electronically, a certified payroll to the public body in charge of the project. The bill also provides that the records become public records upon two business days' notice. The bill excludes an employee's address, telephone number, and Social Security number from public inspection.

Senate Bill 123

This bill amends the Illinois Administrative Procedure Act and the Department of Natural Resources Act. It requires the Department of Natural Resources as soon as practicable to assign a customer identification number to each applicant for a hunting or fishing license. The bill also provides that after the applicant has been assigned a customer identification number, the applicant may use that customer identification number in place of his or her Social Security number on any subsequent application for a hunting or fishing license. Requires the Department to keep a record of the Social Security number of each applicant and to notify each applicant that his or her Social Security number is kept on file with the department. The bill also provides that a licensee's Social Security number shall not appear on the face of his or her hunting or fishing license.

Senate Bill 445

This bill creates the Social Security Numbers Limited Use Act. It prohibits the use of Social Security numbers by persons or entities except for certain uses. The bill also provides that an individual's Social Security number may not be printed on an insurance card. It prohibits private universities and colleges and private business and vocational schools from printing an individual's Social Security number on any card or other document required for the individual to access products or services provided by the institution. Violations of this bill carry criminal penalties. The bill also amends the University of Illinois Act, the Southern Illinois University Management Act, the Chicago State University Law, the Eastern Illinois University Law, the Governors State University Law, the Illinois State University Law, the Northeastern Illinois University Law, the Northern Illinois University Law, the Western Illinois University Law, and the Public Community College Act to prohibit the printing of an individual's Social Security number on any card or other document required for the individual to access products or services provided by the institution. The bill also amends the Consumer Fraud and Deceptive Business Practices Act to repeal a section prohibiting the use of an individual's Social Security number on an insurance card. Amends the State Mandates Act to require implementation without reimbursement.

Senate Bill 1799

This bill amends the Illinois Department of Revenue Law of the Civil Administrative Code. It requires the Illinois Department of Revenue to notify an individual if the Department discovers or reasonably suspects that another person has used that individual's Social Security number.

House Bill 605

This bill updates the Personal Information Protection Act, House Bill 1633. It defines a breach of the security of the system data or written material. Furthermore, it provides that the notice requirements of the Act apply to breaches of written material containing personal information. The bill goes on to state that a data collector shall notify the resident that there has been a breach of the security of the system data or written material within a reasonable time after the discovery of the breach of the system data or written material.

House Bill 3725

This bill creates the Illinois Financial Information Privacy Act, and allows a consumer to direct a financial institution to not share the nonpublic personal information with affiliated companies or with nonaffiliated financial companies with which the financial institution has contracted to provide financial products and services. This is a similar requirement to the opt-in and opt-out data sharing provisions of Gramm-Leach-Bliley, which was passed at the federal level back in 2003.

Senate Bill 235

This bill amends the Illinois Banking Act. It states that a bank may not disclose to any person, except to the customer or his or her duly authorized agent, any financial records or financial information obtained from financial records relating to that customer of that bank unless the financial records are disclosed in response to a lawful subpoena, summons, warrant, citation to discover assets, or court order which meets certain criteria.

Chapter 14: Indiana

Senate Bill 503

This bill prohibits an Indiana state agency from releasing the Social Security number of an individual unless the release is (1) required by state law, federal law, or court order; (2) authorized in writing by the individual; (3) made to comply with the USA Patriot Act or Presidential Executive Order 13224; or (4) made to a commercial entity for permissible uses set forth in the Drivers Privacy Protection Act, the Fair Credit Reporting Act, or the Financial Modernization Act of 1999. Provides that disclosure of the last four digits of a Social Security number is not considered a disclosure of the Social Security number. Requires a state agency to notify an individual of a security breach of the agency's computer system if the individual's unencrypted personal information was or is reasonably believed to have been acquired by an unauthorized person. Makes it a Class D felony to knowingly make a false representation to obtain a Social Security number or for an agency employee to knowingly disclose a Social Security number. Provides that an agency employee who negligently discloses a Social Security number commits a Class A infraction. Requires an individual who prepares a document for recording to certify that the individual reviewed the entire document and took reasonable care to redact Social Security numbers in the document. After December 31, 2007, requires a county recorder or an employee of a county recorder to search documents using redacting technology to redact Social Security numbers before the documents are released for public inspection. Authorizes establishment of a pilot project beginning July 1, 2005, to develop procedures and test technology and equipment for searching recorded documents and redacting Social Security numbers. Requires county recorders to seek federal grants, private funds, and other sources of money to implement redacting technology.

Be it enacted by the General Assembly of the State of Indiana:

SOURCE: IC 4-1-10; (05)SE0503.1.1. --> SECTION 1. IC 4-1-10 IS ADDED TO THE INDIANA CODE AS A NEW CHAPTER TO READ AS FOLLOWS [EFFECTIVE JULY 1, 2005]:

Chapter 10. Release of Social Security Number.

Sec. 1. This chapter applies after June 30, 2006.

Sec. 2. As used in this chapter, "state agency" means an authority, a board, a branch, a commission, a committee, a department, a division, or another instrumentality of the executive, including the administrative, department of state government. Except as provided in subdivision (4), the term does not include the judicial or legislative department of state government. The term

Includes the following:

(1) A state elected official's office

(2) A state educational institution (as defined in IC 20-12-0.5-1)

(3) A body corporate and politic of the state created by state statute.

(4) The Indiana lobby registration commission established by IC 2-7-1.6-1.

Sec. 3. (a) For purposes of this section, disclosure of the last four (4) digits of an individual's Social Security number is not a disclosure of the individual's Social Security number.

(b) Except as provided in section 4 or 5 of this chapter, a state agency may not disclose an individual's Social Security number.

Sec. 4. Unless prohibited by state law, federal law, or court order, the following apply:

(1) A state agency may disclose the Social Security number of an individual to a state, local, or federal agency.

(2) A state law enforcement agency may, for purposes of furthering an investigation, disclose the Social Security number of an

individual to any individual, state, local, or federal agency, or other legal entity.

Sec. 5. A state agency may disclose the Social Security number of an individual if any of the following apply:

(1) The disclosure of the Social Security number is expressly required by state law, federal law, or a court order.

(2) The individual expressly consents in writing to the disclosure of the individual's Social Security number.

(3) The disclosure of the Social Security number is:

(A) made to comply with:

(i) the USA Patriot Act of 2001 (P.L. 107-56);or

(ii) Presidential Executive Order 13224:or

(B) to a commercial entity for the permissible uses set forth in the:

(i) Drivers Privacy Protection Act (18 U.S.C. 2721 et seq.);

(ii) Fair Credit Reporting Act (15 U.S.C. 1681 et seq.); or

(iii) Financial Modernization Act of 1999 (15 U.S.C. 6801 et seq.).

(4) The disclosure of the Social Security number is for the purpose of administration of a state agency employee's or the state agency employee's dependent's health benefits.

Sec. 6. A state agency complies with section 3 of this chapter if the agency:

(1) removes or

(2) completely and permanently obscures: a Social Security number on a public record before disclosing the public record.

Sec. 7. If a state agency releases a Social Security number in violation of this chapter, the agency shall provide notice to the person whose Social Security number was disclosed in the manner set forth in IC 4-1-11.

Sec. 8. An employee of a state agency who knowingly, intentionally, or recklessly discloses a Social Security number in violation of this chapter commits a Class D felony.

Sec. 9. A person who knowingly, intentionally, or recklessly makes a false representation to a state agency to obtain a Social Security number from the state agency commits a Class D felony.

Sec. 10. An employee of a state agency who negligently discloses a Social Security number in violation of this chapter commits a Class A infraction.

Sec. 11. (a) The attorney general may investigate any allegation that a Social Security number was disclosed in violation of this chapter.

(b) If the attorney general determines that there is evidence that a state employee committed a criminal act under section 8 or 9 of this chapter, the attorney general shall report the attorney general's findings to:

(1) the prosecuting attorney in the county where the criminal act occurred; and

(2) the state police department.

Sec. 12. If the attorney general determines that there is evidence that a state employee committed an infraction under section 10 of this chapter, the attorney general:

(1) shall report the attorney general's findings to the appointing authority (as defined in IC 4-2-6-1) of the agency that employs the employee; and

(2) may report the attorney general's findings to the local prosecuting attorney in the county where the infraction occurred.

Sec. 13. The attorney general may adopt rules under IC 4-22-2 that the attorney general considers necessary to carry out this chapter.

SOURCE: IC 4-1-11; (05)SE0503.1.2. --> SECTION 2. IC 4-1-11 IS ADDED TO THE INDIANA CODE AS A NEW CHAPTER TO READ AS FOLLOWS [EFFECTIVE JULY 1, 2005]:

Chapter 11. Notice of Security Breach.

Sec. 1. This chapter applies after June 30, 2006.

Sec. 2. (a) As used in this chapter, "breach of the security of the system" means unauthorized acquisition of computerized data that compromises the security, confidentiality, or integrity of personal information maintained by a state or local agency.

(b) The term does not include the following:

(1) Good faith acquisition of personal information by an agency or employee of the agency for purposes of the agency, if the personal information is not used or subject to further unauthorized disclosure.

(2) Unauthorized acquisition of a portable electronic device on which personal information is stored if access to the device is protected by a password that has not been disclosed.
Sec. 3. (a) As used in this chapter, "personal information" means.

(1) an individual's

(a) first name and last name; or

(b) first initial and last name; and

i. at least (1) of the following data elements:

1. Social Security number

2. Driver's license number or identification card number.

3. Account number, credit card number, debit card number, security code, access code, or password of an individual's financial account

(b) The term does not include the following:

(1) The last four (4) digits of an individual's Social Security number.

(2) Publicly available information that is lawfully made available to the public from records of a federal agency or local agency.

Sec. 4. As used in this section "state agency" has the meaning set forth in IC 4-1-10-2.

Sec. 5. (a) Any state agency that owns or licenses computerized data that includes personal information shall disclose a breach of the security of the system following discovery or notification of the breach to any state resident whose unencrypted personal information was or is reasonably believed to have been acquired by an unauthorized person.

(b) The disclosure of a breach of the security of the system shall be made:

(1) without unreasonable delay; and

(2) consistent with:

a. the legitimate needs of law enforcement, as described in section 7 of this chapter; and

b. any measures necessary to:

i. determine the scope of the breach; and

ii. restore the reasonable integrity of the data system.

Sec. 6. (a) This section applies to a state agency that maintains computerized data that includes personal information that the state agency does not own.

(b) If personal information was or is reasonably believed to have been acquired by an unauthorized person, the state agency shall notify the owner or licensee of the information of a breach of the security of the system immediately following discovery. The agency shall provide the notice to state residents as required under section 5 of this chapter.

Sec. 7 The notification required by this chapter:

(1) may be delayed if a law enforcement agency determines that the notification will impede a criminal investigation.

(2) shall be made after the law enforcement agency determines that it will not compromise the investigation.

Sec. 8. Except as provided in section 9 of this chapter, a state agency may provide the notice required under this chapter in writing; or

(1) by electronic mail, if the individual has provided the state agency with the individual's electronic mail address.

Sec. 9. (a) This section applies if a state agency demonstrates that:

(1) the cost of providing the notice required under this chapter is at least two hundred fifty thousand dollars ($250,000);

(2) the number of persons to be notified is at least five hundred thousand (500,000); or

(3) the agency does not have sufficient contact information; the state agency may use an alternate form of notice set forth in subsection (b).

(b) A state agency may provide the following alternate forms of notice if authorized by subsection (a):

(1) Conspicuous posting of the notice on the state agency's website if the state agency maintains a website.

(2) Notification to major statewide media.

Sec. 10. If a state agency is required to provide notice under this section to more than one thousand (1,000) individuals, the state agency shall notify without unreasonable delay all consumer reporting agencies (as defined in 15 U.S.C. 1681a) of the distribution and content of the notice.

SOURCE: IC 36-2-7.5; (05)SE0503.1.3. --> SECTION 3. IC 36-2-7.5 IS ADDED TO THE INDIANA CODE AS A NEW CHAPTER TO READ AS FOLLOWS [EFFECTIVE JULY 1, 2005]:

Chapter 7.5. Recording Documents Containing Social Security Numbers

Sec. 1. This chapter applies after December 31, 2005.
Sec. 2. As used in this chapter, "redacting technology" refers to technology that has the ability to:

(1) search recorded documents; and

(2) redact Social Security numbers from recorded documents.

Sec. 3. For purposes of this chapter, disclosure of the last four (4) digits of an individual's Social Security number is not a disclosure of the individual's Social Security number.

Sec. 4. A document may not be submitted to the county recorder for recording if the document contains the Social Security number of an individual, unless required by law.

Sec. 5. (a) An individual preparing a document for recording shall affirm, under the penalties for perjury, that the individual has:

(1) reviewed the entire document before submitting the document for recording for the purpose of identifying and, to the extent permitted by law, redacting all Social Security numbers; and

(2) taken reasonable care to redact each Social Security number in the document.

(b) An individual shall make the affirmation required under subsection (a) on a form prescribed by the state board of accounts.
Sec. 6. (a) A county recorder may not accept a document for recording without the completed and executed form described in section 5 of this chapter attached to the document. A form attached to a document under this subsection is considered part of the document for purposes of the fee charged under subsection (b) in accordance with IC 36-2-7-10.

(b) The county recorder shall charge a fee for recording a document under this chapter in accordance with IC 36-2-7-10.

(c) The county recorder shall deposit two dollars ($2) of the fee charged under subsection (b) in the county identification security protection fund established by section 11 of this chapter. This Subsection expires July 1, 2001.

Sec. 7. The state board of accounts shall establish reasonable procedures for a county recorder to follow:

(1) when receiving and reviewing a document submitted for recording; and

(2) in order to comply with this chapter.

Sec. 8. (a) This section applies after December 31, 2007.

(b) To the extent possible, a county recorder may not disclose a recorded document for public inspection under IC 5-14-3 until the county recorder has:

(1) searched the document for a Social Security number; and

(2) to the extent possible, redacted any Social Security numbers contained in the document; using redacting technology.

Sec. 9. A county recorder shall post a notice in the county recorder's office that states the:

(1) duties of

a. an individual preparing a document for recording; and

b. the county recorder; under this chapter, and penalties under section 12 of this chapter.

Sec. 10. A county recorder shall conduct training sessions at least two (2) times each year for the county recorder's employees on the: requirements of this chapter; and procedures to follow in order to comply with this chapter. Sec. 11. (a) As used in this section, "fund" refers to a county identification security protection fund established under subsection (b).

(b) Each county legislative body shall establish an identification security protection fund to be administered by the county recorder. The county fiscal body shall appropriate money from the fund.

(c) A fund consists of money deposited in the fund under section 6(c) of this chapter. Money in a fund does not revert to the county general fund.

(d) A county recorder may use money in the fund only to purchase, upgrade, implement, or maintain redacting technology used in the office of the county recorder.

Sec. 12. (a) This section applies after June 30, 2008.

(b) A county recorder or an employee of a county recorder who discloses a recorded document that contains a Social Security number without having the document searched, to the extent technologically possible, using redacting technology commits a Class A infraction.

SOURCE: ; (05)SE0503.1.4. --> SECTION 4. [EFFECTIVE UPON PASSAGE] (a) The governor may select at least three (3) and not more than six (6) counties for a pilot project beginning July 1, 2005. The governor shall appoint the county recorder to represent each pilot county selected.

(b) The county recorders appointed to the pilot project shall develop procedures and test technology and equipment to fulfill the purposes of IC 36-2-7.5, as added by this act. The state board of accounts shall work with the county recorders appointed under this SECTION in the development of the procedures and testing of technology.

(c) County recorders shall seek federal grants, private funds, and other possible sources of money to implement the redacting technology required by IC 36-2-7.5, as added by this act.

(d) This SECTION expires July 1, 2008.

SOURCE: ; (05)SE0503.1.5. --> SECTION 5. An emergency is declared for this act.

House Bill 1935

This bill makes various changes in the laws concerning access to public records and the collection and protection of personal information.

House Bill 1207

This bill exempts the Indiana Alcohol and Tobacco Commission from statutes that prevent a state agency from compelling an individual to disclose a Social Security number.

House Bill 1073

The bill specifies that: (1) the Indiana Bureau of Motor Vehicles has discretion to withhold certain medical records and evaluations regarding the ability of a driver to operate a motor vehicle safely; and (2) a law enforcement agency has discretion to withhold certain items of personal information contained in the files of the law enforcement agency. It exempts a Social Security number contained in the records of a public agency from disclosure.

Senate Bill 227

The bill prohibits the Indiana Bureau of Motor Vehicles from placing a Social Security number on certain identifying documents without authorization from the holder of the identifying documents. The bill also requires the bureau to adopt rules that do not require the Social Security number of the holder of a commercial driver's license to be contained on the license.

House Bill 114

This bill requires redaction of Social Security numbers, unless required under other law, in documents filed with the county recorder. The bill also requires an instrument that conveys, creates, encumbers, assigns, or otherwise disposes of an interest in or lien on property to have the Social Security numbers redacted before recording and filing unless required by other law. Federal liens are exempt. It reduces the standard for the redaction of Social Security numbers in recorded or filed documents from "to the extent possible" to "to the extent practicable and as permitted by law." The bill adds a culpability standard for the Class A infraction that may be committed when recorded documents containing Social Security numbers are disclosed by the county recorder's office. The bill also provides that a county recorder shall charge a county identification security protection fee for recording or filing a document. Amends the affirmation regarding redacting a Social Security number that must be attached to a document that is recorded or filed.

Chapter 15: Iowa

Iowa's disclosure law provides for the notification of a breach in the security of computerized data of personal information, allows a security alert or block on a consumer report, allows the issuance of an identity theft passport, requires the deletion of certain records relating to dishonored checks, prohibits the collection of certain unauthorized debt obligations, and provides for civil remedies and penalties.

HF 655

An Act relating to identity theft including providing for the notification of a breach in the security of computerized data of personal information, allowing a security alert or block on a consumer report, allowing the issuance of an identity theft passport, requiring the deletion of certain records relating to dishonored checks, prohibiting the collection of certain unauthorized debt obligations, and providing for civil remedies and penalties.

BE IT ENACTED BY THE GENERAL ASSEMBLY OF THE STATE OF IOWA:

Section 1. NEW SECTION. 715C.1 DEFINITIONS.

As used in this chapter unless the context otherwise requires:

1. "Breach of the security of the system" means unauthorized acquisition of computerized data maintained by a person that compromises the security, confidentiality, or integrity of personal information maintained by the person. Good faith acquisition of personal information by an employee or agent of the person for the purposes of the person is not a breach of the security of the system, provided that the personal information is not used for or subject to further unauthorized disclosure.

2. "Consumer" means a natural person.

3. "Consumer report" means the same as defined by the federal Fair Credit Reporting Act, 15 U.S.C. } 1681a.

4. "Consumer reporting agency" means the same as defined by the federal Fair Credit Reporting Act, 15 U.S.C. } 1681a.

5. "Debt collector" means the same as provided in section 537.7102.

6. "File", when used in connection with information on any consumer, means all of the information on that consumer recorded and retained by a consumer reporting agency regardless of how the information is stored.

7. "Personal information" means the same as "identification information" as defined in section 715A.8. "Personal information" does not include publicly available information that is lawfully made available to the general public from federal, state, or local government records.

8. "Security alert" means a notice placed on a consumer file at the request of the consumer that is sent to a recipient of a consumer report involving that consumer file, signifying the fact that the consumer's identity may have been used without the consumer's consent to fraudulently obtain goods or services in the consumer's name.

9. "Security block" means a notice placed on a consumer file that prohibits a consumer reporting agency from releasing a consumer report relating to the extension of credit involving that consumer file without the express authorization of the consumer.

10. "State agency" means any executive, judicial, or legislative department, commission, board, institution, division, bureau, office, agency, or other entity of state government.

Sec. 2. NEW SECTION. 715C.2 NOTIFICATION OF SECURITY BREACH -- REMEDIES.

1. A person that owns or licenses computerized data that includes personal information shall provide notice of any breach of the security of the system following discovery or notification of the breach in the security of the data to any resident of this state whose unencrypted personal information was, or is reasonably believed to have been, acquired by an unauthorized person. The notice shall be made in the most expedient manner possible and without unreasonable delay, consistent with the legitimate needs of law enforcement, as provided in subsection 3, or any measures necessary to determine the scope of the breach and restore the reasonable integrity of the data system. The notice shall include contact information for applicable state and federal services available for victims of identity theft.

2. A person that maintains computerized data that includes personal information that the person does not own shall notify the owner or licensee of the information of any breach of the security of the system maintaining the data immediately following discovery, if the personal information was, or is reasonably believed to have been, acquired by an unauthorized person.

3. The notice required by subsection 1 may be delayed if a law enforcement agency determines that the notification will impede a criminal investigation. The notice required by subsection 1 shall be made after the law enforcement agency determines that such notice will not compromise the investigation.

4. The notice required by subsection 1 shall be provided by one of the following methods:

a. Written notice.

b. Electronic notice, if the notice provided is consistent with the provisions regarding electronic records and signatures required in chapter 554D and 15 U.S.C. } 7001.

c. Substitute notice, if the person demonstrates that the cost of providing notice would exceed two hundred fifty thousand dollars, or that the affected class of subject persons to be notified exceeds five hundred thousand persons, or the person does not have sufficient contact information. Substitute notice shall consist of all of the following:

(1) Electronic mail notice when the person has an electronic mail address for the subject persons.

(2) Conspicuous posting of the notice on the person's internet website, if the person maintains an internet website.

(3) Notification to major statewide media.

5. Notwithstanding subsection 4, a person that maintains its own notification procedures as part of an information security policy for the treatment of personal information and is otherwise consistent with the timing requirements of this section shall be deemed to be in compliance with the notice requirements of subsection 1 if the person notifies subject persons in accordance with the person's policies in the event of a breach of security of the system.

6. a. A person injured by a violation of this section may bring a civil action for an injunction, actual damages, attorney fees, interest, and court costs.

b. The attorney general may bring an action on behalf of an injured person for an injunction, actual damages incurred by the person, attorney fees, interest, and court costs.

c. The rights and remedies available under this section are cumulative to each other and to any other rights and remedies available under law.

7. As used in this section, "person" means a person as defined in section 4.1 that conducts business in this state and includes a state agency.

Sec. 3. NEW SECTION. 715C.3 SECURITY ALERT.

1. REQUESTING ALERT. Upon request by a consumer in writing or by telephone, with proper identification provided by the consumer, a consumer reporting agency shall place a security alert on the consumer's file not later than two business days after the agency receives the request. A consumer may include with the security alert request a telephone number to be used by persons to verify the consumer's identity before entering into a transaction with the consumer. The security alert must remain in effect for not less than ninety days after the date the agency places the security alert on the file. There is no limit on the number of security alerts a consumer may request. At the termination of the security alert, upon written request or telephone authorization by the consumer, and with proper identification provided by the consumer, the agency shall provide the consumer with a copy of the consumer's file.

2. NOTIFICATION OF ALERT.

a. A consumer reporting agency shall send an alert to each person who requests a consumer report if a security alert is in effect for the consumer file involved regardless of whether a full credit report or summary report is requested and shall include a verification telephone number for the consumer if the consumer has provided a telephone number under subsection 1.

b. A person who receives notification of a security alert in connection with a request for a consumer report for the approval of a credit-based application including an application for a new extension of credit, a purchase, lease, or rental agreement for goods, or for an application for a noncredit-related service, shall not lend money, extend credit, or authorize an application without taking reasonable steps to verify the consumer's identity. For the purposes of this section, "extension of credit" does not include an increase in an existing open-end credit plan or any change to or review of an existing credit account.

c. If a consumer has included with a security alert request a specified telephone number to be used for identity verification purposes, a person who receives that telephone number with a security alert shall contact the consumer using that telephone number or take reasonable steps to verify the consumer's identity and confirm that an application for an extension of credit is not the result of identity theft before lending money, extending credit, or completing any purchase, lease, or rental of goods, or approving any noncredit-related services.

3. TOLL-FREE ALERT REQUEST NUMBER. A consumer reporting agency that compiles and maintains files on a nationwide basis as defined by 15 U.S.C. } 1681a(p) shall maintain a toll-free telephone number that will accept security alert requests from consumers twenty-four hours a day, seven days a week, subject to reasonable maintenance or service outages beyond the control of the consumer reporting agency.

4. VIOLATIONS OF ALERT. A creditor, potential creditor, consumer reporting agency, or other entity that violates any provision of this section shall be liable to the victim of an identity theft for all of the documented out-of-pocket expenses caused by the violation committed by such creditor, potential creditor, consumer reporting agency, or other entity and suffered by the victim as a result of the identity theft, plus reasonable attorney fees

and court costs. A violation of this section is an unlawful practice under section 714.16.

Sec. 4. NEW SECTION. 715C.4 SECURITY BLOCK.

1. REQUESTING BLOCK. On written request by a consumer that includes proper identification and a copy of a valid police report or complaint alleging a violation of section 715A.8, a consumer reporting agency shall, within five business days of receipt, place a security block on a consumer's file.

2. DECLINING BLOCK. A consumer reporting agency may decline to block or may rescind any block of consumer information in the exercise of good faith and reasonable judgment, if the consumer reporting agency believes any of the following:

a. The information was blocked due to a misrepresentation of a material fact by the consumer.

b. The information was blocked due to fraud, in which the consumer participated, or of which the consumer had knowledge, and which may for purposes of this section be demonstrated by circumstantial evidence.

c. The consumer agrees that portions of the blocked information or all of the information was blocked in error.

d. The consumer knowingly obtained or should have known that the consumer obtained possession of goods, services, or money as a result of the blocked transaction or transactions.

e. The consumer's report of a violation of section 715A.8 was not authentic.

3. NOTIFICATION OF BLOCK. A consumer reporting agency shall promptly notify a person who requests a consumer report if a

security block is in effect for the consumer file involved in that report and the effective date of the block.

4. RELEASE OF BLOCK.

a. On written request or by telephone and with proper identification provided by a consumer, a consumer reporting agency shall remove a security block not later than the third business day after the date the agency receives the request. The block may be temporarily lifted for a certain predesignated period of time if requested by the consumer.

b. If blocked information is unblocked pursuant to this subsection, the consumer shall be notified in the same manner as consumers are notified of the reinsertion of information pursuant to the federal Fair Credit Reporting Act, 15 U.S.C. } 1681i. The prior presence of the blocked information in the consumer reporting agency's file on the consumer is not evidence of whether the consumer knew or should have known that the consumer obtained possession of any goods, services, or money as described in subsection 2, paragraph "d".

5. FALSE INQUIRIES. A consumer reporting agency shall delete from a consumer report inquiries for consumer reports based upon credit requests that the consumer reporting agency verifies were initiated as a result of a violation of section 715A.8.

6. FEES. A consumer reporting agency may impose a reasonable charge on a consumer for placing a security block on a consumer file.

7. EXEMPTIONS FROM BLOCK. The provisions of this section do not apply to any of the following:

a. A state or local governmental entity, including a law enforcement agency or private collection agency, if the entity or agency is acting under a court order, warrant, subpoena, or administrative subpoena.

b. A consumer reporting agency that acts as a reseller of credit information by assembling and merging information contained in the databases of other consumer reporting agencies, and that does not maintain a permanent database of credit information from which new consumer reports are produced.

c. A check services or fraud prevention services company that issues reports on incidents of fraud or authorizations for the purpose of approving or processing negotiable instruments, electronic funds transfers, or similar payment methods.

d. A demand deposit account information service company that issues reports regarding account closures due to fraud, substantial overdrafts, automatic teller machine abuse, or similar negative information regarding a consumer to inquiring banks or other financial institutions for use only in reviewing a consumer request for a demand deposit account at the inquiring bank or financial institution.

8. VIOLATIONS OF BLOCK. A violation of this section is an unlawful practice under section 714.16.

Sec. 5. NEW SECTION. 715C.5 IDENTITY THEFT PASSPORT.

1. The attorney general, in cooperation with any law enforcement agency, may issue an identity theft passport to a person who meets both of the following requirements:

a. Is a victim of identity theft in this state as described in section 715A.8.

b. Has filed a police report with any law enforcement agency citing that the person is a victim of identity theft.

2. A victim who has filed a report of identity theft with a law enforcement agency may apply for an identity theft passport through the law enforcement agency. The law enforcement agency

shall send a copy of the police report and the application to the attorney general, who shall process the application and supporting report and may issue the victim an identity theft passport in the form of a card or certificate.

3. A victim of identity theft issued an identity theft passport may present the passport to any of the following:

a. A law enforcement agency, to help prevent the victim's arrest or detention for an offense committed by someone other than the victim who is using the victim's identity.

b. A creditor of the victim, to aid in the creditor's investigation and establishment of whether fraudulent charges were made against accounts in the victim's name or whether accounts were opened using the victim's identity.

c. A consumer reporting agency, which shall accept the passport as notice of a dispute and shall include notice of the dispute in all future reports that contain disputed information caused by identity theft.

4. A law enforcement agency, creditor, or consumer reporting agency may accept an identity theft passport issued pursuant to this section and presented by a victim at the discretion of the law enforcement agency, creditor, or consumer reporting agency. A law enforcement agency, creditor, or consumer reporting agency may consider the surrounding circumstances and available information regarding the offense of identity theft pertaining to the victim.

5. An application made with the attorney general under subsection 2, including any supporting documentation, shall be confidential and shall not be a public record subject to disclosure under chapter 22.

6. The attorney general shall adopt rules necessary to implement this section, which shall include a procedure by which the attorney

general shall ensure that an identity theft passport applicant has an identity theft claim that is legitimate and adequately substantiated.

Sec. 6. NEW SECTION. 715C.6 DISHONORED CHECK ELECTRONIC RECORDS -- PENALTY.

1. Any person doing business in this state who accepts a check from a consumer in the ordinary course of business shall delete any electronic records containing information relating to a consumer's dishonored check upon which the person bases a refusal to accept a check from the consumer not later than thirty days after the date that any of the following occur:

a. The consumer and the person doing business agree that the information in the electronic records is incorrect.

b. The consumer presents to the person doing business a report filed by the consumer with a law enforcement agency, or any other written notice by the consumer, stating that the dishonored check was not authorized by the consumer.

2. The attorney general may file an action in district court to seek the assessment of a civil penalty of one hundred dollars for each violation of subsection 1 and may recover reasonable expenses incurred, including attorney fees, investigative costs, witness fees, and deposition expenses.

3. This section shall not apply to electronic records containing information relating to the checking account number or bank routing transit number of a dishonored check.

4. This section shall not apply to a financial institution as defined in section 527.2.

Sec. 7. NEW SECTION. 715C.7 DEBT COLLECTION OF UNAUTHORIZED TRANSACTION.

1. A debt collector shall not collect or attempt to collect an obligation under a check, debit payment, or credit card payment if all of the following conditions apply:

a. The check, debit payment, or credit card payment was dishonored or refused because the obligation was not incurred by a person authorized to use the check, debit, or credit card account.

b. The debt collector has received written notice from a person authorized to use the check, debit, or credit card account that the obligation under the check, debit payment, or credit card payment was not authorized.

c. A person authorized to use the check, debit, or credit card account has filed a report concerning the unauthorized obligation under a check, debit payment, or credit card payment with a law enforcement agency and has provided a copy of the report to the debt collector.

2. This section does not prohibit a debt collector from collecting or attempting to collect an obligation under a check, debit payment, or credit card payment, if the debt collector has credible evidence that the report filed with a law enforcement agency is fraudulent and that the obligation under a check, debit payment, or credit card payment was authorized.

EXPLANATION

This bill provides for certain consumer protections against identity theft including notification of a breach in the security of computerized data of personal information, providing for a security alert or block on a consumer report, and for the issuance of an identity theft passport. The bill requires a person that owns or licenses computerized data that includes personal information to provide notice of any breach of the person's security of the data to those residents of this state whose personal information was or may have been acquired by an unauthorized person. The bill requires a person that maintains computerized data that includes personal information that the person does not own to notify the owner of the data of any breach in the security of the data. A "person" is defined by the bill to include persons that conduct business in this state and state agencies. The notice shall be provided immediately unless a law enforcement agency determines that the notification will impede a criminal investigation. The notice may be made in writing, through electronic means, or by substitute notice, as defined by the bill, and must contain information regarding state and federal services available for victims of identity theft.

The bill provides that a person who is injured by the failure to notify of a security breach required by the bill may file a civil action for an injunction, actual damages, attorney fees, interest, and court costs. The attorney general may also bring a civil action on behalf of an injured person for an injunction, actual damages, attorney fees, and court costs. The bill permits victims of identity theft to request that a security alert be placed on the victim's consumer report, which is more commonly known as a credit report. Before issuing credit on a consumer report containing a security alert, the creditor must take reasonable steps to verify the identity of the person whose consumer report contains the security alert. Failure to verify the identity of the person before issuing credit may result in liability of the creditor for any damages suffered by the person as a result of the credit being issued. A violation is also a consumer fraud under Code section 714.16. The bill requires consumer reporting agencies to maintain a nationwide toll-free telephone number to accept requests for security alerts. The bill permits victims of identity theft to request that a security block be placed on the victim's consumer report. A security block prohibits a consumer reporting agency from releasing the victim's consumer report relating to the extension of credit without the victim's express authorization. A consumer reporting agency may decline to place the block under specific circumstances. With proper identification, the victim may request that the block be temporarily lifted or permanently released. The consumer reporting agency must notify the consumer when a block is placed and when a block is released. A consumer reporting agency may impose a reasonable fee to place a block on a consumer file. Certain entities are exempt from compliance with a security block. Violations are treated as consumer fraud under Code section 714.16. The bill authorizes the attorney general to issue an identity theft passport to a victim of the criminal offense of identity theft, as defined in Code section 715A.8, who has filed a police report with a law enforcement agency. A victim of identity theft may apply for an identity theft passport with the law enforcement agency, which shall send a copy of the police report and application to the attorney general. The identity theft passport shall be in the form of a card or certificate which the victim may present to a law enforcement agency, creditor, or consumer reporting agency to help protect the victim from false criminal charges and fraudulent credit charges. A law enforcement agency, creditor, or consumer reporting agency may use discretion as to whether to accept the identity theft passport after considering surrounding circumstances and available information concerning the commission of identity theft against the victim presenting the passport. An application for an identity theft passport and all supporting documents shall be confidential and not considered a public record under Code chapter 22. The attorney general shall adopt rules necessary to issue the identity theft passports and to ensure that applications for the identity theft passports are legitimate. The bill requires any person doing business in this state to delete any electronic records which contain information about a consumer's dishonored check which has caused the person doing business to refuse to accept other checks from the consumer if the information in the electronic records is incorrect or if the consumer has provided the person doing business with a report filed with a law enforcement agency or other notice that the dishonored check was not authorized by the consumer. The bill provides that the attorney general may seek a civil penalty of up to $100 plus reasonable expenses per violation. The bill prohibits a debt collector from collecting or attempting to collect an obligation under a payment by check, debit, or credit card if the debt collector has received written notice that, and payment was dishonored or refused because, the obligation was not made by a person authorized to use the check, debit, or credit card, and a report of the

unauthorized use has been filed with a law enforcement agency. A debt collector is not prohibited from collecting or attempting to collect an obligation under the bill if the debt collector has credible evidence that the report filed with a law enforcement agency is fraudulent and the obligation was authorized.

Senate Filing 454

Under the bill, the Iowa Supreme Court may prescribe a rule or issue a directive requiring confidentiality of certain categories of personal identification and financial account information filed with the clerk of the district court or the clerk of the State Supreme Court. The bill provides the rule or directive may specify the manner and format in which the confidential information is to be provided to or disseminated by the clerk. The bill also provides that the rule or directive prescribed by the State Supreme Court shall prevail over any other state laws and administrative rules.

Chapter 16: Kansas

The specific data elements that require disclosure according to the laws of the states vary to a certain degree. Kansas Senate Bill 196 is a perfect example of this. Unlike the disclosure laws of the other states, S.B. 196 states that a credit card account number without the associated PIN does rise to the level of requiring disclosure.

An Act Concerning the Protection of Certain Personal Information–Senate Bill 196

HOUSE Substitute for SENATE BILL No. 196

AN ACT concerning protection of certain personal information; restricting disclosure or use of certain information; prohibiting certain acts and providing penalties and remedies for violations; amending K.S.A. 12-4516a, 50-702, 60-4104 and 60-4105 and K.S.A. 2005 Supp. 21-4018, 21-4603d and 22-2410 and repealing the existing sections. *Be it enacted by the Legislature of the State of Kansas:* New Section 1. (a) It shall be unlawful for any person to knowingly and with the intent to defraud, possess or use a scanning device to access, read, obtain, memorize or store, temporarily or permanently, information encoded on the computer chip or magnetic strip or stripe of a payment card. (b) It shall be unlawful for any person to knowingly and with the intent to defraud, possess or use a reencoder to place encoded information on the computer chip or magnetic strip or stripe of a payment card or any electronic medium that allows an authorized transaction to occur. (c) As used in this section: (1) "Scanning device" means a scanner, reader or any other electronic device that is used to access, read, scan, obtain, memorize or store, temporarily or permanently, information encoded on the computer chip or magnetic strip or stripe of a payment card. "Reencoder" means an electronic device that places encoded information from the computer chip, magnetic strip or stripe of a payment card onto the computer chip, magnetic strip or stripe of a different payment card or any electronic medium that allows an authorized transaction to occur. (3) "Payment card"

means a credit card, debit card or any other card that is issued to an authorized user and that allows the user to obtain, purchase or receive goods, services, money or anything else of value. (d) Violation of this section shall be a severity level 6, non-person felony.

(e) This section shall be a part of and supplemental to the Kansas criminal code. New Sec. 2. (a) (1) Unless required by federal law, no document available for public inspection or copying shall contain an individual's Social Security number if such document contains such individual's personal information. "Personal information" shall include, but not be limited to, name, address, phone number or e-mail address. (2) The provisions of paragraph (1) of this subsection shall not apply to documents recorded in the official records of any recorder of deeds of the county or to any documents filed in the official records of the court and shall be included, but not limited to, such documents of any records that when filed constitutes:

(1) A consensual or nonconsensual lien;
(2) an eviction record;
(3) a judgment;
(4) a conviction or arrest;
(5) a bankruptcy;
(6) a secretary of state filing; or
(7) a professional license.

(b) (1) No person, including an individual, firm, corporation, association, partnership, joint venture or other business entity, or any employee or agent therefore, shall solicit, require or use for commercial purposes an individual's Social Security number unless such number is necessary for such person's normal course of business and there is a specific use for such number for which no other identifying number may be used. (2) Paragraph (1) of this subsection does not apply to documents or records that are recorded or required to be open to the public pursuant to state or federal law, or by court rule or order, and this paragraph does not limit access to these documents or records. (3) Paragraph (1) of this subsection does not apply to the collection, use or release of Social Security numbers for the following purposes: (A) Mailing of documents that include Social Security numbers sent as part of an application or enrollment process or to establish, amend or terminate an account, contract or policy or to confirm the accuracy of the Social Security number; (B) internal verification or administrative purposes; (C) investigate or prevent fraud, conduct background checks, conduct social or scientific research, collect a debt, obtain a credit report from or furnish data to a consumer reporting agency pursuant to the fair credit reporting act, 15 U.S.C. §1681, et seq., undertake a permissible purpose enumerated under the Gramm-Leach Bliley Act, 15 U.S.C. §6802 (e), or locate an individual who is missing, a lost relative, or due a benefit, such as pension, insurance or unclaimed property benefit; or(D) otherwise required by state or federal law or regulation. (c) An individual who is aggrieved by a violation of this section may recover a civil penalty of not more than $1,000 for each violation. New Sec. 3. As used in sections 3 and 4, and amendments thereto: (a) "Consumer" means an individual who is a resident of this state. (b) "Encrypted" means transformation of data through the use of algorithmic process into a form in which there is a low probability of assigning meaning without the use of a confidential process or key, or securing the information by another method that renders the data elements unreadable or unusable. (c) "Notice" means: (1) Written notice; (2) electronic notice, if the notice provided is consistent with the provisions regarding electronic records and signatures set forth in 15 U.S.C. 7001; or

(3) substitute notice, if the individual or the commercial entity required to provide notice demonstrates that the cost of providing notice will exceed $100,000, or that the affected class of consumers to be notified exceeds 5,000, or that the individual or the commercial entity does not have sufficient contact information to provide notice. (d) "Redact" means alteration or truncation of data such that no more than the following are accessible as part of the personal information: (1) Five digits of a Social Security number; or

(2) the last four digits of a driver's license number, state identification card number or account number.

(e) "Substitute notice" means: (1) E-mail notice if the individual or the commercial entity has e-mail addresses for the affected class of consumers; (2) conspicuous posting of the notice on the website page of the individual or the commercial entity if the individual or the commercial entity maintains a website; and

(3) notification to major statewide media. (f) "Person" means any individual, partnership, corporation, trust, estate, cooperative, association, government, or governmental subdivision or agency or other entity.

(g) "Personal information" means a consumer's first name or first initial and last name linked to any one or more of the following data elements that relate to the consumer, when the data elements are neither encrypted nor redacted:

(1) Social Security number;

(2) driver's license number or state identification card number; or

(3) financial account number, or credit or debit card number, alone or in combination with any required security code, access code or password that would permit access to a consumer's financial account. The term "personal information" does not include publicly available information that is lawfully made available to the general public from federal, state or local government records.

(h) "Security breach" means the unauthorized access and acquisition of unencrypted or unredacted computerized data that compromises the security, confidentiality or integrity of personal information maintained by an individual or a commercial entity and that causes, or such individual or entity reasonably believes has caused or will cause, identity theft to any consumer. Good faith acquisition of personal information by an employee or agent of an individual or a commercial entity for the purposes of the individual or the commercial entity is not a breach of the security of the system, provided that the personal information is not used for or is not subject to further unauthorized disclosure.

New Sec. 4. (a) A person that conducts business in this state, or a government, governmental subdivision or agency that owns or licenses computerized data that includes personal information shall, when it becomes aware of any breach of the security of the system, conduct in good faith a reasonable and prompt investigation to determine the likelihood that personal information has been or will be misused. If the investigation determines that the misuse of information has occurred or is reasonably likely to occur, the person or government, governmental subdivision or agency shall give notice as soon as possible to the affected Kansas resident. Notice must be made in the most expedient time possible and without unreasonable delay, consistent with the legitimate needs of law enforcement and consistent with any measures necessary to determine the scope of the breach and to restore the reasonable integrity of the computerized data system.

(b) An individual or a commercial entity that maintains computerized data that includes personal information that the individual or the commercial entity does not own or license shall give notice to the owner or licensee of the information of any breach of the security of the data following discovery of a breach, if the personal information was, or is reasonably believed to have been, accessed and acquired by an unauthorized person.

(c) Notice required by this section may be delayed if a law enforcement agency determines that the notice will impede a criminal investigation. Notice required by this section shall be made in good faith, without unreasonable delay and as soon as possible after the law enforcement agency determines that notification will no longer impede the investigation.

(d) Notwithstanding any other provision in this section, an individual or a commercial entity that maintains its own notification procedures as part of an information security policy for the treatment of personal information, and whose procedures are otherwise consistent with the timing requirements of this section, is deemed to be in compliance with the notice requirements of this section if the individual or the commercial entity notifies affected consumers in accordance with its policies in the event of a breach of security of the system.

(e) An individual or a commercial entity that is regulated by state or federal law and that maintains procedures for a breach of the security of the system pursuant to the laws, rules, regulations, guidances or guidelines established by its primary or functional state or federal regulator is deemed to be in compliance with this section. This section does not relieve an individual or a commercial entity from a duty to comply with other requirements of state and federal law regarding the protection and privacy of personal information.

(f) In the event that a person discovers circumstances requiring notification pursuant to this section of more than 1,000 consumers at one time, the person shall also notify, without unreasonable delay, all consumer reporting agencies that compile and maintain files on consumers on a nationwide basis, as defined by 15 U.S.C. §1681a(p), of the timing, distribution and content of the notices.

(g) For violations of this section, except as to insurance companies licensed to do business in this state, the attorney general is empowered to bring an action in law or equity to address violations of this section and for other relief that may be appropriate. The provisions of this section are not exclusive and do not relieve an individual or a commercial entity subject to this section from compliance with all other applicable provisions of law.

(h) For violations of this section by an insurance company licensed to do business in this state, the insurance commissioner shall have the sole authority to enforce the provisions of this section.

S.R. 1824

This bill urges the US Congress to impose prohibitions or limitations on the sale or other dissemination of personal data.

Chapter 17: Kentucky

As of this writing, not all fifty states have disclosure laws. Kentucky does not yet have a data security law with disclosure requirements, or as some would say, a California Senate Bill 1386 type law. Kentucky does have a law regarding the use of Social Security numbers in marriage licenses and in cases involving child support.

House Bill 7 AN ACT relating to consumer protection

Create new sections of KRS Chapter 367 to create definitions related to identity theft; restrict certain uses by businesses of a consumer's Social Security number subject to certain exceptions, to delay the effective date to July 1, 2008, and to make a violation subject to the same remedies, duties, powers and penalties as violations of the Consumer Protection Act; require an agency or business to give notice to a person whose personal information was acquired in a security breach subject to certain exceptions, to make a waiver void and unenforceable, and to declare that a violation is subject to the same remedies, duties, powers and penalties as violations of the Consumer Protection Act; require an agency or business to take certain measures to safeguard against security breaches subject to certain exceptions, and to declare that a violation is subject to the same remedies, duties, powers and penalties as violations of the Consumer Protection Act; declare that the provisions regarding business use of Social Security numbers, security breach notices, and safeguarding against security breaches do not limit the power to enforce criminal or civil statutes or the right to bring civil actions, and to provide venue for civil actions brought by the Attorney General regarding violations; create a new section of KRS Chapter 17 to require a law enforcement agency to take a complaint and provide a copy of the police report to a complainant who has learned or reasonably suspects that his or her identity or personal information has been used without consent in the commission of a criminal offense; create a new section of KRS Chapter 411 to establish an expedited Circuit Court procedure for a person whose identity or personal information has been used without consent in

the commission of a criminal offense to get a determination that he or she is a victim of identity theft, and to require that the court filing fee be the same as for filing a small claims case; create a new section of KRS Chapter 431 to establish an expedited procedure allowing a person who has been charged with a crime because another person used his or her identifying information, and who has been found not guilty or the charges have been dismissed, to make a motion to the Court to redact his or her identifying information from certain records and to establish a procedure restricting access and inspection of those records; create a new section of KRS Chapter 12 to restrict certain uses by agencies of a person's Social Security number, and to prohibit the inclusion of a person's Social Security number in documents filed or recorded with an agency, subject to certain exceptions, to establish a procedure to request redaction of a Social Security number shown in official records on an agency's Internet website subject to certain exceptions, and to delay the effective date to July 1, 2008; create a new section of KRS Chapter 434 to create definitions and establish a Class D felony offense for "phishing," which is using the Internet to induce a person to provide identifying information by representing without authorization that the requester is another person; create a new section of KRS Chapter 411 to provide a civil cause of action against a person who "phishes," to allow injunctive relief, damages up to the greater of actual damages or $25,000 for each violation, treble damages in certain circumstances, and reasonable attorney's fees and court costs to a prevailing plaintiff to subject violations to the remedies, powers, and duties of the Consumer Protection Act, and to establish a statute of limitations; amend KRS 365.720 relating to disposal of records to create a definition for "agency" and delete the definition for "customer"; amend KRS 365.725 to extend the application of the records disposal provisions to agencies and to make the provisions applicable to all records; amend KRS 15.334 to require law enforcement basic training regarding identity theft; amend KRS 411.210 to extend the civil cause of action for victims of certain identity-theft-related crimes to persons whose identity or personal information has been used without consent in the commission of a criminal offense, and to extend the statute of limitations to the later of five years or the date of discovery of the violation or the identity of the perpetrator of the violation; amend KRS 514.160 to provide that the crime of theft of identity applies to use of a live or deceased person's identity, to increase the types of identifying information protected, and to delete the exclusion of credit or debit card fraud crimes; amend KRS 525.080 to provide that the crime of harassing communications applies whether the perpetrator is using the perpetrator's own or another person's identity.

SECTION 1. A NEW SECTION OF KRS CHAPTER 367 IS CREATED TO READ AS FOLLOWS:

As used in Sections 1 to 5 of this Act, unless the context requires otherwise:

(1) "Agency" means any public agency of the executive branch of the Commonwealth of Kentucky or its subdivisions, unless the context requires otherwise;

(2) "Business" means a sole proprietorship, partnership, company, corporation, firm, association, or other group, however organized and whether or not organized to operate at a profit. "Business" shall not include any government or governmental subdivision or agency;

(3) "Consumer" means an individual who is a resident of Kentucky, or his or her legal guardian, or his or her attorney-in-fact specifically appointed for the exercise of rights provided in Sections 1 to 5 of this Act;

(4) "Encrypt" means use of an algorithmic process to transform data into a form in which the data are rendered unreadable or unusable without use of a confidential process or key;

(5) "Person" means any individual, partnership, corporation, company, trust, estate, cooperative, association, or other entity, but

does not include a government or governmental subdivision or agency;

(6) "Personal information" means an individual's first name or first initial and last name, or birth date, in combination with any of the following identifying information of the individual:

(a) Account number;
(b) Code;
(c) Password;
(d) Social Security number;
(e) Tax identification number;
(f) Driver's license number;
(g) Personal identification number;
(h) Credit card number;
(i) Debit card number; or
(j) Medical information.

"Personal information" does not include publicly available information that is lawfully made available to the general public from federal, state, or local government records;

(7) "Records" means any material on which written, drawn, spoken, visual, or electromagnetic information is recorded or preserved, regardless of physical form or characteristics;

(8) "Redact" means rendering data so that it is unreadable or is truncated so that no more than the last four (4) digits of the identification number are accessible as part of the data; and

(9) "Security breach" means unauthorized acquisition, distribution, disclosure, or release of unencrypted or unredacted records or data that compromises the security, confidentiality, or integrity of personal information. "Security breach" also means unauthorized acquisition, distribution, disclosure, or release of encrypted records or data containing personal information along with the confidential process or key to unencrypt the records or

data. Good-faith acquisition of personal information by an employee or agent of the business or agency for the purposes of the business or agency is not a security breach, if the personal information is not used for a purpose unrelated to the business or agency or subject to further unauthorized disclosure.

SECTION 2. A NEW SECTION OF KRS CHAPTER 367 IS CREATED TO READ AS FOLLOWS:

(1) Except as provided in subsection (2) of this section, it shall be unlawful for a business to do any of the following:

(a) Intentionally communicate or otherwise make available to the general public or a nonaffiliated third party a consumer's Social Security number;

(b) Print a consumer's Social Security number on any card required for the consumer to access products or services provided by the business;

(c) Require a consumer to transmit his or her Social Security number over the Internet, unless the connection is secure or the Social Security number is encrypted;

(d) Require a consumer to use his or her Social Security number to access an Internet website, unless a password or unique personal identification number or other authentication device is also required to access the Internet website;

(e) Print a consumer's Social Security number on any materials that are mailed to the consumer, unless state or federal law requires the Social Security number to be on the document to be mailed; or

(f) Disclose a consumer's Social Security number when the party making the disclosure knows or in the exercise of reasonable diligence would have reason to believe that the third party lacks a legitimate purpose for obtaining the consumer's Social Security number.

(2) Subsection (1) of this section shall not apply in the following instances:

(a) When a Social Security number is included in an application or in documents related to an enrollment process, or to establish, amend, or terminate an account, contract, or policy, or to confirm the accuracy of the Social Security number for the purpose of obtaining a consumer report pursuant to 15 U.S.C. sec. 1681b. A Social Security number that is permitted to be mailed under this section may not be printed, in whole or in part, on a postcard or other mailer not requiring an envelope, or visible on the envelope or without the envelope having been opened;

(b) To the collection, use, or release of a Social Security number:

1. For internal verification or administrative purposes;
2. To investigate or prevent fraud;
3. To conduct background checks, as permitted by law;
4. To collect a debt;
5. To undertake a permissible purpose enumerated under or disclosure permitted by the Fair Credit Reporting Act, as amended, 15 U.S.C. sec. 1681 et seq.; or for any purpose set forth in section 502(e) of the Gramm-Leach-Bliley Act, as amended, 15 U.S.C. sec. 6802(e);
6. To locate a person who is due a benefit, such as a pension, insurance, or unclaimed property benefit;
7. To act pursuant to a court order, warrant, subpoena, or when otherwise required by law; or
8. To provide the Social Security number to a federal, state, or local government entity, including a law enforcement agency or court, or their agents or assigns; and

(c) To a Social Security number that has been redacted.

(3) Any waiver of the provisions of this section is contrary to public policy and is void and unenforceable.

(4) All of the remedies, powers, and duties provided by KRS 367.190 to 367.300 and the penalties provided in KRS 367.990 shall apply with equal force and effect to acts or practices declared unlawful by this section.

SECTION 3. A NEW SECTION OF KRS CHAPTER 367 IS CREATED TO READ AS FOLLOWS:

(1) It shall be unlawful for any business or agency that conducts business in Kentucky, and owns or licenses data that include personal information, to fail to notify a resident of Kentucky of a security breach of that resident's personal information, following discovery or notification of an occurrence of a security breach, or when the business or agency has a reasonable belief that a security breach has occurred. The notification shall be made in the most expedient time possible and without unreasonable delay, consistent with the legitimate needs of law enforcement as provided in subsection (3) of this section, or any measures necessary to determine the scope of the security breach and restore the reasonable integrity of the data system.

(2) Any business or agency that maintains data that include personal information that the business or agency does not own shall notify the owner or licensee of the information of any security breach of the information immediately following discovery.

(3) The notice required by this section shall be delayed if the business or agency receives a written request from a law enforcement agency to delay the notice because the notice may impede a criminal investigation. The notice required by this section shall be provided without unreasonable delay after the law enforcement agency communicates to the business or agency its determination that notice will no longer impede the investigation. The request to delay the notice and the

communication to end the delay shall be in writing, or the business or agency shall document the request and communication contemporaneously in writing, and shall include the name of the law enforcement officer and law enforcement agency making the request.

(4) The notice required by subsection (1) of this section shall be clear and conspicuous. The notice shall include a description of the following:

(a) The incident in general terms;

(b) The type of personal information that was subject to the unauthorized acquisition;

(c) The general acts of the business or agency to protect the personal information from further unauthorized acquisition;

(d) A telephone number that the consumer may call for further information and assistance, if one exists; and

(e) A statement that the consumer should remain vigilant by reviewing account statements and monitoring free credit reports.

(5) For purposes of this section, notice to affected consumers shall be provided by at least one (1) of the following methods:

(a) Written notice;

(b) Electronic notice, if the notice provided is consistent with the provisions regarding electronic records and signatures set forth in 15 U.S.C. sec. 7001; or

(c) Substitute notice, if the cost of providing notice would exceed two hundred fifty thousand dollars ($250,000), or the affected class of subject persons to be notified exceeds five hundred thousand (500,000), or that the business or agency does not have sufficient contact information. Substitute notice shall consist of all of the following:

1. E-mail notice when the business or agency has an e-mail address for the subject persons;

2. Conspicuous posting of the notice on the website page of the business or agency , if the business or agency maintains one; and

3. Notification to major statewide media.

(6) Any business or agency that maintains its own notification procedures as part of an information security policy for the treatment of personal information that is substantially consistent with the requirements of this section shall be deemed to be in compliance with the notification requirements of this section if the business or agency notifies subject persons in accordance with its notification procedures in the event of a security breach.

(7) Any waiver of the provisions of this section is contrary to public policy and is void and unenforceable.

(8) This section does not apply to the following:

(a) Any bank or financial institution that is subject to and in compliance with the privacy and security provisions of the Gramm-Leach-Bliley Act, as amended, 15 U.S.C. sec. 6801 et seq;

(b) Any person that is subject to and in compliance with the standards for privacy of individually identifiable health information and the security standards for the protection of electronic health information of the Health Insurance Portability and Accountability Act of 1996, as amended, and regulations adopted thereto, as amended; and

(c) Any consumer reporting agency that is subject to and in compliance with the privacy and security provisions of the federal Fair Credit Reporting Act, 15 U.S.C. sec. 1681 et seq., as amended.

(9) In the event that a business or agency provides notice to more than one thousand (1,000) consumers at one (1) time pursuant to this section, the business or agency shall notify, without unreasonable delay, the Office of Consumer Protection of the Office of the Attorney General and all consumer reporting agencies that compile and maintain files on consumers on a nationwide basis, as defined in 15 U.S.C. sec. 1681a(p), of the timing, distribution, and content of the notice.

(10) The business or agency providing a notice pursuant to this section shall cooperate with reasonable requests from the Office of Consumer Protection of the Office of the Attorney General, consumer reporting agencies, or recipients of the notice, to verify the authenticity of the notice.

(11) All of the remedies, powers, and duties provided by KRS 367.190 to 367.300 and the penalties provided in KRS 367.990 shall apply with equal force and effect to acts or practices declared unlawful by this section.

SECTION 4. A NEW SECTION OF KRS CHAPTER 367 IS CREATED TO READ AS FOLLOWS:

(1) (a) It shall be unlawful for any business or agency that conducts business in Kentucky and maintains or otherwise possesses personal information of a resident of Kentucky, regardless of the form in which the personal information is maintained, to fail to implement and maintain reasonable procedures, including taking any appropriate corrective action, to protect and safeguard against security breaches.

(b) A business may comply with the requirements of this subsection if the actions of the business conform to the requirements for entities subject to the Gramm-Leach-Bliley Act, as amended, 15 U.S.C. sec. 6801 et seq., for safeguarding customer information.

(2) This section does not apply to the following:

(a) Any bank or financial institution that is subject to and in compliance with the privacy and security provision of the Gramm-Leach-Bliley Act, as amended, 15 U.S.C. sec. 6801 et seq;

(b) Any person that is subject to and in compliance with the standards for privacy of individually identifiable health information and the security standards for the protection of electronic health information of the Health Insurance Portability and Accountability Act of 1996, as amended, and regulations adopted thereto, as amended; and

(c) Any consumer reporting agency that is subject to and in compliance with the federal Fair Credit Reporting Act, 15 U.S.C. sec. 1681 et seq., as amended.

(3) All of the remedies, powers, and duties provided by KRS 367.190 to 367.300 and the penalties provided in KRS 367.990 shall apply with equal force and effect to acts or practices declared unlawful by this section.

SECTION 5. A NEW SECTION OF KRS CHAPTER 367 IS CREATED TO READ AS FOLLOWS:

The Attorney General may promulgate administrative regulations necessary for the proper administration and enforcement of Sections 1 to 5 of this Act.

SECTION 6. A NEW SECTION OF KRS CHAPTER 367 IS CREATED TO READ AS FOLLOWS:

(1) Nothing in Sections 1 to 5 of this Act limits the power of any agency of the Commonwealth of Kentucky to enforce criminal or

civil provisions of any chapter of the Kentucky Revised Statutes or the right of any person to bring civil actions granted by any chapter of the Kentucky Revised Statutes or common law and based upon conduct prohibited herein, and nothing in this chapter limits the power of the Commonwealth of Kentucky to punish any person for any conduct which constitutes a criminal offense.

(2) The remedies and penalties provided in Sections 1 to 5 of this Act shall be in addition to any other remedies or penalties for any conduct provided for by common law or statute.

(3) The Attorney General may bring a civil action regarding a violation of Sections 1 to 5 of this Act directly in the Franklin Circuit Court, or in the Circuit Court of any county in which the unlawful conduct occurred or in which an affected consumer resides.

SECTION 7. A NEW SECTION OF KRS CHAPTER 17 IS CREATED TO READ AS FOLLOWS:

(1) A person who has learned or reasonably suspects that his or her identity or personal information has been used, without his or her consent, in violation of KRS 514.160 or any other criminal statute, may make a complaint to any office of the Kentucky State Police, the local law enforcement agency where jurisdiction may lie for investigation and prosecution of the criminal offense, or the local law enforcement agency that has jurisdiction over his or her actual residence.

(2) Regardless of where jurisdiction may lie for investigation and prosecution of the offense, the office of the Kentucky State Police or the local law enforcement agency shall take the complaint, and provide the complainant with a copy of the report form used to take the complaint.

SECTION 8. A NEW SECTION OF KRS CHAPTER 411 IS CREATED TO READ AS FOLLOWS:

(1) For purposes of this section, "identity theft" means the use of an individual's identity or personal information, without that individual's consent, in violation of KRS 514.160 or any other criminal statute.

(2) An individual who reasonably believes that he or she is a victim of identity theft may petition the Circuit Court, in a civil action, for an expedited determination that he or she is a victim of identity theft.

(3) The petition may be filed in the Circuit Court either where the petitioner resides or where related proceedings have been filed.

(4) A petition filed under this section shall be verified by the petitioner and include at least the following:

(a) A description of the facts and circumstances relating to the identity theft;

(b) A statement of the nature of the relief sought by the petitioner;

(c) A copy of the related police report, if any; and

(d) If known, the case number and court of each related proceeding, if any, and the status thereof.

(5) The petitioner shall certify that he or she has served a copy of the petition upon any opposing party or prosecutor for a related proceeding identified in the petition.

(6) A petition may be filed under this section regardless of whether the petitioner is able to identify the person or persons who allegedly engaged in the identity theft.

(7) The court fee for filing a petition under this section shall be the same as the filing fee for small claims filed in the District Court.

(8) The clerk of the court shall provide a copy of the petition to the Commonwealth's attorney and county attorney for the county in which the petition is filed, within three (3) business days of the date the petition is filed.

(9) The Commonwealth's attorney or county attorney, or any party or prosecutor for a related proceeding identified in the petition, may respond to the petition within twenty (20) business days of the date the petition is filed, and may participate in and introduce evidence at a hearing on the petition.

(10) A hearing on a petition filed under this section shall be held within thirty (30) business days of the date the petition is filed.

(11) (a) A judicial determination made pursuant to this section may be based on testimony, affidavits, police reports, or other material, relevant and reliable information, or documentation submitted by the petitioner and other interested parties.

(b) The petitioner is presumed to be a victim of identity theft under this section if a person other than the petitioner is convicted of a criminal offense involving the use of the petitioner's identity or personal information without the petitioner's consent.

(c) The court shall verify the identity of the petitioner. The petitioner shall personally appear before the court and testify under oath.

(12) If the court determines from a preponderance of the evidence that the petitioner is a victim of identity theft, the court shall issue an order:

(a) Declaring that the petitioner is a victim of identity theft;

(b) Describing in general terms the type of personal information and documents involved in the alleged identity theft;

(c) Stating the date of the identity theft, if known;

(d) Stating any known information identifying the person convicted of an offense as stated in paragraph (b) of subsection (11) of this section; and

(e) Making such other orders as are necessary to assist the petitioner in correcting erroneous information that has resulted from the identity theft.

(13) A court may at any time vacate an order issued under this section if the court finds that the petition, or any information submitted in support of the petition, contains a material factual error, material misrepresentation, or fraudulent misrepresentation.

SECTION 9. A NEW SECTION OF KRS CHAPTER 431 IS CREATED TO READ AS FOLLOWS:

(1) An individual who has been charged with a criminal offense as a result of another person or persons using the identifying information of the individual to commit a criminal offense and who has been found not guilty of the offense, or against whom charges have been dismissed, and not in exchange for a guilty plea to another offense, may make a motion, in the District or Circuit Court in which the charges were filed, to redact the movant's identifying information in records as provided in this section, including but not limited to arrest records, fingerprints, photographs, index references, or other data, whether in documentary or electronic form, relating to the arrest, charge, or other matters arising out of the arrest or charge. The motion shall be supported by evidence and the movant's oath that the movant was not the perpetrator of the offenses charged against the movant. The motion is an alternative to any other available remedies.

(2) The motion may be filed at any time following the order of acquittal or dismissal.

(3) (a) Following the filing of the motion, the court may set a date for a hearing.

(b) If the court sets a date for a hearing, it shall notify the following of a reasonable opportunity for a response to the motion:

1. The county or Commonwealth's attorney, as appropriate, or both; and

2. If the criminal charge relates to the abuse or neglect of a child, the Office of General Counsel of the Cabinet for Health and Family Services.

(c) Any hearing on a motion filed pursuant to this section shall be held within thirty (30) days of the filing of the motion.

(4) If the court finds that there are no current charges or proceedings pending in relation to the matter for which the redaction is sought, the court may grant the motion and order the redaction of records in the custody of the court. The court shall order the redaction on a form provided by the Administrative Office of the Courts. The court clerk, Court of Justice, Administrative Office of the Courts, and any other agency of the judicial branch with records relating to the arrest, charge, or other matters arising out of the arrest or charge, that is ordered to redact records, shall certify to the court within sixty (60) days of the entry of the order that the required action has been completed. The court may make such other orders as are necessary to preserve under seal any evidence for future use by law enforcement in the investigation and prosecution of criminal offenses associated with events surrounding the criminal offense the individual was charged with. All orders enforcing the procedure shall be sealed.

(5) The individual whose record is redacted shall not have to disclose the fact of the redaction or any matter relating thereto on an application for employment, credit, or other type of application.

(6) Inspection of the court records subject to the order may thereafter be permitted by the court only upon a motion by the individual who is the subject of the records or by motion of the county or Commonwealth's attorney and only to those persons named in the motion. The records shall be made available as evidence in the prosecution of the person or persons who used the identifying information of the individual.

(7) KRS 523.070 shall not be construed to apply to statements or testimony made in relation to a motion filed pursuant to this section.

SECTION 10. A NEW SECTION OF KRS CHAPTER 12 IS CREATED TO READ AS FOLLOWS:

(1) As used in this section, unless the context requires otherwise, "agency" means any public agency of the executive branch of the Commonwealth or its subdivisions.

(2) Except as provided in subsection (3) of this section, no agency shall do any of the following:

(a) Collect a Social Security number from an individual unless authorized by law to do so or unless the collection of the Social Security number is otherwise necessary for the performance of that agency's duties and responsibilities as prescribed by law. Social Security numbers collected by an agency shall be relevant to the purpose for which collected and shall not be collected until and unless the need for Social Security numbers has been clearly documented;

(b) Fail, when collecting a Social Security number from an individual, to segregate that number on a separate page from the rest of the record, or as otherwise appropriate, in order that the Social Security number can be more easily redacted pursuant to a valid open records request;

(c) Fail, when collecting a Social Security number from an individual, to provide, at the time of or prior to the actual collection of the Social Security number by that agency, that individual, upon request, with a written statement of the purpose or purposes for which the Social Security number is being collected and used;

(d) Use the Social Security number for any purpose other than the purpose stated pursuant to paragraph (c) of this subsection;

(e) Intentionally communicate or otherwise make available to the general public or a nonaffiliated third party a person's Social Security number;

(f) Print an individual's Social Security number on any card required for the individual to access government services;

(g) Require an individual to transmit the individual's Social Security number over the Internet, unless the connection is secure or the Social Security number is encrypted;

(h) Require an individual to use the individual's Social Security number to access an Internet website, unless a password or unique personal identification number or other authentication device is also required to access the Internet website;

(i) Print an individual's Social Security number on any materials that are mailed to the individual, unless state or federal law requires the Social Security number to be on the document to be mailed; or

(j) Disclose an individual's Social Security number when the party making the disclosure knows or in the exercise of reasonable diligence would have reason to believe that the third party lacks a legitimate purpose for obtaining the consumer's Social Security number.

(3) Subsection (2) of this section does not apply in the following circumstances:

(a)When a Social Security number is included in an application or in documents related to an enrollment process, or to establish, amend, or terminate an account, contract, or policy, or to confirm the accuracy of the Social Security number for the purpose of obtaining a consumer report pursuant to 15 U.S.C. sec. 1681b. A Social Security number that is permitted to be mailed under this section may not be printed, in whole or in part, on a postcard or other mailer not requiring an envelope, or visible on the envelope or without the envelope having been opened;

(b)To the collection, use, or release of Social Security numbers:

1. For internal verification or administrative purposes;
2. To investigate or prevent fraud;
3. To conduct background checks, as permitted by law;
4. To collect a debt;
5. To undertake a permissible purpose enumerated under or disclosure permitted by the Fair Credit Reporting Act, as amended, 15 U.S.C. sec. 1681 et seq.; or for any purpose set forth in section 502(e) of the Gramm-Leach-Bliley Act, as amended, 15 U.S.C. sec. 6802(e);
6. To locate a person who is due a benefit, such as a pension, insurance, or unclaimed property benefit; or
7. To act pursuant to a court order, warrant, subpoena, or when otherwise required by law;

(c)To a Social Security number that has been redacted;

(d)To Social Security numbers disclosed to another governmental entity or its agents, assignees, employees, or subcontractors if disclosure is necessary for the governmental entity or its agents, assignees, employees, or subcontractors to perform their duties and responsibilities. The receiving governmental entity and its agents, assignees, employees, and subcontractors shall maintain the confidential status of such numbers;

(e)To Social Security numbers disclosed for a public health purpose pursuant to and in compliance with KRS Chapter 194A or any chapters contained in KRS Title XVIII;

(f)To certified copies of vital records issued pursuant to KRS 213.136;

(g)To vital records or the information contained in vital records that is disclosed pursuant to KRS 213.131;

(h)To any document recorded in the official records of the clerk of the county;

(i)To any document filed in the official records of the courts; or

(j)To Social Security numbers disclosed to or by a law enforcement agency for a law enforcement purpose.

(4)(a) No person preparing or filing a document to be recorded or filed in the official records of an agency may include any person's Social Security number, unless:

1. Otherwise expressly required by law;
2. Otherwise expressly required by the agency pursuant to this section;
3. Otherwise expressly required pursuant to an administrative regulation promulgated by the agency;
4. Otherwise expressly required by court order; or
5. The Social Security number is redacted.

(b) Any loan closing instruction that requires the inclusion of a person's Social Security number on a document to be recorded or filed in the official records of an agency shall be void.

(5) The validity of an instrument as between the parties to the instrument is not affected by the inclusion of a Social Security number on a document recorded or filed with an agency. The agency may not reject an instrument presented for recording or filing because the instrument contains an individual's Social Security number.

(6)(a)Any person has the right to request that an agency remove from a copy of an official record placed on the agency's Internet website available to the general public the person's Social Security number contained in that official record, unless the agency is specifically required or authorized by federal or state statute to place the Social Security number on the agency's Internet website.

(b)The request shall be made in writing, signed by the requester and with the requester's name typed or legibly printed, and delivered in person or by mail, facsimile, or electronic transmission. The request shall identify with specificity the Social Security number to be redacted, the official record that contains the Social Security number, and the location of the Social Security number to be redacted within the official record.

(c)The agency shall have no duty to inquire beyond the written request to verify the identity of a person requesting redaction.

(d)No fee shall be charged for the redaction pursuant to such a request.

(7)An agency shall give notice of the provisions of this section by conspicuously posting signs throughout its offices for public viewing and by conspicuously posting a notice on any Internet website used by the agency that is available to the general public.

(8)Any affected person may petition the Franklin Circuit Court for an order directing compliance with this section.

SECTION 11. A NEW SECTION OF KRS CHAPTER 434 IS CREATED TO READ AS FOLLOWS:

(1)For purposes of this section:

(a)"Electronic mail message" means a message sent to a unique destination that consists of a unique user name or mailbox and a reference to an Internet domain, whether or not displayed, to which such message can be sent or delivered; and

(b)"Identifying information" means specific details that can be used to access a person's financial accounts or to obtain goods or services, including but not limited to such person's Social Security number, driver's license number, bank account number, credit or debit card number, personal identification number, automated or electronic signature, unique biometric data, or account password.

(2)It is a violation of this section to solicit, request, or take any action to induce a person to provide identifying information by means of a Web page, electronic mail message, or otherwise using the Internet, by representing oneself, either directly or by implication, to be another person without the authority or approval of such other person.

(3)Violation of this section is a Class D felony.

(4)In any prosecution for a violation of this section, the Commonwealth is not required to establish, and it is no defense that:

(a)A person other than the defendant who violated this section has not been convicted, apprehended, or identified; or

(b)Some of the acts constituting a violation of this section did not occur in Kentucky or were not a criminal offense or elements of a criminal offense where they did occur.

SECTION 12. A NEW SECTION OF KRS CHAPTER 411 IS CREATED TO READ AS FOLLOWS:

(1)The following persons shall have a cause of action against a person who violates Section 11 of this Act:

(a)Any person who is induced to provide identifying information by means of a Web page, electronic mail message, or otherwise using the Internet, in violation of Section 11 of this Act;

(b)A person engaged in the business of providing Internet access service to the public whose service was used in a violation of Section 11 of this Act;

(c)An owner of a Web page or trademark whose Web page or trademark was used in a violation of Section 11 of this Act; and

(d)The Attorney General.

(2)A person bringing an action under this section may:

(a)Seek injunctive relief to restrain the violator from continuing the violation; and

(b)Recover damages in an amount equal to the greater of:

1. Actual damages arising from the violation; or
2. Twenty-five thousand dollars ($25,000) for each separate violation.

(3)The court may increase an award of damages in an action brought under this section to an amount not to exceed three (3) times the amount allowed under paragraph (b) of subsection (2) of this section, if the defendant has engaged in a pattern or practice of violating Section 11 of this Act.

(4)A plaintiff who prevails in an action filed under this section is entitled to recover reasonable attorney's fees and court costs.

(5)All of the remedies, powers, and duties provided by KRS 367.190 to 367.300 and the penalties provided in KRS 367.990 shall apply with equal force and effect to acts or practices declared unlawful by Section 11 of this Act.

(6)The statute of limitations for cases under the provisions of this section shall be the later of five (5) years from the date of the discovery of the violation of Section 11 of this Act, or five (5) years from the date of discovery of the identity of the perpetrator of the violation.

(7)An interactive computer service provider shall not be held liable or found in violation of Section 11 of this Act for identifying, removing, or disabling access to an Internet Web page or other on-line location that such provider believes in good faith is being used to engage in a violation of this Section 11 of this Act.

Section 13. KRS 365.720 is amended to read as follows:

As used in KRS 367.720 to 365.730, unless the context requires otherwise:

(1) "Agency" means any public agency of the executive branch of the Commonwealth or its subdivisions, unless the context requires otherwise;

(2) "Business" means a sole proprietorship, partnership, corporation, limited liability company, association, or other entity, however organized and whether or not organized to operate at a profit. "Business" shall not mean a bank as defined in 12 U.S.C. sec. 1813(a) or Subtitles 1, 2, and 3 of KRS Chapter 286, a credit union as defined in 12 U.S.C. sec. 1752 or Subtitle 6 of KRS Chapter 286, a savings association as defined in 12 U.S.C. sec. 1813(b), or an association as defined in Subtitle 5 of KRS Chapter 286. The term includes an entity that destroys records;

(3) "Individual" means a natural person;

(4) "Personally identifiable information" means data capable of being associated with a particular person~~[customer]~~ through one (1) or more identifiers, including but not limited to the person's~~[a customer's]~~ name, address, telephone number, electronic mail address, fingerprints, photographs or computerized image, Social Security number, passport number, driver identification number, personal identification card number or code, date of birth, medical information, financial information, tax information, and disability information; and

(5) "Records" means any material, regardless of the physical form, on which information is recorded or preserved by any means, including in written or spoken words, graphically depicted, printed, or electromagnetically transmitted.

Section 14. KRS 365.725 is amended to read as follows:

When a business or agency disposes of, other than by storage, any, the business or agency shall take reasonable steps to destroy, or arrange for the destruction of, that portion of the records containing personally identifiable information by shredding, erasing, or otherwise modifying the personal information in those records to make it unreadable or indecipherable through any means.

Section 15. KRS 15.334 is amended to read as follows:

(1)The Kentucky Law Enforcement Council shall approve mandatory training subjects to be taught to all students attending a law enforcement basic training course that include but are not limited to:

(a) Abuse, neglect, and exploitation of the elderly and other crimes against the elderly, including the use of multidisciplinary teams in the investigation and prosecution of crimes against the elderly;

(b) The dynamics of domestic violence, child physical and sexual abuse, and rape; child development; the effects of abuse and crime on adult and child victims, including the impact of abuse and violence on child development; legal remedies for protection; lethality and risk issues; profiles of offenders and offender treatment; model protocols for addressing domestic violence, rape, and child abuse; available community resources and victim services; and reporting requirements. This training shall be developed in consultation with legal, victim services, victim advocacy, and mental health professionals with expertise in domestic violence, child abuse, and rape;

(c) Human immunodeficiency virus infection and acquired immunodeficiency virus syndrome;

(d) Identification and investigation of, responding to, and reporting bias-related crime, victimization, or intimidation that is a result of or reasonably related to race, color, religion, sex, or national origin; and

(e) Theft of identity and criminal offenses involving identity theft or misuse of another person's identity or personal information.

(2)The council shall develop and approve mandatory professional development training courses to be presented to all certified peace officers. A mandatory professional development training course shall be first taken by a certified peace officer in the training year following its approval by the council and biennially thereafter. A certified peace officer shall be required to take these courses no more than two (2) times in eight (8) years.

(3) The council shall promulgate administrative regulations in accordance with KRS Chapter 13A to establish mandatory basic training and professional development training courses.

(4) The council shall make an annual report by December 31 each year to the Legislative Research Commission that details the subjects and content of mandatory professional development training courses established during the past year and the subjects under consideration for future mandatory training.

Section 16. KRS 411.210 is amended to read as follows:

(1) In addition to pursuing any other remedy, any person whose identity or personal information was used without his or her consent in violation of KRS 514.160 or any other criminal statute-shall have a cause of action, either where the person–resides or the defendant resides, for compensatory and punitive damages against the person who committed the crime–and, if successful, shall be awarded reasonable costs and attorneys' fees.

(2) The statute of limitations for cases under the provisions of this section shall be the later of five (5) years from the date of the discovery that the person's identity or personal information was used without his or her consent in violation of KRS 514.160 or any other criminal statute, or five (5) years from the date of discovery of the identity of the person who committed the crime
Section 17. KRS 514.160 is amended to read as follows:

(1) A person is guilty of the theft of the identity of another when he or she knowingly possesses or uses any current or former identifying information of the other person, whether alive or deceased, or family member or ancestor of the other person, such as that person's or family member's or ancestor's name, address, telephone number, electronic mail address, Social Security number, driver's license number, credit card number, debit card number, bank or other financial institution account numbers, investment account number, identification card number, passport number, electronic identification number, digital signature, birth date, personal identification number or code, and any other information which could be used to identify the person, including unique biometric data, with the intent to represent that he or she is the other person for the purpose of:

(a) Depriving the other person of property;

(b) Obtaining benefits or property to which he or she would otherwise not be entitled;

(c) Making financial or credit transactions using the other person's identity;

(d) Avoiding detection; or

(e) Commercial or political benefit.

(2) Theft of identity is a Class D felony. If the person violating this section is a business that has violated this section on more than one (1) occasion, then that person also violates the Consumer Protection Act, KRS 367.110 to 367.300.

(3) This section shall not apply when a person obtains the identity of another to misrepresent his or her age for the purpose of obtaining alcoholic beverages, tobacco, or another privilege denied to minors.

(4)-Where the offense consists of theft by obtaining or trafficking in the personal identity of another person, the venue of the prosecution may be in either the county where the offense was committed or the county where the other person resides.

(5) A person found guilty of violating any provisions of this section shall forfeit any lawful claim to the identifying information, property, or other realized benefit of the other person as a result of such violation.

Section 18. KRS 525.080 is amended to read as follows:

(1) A person is guilty of harassing communications when with intent to harass, annoy, or alarm another person, whether using his or her own or another person's identity, he or she:

(a) Communicates with a person, anonymously or otherwise, by telephone, telegraph, mail, or any other form of written communication in a manner which causes annoyance or alarm and serves no purpose of legitimate communication; or

(b) Makes a telephone call, whether or not conversation ensues, with no purpose of legitimate communication.

(2) Harassing communications is a Class B misdemeanor.
Section 19. Sections 2 and 10 of this Act take effect on July 1, 2008.

House Bill 111

This bill deletes the requirement in existing law for the inclusion of Social Security numbers on the marriage license, and the requirement for the county clerk to store the Social Security number. The bill also requires a Social Security number, if possessed by a party to a marriage license, to be used as a form of identification. It also permits other forms of identification and requires the Social Security number to be forwarded to the agency responsible for enforcing child support and stored by that agency with a non-identifying numeric, and prohibits the Social Security number from being released to the public.

Chapter 18: Louisiana

Louisiana's disclosure law, Senate Bill 205, also has the exemption from disclosure if, upon investigation, it is determined that the data will not and likely will not be misused. Be very careful to avoid the appearance of a conflict of interest. A company determining that the data they just lost as a result of a security breach will not be misused likely will not stand up to public scrutiny.

The Database Security Breach Notification Law –Senate Bill 205

Pre-filed pursuant to Article III, Section 2(A)(4)(b)(i) of the Constitution of Louisiana.

To enact Chapter 51 of Title 51 of the Louisiana Revised Statutes of 1950, to be comprised of R.S. 51:3071 through 3077, relative to database security; to provide for legislative findings; to provide definitions; to provide for disclosure upon breach in the security of personal information by agencies and persons; to provide for delayed notification in the event of certain criminal investigations; to provide for means of notification; to provide for the recovery of damages; to provide for financial institution compliance in certain cases; and to provide for related matters.

Be it enacted by the Legislature of Louisiana: Section 1. Chapter 51 of Title 51 of the Louisiana Revised Statutes of 1950, comprised of R.S. 51:3071 through 3077, is hereby enacted to read as follows:

CHAPTER 51. DATABASE SECURITY BREACH NOTIFICATION LAW §3071. Short title

This Chapter may be cited as the "Database Security Breach Notification Law."

§3072. Legislative findings. The legislature hereby finds and declares that:

(1) The privacy and financial security of individuals are increasingly at risk due to the ever more widespread collection of personal information.

(2) Credit card transactions, magazine subscriptions, telephone numbers, real estate records, automobile registrations, consumer surveys, warranty registrations, credit reports, and Internet websites are all sources of personal information and form the source material of identity theft.

(3) The crime of identity theft is on the rise in the United States. Criminals who steal personal information use the information to open credit card accounts, write bad checks, buy automobiles, and commit other financial crimes using the identity of another person.

(4) Identity theft is costly to the marketplace and to consumers.

(5) Victims of identity theft must act quickly to minimize the damage; therefore, expeditious notification of possible misuse of a person's personal information is imperative. §3073. Definitions As used in this Chapter, the following terms shall have the following meanings:

(1) "Agency" means the state, a political subdivision of the state, and any officer, agency, board, commission, department or similar body of the state or any political subdivision of the state.

(2) "Breach of the security of the system" means the compromise of the security, confidentiality, or integrity of computerized data that results in, or there is a reasonable basis to conclude has resulted in, the unauthorized acquisition of and access to personal information maintained by an agency or person. Good faith acquisition of personal information by an employee or agent of an agency or person for the purposes of the agency or person is not a breach of the security of the system, provided that the personal information is not used for, or is subject to, unauthorized disclosure.

(3) "Person" means any individual, corporation, partnership, sole proprietorship, joint stock company, joint venture, or any other legal entity.

(4)(a) "Personal information" means an individual's first name or first initial and last name in combination with any one or more of the following data elements, when the name or the data element is not encrypted or redacted:

(i) Social Security number.

(ii) Driver's license number.

(iii) Account number, credit or debit card number, in combination with any required security code, access code, or password that would permit access to an individual's financial account.

(b) "Personal information" shall not include publicly available information that is lawfully made available to the general public from federal, state, or local government records. §3074. Disclosure upon breach in the security of personal information; notification requirements; exemption

A. Any person that conducts business in the state or that owns or licenses computerized data that includes personal information, or any agency that owns or licenses computerized data that includes personal information, shall, following discovery of a breach in the security of the system containing such data, notify any resident of the state whose personal information was, or is reasonably believed to have been, acquired by an unauthorized person.

B. Any agency or person that maintains computerized data that includes personal information that the agency or person does not own shall notify the owner or licensee of the information if the personal information was, or is reasonably believed to have been, acquired by an unauthorized person through a breach of security of the system containing such data, following discovery by the agency or person of a breach of security of the system.

C. The notification required pursuant to Subsections A and B of this Section shall be made in the most expedient time possible and without unreasonable delay, consistent with the legitimate needs of law enforcement, as provided in Subsection D of this Section, or any measures necessary to determine the scope of the breach, prevent further disclosures, and restore the reasonable integrity of the data system.

D. If a law enforcement agency determines that the notification required under this Section would impede a criminal investigation, such notification may be delayed until such law enforcement agency determines that the notification will no longer compromise such investigation.

E. Notification may be provided by one of the following methods:

(1) Written notification.

(2) Electronic notification, if the notification provided is consistent with the provisions regarding electronic records and signatures set forth in 15 U.S.C. 7001.

(3) Substitute notification, if an agency or person demonstrates that the cost of providing notification would exceed two hundred fifty thousand dollars, or that the affected class of persons to be notified exceeds five hundred thousand, or the agency or person does not have sufficient contact information. Substitute notification shall consist of all of the following:

(a) E-mail notification when the agency or person has an e-mail address for the subject persons.

(b) Conspicuous posting of the notification on the Internet site of the agency or person, if an Internet site is maintained.

(c) Notification to major statewide media.

F. Notwithstanding Subsection E of this Section, an agency or person that maintains a notification procedure as part of its information security policy for the treatment of personal information which is otherwise consistent with the timing requirements of this Section shall be deemed to be in compliance with the notification requirements of this Section if the agency or person notifies subject persons in accordance with the policy and procedure in the event of a breach of security of the system.

G. Notification under this title is not required if after a reasonable investigation the person or business determines that there is no reasonable likelihood of harm to customers. §3075. Recovery of damages A civil action may be instituted to recover actual damages resulting from the failure to disclose in a timely manner to a person that there has been a breach of the security system resulting in the disclosure of a person's personal information.

§3076. Financial institution; compliance

A financial institution that is subject to and in compliance with the Federal Interagency Guidance on Response Programs for Unauthorized Access to Customer Information and Customer Notice, issued on March 7, 2005, by the Board of Governors of the Federal Reserve System, the Federal Deposit Insurance Corporation, the office of the comptroller of the currency and the office of thrift supervision, and any revisions, additions, or substitutions relating to said interagency guidance, shall be deemed to be in compliance with this Chapter. §3077. Rulemaking

The provisions of this Chapter shall not take effect until rules are promulgated by the attorney general's office.

Section 2. This Act shall become effective on January 1, 2006; if vetoed by the governor and subsequently approved by the legislature, this Act shall become effective on January 1, 2006, or on

the day following such approval by the legislature, whichever is later.

Senate Bill 338

This bill authorizes the Louisiana State Department of Environmental Quality to restrict access to certain sensitive and personal identification information, such as Social Security numbers, for the purpose of preventing the distribution or dissemination of such information via the Internet by the department or its employees, or by authorized contractors.

House Concurrent Resolution 118

This bill requests that the clerks of the court remove Social Security numbers from documents in the mortgage and conveyance records when making such documents available on the Internet.

House Bill 1464

This bill requires that only the last four digits of a Social Security number appear on mortgage records and notary acts.

House Bill 1149

This bill provides that a health insurance issuer who is in compliance with the Health Insurance Portability and Accountability Act shall be deemed to be in compliance with state laws intended to implement requirements of the Gramm-Leach-Bliley Act provided with respect to personal financial information, including personal health insurance information.

Senate Bill 106

This bill makes it a deceptive and unfair trade practice for a retail business to require an individual's name, address, telephone number, or other personal information when the individual makes payment in cash for a transaction, the subject of which is primarily intended for personal, family, or household use. However, nothing shall prevent a retail business from obtaining such personal information when the consumer makes payment by either credit card or by check. The bill further exempts any cash transaction involving the sale of automobiles, as well as any cash transaction where either state or federal law requires the retail business to obtain a consumer's personal information from the requirements of new law. The bill subjects the violator to any and all actions and penalties associated with the Unfair Trade Practices and Consumer Protection Law.

Senate Bill 137

This bill requires the Louisiana State Department of Justice to create policies and procedures necessary to provide notice to retail businesses relating to deceptive trade practices for requesting certain personal information for cash sales.

Chapter 19: Maine

In addition to the state's main disclosure law, L.D. 1671, Maine has also expanded the requirement to include colleges and universities, identifying them as information brokers that must notify consumers in the event of a security breach. I found the fact that educational institutions were specifically mentioned to be interesting. Colleges and universities are not generally considered to have the most stringent computer security, generally in the name of academic freedom. The statute is L.D. 2017.

Notice of Risk to Personal Data–L.D. 1671

Be it enacted by the People of the State of Maine as follows:

Sec. 1. 10 MRSA c. 210-B is enacted to read:

CHAPTER 210-B

NOTICE OF RISK TO PERSONAL DATA

§1346. Short title

This chapter may be known and cited as "the Notice of Risk to Personal Data Act."

§1347. Definitions

As used in this chapter, unless the context otherwise indicates, the following terms have the following meanings.

1. Business. "Business" means a person, including a corporation, doing business in the State.

2. Encryption. "Encryption" means the disguising of data using generally accepted practices.

3. Personal information. "Personal information" means an individual's last name in combination with one or more of the following data elements, when either the name or the data elements are not encrypted:

A. Social Security number;

B. Driver's license number or state identification number; and

C. Account number or credit or debit card number in combination with any required security code, access code or password that would permit access to an individual's account or financial records as defined in Title 9-B, section 161.

4. Reasonable notification procedures. "Reasonable notification procedures," with respect to a security breach, means procedures that:

A. Use a security program reasonably designed to block unauthorized transactions before they are charged to a customer's account;

B. Provide for notice to be given to a subject person by the owner or licensee of a database or an agent of the owner or licensee after the security program required under paragraph A indicates that the security breach has resulted in fraud or unauthorized transactions, but do not necessarily require notice in other circumstances; and

C. Are subject to examination for compliance with the requirements of this chapter by one or more federal functional regulators, as defined in the federal Gramm-Leach-Bliley Act, 15 United States Code, Section 6809(2), or by the Department of Professional and Financial Regulation, Office of Consumer Credit Regulation with respect to the operation of the security program and the notification procedures.

5. Security breach. "Security breach" means the compromise of the security, confidentiality or integrity of computerized data that results in unauthorized acquisition of and access to personal information maintained by a business or that creates a reasonable basis for the conclusion that such acquisition has occurred. "Security breach" does not include the good faith acquisition of personal information by an employee or agent of a business for the purposes of that business if the personal information is not used or subject to further unauthorized disclosure.

6. Subject person. "Subject person" means a resident of this State whose personal information is stored by a business that has suffered a security breach resulting in the disclosure or possible disclosure of the resident's personal information.

7. Substitute notice. "Substitute notice" means:

A. An e-mail notice, if the business has the e-mail addresses of its customers;

B. A conspicuous posting of the notice on a publicly accessible website of the business; or

C. Publication in major media, including newspapers of general circulation.

8. System. "System" means a computerized data storage system containing personal information.

§1348. Database security

1. Disclosure of security breach to subject person. A business that owns or licenses electronic data containing personal information, following the discovery of a security breach, shall notify the subject person whose unencrypted personal information was, or is reasonably believed to have been, acquired by an unauthorized person.

2. Notification to owner or licensee. A business in possession of electronic data containing personal information that the business does not own or license shall notify the owner or licensee of the personal information if the personal information was, or is reasonably believed to have been, acquired by an unauthorized person through a security breach.

3. Timeliness of notification. Except as provided in subsection 4, notification required pursuant to subsections 1 and 2 must be made as expediently as possible and without unreasonable delay following:

A. The discovery by the business of a security breach; and

B. Any measures necessary to determine the scope of the security breach, prevent further disclosures and restore the reasonable integrity of the system.

4. Delay of notification for law enforcement purposes. Notwithstanding subsections 1 and 2, if a law enforcement agency determines that the notification required under this section would impede a criminal investigation, notification may be delayed until that law enforcement agency determines that the notification will no longer compromise the investigation.

5. Methods of notice. A business is considered to be in compliance with this section if the business provides the subject person with:

A. Written notice by regular, first-class mail; or

B. Substitute notice, if:

(1) The business demonstrates to the Director of the Office of Consumer Credit Regulation within the Department of Professional and Financial Regulation that the cost of providing direct notice would exceed $250,000;

(2) The number of subject persons to be notified exceeds 500,000; or

(3) The business does not have sufficient contact information to notify the subject persons.

Alternative notification procedures. Notwithstanding the requirements of subsections 1 and 2, a business is in compliance with the requirements of this chapter if the business maintains its own reasonable notification procedures as part of a security policy for personal information and notifies subject persons in accordance with that security policy in the event of a security breach.

§1349. Enforcement; penalties

1. Enforcement. The Department of Professional and Financial Regulation, Office of Consumer Credit Regulation is responsible for enforcement of this chapter.

2. Civil violation. A business that violates this chapter commits a civil violation and is subject to the following:

A. A fine of not more than $5,000 per violation, up to a maximum of $25,000 per each day the business is in violation of this chapter;

B. Equitable relief; or

C. Enjoinment from further violations of this chapter.

3. Other rights and remedies. In addition to a civil penalty assessed or relief provided pursuant to subsection 2, a subject person injured by a violation of this chapter may bring a civil action against the business to recover damages.

4. Cumulative effect. The rights and remedies available under this section are cumulative and do not affect or prevent rights and remedies available under federal or state law.

L.D. 692

This bill prohibits the denial of goods or services to an individual because the individual refuses to provide a Social Security number. However, it does not prevent the collection of Social Security numbers when provided for in current law.

Chapter 20: Maryland

Maryland is one of the states that did not have a data breach disclosure law back when the first edition of this book was published. Like nine other states in the two years that have passed, Maryland has since adopted such a law.

HOUSE BILL 90 An Act Concerning Consumer Protection – Personal Identity Protection

FOR the purpose of requiring certain businesses to destroy or arrange for the destruction of records that contain certain personal information in a certain manner; requiring certain businesses that own or license certain personal information of an individual residing in the State to implement and maintain certain security procedures and practices; requiring certain businesses that own or license computerized data that include certain personal information of an individual residing in the State to notify the individual of a breach of the security of a system under certain circumstances; specifying the time at which notification must be given; authorizing notification to be given in a certain manner; requiring the notification to include certain information; requiring certain businesses to give certain notice to certain consumer reporting agencies; requiring certain businesses to provide notice of a breach of the security of a system to the Office of the Attorney General and the Maryland Department of Homeland Security at a certain time; providing that a waiver of certain provisions of this Act is contrary to public policy and is void and unenforceable; providing that compliance with certain provisions of this Act does not relieve a certain business from a duty to comply with certain other requirements of federal or State law; providing that compliance with a federal or State law is deemed to be compliance with this Act with regard to the subject matter of that law under certain circumstances; providing that a violation of this Act is an unfair or deceptive trade practice within the meaning of the Maryland Consumer Protection Act and is subject to certain enforcement and penalty provisions; defining certain terms; providing for a delayed

effective date; and generally relating to the protection of personal information 1 owned or leased by businesses or included in computerized data owned or licensed by businesses.

BY adding to Article – Commercial Law Section 14–3501 through 14–3506 to be under the new subtitle "Subtitle 35. Maryland Personal Information Protection Act" Annotated Code of Maryland (2005 Replacement Volume and 2006 Supplement)

SECTION 1. BE IT ENACTED BY THE GENERAL ASSEMBLY OF MARYLAND, That the Laws of Maryland read as follows:

Article – Commercial Law SUBTITLE 35.MARYLAND PERSONAL INFORMATION PROTECTION ACT. 14–3501.

(A) IN THIS SUBTITLE THE FOLLOWING WORDS HAVE THE MEANINGS INDICATED.

(B) (1) "BUSINESS" MEANS A SOLE PROPRIETORSHIP, PARTNERSHIP, CORPORATION, ASSOCIATION, OR ANY OTHER BUSINESS ENTITY, WHETHER OR NOT ORGANIZED TO OPERATE FOR PROFIT. (2) "BUSINESS" INCLUDES A FINANCIAL INSTITUTION ORGANIZED, CHARTERED, LICENSED, OR OTHERWISE AUTHORIZED UNDER THE LAWS OF THIS STATE, ANY OTHER STATE, THE UNITED STATES, OR ANY OTHER COUNTRY, AND THE PARENT OR SUBSIDIARY OF A FINANCIAL INSTITUTION.

(C) (1) "PERSONAL INFORMATION" MEANS AN INDIVIDUAL'S FIRST NAME OR FIRST INITIAL AND LAST NAME IN COMBINATION WITH ONE OR MORE OF THE FOLLOWING DATA ELEMENTS, WHEN EITHER THE NAME OR THE DATA ELEMENT IS NOT ENCRYPTED, REDACTED, OR SECURED BY ANY OTHER METHOD RENDERING THE ELEMENT UNREADABLE OR UNUSABLE:

(I) A SOCIAL SECURITY NUMBER;

(II) A DRIVER'S LICENSE NUMBER; HOUSE BILL 90 3

(III) A FINANCIAL ACCOUNT NUMBER, 1 INCLUDING A CREDIT CARD NUMBER OR DEBIT CARD NUMBER;

(IV) ANY REQUIRED SECURITY CODE, ACCESS CODE, OR PASSWORD THAT WOULD PERMIT ACCESS TO AN INDIVIDUAL'S FINANCIAL ACCOUNT; OR (V) A CONSUMER REPORT, AS DEFINED IN § 14–1201 OF THIS TITLE. (2) "PERSONAL INFORMATION" DOES NOT INCLUDE PUBLICLY AVAILABLE INFORMATION THAT IS LAWFULLY MADE AVAILABLE TO THE GENERAL PUBLIC FROM FEDERAL, STATE, OR LOCAL GOVERNMENT RECORDS.

(D) "RECORD" MEANS INFORMATION THAT: (1) IS INSCRIBED ON A TANGIBLE MEDIUM; OR (2) IS STORED IN AN ELECTRONIC OR OTHER MEDIUM AND IS RETRIEVABLE IN PERCEIVABLE FORM. 14–3502.

WHEN A BUSINESS IS DESTROYING A RECORD THAT CONTAINS PERSONAL INFORMATION, THE BUSINESS SHALL TAKE ALL REASONABLE STEPS TO DESTROY OR ARRANGE FOR THE DESTRUCTION OF THE RECORD IN A MANNER THAT MAKES THE PERSONAL INFORMATION UNREADABLE OR UNDECIPHERABLE THROUGH ANY MEANS. 14–3503.

(A) TO PROTECT PERSONAL INFORMATION FROM UNAUTHORIZED ACCESS, DESTRUCTION, USE, MODIFICATION, OR DISCLOSURE, A BUSINESS THAT OWNS OR LICENSES PERSONAL INFORMATION OF AN INDIVIDUAL RESIDING IN THE STATE SHALL IMPLEMENT AND MAINTAIN REASONABLE SECURITY

PROCEDURES AND PRACTICES APPROPRIATE TO THE NATURE OF THE PERSONAL INFORMATION.

HOUSE BILL 90 (B) (1) A BUSINESS THAT USES A NONAFFILIATED 1 THIRD PARTY AS A SERVICE TO PERFORM SERVICES FOR THE BUSINESS AND DISCLOSES PERSONAL INFORMATION ABOUT AN INDIVIDUAL RESIDING IN THE STATE UNDER A WRITTEN CONTRACT WITH THE THIRD PARTY SHALL REQUIRE BY CONTRACT THAT THE THIRD PARTY IMPLEMENT AND MAINTAIN REASONABLE SECURITY PROCEDURES AND PRACTICES APPROPRIATE TO THE NATURE OF THE PERSONAL INFORMATION. (2) THIS SUBSECTION SHALL APPLY TO A WRITTEN CONTRACT THAT IS ENTERED INTO ON OR AFTER JANUARY 1, 2009. 14–3504.

(A) IN THIS SECTION: (1) “BREACH OF THE SECURITY OF A SYSTEM” MEANS THE UNAUTHORIZED ACQUISITION OF RECORDS CONTAINING PERSONAL INFORMATION THAT COMPROMISES THE SECURITY, CONFIDENTIALITY, OR INTEGRITY OF THE PERSONAL INFORMATION MAINTAINED BY A BUSINESS; AND (2) “BREACH OF THE SECURITY OF A SYSTEM” DOES NOT INCLUDE THE GOOD–FAITH ACQUISITION OF PERSONAL INFORMATION BY AN EMPLOYEE OR AGENT OF A BUSINESS FOR THE PURPOSES OF THE BUSINESS, PROVIDED THAT THE PERSONAL INFORMATION IS NOT USED OR SUBJECT TO FURTHER UNAUTHORIZED DISCLOSURE.

(B) (1) A BUSINESS THAT OWNS OR LICENSES COMPUTERIZED DATA THAT INCLUDE PERSONAL INFORMATION OF AN INDIVIDUAL RESIDING IN THE STATE SHALL NOTIFY THE INDIVIDUAL OF A BREACH OF THE SECURITY OF A SYSTEM IF, AS A RESULT OF THE BREACH, THE INDIVIDUAL’S PERSONAL INFORMATION:

(I) HAS BEEN ACQUIRED BY AN UNAUTHORIZED PERSON; OR

(II) IS REASONABLY BELIEVED TO HAVE BEEN ACQUIRED BY AN UNAUTHORIZED PERSON.

EXCEPT AS PROVIDED IN SUBSECTION 1 (C) OF THIS SECTION, THE NOTIFICATION REQUIRED UNDER PARAGRAPH (1) OF THIS SUBSECTION SHALL BE GIVEN AS SOON AS PRACTICABLE AFTER THE BUSINESS DISCOVERS OR IS NOTIFIED OF THE BREACH OF THE SECURITY OF A SYSTEM.

(C) (1) THE NOTIFICATION REQUIRED UNDER SUBSECTION (B) OF THIS SECTION MAY BE DELAYED:

(I) IF A LAW ENFORCEMENT AGENCY DETERMINES THAT THE NOTIFICATION WILL IMPEDE A CRIMINAL INVESTIGATION; OR (II) TO DETERMINE THE SCOPE OF THE BREACH OF THE SECURITY OF A SYSTEM AND RESTORE THE INTEGRITY OF THE SYSTEM. (2) IF NOTIFICATION IS DELAYED UNDER ITEM (1)(I) OF THIS SUBSECTION, NOTIFICATION SHALL BE GIVEN AS SOON AS PRACTICABLE AFTER THE LAW ENFORCEMENT AGENCY DETERMINES THAT IT WILL NOT IMPEDE A CRIMINAL INVESTIGATION.

(D) THE NOTIFICATION REQUIRED UNDER SUBSECTION (B) OF THIS SECTION MAY BE GIVEN BY:

(1) WRITTEN NOTICE;

(2) ELECTRONIC NOTICE, IF THE ELECTRONIC NOTICE IS CONSISTENT WITH THE REQUIREMENTS FOR ELECTRONIC RECORDS AND SIGNATURES UNDER 15 U.S.C. § 7001;

(3) TELEPHONIC NOTICE, IF CONTACT IS MADE DIRECTLY WITH THE INDIVIDUALS ENTITLED TO NOTIFICATION UNDER SUBSECTION (B) OF THIS SECTION; OR

(4) SUBSTITUTE NOTICE AS PROVIDED IN SUBSECTION (E) OF THIS SECTION, IF:

(I) THE BUSINESS DEMONSTRATES THAT THE COST OF PROVIDING NOTICE WOULD EXCEED $250,000 OR THAT THE NUMBER OF INDIVIDUALS TO BE NOTIFIED EXCEEDS 500,000;

(II) THE BUSINESS DOES NOT HAVE 1 SUFFICIENT CONTACT INFORMATION OR CONSENT TO SATISFY ITEM (1), (2), OR (3) OF THIS SUBSECTION, FOR ONLY THOSE INDIVIDUALS WITHOUT SUFFICIENT CONTACT INFORMATION OR CONSENT; OR (III) THE BUSINESS IS UNABLE TO IDENTIFY AN INDIVIDUAL ENTITLED TO NOTIFICATION UNDER SUBSECTION (B) OF THIS SECTION, FOR ONLY THOSE UNIDENTIFIABLE AFFECTED INDIVIDUALS. (E) SUBSTITUTE NOTICE UNDER SUBSECTION (D)(4) OF THIS SECTION SHALL CONSIST OF:

(1) ELECTRONICALLY MAILING THE NOTICE TO AN INDIVIDUAL ENTITLED TO NOTIFICATION UNDER SUBSECTION (B) OF THIS SECTION, IF THE BUSINESS HAS AN ELECTRONIC MAIL ADDRESS FOR THE INDIVIDUAL;

(2) CONSPICUOUS POSTING OF THE NOTICE ON THE WEBSITE OF THE BUSINESS, IF ONE IS MAINTAINED; AND

(3) PUBLISHING THE NOTICE, INCLUDING CONTACT INFORMATION FOR THE BUSINESS WHERE AFFECTED

INDIVIDUALS CAN OBTAIN MORE INFORMATION, IN MAJOR STATEWIDE MEDIA.

(F) THE NOTIFICATION REQUIRED UNDER SUBSECTION (B) OF THIS SECTION MUST INCLUDE:

(1) TO THE EXTENT POSSIBLE, A DESCRIPTION OF THE CATEGORIES OF INFORMATION THAT WERE, OR ARE REASONABLY BELIEVED TO HAVE BEEN, ACQUIRED BY A PERSON WITHOUT VALID AUTHORIZATION, INCLUDING WHICH OF THE ELEMENTS OF PERSONAL INFORMATION WERE, OR ARE REASONABLY BELIEVED TO HAVE BEEN, ACQUIRED; (2) CONTACT INFORMATION FOR THE BUSINESS MAKING THE NOTIFICATION, INCLUDING AN ADDRESS AND TOLL–FREE CONTACT TELEPHONE NUMBER;

(3) THE TOLL–FREE TELEPHONE NUMBERS AND ADDRESSES FOR THE MAJOR CONSUMER REPORTING AGENCIES; AND

(4) (I) THE TOLL–FREE TELEPHONE 1 NUMBERS, ADDRESSES, AND WEBSITE ADDRESSES FOR:

1. THE FEDERAL TRADE COMMISSION; AND

2. THE OFFICE OF THE ATTORNEY GENERAL; AND

(II) A STATEMENT THAT AN INDIVIDUAL CAN OBTAIN INFORMATION FROM THESE SOURCES ABOUT STEPS THE INDIVIDUAL CAN TAKE TO AVOID IDENTITY THEFT.

(G) (1) A BUSINESS REQUIRED UNDER SUBSECTIONS OF THIS SECTION TO GIVE NOTICE OF A BREACH OF THE SECURITY OF A SYSTEM TO 1,000 OR MORE INDIVIDUALS SHALL ALSO NOTIFY EACH CONSUMER REPORTING

AGENCY THAT COMPILES AND MAINTAINS FILES ON CONSUMERS ON A NATIONWIDE BASIS, AS DEFINED BY U.S.C. § 1681 (A), OF THE TIMING, DISTRIBUTION, AND CONTENT OF THE NOTICES. (2) THIS SUBSECTION DOES NOT REQUIRE A BUSINESS TO PROVIDE A CONSUMER REPORTING AGENCY WITH THE NAMES OR OTHER PERSONAL INFORMATION OF RECIPIENTS OF NOTICES OF A BREACH OF THE SECURITY OF A SYSTEM.

(H) A BUSINESS SHALL PROVIDE NOTICE OF A BREACH OF THE SECURITY OF A SYSTEM TO THE OFFICE OF THE ATTORNEY GENERAL AND THE MARYLAND DEPARTMENT OF HOMELAND SECURITY WITHIN 72 HOURS AFTER THE BUSINESS BECOMES AWARE OF THE BREACH.

(I) A WAIVER OF ANY PROVISION OF THIS SECTION IS CONTRARY TO PUBLIC POLICY AND IS VOID AND UNENFORCEABLE. (J) COMPLIANCE WITH THIS SECTION DOES NOT RELIEVE A BUSINESS FROM A DUTY TO COMPLY WITH ANY OTHER REQUIREMENTS OF FEDERAL OR STATE LAW RELATING TO THE PROTECTION AND PRIVACY OF PERSONAL INFORMATION. 28 14–3505.

(A) COMPLIANCE WITH A FEDERAL OR 1 STATE LAW IS DEEMED TO BE COMPLIANCE WITH THIS SUBTITLE WITH REGARD TO THE SUBJECT MATTER OF THAT LAW IF THE FEDERAL OR STATE LAW PROVIDES:

(1) AT LEAST THE SAME PROTECTION OF PERSONAL INFORMATION AS THE PROTECTION PROVIDED UNDER THIS SUBTITLE; AND

(2) DISCLOSURE REQUIREMENTS THAT ARE AT LEAST AS STRINGENT AS THE DISCLOSURE REQUIREMENTS UNDER § 14–3504 OF THIS SUBTITLE.

(B) THIS SECTION DOES NOT RELIEVE A BUSINESS FROM A DUTY TO COMPLY WITH ANY OTHER REQUIREMENTS OF FEDERAL OR STATE LAW, RELATING TO THE PROTECTION AND PRIVACY OF PERSONAL INFORMATION 14–3506. A VIOLATION OF THIS SUBTITLE:

(1) IS AN UNFAIR OR DECEPTIVE TRADE PRACTICE WITHIN THE MEANING OF TITLE 13 OF THIS ARTICLE; AND

(2) IS SUBJECT TO THE ENFORCEMENT AND PENALTY PROVISIONS CONTAINED IN TITLE 13 OF THIS ARTICLE. 18 SECTION 2. AND BE IT FURTHER ENACTED, That this Act shall take effect 19 January 1, 2008.

House Bill 313

This bill makes some modifications to the definition of financial institution in a provision requiring a financial institution to provide specified information and assistance to Maryland's Child Support Enforcement Administration. It also establishes that an institution-affiliated party is not required to provide specified information or assistance to the administration under specified circumstances. The bill also provides specified immunity from civil liability or criminal penalty for an institution-affiliated party.

House Bill 598

This bill increases from $5,000 to $25,000 the maximum fine for a person knowingly, willfully, and with fraudulent intent possessing, obtaining, or helping another person to possess or obtain any personal identifying information of an individual without consent, in order to use, sell, or transfer the information to get a benefit, credit, good, service, or other thing of value of a specified value or greater in the name of the individual.

House Bill 56

This bill prohibits the public posting or displaying of an individual's Social Security number under specified circumstances; prohibits the printing of an individual's Social Security number on specified cards under specified circumstances; prohibits a person from requiring an individual to transmit the individual's Social Security number over the Internet under specified circumstances; and prohibits a person from transmitting an individual's Social Security number over the Internet under specified circumstances.

House Bill 388

This bill prohibits an employer from printing or causing to be printed an employee's Social Security number on a wage payment check or specified other wage payment documents. I see this as an opportunity for businesses to adopt unique employee identification numbers. This would provide a reference number to track their employees, while at the same time they would be compliant with this bill and protect their employees' non-public information. The same strategy could be applied to their customer as well. Bear in mind that in most cases, the only time a Social Security number is absolutely required is for tax reporting purposes.

House Bill 646

This law states that any person who intentionally discloses a Social Security number as part of the public record of a marriage license application is guilty of a misdemeanor and on conviction is subject to a fine not exceeding $1,000.

Chapter 21: Massachusetts

This is one of the more comprehensive data breach disclosure laws that I have seen at the state level. It not only covers issues of security breaches, and disclosure, but also security freezes and even trafficking in stolen identities. Do not pose as another person who is a resident of Massachusetts. The first offense carries with it a fine of up to $5,000 along with a prison term of not more than two and one-half years. Second offense, and you are looking at a fine of up to $250,000 along with prison time of not more than five years.

The state requires that companies have and maintain written security policies, and keep a detailed inventory of all personal data, both electronic and paper (physical). Massachusetts also requires encryption of sensitive data of its residents when transmitted over a public network such as the Internet, transmitted wirelessly, and when stored on mobile devices such as laptops.

Mass. Gen. Laws § 93H-1 et seq.

Section 1. (a) As used in this chapter, the following words shall, unless the context clearly requires otherwise, have the following meanings:—

"Agency," any agency, executive office, department, board, commission, bureau, division or authority of the commonwealth, or any of its branches, or of any political subdivision thereof.

"Breach of security," the unauthorized acquisition or unauthorized use of unencrypted data or, encrypted electronic data and the confidential process or key that is capable of compromising the security, confidentiality, or integrity of personal information, maintained by a person or agency that creates a substantial risk of identity theft or fraud against a resident of the commonwealth. A good faith but unauthorized acquisition of personal information by a person or agency, or employee or agent thereof, for the lawful purposes of such person or agency, is not a breach of security unless the personal information is used in an unauthorized manner or subject to further unauthorized disclosure.

"Data" any material upon which written, drawn, spoken, visual, or electromagnetic information or images are recorded or preserved, regardless of physical form or characteristics.

"Electronic," relating to technology having electrical, digital, magnetic, wireless, optical, electromagnetic or similar capabilities.

"Encrypted" transformation of data through the use of a 128-bit or higher algorithmic process into a form in which there is a low probability of assigning meaning without use of a confidential process or key, unless further defined by regulation of the department of consumer affairs and business regulation.

"Notice" shall include:—

(i) written notice;

(ii) electronic notice, if notice provided is consistent with the provisions regarding electronic records and signatures set forth in § 7001 (c) of Title 15 of the United States Code; and chapter 110G; or

(iii) substitute notice, if the person or agency required to provide notice demonstrates that the cost of providing written notice will exceed $250,000, or that the affected class of Massachusetts residents to be notified exceeds 500,000 residents, or that the person or agency does not have sufficient contact information to provide notice.

"Person," a natural person, corporation, association, partnership or other legal entity.

"Personal information" a resident's first name and last name or first initial and last name in combination with any 1 or more of the following data elements that relate to such resident:

(a) Social Security number;

(b) driver's license number or state-issued identification card number; or

(c) financial account number, or credit or debit card number, with or without any required security code, access code, personal identification number or password, that would permit access to a resident's financial account; provided, however, that "Personal information" shall not include information that is lawfully obtained from publicly available information, or from federal, state or local government records lawfully made available to the general public.

"Substitute notice," shall consist of all of the following:—

(i) electronic mail notice, if the person or agency has electronic mail addresses for the members of the affected class of Massachusetts residents;

(ii) clear and conspicuous posting of the notice on the home page of the person or agency if the person or agency maintains a website; and

(iii) publication in or broadcast through media or medium that provides notice throughout the commonwealth.

(b) The department of consumer affairs and business regulation may adopt regulations, from time to time, to revise the definition of "encrypted," as used in this chapter, to reflect applicable technological advancements.

Section 2. When disposing of records, each agency or person shall meet the following minimum standards for proper disposal of records containing personal information:

(a) paper documents containing personal information shall be either redacted, burned, pulverized or shredded so that personal data cannot practicably be read or reconstructed;

(b) electronic media and other non-paper media containing personal information shall be destroyed or erased so that personal information cannot practicably be read or reconstructed.

Any agency or person disposing of personal information may contract with a third party to dispose of personal information in accordance with this chapter. Any third party hired to dispose of material containing personal information shall implement and monitor compliance with policies and procedures that prohibit unauthorized access to or acquisition of or use of personal information during the collection, transportation and disposal of personal information.

Any agency or person who violates the provisions of this chapter shall be subject to a civil fine of not more than $100 per data subject affected, provided said fine shall not exceed $50,000 for each instance of improper disposal. The attorney general may file a civil action in the superior or district court in the name of the commonwealth to recover such penalties.

Section 3. The attorney general may bring an action pursuant to section 4 of chapter 93A against a person or otherwise to remedy violations of this chapter and for other relief that may be appropriate.

H.B 328 An Act Relative To Identity Theft Protection

SECTION 1. Section 50 of chapter 93 of the General Laws, as so appearing, is hereby amended by inserting after the definition "user" the following definition: "Security freeze", a notice, at the request of the consumer and subject to certain exceptions, that prohibits the consumer reporting agency from releasing all or any part of the consumer's credit report or any information derived from it without the express authorization of the consumer. If a security freeze is in place, such a report or information may not be released to a third party without prior express authorization from the consumer. This subdivision does not prevent a consumer reporting agency from advising a third party that a security freeze is in effect with respect to the consumer's credit report.

"Reviewing the account" or "account review" includes activities related to account maintenance, monitoring, credit line increases, and account upgrades and enhancements

SECTION 2. Said chapter 93 is hereby amended by inserting after section 51A the following section:— Section 51B Consumer Report Security Freeze

1) A consumer may elect to place a "security freeze" on his or her credit report by: a) making a request by mail,

b) making a request by telephone by providing certain personal identification, or c) making a request directly to the consumer reporting agency through a secure electronic mail connection if such connection is made available by the agency. Credit reporting agencies shall make a secure electronic mail method of requesting a security freeze available within 180 days of this Act's effective date.

Be it enacted by the Senate and House of Representatives in General Court assembled, and by the authority of the same, as follows:

In the Year Two Thousand and Seven.

AN ACT RELATIVE TO IDENTITY THEFT PROTECTION.

2) A consumer reporting agency shall place a security freeze on a consumer's credit report no later than five business days after receiving a written or telephone request from the consumer or three business days after receiving a secure electronic mail request. Within one year of this Act's effective date, a consumer reporting agency shall place a security freeze on a consumer's credit report no later than 3 business days after receiving a written or telephone request from the consumer or one business day after receiving a secure electronic mail request. Within two years of this Act's effective date, a consumer reporting agency shall place a security freeze on a consumer's credit reporting agency no later than one business day after receiving a written or telephone request.

3) The consumer reporting agency shall send a written confirmation of the security freeze to the consumer within five business days of

placing the freeze and at the same time shall provide the consumer with a unique personal identification number or password to be used by the consumer when providing authorization for the release of his or her credit for a specific party or period of time, or when permanently lifting the freeze.

4) If the consumer wishes to allow his or her credit report to be accessed for a specific party or period of time while a freeze is in place, he or she shall contact the consumer reporting agency via telephone, mail, or secure electronic mail, with a request that the freeze be temporarily lifted, and provide the following:

a) proper identification, b) the unique personal identification number or password provided by the consumer reporting agency pursuant to paragraph (3) of subsection B, and c) the proper information regarding the third party who is to receive the credit report or the time period for which the report shall be available to users of the credit report.

5) A consumer reporting agency that receives a request from a consumer to temporarily lift a freeze on a credit report pursuant to paragraph (4) of subsection (B) shall comply with the request no later than three business days after receiving the request. Within one year of this Act's effective date, a consumer reporting agency shall honor such a request no later than one business day after receiving the request. Within two years of this Act's effective date, a consumer reporting agency shall honor such a request made by electronic mail or by telephone within fifteen minutes of receiving the request.

6) A consumer reporting agency shall develop procedures involving the use of telephone, fax, or, upon the consent of the consumer in the manner required by the Electronic Signatures in Global and National Commerce Act [E-Sign] for legally required notices, by the Internet, e-mail, or other electronic media to receive and process a request from a consumer to temporarily lift a freeze on a

credit report pursuant to paragraph (4) of subsection (B) in an expedited manner.

7) A consumer reporting agency shall remove or temporarily lift a freeze placed on a consumer's credit report only in the following cases: a) upon consumer request, pursuant to paragraph (4) or paragraph (10) of subsection (B); b) if the consumer's credit report was frozen due to a material misrepresentation of fact by the consumer. If a consumer reporting agency intends to remove a freeze upon a consumer's credit report pursuant to this paragraph, the consumer reporting agency shall notify the consumer in writing five business days prior to removing the freeze on the consumer's credit report.

8) If a third party requests access to a consumer credit report on which a security freeze is in effect, and this request is in connection with an application for credit or any other use, and the consumer does not allow his or her credit report to be accessed for that specific party or period of time, the third party may treat the application as incomplete.

9) If a third party requests access to a consumer credit report on which a security freeze is in effect for the purpose of receiving, extending, or otherwise utilizing the credit therein, and not for the sole purpose of account review, the consumer credit report agency must notify the consumer that an attempt has been made to access the credit report.

10) A security freeze shall remain in place until the consumer requests that the security freeze be removed. A consumer reporting agency shall remove a security freeze within three business days of receiving a request for removal from the consumer, who provides both of the following: a) proper identification, and b) the unique personal identification number or password provided by the consumer reporting agency pursuant to paragraph (3) of subsection (B). Not later than one year after the effective date of this Act, a

consumer reporting agency shall remove a security freeze within one business day after receiving such a request.

11) A consumer reporting agency shall require proper identification of the person making a request to place or remove a security freeze.

12) A consumer reporting agency may not suggest or otherwise state or imply to a third party that the consumer's security freeze reflects a negative credit score, history, report or rating.

13) The provisions of this section do not apply to the use of a consumer credit report by any of the following: a) a person, or the person's subsidiary, affiliate, agent, or assignee with which the consumer has or, prior to assignment, had an account, contract, or debtor-creditor relationship for the purposes of reviewing the account or collecting the financial obligation owing for the account, contract, or debt. b) a subsidiary, affiliate, agent, assignee, or prospective assignee of a person to whom access has been granted under paragraph (4) of subsection (B) for purposes of facilitating the extension of credit or other permissible use. c) any person acting pursuant to a court order, warrant, or subpoena. d) a State or local agency which administers a program for establishing and enforcing child support obligations. e) the [state health department] or its agents or assigns acting to investigate fraud. f) the [state tax authority] or its agents or assigns acting to investigate or collect delinquent taxes or unpaid court orders or to fulfill any of its other statutory responsibilities. g) a person for the purposes of prescreening as defined by the federal Fair Credit Reporting Act. h) any person or entity administering a credit file monitoring subscription service to which the consumer has subscribed. i) any person or entity for the purpose of providing a consumer with a copy of his or her credit report upon the consumer's request.

14) A consumer reporting agency shall not charge a consumer any fee to place a security freeze or for temporary or permanent removal of the security freeze on a consumer report. A consumer reporting agency may charge up to $5 for a replacement of the personal

identification number or password provided by the consumer reporting agency when the security freeze was requested. There shall be no such fees if a consumer:— a) provides the consumer reporting agency with a copy of a police incident report or criminal complaint alleging identity theft; b) is 62 years or older; or c) is a person with a disability, as defined in section 1 of chapter 123B, or who is otherwise mentally or physically disabled and as a result of such mental or physical disability is wholly or partially dependent on another person or persons to meet his daily living needs. d) is a veteran of the United States armed services or a person who receives veteran's benefits. Subsection C. Notice of Rights. At any time that a consumer is required to receive a summary of rights required under Section 609 of the federal Fair Credit Reporting Act the following notice shall be included:

Massachusetts Consumers Have the Right to Obtain a Security Freeze. You may obtain a security freeze on your credit report at no charge to protect your privacy and ensure that credit is not granted in your name without your knowledge. You have a right to place a "security freeze" on your credit report pursuant to [State law]. The security freeze will prohibit a consumer reporting agency from releasing any information in your credit report without your express authorization or approval.

The security freeze is designed to prevent credit, loans, and services from being approved in your name without your consent. When you place a security freeze on your credit report, within five business days (and by [date], no later than one business day) you will be provided a personal identification number or password to use if you choose to remove the freeze on your credit report or to temporarily authorize the release of your credit report for a specific party, parties or period of time after the freeze is in place. To provide that authorization, you must contact the consumer reporting agency and provide all of the following:

1. The unique personal identification number or password provided by the consumer reporting agency.

2. Proper identification to verify your identity.
3. The proper information regarding the third party or parties who are to receive the credit report or the period of time for which the report shall be available to users of the credit report.

A consumer reporting agency that receives a request from a consumer to lift temporarily a freeze on a credit report shall comply with the request no later than three business days after receiving the request (By [date] the consumer reporting agency must temporarily lift the freeze within 15 minutes of receiving the request.) A security freeze does not apply to circumstances where you have an existing account relationship and a copy of your report is requested by your existing creditor or its agents or affiliates for certain types of account review, collection, fraud control or similar activities. If you are actively seeking a new credit, loan, utility, telephone, or insurance account, you should understand that the procedures involved in lifting a security freeze may slow your own applications for credit. You should plan ahead and lift a freeze — either completely if you are shopping around, or specifically for a certain creditor — with enough advance notice before you apply for new credit for the lifting to take effect. Until [date], you should lift the freeze at least 3 business days before applying; between [date] and [date] you should lift the freeze at least one business day before applying; and after [date] you should lift the freeze at least 15 minutes before applying for a new account. You have a right to bring a civil action against someone who violates your rights under the credit reporting laws. The action can be brought against a consumer reporting agency or a user of your credit report." Subsection D. Violations; Penalties. If a consumer reporting agency erroneously, whether by accident or design, violates the security freeze by releasing credit information that has been placed under a security freeze, the affected consumer is entitled to:

1) Notification within five business days of the release of the information, including specificity as to the information released and the third party recipient of the information.

2) File a complaint with the Federal Trade Commission and the state Attorney General and the office of Consumer Affairs and Business Regulation.

3) In a civil action against the consumer reporting agency recover:

a) injunctive relief to prevent or restrain further violation of the security freeze, and/or
b) a civil penalty in an amount not to exceed $1,000 for each violation plus any damages available under other civil laws, and
c) reasonable expenses, court costs, investigative costs, and attorney's fees.

4) Each violation of the security freeze shall be counted as a separate incident for purposes of imposing penalties under this section.

SECTION 3. The General Laws are amended to create a new Chapter 66B entitled "Consumer Breach Notification" and providing as follows:— Section 1. Definitions. For the purposes of this chapter, the following terms shall have the following meanings:

1) "Data Collector" may include but is not limited to government agencies, public and private universities, privately and publicly held corporations, financial institutions, retail operators, and any other entity which, for any purpose, whether by automated collection or otherwise, handles, collects, disseminates, or otherwise deals with personal information.

2) "Personal information," means an individual's last name, address, or phone number in combination with any one or more of the following data elements, when either the name or the data elements are not encrypted or redacted, or encrypted with an encryption key that was also acquired:

a) Social Security number.

b) Driver's license number or state identification card number.
c) Account number, credit or debit card number, if circumstances exist wherein such a number could be used without additional identifying information, access codes, or passwords.
d) Account passwords or personal identification numbers (PINs) or other access codes.
e) Biometric data.
f) Any of items (a)-(e) when not in connection with the individual's last name, address or phone number if the information compromised would be sufficient to perform or attempt to perform identity theft against the person whose information was compromised.

"Personal information" does not include publicly available information that is lawfully made available to the general public from federal, state, or local government records and in the possession of a data receiver.

3) "Security Breach", the unauthorized acquisition of computerized or non-computerized data that compromises the security, confidentiality, or integrity of personal information maintained by the data collector. Good faith acquisition of personal information by an employee or agent of the data collector for a legitimate purpose of the data collector is not a breach of the security of the data, provided that the personal information is not used for a purpose unrelated to the data collector or subject to further unauthorized disclosure. Breach of the security of non-computerized data may include but is not limited to unauthorized photocopying, facsimiles, or other paper-based transmittal of documents.

Section 2. Notice of Breach.

1) Any data collector that owns or uses personal information in any form (whether computerized, paper, or otherwise) that includes personal information concerning a Massachusetts resident shall

notify the resident that there has been a breach of the security of the data following discovery or notification of the breach. The disclosure notification shall be made in the most expedient time possible and without unreasonable delay, consistent with the legitimate needs of law enforcement, as provided in paragraph (2) of subsection B, or with any measures necessary to determine the scope of the breach and restore the reasonable integrity, security and confidentiality of the data system.

2) The notification required by this section may be delayed if a law enforcement agency determines in writing that the notification may seriously impede a criminal investigation.

3) For purposes of this section, "notice" to consumers may be provided by one of the following methods:

a) Written notice.

b) Electronic notice, if the notice provided is consistent with the provisions regarding electronic records and signatures, for notices legally required to be in writing, set forth in Section 7001 of Title 15 of the United States Code.

c) Substitute notice, if the agency demonstrates that the cost of providing notice would exceed two hundred fifty thousand dollars ($250,000) or that the affected class of subject persons to be notified exceeds 500,000, or the agency does not have sufficient contact information. Substitute notice shall consist of all of the following:

1. Conspicuous posting of the notice on the Internet site of the agency or person, if the agency or person maintains a public Internet site; and

2. Notification to major statewide media. The notice to media shall include a toll-free phone number where an individual can learn whether or not that individual's personal data is included in the security breach.

4) Content of Notice

Such notice shall include—

a) to the extent possible, a description of the categories of information that was, or is reasonably believed to have been, acquired by an unauthorized person, including social security numbers, driver's license or State identification numbers and financial data;

b) a toll-free number—

1. that the individual may use to contact the agency or person, or the agent of the agency or person; and

2. from which the individual may learn—

(a) what types of information the agency or person maintained about that individual or about individuals in general; and

(b) whether or not the agency or person maintained information about that individual; and

c) the toll-free contact telephone numbers and addresses for the major credit reporting agencies.

5) The notification required by this section may be delayed if a law enforcement agency determines, in writing, that the notification may impede a criminal investigation.

6) Additional Obligation Following Breach — A person required to provide notification under Subsection A shall provide or arrange for the provision of, to each individual to whom notification is provided under subsection and on request and at no cost to such individual, consumer credit reports from at least one of the major credit reporting agencies beginning not later than 2 months following a breach of security and continuing on a quarterly basis for a period of 2 years thereafter.

Subsection C. Remedies.

1) Violations of any provision of this section shall constitute and unfair and deceptive trade practice pursuant to the provisions of chapter ninety-three A. Section 3. Social Security Numbers. No person or data collector operating in the commonwealth shall:

(1) intentionally communicate or otherwise make available to the general public an individual's Social Security number;

(2) print an individual's Social Security number on any card required for the individual to access products or services provided by the person or data collector;

(3) require an individual to transmit his or her Social Security number over the Internet, unless the connection is secure or the Social Security number is encrypted;

(4) require an individual to use his or her Social Security number to access an Internet website, unless a password or unique personal identification number or other authentication device is also required to access the Internet website;

(5) print an individual's Social Security number on any materials that are mailed to the individual, unless required by law;

(6) sell, lease, loan, trade, rent, or otherwise disclose an individual's Social Security number to a third party for any purpose without written consent to the disclosure from the individual.

Section 4. Disposal of Personal Information.

A data collector shall take all reasonable measures to protect against unauthorized access to or use of personal information in connection with, or after its disposal including, but not limited to:

(a) Implementing and monitoring compliance with policies and procedures that require the burning, pulverizing or shredding of papers containing personal information so that the information cannot practicably by read or reconstructed; and

(b) Implementing and monitoring compliance with policies and procedures that require the destruction or erasure of electronic media and other non-paper media containing personal information so that the information cannot practicably by read or reconstructed.

SECTION 4. Penalties

Chapter 266 of the General Laws is hereby amended by striking out Section 37E and inserting in its place the following:—

Section 37E. Use of personal identification of another; identity fraud; penalty; restitution

(a) For purposes of this section, the following words shall have the following meanings:—

"Harass", willfully and maliciously engage in an act directed at a specific person or persons, or at a specific organization or organizations, which act seriously alarms or annoys such person or persons or any person or persons employed by or associated with such organization or organizations, and would cause a reasonable person to suffer substantial emotional distress.

"Identifying information", any name or number that may be used, alone or in conjunction with any other information, to assume the identity of an individual or organization including any name, address, telephone number, driver's license number, social security number, place of employment, employee identification number, tax identification number, mother's maiden name, demand deposit account number, savings account number, credit card number, computer password identification or other identifying information.
"Organization", any corporation, partnership, joint venture, firm,

sole proprietorship, association of individuals, or any other professional or business entity.

"Person with a disability", a person who is mentally retarded, as defined by section one of chapter one hundred and twenty three B or who is otherwise mentally or physically disabled and as a result of such mental or physical disability is wholly or partially dependent on another person or persons to meet his daily living needs. "Pose", to falsely represent oneself, directly or indirectly, as another person, persons, or organization.

"Victim", any person who, or organization that, has suffered financial loss or any entity that provided money, credit, goods, services or anything of value and has suffered financial loss as a direct result of the commission or attempted commission of a violation of this section.

(b) Whoever, with fraudulent intent, knowingly and intentionally poses as another person, living or dead, as a representative of an organization, or as being authorized to act on behalf of an organization, and uses such person's or organization's identifying information to obtain or to attempt to obtain money, credit, goods, services, anything of value, any identification card or other evidence of such person's or organization's identity, to harass another person or organization, to commit an illegal act, or to avoid identification, apprehension or prosecution for a crime shall be guilty of the crime of identity fraud and shall be punished for an initial offense by a fine of not more than $5,000 or imprisonment in a house of correction for not more than two and one-half years, or by both such fine and imprisonment and for a second and subsequent offense by a fine of not more than $25,000 or imprisonment in the state prison for not more than five years or a house of correction for not more than two and one half years, or both such fine and imprisonment.

(c) Whoever, with fraudulent intent, knowingly and intentionally obtains identifying information about another person, living or dead, or an organization, with the intent to pose as such person, or as a representative of such organization, or as being authorized to act on behalf of an organization in order to obtain money, credit, goods, services, anything of value, any identification card or other evidence of such person's or organization's identity, to harass another person or organization, or to avoid identification, apprehension or prosecution for a crime shall be guilty of the crime of identity fraud and shall be punished for an initial offense by a fine of not more than $5,000 or imprisonment in a house of correction for not more than two and one-half years, or by both such fine and imprisonment and for a second and subsequent offense by a fine of not more than $25,000 or imprisonment in the state prison for not more than five years or a house of correction for not more than two and one half years, or both such fine and imprisonment.

(d) Whoever commits an offense described in this section by using the identifying information of a person sixty-five years or older or a person with a disability shall be punished by a fine of not more than $10,000 or imprisonment in the state prison for not more than five years, or in jail for not more than two and one half years, or both and for a second and subsequent offense by a fine of not more than $25,000 or imprisonment in the state prison for not more than ten years or a house of correction for not more than two and one half years, or both such fine and imprisonment.

(e) Whoever knowingly and intentionally manufactures, sells, purchases, transfers, gives, trades, loans, delivers, or possesses five or more items containing the identifying information of the same person or organization, or the identifying information of five or more separate persons or organizations with the intent to commit an offense described in this section or to assist another to commit an offense described in this section shall be guilty of the crime of trafficking in stolen identities and shall be punished by a fine of not more than $25,000 or imprisonment in the state prison for not more than five years, or in jail for not more than two and one half years, or both and for a second and subsequent offense by a fine of not more than $50,000 or imprisonment in the state prison for not more than ten years or a house of correction for not more than two and one half years, or both such fine and imprisonment.

(f) The knowledge or intent of the person alleged to have committed any of the crimes within this section may be proved by direct or circumstantial evidence and the testimony of the individual or a representative on behalf of the organization whose identifying information or item containing identifying information was obtained or used to commit any of the crimes within this section shall not be required to find a person guilty of those crimes.

(g) An offense under this section may be prosecuted in any county in which an element of the offense was committed or in the county of residence of the person or organization whose identifying information was allegedly used in the commission of the crimes of identity fraud or of trafficking in stolen identities as defined in this section.

(h) A person found guilty of violating any provisions of this section shall, in addition to any other punishment, be ordered to make restitution for financial loss sustained by a victim as a result of such violation. Financial loss may include any costs incurred by such victim in correcting the credit history of such victim or any costs incurred in connection with any civil or administrative proceeding to satisfy any debt or other obligation of such victim, including lost wages and attorney's fees.

(i) A victim who reasonably believes that his or her personal identifying information has been unlawfully used in violation of this section may initiate a law enforcement investigation by contacting the local law enforcement agency that has jurisdiction over his or her actual residence or by contacting a local law enforcement agency that has jurisdiction over any location where his or her personal identifying information has been unlawfully used. Said law enforcement agency shall provide the victim with a written report of the incident and may begin an investigation of the facts or, if the suspected crime was committed in a different jurisdiction, refer the

matter to the law enforcement agency where the suspected crime was committed for an investigation of the facts. Nothing in this section shall interfere with the discretion of a local police department to allocate resources for investigations of crimes and a complaint filed under this section shall not be counted as an open case for the purpose compiling open case statistics.

(j) A law enforcement officer may arrest without warrant any person he has probable cause to believe has committed the offense of identity fraud or trafficking in stolen identities as defined in this section.

House Bill 1008

This Bill provides that no insurance company shall disclose any non-public personal information contrary to the provisions of Title V of the federal Financial Services Modernization Act of 1999 (public law 106-102), known as the Gramm-Leach-Bliley Act.

Chapter 22: Michigan

IDENTITY THEFT PROTECTION ACT (EXCERPT)
Act 452 of 2004

445.72 Notice of security breach; requirements.

Sec. 12.

(1) Unless the person or agency determines that the security breach has not or is not likely to cause substantial loss or injury to, or result in identity theft with respect to, 1 or more residents of this state, a person or agency that owns or licenses data that are included in a database that discovers a security breach, or receives notice of a security breach under subsection (2), shall provide a notice of the security breach to each resident of this state who meets 1 or more of the following:

(a) That resident's unencrypted and unredacted personal information was accessed and acquired by an unauthorized person.

(b) That resident's personal information was accessed and acquired in encrypted form by a person with unauthorized access to the encryption key.

(2) Unless the person or agency determines that the security breach has not or is not likely to cause substantial loss or injury to, or result in identity theft with respect to, 1 or more residents of this state, a person or agency that maintains a database that includes data that the person or agency does not own or license that discovers a breach of the security of the database shall provide a notice to the owner or licensor of the information of the security breach.

(3) In determining whether a security breach is not likely to cause substantial loss or injury to, or result in identity theft with respect to, 1 or more residents of this state under subsection (1) or (2), a person or agency shall act with the care an ordinarily prudent

person or agency in like position would exercise under similar circumstances.

(4) A person or agency shall provide any notice required under this section without unreasonable delay. A person or agency may delay providing notice without violating this subsection if either of the following is met:

(a) A delay is necessary in order for the person or agency to take any measures necessary to determine the scope of the security breach and restore the reasonable integrity of the database. However, the agency or person shall provide the notice required under this subsection without unreasonable delay after the person or agency completes the measures necessary to determine the scope of the security breach and restore the reasonable integrity of the database.

(b) A law enforcement agency determines and advises the agency or person that providing a notice will impede a criminal or civil investigation or jeopardize homeland or national security. However, the agency or person shall provide the notice required under this section without unreasonable delay after the law enforcement agency determines that providing the notice will no longer impede the investigation or jeopardize homeland or national security.

(5) Except as provided in subsection (11), an agency or person shall provide any notice required under this section by providing 1 or more of the following to the recipient:

(a) Written notice sent to the recipient at the recipient's postal address in the records of the agency or person.

(b) Written notice sent electronically to the recipient if any of the following are met:

(i) The recipient has expressly consented to receive electronic notice.

(ii) The person or agency has an existing business relationship with the recipient that includes periodic electronic mail communications and based on those communications the person or agency reasonably believes that it has the recipient's current electronic mail address.

(iii) The person or agency conducts its business primarily through internet account transactions or on the internet.

(c) If not otherwise prohibited by state or federal law, notice given by telephone by an individual who represents the person or agency if all of the following are met:

(i) The notice is not given in whole or in part by use of a recorded message.

(ii) The recipient has expressly consented to receive notice by telephone, or if the recipient has not expressly consented to receive notice by telephone, the person or agency also provides notice under subdivision (a) or (b) if the notice by telephone does not result in a live conversation between the individual representing the person or agency and the recipient within 3 business days after the initial attempt to provide telephonic notice.

(d) Substitute notice, if the person or agency demonstrates that the cost of providing notice under subdivision (a), (b), or (c) will exceed $250,000.00 or that the person or agency has to provide notice to more than 500,000 residents of this state. A person or agency provides substitute notice under this subdivision by doing all of the following:

(i) If the person or agency has electronic mail addresses for any of the residents of this state who are entitled to receive the notice, providing electronic notice to those residents.

(ii) If the person or agency maintains a website, conspicuously posting the notice on that website.

(iii) Notifying major statewide media. A notification under this subparagraph shall include a telephone number or a website address that a person may use to obtain additional assistance and information.

(6) A notice under this section shall meet all of the following:

(a) For a notice provided under subsection (5)(a) or (b), be written in a clear and conspicuous manner and contain the content required under subdivisions (c) to (g).

(b) For a notice provided under subsection (5)(c), clearly communicate the content required under subdivisions (c) to (g) to the recipient of the telephone call.

(c) Describe the security breach in general terms.

(d) Describe the type of personal information that is the subject of the unauthorized access or use.

(e) If applicable, generally describe what the agency or person providing the notice has done to protect data from further security breaches.

(f) Include a telephone number where a notice recipient may obtain assistance or additional information.

(g) Remind notice recipients of the need to remain vigilant for incidents of fraud and identity theft.

(7) A person or agency may provide any notice required under this section pursuant to an agreement between that person or agency and another person or agency, if the notice provided pursuant to the agreement does not conflict with any provision of this section.

(8) Except as provided in this subsection, after a person or agency provides a notice under this section, the person or agency shall

notify each consumer reporting agency that compiles and maintains files on consumers on a nationwide basis, as defined in 15 USC 1681a(p), of the security breach without unreasonable delay. A notification under this subsection shall include the number of notices that the person or agency provided to residents of this state and the timing of those notices. This subsection does not apply if either of the following is met:

(a) The person or agency is required under this section to provide notice of a security breach to 1,000 or fewer residents of this state.

(b) The person or agency is subject to title V of the Gramm-Leach-Bliley act, 15 USC 6801 to 6809.

(9) A financial institution that is subject to, and has notification procedures in place that are subject to examination by the financial institution's appropriate regulator for compliance with, the interagency guidance on response programs for unauthorized access to customer information and customer notice prescribed by the board of governors of the federal reserve system and the other federal bank and thrift regulatory agencies, or similar guidance prescribed and adopted by the national credit union administration, and its affiliates, is considered to be in compliance with this section.

(10) A person or agency that is subject to and complies with the health insurance portability and accountability act of 1996, Public Law 104-191, and with regulations promulgated under that act, 45 CFR parts 160 and 164, for the prevention of unauthorized access to customer information and customer notice is considered to be in compliance with this section.

(11) A public utility that sends monthly billing or account statements to the postal address of its customers may provide notice of a security breach to its customers in the manner described in subsection (5), or alternatively by providing all of the following:

(a) As applicable, notice as described in subsection (5)(b).

(b) Notification to the media reasonably calculated to inform the customers of the public utility of the security breach.

(c) Conspicuous posting of the notice of the security breach on the website of the public utility.

(d) Written notice sent in conjunction with the monthly billing or account statement to the customer at the customer's postal address in the records of the public utility.

(12) A person that provides notice of a security breach in the manner described in this section when a security breach has not occurred, with the intent to defraud, is guilty of a misdemeanor punishable by imprisonment for not more than 30 days or a fine of not more than $250.00 for each violation, or both.

(13) Subject to subsection (14), a person that knowingly fails to provide any notice of a security breach required under this section may be ordered to pay a civil fine of not more than $250.00 for each failure to provide notice. The attorney general or a prosecuting attorney may bring an action to recover a civil fine under this section.

(14) The aggregate liability of a person for civil fines under subsection (13) for multiple violations of subsection (13) that arise from the same security breach shall not exceed $750,000.00.

(15) Subsections (12) and (13) do not affect the availability of any civil remedy for a violation of state or federal law.

(16) This section applies to the discovery or notification of a breach of the security of a database that occurs on or after the effective date of the amendatory act that added this section.

(17) This section does not apply to the access or acquisition by a person or agency of federal, state, or local government records or documents lawfully made available to the general public.

(18) This section deals with subject matter that is of statewide concern, and any charter, ordinance, resolution, regulation, rule, or other action by a municipal corporation or other political subdivision of this state to regulate, directly or indirectly, any matter expressly set forth in this section is preempted.

History: Add. 2006, Act 566, Eff. July 2, 2007

Moving on from security breaches and disclosure requirements, next is Michigan's "Identity Theft Protection Act."

Senate Bill 309

A bill to amend 2004 PA 452, entitled "Identity theft protection act," by amending section 11 (MCL 445.71) and by adding section 12.

THE PEOPLE OF THE STATE OF MICHIGAN ENACT:

Sec. 11. (1) A person shall not do any of the following in the conduct of trade or commerce:

(a) Deny credit or public utility service to or reduce the credit limit of a consumer solely because the consumer was a victim of identity theft, if the person had prior knowledge that the consumer was a victim of identity theft. A consumer is presumed to be a victim of identity theft for the purposes of this subdivision if he or she provides both of the following to the person:

(i) A copy of a police report evidencing the claim of the victim of identity theft.

(ii) Either a properly completed copy of a standardized affidavit of identity theft developed and made available by the federal trade commission pursuant to 15 USC 1681g or an affidavit of fact that is acceptable to the person for that purpose.

(b) Solicit to extend credit to a consumer who does not have an existing line of credit, or has not had or applied for a line of credit within the preceding year, through the use of an unsolicited check that includes personal identifying information other than the recipient's name, address, and a partial, encoded, or truncated personal identifying number. In addition to any other penalty or remedy under this act or the Michigan consumer protection act, 1976 PA 331, MCL 445.901 to 445.922, a credit card issuer, financial institution, or other lender that violates this subdivision, and not the consumer, is liable for the amount of the instrument if the instrument is used by an unauthorized user and for any fees assessed to the consumer if the instrument is dishonored.

(c) Solicit to extend credit to a consumer who does not have a current credit card, or has not had or applied for a credit card within the preceding year, through the use of an unsolicited credit card sent to the consumer. In addition to any other penalty or remedy under this act or the Michigan consumer protection act, 1976 PA 331, MCL 445.901 to 445.922, a credit card issuer, financial institution, or other lender that violates this subdivision, and not the consumer, is liable for any charges if the credit card is used by an unauthorized user and for any interest or finance charges assessed to the consumer.

(d) Extend credit to a consumer without exercising reasonable procedures to verify the identity of that consumer. Compliance with regulations issued for depository institutions, and to be issued for other financial institutions, by the United States department of treasury under section 326 of the USA patriot act of 2001, 31 USC 5318, is considered compliance with this subdivision. This subdivision does not apply to a purchase of a credit obligation in an acquisition, merger, purchase of assets, or assumption of liabilities or any change to or review of an existing credit account.

(E) FAIL TO PROVIDE NOTICE TO A PERSON IN VIOLATION OF SECTION 12.

(2) A person who knowingly or intentionally violates subsection (1) is guilty of a misdemeanor punishable by imprisonment for not more than 30 days or a fine of not more than $1,000.00, or both. This subsection does not affect the availability of any civil remedy for a violation of this act, the Michigan consumer protection act, 1976 PA 331, MCL 445.901 to 445.922, or any other state or federal law.

SEC. 12. (1) AN AGENCY OF THIS STATE THAT OWNS OR LICENSES COMPUTERIZED DATA THAT INCLUDE PERSONAL IDENTIFYING INFORMATION SHALL PROVIDE NOTICE OF ANY BREACH OF THE SECURITY OF THE SYSTEM FOLLOWING DISCOVERY OR NOTIFICATION OF THE BREACH IN THE SECURITY OF THE DATA TO A RESIDENT OF THIS STATE WHOSE UNENCRYPTED PERSONAL IDENTIFYING INFORMATION IS ACQUIRED BY AN UNAUTHORIZED PERSON OR IF THE AGENCY REASONABLY BELIEVES THAT AN UNAUTHORIZED PERSON HAS ACQUIRED THAT INFORMATION. THE AGENCY SHALL PROVIDE NOTICE IN THE MOST EXPEDIENT TIME POSSIBLE AND WITHOUT UNREASONABLE DELAY.

(2) AN AGENCY THAT MAINTAINS COMPUTERIZED DATA THAT INCLUDE PERSONAL IDENTIFYING INFORMATION THAT THE AGENCY DOES NOT OWN SHALL PROVIDE NOTICE TO THE OWNER OR LICENSEE OF THE INFORMATION OF ANY BREACH OF THE SECURITY OF THE DATA IMMEDIATELY FOLLOWING DISCOVERY, IF THE PERSONAL IDENTIFYING INFORMATION IS ACQUIRED BY AN UNAUTHORIZED PERSON OR IF THE AGENCY REASONABLY BELIEVES THAT AN UNAUTHORIZED PERSON HAS ACQUIRED THAT INFORMATION.

(3) A PERSON DOING BUSINESS IN THIS STATE THAT OWNS OR LICENSES COMPUTERIZED DATA THAT INCLUDE PERSONAL IDENTIFYING INFORMATION

SHALL PROVIDE NOTICE OF ANY BREACH OF THE SECURITY OF THE SYSTEM FOLLOWING DISCOVERY OR NOTIFICATION OF THE BREACH IN THE SECURITY OF THE DATA TO A RESIDENT OF THIS STATE WHOSE UNENCRYPTED PERSONAL IDENTIFYING INFORMATION IS ACQUIRED BY AN UNAUTHORIZED PERSON OR IF THE PERSON REASONABLY BELIEVES THAT AN UNAUTHORIZED PERSON HAS ACQUIRED THAT INFORMATION. THE PERSON SHALL PROVIDE NOTICE IN THE MOST EXPEDIENT TIME POSSIBLE AND WITHOUT UNREASONABLE DELAY, UNLESS DELAY IS NECESSARY TO DETERMINE THE SCOPE OF THE BREACH AND RESTORE THE REASONABLE INTEGRITY OF THE DATA SYSTEM.

(4) A PERSON DOING BUSINESS IN THIS STATE THAT MAINTAINS COMPUTERIZED DATA THAT INCLUDE PERSONAL IDENTIFYING INFORMATION THAT THE PERSON DOES NOT OWN SHALL PROVIDE NOTICE TO THE OWNER OR LICENSEE OF THE INFORMATION OF ANY BREACH OF THE SECURITY OF THE DATA IMMEDIATELY FOLLOWING DISCOVERY, IF THE PERSONAL IDENTIFYING INFORMATION IS ACQUIRED BY AN UNAUTHORIZED PERSON OR IF THE PERSON REASONABLY BELIEVES THAT AN UNAUTHORIZED PERSON HAS ACQUIRED THAT INFORMATION.

(5) AN AGENCY OR PERSON DOING BUSINESS IN THIS STATE MAY PROVIDE NOTICE UNDER THIS SECTION BY 1 OF THE FOLLOWING METHODS:

(A) WRITTEN NOTICE.

(B) ELECTRONIC NOTICE, IF THE NOTICE PROVIDED IS CONSISTENT WITH THE PROVISIONS REGARDING ELECTRONIC RECORDS AND SIGNATURES SET FORTH IN SECTION 101 OF TITLE I OF THE ELECTRONIC

SIGNATURES IN GLOBAL AND NATIONAL COMMERCE ACT, 15 USC 7001, AND THE AGENCY OR PERSON DOES NOT HAVE SUFFICIENT CONTACT INFORMATION FOR THE INDIVIDUALS, OWNERS, OR LICENSEES IT IS REQUIRED TO NOTIFY UNDER THAT SUBSECTION TO PROVIDE EACH OF THEM WITH WRITTEN NOTICE.

(6) AN AGENCY OR A PERSON DOING BUSINESS IN THIS STATE THAT IS REQUIRED TO PROVIDE NOTICE TO A PERSON UNDER THIS SECTION SHALL NOTIFY THE DEPARTMENT OF ATTORNEY GENERAL, THE COMPUTER CRIMES SECTION OF THE DEPARTMENT OF STATE POLICE, AND ANY LOCAL LAW ENFORCEMENT AGENCY WITH JURISDICTION IN THE CITY, VILLAGE, OR TOWNSHIP WHERE THE AGENCY OR PERSON IS LOCATED.

(7) A PERSON INJURED BY A VIOLATION OF THIS SECTION MAY BRING A CIVIL ACTION IN A COURT OF COMPETENT JURISDICTION TO RECOVER ACTUAL DAMAGES AND REASONABLE ATTORNEY FEES OR SEEK INJUNCTIVE OR ANY OTHER RELIEF AVAILABLE AT LAW OR IN EQUITY.

(8) AS USED IN THIS SECTION:

(A) "AGENCY" MEANS A DEPARTMENT, BOARD, COMMISSION, OFFICE, AGENCY, AUTHORITY, OR OTHER UNIT OF STATE GOVERNMENT. THE TERM INCLUDES A STATE INSTITUTION OF HIGHER EDUCATION.

(B) "BREACH OF THE SECURITY OF THE SYSTEM" MEANS UNAUTHORIZED ACQUISITION OF COMPUTERIZED DATA THAT COMPROMISES THE SECURITY, CONFIDENTIALITY, OR INTEGRITY OF PERSONAL IDENTIFYING INFORMATION MAINTAINED BY AN AGENCY OR A PERSON DOING BUSINESS IN THIS STATE.

THE TERM DOES NOT INCLUDE GOOD FAITH ACQUISITION OF PERSONAL IDENTIFYING INFORMATION BY AN EMPLOYEE OR AGENT OF THE AGENCY OR PERSON RELATED TO THE ACTIVITIES OF THE AGENCY OR PERSON IF THE PERSONAL IDENTIFYING INFORMATION IS NOT USED OR SUBJECT TO FURTHER UNAUTHORIZED DISCLOSURE.

You will find that most data privacy laws of the various states have disclosure and perhaps some kind of fine associated with them. Violate Michigan's Senate Bill 795, and you could face up to ninety-three days behind bars. While the disclosure laws of some other states carry even longer prison terms, I find the inclusion interesting. The specter of being placed behind bars has a more tangible impact on most individuals than laws that only include fines. This is particularly true when said fines would likely be paid by the company, and not be any one individual.

The Social Security Number Privacy Act–Senate Bill 795

Creates the Social Security Number Privacy Act to prohibit a person from disclosing to a third party or publicly displaying all or any part of the Social Security number of an employee, student, or other individual, unless he or she consented to the disclosure in writing or the disclosure was authorized by law. A person who violates the act would be responsible for a civil fine of up to $1,000. A person who knowingly violates the act would be guilty of a misdemeanor punishable by up to ninety-three days imprisonment, a maximum fine of $1,000, or both. Authorizes an individual to bring a civil action against a person who violates the act and recover actual damages or $1,000, whichever is greater, plus reasonable attorneys' fees. "Person" is defined as an individual, partnership, limited liability company, trust, custodian, estate, association, corporation, public or private elementary or secondary school, trade school, vocational school, community or junior college, college, university, or other governmental or legal entity.

Sec. 1. This act shall be known and may be cited as the "Social Security number privacy act."

Sec. 2. As used in this act:

(a) "Child or spousal support" means support for a child or spouse, paid or provided pursuant to state or federal law under a court order or judgment. Support includes, but is not limited to, any of the following:

(i) Expenses for day-to-day care.

(ii) Medical, dental, or other health care.

(iii) Child care expenses.

(iv) Educational expenses.

(v) Expenses in connection with pregnancy or confinement under the paternity act, 1956 PA 205, MCL 722.711 to 722.730.

(vi) Repayment of genetic testing expenses, under the paternity act, 1956 PA 205, MCL 722.711 to 722.730.

(vii) A surcharge paid under section 3a of the support and parenting time enforcement act, 1982 PA 295, MCL552.603a.

(b) "Computer", "computer network", or "computer system" mean those terms as defined in section 2 of 1979 PA 53, MCL 752.792.

(c) "Internet" means that term as defined in 47 U.S.C. 230.

(d) "Mailed" means delivered by United States mail or other delivery service that does not require the signature of recipient indicating actual receipt.

(e) "Person" means an individual, partnership, limited liability company, association, corporation, public or nonpublic elementary or secondary school, trade school, vocational school, community or junior college, college, university, state or local governmental agency or department, or other legal entity.

(d) "Publicly display" means to exhibit, hold up, post, or make visible or set out for open view, including, but not limited to, open view on a computer device, computer network, website, or other electronic medium or device, to members of the public or in a public manner. The term does not include conduct described in section 3(1)(b), (c), or (f).

(e) "Title IV-D agency" means that term as defined in section 2 of the support and parenting time enforcement act, 1982 PA 295, MCL 552.602.

(f) "Vital record" means that term as defined in section 2805 of the public health code, 1978 PA 368, MCL 333.2805.

(g) "Website" means a collection of pages of the world wide web or internet, usually in HTML format, with clickable or hypertext links to enable navigation from one page or section to another, that often uses associated graphics files to provide illustration and may contain other clickable or hypertext links.

Sec. 3. (1) Except as provided in subsection (2), a person shall not intentionally do any of the following with the Social Security number of an employee, student, or other individual:

(a) Publicly display all or more than 4 sequential digits of the Social Security number.

(b) Subject to subsection (3), use all or more than 4 sequential digits of the Social Security number as the primary account number for an individual. However, if the person is using the Social Security number under subdivision (c) and as the primary account number on the effective date of this act, this subdivision does not apply to that person until January 1, 2006.

(c) Visibly print all or more than 4 sequential digits of the Social Security number on any identification badge or card, membership card, or permit or license. However, if a person has implemented or implements a plan or schedule that establishes a specific date by which it will comply with this subdivision, this subdivision does not apply to that person until January 1, 2006, or the completion date specified in that plan or schedule, whichever is earlier.

(d) Require an individual to use or transmit all or more than 4 sequential digits of his or her Social Security number over the internet or a computer system or network unless the connection is secure or the transmission is encrypted.

(e) Require an individual to use or transmit all or more than 4 sequential digits of his or her Social Security number to gain access to an internet website or a computer system or network unless the connection is secure, the transmission is encrypted, or a password or other unique personal identification number or other authentication device is also required to gain access to the internet website or computer system or network.

(f) Include all or more than 4 sequential digits of the Social Security number in or on any document or information mailed or otherwise sent to an individual if it is visible on or, without manipulation, from outside of the envelope or packaging.

(g) Subject to subsection (3), beginning January 1, 2006, include all or more than 4 sequential digits of the Social Security number in any document or information mailed to a person, unless any of the following apply:

(i) State or federal law, rule, regulation, or court order or rule authorizes, permits, or requires that a Social Security number appear in the document.

(ii) The document is sent as part of an application or enrollment process initiated by the individual.

(iii) The document is sent to establish, confirm the status of, service, amend, or terminate an account, contract, policy, or employee or health insurance benefit or to confirm the accuracy of a Social Security number of an individual who has an account, contract, policy, or employee or health insurance benefit.

(iv) The document or information is mailed by a public body under any of the following circumstances:

(A) The document or information is a public record and is mailed in compliance with the freedom of information act, 1976 PA 442, MCL 15.231 to 15.246.

(B) The document or information is a copy of a public record filed or recorded with a county clerk or register of deeds office and is mailed by that office to a person entitled to receive that record.

(C) The document or information is a copy of a vital record recorded as provided by law and is mailed to a person entitled to receive that record.

(v) The document or information is mailed by or at the request of an individual whose Social Security number appears in the document or information or his or her parent or legal guardian.

(vi) The document or information is mailed in a manner or for a purpose consistent with subtitle A of title V of the Gramm-Leach-Bliley act, 15 USC 6801 to 6809; with the health insurance portability and accountability act of 1996, Public Law 104-191; or with section 537 or 539 of the insurance code of 1956, 1956 PA 218, MCL 500.537 and 500.539.

(2) Subsection (1) does not apply to any of the following:

(a) A use of all or more than 4 sequential digits of a Social Security number that is authorized or required by state or federal statute, rule, or regulation, by court order or rule, or pursuant to legal discovery or process.

(b) A use of all or more than 4 sequential digits of a Social Security number by a title IV-D agency, law enforcement agency, court, or prosecutor as part of a criminal investigation or prosecution, or providing all or more than 4 sequential digits of a Social Security number to a title IV-D agency, law enforcement agency, court, or prosecutor as part of a criminal investigation or prosecution.

(3) It is not a violation of subsection (1)(b) or (g) to use all or more than 4 sequential digits of a Social Security number if the use is any of the following:

(a) An administrative use of all or more than 4 sequential digits of the Social Security number in the ordinary course of business, by a person or a vendor or contractor of a person, to do any of the following:

(i) Verify an individual's identity, identify an individual, or do another similar administrative purpose related to an account, transaction, product, service, or employment or proposed account, transaction, product, service, or employment.

(ii) Investigate an individual's claim, credit, criminal, or driving history.

(iii) Detect, prevent, or deter identity theft or another crime.

(iv) Lawfully pursue or enforce a person's legal rights, including, but not limited to, an audit, collection, investigation, or transfer of a tax, employee benefit, debt, claim, receivable, or account or an interest in a receivable or account.

(v) Lawfully investigate, collect, or enforce a child or spousal support obligation or tax liability.

(vi) Provide or administer employee or health insurance or membership benefits, claims, or retirement programs or to administer the ownership of shares of stock or other investments.

(b) A use of all or more than 4 sequential digits of a Social Security number as a primary account number that meets both of the following:

(i) The use began before the effective date of this act.

(ii) The use is ongoing, continuous, and in the ordinary course of business. If the use is stopped for any reason, this subdivision no longer applies.

Sec. 4. (1) Beginning January 1, 2006, a person who obtains 1 or more Social Security numbers in the ordinary course of business shall create a privacy policy that does at least all of the following concerning the Social Security numbers the person possesses or obtains:

(a) Ensures to the extent practicable the confidentiality of the Social Security numbers.

(b) Prohibits unlawful disclosure of the Social Security numbers.

(c) Limits who has access to information or documents that contain the Social Security numbers.

(d) Describes how to properly dispose of documents that contain the Social Security numbers.

(e) Establishes penalties for violation of the privacy policy.

(2) A person that creates a privacy policy under subsection (1) shall publish the privacy policy in an employee handbook, in a procedures manual, or in 1 or more similar documents, which may be made available electronically.

(3) This section does not apply to a person who possesses Social Security numbers in the ordinary course of business and in compliance with the fair credit reporting act, 15 USC 1681 to 1681v, or subtitle A of title V of the Gramm-Leach-Bliley act, 15 USC 6801 to 6809.

Sec. 5. All or more than 4 sequential digits of a Social Security number contained in a public record are exempt from disclosure under the freedom of information act, 1976 PA 442, MCL 15.231 to 15.246, pursuant to section 13(1)(d) of the freedom of information act, 1976 PA 442, MCL 15.243.

Sec. 6. (1) A person who violates section 3 with knowledge that the person's conduct violates this act is guilty of a misdemeanor punishable by imprisonment for not more than 93 days or a fine of not more than $1,000.00, or both.

(2) An individual may bring a civil action against a person who violates section 3 and may recover actual damages. If the person knowingly violates section 3, an individual may recover actual damages or $1,000.00, whichever is greater. If the person knowingly violates section 3, an individual may also recover reasonable attorney fees. Except for good cause, not later than 60 days before filing a civil action, an individual must make a written demand to the person for a violation of section 3 for the amount of his or her actual damages with reasonable documentation of the violation and the actual damages caused by the violation. This subsection does not apply to a person for conduct by an employee or agent of the person in violation of a privacy policy created pursuant to section 4 or in compliance with the fair credit reporting act, 15 USC 1681 to 1681v, or subtitle A of title V of the Gramm-Leach-Bliley act, 15 USC 6801 to 6809, if the person has taken reasonable measures to enforce

its policy and to correct and prevent the reoccurrence of any known violations.

Sec. 7. This act takes effect March 1, 2005.

This act is ordered to take immediate effect.

Senate Bill 657

This bill adds to the list of offenses constituting unlawful trade practices the act of requiring a consumer to disclose his or her Social Security number as a condition to selling goods or providing a service. The bill has an exemption if the purchase, provision, payment, or transaction included an application for or an extension of credit to the consumer or disclosure was required or authorized by applicable state or federal statute, rule, or regulation.

House Bill 4521

This bill provides that an order or judgment entered in an action for divorce or separate maintenance, or any document that is attached to or filed in the case file with the judgment or order, shall not contain personal identifying information unless specifically required by state or federal law, rule, or regulation, or by a court order or rule. This section does not affect an obligation of a person to provide personal identifying information to the friend of the court or another person.

Chapter 23: Minnesota

What I found interesting about Minnesota's disclosure law is the exemption relating to portable devices. S.F. 2118 states that if the data on a portable device is protected by a password, and if the password has not been compromised, you do not have to disclose the breach. I would not want the security of my personal information dependent on the strength of somebody's password. How many people also write down their password so they will not forget it?

S.F. 2118

This bill requires businesses that possess personal data to notify persons whose personal information has been disclosed to unauthorized persons.

A bill for an act relating to commerce; requiring businesses that possess personal data to notify persons whose personal information has been disclosed to unauthorized persons; proposing coding for new law in Minnesota Statutes, chapter 325E. BE IT ENACTED BY THE LEGISLATURE OF THE STATE OF MINNESOTA: Section 1. [325E.61] [DATA WAREHOUSES; NOTICE REQUIRED FOR CERTAIN DISCLOSURES.] Subdivision 1. [DISCLOSURE OF PERSONAL INFORMATION; NOTICE REQUIRED.] (a) Any person or business that conducts business in this state, and that owns or licenses computerized data that includes personal information, shall disclose any breach of the security of the system following discovery or notification of the breach in the security of the data to any resident of this state whose unencrypted personal information was, or is reasonably believed to have been, acquired by an unauthorized person. The disclosure must be made in the most expedient time possible and without unreasonable delay, consistent with the legitimate needs of law enforcement, as provided in paragraph (c), or with any measures necessary to determine the scope of the breach and restore the reasonable integrity of the data system. (b) Any person or business that maintains computerized data that includes personal information that the person or business does not own shall notify

the owner or licensee of the information of any breach of the security of the data immediately following discovery, if the personal information was, or is reasonably believed to have been, acquired by an unauthorized person. (c) The notification required by this section may be delayed if a law enforcement agency determines that the notification will impede a criminal investigation. The notification required by this section must be made after the law enforcement agency determines that it will not compromise the investigation. (d) For purposes of this section, "breach of the security of the system" means unauthorized acquisition of computerized data that compromises the security, confidentiality, or integrity of personal information maintained by the person or business. Unauthorized acquisition of a portable electronic device on which personal information is stored is not a breach of the security of the system when access to the personal information or the device is protected by a password that has not been disclosed, or by another security measure. (e) For purposes of this section, "personal information" means an individual's first name or first initial and last name in combination with any one or more of the following data elements, when the name and the data elements are not encrypted:

(1) Social Security number;

(2) driver's license number or Minnesota identification card number; or

(3) account number or credit or debit card number, in combination with any required security code, access code, or password that would permit access to an individual's financial account.

(f) For purposes of this section, "personal information" does not include publicly available information that is lawfully made available to the general public from federal, state, or local government records.

(g) For purposes of this section, "notice" may be provided by one of the following methods:

(1) written notice;

(2) electronic notice, if the notice provided is consistent with the provisions regarding electronic records and signatures in United States Code, title 15, section 7001; or

(3) substitute notice, if the person or business demonstrates that the cost of providing notice would exceed $250,000, or that the affected class of subject persons to be notified exceeds 500,000, or the person or business does not have sufficient contact information. Substitute notice must consist of all of the following: (i) e-mail notice when the person or business has an e-mail address for the subject persons; (ii) conspicuous posting of the notice on the Website page of the person or business, if the person or business maintains one; and (iii) notification to major statewide media. (h) Notwithstanding paragraph (g), a person or business that maintains its own notification procedures as part of an information security policy for the treatment of personal information and is otherwise consistent with the timing requirements of this section, shall be deemed to be in compliance with the notification requirements of this section if the person or business notifies subject persons in accordance with its policies in the event of a breach of security of the system.

Subd. 2. [WAIVER PROHIBITED.] Any waiver of the provisions of this section is contrary to public policy and is void and unenforceable.

Subd. 3. [REMEDIES AND ENFORCEMENT.] (a) Any person injured by a violation of this section may commence a civil action to recover damages. (b) Any business that violates, proposes to violate, or has violated this section may be enjoined. (c) The rights and remedies available under this section are cumulative to each other and to any other rights and remedies available under law.

S.F. 361

This bill makes technical, conforming, and clarifying changes to the Minnesota Government Data Practices Act; defines terms; classifies, regulating, and reviewing access to and dissemination of certain data. The bill also provides notice of breaches in security; regulates certain fees; provides for the conduct of certain board and council meetings; and modifies provisions regulating motor vehicle and driver applications and records. The bill also regulates disclosure of non-identifying sales tax returns. The bill also contains language specific to vehicle accident reports and procedures; provides for treatment of data held by the comprehensive incident-based reporting system; regulates use of Social Security numbers; classifies certain animal health data; defines terms and regulates data privacy practices for wireless telecommunications; and provides for a review of the handling of genetic information.

S.F. 1117

This bill requires the Minnesota Higher Education Services Office to consider developing data collection procedures and agreements using the students' Social Security numbers to monitor the extent to which students who attend any of the state's post-secondary institutions under reciprocity agreements are employed in Minnesota after graduation.

S.F. 2002

This bill authorizes a consumer to place a security freeze on the consumer's credit report. It also provides notice of this right; provides protections against identity theft; provides Social Security number protections; provides credit monitoring; provides for the adequate destruction of personal records; and provides civil and criminal penalties.

S.F. 3132

This bill relates to data practices and regulates the collection, use, and disclosure of certain data. It also classifies certain data; modifies the powers and duties of certain commissioners; regulates tribal identification cards; authorizes the exchange of certain information; permits the use of a secure subscription service; provides civil remedies; and provides criminal penalties.

Chapter 24: Mississippi

Enacted on July 1, 2011, Mississippi is one of the last states to enact a data breach disclosure law. Like most of the state level data breach laws, Mississippi's HB 583 recognizes encryption as a effective measure to protect data, even breached data, from misuse. Some other states also recognize redaction specifically. HB 583 states "encryption or by any other method or technology that renders the personal information unreadable or unusable." I see that particular wording as being very interesting. It leaves a certain level of interpretation as to the specific method or technology used to render personal information unreadable or unusable.

House Bill 583

AN ACT TO REQUIRE NOTICE OF A BREACH OF SECURITY; TO DEFINE CERTAIN TERMS; TO PROVIDE THAT NOTICE MAY BE DELAYED FOR A REASONABLE PERIOD OF TIME IF NOTICE WILL IMPEDE A CRIMINAL INVESTIGATION OR IMPAIR NATIONAL SECURITY; TO PROVIDE METHODS OF NOTICE; AND FOR RELATED PURPOSES.

BE IT ENACTED BY THE LEGISLATURE OF THE STATE OF MISSISSIPPI:

SECTION 1. (1) This section applies to any person who conducts business in this state and who, in the ordinary course of the person's business functions, owns, licenses or maintains personal information of any resident of this state.

(2) For purposes of this section, the following terms shall have the meanings ascribed unless the context clearly requires otherwise:

(a) "Breach of security" means unauthorized acquisition of electronic files, media, databases or computerized data containing personal information of any resident of this state when access to the personal information has not been secured by encryption or by any other method or technology that renders the personal information unreadable or unusable;

(b) "Personal information" means an individual's first name or first initial and last name in combination with any one or more of the following data elements:

(i) Social security number;

(ii) Driver's license number or state identification card number; or

(iii) An account number or credit or debit card number in combination with any required security code, access code or password that would permit access to an individual's financial account; "personal information" does not include publicly available information that is lawfully made available to the general public from federal, state or local government records or widely distributed media;

(iv) "Affected individual" means any individual who is a resident of this state whose personal information was, or is reasonably believed to have been, intentionally acquired by an unauthorized person through a breach of security.

(3) A person who conducts business in this state shall disclose any breach of security to all affected individuals. The disclosure shall be made without unreasonable delay, subject to the provisions of subsections (4) and (5) of this section and the completion of an investigation by the person to determine the nature and scope of the incident, to identify the affected individuals, or to restore the reasonable integrity of the data system. Notification shall not be required if, after an appropriate investigation, the person reasonably determines that the breach will not likely result in harm to the affected individuals.

(4) Any person who conducts business in this state that maintains computerized data which includes personal information that the person does not own or license shall notify the owner or licensee of the information of any breach of the security of the data as soon as practicable following its discovery, if the personal information was, or is reasonably believed to have been, acquired by an unauthorized person for fraudulent purposes.

(5) Any notification required by this section shall be delayed for a reasonable period of time if a law enforcement agency determines that the notification will impede a criminal investigation or national security and the law enforcement agency has made a request that the notification be delayed. Any such delayed notification shall be made after the law enforcement agency determines that notification will not compromise the criminal investigation or national security and so notifies the person of that determination.

(6) Any notice required by the provisions of this section may be provided by one (1) of the following methods: (a) written notice; (b) telephone notice; (c) electronic notice, if the person's primary means of communication with the affected individuals is by electronic means or if the notice is consistent with the provisions regarding electronic records and signatures set forth in 15 USCS 7001; or (d) substitute notice, provided the person demonstrates that the cost of providing notice in accordance with paragraph (a), (b) or (c) of this subsection would exceed Five Thousand Dollars ($5,000.00), that the affected class of subject persons to be notified exceeds five thousand (5,000) individuals or the person does not have sufficient contact information. Substitute notice shall consist of the following: electronic mail notice when the person has an electronic mail address for the affected individuals; conspicuous posting of the notice on the website of the person if the person maintains one; and notification to major statewide media, including newspapers, radio and television.

(7) Any person who conducts business in this state that maintains its own security breach procedures as part of an information security policy for the treatment of personal information, and otherwise complies with the timing requirements of this section, shall be deemed to be in compliance with the security breach notification requirements of this section if the person notifies affected individuals in accordance with the person's policies in the event of a breach of security. Any person that maintains such a security breach procedure pursuant to the rules, regulations, procedures or guidelines established by the primary or federal functional regulator, as defined in 15 USCS 6809(2), shall be deemed to be in compliance with the security breach notification requirements of this section, provided the person notifies affected individuals in accordance with the policies or the rules, regulations,

procedures or guidelines established by the primary or federal functional regulator in the event of a breach of security of the system.

(8) Failure to comply with the requirements of this section shall constitute an unfair trade practice and shall be enforced by the Attorney General; however, nothing in this section may be construed to create a private right of action.

SECTION 2. This act shall take effect and be in force from and after July 1, 2011.

Senate Bill 2756

Defines and clarifies certain terms; includes the use of computers in the prohibition of exploitation of children; revises penalties; defines certain terms related to computer crimes; revises computer fraud and penalties; creates the offense of cyber-stalking and prescribes penalties for violations; prohibits posting certain messages through electronic media and prescribes penalties for violations; prohibits obtaining personal identity information and prescribes penalties for violations; clarifies where criminal action may be brought; provides for investigations and prosecutions; and provides for additional penalties.

SECTION 1. Section 97-5-31, Mississippi Code of 1972, is amended as follows:

97-5-31. As used in Sections 97-5-33 <u>through</u> 97-5-37, the following words and phrases shall have the meanings given to them in this section:

(a) "Child" means any individual who has not attained the age of eighteen (18) years.

(b) "Sexually explicit conduct" means actual or simulated:

(i) Sexual intercourse, including genital-genital, oral-genital, anal-genital, or oral-anal, whether between persons of the same or opposite sex;

(ii) Bestiality;

(iii) Masturbation;

(iv) Sadistic or masochistic abuse;

(v) Lascivious exhibition of the genitals or pubic area of any person; or

(vi) Fondling or other erotic touching of the genitals, pubic area, buttocks, anus or breast.

(c) "Producing" means producing, directing, manufacturing, issuing, publishing or advertising.

(d) "Visual depiction" includes without limitation developed or undeveloped film and video tape or other visual unaltered reproductions by computer.

(e) "Computer" has the meaning given in Title 18, United States Code, Section 1030.

(f) "Simulated" means any depicting of the genitals or rectal areas that gives the appearance of sexual conduct or incipient sexual conduct.

SECTION 2. Section 97-5-33, Mississippi Code of 1972, is amended as follows:

97-5-33. (1) No person shall, by any means including computer, cause, <u>solicit</u> or knowingly permit any child to engage in sexually explicit conduct or in the simulation of sexually explicit conduct for the purpose of producing any visual depiction of such conduct.

(2) No person shall, by any means including computer, photograph, * * * film, video tape or otherwise depict or record a

child engaging in sexually explicit conduct or in the simulation of sexually explicit conduct.

(3) No person shall, by any means including computer, knowingly send, transport, transmit, ship, mail or receive any photograph, drawing, sketch, film, video tape or other visual depiction of an actual child engaging in sexually explicit conduct.

(4) No person shall, by any means including computer, receive with intent to distribute, distribute for sale, sell or attempt to sell in any manner any photograph, drawing, sketch, film, video tape or other visual depiction of an actual child engaging in sexually explicit conduct.

(5) No person shall, by any means including computer, possess any photograph, drawing, sketch, film, video tape or other visual depiction of an actual child engaging in sexually explicit conduct.

(6) No person shall, by any means including computer, knowingly entice, induce, persuade, seduce, solicit, advise, coerce, or order a child to meet with the defendant or any other person for the purpose of engaging in sexually explicit conduct.

(7) The fact that an undercover operative or law enforcement officer was involved in the detection and investigation of an offense under this section shall not constitute a defense to a prosecution under this section.

(8) For purposes of determining jurisdiction, the offense is committed in this state if all or part of the conduct described in this section occurs in the State of Mississippi or if the transmission that constitutes the offense either originates in this state or is received in this state.

SECTION 3. Section 97-5-35, Mississippi Code of 1972, is amended as follows:

97-5-35. Any person who violates any provision of subsections (1) through (6) of Section 97-5-33 shall be guilty of a felony and upon conviction shall pay a fine of not * * * more than Fifty Thousand Dollars ($50,000.00) and shall be imprisoned for not less than two (2) years nor more than twenty (20) years, or by both such fine and imprisonment. Any person convicted of a second or subsequent violation of subsections (1) through (6) of Section 97-5-33 shall pay a fine of not more than One Hundred Thousand Dollars ($100,000.00) and shall be imprisoned not less than ten (10) years nor more than thirty (30) years, or by both such fine and imprisonment.

SECTION 4. Section 97-45-1, Mississippi Code of 1972, is amended as follows:

97-45-1. For the purposes of this chapter, the following words shall have the meanings ascribed herein unless the context clearly requires otherwise:

(a) "Access" means to program, to execute programs on, to communicate with, store data in, retrieve data from or otherwise make use of any resources, including data or programs, of a computer, computer system or computer network.

(b) "Computer" includes an electronic, magnetic, optical or other high-speed data processing device or system performing logical arithmetic and storage functions and includes any property, data storage facility or communications facility directly related to or operating in conjunction with such device or system. "Computer" shall not include an automated typewriter or typesetter, a machine designed solely for word processing which contains no database intelligence or a portable hand-held calculator nor shall "computer" include any other device which contains components similar to those in computers but in which the components have the sole function of controlling the device for the single purpose for which the device is intended unless the thus controlled device is a processor of data or is a storage of intelligence in which case it too is included.

(c) "Computer network" means a set of related, remotely connected devices and communication facilities including at least one (1) computer system with the capability to transmit data through communication facilities.

(d) "Computer program" means an ordered set of data representing coded instructions or statements that when executed by a computer cause the computer to process data.

(e) "Computer software" means a set of computer programs, procedures and associated documentation concerned with operation of a computer system.

(f) "Computer system" means a set of functionally related, connected or unconnected, computer equipment, devices or computer software.

(g) "Computer services" means providing access to or service or data from a computer, a computer system or a computer network and includes the actual data processing.

(h) "Credible threat" means a threat made with the intent and the apparent ability to carry out the threat so as to cause the person who is the target of the threat to reasonably fear for his or her safety.

(i) "Loss or damage" includes any reasonable cost to any victim, including the cost of responding to an offense, conducting a damage assessment, and restoring the data, program, system, or information to its condition prior to the offense, and any revenue lost, cost incurred or other consequential damages incurred because of interruption of service.

(j) "Device" includes, but is not limited to, an electronic, magnetic, electrochemical, biochemical, hydraulic, optical, or organic object that performs input, output, or storage functions by the manipulation of electronic, magnetic or other impulses.

(k) "Electronic communication" means any transfer of signs, signals, writing, images, sounds, data, or intelligence of any nature, transmitted in whole or in part by a wire, radio, computer, electromagnetic, photoelectric or photo-optical system.

(l) "Electronic mail" means the transmission of information or communication by the use of the Internet, a computer, a facsimile machine, a pager, a cellular telephone, a video recorder or other electronic means sent to a person identified by a unique address or address number and received by that person.

(m) "Emotional distress" means significant mental suffering or distress that may, but does not necessarily, require medical or other professional treatment or counseling.

(n) "Financial instrument" means any check, draft, money order, certificate of deposit, letter of credit, bill of exchange, credit card as defined in Section 97-19-9(b), Mississippi Code of 1972, or marketable security.

(o) "Financial transaction device" means any of the following:

(i) An electronic funds transfer card.

(ii) A credit card.

(iii) A debit card.

(iv) A point-of-sale card.

(v) Any instrument, device, card, plate, code, account number, personal identification number, or a record or copy of a code, account number, or personal identification number or other means of access to a credit account or deposit account, or a driver's license or state identification card used to access a proprietary account, other than access originated solely by a paper instrument, that can be used alone or in conjunction with another access device, for any of the following purposes.

1. Obtaining money, cash refund or credit account credit, goods, services or any other thing of value.

2. Certifying or guaranteeing to a person or business the availability to the device holder of funds on deposit to honor a draft or check payable to the order of that person or business.

3. Providing the device holder access to a deposit account for the purpose of making deposits, withdrawing funds, transferring funds between deposit accounts, obtaining information pertaining to a deposit account or making an electronic funds transfer.

(p) "Intellectual property" includes data, computer programs, computer software, trade secrets, copyrighted materials and confidential or proprietary information in any form or medium when such is stored in, produced by or intended for use or storage with or in a computer, a computer system or a computer network.

(q) "Internet" means that term as defined in Section 230 of Title II of the Communications Act of 1934, Chapter 652, 110 Stat. 137, 47 USCS 230.

(r) "Medical records" includes, but is not limited to, medical and mental health histories, reports, summaries, diagnoses and prognoses, treatment and medication information, notes, entries, and x-rays and other imaging records.

(s) "Personal identity information" means any of the following information of another person:

(i) A Social Security number.

(ii) A driver's license number or state personal identification card number.

(iii) Employment information.

(iv) Information regarding any financial account held by another person including, but not limited to, any of the following:

1. A savings or checking account number.
2. A financial transaction device account number.
3. A stock or other security certificate or account number.
4. A personal information number for an account described in items 1 through 4.

(t) "Post a message" means transferring, sending, posting, publishing, disseminating, or otherwise communicating or attempting to transfer, send, post, publish, disseminate or otherwise communicate information, whether truthful or untruthful, about the victim.

(u) "Property" means property as defined in Section 1-3-45, Mississippi Code of 1972, and shall specifically include, but not be limited to, financial instruments, electronically stored or produced data and computer programs, whether in machine readable or human readable form.

(v) "Proper means" includes:

(i) Discovery by independent invention;

(ii) Discovery by "reverse engineering"; that is, by starting with the known product and working backward to find the method by which it was developed. The acquisition of the known product must be by lawful means;

(iii) Discovery under license or authority of the owner;

(iv) Observation of the property in public use or on public display; or

(v) Discovery in published literature.

(w) "Unconsented contact" means any contact with another individual that is initiated or continued without that individual's consent or in disregard of that individual's expressed desire that the contact be avoided or discontinued. Unconsented contact includes any of the following:

(i) Following or appearing within sight of the victim.

(ii) Approaching or confronting the victim in a public place or on private property.

(iii) Appearing at the victim's workplace or residence.

(iv) Entering onto or remaining on property owned, leased or occupied by the victim.

(v) Contacting the victim by telephone.

(vi) Sending mail or electronic communications to the victim through the use of any medium, including the Internet or a computer, computer program, computer system or computer network.

(vii) Placing an object on, or delivering or having delivered an object to, property owned, leased or occupied by the victim.

(x) "Use" means to make use of, to convert to one's service, to avail oneself of or to employ. In the context of this act, "use" includes to instruct, communicate with, store data in or retrieve data from, or otherwise utilize the logical arithmetic or memory functions of a computer.

(y) "Victim" means the individual who is the target of the conduct elicited by the posted message or a member of that individual's immediate family.

SECTION 5. Section 97-45-3, Mississippi Code of 1972, is amended as follows:

97-45-3. (1) Computer fraud is the accessing or causing to be accessed of any computer, computer system, computer network or any part thereof with the intent to:

(a) Defraud; * * *

(b) Obtain money, property or services by means of false or fraudulent conduct, practices or representations; or through the false or fraudulent alteration, deletion or insertion of programs or data; or

(c) Insert or attach or knowingly create the opportunity for an unknowing and unwanted insertion or attachment of a set of instructions or a computer program into a computer program, computer, computer system, or computer network, that is intended to acquire, alter, damage, delete, disrupt, or destroy property or otherwise use the services of a computer program, computer, computer system or computer network.

(2) Whoever commits the offense of computer fraud shall be punished, upon conviction, by a fine of not more than One Thousand Dollars ($1,000.00), or by imprisonment for not more than six (6) months, or by both such fine and imprisonment. However, when the damage or loss or attempted damage or loss amounts to a value of Five Hundred Dollars ($500.00) or more, the offender may be punished, upon conviction, by a fine of not more than Ten Thousand Dollars ($10,000.00) or by imprisonment for not more than five (5) years, or by both such fine and imprisonment.

SECTION 6. The following shall be codified as Section 97-45-15, Mississippi Code of 1972:

97-45-15. (1) It is unlawful for a person to:

(a) Use in electronic mail or electronic communication any words or language threatening to inflict bodily harm to any person or to that person's child, sibling, spouse or dependent, or physical injury to the property of any person, or for the purpose of extorting money or other things of value from any person.

(b) Electronically mail or electronically communicate to another repeatedly, whether or not conversation ensues, for the purpose of threatening, terrifying or harassing any person.

(c) Electronically mail or electronically communicate to another and to knowingly make any false statement concerning death, injury, illness, disfigurement, indecent conduct, or criminal conduct of the person electronically mailed or of any member of the person's family or household with the intent to threaten, terrify or harass.

(d) Knowingly permit an electronic communication device under the person's control to be used for any purpose prohibited by this section.

(2) Whoever commits the offense of cyber stalking shall be punished, upon conviction:

(a) Except as provided herein, the person is guilty of a felony punishable by imprisonment for not more than two (2) years or a fine of not more than Five Thousand Dollars ($5,000.00), or both.

(b) If any of the following apply, the person is guilty of a felony punishable by imprisonment for not more than five (5) years or a fine of not more than Ten Thousand Dollars ($10,000.00), or both:

(i) The offense is in violation of a restraining order and the person has received actual notice of that restraining order or posting the message is in violation of an injunction or preliminary injunction.

(ii) The offense is in violation of a condition of probation, a condition of parole, a condition of pretrial release or a condition of release on bond pending appeal.

(iii) The offense results in a credible threat being communicated to the victim, a member of the victim's family, or another individual living in the same household as the victim.

(iv) The person has been previously convicted of violating this section or a substantially similar law of another state, a political subdivision of another state, or of the United States.

(3) This section does not apply to any peaceable, nonviolent, or nonthreatening activity intended to express political views or to provide lawful information to others. This section shall not be construed to impair any constitutionally protected activity, including speech, protest or assembly.

SECTION 7. The following shall be codified as Section 97-45-17, Mississippi Code of 1972:

97-45-17. (1) A person shall not post a message for the purpose of causing injury to any person through the use of any medium of communication, including the Internet or a computer, computer program, computer system or computer network, or other electronic medium of communication without the victim's consent, for the purpose of causing injury to any person.

(2) A person who violates this section, upon conviction, shall be guilty of a felony punishable by imprisonment for not more than five (5) years or a fine of not more than Ten Thousand Dollars ($10,000.00), or both.

SECTION 8. The following shall be codified as Section 97-45-19, Mississippi Code of 1972:

97-45-19. (1) A person shall not obtain or attempt to obtain personal identity information of another person with the intent to unlawfully use that information for any of the following purposes without that person's authorization:

(a) To obtain financial credit.

(b) To purchase or otherwise obtain or lease any real or personal property.

(c) To obtain employment.

(d) To obtain access to medical records or information contained in medical records.

(e) To commit any illegal act.

(2) A person who violates this section is guilty of a felony punishable by imprisonment for not more than five (5) years or a fine of not more than Ten Thousand Dollars ($10,000.00), or both.

(3) This section does not prohibit the person from being charged with, convicted of, or sentenced for any other violation of law committed by that person using information obtained in violation of this section.

(4) This section does not apply to a person who obtains or attempts to obtain personal identity information of another person pursuant to the discovery process of a civil action, an administrative proceeding or an arbitration proceeding.

SECTION 9. The following shall be codified as Section 97-45-21, Mississippi Code of 1972:

97-45-21. For purposes of bringing a criminal action under this chapter, a person who causes, by any means, the access of a computer, computer system or computer network in one jurisdiction from another jurisdiction is deemed to have personally accessed the computer, computer system or computer network in each jurisdiction.

SECTION 10. The following shall be codified as Section 97-45-23, Mississippi Code of 1972:

97-45-23. Prosecutions for violations under Title 97, Chapter 45, or Section 97-5-33, may be instituted by the Attorney General, his designee or the district attorney of the district in which the violation occurred, and shall be conducted in the name of the State of Mississippi. In the prosecution of any criminal proceeding in accordance with this subsection by the Attorney General, his designee, and in any proceeding before a grand jury in connection therewith, the Attorney General, or his designee, shall exercise all the powers and perform all the duties which the district attorney would otherwise be authorized or required to exercise or perform. The Attorney General, or his designee, shall have the authority to issue and serve subpoenas in the investigation of any matter which may violate Title 97, Chapter 45, or Section 97-5-33.

SECTION 11. The following shall be codified as Section 97-45-25, Mississippi Code of 1972:

97-45-25. In a proceeding for violations under Title 97, Chapter 45, or Section 97-5-33, the court, in addition to the criminal penalties imposed under this chapter, shall assess against the defendant convicted of such violation double those reasonable costs that are expended by the Office of Attorney General, the district attorney's office, the sheriff's office or police department involved in the investigation of such case, including, but not limited to, the cost of investigators, software and equipment utilized in the investigation, together with costs associated with process service, court reporters and expert witnesses. The Attorney General or district attorney may institute and maintain proceedings in his name for enforcement of payment in the circuit court of the county of residence of the defendant and, if the defendant is a nonresident, such proceedings shall be in the Circuit Court of the First Judicial District of Hinds County, Mississippi. The Attorney General or district attorney shall distribute the property or interest assessed under this section as follows:

(a) Fifty percent (50%) shall be distributed to the unit of state or local government whose officers or employees conducted the investigation into computer fraud or child exploitation which resulted in the arrest or arrests and prosecution. Amounts distributed to units of local government shall be used for training or enforcement purposes relating to detection, investigation or prosecution of computer and financial crimes, including computer fraud or child exploitation.

(b) Where the prosecution was maintained by the district attorney, fifty percent (50%) shall be distributed to the county in which the prosecution was instituted by the district attorney and appropriated to the district attorney for use in training or enforcement purposes relating to detection, investigation or prosecution of computer and financial crimes, including computer fraud or child exploitation. Where a prosecution was maintained by the Attorney General, fifty percent (50%) of the proceeds shall be paid or distributed into the Attorney General's Cyber Crime Central. Where the Attorney General and the district attorney have participated jointly in any part of the proceedings, twenty-five percent (25%) of the property forfeited shall be paid to the county in which the prosecution occurred, and twenty-five percent (25%) shall be paid to the Attorney General's Cyber Crime Central to be used for the purposes as stated in this paragraph.

SECTION 12. If any provision of this act is held by a court to be invalid, such invalidity shall not affect the remaining provisions of this act, and to this end the provisions of this act are declared severable.

SECTION 13. This act shall take effect and be in force from and after July 1, 2003.

Chapter 25: Missouri

I find Missouri interesting in that back in May 2006 the state passed House Concurrent Resolution #10, which urged the US Congress to adopt a comprehensive federal law to protect consumer information from data thieves. Fast forward to 2011, and there still is no national level data breach notification law. Missouri enacted its own state level law.

Definitions—notice to consumer for breach of security, procedure--attorney general may bring action for damages.

407.1500. 1. As used in this section, the following terms mean:

(1) "Breach of security" or "breach," unauthorized access to and unauthorized acquisition of personal information maintained in computerized form by a person that compromises the security, confidentiality, or integrity of the personal information. Good faith acquisition of personal information by a person or that person's employee or agent for a legitimate purpose of that person is not a breach of security, provided that the personal information is not used in violation of applicable law or in a manner that harms or poses an actual threat to the security, confidentiality, or integrity of the personal information;

(2) "Consumer", an individual who is a resident of this state;

(3) "Consumer reporting agency", the same as defined by the federal Fair Credit Reporting Act, 15 U.S.C. Section 1681a;

(4) "Encryption," the use of an algorithmic process to transform data into a form in which the data is rendered unreadable or unusable without the use of a confidential process or key;

(5) "Health insurance information," an individual's health insurance policy number or subscriber identification number, any unique identifier used by a health insurer to identify the individual;

(6) "Medical information,0" any information regarding an individual's medical history, mental or physical condition, or medical treatment or diagnosis by a health care professional;

(7) "Owns or licenses" includes, but is not limited to, personal information that a business retains as part of the internal customer account of the business or for the purpose of using the information in transactions with the person to whom the information relates;

(8) "Person," any individual, corporation, business trust, estate, trust, partnership, limited liability company, association, joint venture, government, governmental subdivision, governmental agency, governmental instrumentality, public corporation, or any other legal or commercial entity;

(9) "Personal information," an individual's first name or first initial and last name in combination with any one or more of the following data elements that relate to the individual if any of the data elements are not encrypted, redacted, or otherwise altered by any method or technology in such a manner that the name or data elements are unreadable or unusable:

(a) Social Security number;

(b) Driver's license number or other unique identification number created or collected by a government body;

(c) Financial account number, credit card number, or debit card number in combination with any required security code, access code, or password that would permit access to an individual's financial account;

(d) Unique electronic identifier or routing code, in combination with any required security code, access code, or password that would permit access to an individual's financial account;

(e) Medical information; or

(f) Health insurance information.

"Personal information" does not include information that is lawfully obtained from publicly available sources, or from federal, state, or local government records lawfully made available to the general public;

(10) "Redacted," altered or truncated such that no more than five digits of a social security number or the last four digits of a driver's license number, state identification card number, or account number is accessible as part of the personal information.

2. (1) Any person that owns or licenses personal information of residents of Missouri or any person that conducts business in Missouri that owns or licenses personal information in any form of a resident of Missouri shall provide notice to the affected consumer that there has been a breach of security following discovery or notification of the breach. The disclosure notification shall be:

(a) Made without unreasonable delay;

(b) Consistent with the legitimate needs of law enforcement, as provided in this section; and

(c) Consistent with any measures necessary to determine sufficient contact information and to determine the scope of the breach and restore the reasonable integrity, security, and confidentiality of the data system.

(2) Any person that maintains or possesses records or data containing personal information of residents of Missouri that the person does not own or license, or any person that conducts business in Missouri that maintains or possesses records or data containing personal information of a resident of Missouri that the person does not own or license, shall notify the owner or licensee of the information of any breach of security immediately following discovery of the breach, consistent with the legitimate needs of law enforcement as provided in this section.

(3) The notice required by this section may be delayed if a law enforcement agency informs the person that notification may impede a criminal investigation or jeopardize national or homeland

security, provided that such request by law enforcement is made in writing or the person documents such request contemporaneously in writing, including the name of the law enforcement officer making the request and the officer's law enforcement agency engaged in the investigation. The notice required by this section shall be provided without unreasonable delay after the law enforcement agency communicates to the person its determination that notice will no longer impede the investigation or jeopardize national or homeland security.

(4) The notice shall at minimum include a description of the following:

(a) The incident in general terms;

(b) The type of personal information that was obtained as a result of the breach of security;

(c) A telephone number that the affected consumer may call for further information and assistance, if one exists;

(d) Contact information for consumer reporting agencies;

(e) Advice that directs the affected consumer to remain vigilant by reviewing account statements and monitoring free credit reports.

(5) Notwithstanding subdivisions (1) and (2) of this subsection, notification is not required if, after an appropriate investigation by the person or after consultation with the relevant federal, state, or local agencies responsible for law enforcement, the person determines that a risk of identity theft or other fraud to any consumer is not reasonably likely to occur as a result of the breach. Such a determination shall be documented in writing and the documentation shall be maintained for five years.

(6) For purposes of this section, notice to affected consumers shall be provided by one of the following methods:

(a) Written notice;

(b) Electronic notice for those consumers for whom the person has a valid email address and who have agreed to receive communications electronically, if the notice provided is consistent with the provisions of 15 U.S.C. Section 7001 regarding electronic records and signatures for notices legally required to be in writing;

(c) Telephonic notice, if such contact is made directly with the affected consumers; or

(d) Substitute notice, if:

a. The person demonstrates that the cost of providing notice would exceed one hundred thousand dollars; or

b. The class of affected consumers to be notified exceeds one hundred fifty thousand; or

c. The person does not have sufficient contact information or consent to satisfy paragraphs (a), (b), or (c) of this subdivision, for only those affected consumers without sufficient contact information or consent; or

d. The person is unable to identify particular affected consumers, for only those unidentifiable consumers.

(7) Substitute notice under paragraph (d) of subdivision (6) of this subsection shall consist of all the following:

(a) Email notice when the person has an electronic mail address for the affected consumer;

(b) Conspicuous posting of the notice or a link to the notice on the Internet website of the person if the person maintains an Internet website; and

(c) Notification to major statewide media.

(8) In the event a person provides notice to more than one thousand consumers at one time pursuant to this section, the person shall notify, without unreasonable delay, the attorney general's office and

all consumer reporting agencies that compile and maintain files on consumers on a nationwide basis, as defined in 15 U.S.C. Section 1681a(p), of the timing, distribution, and content of the notice.

3. (1) A person that maintains its own notice procedures as part of an information security policy for the treatment of personal information, and whose procedures are otherwise consistent with the timing requirements of this section, is deemed to be in compliance with the notice requirements of this section if the person notifies affected consumers in accordance with its policies in the event of a breach of security of the system.

(2) A person that is regulated by state or federal law and that maintains procedures for a breach of the security of the system pursuant to the laws, rules, regulations, guidances, or guidelines established by its primary or functional state or federal regulator is deemed to be in compliance with this section if the person notifies affected consumers in accordance with the maintained procedures when a breach occurs.

(3) A financial institution that is:

(a) Subject to and in compliance with the Federal Interagency Guidance Response Programs for Unauthorized Access to Customer Information and Customer Notice, issued on March 29, 2005, by the board of governors of the Federal Reserve System, the Federal Deposit Insurance Corporation, the Office of the Comptroller of the Currency, and the Office of Thrift Supervision, and any revisions, additions, or substitutions relating to said interagency guidance; or

(b) Subject to and in compliance with the National Credit Union Administration regulations in 12 CFR Part 748; or

(c) Subject to and in compliance with the provisions of Title V of the Gramm-Leach-Bliley Financial Modernization Act of 1999, 15 U.S.C. Sections 6801 to 6809;

shall be deemed to be in compliance with this section.

4. The attorney general shall have exclusive authority to bring an action to obtain actual damages for a willful and knowing violation of this section and may seek a civil penalty not to exceed one hundred fifty thousand dollars per breach of the security of the system or series of breaches of a similar nature that are discovered in a single investigation.

House Concurrent Resolution 10

This bill urges the US Congress to adopt a comprehensive federal law that protects consumer information from data thieves.

Whereas, today 40 million credit cardholders are exposed to the risk of fraud by data thieves; and

Whereas, in 2005, a credit card processing company, CardSystems Solutions, improperly retained masses of data in vulnerable files and data thieves moved in, resulting in approximately 200,000 credit card accounts being reported stolen; and

Whereas, other incidents in 2005 included CitiFinancial disclosing that unencrypted computer tapes for 3.9 million customers were lost by a package deliverer and ChoicePoint, the nation's largest broker of personal information were the target of thieves who were easily able to buy the data of 145,000 consumers; and

Whereas, in the hands of thieves, consumer data becomes liquid assets and must be guarded as such by companies; and

Whereas, with California's passage of a law requiring notice to affected consumers, the entire nation became aware that consumers' assets and identities are increasingly at risk of fraud because of the remarkable success of data thieves

Whereas, several pieces of legislation have been introduced in the United States Congress, including a bill proposing a national requirement for consumer notification with civil penalties for negligent companies, and a comprehensive bill to begin regulating

data merchants by requiring registration with the Federal Trade Commission and to impose stronger safeguards, stop the easy access to Social Security numbers, and help identity theft victims regain their fiscal balance:

Now, therefore, be it resolved that the members of the House of Representatives of the Ninety-third General Assembly, Second Regular Session, the Senate concurring therein, hereby urge the United States Congress to adopt a comprehensive federal law that protects consumer information from data thieves; and

Be it further resolved that the Chief Clerk of the Missouri House of Representatives be instructed to prepare a properly inscribed copy of this resolution for each member of the Missouri Congressional Delegation.

Senate Bill 292

This bill states that no person, other than the cardholder, shall print more than the last five digits of a credit card or debit card account number on a sales receipt provided to the cardholder for merchandise sold in Missouri.

House Bill 337

This bill changes the laws regarding the release of personal information to unauthorized persons.

House Bill 1190

This bill makes personal information that is collected by a county collector including data elements such as an individual's name, address, real estate tax information, financial information or transactions, real estate parcel number, loan number for real estate parcels, or any other personal information, not a public record unless authorized by the county collector.

House Bill 1285

This bill makes some revisions to the definition of "public record" by excluding an individual's personal information collected by municipalities. Personal information includes any financial information, medical history, or criminal or employment history that contains an individual's name, identifying number, or other identifiers assigned to the individual.

House Bill 1248

This bill prohibits both the displaying and posting of financial information over the Internet if consent was not obtained by the individual or entity whose information is being displayed or posted.

House Concurrent Resolution 10

This resolution urges the United States Congress to adopt a comprehensive federal law that protects consumer information from data thieves. This would add a level of uniformity across the country by having a single federal statute that is above the forty-plus state laws.

Chapter 26: Montana

Montana House Bill 732 provides exception from disclosure liabilities if the data was encrypted. The bill also has required the secure destruction of paper that contains confidential personal information.

House Bill 732

This bill adopts and revises laws to implement individual privacy and to prevent identity theft. It requires a consumer reporting agency, such as Experian, to block or expunge information on a report that results from a theft of identity; provides privacy protection provisions for credit card solicitations and renewals and telephone accounts; provides privacy protection for business records by requiring destruction of records; requires businesses to report a breach of computer security; requires a business that has an established business relationship with a customer and that has disclosed certain personal information to third parties to report that information to the customer; and provides remedies and penalties for violation.

Section 1. Section 31-3-115, MCA, is amended to read:

"31-3-115. Adverse information. (1) Whenever a consumer reporting agency prepares an investigative consumer report, ~~no~~ adverse information in the consumer report, ~~(~~other than information ~~which~~ that is a matter of public record~~)~~, may not be included in a subsequent consumer report unless ~~such~~ the adverse information has been verified in the process of making ~~such~~ the subsequent consumer report.

(2) A consumer reporting agency shall block the reporting of any information in the file of a consumer that the consumer identifies as information that resulted from an alleged identity theft, pursuant to 15 U.S.C. 1681c-2."

Section 2. Identity theft impediments -- credit cards -- definition. (1) A credit card issuer that mails an offer or solicitation to receive a

credit card and, in response, receives a completed application for a credit card that lists an address that is different from the address on the offer or solicitation shall verify the change of address by contacting the person to whom the solicitation or offer was mailed, as provided in [section 3].

(2) Notwithstanding any other provision of law, a person to whom an offer or solicitation to receive a credit card is made is not liable for the unauthorized use of a credit card issued in response to that offer or solicitation if the credit card issuer does not verify the change of address pursuant to subsection (1) prior to the issuance of the credit card unless the credit card issuer proves that this person actually incurred the charge on the credit card.

(3) When a credit card issuer receives a written or oral request for a change of the cardholder's billing address and then receives a written or oral request for an additional credit card within 10 days after the requested address change, the credit card issuer may not mail the requested additional credit card to the new address or, alternatively, activate the requested additional credit card unless the credit card issuer has verified the change of address.

(4) (a) Except as provided in subsections (4)(b) through (4)(d), a person, firm, partnership, association, corporation, or limited liability company that accepts credit cards for the transaction of business may not print more than the last five digits of the credit card account number or the expiration date upon any receipt provided to the cardholder.

(b) Subsection (4)(a) applies only to receipts that are electronically printed and does not apply to transactions in which the sole means of recording the person's credit card number is by handwriting or by an imprint or copy of the credit card.

(c) Subsection (4)(a) applies beginning January 1, 2008, with respect to any cash register or other machine or device that electronically prints receipts for credit card transactions that is in use before January 1, 2005.

(d) Subsection (4)(a) applies beginning January 1, 2006, with respect to any cash register or other machine or device that electronically prints receipts for credit card transactions that is first put into use on or after January 1, 2005.

(5) (a) As used in this section, "credit card" means any card, plate, coupon book, or other single credit device existing for the purpose of being used from time to time upon presentation to obtain money, property, labor, or services on credit.

(b) "Credit card" does not mean any of the following:

(i) any single credit device used to obtain telephone property, labor, or services in any transaction with an entity under regulation as a public utility;

(ii) any device that may be used to obtain credit pursuant to an electronic fund transfer, but only if the credit is obtained under an agreement between a consumer and a financial institution to extend credit when the consumer's asset account is overdrawn or to maintain a specified minimum balance in the consumer's asset account;

(iii) any key or card key used at an automated dispensing outlet to obtain or purchase petroleum products that will be used primarily for business rather than personal or family purposes.

Section 3. Identity theft impediments -- credit card renewal -- telephone accounts. (1) A credit card issuer that receives a change of address request, other than for a correction of a typographical error, from a cardholder who orders a replacement credit card within 60 days before or after that request is received shall send to that cardholder a change of address notification that is addressed to the cardholder at the cardholder's previous address of record. If the replacement credit card is requested prior to the effective date of the change of address, the notification must be sent within 30 days of the change of address request. If the replacement credit card is requested after the effective date of the change of address, the notification must be sent within 30 days of the request for the replacement credit card.

(2) Any business entity that provides telephone accounts that receives a change of address request, other than for a correction of a typographical error, from an account holder who orders new service shall send to that account holder a change of address notification that is addressed to the account holder at the account holder's previous address of record. The notification must be sent within 30 days of the request for new service.

(3) The notice required pursuant to subsection (1) or (2) may be given by telephone or electronic mail communication if the credit card issuer or business entity that provides telephone accounts reasonably believes that it has the current telephone number or electronic mail address for the account holder or cardholder who has requested a change of address. If the notification is in writing, it may not contain the consumer's account number, Social Security number, or other personal identifying information but may contain the consumer's name, previous address, and new address of record. For business entities described in subsection (2), the notification may also contain the account holder's telephone number.

(4) A credit card issuer or a business entity that provides telephone accounts is not required to send a change of address notification when a change of address request is made in person by a consumer who has presented valid identification or is made by telephone and the requester has provided a unique alphanumeric password.

(5) As used in this section, the following definitions apply:

(a) "Credit card" has the meaning provided in [section 2].

(b) "Telephone account" means an account with a telecommunications carrier, as defined in 69-3-803.

Section 4. Purpose. The purpose of [sections 4 through 8] is to enhance the protection of individual privacy and to impede identity theft as prohibited by 45-6-332.

Section 5. Definitions. As used in [sections 4 through 8], unless the context requires otherwise, the following definitions apply:

(1) (a) "Business" means a sole proprietorship, partnership, corporation, association, or other group, however organized and whether or not organized to operate at a profit, including a financial institution organized, chartered, or holding a license or authorization certificate under the law of this state, any other state, the United States, or of any other country or the parent or the subsidiary of a financial institution. The term includes an entity that destroys records. The term also includes industries regulated by the public service commission or under Title 30, chapter 10.

(b) The term does not include industries regulated under Title 33.

(2) "Customer" means an individual who provides personal information to a business for the purpose of purchasing or leasing a product or obtaining a service from the business.

(3) "Individual" means a natural person.

(4) "Personal information" means an individual's name, signature, address, or telephone number, in combination with one or more additional pieces of information about the individual, consisting of the individual's passport number, driver's license or state identification number, insurance policy number, bank account number, credit card number, debit card number, passwords or personal identification numbers required to obtain access to the individual's finances, or any other financial information as provided

by rule. A Social Security number, in and of itself, constitutes personal information.

(5) (a) "Records" means any material, regardless of the physical form, on which personal information is recorded.

(b) The term does not include publicly available directories containing personal information an individual has voluntarily consented to have publicly disseminated or listed, such as name, address, or telephone number.

Section 6. Record destruction. A business shall take all reasonable steps to destroy or arrange for the destruction of a customer's records within its custody or control containing personal information that is no longer necessary to be retained by the business by shredding, erasing, or otherwise modifying the personal information in those records to make it unreadable or undecipherable.

Section 7. Computer security breach. (1) Any person or business that conducts business in Montana and that owns or licenses computerized data that includes personal information shall disclose any breach of the security of the data system following discovery or notification of the breach to any resident of Montana whose unencrypted personal information was or is reasonably believed to have been acquired by an unauthorized person. The disclosure must be made without unreasonable delay, consistent with the legitimate needs of law enforcement, as provided in subsection (3), or consistent with any measures necessary to determine the scope of the breach and restore the reasonable integrity of the data system.

(2) Any person or business that maintains computerized data that includes personal information that the person or business does not own shall notify the owner or licensee of the information of any breach of the security of the data system immediately following

discovery if the personal information was, or is reasonably believed to have been acquired by an unauthorized person.

(3) The notification required by this section may be delayed if a law enforcement agency determines that the notification will impede a criminal investigation and requests a delay in notification. The notification required by this section must be made after the law enforcement agency determines that it will not compromise the investigation.

(4) For purposes of this section, the following definitions apply:

(a) "Breach of the security of the data system" means unauthorized acquisition of computerized data that materially compromises the security, confidentiality, or integrity of personal information maintained by the person or business and causes or is reasonably believed to cause loss or injury to a Montana resident. Good faith acquisition of personal information by an employee or agent of the person or business for the purposes of the person or business is not a breach of the security of the data system, provided that the personal information is not used or subject to further unauthorized disclosure.

(b) (i) "Personal information" means an individual's first name or first initial and last name in combination with any one or more of the following data elements, when either the name or the data elements are not encrypted:

(A) Social Security number;

(B) driver's license number or state identification card number;

(C) account number or credit or debit card number, in combination with any required security code, access code, or password that would permit access to an individual's financial account.

(ii) Personal information does not include publicly available information that is lawfully made available to the general public from federal, state, or local government records.

(5) (a) For purposes of this section, notice may be provided by one of the following methods:

(i) written notice;

(ii) electronic notice, if the notice provided is consistent with the provisions regarding electronic records and signatures set forth in 15 U.S.C. 7001;

(iii) telephonic notice; or

(iv) substitute notice, if the person or business demonstrates that:

(A) the cost of providing notice would exceed $250,000;

(B) the affected class of subject persons to be notified exceeds 500,000; or

(C) the person or business does not have sufficient contact information.

(b) Substitute notice must consist of the following:

(i) an electronic mail notice when the person or business has an electronic mail address for the subject persons; and

(ii) conspicuous posting of the notice on the website page of the person or business if the person or business maintains one; or

(iii) notification to applicable local or statewide media.

(6) Notwithstanding subsection (5), a person or business that maintains its own notification procedures as part of an information

security policy for the treatment of personal information and that does not unreasonably delay notice is considered to be in compliance with the notification requirements of this section if the person or business notifies subject persons in accordance with its policies in the event of a breach of security of the data system.

(7) If a business discloses a security breach to any individual pursuant to this section and gives a notice to the individual that suggests, indicates, or implies to the individual that the individual may obtain a copy of the file on the individual from a consumer credit reporting agency, the business shall coordinate with the consumer reporting agency as to the timing, content, and distribution of the notice to the individual. The coordination may not unreasonably delay the notice to the affected individuals.

Section 8. Department to restrain unlawful acts -- penalty. (1) Whenever the department has reason to believe that a person has violated [sections 2 through 8] and that proceeding would be in the public interest, the department may bring an action in the name of the state against the person to restrain by temporary or permanent injunction or temporary restraining order the use of the unlawful method, act, or practice upon giving appropriate notice to that person, pursuant to 30-14-111(2).

(2) The provisions of 30-14-111(3) and (4) and 30-14-112 through 30-14-115 apply to [sections 2 through 8].

(3) A violation of [sections 2 through 8] is a violation of 30-14-103, and the penalties for a violation of [sections 2 through 8] are as provided in 30-14-142.

Section 9. Computer security breach. (1) Any licensee or insurance-support organization that conducts business in Montana and that owns or licenses computerized data that includes personal information shall provide notice of any breach of the security of the system following discovery or notice of the breach of the security of the system to any individual whose unencrypted personal information was or is reasonably believed to have been acquired by an unauthorized person. The notice must be made without unreasonable delay, consistent with the legitimate needs of law enforcement, as provided in subsection (3), or consistent with any measures necessary to determine the scope of the breach and restore the reasonable integrity of the data system.

(2) Any person to whom personal information is disclosed in order for the person to perform an insurance function pursuant to this part that maintains computerized data that includes personal information shall notify the licensee or insurance-support organization of any breach of the security of the system in which the data is maintained immediately following discovery of the breach of the security of the system if the personal information was or is reasonably believed to have been acquired by an unauthorized person.

(3) The notice required by this section may be delayed if a law enforcement agency determines that the notice will impede a criminal investigation and requests a delay of notice. The notice required by this section must be made after the law enforcement agency determines that the notice will not compromise the investigation.

(4) Licensees, insurance-support organizations, and persons to whom personal information is disclosed pursuant to this part shall develop and maintain an information security policy for the safeguarding of personal information and security breach notice procedures that provide expedient notice to individuals as provided in subsection (1).

(5) For purposes of this section, the following definitions apply:

(a) "Breach of the security of the system" means unauthorized acquisition of computerized data that compromises the security, confidentiality, or integrity of personal information maintained by a licensee, insurance-support organization, or person to whom information is disclosed pursuant to this part. Acquisition of personal information by a licensee, insurance-support organization, or employee or agent of a person as authorized pursuant to this part is not a breach of the security of the system.

(b) (i) "Personal information" means an individual's first name or first initial and last name in combination with any one or more of the following data elements, when the name and the data elements are not encrypted:

(A) Social Security number;

(B) driver's license number or state identification number;

(C) account number or credit or debit card number, in combination with any required security code, access code, or password that would permit access to an individual's financial account.

(ii) Personal information does not include publicly available information that is lawfully made available to the general public from federal, state, or local government records.

Section 10. Codification instruction. (1) [Sections 2 through 8] are intended to be codified as an integral part of Title 30, chapter 14, and the provisions of Title 30, chapter 14, apply to [sections 2 through 8].

(2) [Section 9] is intended to be codified as an integral part of Title 33, chapter 19, part 3, and the provisions of Title 33, chapter 19, part 3, apply to [section 9].

Section 11. Severability. If a part of [this act] is invalid, all valid parts that are severable from the invalid part remain in effect. If a part of [this act] is invalid in one or more of its applications, the part remains in effect in all valid applications that are severable from the invalid applications.

Section 12. Effective date. (1) Except as provided in subsection (2), [this act] is effective March 1, 2006.

Chapter 27: Nebraska

Nebraska's Financial Data Protection and Consumer Notification of Data Security Breach Act of 2006 provides that an individual or commercial entity (defined in the bill to include government, governmental subdivision, and agency) that owns or licenses computerized data that includes personal information about any Nebraska residents is to give notice to the affected Nebraskans following a security breach of the computerized data system if an investigation determines that the use of information about a Nebraska resident for an unauthorized purpose has occurred or is reasonably likely to occur; and authorizes the attorney general to issue subpoenas and seek and recover damages for Nebraska residents injured by violations.

L.B. 876

Uniform Commercial Code, Reissue Revised Statutes Of Nebraska; to adopt the Financial Data Protection and Consumer Notification of Data Security Breach Act of 2006; to change provisions relating to state-chartered bank loan limits; to change Community development investment conditions; to change provisions relating to the reorganization of nationally-chartered banks as state-chartered banks; to revise powers of state-chartered banks, building and loan associations, and credit unions; to change and provide enforcement powers and procedures under the Nebraska Sale of Checks and Funds Transmission Act; to provide for a transaction exempt from registration under the Securities Act of Nebraska; to change provisions relating to bankers banks; to change provisions, provide enforcement powers and procedures, and change administrative fines under the Mortgage Bankers Registration and Licensing Act; to change provisions relating to the Delayed Deposit Services Licensing Act; to change provisions relating to installment sales and loans and to define terms; to change requirements relating to charges, loan fees, and the writing of loans or other products or services as prescribed; to change provisions relating to the sale of trust property; to eliminate obsolete provisions; to change provisions relating to the effectiveness of certain secured

transactions; to harmonize provisions; to provide operative dates; to repeal the original sections; and to declare an emergency. Be it enacted by the people of the State of Nebraska, Section1. Sections1 to 7 of this act shall be known and may be cited as the Financial Data Protection and Consumer Notification of Data Security Breach Act of 2006.

Sec. 2. For purposes of the Financial Data Protection and Consumer Notification of Data Security Breach Act of 2006: (1) Breach of the security of the system means the unauthorized acquisition of unencrypted computerized data that compromises the security, confidentiality, or integrity of personal information maintained by an individual or a commercial entity. Good faith acquisition of personal information by an employee or agent of an individual or a commercial entity for the purposes of the individual or the commercial entity is not a breach of the security of the system if the personal information is not used or subject to further unauthorized disclosure. Acquisition of personal information pursuant to a search warrant, subpoena, or other court order or

Pursuant to a subpoena or order of a state agency is not a breach of the security of the system; (2) Commercial entity includes a corporation, business trust, estate, trust, partnership, limited partnership, limited liability partnership, limited liability company, association, organization, joint venture, government, governmental subdivision, agency, or instrumentality, or any other legal entity, whether for profit or not for profit;(3) Encrypted means converted by use of an algorithmic process to transform data into a form in which the data is rendered unreadable or unusable without use of a confidential process or key;(4) Notice means:

(a) Written notice;

(b) Telephonic notice;

(c) Electronic notice, if the notice provided is consistent with the provisions regarding electronic records and signatures set forth in

15 U.S.C.7001, as such section existed on January 1, 2006;-1-LB 876LB 876(d) Substitute notice, if the individual or commercial entity required to provide notice demonstrates that the cost of providing notice will exceed seventy-five thousand dollars, that the affected class of Nebraska residents to be notified exceeds one hundred thousand residents, or that the individual or commercial entity does not have sufficient contact information to provide notice. Substitute notice under this subdivision requires all of the following: (i) Electronic mail notice if the individual or commercial entity has electronic mail addresses for the members of the affected class of Nebraska residents; (ii) Conspicuous posting of the notice on the website of the individual or commercial entity if the individual or commercial entity maintains a website; and (iii) Notice to major statewide media outlets; or (e)Substitute notice, if the individual or commercial entity required to provide notice has ten employees or fewer and demonstrates that the cost of providing notice will exceed ten thousand dollars. Substitute notice under this subdivision requires all of the following: (i) Electronic mail notice if the individual or commercial entity has electronic mail addresses for the members of the affected class of Nebraska residents;(ii) Notification by a paid advertisement in a local newspaper that is distributed in the geographic area in which the individual or commercial entity is located, which advertisement shall be of sufficient size that it covers at least one-quarter of a page in the newspaper and shall be published in the newspaper at least once a week for three consecutive weeks; (iii) Conspicuous posting of the notice on the website of the individual or commercial entity if the individual or commercial entity maintains a website; and(iv) Notification to major media outlets in the geographic area in which the individual or commercial entity is located;(5) Personal information means a Nebraska resident's first name or first initial and last name in combination with any one or more of the following data elements that relate to the resident if either the name or the data elements are not encrypted, redacted, or otherwise altered by any method or technology in such a manner that the name or data elements are unreadable:

(a) Social security number;

(b) Motor vehicle operator's license number or state identification card number;

(c) Account number or credit or debit card number, in combination with any required security code, access code, or password that would permit access to a resident's financial account;

(d) Unique electronic identification number or routing code, in combination with any required security code, access code, or password; or

(e) Unique biometric data, such as a fingerprint, voice print, or retina or iris image, or other unique physical representation. Personal information does not include publicly available information that is lawfully made available to the general public from federal, state, or local government records; and(6) Redact means to alter or truncate data such that no more than the last four digits of a social security number, motor vehicle operator's license number, state identification card number, or account number is accessible as part of the personal information.

Sec.3. (1) An individual or a commercial entity that conducts business in Nebraska and that owns or licenses computerized data that includes personal information about a resident of Nebraska shall, when it becomes aware of a breach of the security of the system, conduct in good faith a reasonable and prompt investigation to determine the likelihood that personal information has been or will be used for an unauthorized purpose. If the investigation determines that the use of information about a Nebraska resident for an unauthorized purpose has occurred or is reasonably likely to occur, the individual or commercial entity shall give notice to the affected Nebraska resident. Notice shall be made as soon as possible and without unreasonable delay, consistent with the legitimate needs of law enforcement and consistent with any measures necessary to determine the scope of the breach and to restore the reasonable integrity of the computerized data system.(2) An individual or a commercial entity that maintains computerized data that includes personal information that the individual or commercial entity does not own or license shall give notice to and cooperate with the owner or licensee of the information of any breach of the security of the system when it becomes aware of a breach if use of personal information about a Nebraska resident for an unauthorized purpose occurred or is reasonably-2-LB 876LB 876 likely to occur. Cooperation includes, but is not limited to, sharing with the owner or licensee information relevant to the breach, not including information proprietary to the individual or commercial entity. (3)Notice required by this section may be delayed if a law enforcement agency determines that the notice will impede a criminal investigation. Notice shall be made in good faith, without unreasonable delay, and as soon as possible after the law enforcement agency determines that notification will no longer impede the investigation.

Sec. 4. (1) An individual or a commercial entity that maintains its own notice procedures which are part of an information security policy for the treatment of personal information and which are otherwise consistent with the timing requirements of section 3 of this act, is deemed to be in compliance with the notice requirements of section 3 of this act if the individual or the commercial entity notifies affected Nebraska residents in accordance with its notice procedures in the event of a breach of the security of the system. (2) An individual or a commercial entity that is regulated by state or federal law and that maintains procedures for a breach of the security of the system pursuant to the laws, rules, regulations, guidances, or guidelines established by its primary or functional state or federal regulator is deemed to be in compliance with section 3 of this act if the individual or commercial entity notifies affected Nebraska residents in accordance with the maintained procedures in the event of a breach of the security of the system.

Sec.5. Any waiver of the provisions of the Financial Data Protection and Consumer Notification of Data Security Breach Act of 2006 is contrary to public policy and is void and unenforceable.

Sec. 6. For purposes of the Financial Data Protection and Consumer Notification of Data Security Breach Act of 2006, the Attorney General may issue subpoenas and seek and recover direct economic damages for each affected Nebraska resident injured by a violation of the act.

Sec. 7. The Financial Data Protection and Consumer Notification of Data Security Breach Act of 2006 applies to the discovery of or notification pertaining to a breach of the security of the system that occurs on or after the operative date of this section.

Sec. 8. Section 8-141, Revised Statutes Cumulative Supplement, 2004, is amended to read:8-141 (1) No bank shall directly or indirectly loan to any single corporation, limited liability company, firm, or individual, including in such loans all loans made to the several members or shareholders of such firm, limited liability company, or corporation, for the use and benefit of such corporation, limited liability company, firm, or individual, more than twenty-five percent of the paid-up capital, surplus, and capital notes and debentures or fifteen percent of the unimpaired capital and unimpaired surplus of such bank, whichever is greater. Such limitations shall be subject to the following exceptions:(a) Obligations of any person, partnership, limited liability company, association, or corporation in the form of notes or drafts secured by shipping documents or instruments transferring or securing title covering livestock or giving alien on livestock, when the market value of the livestock securing the obligation is not at any time less than one hundred fifteen percent of the face amount of the notes covered by such documents, shall be subject under this section to a limitation of ten percent of such capital, surplus, and capital notes and debentures or ten percent of such unimpaired capital and unimpaired surplus, whichever is greater, in addition to such twenty-five percent of such capital and surplus or such fifteen percent of such unimpaired capital and unimpaired surplus;(b) Obligations of any person, partnership, limited liability company, association, or corporation secured by not less than a like amount of bonds or notes of the United States issued since April 24, 1917, or certificates of indebtedness of the United States, treasury bills of the United States, or obligations fully guaranteed both as to principal and interest by the United States shall be subject under this section to a limitation of ten percent of such capital, surplus, and capital notes and debentures or ten percent of such unimpaired capital and unimpaired surplus, whichever is greater, in addition to such twenty-five percent of such capital and surplus or such fifteen percent of such unimpaired capital and unimpaired surplus;(c) Obligations of any person, partnership, limited liability company, association, or corporation which are secured by negotiable warehouse receipts in an amount not less than one hundred fifteen percent of the face amount of the note or notes secured by such documents shall be subject under this section to a limitation of ten percent of such capital, surplus, and capital notes and debentures or ten percent of such unimpaired capital and-3-LB 876LB 876unimpairedsurplus,whicheverisgreater,inadditiontosuchtwenty-fivepercent of such capital and surplus or such fifteen percent of such unimpaired capital and unimpaired surplus; or(d) Obligations of any person, partnership, limited liability company, association, or corporation which are secured by readily marketable collateral having a market value, as determined by reliable and continuously available price quotations, in an amount at least equal to the face amount of the note or notes secured by such collateral, shall be subject under this section to a limitation of ten percent of such capital, surplus, and capital notes and debentures or ten percent of such unimpaired capital and unimpaired surplus, whichever is greater, in addition to such twenty-five percent of such capital and surplus or such fifteen percent of such unimpaired capital and unimpaired surplus. (2) For purposes of this section, the discounting of bills of exchange, drawn in good faith against actually existing values, and the discounting of commercial paper actually owned by the persons negotiating the same shall not be considered as the lending of money. Loans or obligations shall not be subject to any limitation under this section, based upon such capital and surplus or such unimpaired capital and unimpaired surplus, to the extent that they are secured or covered by guaranties, or by commitments or agreements to take over or to purchase the same, made by any federal reserve bank or by the United States Government or any authorized agency thereof, including any corporation wholly owned directly or indirectly by the United States, or general obligations of any state of the United States or any political subdivision thereof. The phrase general obligation of any state or any political sub-division thereof means an obligation supported by the full faith and credit of an obligor possessing general powers of taxation, including property taxation, but does not include municipal revenue bonds and sanitary and improvement district warrants which are subject to the limitations set forth in this section. Any bank may subscribe to, invest in, purchase, and own single-family mortgages secured by the Federal Housing Administration or the United States Department of Veterans Affairs and mortgage-backed certificates of the Government National Mortgage Association which are guaranteed as to payment of principal and interest by the Government National Mortgage Association. Such mortgages and certificates shall not be subject under this section to any limitation based upon such capital and surplus or such unimpaired capital and unimpaired surplus. Obligations representing loans to any national banking association or to any banking institution organized under the laws of any state, when such loans are approved by the Director of Banking and Finance by regulation or otherwise, shall not be subject under this section to any limitation based upon such capital and surplus or such unimpaired capital and unimpaired surplus. Loans or extensions of credit secured by a segregated deposit account in the lending banks hall not be subject under this section to any limitation based on such capital and surplus or such unimpaired capital and unimpaired surplus. The department may adopt and promulgate rules and regulations governing the terms and conditions of such security interest and segregated deposit account. For the purpose of determining lending limits, partnerships shall not be treated as separate entities. Each individual shall be charged with his or her personal debt plus the debt of every partnership in which he or she is a partner, except that for purposes of this section (a) an individual shall only be charged with the debt of any limited partnership in which he or she is a partner to the extent that the terms of the limited partnership agreement provide that such individual is to be held liable for the debts or actions of such limited partnership and (b) no individual shall be charged with the debt of any general partnership in which he or she is a partner beyond the extent to which (I)his or her liability for such partnership debt is limited by the terms of a contract or other written agreement between the bank and such individual and (ii) any personal debt of such individual is incurred for the use and benefit of such general partnership.(3) A loan made within lending limits at the initial time the loan was made may be renewed, extended, or serviced without regard to changes in the lending limit of a bank following the initial extension of the loan if (a) the renewal, extension, or servicing of the loan does not result in the extension of funds beyond the initial amount of the loan or (b) the accrued interest on the loan is not added to the original amount of the loan in the process of renewal, extension, or servicing. (4) Any bank may purchase or take an interest in life insurance contracts for any purpose incidental to the business of banking. A bank's purchase of any life insurance contract, as measured by its cash surrender value, from any one life insurance company shall not at any time exceed twenty-five percent of the paid-up capital, surplus, and capital notesand-4-LB 876LB 876debentures of such bank or fifteen percent of the paid-up capital, surplus, undivided profits, and capital notes and debentures of such bank, whichever is greater. A bank's purchase of life insurance contracts, as measured by their cash surrender values, in the aggregate from all life insurance companies shall not at anytime exceed thirty-five percent of the paid-up capital, surplus ,undivided profits, and capital notes and debentures of such bank. The limitations under this subsection on a bank's purchase of life insurance contracts, in the aggregate from all life insurance companies, shall not apply to any contract purchased prior to April 5, 1994.(5) For purposes of this section, unimpaired capital and unimpaired surplus means(a) the bank's tier1 and tier 2capital included in the bank's risk-based capital under the capital guidelines of the appropriate federal banking agency, based on the bank's most recent consolidated report of condition filed under 12 U.S.C. 1817(a)(3), and (b) the balance of the bank's allowance for loan and lease losses not included in the bank's tier 2 capital for purposes of the calculation of risk-based capital by the appropriate federal banking agency, based on the bank's most recent consolidated report of condition filed under 12 U.S.C. 1817(a)(3). Notwithstanding the provisions of section 8-1,140, the department may, by order, deny or limit the inclusion of goodwill in the calculation of a bank's unimpaired capital and unimpaired surplus or in the calculation of a bank's paid-up capital and surplus.

Sec. 9. Section 8-148.04, Reissue Revised Statutes of Nebraska, is amended to read:8-148.04 (1) Any bank may make a community development investment or investments either directly or through purchasing an equity interest in or an evidence of indebtedness of an entity primarily engaged in making community development investments, if the following conditions are satisfied:(a) The investments An investment under this subsection do does not expose the bank to unlimited liability;(b)The bank's aggregate investment in any one entity under this subsection does not exceed five percent of its capital and surplus and its aggregate investments under this subsection do not exceed ten percent of its capital and surplus. If the bank's investment in any one entity will exceed five percent of its capital and surplus, the prior written approval of the department must be obtained; and(c) All investments made under this subsection are accounted for on the bank's books under "Other Assets".(2)Nothing in this section shall prevent a bank from charging off as a contribution an investment made pursuant to subsection (1) of this section.(3)Such subscription, investment, possession, or ownership shall not be subject to sections 8-148, 8-149, and 8-150.(4) For purposes of this section, community development investments means investments of a predominantly civic, community, or public nature and not merely private and entrepreneurial.

Sec.10.Section8-178, Revised Statutes Cumulative Supplement, 2004, is amended to read :8 178 Any national banking association located and doing business within the State of Nebraska which follows the procedure prescribed by the laws of the United States may convert into a state bank or merge or consolidate with a state bank upon a vote of the holders of at least two-thirds of the capital stock of such state bank when the resulting state bank meets the requirements of the state law as to the formation of a new state bank. If the national banking association has been further chartered to conduct a trust company business within a trust department of the bank, the trust department to be converted shall meet the requirements of state law as to the formation of a trust company business within a trust department of a state bank. The public hearing requirement of subdivision (1) of section 8-115.01 and the rules and regulations of the department shall only be required only if (1) after publishing a notice of the proposed conversion in a newspaper of general circulation in the county where the main office of the national bank is located, the expense of which shall be paid by the applicant bank, the director receives an objection to the conversion within fifteen days after such publication or (2) in the discretion of the director, the condition of the bank warrants a hearing. If the national bank has been further chartered to conduct a trust company business within a trust department of the bank, the notice of the proposed conversion of the national bank shall include notice that the trust department will be converted in connection with the national bank conversion.

Sec.11.Section8-179, Reissue Revised Statutes of Nebraska, is amended to read:-5-LB 876LB 8768-179 (1) The resulting state bank shall file a statement with the department, under the oath of its president or cashier, (a) showing that the procedure prescribed by the laws of the United States and by this state have been followed, and (b) setting forth in the statement the matter prescribed by sections 8-121and8-1901to8 1903, and(c) if the national bank has been further chartered to conduct a trust company business within a trust department of the bank, setting forth the matter prescribed by sections 8-159 to 8-162.01.Upon payment of all applicable fees, pay the fees prescribed therein, and thereupon the department shall issue to such corporation the certificate provided for in section8-122, and a charter to transact the business provided for in its articles of incorporation, and, if applicable, a charter to conduct a trust company business within a trust department of the bank.(2) The department may accept good assets of any such national bank, worth not less than par, in lieu of the payment otherwise provided by law for the stock of such resulting bank. When the parties requesting the conversion, merger, or consolidation are officers or directors of either the national bank or of the state bank, they shall be accepted without investigation as parties of integrity and responsibility. Unless the resulting bank is at a different location than the former national or state bank, the department shall recognize the public necessity, convenience, and advantage of permitting the resulting bank and, if applicable, the trust company business within a trust department of the bank, to engage in business.

Sec.12.Section8-1,140, Revised Statutes Supplement, 2005, is amended to read:8-1,140 Notwithstanding any of the other provisions of the Nebraska Banking Act or any other Nebraska statute, any bank incorporated under the laws of this state and organized under the provisions of the act, or under the laws of this state as they existed prior to May 9, 1933, shall directly, or indirectly through a subsidiary or subsidiaries, have all the rights, powers, privileges, benefits, and immunities which may be exercised as of March 23, 2005 the operative date of this section, by a federally chartered bank doing business in Nebraska, including the exercise of all powers and activities that are permitted for a financial subsidiary of a federally chartered bank. Such rights, powers, privileges, benefits, and immunities shall not relieve such bank from payment of state taxes assessed under any applicable laws of this state.

Sec.13. Section 8-355, Revised Statutes Supplement, 2005, is amended to read:8-355 Notwithstanding any of the provisions of Chapter 8, article3, or any other Nebraska statute, except as provided in section8 345.02,any association incorporated under the laws of the State of Nebraska and organized under the provisions of such article shall have all the rights, powers, privileges, benefits, and immunities which may be exercised as of March 23, 2005 the operative date of this section, by a federal savings and loan association doing business in Nebraska. Such rights, powers, privileges, benefits, and immunities shall not relieve such association from payment of state taxes assessed under any applicable laws of this state.

Sec. 14. Section 8-1001.01, Revised Statutes Cumulative Supplement,2004, is amended to read:8-1001.01 Sections 8-1001 to 8-1014 and sections 18 and 19 of this act shall be known and may be cited as the Nebraska Sale of Checks and Funds Transmission Act.

Sec.15.Section8-1008,Revised Statutes Cumulative Supplement,2004, is amended to read:8-1008(1)After a license has been granted, the licensee shall maintain the bond or securities in the amount prescribed by section 8-1006, as follows:(a) (1) Each licensee who does not have on file or deposit a bond or securities in the undiminished sum of two hundred fifty thousand dollars shall file semiannual reports with the director setting forth the locations at which the licensee sells checks in this state as of January 1 and July 1 in each year with the report for each such date being due on or before the fifteenth day thereafter. The licensee shall not be required to list on such reports those agents which are exempted by the provisions of section 8-1003.

Within ten days following the filing of such reports, the principal sum of the bond or securities shall be increased to reflect any increase in the number of locations and may be decreased to reflect any decrease in the number of locations; and (b) (2) If the director finds at any time that any bond required by the Nebraska Sale of Checks and Funds Transmission Act is insecure, insufficient, or exhausted, an additional bond to be approved by the director-6-LB 876LB 876shall be filed by the licensee within ten days after written demand therefore by the director. (2) Until July 1, 2005, a licensee licensed prior to July 16, 2004, may maintain the bond or securities amount such licensee was originally licensed under.

Sec.16.Section8-1010,RevisedStatutesCumulativeSupplement,2004, is amended to read:8-1010 Each licensee may conduct business at one or more locations within this state and through or by means of such employees, agents, or representatives as the licensee may designate and appoint from time to time. In addition to any reports which may be required by subdivision (1)(a) (1) of section 8-1008, each licensee shall notify the Department of Banking and Finance annually on or before July 1 of each year of all such locations except for agents which are exempted under section 8-1003. No license under the Nebraska Sale of Checks and Funds Transmission Act shall be required of any employee, agent, or representative who is acting for or in behalf of a licensee in the sale of checks of which the licensee is the issuer.

Sec.17.Section8-1012,Revised Statutes Cumulative Supplement, 2004, is amended to read: 81012(1) The director may, following a hearing under the Administrative Procedure Act, suspend or revoke a license issued under the Nebraska Sale of Checks and Funds Transmission Act on any ground on which he or she may refuse to grant a license or for violation of the Nebraska Sale of Checks and Funds Transmission Act, for failure to pay an annual fee, or for the failure or refusal of a licensee to comply with any order, decision, or finding of the director made pursuant to the act. In furtherance of the provisions of this section, the director, if he or she has reasonable cause to believe that the grounds for revocation exist, may investigate the business, books, and records of the licensee.(2)Except as provided in this section, a license shall not be revoked or suspended except after notice and a hearing in accordance with the Administrative Procedure Act.(3)A licensee may voluntarily surrender a license by delivering to the director written notice of the surrender but a surrender shall not affect civil or criminal liability for acts committed before the surrender or liability for any fines which may be levied against the licensee or any of its officers, directors, shareholders, partners, or members for acts committed before the surrender. (4) (a) If a licensee fails to renew its license as required by section8 1009 and does not voluntarily surrender the license pursuant to this section, the Department of Banking and Finance may issue a notice of expiration of the license to the licensee in lieu of revocation proceedings.(b) If a licensee fails to maintain a surety bond as required by section8-1008,the department may issue a notice of cancellation of the license in lieu of revocation proceedings.(5) Revocation, suspension, surrender, cancellation, or expiration of a license shall not impair or affect the obligation of a preexisting lawful contract between the licensee and any person.(6) Revocation, suspension, cancellation, or expiration of a license shall not affect civil or criminal liability for acts committed before the revocation, suspension, cancellation, or expiration or liability for any fines which may be levied against the licensee or any of its officers, directors, shareholders, partners, or members for acts committed before the revocation, suspension, cancellation, or expiration.

Sec.18. (1) The Department of Banking and Finance may order any person to cease and desist whenever the department determines that the person has violated any provision of the Nebraska Sale of Checks and Funds Transmission Act. Upon entry of a cease and desist order, the director shall promptly notify the affected person that such order has been entered, of the reasons for such order, and that upon receipt, within fifteen business days after the date of the order, of written request from the affected person a hearing will be scheduled within thirty business days after the date of receipt of the written request, unless the parties consent to a later date or the hearing officer sets a later date for good cause. If a hearing is not requested and none is ordered by the director, the order shall remain in effect until it is modified or vacated.(2) The director may vacate or modify a cease and desist order if he or she finds that the conditions which caused its entry have changed or that it is otherwise in the public interest to do so.(3) A person aggrieved by a cease and desist order.

L.B. 1113

This bill deletes references to Social Security numbers in dissolutions of marriage, domestic relations orders, paternity orders, child support orders, and foreign support orders.

I would advise any company to work with an attorney who specializes in data privacy laws prior to posting their company's privacy policy on their website. A poorly worded privacy policy can actually be a liability for a company, not to mention may be out of compliance with a given state's law. Case in point, Nebraska L.B. 118.

L.B. 118

This bill provides that a person engages in a deceptive trade practice when, in the course of his or her business, vocation, or occupation, he or she makes a false or misleading statement in a privacy policy, published on the Internet or otherwise distributed or published, regarding the use of personal information submitted by members of the public.

L.B. 156

This bill provides some clarification around the circumstances under which a financial institution or other entity would be required to disclose customer records or information they deem confidential. It requires a financial institution or other entity when dealing with a law enforcement agency or state agency to be presented with (a) a lawful subpoena, summons, or warrant issued by a court of competent jurisdiction to a law enforcement agency, or (b) a lawful subpoena issued under the laws of this state by a government agency exercising investigatory or adjudicative functions with respect to a matter within the agency's jurisdiction. The bill also recognizes the ability of a financial institution or other entity to disclose customer records or information deemed to be confidential pursuant to a statute which, by its terms or by rules or regulations adopted and promulgated there under, requires the disclosure in a fashion other than by subpoena, summons, warrant, or court order.

Chapter 28: Nevada

Nevada's Senate Bill 297 makes it illegal to possess devices that can unlawfully capture personally identifiable information. What could be considered hacker paraphernalia would also have legitimate uses. On the other hand, I have yet to find anybody who smokes tobacco through a water pipe.

Nevada requires businesses to be PCI compliant if they accept credit/debit card payments. The State also requires encryption when personal data – as defined by statute – is electronically transmitted outside of a secure facility. Voice and fax transmissions are excluded. The text of Nevada's primary data breach disclosure law is below.

GENERAL PROVISIONS

NRS 603A.010 Definitions. As used in this chapter, unless the context otherwise requires, the words and terms defined in NRS 603A.020, 603A.030 and 603A.040 have the meanings ascribed to them in those sections.

(Added to NRS by 2005, 2503)

NRS 603A.020 "Breach of the security of the system data" defined. "Breach of the security of the system data" means unauthorized acquisition of computerized data that materially compromises the security, confidentiality or integrity of personal information maintained by the data collector. The term does not include the good faith acquisition of personal information by an employee or agent of the data collector for a legitimate purpose of the data collector, so long as the personal information is not used for a purpose unrelated to the data collector or subject to further unauthorized disclosure.

(Added to NRS by 2005, 2503)

NRS 603A.030 "Data collector" defined. "Data collector" means any governmental agency, institution of higher education, corporation,

financial institution or retail operator or any other type of business entity or association that, for any purpose, whether by automated collection or otherwise, handles, collects, disseminates or otherwise deals with nonpublic personal information.

(Added to NRS by 2005, 2504)

NRS 603A.040 "Personal information" defined. "Personal information" means a natural person's first name or first initial and last name in combination with any one or more of the following data elements, when the name and data elements are not encrypted:

1. Social Security number.

2. Driver's license number or identification card number.

3. Account number, credit card number or debit card number, in combination with any required security code, access code or password that would permit access to the person's financial account.

☐ The term does not include publicly available information that is lawfully made available to the general public.

(Added to NRS by 2005, 2504; A 2005, 22nd Special Session, 109)

APPLICABILITY

NRS 603A.100 Waiver of provisions of chapter prohibited. Any waiver of the provisions of this chapter is contrary to public policy, void and unenforceable.

(Added to NRS by 2005, 2506)

REGULATION OF BUSINESS PRACTICES

NRS 603A.200 Destruction of certain records.

1. A business that maintains records which contain personal information concerning the customers of the business shall take reasonable measures to ensure the destruction of those records when the business decides that it will no longer maintain the records.

2. As used in this section:

(a) "Business" means a proprietorship, corporation, partnership, association, trust, unincorporated organization or other enterprise doing business in this State.

(b) "Reasonable measures to ensure the destruction" means any method that modifies the records containing the personal information in such a way as to render the personal information contained in the records unreadable or undecipherable, including, without limitation:

(1) Shredding of the record containing the personal information; or

(2) Erasing of the personal information from the records.

(Added to NRS by 2005, 2504)

NRS 603A.210 Security measures.

1. A data collector that maintains records which contain personal information of a resident of this State shall implement and maintain reasonable security measures to protect those records from unauthorized access, acquisition, destruction, use, modification or disclosure.

2. A contract for the disclosure of the personal information of a resident of this State which is maintained by a data collector must include a provision requiring the person to whom the information is disclosed to implement and maintain reasonable security measures

to protect those records from unauthorized access, acquisition, destruction, use, modification or disclosure.

3. If a state or federal law requires a data collector to provide greater protection to records that contain personal information of a resident of this State which are maintained by the data collector and the data collector is in compliance with the provisions of that state or federal law, the data collector shall be deemed to be in compliance with the provisions of this section.

(Added to NRS by 2005, 2504)

NRS 603A.220 Disclosure of breach of security of system data; methods of disclosure.

1. Any data collector that owns or licenses computerized data which includes personal information shall disclose any breach of the security of the system data following discovery or notification of the breach to any resident of this State whose unencrypted personal information was, or is reasonably believed to have been, acquired by an unauthorized person. The disclosure must be made in the most expedient time possible and without unreasonable delay, consistent with the legitimate needs of law enforcement, as provided in subsection 3, or any measures necessary to determine the scope of the breach and restore the reasonable integrity of the system data.

2. Any data collector that maintains computerized data which includes personal information that the data collector does not own shall notify the owner or licensee of the information of any breach of the security of the system data immediately following discovery if the personal information was, or is reasonably believed to have been, acquired by an unauthorized person.

3. The notification required by this section may be delayed if a law enforcement agency determines that the notification will impede a criminal investigation. The notification required by this section

must be made after the law enforcement agency determines that the notification will not compromise the investigation.

4. For purposes of this section, except as otherwise provided in subsection 5, the notification required by this section may be provided by one of the following methods:

(a) Written notification.

(b) Electronic notification, if the notification provided is consistent with the provisions of the Electronic Signatures in Global and National Commerce Act, 15 U.S.C. §§7001 et seq.

(c) Substitute notification, if the data collector demonstrates that the cost of providing notification would exceed $250,000, the affected class of subject persons to be notified exceeds 500,000 or the data collector does not have sufficient contact information. Substitute notification must consist of all the following:

(1) Notification by electronic mail when the data collector has electronic mail addresses for the subject persons.

(2) Conspicuous posting of the notification on the Internet website of the data collector, if the data collector maintains an Internet website.

(3) Notification to major statewide media.

5. A data collector which:

(a) Maintains its own notification policies and procedures as part of an information security policy for the treatment of personal information that is otherwise consistent with the timing requirements of this section shall be deemed to be in compliance with the notification requirements of this section if the data collector notifies subject persons in accordance with its policies and procedures in the event of a breach of the security of the system data.

(b) Is subject to and complies with the privacy and security provisions of the Gramm-Leach-Bliley Act, 15 U.S.C. §§6801 et seq., shall be deemed to be in compliance with the notification requirements of this section.

6. If a data collector determines that notification is required to be given pursuant to the provisions of this section to more than 1,000 persons at any one time, the data collector shall also notify, without unreasonable delay, any consumer reporting agency, as that term is defined in 15 U.S.C. §1681a(p), that compiles and maintains files on consumers on a nationwide basis, of the time the notification is distributed and the content of the notification.

(Added to NRS by 2005, 2504)

REMEDIES AND PENALTIES

NRS 603A.900 Civil action. A data collector that provides the notification required pursuant to NRS 603A.220 may commence an action for damages against a person that unlawfully obtained or benefited from personal information obtained from records maintained by the data collector. A data collector that prevails in such an action may be awarded damages which may include, without limitation, the reasonable costs of notification, reasonable attorney's fees and costs and punitive damages when appropriate. The costs of notification include, without limitation, labor, materials, postage and any other costs reasonably related to providing the notification.

(Added to NRS by 2005, 2506)

NRS 603A.910 Restitution. In addition to any other penalty provided by law for the breach of the security of the system data maintained by a data collector, the court may order a person who is convicted of

unlawfully obtaining or benefiting from personal information obtained as a result of such breach to pay restitution to the data collector for the reasonable costs incurred by the data collector in providing the notification required pursuant to NRS 603A.220, including, without limitation, labor, materials, postage and any other costs reasonably related to providing such notification.

(Added to NRS by 2005, 2506)

NRS 603A.920 Injunction. If the Attorney General or a district attorney of any county has reason to believe that any person is violating, proposes to violate or has violated the provisions of this chapter, he may bring an action against that person to obtain a temporary or permanent injunction against the violation.

(Added to NRS by 2005, 2506)

Senate Bill 297

This bill relates to personal identifying information; makes various changes relating to personal identifying information; prohibits a person from unlawfully possessing or using a scanning device or reencoder to acquire certain personal identifying information; clarifies the applicability of certain crimes relating to personal identifying information; prohibits a public officer or public employee from committing certain unlawful acts relating to personal identifying information; restricts the type of credit card or debit card information that may be printed electronically on a receipt; and provides penalties.

Section 1. Chapter 205 of NRS is hereby amended by adding thereto the provisions set forth as sections 2 to 19, inclusive, of this act.

Sec. 2. As used in sections 2 to 9, inclusive, of this act, unless the context otherwise requires, the words and terms defined in sections 3, 4 and 5 of this act have the meanings ascribed to them in those sections.

Sec. 3. "Payment card" means a credit card, charge card, debit card or any other card that:

1. Is issued to an authorized card user; and
2. Allows the user to obtain, purchase or receive credit, money, a good, a service or anything of value.

Sec. 4. "Reencoder" means an electronic device that places encoded information from the magnetic strip or stripe of a payment card onto the magnetic strip or stripe of a different payment card.

Sec. 5. "Scanning device" means a scanner, reader or any other electronic device that is used to access, read, scan, obtain, memorize or store, temporarily or permanently, information encoded on the magnetic strip or stripe of a payment card.

Sec. 6. 1. A person shall not:

(a) Use a scanning device to access, read, obtain, memorize or store, temporarily or permanently, information encoded on the magnetic strip or stripe of a payment card:

(1) Without the permission of the authorized user of the payment card; and

(2) With the intent to defraud the authorized user, the issuer of the payment card or any other person.

(b) Use a reencoder to place information encoded on the magnetic strip or stripe of a payment card onto the magnetic strip or stripe of a different card:

(1) Without the permission of the authorized user of the card from which the information is being reencoded; and

(2) With the intent to defraud the authorized user, the issuer of the payment card or any other person.

2. A person who violates any provision of this section is guilty of a category B felony and shall be punished by imprisonment in the state prison for a minimum term of not less than 1 year and a maximum term of not more than 20 years, and may be further punished by a fine of not more than $100,000.

3. In addition to any other penalty, the court shall order a person who violates any provision of this section to pay restitution, including, without limitation, any attorney's fees and costs incurred to:

(a) Repair the credit history or rating of each person who is a victim of the violation; and

(b) Satisfy a debt, lien or other obligation incurred by each person who is a victim of the violation.

Sec. 7. 1. A person shall not possess a scanning device or reencoder with the intent to use the scanning device or reencoder for an unlawful purpose.

2. A person who violates any provision of this section is guilty of a category C felony and shall be punished as provided in NRS 193.130.

Sec. 8. The provisions of sections 2 to 9, inclusive, of this act do not apply to any person who, without the intent to defraud or commit an unlawful act, possesses or uses a scanning device or reencoder:

1. In the ordinary course of his business or employment; or

2. Pursuant to a financial transaction entered into with an authorized user of a payment card who has given permission for the financial transaction.

Sec. 9. In any prosecution for a violation of any provision of sections 2 to 9, inclusive, of this act, the State is not required to establish and it is no defense that:

1. An accessory has not been convicted, apprehended or identified; or

2. Some of the acts constituting elements of the crime did not occur in this state or that where such acts did occur they were not a crime or elements of a crime.

Sec. 10. As used in NRS 205.463 and 205.465 and sections 10 to 19, inclusive, of this act, unless the context otherwise requires, the words and terms defined in sections 11 to 15, inclusive, of this act have the meanings ascribed to them in those sections.

Sec. 11. "Document" includes, without limitation, a photocopy print, photostat and other replica of a document.

Sec. 12. "Personal identifying information" means any information designed, commonly used or capable of being used, alone or in conjunction with any other information, to identify a living or deceased person, including, without limitation:

1. The name, driver's license number, Social Security number, savings account number, credit card number, debit card number, date of birth, place of employment and maiden name of the mother of a person; and

2. The fingerprints, voiceprint, retina image and iris image of a person.

Sec. 13. "Public body" means:

1. The State of Nevada, or any agency, instrumentality or corporation thereof;

2. The University and Community College System of Nevada;

3. Any municipality, county, school district or other type of district, or a city or town, incorporated or unincorporated; or
4. Any other body corporate and politic comprising a political subdivision of this state or acting on behalf thereof.

Sec. 14. "Public employee" means any person who is an employee or independent contractor of a public body.

Sec. 15. "Public officer" means a person who:

1. Is elected or appointed to a position which is established by the Constitution or a statute of this state, or by a charter or ordinance of a political subdivision of this state; or

2. Otherwise serves as an officer for a public body.

Sec. 16. A person who violates any provision of NRS 205.463 and 205.465 and sections 10 to 19, inclusive, of this act may be prosecuted for the violation whether or not the person whose personal identifying information forms a part of the violation is living or deceased during the course of the violation or the prosecution.

Sec. 17. 1. A public officer or public employee who knowingly:

(a) Obtains any personal identifying information of another person from any document, file, database, source or process used by a public body to collect, store, maintain, transfer, reproduce, manage or administer personal identifying information; and

(b) Uses the personal identifying information to harm that other person or for any unlawful purpose, including, without limitation, to obtain credit, a good, a service or anything of value in the name of that person, is guilty of a category B felony and shall be punished by imprisonment in the state prison for a minimum term of not less than 5 years and a maximum term of not more than 20 years, and may be further punished by a fine of not more than $100,000.

2. In addition to any other penalty, the court shall order a public officer or public employee convicted of violating subsection 1 to pay restitution, including, without limitation, any attorney's fees and costs incurred to:

(a) Repair the credit history or rating of the person whose personal identifying information the public officer or public employee obtained and used in violation of subsection 1; and

(b) Satisfy a debt, lien or other obligation incurred by the person whose personal identifying information the public officer or public employee obtained and used in violation of subsection 1.

3. A public officer or public employee who knowingly:

(a) Obtains any personal identifying information of another person from any document, file, database, source or process used by a public body to collect, store, maintain, transfer, reproduce, manage or administer personal identifying information; and

(b) Possesses, sells or transfers the personal identifying information for the purpose of establishing a false status, occupation, membership, license or identity for himself or any other person, is guilty of a category C felony and shall be punished as provided in NRS 193.130.

4. A public officer or public employee who knowingly aids another public officer or public employee to commit a violation of any provision of this section is guilty of a category C felony and shall be punished as provided in NRS 193.130.

5. The provisions of this section do not prohibit the possession or use of any personal identifying information by officers of local police, sheriff and metropolitan police departments and by agents

of the Investigation Division of the Department of Public Safety while engaged in undercover investigations related to the lawful discharge of their duties.

Sec. 18. The provisions of NRS 205.463 and 205.465 and sections 10 to 19, inclusive, of this act do not apply to any person who, without the intent to defraud or commit an unlawful act, possesses or uses any personal identifying information of another person:
1. In the ordinary course of his business or employment; or

2. Pursuant to a financial transaction entered into with an authorized user of a payment card who has given permission for the financial transaction.

Sec. 19. In any prosecution for a violation of any provision of NRS 205.463 and 205.465 and sections 10 to 19, inclusive, of this act, the State is not required to establish and it is no defense that:

1. An accessory has not been convicted, apprehended or identified; or

2. Some of the acts constituting elements of the crime did not occur in this state or that where such acts did occur they were not a crime or elements of a crime.

Sec. 20. NRS 205.463 is hereby amended to read as follows:

205.463 1. Except as otherwise provided in subsection 2, a person who knowingly:

(a) Obtains any personal identifying information of another person; and

(b) Uses the personal identifying information to harm that other person or for any unlawful purpose, including, without limitation, to obtain credit, a good, a service or anything of value in the name of that person, is guilty of a category B felony and shall be punished

by imprisonment in the state prison for a minimum term of not less than 1 year and a maximum term of not more than 20 years, and may be further punished by a fine of not more than $100,000.
2. A person who knowingly:

(a) Obtains any personal identifying information of another person; and

(b) Uses the personal identifying information to avoid or delay being prosecuted for an unlawful act, is guilty of a category E felony and shall be punished as provided in NRS 193.130.

3. In addition to any other penalty, the court shall order a person convicted of violating subsection 1 to pay restitution, including, without limitation, any attorney's fees and costs incurred to:

(a) Repair the credit history or rating of the person whose personal identifying information he obtained and used in violation of subsection 1; and

(b) Satisfy a debt, lien or other obligation incurred by the person whose personal identifying information he obtained and used in violation of subsection 1.

[4. As used in this section, "personal identifying information" has the meaning ascribed to it in NRS 205.465.]

Sec. 21. NRS 205.465 is hereby amended to read as follows: 205.465

1. It is unlawful for a person to possess, sell or transfer any document or personal identifying information for the purpose of establishing a false status, occupation, membership, license or identity for himself or any other person.

2. A person who:

(a) Sells or transfers any such document or personal identifying information in violation of subsection 1; or

(b) Possesses any such document or personal identifying information in violation of subsection 1 to commit any of the crimes set forth in NRS 205.085 to 205.217, inclusive, 205.473 to 205.513, inclusive, or 205.610 to 205.810, inclusive is guilty of a category C felony and shall be punished as provided in NRS 193.130.

3. Except as otherwise provided in subsection 2, a person who possesses any such document or personal identifying information in violation of subsection 1 is guilty of a misdemeanor.

4. Subsection 1 does not:

(a) Preclude the adoption by a city or county of an ordinance prohibiting the possession of any such document or personal identifying information; or

(b) Prohibit the possession or use of any such document or personal identifying information by officers of local police, sheriff and metropolitan police departments and by agents of the Investigation Division of the Department of Public Safety while engaged in undercover investigations related to the lawful discharge of their duties.

[5. As used in this section:

(a) "Document" includes, without limitation, a photocopy print, photostat and other replica of a document.

(b) "Personal identifying information" means any information designed, commonly used or capable of being used, alone or in conjunction with any other information, to identify a person, including, without limitation:

(1) The name, driver's license number, Social Security number, savings account number, credit card number, debit card number, date of birth, place of employment and maiden name of the mother of a person; and

(2) The fingerprints, voiceprint, retina image and iris image of a person.

Sec. 22. Chapter 597 of NRS is hereby amended by adding thereto a new section to read as follows:

1. Except as otherwise provided in this section, if a person accepts credit cards or debit cards for the transaction of business, the person shall not do any of the following:

(a) Print the expiration date of the credit card or debit card on any receipt provided to the cardholder.

(b) Print more than the last five digits of the account number of the credit card or debit card on any receipt provided to the cardholder.

2. This section:

(a) Applies only to receipts that are electronically printed

(b) Does not apply to transactions in which the only means of recording the credit card or debit card number is:

(1) By handwriting the credit card or debit card number; or

(2) By imprinting or copying the credit card or debit card.

3. If any cash register or other machine or device that electronically prints receipts for credit card or debit card transactions was first put into use before October 1, 2003, the provisions of this section do not apply to any transaction that occurs with regard to that cash register or other machine or device before January 1, 2008.

4. As used in this section:

(a) "Credit card" means any instrument or device, whether known as a credit card, credit plate, or by any other name, issued with or without fee by an issuer for the use of the cardholder in obtaining money, property, goods, services or anything else of value on credit.

(b) "Debit card" means any instrument or device, whether known as a debit card or by any other name, that is issued with or without a fee by an issuer for the use of the cardholder in obtaining money, property, goods, services or anything else of value, subject to the issuer removing money from the checking account or savings account of the cardholder.

A.B. 334

This bill requires a governmental entity, except in certain circumstances, to ensure that Social Security numbers in its books and records are maintained in a confidential manner, and it prohibits the inclusion of Social Security numbers in certain documents that are recorded, filed, or otherwise submitted to a governmental agency. The bill also requires a governmental agency or certain persons who do business in this state that own, license, or maintain computerized data to notify certain persons if personal information included in that data was, or is reasonably believed to have been, acquired by an unauthorized person. It also expands the types of prohibited computer contaminants to include spyware.

Senate Bill 347

This bill relates to personal identifying information. It prohibits the establishment or possession of a financial forgery laboratory; it enhances the penalties for crimes involving personal identifying information that are committed against older persons and vulnerable persons. The bill requires the issuer of a credit card to provide a notice including certain information concerning its policies regarding identity theft and the rights of cardholders when issuing a credit card to a cardholder. The bill also requires data collectors to provide notification concerning any breach of security involving system data.

Senate Bill 164

This bill protects the confidentiality of certain personal identifying information of parents and children involved in paternity cases by removing the requirement that the court include such information in its orders, which are available to the public. The bill states, however, that the court must continue to obtain and provide certain personal identifying information to the Welfare Division and must ensure that the Social Security numbers of parents and children that are placed in the court's records are kept confidential unless otherwise required by statute.

Chapter 29: New Hampshire

Like many other states, New Hampshire's House Bill 1660 provides for an exemption to the disclosure requirement if, upon an investigation, misuse has not, and likely will not, occur. It does state, however, that if, upon an investigation, it cannot be determined if misuse will occur, disclosure is still required. I find that to be more honest, as I do not believe it truly can be determined what a hacker will do with the data they have stolen.

An Act Regulating Identity Theft–House Bill 1660

This bill requires that a person engaged in business in the state of New Hampshire to notify consumers of any security breach that compromises the confidentiality of their personal information.

STATE OF NEW HAMPSHIRE

In the Year of Our Lord Two Thousand Six

AN ACT regulating identity theft.

Be it Enacted by the Senate and House of Representatives in General Court convened:

242:1 New Subdivision; Right to Privacy; Notice of Security Breach. Amend RSA 359-C by inserting after section 18 the following new subdivision:

Notice of Security Breach

359-C:19 Definitions. In this subdivision:

I. "Computerized data" means personal information stored in an electronic format.

II. "Encrypted" means the transformation of data through the use of an algorithmic process into a form for which there is a low probability of assigning meaning without use of a confidential process or key, or securing the information by another method that renders the data elements completely unreadable or unusable. Data shall not be considered to be encrypted for purposes of this subdivision if it is acquired in combination with any required key, security code, access code, or password that would permit access to the encrypted data.

III. "Person" means an individual, corporation, trust, partnership, incorporated or unincorporated association, limited liability company, or other form of entity, or any agency, authority, board, court, department, division, commission, institution, bureau, or other state governmental entity, or any political subdivision of the state.

IV.(a) "Personal information" means an individual's first name or initial and last name in combination with any one or more of the following data elements, when either the name or the data elements are not encrypted:

(1) Social Security number.

(2) Driver's license number or other government identification number.

(3) Account number, credit card number, or debit card number, in combination with any required security code, access code, or password that would permit access to an individual's financial account.

(b) "Personal information" shall not include information that is lawfully made available to the general public from federal, state, or local government records.

V. "Security breach" means unauthorized acquisition of computerized data that compromises the security or confidentiality of personal information maintained by a person doing business in this state. Good faith acquisition of personal information by an employee or agent of a person for the purposes of the person's business shall not be considered a security breach, provided that the personal information is not used or subject to further unauthorized disclosure.

359-C:20 Notification of Security Breach Required.

I.(a) Any person doing business in this state who owns or licenses computerized data that includes personal information shall, when it becomes aware of a security breach, promptly determine the likelihood that the information has been or will be misused. If the determination is that misuse of the information has occurred or is reasonably likely to occur, or if a determination cannot be made, the person shall notify the affected individuals as soon as possible as required under this subdivision.

(b) Any person engaged in trade or commerce that is subject to RSA 358-A:3, I shall also notify the regulator which has primary regulatory authority over such trade or commerce. All other persons shall notify the New Hampshire attorney general's office. The notice shall include the anticipated date of the notice to the individuals and the approximate number of individuals in this state who will be notified. Nothing in this section shall be construed to require the person to provide to any regulator or the New Hampshire attorney general's office the names of the individuals entitled to receive the notice or any personal information relating to them. The disclosure shall be made to affected individuals as quickly as possible, after the determination required under this section.

(c) Any person or business that maintains computerized data that includes personal information that the person or business does not own shall notify and cooperate with the owner or licensee of the information of any breach of the security of the data immediately following discovery, if the personal information was acquired by an unauthorized person. Cooperation includes sharing with the owner or licensee information relevant to the breach; except that such cooperation shall not be deemed to require the disclosure of confidential or business information or trade secrets.

II. Notification pursuant to paragraph I may be delayed if a law enforcement agency, or national or homeland security agency determines that the notification will impede a criminal investigation or jeopardize national or homeland security.

III. The notice required under this section shall be provided by one of the following methods:

(a) Written notice.

(b) Electronic notice, if the agency or business' primary means of communication with affected individuals is by electronic means.

(c) Telephonic notice, provided that a log of each such notification is kept by the person or business who notifies affected persons.

(d) Substitute notice, if the person demonstrates that the cost of providing notice would exceed $5,000, that the affected class of subject individuals to be notified exceeds 1,000, or the person does not have sufficient contact information or consent to provide notice pursuant to subparagraphs I(a)-I(c). Substitute notice shall consist of all of the following:

(1) E-mail notice when the person has an e-mail address for the affected individuals.

(2) Conspicuous posting of the notice on the person's business website, if the person maintains one.

(3) Notification to major statewide media.

(e) Notice pursuant to the person's internal notification procedures maintained as part of an information security policy for the treatment of personal information.

IV. Notice under this section shall include at a minimum:

(a) A description of the incident in general terms.

(b) The approximate date of breach.

(c) The type of personal information obtained as a result of the security breach.

(d) The telephonic contact information of the person subject to this section.

V. Any person engaged in trade or commerce that is subject to RSA 358-A:3, I which maintains procedures for security breach notification pursuant to the laws, rules, regulations, guidances, or guidelines issued by a state or federal regulator shall be deemed to be in compliance with this subdivision if it acts in accordance with such laws, rules, regulations, guidances, or guidelines.

VI. (a) If a person is required to notify more than 1,000 consumers of a breach of security pursuant to this section, the person shall also notify, without unreasonable delay, all consumer reporting agencies that compile and maintain files on consumers on a nationwide basis, as defined by 15 U.S.C. section 1681a(p), of the anticipated date of the notification to the consumers, the approximate number of consumers who will be notified, and the content of the notice. Nothing in this paragraph shall be construed to require the person to provide to any consumer reporting agency the names of the consumers entitled to receive the notice or any personal information relating to them.

(b) Subparagraph (a) shall not apply to a person who is subject to Title V of the Gramm, Leach-Bliley Act, 15 U.S.C. section 6801 et seq.

359-C:21 Violation.

I. Any person injured by any violation under this subdivision may bring an action for damages and for such equitable relief, including an injunction, as the court deems necessary and proper. If the court finds for the plaintiff, recovery shall be in the amount of actual damages. If the court finds that the act or practice was a willful or knowing violation of this chapter, it shall award as much as 3 times, but not less than 2 times, such amount. In addition, a prevailing plaintiff shall be awarded the costs of the suit and reasonable attorney's fees, as determined by the court. Any attempted waiver of the right to the damages set forth in this paragraph shall be void and unenforceable. Injunctive relief shall be available to private individuals under this chapter without bond, subject to the discretion of the court.

II. The New Hampshire attorney general's office shall enforce the provisions of this subdivision pursuant to RSA 358-A:4.

III. The burden shall be on the person responsible for the determination under RSA 359-C:20, I to demonstrate compliance with this subdivision.

242:2 Effective Date. This act shall take effect January 1, 2007.

House Bill 384

This bill provides that financial affidavits in domestic relations cases are confidential and accessible only to the parties, their attorneys, the guardian, and certain state and federal officials. It also establishes a private right of action under RSA 359-C, the Right to Privacy Act.

Senate Bill 319

This bill prohibits, with certain limited exceptions, a person from filing with the registry of deeds a document that includes an individual's Social Security number or financial information.

House Bill 269

This bill makes "pretexting," the act of using a false pretense to obtain personally identifiable information about another individual, a violation, subject to a fine, and establishes a private cause of action for those injured by pretexting.

House Bill 745

This bill prohibits any public or private entity from using a secret database that contains personally identifiable information and does not provide the person an opportunity to review the accuracy of such information.

Chapter 30: New Jersey

A person who knowingly violates New Jersey's Senate Bill 2665 can face fines up to $5,000 plus court and attorneys' fees and up to fifteen days behind bars. The law also allows consumers to place a freeze on their account with the credit bureaus. I like that more and more states are passing laws empowering consumers with a certain amount of ownership over the personal information the major credit bureaus have about us.

The Identity Theft Prevention Act: Assembly, # 4001

Be It Enacted *by the Senate and General Assembly of the State of New Jersey:*

1. (New section) This act shall be known and may be cited as the "Identity Theft Prevention Act."

2. (New section) The Legislature finds and declares that:

a. The crime of identity theft has become one of the major law enforcement challenges of the new economy, as vast quantities of sensitive, personal information are now vulnerable to criminal interception and misuse; and

b. A number of indicators reveal that, despite increased public awareness of the crime, incidents of identity theft continue to rise; and

c. An integral part of many identity crimes involves the interception of personal financial data or the fraudulent acquisition of credit cards or other financial products in another person's name; and

d. Identity theft is an act that violates the privacy of our citizens and ruins their good names: victims can suffer restricted access to credit and diminished employment opportunities, and may spend years repairing damage to credit histories; and

e. Credit reporting agencies and issuers of credit should have uniform reporting requirements and effective fraud alerts to assist identity theft victims in repairing and protecting their credit; and

f. The Social Security number is the most frequently used record keeping number in the United States. Social Security numbers are used for employee files, medical records, health insurance accounts, credit and banking accounts, university ID cards and many other purposes; and

g. Social Security numbers are frequently used as identification numbers in many computer files, giving access to information an individual may want kept private and allowing an easy way of linking data bases. Therefore, it is wise to limit access to an individual's Social Security number whenever possible; and,

h. It is therefore a valid public purpose for the New Jersey Legislature to ensure that the Social Security numbers of the citizens of the State of New Jersey are less accessible in order to detect and prevent identity theft and to enact certain other protections and remedies related thereto and thereby further the public safety.

3. (New section) a. A person who reasonably believes or reasonably suspects that he has been the victim of identity theft in violation of N.J.S.2C:21-1, section 1 of P.L.1983, c.565 (C.2C:21-2.1) or N.J.S.2C:21-17 may contact the local law enforcement agency in the jurisdiction where he resides, which shall take a police report of the matter and provide the complainant with a copy of that report. Notwithstanding the fact that jurisdiction may lie elsewhere for investigation and prosecution of a crime of identity theft, the local law enforcement agency shall take the complaint and provide the complainant with a copy of the complaint and may refer the complaint to a law enforcement agency in that different jurisdiction.
b. Nothing in this section shall interfere with the discretion of a local law enforcement agency to allocate resources for investigations of crimes. A complaint filed under this section is not

required to be counted as an open case for purposes such as compiling open case statistics.

4. Section 3 of P.L.1997, c.172 (C.56:11-30) is amended to read as follows:

3. As used in this act:

"Adverse action" has the same meaning as in subsection (k) of section 603 of the federal "Fair Credit Reporting Act," 15 U.S.C. s.1681a.

"Consumer" means an individual.

"Consumer report" (1) means any written, oral or other communication of any information by a consumer reporting agency bearing on a consumer's credit worthiness, credit standing, credit capacity, character, general reputation, personal characteristics or mode of living which is used or expected to be used or collected in whole or in part for the purpose of serving as a factor in establishing the consumer's eligibility for:

(a) credit or insurance to be used primarily for personal, family or household purposes;

(b) employment purposes; or

(c) any other purpose authorized under section 4 of this act.

(2) The term "consumer report" does not include:

(a) any:

(i) report containing information solely on transactions or experiences between the consumer and the person making the report;

(ii) communication of that information among persons related by common ownership or affiliated by corporate control; or

(iii) communication of other information among persons related by common ownership or affiliated by corporate control, if it is clearly and conspicuously disclosed to the consumer that the information may be communicated among those persons and the consumer is given the opportunity, before the time that the information is initially communicated, to direct that the information not be communicated among those persons;

(b) any authorization or approval of a specific extension of credit directly or indirectly by the issuer of a credit card or similar device;

(c) any report in which a person, who has been requested by a third party to make a specific extension of credit directly or indirectly to a consumer, conveys his decision with respect to that request, if the third party advises the consumer of the name and address of the person to whom the request was made, and the person makes the disclosures to the consumer required under 15 U.S.C. s.1681m; or

(d) communication excluded from the definition of consumer report pursuant to subsection (o) of section 603 of the federal "Fair Credit Reporting Act," 15 U.S.C. s.1681a.

"Consumer reporting agency" means any person which, for monetary fees, dues, or on a cooperative nonprofit basis, regularly engages, in whole or in part, in the practice of assembling or evaluating consumer credit information or other information on consumers for the purpose of furnishing consumer reports to third parties, and which uses any means or facility for the purpose of preparing or furnishing consumer reports.

"Director" means the Director of the Division of Consumer Affairs in the Department of Law and Public Safety.

"Division" means the Division of Consumer Affairs in the Department of Law and Public Safety.

"Employment purposes" means, when used in connection with a consumer report, a report used for the purpose of evaluating a consumer for employment, promotion, reassignment or retention as an employee.

"File" means, when used in connection with information on any consumer, all of the information on that consumer recorded and retained by a consumer reporting agency regardless of how the information is stored.

"Investigative consumer report" means a consumer report or a portion thereof in which information on a consumer's character, general reputation, personal characteristics or mode of living is obtained through personal interviews with neighbors, friends or associates of the consumer who is the subject of the report or with others with whom the consumer is acquainted or who may have knowledge concerning any of those items of information. However, this information shall not include specific factual information on a consumer's credit record obtained directly from a creditor of the consumer or from a consumer reporting agency when the information was obtained directly from a creditor of the consumer or from the consumer.

"Medical information" means information or records obtained, with the consent of the individual to whom it relates, from licensed physicians or medical practitioners, hospitals, clinics, or other medical or medically related facilities.

"Security freeze" means a notice placed in a consumer's consumer report, at the request of the consumer and subject to certain exceptions, that prohibits the consumer reporting agency from releasing the report or any information from it without the express authorization of the consumer, but does not prevent a consumer reporting agency from advising a third party that a security freeze is in effect with respect to the consumer report.

(cf: P.L.1997, c.172, s.3)

5. (New section) a. A consumer may elect to place a security freeze on his consumer report by:

(1) making a request in writing by certified mail or overnight mail to a consumer reporting agency; or

(2) making a request directly to the consumer reporting agency through a secure electronic mail connection, if an electronic mail connection is provided by the consumer reporting agency.

b. A consumer reporting agency shall place a security freeze on a consumer report no later than five business days after receiving a written request from the consumer.

c. The consumer reporting agency shall send a written confirmation of the security freeze to the consumer within five business days of placing the freeze and at the same time shall provide the consumer with a unique personal identification number or password to be used by the consumer when providing authorization for the release of his credit for a specific party or period of time.

d. If the consumer wishes to allow his consumer report to be accessed for a specific party or period of time while a freeze is in place, he shall contact the consumer reporting agency via certified or overnight mail or secure electronic mail and request that the freeze be temporarily lifted, and provide all of the following:

(1) Information generally deemed sufficient to identify a person;

(2) The unique personal identification number or password provided by the consumer reporting agency pursuant to subsection c. of this section; and

(3) The proper information regarding the third party who is to receive the consumer report or the time period for which the consumer report shall be available to users of the consumer report.

e. A consumer reporting agency that receives a request from a consumer to temporarily lift a freeze on a consumer report pursuant to subsection d. of this section shall comply with the request no later than three business days after receiving the request.

f. A consumer reporting agency shall develop procedures involving the use of telephone, fax, the Internet, or other electronic media to receive and process a request from a consumer to temporarily lift a freeze on a consumer report pursuant to subsection d. of this section in an expedited manner. The director shall promulgate regulations necessary to allow the use of electronic media to receive and process a request from a consumer to temporarily lift a security freeze pursuant to subsection d. of this section as quickly as possible, with the goal of processing a request within 15 minutes of that request.

g. A consumer reporting agency shall remove or temporarily lift a freeze placed on a consumer report only in the following cases:

(1) Upon consumer request, pursuant to subsection d. or j. of this section; or

(2) If the consumer report was frozen due to a material misrepresentation of fact by the consumer. If a consumer reporting agency intends to remove a freeze upon a consumer report pursuant to this paragraph, the consumer reporting agency shall notify the consumer in writing at least five business days prior to removing the freeze on the consumer report.

h. If a third party requests access to a consumer report on which a security freeze is in effect, and this request is in connection with an application for credit or any other use, and the consumer does not allow his consumer report to be accessed for that specific party or period of time, the third party may treat the application as incomplete.

i. (1) At any time that a consumer is required to receive a summary of rights required under section 609 of the federal "Fair Credit Reporting Act," 15 U.S.C. s.1681g, the following notice shall be included:

New Jersey Consumers Have the Right to Obtain a Security Freeze

You may obtain a security freeze on your credit report to protect your privacy and ensure that credit is not granted in your name without your knowledge. You have a right to place a "security freeze" on your credit report pursuant to New Jersey law.

The security freeze will prohibit a consumer reporting agency from releasing any information in your credit report without your express authorization or approval.

The security freeze is designed to prevent credit, loans, and services from being approved in your name without your consent. When you place a security freeze on your credit report, within five business days you will be provided a personal identification number or password to use if you choose to remove the freeze on your credit report or to temporarily authorize the release of your credit report for a specific party, parties, or period of time after the freeze is in place. To provide that authorization, you must contact the consumer reporting agency and provide all of the following:

(i) The unique personal identification number or password provided by the consumer reporting agency;

(ii) Proper identification to verify your identity; and

(iii) The proper information regarding the third party or parties who are to receive the credit report or the period of time for which the report shall be available to users of the credit report.

A consumer reporting agency that receives a request from a consumer to lift temporarily a freeze on a credit report shall comply with the request no later than three business days or less, as provided by regulation, after receiving the request.

A security freeze does not apply to circumstances in which you have an existing account relationship and a copy of your report is requested by your existing creditor or its agents or affiliates for certain types of account review, collection, fraud control or similar activities.

If you are actively seeking credit, you should understand that the procedures involved in lifting a security freeze may slow your own applications for credit. You should plan ahead and lift a freeze, either completely if you are shopping around, or specifically for a certain creditor, a few days before actually applying for new credit.

You have a right to bring a civil action against someone who violates your rights under the credit reporting laws. The action can be brought against a consumer reporting agency or a user of your credit report.

(2) If a consumer requests information about a security freeze, he shall be provided with the notice provided in paragraph (1) of this subsection and with any other information, as prescribed by the director by regulation, about how to place, temporarily lift and permanently lift a security freeze.

j. A security freeze shall remain in place until the consumer requests that the security freeze be removed. A consumer reporting agency shall remove a security freeze within three business days of receiving a request for removal from the consumer, who provides the following:

(1) Proper identification; and

(2) The unique personal identification number or password provided by the consumer reporting agency pursuant to subsection c. of this section.

k. A consumer reporting agency shall require proper identification of the person making a request to place or remove a security freeze.

l. The provisions of this section do not apply to the use of a consumer report by the following:

(1) A person, or subsidiary, affiliate, or agent of that person, or an assignee of a financial obligation owing by the consumer to that person, or a prospective assignee of a financial obligation owing by the consumer to that person in conjunction with the proposed purchase of the financial obligation, with which the consumer has or had prior to assignment an account or contract, including a demand deposit account, or to whom the consumer issued a negotiable instrument, for the purposes of reviewing the account or collecting the financial obligation owing for the account, contract, or negotiable instrument. For purposes of this paragraph, "reviewing the account" includes activities related to account maintenance, monitoring, credit line increases, and account upgrades and enhancements;

(2) A subsidiary, affiliate, agent, assignee, or prospective assignee of a person to whom access has been granted under subsection d. of this section, for purposes of facilitating the extension of credit or other permissible use [1][.];[1]

(3) Any State or local agency, law enforcement agency, trial court, or private collection agency acting pursuant to a court order, warrant, or subpoena;

(4) The Division of Taxation in the Department of the Treasury for the purpose of enforcing the tax laws of this State;

(5) A State or local child support enforcement agency; [1][or][1]

(6) The use of credit information for the purposes of prescreening as provided for by the federal "Fair Credit Reporting Act," 15 U.S.C. s.1681 et seq. [1];

(7) Any person or entity administering a credit file monitoring subscription service to which the consumer has subscribed; or

(8) Any person or entity for the purpose of providing a consumer with a copy of the consumer's credit report upon the consumer's request.[1]

m. (1) A consumer reporting agency shall not charge a consumer any fee to place a security freeze on that consumer's consumer report.

(2) A consumer reporting agency may charge a reasonable fee, not to exceed $5, to a consumer who elects to remove or temporarily lift a security freeze on that consumer's consumer report.

(3) A consumer may be charged a reasonable fee, not to exceed $5, if the consumer fails to retain the original personal identification number provided by the consumer reporting agency and must be reissued the same or a new personal identification number.

6. (New section) If a security freeze is in place, a consumer reporting agency shall not change any of the following official information in a consumer report without sending a written confirmation of the change to the consumer within 30 days of the change being posted to the consumer's file: name; date of birth; Social Security number; or address. Written confirmation is not required for technical modifications of a consumer's official information, including name and street abbreviations, complete spellings, or transposition of numbers or letters. In the case of an address change, the written confirmation shall be sent to both the new address and to the former address.

7. (New section) The provisions of sections 4 through 9 of this amendatory and supplementary act shall not apply to a consumer reporting agency that acts only as a reseller of credit information by assembling and merging information contained in the data base of another consumer reporting agency or multiple consumer reporting agencies, and does not maintain a permanent data base of credit information from which new consumer reports are produced, except that such a reseller of credit information shall honor any security freeze placed on a consumer report by another consumer reporting agency.

8. (New section) The following entities are not required to place a security freeze in a consumer report, pursuant to section 5 of this amendatory and supplementary act:

a. A check services company or fraud prevention services company, which issues reports on incidents of fraud or authorizations for the purpose of approving or processing negotiable instruments, electronic funds transfers, or similar methods of payments; and

b. A demand deposit account information service company, which issues reports regarding account closures due to fraud, substantial overdrafts, ATM abuse, or similar negative information regarding a consumer, to inquiring banks or other financial institutions for use only in reviewing a consumer request for a demand deposit account at the inquiring bank or financial institution.

9. (New section) a. Any person who willfully fails to comply with the requirements of sections 4 through 9 of this amendatory and supplementary act shall be liable to a consumer as provided in section 11 of P.L.1997, c.172 (C.56:11-38).

b. Any person who is negligent in failing to comply with the requirements of sections 4 through 9 of this amendatory and supplementary act shall be liable to a consumer as provided in section 12 of P.L.1997, c.172 (C.56:11-39).

10. (New section) As used in sections 10 through 15 of this amendatory and supplementary act:

"Breach of security" means unauthorized access to electronic files, media or data containing personal information that compromises the security, confidentiality or integrity of personal information when access to the personal information has not been secured by encryption or by any other method or technology that renders the personal information unreadable or unusable. Good faith acquisition of personal information by an employee or agent of the business for a legitimate business purpose is not a breach of security, provided that the personal information is not used for a purpose unrelated to the business or subject to further unauthorized disclosure.

"Business" means a sole proprietorship, partnership, corporation, association, or other entity, however organized and whether or not organized to operate at a profit, including a financial institution organized, chartered, or holding a license or authorization certificate under the law of this State, any other state, the United States, or of any other country, or the parent or the subsidiary of a financial institution.

"Communicate" means to send a written or other tangible record or to transmit a record by any means agreed upon by the persons sending and receiving the record.

"Customer" means an individual who provides personal information to a business.

"Individual" means a natural person.

"Internet" means the international computer network of both federal and non-federal interoperable packet switched data networks.

"Personal information" means an individual's first name or first initial and last name linked with any one or more of the following data elements: (1) Social Security number; (2) driver's license number or State identification card number; or (3) account number or credit or debit card number, in combination with any required security code, access code, or password that would permit access to an individual's financial account. Dissociated data that, if linked, would constitute personal information is personal information if the means to link the dissociated data were accessed in connection with access to the dissociated data.

For the purposes of sections 10 through 15 of this amendatory and supplementary act, personal information shall not include publicly available information that is lawfully made available to the general public from federal, state or local government records, or widely distributed media.

"Private entity" means any individual, corporation, company, partnership, firm, association, or other entity, other than a public entity.

"Public entity" includes the State, and any county, municipality, district, public authority, public agency, and any other political subdivision or public body in the State. For the purposes of sections 10 through 15 of this amendatory and supplementary act, public entity does not include the federal government.

"Publicly post" or "publicly display" means to intentionally communicate or otherwise make available to the general public.

"Records" means any material, regardless of the physical form, on which information is recorded or preserved by any means, including written or spoken words, graphically depicted, printed, or electromagnetically transmitted. Records does not include publicly available directories containing information an individual has voluntarily consented to have publicly disseminated or listed.

11. (New section) A business or public entity shall destroy, or arrange for the destruction of, a customer's records within its custody or control containing personal information, which is no longer to be retained by the business or public entity, by shredding, erasing, or otherwise modifying the personal information in those records to make it unreadable, undecipherable or nonreconstructable through generally available means.

12. (New section) a. Any business that conducts business in New Jersey, or any public entity that compiles or maintains computerized records that include personal information, shall disclose any breach of security of those computerized records following discovery or notification of the breach to any customer who is a resident of New Jersey whose personal information was, or is reasonably believed to have been, accessed by an unauthorized person. The disclosure to a [1][consumer] customer[1] shall be made in the most expedient time possible and without unreasonable delay, consistent with the legitimate needs of law enforcement, as provided in subsection c. of this section, or any measures necessary to determine the scope of the breach and restore the reasonable integrity of the data system. Disclosure of a breach of security to a customer shall not be required under this section if the business or public entity establishes that misuse of the information is not reasonably possible. Any determination shall be documented in writing and retained for five years.

b. Any business or public entity that compiles or maintains computerized records that include personal information on behalf of another business or public entity shall notify that business or public entity, who shall notify its New Jersey customers, as provided in subsection a. of this section, of any breach of security of the computerized records immediately following discovery, if the personal information was, or is reasonably believed to have been, accessed by an unauthorized person.

c. (1) Any business or public entity required under this section to disclose a breach of security of a customer's personal information shall, in advance of the disclosure to the customer, report the breach of security and any information pertaining to the breach to the Division of State Police in the Department of Law and Public Safety for investigation or handling, which may include dissemination or referral to other appropriate law enforcement entities.

(2) The notification required by this section shall be delayed if a law enforcement agency determines that the notification will impede a criminal or civil investigation and that agency has made a request that the notification be delayed. The notification required by this section shall be made after the law enforcement agency determines that its disclosure will not compromise the investigation and notifies that business or public entity.

d. For purposes of this section, notice may be provided by one of the following methods:

(1) Written notice;

(2) Electronic notice, if the notice provided is consistent with the provisions regarding electronic records and signatures set forth in section 101 of the federal "Electronic Signatures in Global and National Commerce Act" (15 U.S.C. s.7001); or

(3) Substitute notice, if the business or public entity demonstrates that the cost of providing notice would exceed $250,000, or that the affected class of subject persons to be notified exceeds 500,000, or the business or public entity does not have sufficient contact information. Substitute notice shall consist of all of the following:

(a) E-mail notice when the business or public entity has an e-mail address;

(b) Conspicuous posting of the notice on the Internet website page of the business or public entity, if the business or public entity maintains one; and

(c) Notification to major Statewide media.

e. Notwithstanding subsection d. of this section, a business or public entity that maintains its own notification procedures as part of an information security policy for the treatment of personal information, and is otherwise consistent with the requirements of this section, shall be deemed to be in compliance with the notification requirements of this section if the business or public entity notifies subject customers in accordance with its policies in the event of a breach of security of the system.

f. In addition to any other disclosure or notification required under this section, in the event that a business or public entity discovers circumstances requiring notification pursuant to this section of more than 1,000 persons at one time, the business or public entity shall also notify, without unreasonable delay, all consumer reporting agencies that compile or maintain files on consumers on a nationwide basis, as defined by subsection (p) of section 603 of the federal "Fair Credit Reporting Act" (15 U.S.C. s.1681a), of the timing, distribution and content of the notices.

13. (New section) a. No person, including any public or private entity, shall:

(1) Publicly post or publicly display an individual's Social Security number, or any four or more consecutive numbers taken from the individual's Social Security number;

(2) Print an individual's Social Security number on any materials that are mailed to the individual, unless State or federal law requires the Social Security number to be on the document to be mailed;

(3) Print an individual's Social Security number on any card required for the individual to access products or services provided by the entity;

(4) Intentionally communicate or otherwise make available to the general public an individual's Social Security number;

(5) Require an individual to transmit his Social Security number over the Internet, unless the connection is secure or the Social Security number is encrypted; or

(6) Require an individual to use his Social Security number to access an Internet website, unless a password or unique personal identification number or other authentication device is also required to access the Internet website.

b. Nothing in this section shall prevent a public or private entity from using a Social Security number for internal verification and administrative purposes, so long as the use does not require the release of the Social Security number to persons not designated by the entity to perform associated functions allowed or authorized by law.

c. Nothing in this section shall prevent the collection, use or release of a Social Security number, as required by State or federal law.

d. Notwithstanding this section, Social Security numbers may be included in applications and forms sent by mail, including documents sent as part of an application or enrollment process, or to establish, amend or terminate an account, contract or policy, or to confirm the accuracy of the Social Security number. A Social Security number that is permitted to be mailed under this subsection may not be printed, in whole or in part, on a postcard or other mailer not requiring an envelope, or visible on the envelope or without the envelope having been open.

e. Nothing in this section shall apply to documents that are recorded or required to be open to the public pursuant to Title 47 of the Revised Statutes. This section shall not apply to records that are required by statute, case law, or New Jersey Court Rules, to be

made available to the public by entities provided for in Article VI of the New Jersey Constitution.

f. Nothing in this section shall apply to the interactive computer service provider's transmissions or routing or intermediate temporary storage or caching of an image, information or data that is otherwise subject to this section.

14. (New section) The Director of the Division of Consumer Affairs in the Department of Law and Public Safety, in consultation with the Commissioner of Banking and Insurance, shall promulgate regulations pursuant to the "Administrative Procedure Act," P.L.1968, c.410 (C.52:14B-1 et seq.), necessary to effectuate sections 4 through 15 of this amendatory and supplementary act.

15. (New section) It shall be an unlawful practice and a violation of P.L.1960, c.39 (C.56:8-1 et seq.) to willfully, knowingly or recklessly violate sections 10 through 13 of this amendatory and supplementary act.

16. This act shall take effect on [1][the 180th day after] January 1 next following[1] enactment, except that section 3 of this act shall take effect immediately.

Senate Bill 2665

Allows victims of identity theft to obtain an official incident record from their local law enforcement agency if the victim has learned or reasonably suspects that he has been a victim of identity theft. The victim may contact his local law enforcement agency to make a complaint and to obtain a copy of the police report. Establishes a procedure whereby a victim of identity theft could obtain a factual determination of innocence and access a statewide identity theft registry. After an order has been issued, the court may order that the name and personal identifying information of the victim contained in court records, files, and indexes be deleted, sealed, or labeled to show that the data is impersonated and does not reflect the defendant's identity. Requires the Administrative Office of the Courts (AOC) to establish and maintain a database of persons who have been victims of identity theft and have received determinations of factual innocence. Access to the database would be limited to criminal justice agencies, victims of identity theft, and any other persons and agencies authorized by the victims. The AOC would also be required to establish a toll-free number to provide access information to victims of identity theft. Amends and supplements the New Jersey Fair Credit Reporting Act, to require that a consumer reporting agency place a security freeze on a consumer credit report within five business days of receiving a request to do so either in writing by certified mail or by a telephone request with certain accompanying personal identifying information, or within three business days of receiving a secure electronic mail request, and prohibits the release of information from the report while the freeze is in place, except as provided by the bill. Provides that the consumer reporting agency shall provide notice to a consumer of the availability and mechanics of the security freeze in a notice, the form of which is provided in the bill, at any time a consumer is required to receive a summary of rights under Section 609 of the federal Fair Credit Reporting Act. It also requires a consumer reporting agency to provide a consumer with an identification number to be used for temporarily lifting a freeze upon a consumer credit report or authorizing the subsequent release of information from a consumer credit report that is subject to a security freeze. Further, the bill stipulates that a security freeze shall remain in place until either the consumer requests to have the security freeze removed or upon discovery by the consumer reporting agency that the consumer's credit report was frozen due to a material misrepresentation by the consumer. Also, if a third party requests access to a consumer credit report on which a security freeze is in effect, and this request is in connection with an application for credit or any other benefit, and the consumer does not allow the report to be accessed, the third party may treat the application as incomplete. A consumer reporting agency that negligently or willfully violates the security freeze sections of the bill shall notify the consumer of the misconduct within five business days and may be subject to civil and injunctive penalties. Any data collector that owns or uses personal information concerning a New Jersey resident shall notify the resident that there has been a security breach related to the data following discovery or notification of the breach. The disclosure notifications shall be made in the most expedient time possible and without unreasonable delay, consistent with the legitimate needs of law enforcement. The disclosure may be delayed, however, if a law enforcement agency determines that notification will impede a criminal investigation. Any data collector that maintains computerized data that includes personal information the data collector does not own shall notify the owner or licensee of the information of any breach of the security of the system immediately following discovery. Any individual injured by a violation of the security breach section of the bill may institute a civil action to recover damages or injunctive relief. Requires any business that conducts business in New Jersey and any business that maintains or otherwise possesses personal information of New Jersey residents must take all reasonable measures to protect against unauthorized access to or use of that information in connection with or after its disposal. Further, the procedures used in the destruction and disposal of the personal records must be comprehensively described and classified as official policy in the writings of the business entity. A violation of the destruction of records provisions of the bill shall be punishable by a civil penalty not to exceed $3,000 for each violation, injunctive relief, and actual damages, costs, and reasonable attorneys' fees. Prohibits any person, including a public or private entity from: (1) intentionally communicating or otherwise making available to the public an individual's Social Security number; (2) printing an individual's Social Security number on any card required for the individual to access products or services provided by the person; (3) requiring an individual to transmit his or her Social Security number over the Internet, unless the connection is secure or the Social Security number is encrypted; (4) requiring an individual to use his or her Social Security number to access an Internet website, unless a password or unique personal identification number or other authentication device is also required to access the Internet website; (5) printing an individual's Social Security number on any materials that are mailed to the individual, unless state or federal law requires the Social Security number to be on the document to be mailed; (6) selling, leasing, loaning, trading, renting, or otherwise disclosing an individual's Social Security number to a third party for any purpose without written consent to the disclosure from the individual; or (7) refusing to do business with an individual because the individual will not consent to the receipt by that person of the Social

Security number of that individual, unless that person is expressly required under state or federal law, in connection with doing business with an individual, to submit to the state or federal government, as applicable, that individual's Social Security number. Unauthorized use of a Social Security number is punishable by a $3,000 fine for a negligent violation, and a $5,000 fine or up to fifteen days imprisonment, or both, for knowingly violating this section. An aggrieved individual may recover actual damages or $5,000, whichever is greater, plus reasonable attorneys' fees and court costs.

Senate Bill 1636

This bill prohibits public or independent institutions of higher education in the state of New Jersey from displaying any student's Social Security number to identify that student for posting or public listing of grades, on class rosters or other lists provided to teachers, on student identification cards, in student directories or similar listings, unless otherwise required in accordance with applicable state or federal law.

Assembly Bill 2047

This bill prohibits any person, including any public or private entity, from printing or displaying in any manner an individual's Social Security number on any document intended for public recording with any county recording authority. The bill also provides that, in the case of certain documents, the county recording authority is authorized to delete, strike, obliterate, or otherwise expunge a Social Security number that appears on the document without invalidating it. As specified in the bill, the fact that such a document is recorded without deleting, striking, obliterating, or otherwise expunging that Social Security number shall not render the document invalid, void, voidable, or in any way defective. Court documents, tax documents, documents that constitute non-consensual liens against an individual, documents required to contain a Social Security number by law, and documents filed with the County Surrogate are exempt and county recording authorities, therefore, may not make any changes on them.

Assembly Bill 4413

This bill prohibits a retail sales establishment from retaining or storing the full magnetic-stripe data, including Visa Card Verification Value 2 or MasterCard Card Validation Code 2, obtained from a credit card, debit card, or access device on any system components after a response to the retail sales establishment's authorization request has been received. However, notwithstanding the above, a retail sales establishment may retain the account number, expiration date, and name contained on the credit card.

The bill also provides that a business or public entity that is required to provide notice of a breach of security of computerized records to a customer pursuant to subsection a. or b. of section 12 of P.L.2005, c.226 (C.56:8-163) will be liable to a financial institution for the costs incurred by that financial institution in protecting the personal information of a customer or providing financial services to that customer as a result of a potential or actual breach of security of the computerized records of the business or public entity, including, but not limited to:

- the cancellation or re-issuance by any financial institution of any credit card, debit card, or access device;
- the closure of any deposit, transaction, share draft, or other account and any action to stop payments or block transactions with respect to a customer's account;
- the opening or re-opening of any deposit, transaction, share draft, or other account for any customer of the financial institution; and
- any refund or credit made to any customer of the financial institution as a result of a breach of security.

The bill also adds a definition of "financial institution" to the "Identity Theft Prevention Act." It defines a financial institution as a bank, savings bank, savings and loan association, mutual savings bank, or credit union organized, chartered, or holding a license or authorization certificate under the law of this State, any other state, the United

States, or of any other country, or the parent or the subsidiary of a financial institution. The term also includes any person who issues an access device and agrees with a consumer to provide electronic fund transfer services.

Chapter 31: New Mexico

New Mexico does not have a bill specific to disclosure. The state does, however, have a bill placing limitations on the number of digits of a Social Security number that may be printed on a business receipt.

Senate Bill 4531

This bill prohibits businesses printing charge card, credit card, or debit card slips for the transaction of business from printing more than five digits of such an account number or expiration date on a sales receipt. It also prohibits a person from selling a cash register or other machine or device that electronically prints receipts of charge card, credit card, or debit card transactions that cannot be programmed or operated to produce with five or fewer of the respective account numbers and no expiration date printed on the receipt either.

House Bill 612

This bill relates to financial privacy; requires consent for sharing certain financial information; provides penalties. The penalties can be as high as $2,500 per individual but not to exceed $500,000 for any single incident. While there is no possibility of incarceration associated with the bill, the financial penalties are high.

House Bill 279

While not a data breach disclosure law, H.B. 279 does place some restrictions on the use of non-public consumer information. This bill relates to public utilities and prohibits the disclosure of consumer information. The bill also states that a public utility or its employees or agents shall not sell or disclose consumers' non-public personal information without the customers' permission or unless it is in accordance with standardized credit reporting practices or other reporting requirements imposed on the public utility.

PROHIBITING THE DISCLOSURE OF CONSUMER INFORMATION. BE IT ENACTED BY THE LEGISLATURE OF THE STATE OF NEW MEXICO:

Section 1. A new section of Chapter 62, Article 8 NMSA 1978 is enacted to read:

"CONSUMER INFORMATION DISCLOSURE PROHIBITED.--

A. A public utility, as defined pursuant to Section 62-3-3 NMSA 1978, or its employees or agents shall not sell or disclose consumers' nonpublic personal information without the customer's permission or unless it is in accordance with standardized credit reporting practices, pursuant to the provisions of Chapter 56, Article 3 NMSA 1978 or the federal Fair Credit Reporting Act or other reporting requirements imposed on the public utility.

B. Exempted from the provisions of this section are:

(1) the public regulation commission pursuant to the Public Utility Act and the Public Regulation Commission Act and rules adopted pursuant to those acts; or

(2) an action by a government agency or an officer, employee or agent of an agency acting on behalf of the agency to obtain telephone records in connection with the performance of the official duties of the agency."

Section 2. EFFECTIVE DATE.--The effective date of the provisions of this act is July 1, 2007.

Chapter 32: New York

New York Assembly Bill 4254 requires that a state agency or business that owns or licenses a computerized database that includes non-public personal information shall disclose any breach of security of such system to any resident of the state whose unencrypted personal information may have been acquired by an unauthorized person. Also provides enforcement provisions.

Information Security Breach and Notification Act–Assembly Bill 4254

NEW YORK 228TH ANNUAL LEGISLATIVE SESSION
ASSEMBLY BILL 4254
STATE OF NEW YORK
4254--A
CAL. NO. 196
2005-2006 REGULAR SESSIONS
IN ASSEMBLY
FEBRUARY 9, 2005

SYNOPSIS: AN ACT to amend the state technology law and the general business law, in relation to enacting the "information security breach and notification act"

Section 1. Short title. This act shall be known and may be cited as the "information security breach and notification act".

Section 2. Legislative Intent. The legislature finds that identity theft and security breaches have affected thousands statewide and millions of people nationwide. The legislature also finds that affected persons are hindered by a lack of information regarding breaches, and that the impact of exposing information that should be held private can be far reaching. In addition, the Legislature finds that state residents deserve a right to know when they have been exposed to identity theft. The legislature further finds that affected state residents deserve an advocate who can speak and take

action on their behalf because recovering from identity theft can, and sometimes does, take many years. Therefore, the legislature enacts the information security breach and notification act which will guarantee state residents the right to know what information was exposed during a breach, so that they can take the necessary steps to both prevent and repair any damage they may incur because of a public or private sector entity's failure to make proper notification.

Section 3. The state technology law is amended by adding a new section 208 to read as follows:

SECTION 208. NOTIFICATION; PERSON WITHOUT VALID AUTHORIZATION HAS ACQUIRED PRIVATE INFORMATION. 1. AS USED IN THIS SECTION, THE FOLLOWING TERMS SHALL HAVE THE FOLLOWING MEANINGS: <A] [A> (A) "PRIVATE INFORMATION" SHALL MEAN PERSONAL INFORMATION IN COMBINATION WITH ANY ONE OR MORE OF THE FOLLOWING DATA ELEMENTS, WHEN EITHER THE PERSONAL INFORMATION OR THE DATA ELEMENT IS NOT ENCRYPTED OR ENCRYPTED WITH AN ENCRYPTION KEY THAT HAS ALSO BEEN ACQUIRED:

(1) SOCIAL SECURITY NUMBER;

(2) DRIVER'S LICENSE NUMBER OR NON-DRIVER IDENTIFICATION CARD NUMBER; OR

(3) ACCOUNT NUMBER, CREDIT OR DEBIT CARD NUMBER, IN COMBINATION WITH ANY REQUIRED SECURITY CODE, ACCESS CODE, OR PASSWORD WHICH WOULD PERMIT ACCESS TO AN INDIVIDUAL'S FINANCIAL ACCOUNT. "PRIVATE INFORMATION" DOES NOT INCLUDE PUBLICLY AVAILABLE INFORMATION THAT IS LAWFULLY MADE AVAILABLE TO THE GENERAL

PUBLIC FROM FEDERAL, STATE, OR LOCAL GOVERNMENT RECORDS.

(B) "BREACH OF THE SECURITY OF THE SYSTEM" SHALL MEAN UNAUTHORIZED ACQUISITION OR ACQUISITION WITHOUT VALID AUTHORIZATION OF COMPUTERIZED DATA WHICH COMPROMISES THE SECURITY, CONFIDENTIALITY, OR INTEGRITY OF PERSONAL INFORMATION MAINTAINED BY A STATE ENTITY. GOOD FAITH ACQUISITION OF PERSONAL INFORMATION BY AN EMPLOYEE OR AGENT OF A STATE ENTITY FOR THE PURPOSES OF THE AGENCY IS NOT A BREACH OF THE SECURITY OF THE SYSTEM, PROVIDED THAT THE PRIVATE INFORMATION IS NOT USED OR SUBJECT TO UNAUTHORIZED DISCLOSURE.

(C) "STATE ENTITY" SHALL MEAN ANY STATE BOARD, BUREAU, DIVISION, COMMITTEE, COMMISSION, COUNCIL, DEPARTMENT, PUBLIC AUTHORITY, PUBLIC BENEFIT CORPORATION, OFFICE OR OTHER GOVERNMENTAL ENTITY PERFORMING A GOVERNMENTAL OR PROPRIETARY FUNCTION FOR THE STATE OF NEW YORK, EXCEPT:

(1) THE JUDICIARY; AND

(2) ALL CITIES, COUNTIES, MUNICIPALITIES, VILLAGES, TOWNS, AND OTHER LOCAL AGENCIES. (D) "CONSUMER REPORTING AGENCY" SHALL MEAN ANY PERSON WHICH, FOR MONETARY FEES, DUES, OR ON A COOPERATIVE NONPROFIT BASIS, REGULARLY ENGAGES IN WHOLE OR IN PART IN THE PRACTICE OF ASSEMBLING OR EVALUATING CONSUMER CREDIT INFORMATION OR OTHER INFORMATION ON CONSUMERS FOR THE PURPOSE OF FURNISHING CONSUMER REPORTS TO THIRD PARTIES, AND WHICH USES ANY MEANS OR FACILITY OF INTERSTATE

COMMERCE FOR THE PURPOSE OF PREPARING OR FURNISHING CONSUMER REPORTS. A LIST OF CONSUMER REPORTING AGENCIES SHALL BE COMPILED BY THE STATE ATTORNEY GENERAL AND FURNISHED UPON REQUEST TO STATE ENTITIES REQUIRED TO MAKE A NOTIFICATION UNDER SUBDIVISION TWO OF THIS SECTION.

2. ANY STATE ENTITY THAT OWNS OR LICENSES COMPUTERIZED DATA THAT INCLUDES PRIVATE INFORMATION SHALL DISCLOSE ANY BREACH OF THE SECURITY OF THE SYSTEM FOLLOWING DISCOVERY OR NOTIFICATION OF THE BREACH IN THE SECURITY OF THE SYSTEM TO ANY RESIDENT OF NEW YORK STATE WHOSE PRIVATE INFORMATION WAS, OR IS REASONABLY BELIEVED TO HAVE BEEN, ACQUIRED BY A PERSON WITHOUT VALID AUTHORIZATION. THE DISCLOSURE SHALL BE MADE IN THE MOST EXPEDIENT TIME POSSIBLE AND WITHOUT UNREASONABLE DELAY, CONSISTENT WITH THE LEGITIMATE NEEDS OF LAW ENFORCEMENT, AS PROVIDED IN SUBDIVISION FOUR OF THIS SECTION, OR ANY MEASURES NECESSARY TO DETERMINE THE SCOPE OF THE BREACH AND RESTORE THE REASONABLE INTEGRITY OF THE DATA SYSTEM.

3. ANY STATE ENTITY THAT MAINTAINS COMPUTERIZED DATA THAT INCLUDES PRIVATE INFORMATION WHICH SUCH AGENCY DOES NOT OWN SHALL NOTIFY THE OWNER OR LICENSEE OF THE INFORMATION OF ANY BREACH OF THE SECURITY OF THE SYSTEM IMMEDIATELY FOLLOWING DISCOVERY, IF THE PRIVATE INFORMATION WAS, OR IS REASONABLY BELIEVED TO HAVE BEEN, ACQUIRED BY A PERSON WITHOUT VALID AUTHORIZATION.

4. THE NOTIFICATION REQUIRED BY THIS SECTION MAY BE DELAYED IF A LAW ENFORCEMENT AGENCY

DETERMINES THAT SUCH NOTIFICATION IMPEDES A CRIMINAL INVESTIGATION. THE NOTIFICATION REQUIRED BY THIS SECTION SHALL BE MADE AFTER SUCH LAW ENFORCEMENT AGENCY DETERMINES THAT SUCH NOTIFICATION DOES NOT COMPROMISE SUCH INVESTIGATION.

5. THE NOTICE REQUIRED BY THIS SECTION SHALL BE DIRECTLY PROVIDED TO THE AFFECTED PERSONS BY ONE OF THE FOLLOWING METHODS:

(A) WRITTEN NOTICE;

(B) ELECTRONIC NOTICE, PROVIDED THAT THE PERSON TO WHOM NOTICE IS REQUIRED HAS EXPRESSLY CONSENTED TO RECEIVING SAID NOTICE IN ELECTRONIC FORM AND A LOG OF EACH SUCH NOTIFICATION IS KEPT BY THE STATE ENTITY WHO NOTIFIES AFFECTED PERSONS IN SUCH FORM; PROVIDED FURTHER, HOWEVER, THAT IN NO CASE SHALL ANY PERSON OR BUSINESS REQUIRE A PERSON TO CONSENT TO ACCEPTING SAID NOTICE IN SAID FORM AS A CONDITION OF ESTABLISHING ANY BUSINESS RELATIONSHIP OR ENGAGING IN ANY TRANSACTION; (C) SUBSTITUTE NOTICE, IF A STATE ENTITY DEMONSTRATES TO THE STATE ATTORNEY GENERAL THAT THE COST OF PROVIDING NOTICE WOULD EXCEED TWO HUNDRED FIFTY THOUSAND DOLLARS, OR THAT THE AFFECTED CLASS OF SUBJECT PERSONS TO BE NOTIFIED EXCEEDS FIVE HUNDRED THOUSAND, OR SUCH AGENCY DOES NOT HAVE SUFFICIENT CONTACT INFORMATION. SUBSTITUTE NOTICE SHALL CONSIST OF ALL OF THE FOLLOWING:

(1) E-MAIL NOTICE WHEN SUCH STATE ENTITY HAS AN E-MAIL ADDRESS FOR THE SUBJECT PERSONS;

(2) CONSPICUOUS POSTING OF THE NOTICE ON SUCH STATE ENTITY'S WEBSITE PAGE, IF SUCH AGENCY MAINTAINS ONE; AND

(3) NOTIFICATION TO MAJOR STATEWIDE MEDIA.

REGARDLESS OF THE METHOD BY WHICH NOTICE IS PROVIDED, SUCH NOTICE SHALL INCLUDE CONTACT INFORMATION FOR THE PERSON OR BUSINESS MAKING THE NOTIFICATION AND A DESCRIPTION OF THE CATEGORIES OF INFORMATION THAT WERE, OR ARE REASONABLY BELIEVED TO HAVE BEEN, ACQUIRED BY A PERSON WITHOUT VALID AUTHORIZATION, INCLUDING SPECIFICATION OF WHICH OF THE ELEMENTS OF PERSONAL INFORMATION AND PRIVATE INFORMATION WERE, OR ARE REASONABLY BELIEVED TO HAVE BEEN, SO ACQUIRED.

(A) IN THE EVENT THAT ANY NEW YORK RESIDENTS ARE TO BE NOTIFIED AT ONE TIME, THE PERSON OR BUSINESS SHALL NOTIFY THE STATE ATTORNEY GENERAL, THE CONSUMER PROTECTION BOARD, AND THE STATE OFFICE OF CYBER SECURITY AND CRITICAL INFRASTRUCTURE COORDINATION AS TO THE TIMING, CONTENT AND DISTRIBUTION OF THE NOTICES AND APPROXIMATE NUMBER OF AFFECTED PERSONS. SUCH NOTICE SHALL BE MADE WITHOUT DELAYING NOTICE TO AFFECTED NEW YORK RESIDENTS. IN THE EVENT THAT MORE THAN FIVE THOUSAND NEW YORK RESIDENTS ARE TO BE NOTIFIED AT ONE TIME, THE PERSON OR BUSINESS SHALL ALSO NOTIFY CONSUMER REPORTING AGENCIES AS TO THE TIMING, CONTENT AND DISTRIBUTION OF THE NOTICES AND APPROXIMATE NUMBER OF AFFECTED PERSONS. SUCH NOTICE SHALL BE MADE WITHOUT DELAYING NOTICE TO AFFECTED NEW YORK RESIDENTS.

ANY ENTITY LISTED IN SUBPARAGRAPH TWO OF PARAGRAPH (C) OF SUBDIVISION ONE OF THIS SECTION SHALL ADOPT A NOTIFICATION POLICY NO MORE THAN ONE HUNDRED TWENTY DAYS AFTER THE EFFECTIVE DATE OF THIS SECTION. SUCH ENTITY MAY DEVELOP A NOTIFICATION POLICY WHICH IS CONSISTENT WITH THIS SECTION OR ALTERNATIVELY SHALL ADOPT A LOCAL LAW WHICH IS CONSISTENT WITH THIS SECTION.

Section 4. The general business law is amended by adding a new article 39F to read as follows:

ARTICLE 39-F NOTIFICATION OF UNAUTHORIZED ACQUISITION OF PRIVATE INFORMATION SECTION 899-AA. NOTIFICATION; PERSON WITHOUT VALID AUTHORIZATION HAS ACQUIRED PRIVATE INFORMATION. SECTION 899-AA. NOTIFICATION; PERSON WITHOUT VALID AUTHORIZATION HAS ACQUIRED PRIVATE INFORMATION. 1. AS USED IN THIS SECTION, THE FOLLOWING TERMS SHALL HAVE THE FOLLOWING MEANINGS:

(A) "PERSONAL INFORMATION" SHALL MEAN ANY INFORMATION CONCERNING A NATURAL PERSON WHICH, BECAUSE OF NAME, NUMBER, PERSONAL MARK, OR OTHER IDENTIFIER, CAN BE USED TO IDENTIFY SUCH NATURAL PERSON;

(B) "PRIVATE INFORMATION" SHALL MEAN PERSONAL INFORMATION CONSISTING OF ANY INFORMATION IN COMBINATION WITH ANY ONE OR MORE OF THE FOLLOWING DATA ELEMENTS, WHEN EITHER THE PERSONAL INFORMATION OR THE DATA ELEMENT IS NOT ENCRYPTED, OR ENCRYPTED WITH AN ENCRYPTION KEY THAT HAS ALSO BEEN ACQUIRED:

(1) SOCIAL SECURITY NUMBER;

(2) DRIVER'S LICENSE NUMBER OR NON-DRIVER IDENTIFICATION CARD NUMBER; OR

(3) ACCOUNT NUMBER, CREDIT OR DEBIT CARD NUMBER, IN COMBINATION WITH ANY REQUIRED SECURITY CODE, ACCESS CODE, OR PASSWORD THAT WOULD PERMIT ACCESS TO AN INDIVIDUAL'S FINANCIAL ACCOUNT; "PRIVATE INFORMATION" DOES NOT INCLUDE PUBLICLY AVAILABLE INFORMATION WHICH IS LAWFULLY MADE AVAILABLE TO THE GENERAL PUBLIC FROM FEDERAL, STATE, OR LOCAL GOVERNMENT RECORDS.

(C) "BREACH OF THE SECURITY OF THE SYSTEM" SHALL MEAN UNAUTHORIZED ACQUISITION OR ACQUISITION WITHOUT VALID AUTHORIZATION OF COMPUTERIZED DATA THAT COMPROMISES THE SECURITY, CONFIDENTIALITY, OR INTEGRITY OF PERSONAL INFORMATION MAINTAINED BY A BUSINESS. GOOD FAITH ACQUISITION OF PERSONAL INFORMATION BY AN EMPLOYEE OR AGENT OF THE BUSINESS FOR THE PURPOSES OF THE BUSINESS IS NOT A BREACH OF THE SECURITY OF THE SYSTEM, PROVIDED THAT THE PRIVATE INFORMATION IS NOT USED OR SUBJECT TO UNAUTHORIZED DISCLOSURE.

(D) "CONSUMER REPORTING AGENCY" SHALL MEAN ANY PERSON WHICH, FOR MONETARY FEES, DUES, OR ON A COOPERATIVE NONPROFIT BASIS, REGULARLY ENGAGES IN WHOLE OR IN PART IN THE PRACTICE OF ASSEMBLING OR EVALUATING CONSUMER CREDIT INFORMATION OR OTHER INFORMATION ON CONSUMERS FOR THE PURPOSE OF FURNISHING CONSUMER REPORTS TO THIRD PARTIES, AND WHICH USES ANY MEANS OR FACILITY OF INTERSTATE COMMERCE FOR THE PURPOSE OF PREPARING OR FURNISHING CONSUMER REPORTS. A LIST OF

CONSUMER REPORTING AGENCIES SHALL BE COMPILED BY THE STATE ATTORNEY GENERAL AND FURNISHED UPON REQUEST TO ANY PERSON OR BUSINESS REQUIRED TO MAKE A NOTIFICATION UNDER SUBDIVISION TWO OF THIS SECTION. 2. ANY PERSON OR BUSINESS WHICH CONDUCTS BUSINESS IN NEW YORK STATE, AND WHICH OWNS OR LICENSES COMPUTERIZED DATA WHICH INCLUDES PRIVATE INFORMATION SHALL DISCLOSE ANY BREACH OF THE SECURITY OF THE SYSTEM FOLLOWING DISCOVERY OR NOTIFICATION OF THE BREACH IN THE SECURITY OF THE SYSTEM TO ANY RESIDENT OF NEW YORK STATE WHOSE PRIVATE INFORMATION WAS, OR IS REASONABLY BELIEVED TO HAVE BEEN, ACQUIRED BY A PERSON WITHOUT VALID AUTHORIZATION. THE DISCLOSURE SHALL BE MADE IN THE MOST EXPEDIENT TIME POSSIBLE AND WITHOUT UNREASONABLE DELAY, CONSISTENT WITH THE LEGITIMATE NEEDS OF LAW ENFORCEMENT, AS PROVIDED IN SUBDIVISION FOUR OF THIS SECTION, OR ANY MEASURES NECESSARY TO DETERMINE THE SCOPE OF THE BREACH AND RESTORE THE REASONABLE INTEGRITY OF THE SYSTEM. 3. ANY PERSON OR BUSINESS WHICH MAINTAINS COMPUTERIZED DATA WHICH INCLUDES PRIVATE INFORMATION WHICH SUCH PERSON OR BUSINESS DOES NOT OWN SHALL NOTIFY THE OWNER OR LICENSEE OF THE INFORMATION OF ANY BREACH OF THE SECURITY OF THE SYSTEM IMMEDIATELY FOLLOWING DISCOVERY, IF THE PRIVATE INFORMATION WAS, OR IS REASONABLY BELIEVED TO HAVE BEEN, ACQUIRED BY A PERSON WITHOUT VALID AUTHORIZATION. THE NOTIFICATION REQUIRED BY THIS SECTION MAY BE DELAYED IF A LAW ENFORCEMENT AGENCY DETERMINES THAT SUCH NOTIFICATION IMPEDES A CRIMINAL INVESTIGATION. THE NOTIFICATION REQUIRED BY THIS SECTION SHALL BE MADE AFTER SUCH LAW ENFORCEMENT AGENCY

DETERMINES THAT SUCH NOTIFICATION DOES NOT COMPROMISE SUCH INVESTIGATION. THE NOTICE REQUIRED BY THIS SECTION SHALL BE DIRECTLY PROVIDED TO THE AFFECTED PERSONS BY ONE OF THE FOLLOWING METHODS:

(A) WRITTEN NOTICE;

(B) ELECTRONIC NOTICE, PROVIDED THAT THE PERSON TO WHOM NOTICE IS REQUIRED HAS EXPRESSLY CONSENTED TO RECEIVING SAID NOTICE IN ELECTRONIC FORM AND A LOG OF EACH SUCH NOTIFICATION IS KEPT BY THE PERSON OR BUSINESS WHO NOTIFIES AFFECTED PERSONS IN SUCH FORM; PROVIDED FURTHER, HOWEVER, THAT IN NO CASE SHALL ANY PERSON OR BUSINESS REQUIRE A PERSON TO CONSENT TO ACCEPTING SAID NOTICE IN SAID FORM AS A CONDITION OF ESTABLISHING ANY BUSINESS RELATIONSHIP OR ENGAGING IN ANY TRANSACTION.

(C) TELEPHONE NOTIFICATION PROVIDED THAT A LOG OF EACH SUCH NOTIFICATION IS KEPT BY THE PERSON OR BUSINESS WHO NOTIFIES AFFECTED PERSONS; OR

(D) SUBSTITUTE NOTICE, IF A BUSINESS DEMONSTRATES TO THE STATE ATTORNEY GENERAL THAT THE COST OF PROVIDING NOTICE WOULD EXCEED TWO HUNDRED FIFTY THOUSAND DOLLARS, OR THAT THE AFFECTED CLASS OF SUBJECT PERSONS TO BE NOTIFIED EXCEEDS FIVE HUNDRED THOUSAND, OR SUCH BUSINESS DOES NOT HAVE SUFFICIENT CONTACT INFORMATION. SUBSTITUTE NOTICE SHALL CONSIST OF ALL OF THE FOLLOWING:

(1) E-MAIL NOTICE WHEN SUCH BUSINESS HAS AN E-MAIL ADDRESS FOR THE SUBJECT PERSONS;

(2) CONSPICUOUS POSTING OF THE NOTICE ON SUCH BUSINESS'S WEBSITE PAGE, IF SUCH BUSINESS MAINTAINS ONE; AND

(3) NOTIFICATION TO MAJOR STATEWIDE MEDIA.

(A) WHENEVER THE ATTORNEY GENERAL SHALL BELIEVE FROM EVIDENCE SATISFACTORY TO HIM THAT THERE IS A VIOLATION OF THIS ARTICLE HE MAY BRING AN ACTION IN THE NAME AND ON BEHALF OF THE PEOPLE OF THE STATE OF NEW YORK, IN A COURT OF JUSTICE HAVING JURISDICTION TO ISSUE AN INJUNCTION, TO ENJOIN AND RESTRAIN THE CONTINUATION OF SUCH VIOLATION. IN SUCH ACTION, PRELIMINARY RELIEF MAY BE GRANTED UNDER ARTICLE SIXTY-THREE OF THE CIVIL PRACTICE LAW AND RULES. IN SUCH ACTION THE COURT MAY AWARD DAMAGES FOR ACTUAL COSTS OR LOSSES INCURRED BY A PERSON ENTITLED TO NOTICE PURSUANT TO THIS ARTICLE, INCLUDING CONSEQUENTIAL FINANCIAL LOSSES. WHENEVER THE COURT SHALL DETERMINE IN SUCH ACTION THAT A PERSON OR BUSINESS VIOLATED THIS ARTICLE KNOWINGLY OR RECKLESSLY, THE COURT MAY IMPOSE A CIVIL PENALTY OF THE GREATER OF FIVE THOUSAND DOLLARS OR UP TO TEN DOLLARS PER INSTANCE OF FAILED NOTIFICATION, PROVIDED THAT THE LATTER AMOUNT SHALL NOT EXCEED ONE HUNDRED FIFTY THOUSAND DOLLARS.

(B) THE REMEDIES PROVIDED BY THIS SECTION SHALL BE IN ADDITION TO ANY OTHER LAWFUL REMEDY AVAILABLE.

(C) NO ACTION MAY BE BROUGHT UNDER THE PROVISIONS OF THIS SECTION UNLESS SUCH ACTION IS COMMENCED WITHIN TWO YEARS IMMEDIATELY AFTER THE DATE OF THE ACT COMPLAINED OF OR THE DATE

OF DISCOVERY OF SUCH ACT. REGARDLESS OF THE METHOD BY WHICH NOTICE IS PROVIDED, SUCH NOTICE SHALL INCLUDE CONTACT INFORMATION FOR THE PERSON OR BUSINESS MAKING THE NOTIFICATION AND A DESCRIPTION OF THE CATEGORIES OF INFORMATION THAT WERE, OR ARE REASONABLY BELIEVED TO HAVE BEEN, ACQUIRED BY A PERSON WITHOUT VALID AUTHORIZATION, INCLUDING SPECIFICATION OF WHICH OF THE ELEMENTS OF PERSONAL INFORMATION AND PRIVATE INFORMATION WERE, OR ARE REASONABLY BELIEVED TO HAVE BEEN, SO ACQUIRED. (A) IN THE EVENT THAT ANY NEW YORK RESIDENTS ARE TO BE NOTIFIED AT ONE TIME, THE PERSON OR BUSINESS SHALL NOTIFY THE STATE ATTORNEY GENERAL, THE CONSUMER PROTECTION BOARD, AND THE STATE OFFICE OF CYBER SECURITY AND CRITICAL INFRASTRUCTURE COORDINATION AS TO THE TIMING, CONTENT AND DISTRIBUTION OF THE NOTICES AND APPROXIMATE NUMBER OF AFFECTED PERSONS. SUCH NOTICE SHALL BE MADE WITHOUT DELAYING NOTICE TO AFFECTED NEW YORK RESIDENTS. (B) IN THE EVENT THAT MORE THAN FIVE THOUSAND NEW YORK RESIDENTS ARE TO BE NOTIFIED AT ONE TIME, THE PERSON OR BUSINESS SHALL ALSO NOTIFY CONSUMER REPORTING AGENCIES AS TO THE TIMING, CONTENT AND DISTRIBUTION OF THE NOTICES AND APPROXIMATE NUMBER OF AFFECTED PERSONS. SUCH NOTICE SHALL BE MADE WITHOUT DELAYING NOTICE TO AFFECTED NEW YORK RESIDENTS.

THE PROVISIONS OF THIS SECTION SHALL BE EXCLUSIVE AND SHALL PREEMPT ANY PROVISIONS OF LOCAL LAW, ORDINANCE OR CODE, AND NO LOCALITY SHALL IMPOSE REQUIREMENTS THAT ARE INCONSISTENT WITH OR MORE RESTRICTIVE THAN THOSE SET FORTH IN THIS SECTION.

Assembly Bill 5150

The bill prohibits businesses from printing the expiration date and more than the last five numbers of a credit or debit card on any receipt given to the cardholder. The law applies only to electronically printed receipts. Any new credit and debit card machines placed into service on or after January 1, 2004, must comply with the new law. Credit and debit card machines in use before January 1 must conform with the new law by January 1, 2007. Violations of the new law carry a maximum civil fine of $4,500.

Anti-Phishing Act of 2005–Senate Bill 5370

This bill prohibits the misuse of the Internet to obtain identifying information by misrepresenting oneself as a business, sometimes called phishing. It also authorizes the attorney general, Internet service providers, and those owning a web page or trademark, who are adversely affected by such conduct, to bring an action for injunctive relief and damages.

Disposal of Personal Records Law–Senate Bill 5178

This bill relates to the disposal of records that contain personal information. It requires any business to properly dispose of records containing personal information to prevent unauthorized persons from having access to the personal information of clients and consumers. It states that shredding is an appropriate method, and actions consistent with commonly accepted industry practices to ensure that no unauthorized person will have access to the data.

Senate Bill 279

This bill gives consumers the option to prohibit the rental, sale, exchange or other availability of personal information possessed by an issuer of a credit card, charge card or debit card. The bill also requires notice of such option be given to cardholders by credit card, charge card and debit card issuers in existing bill mailings and in credit card and debit card agreements and renewals thereof; limits any effect on credit card registration services.

Senate Bill 5047

This bill prohibits the use of inmate labor to be used to access, collect or process personal information relating to a natural person residing in this state. The bill also provides for a civil penalty of not more than $1,500 for a first violation and not more than $2,500 for a second or subsequent violation. Considering that accessing a person's personal information is considered to be a position of trust, I would not want inmates being given access to personal information.

Assembly Bill 2243

This bill makes provisions for privacy in banking, insurance, and other financial transactions. The bill forbids the disclosure of personal information without the prior consent granted by the customer to the financial institution. The bill also requires written notice of privacy policies and practices be given to customers; requires security and confidentiality safeguards; and it also prohibits the disclosure of account number or access code information.

Senate Bill 4129

This bill requires employers to provide notice of the outsourcing of jobs prior to such outsourcing; prohibits any governmental agency from engaging in the practice of outsourcing jobs. The bill also requires consumers to be made aware and to provide consent if such consumers' non-public personal information is going to be disclosed to non-affiliated third parties by any corporation or other business entity. The bill also requires ratification by the legislature of procurement contracts between the State, through the governor, and any multi-national trade organization or corporation; and defines applicable terms.

Assembly Bill 3295

This bill enacts the Electronic Fund Transfer Privacy Act; and provides privacy protection for consumers engaging in electronic fund transfer transactions by limiting the disclosure of personal information about any consumer involved in such and limiting the circumstances in which government authority may get such information.

Assembly Bill 3189

This bill enacts the Financial Information New York Privacy Act and states that financial institutions are to obtain consent from consumers prior to disclosing non-public personal information.

Chapter 33: North Carolina

North Carolina's House Bill 1048 has a provision in it that allows consumers to place a freeze on their accounts with the credit bureaus. This is a good way to deter identity theft. North Carolina also passed an update of HB 1048, which is HB 1248. The text of both statutes is below.

The identity theft protection act of 2005- Senate Bill 1048

SECTION 1. Chapter 75 of the General Statutes is amended by adding a new Article to read:

"§7560. Title.

This Article shall be known and may be cited as the "Identity Theft Protection Act".

"§7561. Definitions.

The following definitions apply in this Article:

(1) "Business". – A sole proprietorship, partnership, corporation, association, or other group, however organized and whether or not organized to operate at a profit. The term includes a financial institution organized, chartered, or holding a license or authorization certificate under the laws of this State, any other state, the United States, or any other country, or the parent or the subsidiary of any such financial institution. Business shall not include any government or governmental subdivision or agency.

(2) "Consumer". – An individual.

(3) "Consumer reporting agency". – Any person who, for monetary fees, dues, or on a cooperative nonprofit basis, regularly engages in whole or in part in the practice of assembling or evaluating consumer credit information or other information on consumers for the purpose of furnishing consumer reports to third parties.

(4) "Consumer report" or "credit report". – Any written, oral, or other communication of any information by a consumer reporting agency bearing on a consumer's creditworthiness, credit standing, credit capacity, character, general reputation, personal characteristics, or mode of living which is used or expected to be used or collected in whole or in part for the purpose of serving as a factor in establishing the consumer's eligibility for any of the following:

a. Credit to be used primarily for personal, family, or household purposes.

b. Employment purposes.

c. Any other purpose authorized under 15 U.S.C. §1681(b).

(5) "Credit card". – Has the same meaning as in section 103 of the Truth in Lending Act (15 U.S.C. §160, et seq.).

(6) "Debit card". – Any card or device issued by a financial institution to a consumer for use in initiating an electronic fund transfer from the account holding assets of the consumer at such financial institution, for the purpose of transferring money between accounts or obtaining money, property, labor, or services.

(7) "Disposal" includes the following:

a. The discarding or abandonment of records containing personal information.

b. The sale, donation, discarding, or transfer of any medium, including computer equipment or computer media, containing records of personal information, or other non-paper media upon which records of personal information are stored, or other equipment for non-paper storage of information.

(8) "Encryption". – The use of an algorithmic process to transform data into a form in which the data is rendered unreadable or unusable without use of a confidential process or key.

(9) "Person". – Any individual, partnership, corporation, trust, estate, cooperative, association, government, or governmental subdivision or agency, or other entity.

(10) "Personal information". – A person's first name or first initial and last name in combination with identifying information as defined in G.S. 14113.20(b). Personal information does not include publicly available directories containing information an individual has voluntarily consented to have publicly disseminated or listed, including name, address, and telephone number, and does not include information made lawfully available to the general public from federal, state, or local government records.

(11) "Proper identification". – Information generally deemed sufficient to identify a person. If a person is unable to reasonably identify himself or herself with the information described above, a consumer reporting agency may require additional information concerning the consumer's employment and personal or family history in order to verify the consumer's identity.

(12) "Records". – Any material on which written, drawn, spoken, visual, or electromagnetic information is recorded or preserved, regardless of physical form or characteristics.

(13) "Redaction". – The rendering of data so that it is unreadable or is truncated so that no more than the last four digits of the identification number is accessible as part of the data.

(14) "Security breach". – An incident of unauthorized access to and acquisition of unencrypted and unredacted records or data containing personal information where illegal use of the personal information has occurred or is reasonably likely to occur or that creates a material risk of harm to a consumer. Any incident of

unauthorized access to and acquisition of encrypted records or data containing personal information along with the confidential process or key shall constitute a security breach. Good faith acquisition of personal information by an employee or agent of the business for a legitimate purpose is not a security breach, provided that the personal information is not used for a purpose other than a lawful purpose of the business and is not subject to further unauthorized disclosure.

(15) "Security freeze". – Notice placed in a credit report, at the request of the consumer and subject to certain exceptions, that prohibits the consumer reporting agency from releasing all or any part of the consumer's credit report or any information derived from it without the express authorization of the consumer.

"§7562. Social Security number protection.

(a) Except as provided in subsection (b) of this section, a business may not do any of the following:

(1) Intentionally communicate or otherwise make available to the general public an individual's Social Security number.

(2) Intentionally print or imbed an individual's Social Security number on any card required for the individual to access products or services provided by the person or entity.

(3) Require an individual to transmit his or her Social Security number over the Internet, unless the connection is secure or the Social Security number is encrypted.

(4) Require an individual to use his or her Social Security number to access an Internet website, unless a password or unique personal identification number or other authentication device is also required to access the Internet website.

(5) Print an individual's Social Security number on any materials that are mailed to the individual, unless state or federal law requires the Social Security number to be on the document to be mailed.

(6) Sell, lease, loan, trade, rent, or otherwise intentionally disclose an individual's Social Security number to a third party without written consent to the disclosure from the individual, when the party making the disclosure knows or in the exercise of reasonable diligence would have reason to believe that the third party lacks a legitimate purpose for obtaining the individual's Social Security number.

(b) Subsection (a) of this section shall not apply in the following instances:

(1) When a Social Security number is included in an application or in documents related to an enrollment process, or to establish, amend, or terminate an account, contract, or policy; or to confirm the accuracy of the Social Security number for the purpose of obtaining a credit report pursuant to 15 U.S.C. §1681(b)(2). A Social Security number that is permitted to be mailed under this section may not be printed, in whole or in part, on a postcard or other mailer not requiring an envelope, or visible on the envelope or without the envelope having been opened.

(2) To the collection, use, or release of a Social Security number for internal verification or administrative purposes.

(3) To the opening of an account or the provision of or payment for a product or service authorized by an individual.

(4) To the collection, use, or release of a Social Security number to investigate or prevent fraud, conduct background checks, conduct social or scientific research, collect a debt, obtain a credit report from or furnish data to a consumer reporting agency pursuant to the Fair Credit Reporting Act, 15 U.S.C. §1681, et seq., undertake a permissible purpose enumerated under Gramm Leach Bliley, 12

C.F.R. §216.1315, or locate an individual who is missing, a lost relative, or due a benefit, such as a pension, insurance, or unclaimed property benefit.

(5) To a business acting pursuant to a court order, warrant, subpoena, or when otherwise required by law.

(6) To a business providing the Social Security number to a federal, state, or local government entity, including a law enforcement agency, court, or their agents or assigns.

(7) To a Social Security number that has been redacted.

(c) A business covered by this section shall make reasonable efforts to cooperate, through systems testing and other means, to ensure that the requirements of this Article are implemented.

(d) A violation of this section is a violation of G.S. 751.1.

"§7563. Security freeze.

(a) A consumer may place a security freeze on the consumer's credit report by making a request in writing by certified mail to a consumer reporting agency. A security freeze shall prohibit, subject to exceptions in subsection (l) of this section, the consumer reporting agency from releasing the consumer's credit report or any information from it without the express authorization of the consumer. When a security freeze is in place, a consumer reporting agency may not release the consumer's credit report or information to a third party without prior express authorization from the consumer. This subsection does not prevent a consumer reporting agency from advising a third party that a security freeze is in effect with respect to the consumer's credit report.

(b) A consumer reporting agency shall place a security freeze on a consumer's credit report no later than five business days after receiving a written request from the consumer.

(c) The consumer reporting agency shall send a written confirmation of the security freeze to the consumer within 10 business days of placing the freeze and at the same time shall provide the consumer with a unique personal identification number or password, other than the consumer's Social Security number, to be used by the consumer when providing authorization for the release of the consumer's credit report for a specific period of time.

(d) If the consumer wishes to allow the consumer's credit report to be accessed for a specific period of time while a freeze is in place, the consumer shall contact the consumer reporting agency, request that the freeze be temporarily lifted, and provide all of the following:

(1) Proper identification.

(2) The unique personal identification number or password provided by the consumer reporting agency pursuant to subsection (c) of this section.

(3) The proper information regarding the time period for which the report shall be available to users of the credit report.

(e) A consumer reporting agency may develop procedures involving the use of telephone, fax, the Internet, or other electronic media to receive and process a request from a consumer to temporarily lift a freeze on a credit report pursuant to subsection (d) of this section in an expedited manner.

(f) A consumer reporting agency that receives a request from a consumer to temporarily lift a freeze on a credit report pursuant to subsection (d) of this section shall comply with the request no later than three business days after receiving the request.

(g) A consumer reporting agency shall remove or temporarily lift a freeze placed on a consumer's credit report only in the following cases:

(1) Upon the consumer's request, pursuant to subsections (d) or (j) of this section.

(2) If the consumer's credit report was frozen due to a material misrepresentation of fact by the consumer. If a consumer reporting agency intends to remove a freeze upon a consumer's credit report pursuant to this subdivision, the consumer reporting agency shall notify the consumer in writing prior to removing the freeze on the consumer's credit report.

(h) If a third party requests access to a consumer credit report on which a security freeze is in effect and this request is in connection with an application for credit or any other use and the consumer does not allow the consumer's credit report to be accessed for that specific period of time, the third party may treat the application as incomplete.

(i) If a consumer requests a security freeze pursuant to this section, the consumer reporting agency shall disclose to the consumer the process of placing and temporarily lifting a security freeze and the process for allowing access to information from the consumer's credit report for a specific period of time while the security freeze is in place.

(j) A security freeze shall remain in place until the consumer requests that the security freeze be removed. A consumer reporting agency shall remove a security freeze within three business days of receiving a request for removal from the consumer, who provides all of the following:

(1) Proper identification.

(2) The unique personal identification number or password provided by the consumer reporting agency pursuant to subsection (c) of this section.

(k) A consumer reporting agency shall require proper identification of the person making a request to place or remove a security freeze.

(l) The provisions of this section do not apply to the use of a consumer credit report by any of the following:

(1) A person, or the person's subsidiary, affiliate, agent, subcontractor, or assignee with whom the consumer has, or prior to assignment had, an account, contract, or debtor/creditor relationship for the purposes of reviewing the active account or collecting the financial obligation owing for the account, contract, or debt.

(2) A subsidiary, affiliate, agent, assignee, or prospective assignee of a person to whom access has been granted under subsection (d) of this section for purposes of facilitating the extension of credit or other permissible use.

(3) Any person acting pursuant to a court order, warrant, or subpoena.

(4) A state or local agency, or its agents or assigns, which administers a program for establishing and enforcing child support obligations.

(5) A state or local agency, or its agents or assigns, acting to investigate fraud, including Medicaid fraud, or acting to investigate or collect delinquent taxes or assessments, including interest and penalties, unpaid court orders, or to fulfill any of its other statutory responsibilities.

(6) A federal, state, or local governmental entity, including law enforcement agency, court, or their agent or assigns.

(7) A person for the purposes of prescreening as defined by the Fair Credit Reporting Act, 15 U.S.C. §1681, et seq.

(8) Any person for the sole purpose of providing for a credit file monitoring subscription service to which the consumer has subscribed.

(9) A consumer reporting agency for the purpose of providing a consumer with a copy of the consumer's credit report upon the consumer's request.

(10) Any depository financial institution for checking, savings, and investment accounts.

(11) Any property and casualty insurance company for use in setting or adjusting a rate, adjusting a claim, or underwriting for property and casualty insurance purposes.

(m) If a security freeze is in place, a consumer reporting agency shall not change any of the following official information in a credit report without sending a written confirmation of the change to the consumer within 30 days of the change being posted to the consumer's file: name, date of birth, Social Security number, and address. Written confirmation is not required for technical modifications of a consumer's official information, including name and street abbreviations, complete spellings, or transposition of numbers or letters. In the case of an address change, the written confirmation shall be sent to both the new address and the former address.

(n) The following persons are not required to place in a credit report a security freeze pursuant to this section provided, however, that any person that is not required to place a security freeze on a credit report under the provisions of subdivision (3) of this subsection shall be subject to any security freeze placed on a credit report by another consumer reporting agency from which it obtains information:

(1) A check services or fraud prevention services company, which reports on incidents of fraud or issues authorizations for the

purpose of approving or processing negotiable instruments, electronic fund transfers, or similar methods of payment.

(2) A deposit account information service company, which issues reports regarding account closures due to fraud, substantial overdrafts, ATM abuse, or other similar negative information regarding a consumer to inquiring banks or other financial institutions for use only in reviewing a consumer request for a deposit account at the inquiring bank or financial institution.

(3) A consumer reporting agency that does all of the following:

a. Acts only to resell credit information by assembling and merging information contained in a database of one or more credit reporting agencies.

b. Does not maintain a permanent database of credit information from which new credit reports are produced.

(o) This section does not prevent a consumer reporting agency from charging a fee of no more than ten dollars ($10.00) to a consumer for each freeze, removal of the freeze, or temporary lifting of the freeze for a period of time, regarding access to a consumer credit report, except that a consumer reporting agency may not charge any fee to a victim of identity theft who has submitted a copy of a valid investigative or incident report or complaint with a law enforcement agency about the unlawful use of the victim's identifying information by another person.

(p) At any time that a consumer is required to receive a summary of rights required under section 609 of the federal Fair Credit Reporting Act, the following notice shall be included:

"North Carolina Consumers Have the Right to Obtain a Security Freeze.

You have a right to place a "security freeze" on your credit report pursuant to North Carolina law. The security freeze will prohibit a consumer reporting agency from releasing any information in your credit report without your express authorization. A security freeze must be requested in writing by certified mail.

The security freeze is designed to prevent credit, loans, and services from being approved in your name without your consent. However, you should be aware that using a security freeze to take control over who gains access to the personal and financial information in your credit report may delay, interfere with, or prohibit the timely approval of any subsequent request or application you make regarding new loans, credit, mortgage, insurance, rental housing, employment, investment, license, cellular phone, utilities, digital signature, Internet credit card transactions, or other services, including an extension of credit at point of sale.

The freeze will be placed within five business days. When you place a security freeze on your credit report, within 10 business days, you will be provided a personal identification number or a password to use when you want to remove or lift temporarily the security freeze. A freeze does not apply when you have an existing account relationship and a copy of your report is requested by your existing creditor or its agents or affiliates for certain types of account review, collection, fraud control, or similar activities.

You should plan ahead and lift a freeze if you are actively seeking credit or services as a security freeze may slow your applications, as mentioned above.

You can remove a freeze or authorize temporary access for a specific period of time by contacting the consumer reporting agency and providing all of the following:

(1) Your personal identification number or password,

(2) Proper identification to verify your identity, and

(3) Proper information regarding the period of time you want your report available to users of the credit report.

A consumer reporting agency that receives a request from you to temporarily lift a freeze on a credit report shall comply with the request no later than three business days after receiving the request. A consumer reporting agency may charge you up to ten dollars ($10.00) for each time you freeze, remove the freeze, or temporarily lift the freeze for a period of time, except a consumer reporting agency may not charge any amount to a victim of identity theft who has submitted a copy of a valid investigative or incident report or complaint with a law enforcement agency about the unlawful use of the victim's identifying information by another person.

You have a right to bring a civil action against someone who violates your rights under the credit reporting laws. The action can be brought against a consumer reporting agency or a user of your credit report."

(q) A violation of this section is a violation of G.S. 751.1.

"§7564. Destruction of personal information records.

(a) Any business that conducts business in North Carolina and any business that maintains or otherwise possesses personal information of a resident of North Carolina must take reasonable measures to protect against unauthorized access to or use of the information in connection with or after its disposal.

(b) The reasonable measures must include:

(1) Implementing and monitoring compliance with policies and procedures that require the burning, pulverizing, or shredding of papers containing personal information so that information cannot be practicably read or reconstructed.

(2) Implementing and monitoring compliance with policies and procedures that require the destruction or erasure of electronic media and other nonpaper media containing personal information so that the information cannot practicably be read or reconstructed.

(3) Describing procedures relating to the adequate destruction or proper disposal of personal records as official policy in the writings of the business entity.

(c) A business may, after due diligence, enter into a written contract with, and monitor compliance by, another party engaged in the business of record destruction to destroy personal information in a manner consistent with this section. Due diligence should ordinarily include one or more of the following:

(1) Reviewing an independent audit of the disposal business's operations or its compliance with this statute or its equivalent.

(2) Obtaining information about the disposal business from several references or other reliable sources and requiring that the disposal business be certified by a recognized trade association or similar third party with a reputation for high standards of quality review.

(3) Reviewing and evaluating the disposal business's information security policies or procedures or taking other appropriate measures to determine the competency and integrity of the disposal business.

(d) A disposal business that conducts business in North Carolina or disposes of personal information of residents of North Carolina must take all reasonable measures to dispose of records containing personal information by implementing and monitoring compliance with policies and procedures that protect against unauthorized access to or use of personal information during or after the collection and transportation and disposing of such information.

(e) This section does not apply to any of the following:

(1) Any bank or financial institution that is subject to and in compliance with the privacy and security provision of the Gramm Leach Bliley Act, 15 U.S.C. §6801, et seq., as amended.

(2) Any health insurer or health care facility that is subject to and in compliance with the standards for privacy of individually identifiable health information and the security standards for the protection of electronic health information of the Health Insurance Portability and Accountability Act of 1996.

(3) Any consumer reporting agency that is subject to and in compliance with the Federal Credit Reporting Act, 15 U.S.C. §1681, et seq., as amended.

(f) A violation of this section is a violation of G.S. 751.1, but any damages assessed against a business because of the acts or omissions of its nonmanagerial employees shall not be trebled as provided in G.S. 7516 unless the business was negligent in the training, supervision, or monitoring of those employees. No private right of action may be brought by an individual for a violation of this section unless such individual is injured as a result of the violation.

"§7565. Protection from security breaches.

(a) Any business that owns or licenses personal information of residents of North Carolina or any business that conducts business in North Carolina that owns or licenses personal information in any form (whether computerized, paper, or otherwise) shall provide notice to the affected person that there has been a security breach following discovery or notification of the breach. The disclosure notification shall be made without unreasonable delay, consistent with the legitimate needs of law enforcement, as provided in subsection (c) of this section, and consistent with any measures necessary to determine sufficient contact information, determine the scope of the breach and restore the reasonable integrity, security, and confidentiality of the data system. For the purposes of this section, personal information shall not include electronic identification numbers, electronic mail names or addresses, Internet account numbers, Internet identification names, parent's legal surname prior to marriage, or a password unless this information would permit access to a person's financial account or resources.

(b) Any business that maintains or possesses records or data containing personal information of residents of North Carolina that the business does not own or license, or any business that conducts business in North Carolina that maintains or possesses records or data containing personal information that the business does not own or license shall notify the owner or licensee of the information of any security breach immediately following discovery of the breach, consistent with the legitimate needs of law enforcement as provided in subsection (c) of this section.

(c) The notice required by this section shall be delayed if a law enforcement agency informs the business that notification may impede a criminal investigation or jeopardize national or homeland security, provided that such request is made in writing or the business documents such request contemporaneously in writing, including the name of the law enforcement officer making the request and the officer's law enforcement agency engaged in the investigation. The notice required by this section shall be provided without unreasonable delay after the law enforcement agency communicates to the business its determination that notice will no longer impede the investigation or jeopardize national or homeland security.

(d) The notice shall be clear and conspicuous. The notice shall include a description of the following:

(1) The incident in general terms.

(2) The type of personal information that was subject to the unauthorized access and acquisition.

(3) The general acts of the business to protect the personal information from further unauthorized access.

(4) A telephone number that the person may call for further information and assistance, if one exists.

(5) Advice that directs the person to remain vigilant by reviewing account statements and monitoring free credit reports.

(e) For purposes of this section, notice to affected persons may be provided by one of the following methods:

(1) Written notice.

(2) Electronic notice, for those persons for whom it has a valid e-mail address and who have agreed to receive communications electronically if the notice provided is consistent with the provisions regarding electronic records and signatures for notices legally required to be in writing set forth in 15 U.S.C. §7001.

(3) Telephonic notice provided that contact is made directly with the affected persons.

(4) Substitute notice, if the business demonstrates that the cost of providing notice would exceed two hundred fifty thousand dollars ($250,000) or that the affected class of subject persons to be notified exceeds 500,000, or if the business does not have sufficient contact information or consent to satisfy subdivisions (1), (2), or (3) of this subsection, for only those affected persons without sufficient contact information or consent, or if the business is unable to identify particular affected persons, for only those unidentifiable affected persons. Substitute notice shall consist of all the following:

a. Email notice when the business has an electronic mail address for the subject persons.

b. Conspicuous posting of the notice on the website page of the business, if one is maintained.

c. Notification to major statewide media.

(f) In the event a business provides notice to more than 1,000 persons at one time pursuant to this section, the business shall notify, without unreasonable delay, the Consumer Protection Division of the Attorney General's Office and all consumer reporting agencies that compile and maintain files on consumers on a nationwide basis, as defined in 15 U.S.C. §1681a(p), of the timing, distribution, and content of the notice.

(g) Any waiver of the provisions of this Article is contrary to public policy and is void and unenforceable.

(h) A financial institution that is subject to and in compliance with the Federal Interagency Guidance Response Programs for Unauthorized Access to Consumer Information and Customer Notice, issued on March 7, 2005, by the Board of Governors of the Federal Reserve System, the Federal Deposit Insurance Corporation, the Office of the Comptroller of the Currency, and the Office of Thrift Supervision, and any revisions, additions, or substitutions relating to said interagency guidance, shall be deemed to be in compliance with this section.

(i) A violation of this section is a violation of G.S. 751.1. No private right of action may be brought by an individual for a violation of this section unless such individual is injured as a result of the violation.

(j) Causes of action arising under this Article may not be assigned."

SECTION 2. G.S. 14113.21 reads as rewritten:

"§14113.21. Venue of offenses.

In any criminal proceeding brought under G.S. 14113.20, the crime is considered to be committed in ~~any county in which~~ the county where the victim resides, where the perpetrator resides, where any part of the financial identity fraud took place, or in any other county instrumental to the completion of the offense, regardless of whether the defendant was ever actually present in that county."

SECTION 3. Article 19C of Chapter 14 of the General Statutes is amended by adding a new section to read:

"§14113.21A. Investigation of offenses.

(a) A person who has learned or reasonably suspects that the person has been the victim of identity theft may contact the local law enforcement agency that has jurisdiction over the person's actual residence. Notwithstanding the fact that jurisdiction may lie elsewhere for investigation and prosecution of a crime of identity theft, the local law enforcement agency may take the complaint, issue an incident report, and provide the complainant with a copy of the report and may refer the report to a law enforcement agency in that different jurisdiction.

(b) Nothing in this section interferes with the discretion of a local law enforcement agency to allocate resources for investigations of crimes. A complaint filed or report issued under this section is not required to be counted as an open case for purposes of compiling open case statistics."

SECTION 4. Chapter 132 of the General Statutes is amended by adding a new section to read:

"§1321.8. Social Security numbers and other personal identifying information.

(a) The General Assembly finds the following:

(1) The Social Security number can be used as a tool to perpetuate fraud against a person and to acquire sensitive personal, financial, medical, and familial information, the release of which could cause great financial or personal harm to an individual. While the Social Security number was intended to be used solely for the administration of the federal Social Security System, over time this unique numeric identifier has been used extensively for identity verification purposes and other legitimate consensual purposes.

(2) Although there are legitimate reasons for State and local government agencies to collect Social Security numbers and other personal identifying information from individuals, government should collect the information only for legitimate purposes or when required by law.

(3) When State and local government agencies possess Social Security numbers or other personal identifying information, the governments should minimize the instances this information is disseminated either internally within government or externally with the general public.

(b) Except as provided in subsections (c) and (d) of this section, no agency of the State or its political subdivisions, or any agent or employee of a government agency, shall do any of the following:

(1) Collect a Social Security number from an individual unless authorized by law to do so or unless the collection of the Social Security number is otherwise imperative for the performance of that agency's duties and responsibilities as prescribed by law. Social Security numbers collected by an agency must be relevant to the purpose for which collected and shall not be collected until and unless the need for Social Security numbers has been clearly documented.

(2) Fail, when collecting a Social Security number from an individual, to segregate that number on a separate page from the rest of the record, or as otherwise appropriate, in order that the Social Security number can be more easily redacted pursuant to a valid public records request.

(3) Fail, when collecting a Social Security number from an individual, to provide, at the time of or prior to the actual collection of the Social Security number by that agency, that individual, upon request, with a statement of the purpose or purposes for which the Social Security number is being collected and used.

(4) Use the Social Security number for any purpose other than the purpose stated.

(5) Intentionally communicate or otherwise make available to the general public a person's Social Security number or other identifying information. "Identifying information", as used in this subdivision, shall have the same meaning as in G.S. 14113.20(b), except it shall not include electronic identification numbers, electronic mail names or addresses, Internet account numbers, Internet identification names, parent's legal surname prior to marriage, or drivers license numbers appearing on law enforcement records.

(6) Intentionally print or imbed an individual's Social Security number on any card required for the individual to access government services.

(7) Require an individual to transmit the individual's Social Security number over the Internet, unless the connection is secure or the Social Security number is encrypted.

(8) Require an individual to use the individual's Social Security number to access an Internet website, unless a password or unique personal identification number or other authentication device is also required to access the Internet website.

(9) Print an individual's Social Security number on any materials that are mailed to the individual, unless state or federal law required that the Social Security number be on the document to be mailed. A Social Security number that is permitted to be mailed under this subdivision may not be printed, in whole or in part, on a postcard or other mailer not requiring an envelope, or visible on the envelope or without the envelope having been opened.

(c) Subsection (b) of this section does not apply in the following circumstances:

(1) To Social Security numbers or other identifying information disclosed to another governmental entity or its agents, employees, or contractors if disclosure is necessary for the receiving entity to perform its duties and responsibilities. The receiving governmental entity and its agents, employees, and contractors shall maintain the confidential and exempt status of such numbers.

(2) To Social Security numbers or other identifying information disclosed pursuant to a court order, warrant, or subpoena.

(3) To Social Security numbers or other identifying information disclosed for public health purposes pursuant to and in compliance with Chapter 130A of the General Statutes.

(4) To Social Security numbers or other identifying information that have been redacted.

(5) To certified copies of vital records issued by the State Registrar and other authorized officials pursuant to G.S. 130A93(c). The State Registrar may disclose any identifying information other than Social Security numbers on any uncertified vital record.

(6) To any recorded document in the official records of the register of deeds of the county.

(7) To any document filed in the official records of the courts.

(d) No person preparing or filing a document to be recorded or filed in the official records by the register of deeds or of the courts may include any person's Social Security, employer taxpayer identification, driver's license, state identification, passport, checking account, savings account, credit card, or debit card number, or personal identification (PIN) code or passwords in that document, unless otherwise expressly required by law or court order, adopted by the State Registrar on records of vital events, or redacted. Any loan closing instruction that requires the inclusion of a person's Social Security number on a document to be recorded shall be void. Any person who violates this subsection shall be guilty of an infraction, punishable by a fine not to exceed five hundred dollars ($500.00) for each violation.

(e) The validity of an instrument as between the parties to the instrument is not affected by the inclusion of personal information on a document recorded or filed with the official records of the register of deeds. The register of deeds may not reject an instrument presented for recording because the instrument contains an individual's personal information.

(f) Any person has the right to request that a register of deeds or clerk of court remove, from an image or copy of an official record placed on a register of deeds' or court's Internet website available to the general public or an Internet website available to the general public used by a register of deeds or court to display public records by the register of deeds or clerk of court, the person's Social Security, employer taxpayer identification, driver's license, state identification, passport, checking account, savings account, credit card, or debit card number, or personal identification (PIN) code or passwords contained in that official record. The request must be made in writing, legibly signed by the requester, and delivered by mail, facsimile, or electronic transmission, or delivered in person to the register of deeds or clerk of court. The request must specify the personal information to be redacted, information that identifies the document that contains the personal information and unique information that identifies the location within the document that contains the Social Security, employer taxpayer identification, driver's license, state identification, passport, checking account, savings account, credit card, or debit card number, or personal identification (PIN) code or passwords to be redacted. The request for redaction shall be considered a public record with access restricted to the register of deeds, the clerk of court, their staff, or upon order of the court. The register of deeds or clerk of court shall have no duty to inquire beyond the written request to verify the identity of a person requesting redaction and shall have no duty to remove redaction for any reason upon subsequent request by an individual or by order of the court, if impossible to do so. No fee will be charged for the redaction pursuant to such request. Any person who requests a redaction without proper authority to do so shall be guilty of an infraction, punishable by a fine not to exceed five hundred dollars ($500.00) for each violation.

(g) A register of deeds or clerk of court shall immediately and conspicuously post signs throughout his or her offices for public viewing and shall immediately and conspicuously post a notice on any Internet website available to the general public used by a register of deeds or clerk of court a notice stating, in substantially similar form, the following:

(1) Any person preparing or filing a document for recordation or filing in the official records may not include a Social Security, employer taxpayer identification, driver's license, state identification, passport, checking account, savings account, credit card, or debit card number, or personal identification (PIN) code or passwords in the document, unless expressly required by law or court order, adopted by the State Registrar on records of vital events, or redacted so that no more than the last four digits of the identification number is included.

(2) Any person has a right to request a register of deeds or clerk of court to remove, from an image or copy of an official record placed on a register of deeds' or clerk of court's Internet website available to the general public or on an Internet website available to the

general public used by a register of deeds or clerk of court to display public records, any Social Security, employer taxpayer identification, driver's license, state identification, passport, checking account, savings account, credit card, or debit card number, or personal identification (PIN) code or passwords contained in an official record. The request must be made in writing and delivered by mail, facsimile, or electronic transmission, or delivered in person, to the register of deeds or clerk of court. The request must specify the personal information to be redacted, information that identifies the document that contains the personal information and unique information that identifies the location within the document that contains the Social Security, employer taxpayer identification, driver's license, state identification, passport, checking account, savings account, credit card, or debit card number, or personal identification (PIN) code or passwords to be redacted. No fee will be charged for the redaction pursuant to such a request. Any person who requests a redaction without proper authority to do so shall be guilty of an infraction, punishable by a fine not to exceed five hundred dollars ($500.00) for each violation.

(h) Any affected person may petition the court for an order directing compliance with this section. No liability shall accrue to a register of deeds or clerk of court or to his or her agent for any action related to provisions of this section or for any claims or damages that might result from a Social Security number or other identifying information on the public record or on a register of deeds' or clerk of court's Internet website available to the general public or an Internet website available to the general public used by a register of deeds or clerk of court."

SECTION 5. Chapter 120 of the General Statutes is amended by adding a new Article to read:

"Article 30.

"Miscellaneous.

"§12061. Report by State agencies to the General Assembly on ways to reduce incidence of identity theft.

Agencies of the State shall evaluate and report annually by January 1 to the General Assembly about the agency's efforts to reduce the dissemination of personal identifying information, as defined in G.S. 14113.20(b). The evaluation shall include the review of public forms, the use of random personal identification numbers, restriction of access to personal identifying information, and reduction of use of personal identifying information when it is not necessary. Special attention shall be given to the use, collection, and dissemination of Social Security numbers. If the collection of a Social Security number is found to be unwarranted, the State agency shall immediately discontinue the collection of Social Security numbers for that purpose."

SECTION 6. G.S. 14113.20 reads as rewritten:

"§14113.20. Identity theft.

(a) A person who knowingly obtains, possesses, or uses identifying information of another person, living or dead, with the intent to fraudulently represent that the person is the other person for the purposes of making financial or credit transactions in the other person's name, to obtain anything of value, benefit, or advantage, or for the purpose of avoiding legal consequences is guilty of a felony punishable as provided in G.S. 14113.22(a).

(b) The term "identifying information" as used in this Article includes the following:

(1) Social Security or employer taxpayer identification numbers.

(2) Drivers license, State identification card, or passport numbers.

(3) Checking account numbers.

(4) Savings account numbers.

(5) Credit card numbers.

(6) Debit card numbers.

(7) Personal Identification (PIN) Code as defined in G.S. 14113.8(6).

(8) Electronic identification numbers, electronic mail names or addresses, Internet account numbers, or Internet identification names.

(9) Digital signatures.

(10) Any other numbers or information that can be used to access a person's financial resources.

(11) Biometric data.

(12) Fingerprints.

(13) Passwords.

(14) Parent's legal surname prior to marriage.

(c) It shall not be a violation under this Article for a person to do any of the following:

(1) Lawfully obtain credit information in the course of a bona fide consumer or commercial transaction.

(2) Lawfully exercise, in good faith, a security interest or a right of offset by a creditor or financial institution.

(3) Lawfully comply, in good faith, with any warrant, court order, levy, garnishment, attachment, or other judicial or administrative order, decree, or directive, when any party is required to do so."

SECTION 7. The Revisor of Statutes shall make the following technical and conforming corrections:

(1) Rename Article 19C of Chapter 14 of the General Statutes from "Financial Identity Fraud" to "Identity Theft".

(2) Replace the phrase "financial identity fraud" with the phrase "identity theft" wherever the terms appear throughout Article 19C of Chapter 14 of the General Statutes.

SECTION 8. G.S. 15A147(a) reads as rewritten:

"§15A147. Expunction of records when charges are dismissed or there are findings of not guilty as a result of identity theft.

(a) If any person is named in a charge for an infraction or a crime, either a misdemeanor or a felony, as a result of another person using the identifying information of the named person and the charge against the named person is dismissed, a finding of not guilty is entered, or the conviction is set aside, the named person may apply by petition or written motion to the court where the charge was last pending on a form approved by the Administrative Office of the Courts supplied by the clerk of court for an order to expunge from all official records any entries relating to the person's apprehension, charge, or trial. The court, after notice to the district attorney, shall hold a hearing on the motion or petition and, upon finding that the person's identity was used without permission and the charges were dismissed or the person was found not guilty, the court shall order the expunction."

SECTION 9. G.S. 1539.2C reads as rewritten:

"§1539.2C. Damages for identity theft.

(a) Any person whose property or person is injured by reason of an act made unlawful by Article 19C of Chapter 14 of the General Statutes may sue for civil damages. Damages may be in an amount

of up to five thousand dollars ($5,000) but no less than five hundred dollars ($500.00) for each incident, or three times the amount of actual damages, whichever amount is greater. A person seeking damages as set forth in this section may also institute a civil action to enjoin and restrain future acts that would constitute a violation of this section. The court, in an action brought under this section, may award reasonable attorneys' fees to the prevailing party."

SECTION 10. The provisions of this act are severable. If any phrase, clause, sentence, provision, or section is declared to be invalid or preempted by federal law or regulation, the validity of the remainder of this act shall not be affected thereby.

SECTION 11. G.S. 7562(a)(2), (3), (4), and (5), as enacted in Section 1 of this act, become effective October 1, 2006. G.S. 1321.8(b)(6), (7), (8), and (9), as enacted in Section 4 of this act, become effective July 1, 2007. Section 6 of this act becomes effective December 1, 2005, and applies to offenses committed, and to causes of action arising, on or after that date. The remainder of this act becomes effective December 1, 2005.

In the General Assembly read three times and ratified this the 23rd day of August, 2005.

House Bill 1248

This bill amends the Identity Theft Protection Act of 2005, relating to security breaches and publishing Social Security numbers.

AN ACT AMENDING THE IDENTITY THEFT PROTECTION ACT OF 2005.

The General Assembly of North Carolina enacts:

SECTION 1. G.S. 132-1.10 is amended by adding the following new subsection to read:

"(c1) If an agency of the State or its political subdivisions, or any agent or employee of a government agency, experiences a security breach, as defined in Article 2A of Chapter 75 of the General Statutes, the agency shall comply with the requirements of G.S. 75-65."

SECTION 2. G.S. 132-1.10(b)(5) reads as rewritten:

"(b) Except as provided in subsections (c) and (d) of this section, no agency of the State or its political subdivisions, or any agent or employee of a government agency, shall do any of the following:

...

(5) Intentionally communicate or otherwise make available to the general public a person's Social Security number or other identifying information. "Identifying information", as used in this subdivision, shall have the same meaning as in G.S. 14-113.20(b), except it shall not include electronic identification numbers, electronic mail names or addresses, Internet account numbers, Internet identification names, parent's legal surname prior to marriage, or drivers license numbers appearing on law enforcement records. Identifying information shall be confidential and not be a public record under this Chapter. A record, with identifying information removed or redacted, is a public record if it would otherwise be a public record under this Chapter but for the identifying information. The presence of identifying information in a public record does not change the nature of the public record. If all other public records requirements are met under this Chapter, the agency of the State or its political subdivisions shall respond to a public records request, even if the records contain identifying information, as promptly as possible, by providing the public record with the identifying information removed or redacted."

SECTION 3. G.S. 132-1.10(d) reads as rewritten:

"(d) No person preparing or filing a document to be recorded or filed in the official records ~~by~~ of the register of deeds, the Department of the Secretary of State, or of the courts may include any person's Social Security, employer taxpayer identification, drivers license, state identification, passport, checking account, savings account, credit card, or debit card number, or personal identification (PIN) code or passwords in that document, unless otherwise expressly required by law or court order, adopted by the State Registrar on records of vital events, or redacted. Any loan closing instruction that requires the inclusion of a person's Social Security number on a document to be recorded shall be void. Any person who violates this subsection shall be guilty of an infraction, punishable by a fine not to exceed five hundred dollars ($500.00) for each violation."

SECTION 4. G.S. 132-1.10(e) reads as rewritten:

"(e) The validity of an instrument as between the parties to the instrument is not affected by the inclusion of personal information on a document recorded or filed with the official records of the register of deeds or the Department of the Secretary of State. The register of deeds or the Department of the Secretary of State may not reject an instrument presented for recording because the instrument contains an individual's personal information."

SECTION 5. G.S. 132-1.10(f) reads as rewritten:

"(f) Any person has the right to request that the Department of the Secretary of State, a register of deeds or clerk of court remove, from an image or copy of an official record placed on the Department of the Secretary of State's, a register of deeds' or court's Internet Website available to the general public or an Internet website available to the general public used by the Department of the Secretary of State, a register of deeds or court to display public records by the Department of the Secretary of State, the register of deeds or clerk of court, the person's Social Security, employer taxpayer identification, driver's license, state identification, passport, checking account, savings account, credit card, or debit card number, or personal identification (PIN) code or passwords contained in that official record. The request must be made in writing, legibly signed by the requester, and delivered by mail, facsimile, or electronic transmission, or delivered in person to the Department of the Secretary of State, the register of deeds or clerk of court. The request must specify the personal information to be redacted, information that identifies the document that contains the personal information and unique information that identifies the location within the document that contains the Social Security, employer taxpayer identification, driver's license, state identification, passport, checking account, savings account, credit card, or debit card number, or personal identification (PIN) code or passwords to be redacted. The request for redaction shall be considered a public record with access restricted to the Department of the Secretary of State, the register of deeds, the clerk of court, their staff, or upon order of the court. The Department of the Secretary of State, the register of deeds or clerk of court shall have no duty to inquire beyond the written request to verify the identity of a person requesting redaction and shall have no duty to remove redaction for any reason upon subsequent request by an individual or by order of the court, if impossible to do so. No fee will be charged for the redaction pursuant to such request. Any person who requests a redaction without proper authority to do so shall be guilty of an infraction, punishable by a fine not to exceed five hundred dollars ($500.00) for each violation."

SECTION 6. G.S. 132-1.10(g) reads as rewritten:

"(g) ~~A~~ The Department of the Secretary of State, a register of deeds or clerk of court shall immediately and conspicuously post signs throughout his or her offices for public viewing and shall immediately and conspicuously post a notice on any Internet website available to the general public used by the Department of the Secretary of State, a register of deeds or clerk of court a notice stating, in substantially similar form, the following:

(1) Any person preparing or filing a document for recordation or filing in the official records may not include a Social Security, employer taxpayer identification, driver's license, state identification, passport, checking account, savings account, credit card, or debit card number, or personal identification (PIN) code or passwords in the document, unless expressly required by law or court order, adopted by the State Registrar on records of vital events, or redacted so that no more than the last four digits of the identification number is included.

(2) Any person has a right to request the Department of the Secretary of State, a register of deeds or clerk of court to remove, from an image or copy of an official record placed on the Department of the Secretary of State's, a register of deeds' or clerk of court's Internet website available to the general public or on an Internet website available to the general public used by the Department of the Secretary of State, a register of deeds or clerk of court to display public records, any Social Security, employer taxpayer identification, driver's license, state identification, passport, checking account, savings account, credit card, or debit card number, or personal identification (PIN) code or passwords contained in an official record. The request must be made in writing and delivered by mail, facsimile, or electronic transmission, or delivered in person, to the Department of the Secretary of State, the register of deeds or clerk of court. The request must specify the personal information to be redacted, information that identifies the document that contains the personal information and unique information that identifies the location within the document that contains the Social Security, employer taxpayer identification, driver's license, state identification, passport, checking account, savings account, credit card, or debit card number, or personal identification (PIN) code or passwords to be redacted. No fee will be charged for the redaction pursuant to such a request. Any person who requests a redaction without proper authority to do so shall be guilty of an infraction, punishable by a fine not to exceed five hundred dollars ($500.00) for each violation."

SECTION 7. G.S. 132-1.10(h) reads as rewritten:

"(h) Any affected person may petition the court for an order directing compliance with this section. No liability shall accrue to the Department of the Secretary of State, a register of deeds or clerk of court or to their agents for any action related to provisions of this section or for any claims or damages that might result from a Social Security number or other identifying information on the public record or on the Department of the Secretary of State's, a register of deeds' or clerk of court's Internet website available to the general public or an Internet website available to the general public used by the Department of the Secretary of State, a register of deeds or clerk of court."

SECTION 8. The provisions of G.S. 132-1.10(b)(5) shall not apply to identifying information accessible on the Internet website of the Department of the Secretary of State or by magnetic tapes, electronic data feeds, or electronic file transfers of all records or updates of records on file with the Secretary of State until July 1, 2007. Notwithstanding the exemption provided by this section, the Department of the Secretary of State shall, whenever funds are made available, make it a priority to first remove identifying information contained in Uniform Commercial Code financing statements filed with the Department of the Secretary of State under Chapter 25 of the General Statutes no later than June 30, 2007.

SECTION 9. The Department of the Secretary of State shall study the alternatives and costs for redacting identifying information contained in the records of the Department of the Secretary of State, including the Internet website of the Department, and shall report the results of its study to the Office of State Budget and Management and to the House and Senate co-chairs of the Joint Appropriations Subcommittee on General Government on or before February 1, 2007. This study shall focus on the most expeditious, cost-effective method of redacting identifying information on or before January 1, 2007.

SECTION 10. Section 1 of this act becomes effective October 1, 2006. Sections 5 through 7 of this act are effective when the act becomes law and expire on July 1, 2007. The remainder of this act is effective when the act becomes law. In the General Assembly read three times and ratified this the 18th day of July, 2006.

House Bill 357

This bill prohibits a person who accepts credit, charge, or debit cards for the transaction of business from printing more than five digits of a credit card, charge card, or debit card account number or an expiration date on a sales receipt. It also prohibits a person from selling a cash register or other machine or device that electronically prints receipts of credit, charge, or debit card transactions that cannot be programmed or operated to produce a receipt with five or fewer digits of the credit, charge, or debit card account number and no expiration date printed on the receipt.

Consumer and Customer Privacy Act–Senate Bill 966

This bill requires that insurers implement safeguards for the protection of customer information, pursuant to the provisions of the Gramm-Leach-Bliley Act.

The purpose of S.B. 966 is to establish standards for developing and implementing administrative, technical, and physical safeguards to protect the security, confidentiality, and integrity of customer information, as required by sections 501, 505(b), and 507 of the federal Gramm-Leach-Bliley Act (Public Law 106-102), codified as 15 U.S.C. §§6801, 6805(b), and 6807. The purpose is also to provide privacy and security protection consistent with federal regulations governing the privacy and security of medical records when this part is consistent with those federal regulations. In those instances in which this part and the federal regulations are inconsistent and this part provides privacy and security protection beyond that offered by the federal regulations, the purpose of this part is to provide that additional privacy and security protection.

Chapter 34: North Dakota

Commit cyber crime in violation of North Dakota's Senate Bill 2251, and you could be found guilty of a Class C felony. Commit subsequent violations, and you could be found guilty of a Class A felony. In short, "Don't do the crime if you can't do the time."

Senate Bill 2251

This bill relates to requiring the disclosure to consumers of a breach in security by businesses maintaining personal information in electronic form. It also relates to the unauthorized use of personally identifying information, penalties, and prosecution of offenses in multiple counties; the jurisdiction for offenses that involve conduct outside this state; and provides a penalty.

Fifty-ninth Legislative Assembly of North Dakota

In Regular Session Commencing Tuesday, January 4, 2005

SENATE BILL NO. 2251

AN ACT to create and enact chapter 51-30 of the North Dakota Century Code, relating to requiring disclosure to consumers of a breach in security by businesses maintaining personal information in electronic form; to amend and reenact sections 12.1-23-11 and 12.1-23-12 of the North Dakota Century Code, relating to the unauthorized use of personal identifying information, penalties, prosecution of offenses in multiple counties, and jurisdiction in offenses involving conduct outside this state; to provide a penalty; to provide an effective date; and to declare an emergency.

BE IT ENACTED BY THE LEGISLATIVE ASSEMBLY OF NORTH DAKOTA:

SECTION 1. AMENDMENT. **Section 12.1-23-11 of the North Dakota Century Code is amended and reenacted as follows:**

12.1-23-11. Unauthorized use of personal identifying information - Penalty.

1. As used in this section, "personal identifying information" means any of the following information:

a. An individual's name;

b. An individual's address;

c. An individual's telephone number;

d. The distinguishing operator's license number assigned to an individual by the department of transportation under section 39-04-14 39-06-14;

e. An individual's Social Security number;

f. An individual's employer or place of employment;

g. An identification number assigned to the individual by the individual's employer;

h. The maiden name of the individual's mother; or

i. The identifying number of a depository account in a financial institution; or

j. An individual's birth, death, or marriage certificate.

2. A person is guilty of a class C felony an offense if the person uses or attempts to use any personal identifying information of an individual, living or deceased, to obtain credit, money, goods, services, or anything else of value without the authorization or consent of the individual and by representing that person is the individual or is acting with the authorization or consent of the individual. The offense is a class B felony if the credit, money,

goods, services, or anything else of value exceeds one thousand dollars in value, otherwise the offense is a class C felony. A second or subsequent offense is a class A felony.

3. A violation of this section, of a law of another state, or of federal law that is equivalent to this section and which resulted in a plea or finding of guilt must be considered a prior offense. The prior offense must be alleged in the complaint, information, or indictment.

The plea or finding of guilt for the prior offense must have occurred before the date of the commission of the offense or offenses charged in the complaint, information, or indictment.

4. A prosecution for a violation of this section must be commenced within six years after discovery by the victim of the offense of the facts constituting the violation.

5. When a person commits violations of this section in more than one county involving either one or more victims or the commission of acts constituting an element of the offense, the multiple offenses may be consolidated for commencement of prosecution in any county where one of the offenses was committed.

SECTION 2. AMENDMENT. Section 12.1-23-12 of the North Dakota Century Code is amended and reenacted as follows:

12.1-23-12. Jurisdiction - Conduct outside this state. Notwithstanding section 29-03-01.1, a person who, while outside this state and by use of deception, obtains, deprives, or conspires, solicits, or attempts to obtain the property of a person within this state or to deprive such person of property is subject to prosecution under this chapter in the courts of this state. The Except as provided in section12.1-23-11, the venue is in the county in which the victim resides or any other county in which any part of the crime occurred.

SECTION 3. Chapter 51-30 of the North Dakota Century Code is created and enacted as follows:

51-30-01. Definitions. In this chapter, unless the context or subject matter otherwise requires:

1. "Breach of the security system" means unauthorized acquisition of computerized data when access to personal information has not been secured by encryption or by any other method or technology that renders the electronic files, media, or data bases unreadable or unusable. Good-faith acquisition of personal information by an employee or agent of the person is not a breach of the security of the system, if the personal information is not used or subject to further unauthorized disclosure.

2. a. "Personal information" means an individual's first name or first initial and last name in combination with any of the following data elements, when the name and the data elements are not encrypted:

(1) The individual's Social Security number;

(2) The operator's license number assigned to an individual by the department of transportation under section 39-06-14;

(3) A nondriver color photo identification card number assigned to the individual by the department of transportation under section 39-06-03.1;

(4) The individual's financial institution account number, credit card number, or debit card number in combination with any required security code, access code or password that would permit access to an individual's financial accounts;

(5) The individual's date of birth;

(6) The maiden name of the individual's mother;

(7) An identification number assigned to the individual by the individual's employer; or

(8) The individual's digitized or other electronic signature.

b. "Personal information" does not include publicly available information that is lawfully made available to the general public from federal, state, or local government records.

51-30-02. Notice to consumers. Any person that conducts business in this state, and that owns or licenses computerized data that includes personal information, shall disclose any breach of the security of the system following discovery or notification of the breach in the security of the data to any resident of the state whose unencrypted personal information was, or is reasonably believed to have been, acquired by an unauthorized person. The disclosure must be made in the most expedient time possible and without unreasonable delay, consistent with the legitimate needs of law enforcement, as provided in section 51-30-04, or any measures necessary to determine the scope of the breach and to restore the integrity of the data system.

51-30-03. Notice to owner or licensee of personal information. Any person that maintains computerized data that includes personal information that the person does not own shall notify the owner or licensee of the information of the breach of the security of the data immediately following the discovery, if the personal information was, or is reasonably believed to have been, acquired by an unauthorized person.

51-30-04. Delayed notice. The notification required by this chapter may be delayed if a law enforcement agency determines that the notification will impede a criminal investigation. The notification required by this chapter must be made after the law enforcement agency determines that the notification will not compromise the investigation.

51-30-05. Method of notice. Notice under this chapter may be provided by one of the following methods:

1. Written notice;

2. Electronic notice, if the notice provided is consistent with the provisions regarding electronic records and signatures set forth in section 7001 of title 15 of the United States Code; or

3. Substitute notice, if the person demonstrates that the cost of providing notice would exceed two hundred fifty thousand dollars, or that the affected class of subject persons to be notified exceeds five hundred thousand, or the person does not have sufficient contact information. Substitute notice consists of the following:

a. E-mail notice when the person has an e-mail address for the subject persons;

b. Conspicuous posting of the notice on the person's website page, if the person maintains one; and

c. Notification to major statewide media.

51-30-06. Alternate compliance. Notwithstanding section 51-30-05, a person that maintains its own notification procedures as part of an information security policy for the treatment of personal information and is otherwise consistent with the timing requirements of this chapter is deemed to be in compliance with the notification requirements of this chapter if the person notifies subject individuals in accordance with its policies in the event of a breach of security of the system. A financial institution, trust company, or credit union that is subject to, examined for, and in compliance with the federal interagency guidance on response programs for unauthorized access to customer information and customer notice is deemed to be in compliance with this chapter.

51-30-07. Enforcement - Powers - Remedies - Penalties. The attorney general may enforce this chapter. The attorney general, in enforcing this chapter, has all the powers provided in chapter 51-15 and may seek all the remedies in chapter 51-15. A violation of this chapter is deemed a violation of chapter 51-15. The remedies, duties, prohibitions, and penalties of this chapter are not exclusive and are in addition to all other causes of action, remedies, and penalties under chapter 51-15, or otherwise provided by law.

House Bill 1179

This bill prohibits an insurance company, non-profit health service corporation, or health maintenance organization from disclosing non-public personal information to non-affiliated third parties.

House Bill 1478

This bill relates to disclosure of financial information, and relates to financial institution customer privacy definitions and exceptions.

Chapter 35: Ohio

In Ohio's House Bill 104, if the data of more than 1,000 Ohio residents is breached, in addition to notifying the consumers, all consumer reporting agencies that compile and maintain files on them must be notified as well. This will afford the affected consumers a certain degree of protection against misuse of their personal information.

House Bill 104

This bill requires an Ohio state agency, person, or business to contact individuals if unencrypted personal information about those individuals that is maintained on their computers was obtained by unauthorized persons.

This bill is to amend sections 1345.51 and 1347.01 and to enact sections 1347.12, 1349.19, 1349.191, and 1349.192 of the Revised Code to require a state agency, an agency of a political subdivision, or a person, including a business entity that does business in Ohio, to contact individuals residing in Ohio if unencrypted or unredacted personal information about those individuals that is included in computerized data owned or licensed by the agency, person, or business entity is accessed and acquired by unauthorized persons and causes or reasonably is believed will create a material risk of the commission of the offense of identity fraud or other fraud to the individual, and to authorize the attorney general to investigate and enforce compliance with the requirements.

Be it enacted by the General Assembly of the State of Ohio:

SECTION 1. That sections 1345.51 and 1347.01 be amended and sections 1347.12, 1349.19, 1349.191, and 1349.192 of the Revised Code be enacted to read as follows:

Sec. 1345.51. There is hereby created in the state treasury the consumer protection enforcement fund. The fund shall include civil penalties ordered pursuant to divisions (A) and (D) of section 1345.07 of the Revised Code and paid as provided in division (G) of

that section, all civil penalties assessed under division (A) of section 1349.192 of the Revised Code, all costs awarded to the attorney general and all penalties imposed under section 4549.48 of the Revised Code, and all money unclaimed under section 4549.50 of the Revised Code. The money in the consumer protection enforcement fund shall be used for the sole purpose of paying expenses incurred by the consumer protection section of the office of the attorney general.

Sec. 1347.01. As used in this chapter, except as otherwise provided:

(A) "State agency" means the office of any elected state officer and any agency, board, commission, department, division, or educational institution of the state.

(B) "Local agency" means any municipal corporation, school district, special purpose district, or township of the state or any elected officer or board, bureau, commission, department, division, institution, or instrumentality of a county.

(C) "Special purpose district" means any geographic or political jurisdiction that is created by statute to perform a limited and specific function, and includes, but is not limited to, library districts, conservancy districts, metropolitan housing authorities, park districts, port authorities, regional airport authorities, regional transit authorities, regional water and sewer districts, sanitary districts, soil and water conservation districts, and regional planning agencies.

(D) "Maintains" means state or local agency ownership of, control over, responsibility for, or accountability for systems and includes, but is not limited to, state or local agency depositing of information with a data processing center for storage, processing, or dissemination. An agency "maintains" all systems of records that are required by law to be kept by the agency.

(E) "Personal information" means any information that describes anything about a person, or that indicates actions done by or to a person, or that indicates that a person possesses certain personal characteristics, and that contains, and can be retrieved from a system by, a name, identifying number, symbol, or other identifier assigned to a person.

(F) "System" means any collection or group of related records that are kept in an organized manner and that are maintained by a state or local agency, and from which personal information is retrieved by the name of the person or by some identifying number, symbol, or other identifier assigned to the person. "System" includes both records that are manually stored and records that are stored using electronic data processing equipment. "System" does not include collected archival records in the custody of or administered under the authority of the Ohio historical society, published directories, reference materials or newsletters, or routine information that is maintained for the purpose of internal office administration, the use of which would not adversely affect a person.

(G) "Interconnection of systems" means a linking of systems that belong to more than one agency, or to an agency and other organizations, which linking of systems results in a system that permits each agency or organization involved in the linking to have unrestricted access to the systems of the other agencies and organizations.

(H) "Combination of systems" means a unification of systems that belong to more than one agency, or to an agency and another organization, into a single system in which the records that belong to each agency or organization may or may not be obtainable by the others.

Sec. 1347.12. (A) As used in this section:

(1) "Agency of a political subdivision" means each organized body, office, or agency established by a political subdivision for the exercise of any function of the political subdivision.

(2)(a) "Breach of the security of the system" means unauthorized access to and acquisition of computerized data that compromises the security or confidentiality of personal information owned or licensed by a state agency or an agency of a political subdivision and that causes, reasonably is believed to have caused, or reasonably is believed will cause a material risk of identity theft or other fraud to the person or property of a resident of this state.

(b) For purposes of division (A)(2)(a) of this section:

(i) Good faith acquisition of personal information by an employee or agent of the state agency or agency of the political subdivision for the purposes of the agency is not a breach of the security of the system, provided that the personal information is not used for an unlawful purpose or subject to further unauthorized disclosure.

(ii) Acquisition of personal information pursuant to a search warrant, subpoena, or other court order, or pursuant to a subpoena, order, or duty of a regulatory state agency, is not a breach of the security of the system.

(3) "Consumer reporting agency that compiles and maintains files on consumers on a nationwide basis" means a consumer reporting agency that regularly engages in the practice of assembling or evaluating, and maintaining, for the purpose of furnishing consumer reports to third parties bearing on a consumer's creditworthiness, credit standing, or credit capacity, each of the following regarding consumers residing nationwide:

(a) Public record information;

(b) Credit account information from persons who furnish that information regularly and in the ordinary course of business.

(4) "Encryption" means the use of an algorithmic process to transform data into a form in which there is a low probability of assigning meaning without use of a confidential process or key.

(5) "Individual" means a natural person.

(6)(a) "Personal information" means, notwithstanding section 1347.01 of the Revised Code, an individual's name, consisting of the individual's first name or first initial and last name, in combination with and linked to any one or more of the following data elements, when the data elements are not encrypted, redacted, or altered by any method or technology in such a manner that the data elements are unreadable:

(i) Social Security number;

(ii) Driver's license number or state identification card number;

(iii) Account number or credit or debit card number, in combination with and linked to any required security code, access code, or password that would permit access to an individual's financial account.

(b) "Personal information" does not include publicly available information that is lawfully made available to the general public from federal, state, or local government records or any of the following media that are widely distributed:

(i) Any news, editorial, or advertising statement published in any bona fide newspaper, journal, or magazine, or broadcast over radio or television;

(ii) Any gathering or furnishing of information or news by any bona fide reporter, correspondent, or news bureau to news media described in division (A)(6)(b)(i) of this section;

(iii) Any publication designed for and distributed to members of any bona fide association or charitable or fraternal nonprofit corporation;

(iv) Any type of media similar in nature to any item, entity, or activity identified in division (A)(6)(b)(i), (ii), or (iii) of this section.

(7) "Political subdivision" has the same meaning as in section 2744.01 of the Revised Code.

(8) "Record" means any information that is stored in an electronic medium and is retrievable in perceivable form. "Record" does not include any publicly available directory containing information an individual voluntarily has consented to have publicly disseminated or listed, such as name, address, or telephone number.

(9) "Redacted" means altered or truncated so that no more than the last four digits of a Social Security number, driver's license number, state identification card number, account number, or credit or debit card number is accessible as part of the data.

(10) "State agency" has the same meaning as in section 1.60 of the Revised Code.

(11) "System" means, notwithstanding section 1347.01 of the Revised Code, any collection or group of related records that are kept in an organized manner, that are maintained by a state agency or an agency of a political subdivision, and from which personal information is retrieved by the name of the individual or by some identifying number, symbol, or other identifier assigned to the individual. "System" does not include any collected archival records in the custody of or administered under the authority of the Ohio historical society, any published directory, any reference material or newsletter, or any routine information that is maintained for the purpose of internal office administration of the agency, if the use of the directory, material, newsletter, or information would not adversely affect an individual and if there has been no unauthorized external breach of the directory, material, newsletter, or information.

(B)(1) Any state agency or agency of a political subdivision that owns or licenses computerized data that includes personal information shall disclose any breach of the security of the system, following its discovery or notification of the breach of the security of the system, to any resident of this state whose personal information was, or reasonably is believed to have been, accessed and acquired by an unauthorized person if the access and acquisition by the unauthorized person causes or reasonably is believed will cause a material risk of identity theft or other fraud to the resident. The disclosure described in this division may be made pursuant to any provision of a contract entered into by the state agency or agency of a political subdivision with any person or another state agency or agency of a political subdivision prior to the date the breach of the security of the system occurred if that contract does not conflict with any provision of this section. For purposes of this section, a resident of this state is an individual whose principal mailing address as reflected in the records of the state agency or agency of a political subdivision is in this state.

(2) The state agency or agency of a political subdivision shall make the disclosure described in division (B)(1) of this section in the most expedient time possible but not later than forty-five days following its discovery or notification of the breach in the security of the system, subject to the legitimate needs of law enforcement activities described in division (D) of this section and consistent with any measures necessary to determine the scope of the breach, including which residents' personal information was accessed and acquired, and to restore the reasonable integrity of the data system.

(C) Any state agency or agency of a political subdivision that, on behalf of or at the direction of another state agency or agency of a political subdivision, is the custodian of or stores computerized data that includes personal information shall notify that other state agency or agency of a political subdivision of any breach of the security of the system in an expeditious manner, if the personal information was, or reasonably is believed to have been, accessed and acquired by an unauthorized person and if the access and acquisition by the unauthorized person causes or reasonably is believed will cause a material risk of identity theft or other fraud to a resident of this state.

(D) The state agency or agency of a political subdivision may delay the disclosure or notification required by division (B), (C), or (F) of this section if a law enforcement agency determines that the disclosure or notification will impede a criminal investigation or jeopardize homeland or national security, in which case, the state agency or agency of a political subdivision shall make the disclosure or notification after the law enforcement agency determines that disclosure or notification will not compromise the investigation or jeopardize homeland or national security.

(E) For purposes of this section, a state agency or agency of a political subdivision may disclose or make a notification by any of the following methods:

(1) Written notice;

(2) Electronic notice, if the state agency's or agency of a political subdivision's primary method of communication with the resident to whom the disclosure must be made is by electronic means;

(3) Telephone notice;

(4) Substitute notice in accordance with this division, if the state agency or agency of a political subdivision required to disclose demonstrates that the agency does not have sufficient contact information to provide notice in a manner described in division (E)(1), (2), or (3) of this section, or that the cost of providing disclosure or notice to residents to whom disclosure or notification is required would exceed two hundred fifty thousand dollars, or that the affected class of subject residents to whom disclosure or notification is required exceeds five hundred thousand persons. Substitute notice under this division shall consist of all of the following:

(a) Electronic mail notice if the state agency or agency of a political subdivision has an electronic mail address for the resident to whom the disclosure must be made;

(b) Conspicuous posting of the disclosure or notice on the state agency's or agency of a political subdivision's website, if the agency maintains one;

(c) Notification to major media outlets, to the extent that the cumulative total of the readership, viewing audience, or listening audience of all of the outlets so notified equals or exceeds seventy-five per cent of the population of this state.

(5) Substitute notice in accordance with this division, if the state agency or agency of a political subdivision required to disclose demonstrates that the agency has ten employees or fewer and that the cost of providing the disclosures or notices to residents to whom disclosure or notification is required will exceed ten thousand dollars. Substitute notice under this division shall consist of all of the following:

(a) Notification by a paid advertisement in a local newspaper that is distributed in the geographic area in which the state agency or agency of a political subdivision is located, which advertisement shall be of sufficient size that it covers at least one-quarter of a page in the newspaper and shall be published in the newspaper at least once a week for three consecutive weeks;

(b) Conspicuous posting of the disclosure or notice on the state agency's or agency of a political subdivision's website, if the agency maintains one;

(c) Notification to major media outlets in the geographic area in which the state agency or agency of a political subdivision is located.

(F) If a state agency or agency of a political subdivision discovers circumstances that require disclosure under this section to more than one thousand residents of this state involved in a single occurrence of a breach of the security of the system, the state agency or agency of a political subdivision shall notify, without unreasonable delay, all consumer reporting agencies that compile and maintain files on consumers on a nationwide basis of the timing, distribution, and content of the disclosure given by the state agency or agency of a political subdivision to the residents of this state. In no case shall a state agency or agency of a political subdivision that is required to make a notification required by this division delay any disclosure or notification required by division (B) or (C) of this section in order to make the notification required by this division.

(G) The attorney general, pursuant to sections 1349.191 and 1349.192 of the Revised Code, may conduct an investigation and bring a civil action upon an alleged failure by a state agency or agency of a political subdivision to comply with the requirements of this section.

Sec. 1349.19. (A) As used in this section:

(1)(a) "Breach of the security of the system" means unauthorized access to and acquisition of computerized data that compromises the security or confidentiality of personal information owned or licensed by a person and that causes, reasonably is believed to have caused, or reasonably is believed will cause a material risk of identity theft or other fraud to the person or property of a resident of this state.

(b) For purposes of division (A)(1)(a) of this section:

(i) Good faith acquisition of personal information by an employee or agent of the person for the purposes of the person is not a breach of the security of the system, provided that the personal information is not used for an unlawful purpose or subject to further unauthorized disclosure.

(ii) Acquisition of personal information pursuant to a search warrant, subpoena, or other court order, or pursuant to a subpoena, order, or duty of a regulatory state agency, is not a breach of the security of the system.

(2) "Business entity" means a sole proprietorship, partnership, corporation, association, or other group, however organized and whether operating for profit or not for profit, including a financial institution organized, chartered, or holding a license authorizing operation under the laws of this state, any other state, the United States, or any other country, or the parent or subsidiary of a financial institution.

(3) "Consumer reporting agency that compiles and maintains files on consumers on a nationwide basis" means a consumer reporting agency that regularly engages in the practice of assembling or evaluating, and maintaining, for the purpose of furnishing consumer reports to third parties bearing on a consumer's creditworthiness, credit standing, or credit capacity, each of the following regarding consumers residing nationwide:

(a) Public record information;

(b) Credit account information from persons who furnish that information regularly and in the ordinary course of business.

(4) "Encryption" means the use of an algorithmic process to transform data into a form in which there is a low probability of assigning meaning without use of a confidential process or key.

(5) "Individual" means a natural person.

(6) "Person" has the same meaning as in section 1.59 of the Revised Code, except that "person" includes a business entity only if the business entity conducts business in this state.

(7)(a) "Personal information" means an individual's name, consisting of the individual's first name or first initial and last name, in combination with and linked to any one or more of the following data elements, when the data elements are not encrypted, redacted, or altered by any method or technology in such a manner that the data elements are unreadable:

(i) Social Security number;

(ii) Driver's license number or state identification card number;

(iii) Account number or credit or debit card number, in combination with and linked to any required security code, access code, or password that would permit access to an individual's financial account.

(b) "Personal information" does not include publicly available information that is lawfully made available to the general public from federal, state, or local government records or any of the following media that are widely distributed:

(i) Any news, editorial, or advertising statement published in any bona fide newspaper, journal, or magazine, or broadcast over radio or television;

(ii) Any gathering or furnishing of information or news by any bona fide reporter, correspondent, or news bureau to news media described in division (A)(7)(b)(i) of this section;

(iii) Any publication designed for and distributed to members of any bona fide association or charitable or fraternal nonprofit corporation;

(iv) Any type of media similar in nature to any item, entity, or activity identified in division (A)(7)(b)(i), (ii), or (iii) of this section.

(8) "Record" means any information that is stored in an electronic medium and is retrievable in perceivable form. "Record" does not include any publicly available directory containing information an individual voluntarily has consented to have publicly disseminated or listed, such as name, address, or telephone number.

(9) "Redacted" means altered or truncated so that no more than the last four digits of a Social Security number, driver's license number, state identification card number, account number, or credit or debit card number is accessible as part of the data.

(10) "System" means any collection or group of related records that are kept in an organized manner, that are maintained by a person, and from which personal information is retrieved by the name of the individual or by some identifying number, symbol, or other identifier assigned to the individual. "System" does not include any published directory, any reference material or newsletter, or any routine information that is maintained for the purpose of internal office administration of the person, if the use of the directory, material, newsletter, or information would not adversely affect an individual, and there has been no unauthorized external breach of the directory, material, newsletter, or information.

(B)(1) Any person that owns or licenses computerized data that includes personal information shall disclose any breach of the security of the system, following its discovery or notification of the breach of the security of the system, to any resident of this state whose personal information was, or reasonably is believed to have been, accessed and acquired by an unauthorized person if the access and acquisition by the unauthorized person causes or reasonably is believed will cause a material risk of identity theft or other fraud to the resident. The disclosure described in this division may be made pursuant to any provision of a contract entered into by the person with another person prior to the date the breach of the security of the system occurred if that contract does not conflict with any provision of this section and does not waive any provision of this section. For purposes of this section, a resident of this state is an individual whose principal mailing address as reflected in the records of the person is in this state.

(2) The person shall make the disclosure described in division (B)(1) of this section in the most expedient time possible but not later than forty-five days following its discovery or notification of the breach in the security of the system, subject to the legitimate needs of law enforcement activities described in division (D) of this section and consistent with any measures necessary to determine the scope of the breach, including which residents' personal information was accessed and acquired, and to restore the reasonable integrity of the data system.

(C) Any person that, on behalf of or at the direction of another person or on behalf of or at the direction of any governmental entity, is the custodian of or stores computerized data that includes personal information shall notify that other person or governmental entity of any breach of the security of the system in an expeditious manner, if the personal information was, or reasonably is believed to have been, accessed and acquired by an unauthorized person and if the access and acquisition by the unauthorized person causes or reasonably is believed will cause a material risk of identity theft or other fraud to a resident of this state.

(D) The person may delay the disclosure or notification required by division (B), (C), or (G) of this section if a law enforcement agency determines that the disclosure or notification will impede a criminal investigation or jeopardize homeland or national security, in which case, the person shall make the disclosure or notification after the law enforcement agency determines that disclosure or notification will not compromise the investigation or jeopardize homeland or national security.

(E) For purposes of this section, a person may disclose or make a notification by any of the following methods:

(1) Written notice;

(2) Electronic notice, if the person's primary method of communication with the resident to whom the disclosure must be made is by electronic means;

(3) Telephone notice;

(4) Substitute notice in accordance with this division, if the person required to disclose demonstrates that the person does not have sufficient contact information to provide notice in a manner described in division (E)(1), (2), or (3) of this section, or that the cost of providing disclosure or notice to residents to whom disclosure or notification is required would exceed two hundred fifty thousand dollars, or that the affected class of subject residents to whom disclosure or notification is required exceeds five hundred thousand persons. Substitute notice under this division shall consist of all of the following:

(a) Electronic mail notice if the person has an electronic mail address for the resident to whom the disclosure must be made;

(b) Conspicuous posting of the disclosure or notice on the person's website, if the person maintains one;

(c) Notification to major media outlets, to the extent that the cumulative total of the readership, viewing audience, or listening audience of all of the outlets so notified equals or exceeds seventy-five per cent of the population of this state.

(5) Substitute notice in accordance with this division, if the person required to disclose demonstrates that the person is a business entity with ten employees or fewer and that the cost of providing the disclosures or notices to residents to whom disclosure or

notification is required will exceed ten thousand dollars. Substitute notice under this division shall consist of all of the following:

(a) Notification by a paid advertisement in a local newspaper that is distributed in the geographic area in which the business entity is located, which advertisement shall be of sufficient size that it covers at least one-quarter of a page in the newspaper and shall be published in the newspaper at least once a week for three consecutive weeks;

(b) Conspicuous posting of the disclosure or notice on the business entity's website, if the entity maintains one;

(c) Notification to major media outlets in the geographic area in which the business entity is located.

(F)(1) A financial institution, trust company, or credit union or any affiliate of a financial institution, trust company, or credit union that is required by federal law, including, but not limited to, any federal statute, regulation, regulatory guidance, or other regulatory action, to notify its customers of an information security breach with respect to information about those customers and that is subject to examination by its functional government regulatory agency for compliance with the applicable federal law, is exempt from the requirements of this section.

(2) This section does not apply to any person or entity that is regulated by sections 1171 to 1179 of the "Social Security Act," chapter 531, 49 Stat. 620 (1935), 42 U.S.C. 1320d to 1320d-8, and any corresponding regulations in 45 C.F.R. Parts 160 and 164.

(G) If a person discovers circumstances that require disclosure under this section to more than one thousand residents of this state involved in a single occurrence of a breach of the security of the system, the person shall notify, without unreasonable delay, all consumer reporting agencies that compile and maintain files on consumers on a nationwide basis of the timing, distribution, and content of the disclosure given by the person to the residents of this state. In no case shall a person that is required to make a notification required by this division delay any disclosure or notification required by division (B) or (C) of this section in order to make the notification required by this division.

(H) Any waiver of this section is contrary to public policy and is void and unenforceable.

(I) The attorney general may conduct pursuant to sections 1349.191 and 1349.192 of the Revised Code an investigation and bring a civil action upon an alleged failure by a person to comply with the requirements of this section.

Sec. 1349.191. (A) As used in this section and section 1349.192 of the Revised Code:

(1) "Agency of a political subdivision" has the same meaning as in section 1347.12 of the Revised Code.

(2) "Business" has the same meaning as in section 1349.19 of the Revised Code.

(3) "State agency" has the same meaning as in section 1.60 of the Revised Code.

(B) The attorney general may conduct an investigation if the attorney general, based on complaints or the attorney general's own inquiries, has reason to believe that a state agency or an agency of a political subdivision has failed or is failing to comply with section 1347.12 of the Revised Code or that a person has failed or is failing to comply with section 1349.19 of the Revised Code.

(C) In any investigation conducted pursuant to this section, the attorney general may administer oaths, subpoena witnesses, adduce evidence, and subpoena the production of any book, document, record, or other relevant matter.

(D)(1) If the attorney general under division (C) of this section subpoenas the production of any relevant matter that is located outside this state, the attorney general may designate a representative, including an official of the state in which that relevant matter is located, to inspect the relevant matter on the attorney general's behalf. The attorney general may carry out similar requests received from officials of other states.

(2) Any person who is subpoenaed to produce relevant matter pursuant to division (C) of this section shall make that relevant matter available at a convenient location within this state or the state of the representative designated under division (D)(1) of this section.

(E) Any person who is subpoenaed as a witness or to produce relevant matter pursuant to division (C) of this section may file in the court of common pleas of Franklin county, the county in this state in which the person resides, or the county in this state in which the person's principal place of business is located a petition to extend for good cause shown the date on which the subpoena is to be returned or to modify or quash for good cause shown that subpoena. The person may file the petition at any time prior to the date specified for the return of the subpoena or within twenty days after the service of the subpoena, whichever is earlier.

(F) Any person who is subpoenaed as a witness or to produce relevant matter pursuant to division (C) of this section shall comply with the terms of the subpoena unless the court orders otherwise prior to the date specified for the return of the subpoena or, if applicable, that date as extended. If a person fails without lawful excuse to obey a subpoena, the attorney general may apply to the court of common pleas for an order that does one or more of the following:

(1) Compels the requested discovery;

(2) Adjudges the person in contempt of court;

(3) Grants injunctive relief to restrain the person from failing to comply with section 1347.12 or 1349.19 of the Revised Code, whichever is applicable;

(4) Grants injunctive relief to preserve or restore the status quo;

(5) Grants other relief that may be required until the person obeys the subpoena.

(G) The court shall impose a civil penalty on any person who violates an order of a court issued under division (F) of this section in the same manner as the imposition of a civil penalty under section 1349.192 of the Revised Code for a failure to comply with section 1347.12 or 1349.19 of the Revised Code, whichever is applicable.

Sec. 1349.192. (A)(1) The attorney general shall have the exclusive authority to bring a civil action in a court of common pleas for appropriate relief under this section, including a temporary restraining order, preliminary or permanent injunction, and civil penalties, if it appears that a state agency or an agency of a political subdivision has failed or is failing to comply with section 1347.12 of the Revised Code or that a person has failed or is failing to comply with section 1349.19 of the Revised Code. Upon its finding that a state agency or an agency of a political subdivision has failed to comply with section 1347.12 of the Revised Code or that a person has failed to comply with section 1349.19 of the Revised Code, the court shall impose a civil penalty upon the state agency, agency of a political subdivision, or person as follows:

(a) For each day that the state agency, agency of a political subdivision, or person has intentionally or recklessly failed to comply with the applicable section, subject to divisions (A)(1)(b) and (c) of this section, a civil penalty of up to one thousand dollars for each day the agency or person fails to comply with the section;

(b) If the state agency, agency of a political subdivision, or person has intentionally or recklessly failed to comply with the applicable section for more than sixty days, subject to division (A)(1)(c) of this section, a civil penalty in the amount specified in division (A)(1)(a) of this section for each day of the first sixty days that the agency or person fails to comply with the section and, for each day commencing with the sixty-first day that the state agency, agency of a political subdivision, or person has failed to comply with the section, a civil penalty of up to five thousand dollars for each such day the agency or person fails to comply with the section;

(c) If the state agency, agency of a political subdivision, or person has intentionally or recklessly failed to comply with the applicable section for more than ninety days, a civil penalty in the amount specified in division (A)(1)(a) of this section for each day of the first sixty days that the agency or person fails to comply with the section, a civil penalty of up to five thousand dollars for each day commencing with the sixty-first day and continuing through the ninetieth day that the agency or person fails to comply with the section, and, for each day commencing with the ninety-first day that the state agency, agency of a political subdivision, or person has failed to comply with the section, a civil penalty of up to ten thousand dollars for each such day the agency or person fails to comply with the section.

(2) Any civil penalty that is assessed under division (A)(1) of this section shall be deposited into the consumer protection enforcement fund created by section 1345.51 of the Revised Code.

(3) In determining the appropriate civil penalty to assess under division (A)(1) of this section, the court shall consider all relevant factors, including the following:

(a) If the defendant in the civil action is a state agency, an agency of a political subdivision, or a person that is a business entity, whether or not the high managerial officer, agent, or employee of the agency or business entity having supervisory responsibility for compliance

with section 1347.12 or 1349.19 of the Revised Code, whichever is applicable, acted in bad faith in failing to comply with the section.

(b) If the defendant in the civil action is a person other than a business entity, whether or not the person acted in bad faith in failing to comply with section 1349.19 of the Revised Code.

(B) Any state agency or agency of a political subdivision that is found by the court to have failed to comply with section 1347.12 of the Revised Code or any person that is found by the court to have failed to comply with section 1349.19 of the Revised Code shall be liable to the attorney general for the attorney general's costs in conducting an investigation under section 1349.191 of the Revised Code and bringing an action under this section.

(C) The rights and remedies that are provided under this section are in addition to any other rights or remedies that are provided by law.

SECTION 2. That existing sections 1345.51 and 1347.01 of the Revised Code are hereby repealed.

SECTION 3. This act deals with subject matter that is of statewide concern. It is the intent of the General Assembly that this act supersede and preempt all rules, regulations, resolutions, codes, and ordinances of all counties, municipal corporations, townships, and agencies of counties, municipal corporations, and townships that pertain to matters that are expressly set forth or regulated under this act.

House Bill 306

This bill eliminates the authority of the Ohio Division of Liquor Control to order liquor permit holders to stop selling intoxicating liquor to certain persons. It authorizes the division to share Social Security numbers with other state agencies for specific purposes and to seek BCII or FBI criminal records checks.

House Bill 122

This bill prohibits the claiming and payment of a lottery prize award with a value in excess of $599 until the beneficial owner's name, address, and Social Security number are disclosed to the State Lottery Commission. This bill would have interesting implications for persons who are in this country illegally, sometimes referred to as "undocumented immigrants." By their nature, such individuals would either not have a Social Security number, or would have one that would actually belong to somebody else that is here legally.

House Bill 279

This bill prohibits the inclusion of an individual's Social Security number on documents submitted for recording in the office of the county recorder and creates an affirmative defense to associated civil liability of a good faith effort to comply with the non-inclusion requirement.

Chapter 36: Oklahoma

§74-3113.1. Disclosure of breach of security of computerized personal information.

A. Any state agency, board, commission or other unit or subdivision of state government that owns or licenses computerized data that includes personal information shall disclose any breach of the security of the system following discovery or notification of the breach in the security of the data to any resident of Oklahoma whose unencrypted personal information was, or is reasonably believed to have been, acquired by an unauthorized person. The disclosure shall be made in the most expedient time possible and without unreasonable delay, consistent with the legitimate needs of law enforcement, as provided in subsection C of this section, or any measures necessary to determine the scope of the breach and restore the reasonable integrity of the data system.

B. Any state agency, board, commission or other unit or subdivision of state government that maintains computerized data that includes personal information that the state agency, board, commission or other unit or subdivision of state government does not own shall notify the owner or licensee of the information of any breach of the security of the data immediately following discovery, if the personal information was, or is reasonably believed to have been, acquired by an unauthorized person.

C. The notification required by this section may be delayed if a law enforcement agency determines that the notification will impede a criminal investigation. The notification required by this section shall be made after the law enforcement agency determines that it will not compromise the investigation.

D. As used in this section:

1. "Breach of the security of the system" means unauthorized acquisition of computerized data that compromises the security,

confidentiality, or integrity of personal information maintained by the state agency, board, commission or other unit or subdivision of state government. Good faith acquisition of personal information by an employee or agent of the state agency, board, commission or other unit or subdivision of state government for the purposes of that entity shall not be a breach of the security of the system, provided that the personal information is not used or subject to further unauthorized disclosure;

2. "Personal information" means the first name or first initial and last name of an individual in combination with any one or more of the following data elements, when either the name or the data elements are not encrypted:

a. social security number,

b. driver license number, or

c. account number, credit or debit card number, in combination with any required security code, access code, or password that would permit access to the financial account of an individual.

Personal information shall not include publicly available information that is lawfully made available to the general public from federal, state, or local public records; and

3. "Notice" means one of the following methods:

a. written notice,

b. electronic notice, if the notice provided is consistent with the provisions regarding electronic records and signatures set forth in Section 7001 of Title 15 of the United States Code, and

c. substitute notice, if the agency demonstrates that the cost of providing notice would exceed Two Hundred Fifty Thousand Dollars ($250,000.00), or that the affected class of subject persons to

be notified exceeds five hundred thousand (500,000), or the agency does not have sufficient contact information. Substitute notice shall consist of all of the following:

(1) e-mail notice when the agency has an e-mail address for the subject persons,

(2) conspicuous posting of the notice on the agency's website page, if the agency maintains one, and

(3) notification to major statewide media.

E. Notwithstanding paragraph 3 of subsection D of this section, a state agency, board, commission or other unit or subdivision of state government that maintains its own notification procedures as part of an information security policy for the treatment of personal information and is otherwise consistent with the timing requirements of this section shall be deemed to be in compliance with the notification requirements of this section if it notifies subject persons in accordance with its policies in the event of a breach of security of the system.

Added by Laws 2006, c. 298, § 1, emerg. eff. June 8, 2006.

Oklahoma House Bill 2357 is specific to government agencies that have a security breach, and does not mention private-sector businesses. I found that to be unique among all the state-level disclosure laws I have researched.

House Bill 2357

This bill requires government agencies to notify persons of a breach of computer systems that results in the unauthorized release of personal information.

BE IT ENACTED BY THE PEOPLE OF THE STATE OF OKLAHOMA:

SECTION 1. NEW LAW A new section of law to be codified in the Oklahoma Statutes as Section 3113.1 of Title 74, unless there is created a duplication in numbering, reads as follows:

A. Any state agency, board, commission or other unit or subdivision of state government that owns or licenses computerized data that includes personal information shall disclose any breach of the security of the system following discovery or notification of the breach in the security of the data to any resident of Oklahoma whose unencrypted personal information was, or is reasonably believed to have been, acquired by an unauthorized person. The disclosure shall be made in the most expedient time possible and without unreasonable delay, consistent with the legitimate needs of law enforcement, as provided in subsection C of this section, or any measures necessary to determine the scope of the breach and restore the reasonable integrity of the data system.

B. Any state agency, board, commission or other unit or subdivision of state government that maintains computerized data that includes personal information that the state agency, board, commission or other unit or subdivision of state government does not own shall notify the owner or licensee of the information of any breach of the security of the data immediately following discovery, if the personal information was, or is reasonably believed to have been, acquired by an unauthorized person.

C. The notification required by this section may be delayed if a law enforcement agency determines that the notification will impede a criminal investigation. The notification required by this section shall be made after the law enforcement agency determines that it will not compromise the investigation.

D. As used in this section:

1. "Breach of the security of the system" means unauthorized acquisition of computerized data that compromises the security, confidentiality, or integrity of personal information maintained by the state agency, board, commission or other unit or subdivision of state government. Good faith acquisition of personal information by an employee or agent of the state agency, board, commission or other unit or subdivision of state government for the purposes of that entity shall not be a breach of the security of the system, provided that the personal information is not used or subject to further unauthorized disclosure;

2. "Personal information" means the first name or first initial and last name of an individual in combination with any one or more of the following data elements, when either the name or the data elements are not encrypted:

a. Social Security number,

b. driver license number, or

c. account number, credit or debit card number, in combination with any required security code, access code, or password that would permit access to the financial account of an individual.

Personal information shall not include publicly available information that is lawfully made available to the general public from federal, state, or local public records; and

3. "Notice" means one of the following methods:

a. written notice,

b. electronic notice, if the notice provided is consistent with the provisions regarding electronic records and signatures set forth in Section 7001 of Title 15 of the United States Code, and

c. substitute notice, if the agency demonstrates that the cost of providing notice would exceed Two Hundred Fifty Thousand Dollars ($250,000.00), or that the affected class of subject persons to be notified exceeds five hundred thousand (500,000), or the agency does not have sufficient contact information. Substitute notice shall consist of all of the following:

(1) e-mail notice when the agency has an e-mail address for the subject persons,

(2) conspicuous posting of the notice on the agency's website page, if the agency maintains one, and

(3) notification to major statewide media.

E. Notwithstanding paragraph 3 of subsection D of this section, a state agency, board, commission or other unit or subdivision of state government that maintains its own notification procedures as part of an information security policy for the treatment of personal information and is otherwise consistent with the timing requirements of this section shall be deemed to be in compliance with the notification requirements of this section if it notifies subject persons in accordance with its policies in the event of a breach of security of the system.

SECTION 2. It being immediately necessary for the preservation of the public peace, health and safety, an emergency is hereby declared to exist, by reason whereof this act shall take effect and be in full force from and after its passage and approval.

House Bill 2396

This bill relates to the Oklahoma Open Records Act and adds Social Security numbers to the list of information public bodies may keep confidential.

House Bill 1533

This bill states that any contract entered into by the Department of Central Services that involves a customer service call center shall prohibit the sending of any personal information of a person to any location outside the United States without the written consent of the person.

Chapter 37: Oregon

Senate Bill 583

Relating to the Oregon Consumer Theft Protection Act; limiting expenditures; and declaring an emergency.

Be It Enacted by the People of the State of Oregon:

SECTION 1. This 2007 Act shall be known as the Oregon Consumer Identity Theft Protection Act.

SECTION 2. As used in this 2007 Act:

(1)(a) "Breach of security" means unauthorized acquisition of computerized data that materially compromises the security, confidentiality or integrity of personal information maintained by the person.

(b) "Breach of security" does not include good-faith acquisition of personal information by a person or that person's employee or agent for a legitimate purpose of that person if the personal information is not used in violation of applicable law or in a manner that harms or poses an actual threat to the security, confidentiality or integrity of the personal information.

(2) "Consumer" means an individual who is also a resident of this state.

(3) "Consumer report" means a consumer report as described in section 603(d) of the federal Fair Credit Reporting Act (15 U.S.C. 1681a(d)), as that Act existed on the effective date of this 2007 Act, that is compiled and maintained by a consumer reporting agency.

(4) "Consumer reporting agency" means a consumer reporting agency as described in section 603(p) of the federal Fair Credit Reporting Act (15 U.S.C. 1681a(p)) as that Act existed on the effective date of this 2007 Act.

(5) "Debt" means any obligation or alleged obligation arising out of a consumer transaction, as defined in ORS 646.639.

(6) "Encryption" means the use of an algorithmic process to transform data into a form in which the data is rendered unreadable or unusable without the use of a confidential process or key.

(7) "Extension of credit" means the right to defer payment of debt or to incur debt and defer its payment offered or granted primarily for personal, family or household purposes.

(8) "Identity theft" has the meaning set forth in ORS 165.800.

(9) "Identity theft declaration" means a completed and signed statement documenting alleged identity theft, using the form available from the Federal Trade Commission, or another substantially similar form.

(10) "Person" means any individual, private or public corporation, partnership, cooperative, association, estate, limited liability company, organization or other entity, whether or not organized to operate at a profit, or a public body as defined in ORS 174.109.

(11) "Personal information":

(a) Means a consumer's first name or first initial and last name in combination with any one or more of the following data elements, when the data elements are not rendered unusable through encryption, redaction or other methods, or when the data elements are encrypted and the encryption key has also been acquired:

(A) Social Security number;

(B) Driver license number or state identification card number issued by the Department of Transportation;

(C) Passport number or other United States issued identification number; or

(D) Financial account number, credit or debit card number, in combination with any required security code, access code or password that would permit access to a consumer's financial account.

(b) Means any of the data elements or any combination of the data elements described in paragraph (a) of this subsection when not combined with the consumer's first name or first initial and last name and when the data elements are not rendered unusable through encryption, redaction or other methods, if the information obtained would be sufficient to permit a person to commit identity theft against the consumer whose information was compromised.

(c) Does not include information, other than a Social Security number, in a federal, state or local government record that is lawfully made available to the public.

(12) "Redacted" means altered or truncated so that no more than the last four digits of a Social Security number, driver license number, state identification card number, account number or credit or debit card number is accessible as part of the data.

(13) "Security freeze" means a notice placed in a consumer report, at the request of a consumer and subject to certain exemptions, that prohibits the consumer reporting agency from releasing the consumer report for the extension of credit unless the consumer has temporarily lifted or removed the freeze.

SECTION 3. (1) Any person that owns, maintains or otherwise possesses data that includes a consumer's personal information that is used in the course of the person's business, vocation, occupation or volunteer activities and was subject to a breach of security shall give notice of the breach of security following discovery of such breach of security, or receipt of notification under subsection (2) of this section, to any consumer whose personal information was included in the information that was breached. The disclosure notification shall be made in the most expeditious time possible and without unreasonable delay, consistent with the legitimate needs of law enforcement as provided in subsection (3) of this section, and consistent with any measures necessary to determine sufficient contact information for the consumers, determine the scope of the breach and restore the reasonable integrity, security and confidentiality of the data.

(2) Any person that maintains or otherwise possesses personal information on behalf of another person shall notify the owner or licensor of the information of any breach of security immediately following discovery of such breach of security if a consumer's personal information was included in the information that was breached.

(3) The notification to the consumer required by this section may be delayed if a law enforcement agency determines that the notification will impede a criminal investigation and that agency has made a written request that the notification be delayed. The notification required by this section shall be made after that law enforcement agency determines that its disclosure will not compromise the investigation and notifies the person in writing.

(4) For purposes of this section, notification to the consumer may be provided by one of the following methods:

(a) Written notice.

(b) Electronic notice if the person's customary method of communication with the consumer is by electronic means or is consistent with the provisions regarding electronic records and signatures set forth in the Electronic Signatures in Global and National Commerce Act (15 U.S.C. 7001) as that Act existed on the effective date of this 2007 Act.

(c) Telephone notice, provided that contact is made directly with the affected consumer.

(d) Substitute notice, if the person demonstrates that the cost of providing notice would exceed $250,000, that the affected class of consumers to be notified exceeds 350,000, or if the person does not have sufficient contact information to provide notice. Substitute notice consists of the following:

(A) Conspicuous posting of the notice or a link to the notice on the Internet home page of the person if the person maintains one; and

(B) Notification to major statewide television and newspaper media.

(5) Notice under this section shall include at a minimum:

(a) A description of the incident in general terms;

(b) The approximate date of the breach of security;

(c) The type of personal information obtained as a result of the breach of security;

(d) Contact information of the person subject to this section;

(e) Contact information for national consumer reporting agencies; and

(f) Advice to the consumer to report suspected identity theft to law enforcement, including the Federal Trade Commission.

(6) If a person discovers a breach of security affecting more than 1,000 consumers that requires disclosure under this section, the person shall notify, without unreasonable delay, all consumer reporting agencies that compile and maintain reports on consumers on a nationwide basis of the timing, distribution and content of the

notification given by the person to the consumers. In no case shall a person that is required to make a notification required by this section delay any notification in order to make the notification to the consumer reporting agencies. The person shall include the police report number, if available, in its notification to the consumer reporting agencies.

(7) Notwithstanding subsection (1) of this section, notification is not required if, after an appropriate investigation or after consultation with relevant federal, state or local agencies responsible for law enforcement, the person determines that no reasonable likelihood of harm to the consumers whose personal information has been acquired has resulted or will result from the breach. Such a determination must be documented in writing and the documentation must be maintained for five years.

(8) This section does not apply to:

(a) A person that complies with the notification requirements or breach of security procedures that provide greater protection to personal information and at least as thorough disclosure requirements pursuant to the rules, regulations, procedures, guidance or guidelines established by the person's primary or functional federal regulator.

(b) A person that complies with a state or federal law that provides greater protection to personal information and at least as thorough disclosure requirements for breach of security of personal information than that provided by this section.

(c) A person that is subject to and complies with regulations promulgated pursuant to Title V of the Gramm-Leach-Bliley Act of 1999 (15 U.S.C. 6801 to 6809) as that Act existed on the effective date of this 2007 Act.

<u>SECTION 4.</u> (1) A consumer may elect to place a security freeze on the consumer's consumer report by sending a written request to a

consumer reporting agency at an address designated by the agency to receive such requests, or a secure electronic request at a website designated by the agency to receive such requests if such method is made available by the consumer reporting agency at the agency's discretion.

(2) If the consumer is the victim of identity theft or has reported to a law enforcement agency the theft of personal information, the consumer may include a copy of the police report, incident report or identity theft declaration.

(3) The consumer must provide proper identification and any fee authorized by section 6 of this 2007 Act.

(4) Except as provided in section 8 of this 2007 Act, if a security freeze is in place, information from a consumer report may not be released without prior express authorization from the consumer.

(5) This section does not prevent a consumer reporting agency from advising a third party that a security freeze is in effect with respect to the consumer report.

<u>SECTION 5.</u> (1) A consumer reporting agency shall place a security freeze on a consumer report no later than five business days after receiving from the consumer:

(a) The request described in section 4 (1) of this 2007 Act;
(b) Proper identification; and
(c) A fee, if applicable.

(2) The consumer reporting agency shall send a written confirmation of the security freeze to the consumer, to the last known address for the consumer as contained in the consumer report maintained by the consumer reporting agency, within ten business days after placing the freeze and, with the confirmation, shall provide the consumer with a unique personal identification number or password or similar device to be used by the consumer

when providing authorization for release of the consumer's consumer report for a specific period of time or for permanently removing the security freeze. The consumer reporting agency shall also include with such written confirmation information regarding the process of lifting a freeze, and the process of temporarily lifting a freeze for allowing access to information from the consumer's credit report for a period of time while the freeze is in place.

(3) If a consumer wishes to allow the consumer's consumer report to be accessed for a specific period of time while a freeze is in effect, the consumer shall contact the consumer reporting agency using a point of contact designated by the consumer reporting agency, request that the freeze be temporarily lifted and provide the following:

(a) Proper identification;

(b) The unique personal identification number or password or similar device provided by the consumer reporting agency pursuant to subsection (2) of this section;

(c) The information regarding the time period for which the consumer report shall be available to users of the credit report; and

(d) A fee, if applicable.

(4) A consumer reporting agency that receives a request from the consumer to temporarily lift a freeze on a credit report pursuant to subsection (3) of this section shall comply with the request no later than three business days after receiving from the consumer:

(a) Proper identification;

(b) The unique personal identification number or password or similar device provided by the consumer reporting agency pursuant to subsection (2) of this section;

(c) The information regarding the time period for which the consumer report shall be available; and

(d) A fee, if applicable.

(5) A security freeze shall remain in place until the consumer requests, using a point of contact designated by the consumer reporting agency, that the security freeze be removed. A consumer reporting agency shall remove a security freeze within three business days of receiving a request for removal from the consumer, who provides:

(a) Proper identification;

(b) The unique personal identification number or password or similar device provided by the consumer reporting agency pursuant to subsection (2) of this section; and

(c) A fee, if applicable.

(6) No later than December 31, 2008, the Director of the Department of Consumer and Business Services shall report to the chairs of the legislative committees that considered this 2007 Act concerning the minimum amount of time necessary, using current technology, to place, temporarily lift or remove a freeze on a consumer report, and to verify a consumer's identity. If the chair of any legislative committee is vacant at the time of making the report, the report shall also be made to the President of the Senate and the Speaker of the House of Representatives.

SECTION 6. (1) A consumer reporting agency may not charge a fee to a consumer who is the victim of identity theft or who has reported to a law enforcement agency the theft of personal information, provided the consumer has submitted to the consumer reporting agency a copy of a valid police report, incident report or identity theft declaration.

(2) A consumer reporting agency may charge a reasonable fee of no more than $10 to a consumer, other than a consumer described in subsection (1) of this section, for each freeze, temporary lift of the freeze, removal of the freeze or replacing a lost personal identification number or password previously provided to the consumer, regarding access to a consumer credit report.

SECTION 7. A consumer reporting agency shall temporarily lift or remove a freeze placed on a consumer's credit report only in the following cases:

(1) Upon the consumer's request, pursuant to section 5 (3) or (5) of this 2007 Act.

(2) If the consumer's credit report was frozen due to a material misrepresentation of fact by the consumer, the consumer reporting agency may remove the security freeze. If a consumer reporting agency intends to remove a freeze upon a consumer's credit report pursuant to this subsection, the consumer reporting agency shall notify the consumer in writing at least five business days prior to removing the freeze placed on the consumer report.

SECTION 8. The provisions of sections 4 to 6 of this 2007 Act do not apply to the use of a consumer report by or for any of the following:

(1) A person, or the person's subsidiary, affiliate, agent or assignee with which the consumer has or, prior to assignment, had an account, contract or debtor-creditor relationship for the purposes of reviewing the account or collecting the financial obligation owing for the account, contract or debtor-creditor relationship. For purposes of this subsection, "reviewing the account" includes activities related to account maintenance, monitoring, credit line increases and account upgrades and enhancements;

(2) Any person acting pursuant to a judgment, court order, warrant or subpoena;

(3) A federal, state or local governmental entity, including a law enforcement agency or court, or their agents or assignees, acting to investigate fraud or acting to investigate or collect delinquent taxes or unpaid judgments or court orders or to fulfill their statutory or regulatory duties provided such responsibilities are consistent with a permissible purpose under section 604 of the federal Fair Credit Reporting Act (15 U.S.C. 1681b) as that Act existed on the effective date of this 2007 Act;

(4) The use of credit information for the purposes of prescreening as provided by the federal Fair Credit Reporting Act (15 U.S.C. 1681 et seq.) as that Act existed on the effective date of this 2007 Act;

(5) Any person for the sole purpose of providing a credit file monitoring subscription service, or similar service to which the consumer has subscribed;

(6) A consumer reporting agency for the sole purpose of providing a consumer with a copy of the consumer's consumer report upon the consumer's request;

(7) Any person or entity for the use of setting or adjusting rates, for claims handling or underwriting for insurance purposes, to the extent permitted by law;

(8) A subsidiary, affiliate, agent, assignee or prospective assignee of a person to whom access has been granted under section 5 (3) of this 2007 Act for purposes of facilitating the extension of credit or other permissible use;

(9) A child support agency acting pursuant to Title IV-D of the Social Security Act (42 U.S.C. 651 et seq.) as that Act existed on the effective date of this 2007 Act; and

(10) A person for the sole purpose of screening an applicant for a residential dwelling unit as described in ORS 90.295 (1).

SECTION 9. If a third party requests access to a consumer report on which a security freeze is in effect, the request is in connection with an application for credit or any other use, the consumer does not allow the consumer's consumer report to be accessed for that period of time, and the third party cannot obtain the consumer report through section 8 of this 2007 Act, the third party may treat the application as incomplete.

SECTION 10. (1) If a security freeze is in place, a consumer reporting agency shall not change any of the following official information in a consumer credit report without sending a written confirmation of the change to the consumer within 30 days of the change being posted to the consumer's report: name, date of birth, Social Security number and address. Written confirmation is not required for technical modifications of a consumer's official information, including name and street abbreviations, complete spellings or transposition of numbers or letters. In the case of an address change, the written confirmation shall be sent to both the new address and to the former address.

(2) The following entities are not required to place a security freeze on a credit report:

(a) A consumer reporting agency that acts only as a reseller of credit information by assembling and merging information contained in the database of another consumer reporting agency or multiple consumer reporting agencies, and does not maintain a database of credit information from which new consumer credit reports are produced. However, a consumer reporting agency acting as a reseller shall honor any security freeze placed on a consumer report by another consumer reporting agency.

(b) A check services or fraud prevention services company that issues reports on incidents of fraud or authorizations for the purpose of approving or processing negotiable instruments, electronic funds transfers or similar methods of payments.

(c) A deposit account information service company that issues reports regarding account closures due to fraud, substantial overdrafts, ATM abuse or similar negative information regarding a consumer, to inquiring banks or other financial institutions for use only in reviewing a consumer request for a deposit account at the inquiring bank or financial institution.

SECTION 11. (1) Except as otherwise specifically provided by law a person shall not:

(a) Print a consumer's Social Security number on any materials not requested by the consumer or part of the documentation of a transaction or service requested by the consumer that are mailed to the consumer unless redacted;

(b) Print a consumer's Social Security number on any card required for the consumer to access products or services provided by the person; or

(c) Publicly post or publicly display a consumer's Social Security number unless redacted. As used in this paragraph, "publicly post or publicly display" means to communicate or otherwise make available to the public.

(2) This section does not prevent the collection, use, or release of a Social Security number as required by state or federal law, including statute, Oregon Rules of Civil Procedure or rule adopted by the Chief Justice of the Supreme Court, the Chief Judge of the Court of Appeals or the judge of the Oregon Tax Court, or the use or printing of a Social Security number for internal verification or administrative purposes or for enforcement of a judgment or court order.

(3) This section does not apply to records that are required by state or federal law, including statute, Oregon Rules of Civil Procedure or rule adopted by the Chief Justice of the Supreme Court, the Chief Judge of the Court of Appeals or the judge of the Oregon Tax Court, to be made available to the public.

(4) This section does not apply to a Social Security number in any of the following records or copies of records in any form or storage medium maintained or otherwise possessed by a court, the State Court Administrator or the Secretary of State:

(a) A record received on or before the effective date of this 2007 Act;

(b) A record received after the effective date of this 2007 Act if, by state or federal statute or rule, the person that submitted the record could have caused the record to be filed or maintained in a manner that protected the Social Security number from public disclosure; or

(c) A record, regardless of the date created or received, that is:

(A) An accusatory instrument charging a violation or crime;
(B) A record of oral proceedings in a court;
(C) An exhibit offered as evidence in a proceeding; or
(D) A judgment or court order.

SECTION 12. (1) Any person that owns, maintains or otherwise possesses data that includes a consumer's personal information that is used in the course of the person's business, vocation, occupation or volunteer activities must develop, implement and maintain reasonable safeguards to protect the security, confidentiality and integrity of the personal information, including disposal of the data.

(2) The following shall be deemed in compliance with subsection (1) of this section:

(a) A person that complies with a state or federal law providing greater protection to personal information than that provided by this section.

(b) A person that is subject to and complies with regulations promulgated pursuant to Title V of the Gramm-Leach-Bliley Act of 1999 (15 U.S.C. 6801 to 6809) as that Act existed on the effective date of this 2007 Act.

(c) A person that is subject to and complies with regulations implementing the Health Insurance Portability and Accountability Act of 1996 (45 C.F.R. parts 160 and 164) as that Act existed on the effective date of this 2007 Act.

(d) A person that implements an information security program that includes the following:

(A) Administrative safeguards such as the following, in which the person:

(i) Designates one or more employees to coordinate the security program;

(ii) Identifies reasonably foreseeable internal and external risks;

(iii) Assesses the sufficiency of safeguards in place to control the identified risks;

(iv) Trains and manages employees in the security program practices and procedures;

(v) Selects service providers capable of maintaining appropriate safeguards, and requires those safeguards by contract; and

(vi) Adjusts the security program in light of business changes or new circumstances;

(B) Technical safeguards such as the following, in which the person:

(i) Assesses risks in network and software design;

(ii) Assesses risks in information processing, transmission and storage;

(iii) Detects, prevents and responds to attacks or system failures; and

(iv) Regularly tests and monitors the effectiveness of key controls, systems and procedures; and

(C) Physical safeguards such as the following, in which the person:

(i) Assesses risks of information storage and disposal;

(ii) Detects, prevents and responds to intrusions;

(iii) Protects against unauthorized access to or use of personal information during or after the collection, transportation and destruction or disposal of the information; and

(iv) Disposes of personal information after it is no longer needed for business purposes or as required by local, state or federal law by burning, pulverizing, shredding or modifying a physical record and by destroying or erasing electronic media so that the information cannot be read or reconstructed.

(3) A person complies with subsection (2)(d)(C)(iv) of this section if the person contracts with another person engaged in the business of record destruction to dispose of personal information in a manner consistent with subsection (2)(d)(C)(iv) of this section.

(4) Notwithstanding subsection (2) of this section, a person that is an owner of a small business as defined in ORS 285B.123 (3) complies with subsection (1) of this section if the person's information security and disposal program contains administrative, technical and physical safeguards and disposal measures appropriate to the size and complexity of the small business, the nature and scope of its activities, and the sensitivity of the personal information collected from or about consumers.
SECTION 13. (1) The Director of the Department of Consumer and Business Services may:

(a) Make such public or private investigations within or outside this state as the director deems necessary to determine whether a person has violated any provision of this 2007 Act, or to aid in the enforcement of this 2007 Act.

(b) Require or permit a person to file a statement in writing, under oath or otherwise as the director determines, as to all the facts and circumstances concerning the matter to be investigated.

(c) Administer oaths and affirmations, subpoena witnesses, compel attendance, take evidence and require the production of books, papers, correspondence, memoranda, agreements or other documents or records that the director deems relevant or material to the inquiry. Each witness who appears before the director under a subpoena shall receive the fees and mileage provided for witnesses in ORS 44.415 (2).

(2) If a person fails to comply with a subpoena so issued or a party or witness refuses to testify on any matters, the judge of the circuit court or of any county, on the application of the director, shall compel obedience by proceedings for contempt as in the case of disobedience of the requirements of a subpoena issued from such court or a refusal to testify therein.

(3) If the director has reason to believe that any person has engaged or is engaging in any violation of this 2007 Act, the director may issue an order, subject to ORS chapter 183, directed to the person to cease and desist from the violation, or require the person to pay compensation to consumers injured by the violation. The director may order compensation to consumers only upon a finding that enforcement of the rights of the consumers by private civil action would be so burdensome or expensive as to be impractical.

(4)(a) In addition to all other penalties and enforcement provisions provided by law, any person who violates or who procures, aids or abets in the violation of this 2007 Act shall be subject to a penalty of not more than $1,000 for every violation, which shall be paid to the General Fund of the State Treasury.

(b) Every violation is a separate offense and, in the case of a continuing violation, each day's continuance is a separate violation, but the maximum penalty for any occurrence shall not exceed $500,000.

(c) Civil penalties under this section shall be imposed as provided in ORS 183.745.

SECTION 14. In accordance with ORS chapter 183, the Director of the Department of Consumer and Business Services may adopt rules for the purpose of carrying out the provisions of this 2007 Act.

SECTION 15. Notwithstanding ORS 705.145 (2), (3) and (5), the Director of the Department of Consumer and Business Services can allocate as deemed appropriate the moneys derived pursuant to ORS 646.382 to 646.398, 650.005 to 650.100, 697.005 to 697.095, 697.602 to 697.842, 705.350 and 717.200 to 717.320 and 731.804 and ORS chapters 59, 645, 706 to 716, 722, 723, 725 and 726 to implement this 2007 Act.

SECTION 16. Section 12 of this 2007 Act becomes operative on January 1, 2008.

SECTION 17. Notwithstanding any other law limiting expenditures, the limitation on expenditures established by section 1, chapter 215, Oregon Laws 2007 (Enrolled House Bill 5014), for the biennium beginning July 1, 2007, as the maximum limit for payment of expenses from fees, money or other revenues, including Miscellaneous Receipts, but excluding lottery funds and federal funds, collected or received by the Department of Consumer and Business Services, is increased by $202,017 for the purpose of carrying out the provisions of this 2007 Act.

SECTION 18. This 2007 Act being necessary for the immediate preservation of the public peace, health and safety, an emergency is declared to exist, and this 2007 Act takes effect October 1, 2007.

Approved by the Governor July 12, 2007

Filed in the office of Secretary of State July 16, 2007

Effective date October 1, 2007

Oregon's Senate Bill 978 has restrictions surrounding when confidential personal information may be disclosed. It does not speak to any requirements in the event of an unauthorized disclosure that was a result of a breach of computer security.

Relating to Disclosure of Information–Senate Bill 978

This bill prohibits the disclosure of public records relating to criminal investigation or prosecution or to confinement of persons convicted of crimes unless personal identifiers have been deleted. It also increases the punishment for identity theft if personal information transferred relates to specified persons.

SECTION 1. ORS 135.815 is amended to read: 135.815. (1) Except as otherwise provided in ORS 135.855 and 135.873, the district attorney shall disclose to a represented defendant the following material and information within the possession or control of the district attorney:

(a) The names and addresses of persons whom the district attorney intends to call as witnesses at any stage of the trial, together with their relevant written or recorded statements or memoranda of any oral statements of such persons.

(b) Any written or recorded statements or memoranda of any oral statements made by the defendant, or made by a codefendant if the trial is to be a joint one.

(c) Any reports or statements of experts, made in connection with the particular case, including results of physical or mental examinations and of scientific tests, experiments or comparisons which the district attorney intends to offer in evidence at the trial.

(d) Any books, papers, documents, photographs or tangible objects:

(A) Which the district attorney intends to offer in evidence at the trial; or

(B) Which were obtained from or belong to the defendant.

(e) If actually known to the district attorney, any record of prior criminal convictions of persons whom the district attorney intends to call as witnesses at the trial; and the district attorney shall make a good faith effort to determine if such convictions have occurred.

(f) All prior convictions of the defendant known to the state that would affect the determination of the defendant's criminal history for sentencing under rules of the Oregon Criminal Justice Commission.

(2)(a) If a defendant is not represented by a lawyer, the district attorney shall disclose to the defendant all of the information described in subsection (1) of this section except for the { - addresses and telephone numbers - } { + personal identifiers + } of the victim and any witnesses.

(b) Notwithstanding paragraph (a) of this subsection, the district attorney shall disclose the { - addresses and telephone numbers - } { + personal identifiers + } of the victim and any witnesses if the trial court orders the disclosure. A trial court shall order the district attorney to disclose the { - addresses and telephone numbers - } { + personal identifiers + } of the victim and any witnesses if the trial court finds that:

(A) The defendant has requested the information; and

(B)(i) The victim or witness is a business or institution and disclosure of the information would not represent a risk of harm to the victim or witness; or

(ii) The need for the information cannot reasonably be met by other means.

(3)(a) Unless authorized by the trial court to disclose the information, a lawyer representing a defendant, or a representative of the lawyer, may not disclose to the defendant { - the address or telephone number - } { + personal identifiers + } of a victim or witness obtained under subsection (1) of this section.

(b) The trial court shall order the lawyer, or representative of the lawyer, to disclose to the defendant the { - address and telephone number - } { + personal identifiers + } of a victim or witness if the court finds that:

(A) The defendant's lawyer has requested the district attorney to disclose the information to the defendant;

(B) The district attorney has refused to disclose the information to the defendant; and

(C) The need for the information cannot reasonably be met by other means.

(4) As used in this section:

{ + (a) 'Personal identifiers' means a person's address, telephone number, Social Security number and date of birth and the identifying number of a person's depository account at a financial institution, as defined in ORS 706.008, or credit card account. + } { - (a) - } { + (b) + } 'Representative of the lawyer' has the meaning given that term in ORS 40.225. { - (b) - } { + (c) + } 'Represented defendant' means a defendant who is represented by a lawyer in a criminal action.

Senate Bill 643

This bill allows a state institution of higher education to contract with a private contractor to provide the service of facilitating disbursement of funds to students. It also imposes conditions if a student's personally identifiable information is necessary to administer disbursement.

House Bill 2103

This bill prohibits a person from selling, leasing, or renting a payment processing system that provides a customer receipt with more information about a customer than the customer's name and last five digits of the customer's credit or debit card number. It prohibits a person from creating customer receipts with more information about a customer than the customer's name and last five digits of customer's credit or debit card number. The bill requires a person who creates or retains a copy of a receipt that contains more information than the customer's name and last five numbers of credit or debit card to destroy receipt within a certain time. It authorizes the attorney general or district attorney to bring action to prevent violations; imposes civil penalty for violation of order or injunction; increases the civil penalty for unlawful credit or debit card solicitations; and allows for the awarding of attorneys' fees by the court.

Chapter 38: Pennsylvania

What I found to be very interesting about Pennsylvania's disclosure law is their part of encryption keys. While the law does provide for an exemption to the disclosure requirement if the data was encrypted, that exemption is nullified if the encryption keys are also compromised. The management of encryption keys, their storage, and their protection, is often an issue. From a standpoint of providing a high degree of protection of encrypted data, I find this to be a very interesting provision.

Senate Bill 712

This bill provides for the notification of residents whose personal information data was or may have been disclosed due to a security system breach, and imposing penalties.

The General Assembly of the Commonwealth of Pennsylvania hereby enacts as follows: Section 1. Short title. This act shall be known and may be cited as the Breach of Personal Information Notification Act. Section 2. Definitions. The following words and phrases when used in this act shall have the meanings given to them in this section unless the context clearly indicates otherwise: "Breach of the security of the system." The unauthorized access and acquisition of computerized data that MATERIALLY compromises the security or confidentiality of personal information maintained by the entity as part of a database of personal information regarding multiple individuals and that causes or the entity reasonably believes has caused or will cause loss or injury to any resident of this Commonwealth. Good faith acquisition of personal information by an employee or agent of the entity for the purposes of the entity is not a breach of the security of the system if the personal information is not used for a purpose other than the lawful purpose of the entity and is not subject to further unauthorized disclosure. "Business." A sole proprietorship, partnership, corporation, association or other group, however organized and whether or not organized to operate at a profit, including a financial institution organized, chartered or holding a

license or authorization certificate under the laws of this Commonwealth, any other state, the United States or any other country, or the parent or the subsidiary of a financial institution. The term includes an entity that destroys records. "Encryption." The use of an algorithmic process to transform data into a form in which there is a low probability of assigning meaning without use of a confidential process or key.

"Entity." A State agency, a political subdivision of the Commonwealth or an individual or a business doing business in this Commonwealth. "Individual." A natural person. "Notice." May be provided by one ANY of the following methods of notification:

(1) Written or telephonic notice to the last known home address or telephone number for the individual.

(2) TELEPHONIC NOTICE IF THE CUSTOMER CAN BE REASONABLY EXPECTED TO RECEIVE IT AND THE NOTICE IS GIVEN IN A CLEAR AND CONSPICUOUS MANNER, DESCRIBES THE INCIDENT IN GENERAL TERMS AND VERIFIES PERSONAL INFORMATION BUT DOES NOT REQUIRE THE CUSTOMER TO PROVIDE PERSONAL INFORMATION AND THE CUSTOMER IS PROVIDED WITH A TELEPHONE NUMBER TO CALL OR INTERNET WEBSITE TO VISIT FOR FURTHER INFORMATION OR ASSISTANCE.

(2) Electronic

(3) E-MAIL notice, if a prior business relationship exists and the person or entity has a valid electronic mail E-MAIL address for the individual.

(4) (i) Substitute notice, if the entity demonstrates one of the following:

(A) The cost of providing notice would exceed $250,000 $100,000.

(B) The affected class of subject persons to be notified exceeds 500,000 175,000.

(C) The entity does not have sufficient contact information. (ii) Substitute notice shall consist of all of the following:

(A) E-mail notice when the entity has an e-mail address for the subject persons.

(B) Conspicuous posting of the notice on the entity's Internet website, if the entity maintains one.

(C) Notification to major Statewide media. "Personal information."

(1) An individual's first name or first initial and last name in combination with and linked to any one or more of the following data elements, when the name and data elements are not encrypted or redacted:

(i) Social Security number.

(ii) Driver's license number or a State identification card number issued in lieu of a driver's license.

(iii) Financial account number, credit or debit card number, in combination with any required security code, access code or password that would permit access to an individual's financial account.

(2) The term does not include publicly available information that is lawfully made available to the general public from Federal, State or local government records. "Records." Any material, regardless of the physical form, on which information is recorded or preserved by any means, including in written or spoken words, graphically depicted, printed or electromagnetically transmitted. The term does not include publicly available directories containing information an individual has voluntarily consented to have publicly disseminated

or listed, such as name, address or telephone number. "Redact." The term includes, but is not limited to, alteration or truncation such that no more than the last four digits of a Social Security number, driver's license number,

State identification card number or account number is accessible as part of the data. "State agency." Any agency, board, commission, authority or department of the Commonwealth and the General Assembly.

Section 3. Disclosure of computerized data NOTIFICATION OF BREACH.

(a) General rule.--An entity, or a vendor on behalf of another entity, that maintains, stores, manages, owns or licenses THAT MAINTAINS, STORES OR MANAGES computerized data that includes personal information shall disclose PROVIDE NOTICE OF any breach of the security of the system following discovery or notification of the breach of the security of the system to any resident of this Commonwealth whose unencrypted and unredacted personal information was or is reasonably believed to have been accessed and acquired by an unauthorized person. Except as provided in section 5 4 or in order to take any measures necessary to determine the scope of the breach and to restore the reasonable integrity of the data system, the disclosure NOTICE shall be made without unreasonable delay. FOR THE PURPOSE OF THIS SECTION, A RESIDENT OF THIS COMMONWEALTH MAY BE DETERMINED TO BE AN INDIVIDUAL WHOSE PRINCIPAL MAILING ADDRESS, AS REFLECTED IN THE COMPUTERIZED DATA WHICH IS MAINTAINED, STORED OR MANAGED BY THE ENTITY, IS IN THIS COMMONWEALTH.

(b) Encrypted information.--An entity must disclose PROVIDE NOTICE OF the breach if encrypted information is accessed and acquired in an unencrypted form, if the security breach is linked to a breach of the security of the encryption or if the security breach involves a person with access to the encryption key.

(C) VENDOR NOTIFICATION.--A VENDOR THAT MAINTAINS, STORES OR MANAGES COMPUTERIZED DATA ON BEHALF OF ANOTHER ENTITY SHALL PROVIDE NOTICE OF ANY BREACH OF THE SECURITY SYSTEM FOLLOWING DISCOVERY BY THE VENDOR TO THE ENTITY ON WHOSE BEHALF THE VENDOR MAINTAINS, STORES OR MANAGES THE DATA. THE ENTITY SHALL BE RESPONSIBLE FOR MAKING THE DETERMINATIONS AND DISCHARGING ANY REMAINING DUTIES UNDER THIS ACT.

Section 4. Disclosure of maintained computerized data.

An entity that maintains computerized data that includes personal information that the entity does not own or license shall notify the owner or licensee of the information of any breach of the security of the data immediately following discovery, if the personal information was or is reasonably believed to have been accessed and acquired by an unauthorized person. Section 5 4. Exceptions. The notification required by this act may be delayed if a law enforcement agency determines and advises the entity in writing specifically referencing this section that the notification will impede a criminal or civil investigation. The notification required by this act shall be made after the law enforcement agency determines that it will not compromise the investigation or national or homeland security. Section 6 5. Notification of consumer reporting agencies. When an entity provides notification under this act to more than 1,000 persons at one time, the entity shall also notify, without unreasonable delay, all consumer reporting agencies that compile and maintain files on consumers on a nationwide basis, as defined in section 603 of the Fair Credit Reporting Act (Public Law 91-508, 15 U.S.C. §1681a), of the timing, distribution and number of notices. Section 7 6. Preemption. This act deals with subject matter that is of Statewide concern, and it is the intent of the General Assembly that this act shall supersede and preempt all rules, regulations, codes, statutes or ordinances of all cities, counties, municipalities and other local agencies within this Commonwealth regarding the matters expressly set forth in this act.

Section 8 7. Notice exemption. (a) Information privacy or security policy.--An entity that maintains its own notification procedures as part of an information privacy or security policy for the treatment of personal information and is consistent with the notice requirements of this act shall be deemed to be in compliance with the notification requirements of this act if it notifies subject persons in accordance with its policies in the event of a breach of security of the system.

(b) Compliance with Federal requirements.-- (1) A financial institution that complies with the notification requirements prescribed by the Federal Interagency Guidance on Response Programs for Unauthorized Access to Customer Information and Customer Notice is deemed to be in compliance with this act. (2) An entity that complies with the notification requirements or procedures pursuant to the rules, regulations, procedures or guidelines established by the entity's primary or functional Federal regulator shall be in compliance with this act. Section 9 8. Civil relief. A willful and knowing violation of this act shall be deemed to be an unfair or deceptive act or practice in violation of the act of December 17, 1968 (P.L.1224, No.387), known as the Unfair Trade Practices and Consumer Protection Law. The Office of Attorney General shall have exclusive authority to bring an action under the Unfair Trade Practices and Consumer Protection Law for a violation of this act. Section 10 29. Applicability. This act shall apply to the discovery or notification of a breach in the security of personal information data that occurs on or after the effective date of this section.

Relating to confidentiality of Social Security numbers - Senate Bill 703

The General Assembly of the Commonwealth of Pennsylvania hereby enacts as follows:

Section 1. Privacy of Social Security numbers.

(a) General rule.--A person or entity or State agency or political subdivision shall not do any of the following:

(1) Publicly post or publicly display in any manner an individual's Social Security number. "Publicly post" or "publicly display" means to intentionally communicate or otherwise make available to the general public.

(2) Print an individual's Social Security number on any card required for the individual to access products or services provided by the person, entity or State agency or political subdivision.

(3) Require an individual to transmit his or her Social Security number over the Internet unless the connection is secure or the Social Security number is encrypted.

(4) Require an individual to use his or her Social Security number to access an Internet World Wide website unless a password or unique personal identification number or other authentication device is also required to access the World Wide website.

(5) Print an individual's Social Security number on any materials that are mailed to the individual unless Federal or State law requires the Social Security number to be on the document to be mailed. Notwithstanding this provision, applications and forms sent by mail may include Social Security numbers.

(b) Exception.--Except as provided in subsection (c), subsection (a) applies only to the use of Social Security numbers on or after July 1, 2003 2006.

(c) Use prior to July 1, 2003 2006.--A person or entity, not <-- including a State agency or political subdivision, that has used, prior to July 1, 2003 2006, an individual's Social Security number in a manner inconsistent with subsection (a) may continue using that individual's Social Security number in that manner on or after July 1, 2003 2006, if all of the following conditions are met:

(1) The use of the Social Security number is continuous. If the use is stopped for any reason, subsection (a) shall apply.

(2) The individual is provided an annual disclosure, commencing in the year 2003 2006, that informs the individual that he or she has the right to stop the use of his or her Social Security number in a manner prohibited by subsection (a).

(3) A written request by an individual to stop the use of his or her Social Security number in a manner prohibited by subsection (a) shall be implemented within 30 days of the receipt of the request. There shall be no fee or charge for implementing the request.

(4) A person or entity or State agency or political subdivision shall not deny services to an individual because the individual makes a written request pursuant to this subsection.

(d) Internal verification.--This section does not prevent the collection, use or release of a Social Security number as required by Federal or State law or the use of a Social Security number for internal verification or administrative purposes., administrative purposes or for law enforcement investigations.

(e) Penalty – Actions in violation of this act shall be deemed a summary offense and shall be punishable by a fine of not less than $50 and not more than $500. Fines under this section shall be

distributed equally between the individual whose Social Security number was unlawfully disclosed or requested and the office of the Attorney General for future identity theft prevention.

Section 2. Applicability. The provisions of this act shall not apply to:

(1) A financial institution, as defined by Section 509(3) of the Gramm-Leach-Bliley Act (Public Law 106-102, 15 U.S.C. §6809(3)) or regulations adopted by agencies as designated by Section 504(A) of the Gramm-Leach-Bliley Act subject to Title V of the Gramm-Leach-Bliley Act

(2) A covered entity, as defined by regulations promulgated at 45 CFR PTS. 160 (related to general administration requirements) and 164 relating to security and privacy) pursuant to subtitle of the health insurance portability and accountability act of 1996. (Public Law 104-191, 42 U.S.C. 110 STAT. 1936).

(3) An entity subject to the Fair Credit Report Act. (PUBLIC LAW 91-508, 15 U.S.C. §1681, ET SEQ.).Section 2 3. Effective date. This act shall take effect JULY 1, 2006.

H.R. 529

This bill urges the president and Congress of the United States to amend the provision of law that requires applicants for hunting and fishing licenses to provide their Social Security numbers or other identifying numbers by exempting applicants age sixteen and under.

House Bill 2460

This bill limits the availability of an individual's Social Security number under certain circumstances in an attempt to reduce identity theft.

House Bill 1893

This bill prohibits the Commonwealth of Pennsylvania and its political subdivisions from collecting and using Social Security numbers under certain circumstances, and provides for enforcement by the state attorney general.

Chapter 39: Rhode Island

In addition to their disclosure law, Rhode Island is one of several states that allows consumers to place a freeze on their credit report if their personal information has been stolen.

Identity Theft Protection: H 6191

SECTION 1. Title 11 of the General Laws entitled "Criminal Offenses" is hereby amended by adding thereto the following chapter:

CHAPTER 49.2

IDENTITY THEFT PROTECTION

11-49.2-1. Short title. – This chapter shall be known and may be cited as the "Rhode Island Identity Theft Protection Act of 2005."

11-49.2-2. Legislative findings. – It is hereby found and declared as follows:

(1) There is a growing concern regarding the possible theft of an individual's identity and a resulting need for measures to protect the privacy of personal information. It is the intent of the general assembly to ensure that personal information about Rhode Island residents is protected.

To that end, the purpose of this chapter is to require businesses that own or license personal information about Rhode Islanders to provide reasonable security for that information. For the purpose of this chapter, the phrase "owns or licenses" is intended to include, but is not limited to, personal information that a business retains as part of the business' internal customer account or for the purpose of using that information in transactions with the person to whom the information relates.

(2) A business that owns or licenses computerized unencrypted personal information about a Rhode Island resident shall implement and maintain reasonable security procedures and practices appropriate to the nature of the information, to protect the personal information from unauthorized access, destruction, use, modification, or disclosure.

(3) A business that discloses computerized unencrypted personal information about a Rhode Island resident pursuant to a contract with a nonaffiliated third-party shall require by contract that the third-party implement and maintain reasonable security procedures and practices appropriate to the nature of the information, to protect the personal information from unauthorized access, destruction, use, modification, or disclosure.

11-49.2-3. Notification of breach. -- (a) Any state agency or person that owns, maintains or licenses computerized data that includes personal information, shall disclose any breach of the security of the system which poses a significant risk of identity theft following discovery or notification of the breach in the security of the data to any resident of Rhode Island whose unencrypted personal information was, or is reasonably believed to have been, acquired by an unauthorized person or a person without authority, to acquire said information. The disclosure shall be made in the most expedient time possible and without unreasonable delay, consistent with the legitimate needs of law enforcement, as provided in subdivision (c), or any measures necessary to determine the scope of the breach and restore the reasonable integrity of the data system.

(b) Any state agency or person that maintains computerized unencrypted data that includes personal information that the state agency or person does not own shall notify the owner or licensee of the information of any breach of the security of the data which poses a significant risk of identity theft immediately, following discovery, if the personal information was, or is reasonably believed to have been, acquired by an unauthorized person. (c) The notification required by this section may be delayed if a law enforcement agency determines that the notification will impede a criminal investigation. The notification required by this section shall be made after the law enforcement agency determines that it will not compromise the investigation. (d) The notification must be prompt and reasonable following the determination of the breach unless otherwise provided in this section. Any state agency or person required to make notification under this section and who fails to do so promptly following the determination of a breach or receipt of notice from law enforcement as provided for is subsection (c) is liable for a fine as set forth in section 11-49.2-6.11-49.2-4. Notification of breach – Consultation with law enforcement. – Notification of a breach is not required if, after an appropriate investigation or after consultation with relevant federal, state, or local law enforcement agencies, a determination is made that the breach has not and will not likely result in a significant risk of identity theft to the individuals whose personal information has been acquired.

11-49.2-5. Definitions. – The following definitions apply to this section: (a) "Person" shall include any individual, partnership association, corporation or joint venture.

(b) For purposes for this section, "breach of the security of the system" means unauthorized acquisition of unencrypted computerized data that compromises the security, confidentiality, or integrity of personal information maintained by the state agency or person. Good faith acquisition of personal information by an employee or agent of the agency for the purposes of the agency is not a breach of the security of the system; provided, that the personal information is not used or subject to further unauthorized disclosure. (c) For purposes of this section, "personal information" means an individual's first name or first initial and last name in combination with any one or more of the following data elements, when either the name or the data elements are not encrypted:

(1) Social Security number;
(2) Driver's license number or Rhode Island Identification Card number;

(3) Account number, credit or debit card number, in combination with any required security code, access code, or password that would permit access to an individual's financial account.

(d) For purposes of this section, "notice" may be provided by one of the following methods:

(1) Written notice; (2) Electronic notice, if the notice provided is consistent with the provisions regarding electronic records and signatures set for the in Section 7001 of Title 15 of the United States Code; (3) Substitute notice, if the state agency or person demonstrates that the cost of providing notice would exceed twenty five thousand dollars ($25,000), or that the affected class of subject persons to be notified exceeds fifty thousand (50,000), or the state agency or person does not have sufficient contact information. Substitute notice shall consist of all of the following: (A) E-mail notice when the state agency or person has an e-mail address for the subject persons; (B) Conspicuous posting of the notice on the state agency's or person's website page, if the state agency or person maintains one; (C) Notification to major statewide media.

11-49.2-6. Penalties for violation. – (a) Each violation of this chapter is a civil violation for which a penalty of not more than a hundred dollars ($100) per occurrence and not more than twenty-five thousand dollars ($25,000) may be adjudged against a defendant.

(b) No Waiver of Notification – Any waiver of a provision of this section is contrary to public policy and is void and unenforceable. 11-49.2-7. Agencies with security breach procedures. – Any state agency or person that maintains its own security breach procedures as part of an information security policy for the treatment of personal information and otherwise complies with the timing requirements of section 11-49.2-3, shall be deemed to be in compliance with the security breach notification requirements of section 11-49.2-3, provided such person notifies subject persons in accordance with such person's policies in the event of a breach of security. Any person that maintains such a security breach procedure pursuant to the rules, regulations, procedures or guidelines established by the

primary or functional regulator, as defined in 15 USC 6809(2), shall be deemed to be in compliance with the security breach notification requirements of this section, provided such person notifies subject persons in accordance with the policies or the rules, regulations, procedures or guidelines established by the primary or functional regulator in the event of a breach of security of the system. A financial institution, trust company, credit union or its affiliates that is subject to and examined for, and found in compliance with the Federal Interagency Guidelines on Response Programs for Unauthorized Access to Customer Information and Customer Notice shall be deemed in compliance with this chapter. A provider of health care, health care service plan, health insurer, or a covered entity governed by the medical privacy and security rules issued by the federal Department of Health and Human Services, Parts 160 and 164 of Title 45 of the Code of Federal Regulations, established pursuant to the Health Insurance Portability and Accountability Act of 1996 (HIPAA) shall be deemed in compliance with this chapter. SECTION 2. This act shall take effect on March 1, 2006.

The Consumer Empowerment and Identity Theft Prevention Act of 2006–House Bill 7148

Creates the Consumer Empowerment and Identity Theft Prevention Act of 2006 and provides protection for Social Security numbers.

This bill created the consumer Empowerment and Identity Theft Prevention Act of 2006. This act allows consumers, including business consumers, to put a security freeze on their credit and provides for the lifting of the freeze of credit, notice requirements, and guidelines for the consumer reporting agency, disclosures, and penalties.

House Bill 6811

This bill makes unlawful certain modifications to computer settings, control of another's computer, and deceptive sales of software. The act also provides for a civil action for violations under this chapter.

House Bill 7066

This bill prohibits any person, firm, corporation, or other business entity that offers discount cards for purchases made at any business maintained by the offer or from requiring that a person who applies for a discount card furnish his or her Social Security number or motor vehicle operator's license as a condition precedent to the application for the consumer discount card.

House Bill 5103

This bill establishes rules of disclosure of personal information about insurers, by businesses to third parties, rules of notification to consumers of breaches in the security protecting consumer identification information as well as civil penalties and damages for violation of the disclosure and notification rules.

Senate Bill 464

This bill establishes rules concerning the disclosure of personal information about insurers, by businesses to third parties, rules of notification to consumers of breaches in the security protecting consumer identification information as well as civil penalties and damages for violation of the disclosure and notification rules.

House Bill 5223

This bill establishes rules surrounding the disclosure of personal information about insurers, by businesses to third parties, rules of notification to consumers of breaches in the security protecting consumer identification information as well as civil penalties and damages for violation of the disclosure and notification rules.

Chapter 40: South Carolina

South Carolina is another one of the nine states that have adopted their own data breach disclosure laws in the 2007–2008 timeframe. While the data breach laws do vary among the individual states, businesses with a multi-state clientele are adopting data security policies

House Bill 3035

TO AMEND THE CODE OF LAWS OF SOUTH CAROLINA, 1976, SO AS TO ENACT THE "IDENTITY THEFT PROTECTION ACT", BY ADDING CHAPTER 20 TO TITLE 37 PROVIDING FOR PROTECTIONS IN CONNECTION WITH CONSUMER CREDIT-REPORTING AGENCIES AND WITH THE USE AND COMMUNICATION OF A CONSUMER'S SOCIAL SECURITY NUMBER, IMPOSITION OF A SECURITY FREEZE ON A CONSUMER'S CREDIT REPORT, PRESCRIPTION OF MEASURES FOR DISPOSAL OF PERSONAL IDENTIFYING INFORMATION AND DISCLOSURE OF UNAUTHORIZED ACCESS TO PERSONAL IDENTIFYING INFORMATION, AND CIVIL DAMAGES, INCLUDING ATTORNEY'S FEES AND COSTS AND INJUNCTIVE RELIEF; BY REDESIGNATING THE FAMILY PRIVACY PROTECTION ACT OF CHAPTER 2, TITLE 30, AS ARTICLE 1 AND BY ADDING ARTICLE 3 PROVIDING FOR PROTECTION OF PERSONAL IDENTIFYING INFORMATION PRIVACY IN CONNECTION WITH A PUBLIC BODY AND ITS USE AND COMMUNICATION OF A RESIDENT'S SOCIAL SECURITY NUMBER, PRESCRIPTION FOR DISCLOSURE OF SOCIAL SECURITY INFORMATION AND IDENTIFYING INFORMATION BY AND TO CERTAIN PUBLIC BODIES, PROHIBITION OF REQUIRING THE USE OF PERSONAL IDENTIFYING INFORMATION ON A MORTGAGE AND IN PREPARATION OF DOCUMENTS FOR PUBLIC FILING; AND PROCEDURE FOR REDACTING CERTAIN PERSONAL IDENTIFYING INFORMATION FROM PUBLIC RECORDS; BY ADDING SECTION 16-13-540

SO AS TO PROVIDE FOR THE EXPUNCTION OF THE CRIMINAL RECORD OF A NAMED INDIVIDUAL INCURRED AS A RESULT OF THE UNLAWFUL USE OF HIS IDENTIFYING INFORMATION; BY ADDING SECTION 16-13-550 SO AS TO PROVIDE FOR REPORTING OF THE CRIME OF FINANCIAL IDENTITY FRAUD TO THE LOCAL LAW ENFORCEMENT AGENCY AND REFERENCE BY THE LOCAL AGENCY TO THE AGENCY WITH JURISDICTION TO INVESTIGATE AND PROSECUTE; BY AMENDING SECTION 16-13-510, AS AMENDED, RELATING TO THE OFFENSE OF FINANCIAL IDENTITY FRAUD, SO AS TO INCLUDE THE USE OF ANOTHER'S INFORMATION TO OBTAIN ANYTHING OF VALUE, INCLUDING CREDIT, TO AVOID LEGAL CONSEQUENCES, OR TO OBTAIN EMPLOYMENT, AND TO PROVIDE, FOR EXCEPTIONS, TO FURTHER DEFINE "IDENTIFYING INFORMATION", AND TO PROVIDE FOR CRIMINAL PENALTIES, INCLUDING RESTITUTION; BY AMENDING SECTION 16-13-520, RELATING TO PROSECUTION OF THE CRIME OF FINANCIAL IDENTITY FRAUD, SO AS TO FURTHER PROVIDE FOR THE COUNTY IN WHICH THE CRIME IS CONSIDERED TO HAVE BEEN COMMITTED; BY ADDING SECTION 1-11-490 SO AS TO PROVIDE FOR DISCLOSURE BY AN AGENCY OF THIS STATE OF UNAUTHORIZED ACCESS TO THE PERSONAL IDENTIFYING INFORMATION OF A RESIDENT WHOSE INFORMATION THE AGENCY OWNS OR LICENSES AND TO PROVIDE FOR CIVIL DAMAGES, ATTORNEY'S FEES, AND INJUNCTIVE RELIEF; AND TO PROVIDE VARIOUS EFFECTIVE DATES.

Be it enacted by the General Assembly of the State of South Carolina:

SECTION 1. This act may be cited as the "Identity Theft Protection Act".

SECTION 2. Title 37 of the 1976 Code is amended by adding:

"CHAPTER 20

Identity Theft Protection

Section 37-20-10. For purposes of this chapter:

(1) 'Consumer' means an individual residing in the State of South Carolina who undertakes a transaction for personal, family, or household purposes.

(2) 'Consumer credit-reporting agency' means a person that, for monetary fees or dues, or on a cooperative nonprofit basis, regularly engages in whole or in part in the practice of assembling or evaluating consumer credit information or other information about consumers for the purpose of furnishing consumer reports to third parties.

(3) 'Consumer report' or 'credit report' means any written, oral, electronic, or other communication of information by a consumer credit-reporting agency regarding a consumer's creditworthiness, credit standing, credit capacity, character, debts, general reputation, personal characteristics, or mode of living that is used or expected to be used or collected in whole or in part for the purpose of establishing a consumer's eligibility for any of the following:

(a) credit to be used primarily for personal, family, or household purposes;

(b) employment purposes means the use of a consumer report for the purpose of evaluating a consumer for employment, promotion, reassignment, or retention as an employee;

(c) any other purpose authorized pursuant to 15 U.S.C. Section 168lb.

'Consumer report' or 'credit report' does not include a report containing information as to a transaction between the consumer and the person making the report; an authorization or approval by the issuer of a credit card or similar device, directly or indirectly, of a specific extension of credit; or a report in which a person conveys an adverse decision in response to a request from a third party to make a specific extension of credit, directly or indirectly, to the consumer, if the third party advises the consumer of the name and address of the person to whom the request was made and the person makes the required disclosures to the consumer pursuant to the provisions of the federal 'Fair Credit Reporting Act'.

(4) 'Credit card' has the same meaning as in Section 103 of the Truth in Lending Act, 15 U.S.C. Section 160 and includes a lender credit card, as defined in Section 37-1-301(16) and a seller credit card, as defined in Section 37-1-301(26).

(5) 'Creditworthiness' means an entry in a consumer's credit file that affects the ability of a consumer to obtain and retain credit, employment, business or professional licenses, investment opportunities, or insurance. Entries affecting creditworthiness include, but are not limited to, payment information, defaults, judgments, liens, bankruptcies, collections, records of arrest and indictments, and multiple credit inquiries.

(6) 'Debit card' means a card or device issued by a financial institution to a consumer for use in initiating an electronic fund transfer from the account holding assets of the consumer at that financial institution, for the purpose of transferring money between accounts or obtaining money, property, labor, or services.

(7) 'Disposal' means the:

(a) discarding or abandonment of records containing personal identifying information; or

(b) sale, donation, discarding, or transfer of any medium, including computer equipment or computer media, containing records of personal identifying information, other nonpaper media upon which records of personal identifying information are stored, or other equipment for nonpaper storage of information.

(8) 'Person' means an individual, sole proprietorship, partnership, corporation, trust, estate, cooperative, association, government or governmental subdivision or agency, or other entity.

(9) 'Personal identifying information' means an individual's first name or first initial and last name in combination with identifying information as defined in Section 16-13-510(C). 'Personal identifying information' does not include publicly available directories containing information an individual has voluntarily consented to have publicly disseminated or listed, including name, address, and telephone number.

(10) 'Proper identification' means information generally considered sufficient to identify a person. If a person is unable reasonably to identify himself or herself with the information described in item (9), a consumer reporting agency may require additional information concerning the consumer's employment and personal or family history in order to verify the consumer's identity.

(11) 'Records' means material on which written, drawn, spoken, visual, or electromagnetic information is recorded or preserved, regardless of physical form or characteristics.

(12) 'Security breach' means an incident of unauthorized access to, and acquisition of, records or data containing personal identifying information that compromises the security, confidentiality, or integrity of personal identifying information maintained by a person. Good faith acquisition of personal identifying information by an employee or agent of the person for a legitimate purpose is not a security breach, if the personal identifying information is not used for a purpose other than a lawful purpose of the person and is not subject to further unauthorized disclosure.

(13) 'Security freeze' means a notice placed in a consumer credit report, at the request of the consumer and subject to certain exceptions, that prohibits the consumer credit-reporting agency from releasing a credit report containing all or any part of the consumer's credit report or any information derived from it without the express authorization of the consumer.

Section 37-20-20. (A) Except as provided in subsection (B) of this section, a person may not:

(1) intentionally communicate or otherwise make available to the general public a consumer's social security number or a portion of it containing six digits or more;

(2) intentionally print or imbed a consumer's social security number or any portion of it containing six digits or more on any card required for the consumer to access products or services provided by the person;

(3) require a consumer to transmit his social security number or a portion of it containing six digits or more over the Internet, unless the connection is secure or the social security number is encrypted;

(4) require a consumer to use his social security number or a portion of it containing six digits or more to access an Internet website, unless a password or unique personal identification number or other authentication device is also required to access the Internet website;

(5) print a consumer's social security number or a portion of it containing six digits or more on materials that are mailed to the individual, unless state or federal law requires the social security number to be on the document to be mailed;

(6) sell, lease, loan, trade, rent, or otherwise intentionally disclose a consumer's social security number or a portion of it containing six digits or more to a third party without written consent to the

disclosure from the consumer, unless the third party seeking disclosure of the social security number does so for a legitimate business purpose. A legitimate business purpose of the third party includes locating an individual to provide a benefit to that individual, such as a pension, insurance, or unclaimed property benefit, or to find an individual who is missing or a lost relative, or to serve civil process. A legitimate purpose of the third party does not include the bulk purchase or rental of social security numbers or use in marketing.

(B) This section does not apply:

(1) if a social security number is included in an application or in documents related to an enrollment process, or to establish an account, contract, or policy, or to confirm the accuracy of the social security number for the purpose of obtaining a credit report pursuant to the federal Fair Credit Reporting Act. A social security number that is permitted to be mailed pursuant to this section may not be printed, in whole or in part, on a postcard or other mailer not requiring an envelope or may not be visible on or through the envelope;

(2) to the collection, use, or release of a social security number for internal verification or administrative purposes;

(3) to the opening of an account or the provision of or payment for a product or service authorized by a consumer;

(4) to the collection, use, or release of a social security number to investigate or prevent fraud, conduct background checks, conduct social or scientific research, collect a debt, or obtain a credit report from or furnish data to a consumer reporting agency, pursuant to the federal Fair Credit Reporting Act;

(5) to a person acting pursuant to a court order, warrant, subpoena, or other legal process;

(6) to a person providing the social security number to a federal, state, or local government entity, including a law enforcement agency or court, or their agents or assigns.

(C) A violation of this section is a violation of Section 37-20-60.

Section 37-20-30. (A) A consumer who has reason to believe he is the victim of financial identify fraud, as evidenced by a copy of a valid police report, investigative report, or complaint made pursuant to Section 16-13-510, may place a security freeze on his credit report by making a request in writing by certified mail to a consumer credit-reporting agency. A security freeze prohibits the consumer credit-reporting agency from releasing the consumer's credit report or information from it without the express authorization of the consumer. If a security freeze is in place, a consumer credit-reporting agency may not release the consumer's credit report or information to a third party without prior express authorization from the consumer. This subsection does not prevent a consumer credit-reporting agency from advising a third party that a security freeze is in effect with respect to the consumer's credit report.

(B) A consumer credit-reporting agency shall place a security freeze on a consumer's credit report no later than five business days after receiving a written request from the consumer.

(C) The consumer credit-reporting agency shall send a written confirmation of the security freeze to the consumer within ten business days of placing the freeze and, at the same time, provide the consumer with a unique personal identification number or password, other than the consumer's social security number, to be used by the consumer when providing authorization for the release of the consumer's credit report for a specific period of time.

(D) If the consumer wishes to allow the consumer's credit report to be accessed for a specific period of time while a freeze is in place, the consumer shall communicate to the consumer credit-reporting agency:

(1) proper identification;

(2) the unique personal identification number or password provided by the consumer credit-reporting agency pursuant to subsection (C) of this section;

(3) the request that the freeze be lifted temporarily and proper information regarding the time period for which the report must be available to users of the credit report or to only a properly identified user.

(E) A consumer credit-reporting agency may develop procedures involving the use of telephone, facsimile machine, the Internet, or another electronic medium to receive and process a request from a consumer to temporarily lift a freeze on a credit report pursuant to this section.

(F) A consumer credit-reporting agency that receives a request from a consumer to lift temporarily a freeze on a credit report pursuant to this section shall comply with the request no later than three business days after receiving the request.

(G) A consumer credit-reporting agency shall remove or lift temporarily a freeze placed on a consumer's credit report only:

(1) upon the consumer's request, pursuant to this section;

(2) if the consumer's credit report was frozen due to a material misrepresentation of fact by the consumer. If a consumer credit-reporting agency intends to remove a freeze upon a consumer's credit report pursuant to this item, the consumer credit-reporting agency shall notify the consumer in writing five business days before removing the freeze on the consumer's credit report.

(H) If a third party requests access to a consumer credit report on which a security freeze is in effect and this request is in connection with an application for credit or other use and the consumer does not allow the consumer's credit report to be accessed for that specific period of time, the third party may treat the application as incomplete.

(I) If a consumer requests a security freeze pursuant to this section, the consumer credit-reporting agency shall disclose to the consumer the process for placing and temporarily lifting a security freeze and the process for allowing access to information from the consumer's credit report for a specific period of time while the security freeze is in place.

(J) A security freeze must remain in place until the consumer requests that the security freeze be removed. A consumer credit-reporting agency shall remove a security freeze within three business days of receiving a request for removal from the consumer, who provides:

(1) proper identification;

(2) the unique personal identification number or password provided by the consumer credit-reporting agency pursuant to subsection (C) of this section.

(K) A consumer credit-reporting agency shall require proper identification of the person making a request to place or remove a security freeze.

(L) If a security freeze is in place, a consumer credit-reporting agency may not change any of the following official information in a credit report without sending a written confirmation of the change to the consumer within thirty days of the change being posted to the consumer's file: name, date of birth, social security number, and address. Written confirmation is not required for technical modifications of a consumer's official information, including name and street abbreviations, complete spellings, or transposition of numbers or letters. In the case of an address change, the written confirmation must be sent to both the new address and the former address.

(M) The provisions of this section do not apply to the use of a consumer credit report by a:

(1) person, or the person's subsidiary, affiliate, agent, subcontractor, or assignee with which the consumer has, or before assignment had, an account, contract, or debtor-creditor relationship for the purposes of reviewing the account or collecting the financial obligation owing for the account, contract, or debt;

(2) subsidiary, affiliate, agent, assignee, or prospective assignee of a person to whom access has been granted pursuant to subsection (D) of this section for purposes of facilitating the extension of credit or other permissible use;

(3) person acting pursuant to a court order, warrant, or subpoena;

(4) state or local agency, or its agents or assigns, which administers a program for establishing and enforcing child support obligations;

(5) state or local agency, or its agents or assigns, acting to investigate fraud, including Medicaid fraud, or acting to investigate or collect delinquent taxes or assessments, including interest and penalties, unpaid court orders or to fulfill any of its other statutory responsibilities;

(6) federal, state, or local governmental entity, including law enforcement agency or court, their agent or assigns;

(7) person for the purposes of prescreening as defined by the federal Fair Credit Reporting Act;

(8) person for the sole purpose of providing for a credit file monitoring subscription service to which the consumer has subscribed;

(9) consumer reporting agency for the purpose of providing a consumer with a copy of the consumer's credit report upon the consumer's request;

(10) depository financial institution for checking, savings, and investment accounts.

(N) The following persons are not required to place in a credit report a security freeze pursuant to this section; except that any person exempt pursuant to the provisions of item (3) of this subsection is subject to a security freeze placed on a credit report by another consumer credit-reporting agency from which it obtains information:

(1) a check services or fraud prevention services company, which reports on incidents of fraud or issues authorizations for the purpose of approving or processing negotiable instruments, electronic fund transfers, or similar methods of payments;

(2) a deposit account information service company, which issues reports regarding account closures due to fraud, substantial overdrafts, ATM abuse, or other similar negative information regarding a consumer to inquiring banks or other financial institutions for use only in reviewing a consumer request for a deposit account at the inquiring bank or financial institution;

(3) a consumer reporting agency that:

(a) acts only to resell credit information by assembling and merging information contained in a database of one or more credit-reporting agencies; and

(b) does not maintain a permanent database of credit information from which new credit reports are produced.

(O) A consumer credit-reporting agency may not charge a fee to a victim of identity theft who has submitted a copy of a valid investigative or incident report or complaint with a law enforcement agency about the unlawful use of the victim's personal identifying information by another person.

(P) At any time that a consumer is required to receive a summary of rights required pursuant to Section 609 of the federal Fair Credit Reporting Act, the following notice must be included: 'South Carolina Consumers Have the Right to Obtain a Security Freeze. You have a right to place a security freeze on your credit report pursuant to South Carolina law. The security freeze prohibits a consumer credit-reporting agency from releasing information in your credit report without your express authorization. A security freeze must be requested in writing by certified mail. The security freeze is designed to prevent credit, loans, and services from being approved in your name without your consent. However, you should be aware that using a security freeze to take control over who gains access to the personal and financial information in your credit report may delay, interfere with, or prohibit the timely approval of a later request or application you make regarding new loans, credit, mortgage, insurance, rental housing, employment, investment, license, cellular phone, utilities, digital signature, Internet credit card transactions, or other services, including an extension of credit at point of sale. You can remove a freeze or authorize temporary access for a specific period of time by contacting the consumer reporting agency and providing all of the following:

(1) your personal identification number or password provided to you by the agency;

(2) proper identification to verify your identity; and

(3) proper information regarding the period of time you want your report available to users of the credit report. The consumer credit-reporting agency may not charge any amount to a victim of identity theft who has submitted a copy of a valid investigative or incident report or complaint with a law enforcement agency about the unlawful use of the victim's identifying information by another

person. You have a right to bring a civil action against a consumer credit-reporting agency who violates your rights pursuant to the credit reporting laws.'

(Q)(1) A consumer credit-reporting agency that willfully violates a provision of this section is liable for three times the amount of actual damages or one thousand dollars for each incident, whichever is greater, as well as reasonable attorney's fees and costs.

(2) A consumer credit-reporting agency that negligently violates this section is liable for the greater of actual damages or one thousand dollars for each incident, as well as reasonable attorney's fees and costs.

(3) In addition to the damages assessed pursuant to items (1) and (2), if the injury is to the consumer's creditworthiness, credit standing, credit capacity, character, general reputation, employment options, or eligibility for insurance, and results from the failure to place and enforce the security freeze and the failure is not corrected by the consumer credit-reporting agency within ten days after the entry of a judgment for damages, the assessed damages must be increased to one thousand dollars each day until the security freeze is imposed.

Section 37-20-40. (A) A person conducting business in this State and owning, licensing, maintaining, or otherwise possessing personal identifying information of a consumer resident of this State, in any form, must take all reasonable measures to protect against unauthorized access to or use of the information in connection with or after its disposal.

(B) The reasonable measures must include:

(1) implementing and monitoring compliance with policies and procedures that require:

(a) burning, pulverizing, or shredding of papers containing personal identifying information so that information cannot be practicably read or reconstructed; and

(b) destruction or erasure of electronic media and other nonpaper media containing personal identifying information so that the information cannot practicably be read or reconstructed; and

(2) describing procedures relating to the adequate destruction or proper disposal of personal records as official policy in the writings of the business entity.

(C) A person, after due diligence, may enter into a written contract with, and must monitor compliance by, another party engaged in the business of record destruction to destroy personal identifying information in a manner consistent with this section. Due diligence ordinarily includes one or more of the following:

(1) reviewing an independent audit of the disposal business's operations or its compliance with this statute or its equivalent;

(2) obtaining information about the disposal business from several references or other reliable sources and requiring that the disposal business be certified by a recognized trade association or similar third party with a reputation for high standards of quality review;

(3) reviewing and evaluating the disposal business's information security policies or procedures or taking other appropriate measures to determine the competency and integrity of the disposal business.

(D) A disposal business that conducts business in this State or disposes of personal identifying information of residents of this State must take all reasonable measures to dispose of records containing personal identifying information by implementing and monitoring compliance with policies and procedures that protect against unauthorized access to or use of personal identifying information during or after the collection and transportation and disposing of the information.

(E) This section does not apply to:

(1) a bank or financial institution that is subject to and in compliance with the privacy and security provision of the Gramm-Leach-Bliley Act;

(2) a health insurer that is subject to and in compliance with the standards for privacy of individually identifiable health information and the security standards for the protection of electronic health information of the Health Insurance Portability and Accountability Act of 1996;

(3) a consumer credit reporting agency that is subject to and in compliance with the federal Fair Credit Reporting Act.

(F) A violation of this section is a violation of Section 37-20-60.
Section 37-20-50. (A) A person conducting business in this State owning, licensing, maintaining, or otherwise possessing personal identifying information of consumer residents of this State, in any form, must provide notice to the affected resident of a security breach following discovery or notification of the breach. The disclosure notification must be made without unreasonable delay, consistent with the legitimate needs of law enforcement, as provided in subsection (B) of this section, or with measures necessary to determine the scope of the breach and restore the reasonable integrity, security, and confidentiality of the data system.

(B) The notice required by this section may be delayed if a law enforcement agency determines in writing that notification may impede a criminal investigation or jeopardize national or homeland security. The notice required by this section must be provided immediately after the law enforcement agency determines that notice will no longer impede the investigation or jeopardize national or homeland security.

(C) The notice must be clear and conspicuous. The notice must include a description of the following:

(1) the incident in general terms;

(2) the type of consumer resident's personal identifying information that was subject to the unauthorized access and acquisition;

(3) the acts of the person to protect the personal identifying information from further unauthorized access;

(4) a telephone number that the consumer resident may call for further information and assistance;

(5) advice that directs the consumer resident to remain vigilant over the next twelve to twenty-four months by reviewing account statements and monitoring free credit reports.

(D) For purposes of this section, notice to affected consumer residents may be provided by one of the following methods:

(1) written notice;

(2) electronic notice, for those consumer residents for whom it has a valid e-mail address and who have agreed to receive communications electronically, if the notice provided is consistent with the provisions regarding electronic records and signatures for notices legally required to be in writing set forth in Section 7001 of Title 15 of the United State Code and Chapter 6 of Title 26 of the 1976 Code;

(3) substitute notice, if the person demonstrates that the cost of providing notice would exceed two hundred fifty thousand dollars or that the affected class of subject consumer residents to be notified exceeds five hundred thousand, or if the person does not have sufficient contact information for only those affected consumer residents without sufficient contact information, or if the person is

unable to identify particular affected consumer residents, for only those unidentifiable affected consumer residents. Substitute notice must consist of all the following:

(a) e-mail notice when the person has an electronic mail address for the subject consumer residents;

(b) conspicuous posting of the notice on the person's website page, if one is maintained;

(c) notification to major statewide media.

(E) If a person provides notice to more than one thousand consumers residents at one time pursuant to this section, the person shall notify, without unreasonable delay, the South Carolina Department of Consumer Affairs and all consumer reporting agencies that compile and maintain files on consumers on a nationwide basis as defined in 15 U.S.C. Section 1681a(p), of the timing, distribution, and content of the notice.

(F) A financial institution that is subject to and in compliance with the Federal Interagency Guidance Response Programs for Unauthorized Access to Consumer Information and Customer Notice, issued on March 7, 2005, by the Board of Governors of the Federal Reserve System, the Federal Deposit Insurance Corporation, the Office of the Comptroller of the Currency, and the Office of Thrift Supervision, and any revisions, additions, or substitutions relating to that interagency guidance, is considered to be in compliance with this section.

(G) A violation of this section is a violation of Section 37-20-60.

Section 37-20-60. Except as provided in Section 37-20-30(Q), a consumer whose property or person is injured by reason of an act made unlawful by this chapter may sue for civil damages in an amount of up to five thousand dollars, but no less than five hundred dollars for each incident, or three times the amount of actual damages, whichever amount is greater. A consumer seeking damages as set forth in this section also may institute a civil action to enjoin and restrain future acts that would constitute a violation of this chapter. The court, in an action brought pursuant to this chapter, may award reasonable attorney's fees and costs to the prevailing party.

Section 37-20-70. The provisions of this chapter are cumulative, and an action taken pursuant to this chapter is not an election to take that action to the exclusion of other action authorized by law."

SECTION 3. A. Chapter 2 of Title 30 of the 1976 Code is redesignated as "Article 1, Family Privacy Protection Act".

B. Chapter 2 of Title 30 of the 1976 Code is amended by adding:

"Article 3

Personal Identifying Information Privacy Protection

Section 30-2-300. The General Assembly finds:

(1) The social security number can be used as a tool to perpetuate fraud against an individual and to acquire sensitive personal, financial, medical, and familial information, the release of which could cause great financial or personal harm to the individual. While the social security number was intended to be used solely for the administration of the federal Social Security System, over time this unique numeric identifier has been used extensively for identity verification purposes and other legitimate consensual purposes.

(2) Although there are legitimate reasons for State and local government entities to collect social security numbers and other personal identifying information from individuals, government should collect the information only for legitimate purposes or when required by law.

(3) When State and local government entities possess social security numbers or other personal identifying information, the governments should minimize the instances this information is disseminated either internally within government or externally with the general public.

Section 30-2-310. Except as provided in Sections 30-2-320 and 30-2-330 of this article, a public body, as defined in Section 30-1-10(B) may not:

(1) collect a social security number or any portion of it containing six digits or more from an individual unless authorized by law to do so or unless the collection of the social security number is otherwise imperative for the performance of that body's duties and responsibilities as prescribed by law. Social security numbers collected by a public body must be relevant to the purpose for which collected and must not be collected until and unless the need for social security numbers has been clearly documented;

(2) fail, when collecting a social security number or portion of it containing six digits or more from an individual, to segregate that number on a separate page from the rest of the record, or as otherwise appropriate, so that the social security number may be easily redacted pursuant to a public records request;

(3) fail, when collecting a social security number or any portion of it containing six digits or more from an individual, to provide, at the time of or before the actual collection of the social security number by that public body, upon request of the individual, a statement of the purpose or purposes for which the social security number is being collected and used;

(4) use the social security number or a portion of it containing six digits or more for any purpose other than the purpose stated;

(5) intentionally communicate or otherwise make available to the general public an individual's social security number or a portion of

it containing six digits or more or other personal identifying information. 'Personal identifying information', as used in this section, has the same meaning as 'identifying information' in Section 16-13-510, except that it does not include electronic identification names, including electronic mail addresses, or parent's legal surname before marriage;

(6) intentionally print or imbed an individual's social security number or a portion of it containing six digits or more on any card required for the individual to access government services;

(7) require an individual to transmit the individual's social security number or a portion of it containing six digits or more over the Internet, unless the connection is secure or the social security number is encrypted;

(8) require an individual to use the individual's social security number or a portion of it containing six digits or more to access an Internet website, unless a password or unique personal identification number or other authentication device is also required to access the Internet website;

(9) print an individual's social security number or a portion of it containing six digits or more on materials that are mailed to the individual, unless state or federal law requires the social security number be on the mailed document.

Section 30-2-320. Social security numbers and identifying information may be disclosed:

(1) to another governmental entity or its agents, employees, or contractors, if disclosure is necessary for the receiving entity to perform its duties and responsibilities. The receiving governmental entity and its agents, employees, and contractors shall maintain the confidential and exempt status of those numbers;

(2) pursuant to a court order, warrant, or subpoena;

(3) for public health purposes;

(4) on certified copies of vital records issued by the Director of the Department of Health and Environmental Control as the State Registrar, pursuant to Section 44-63-30 and authorized officials pursuant to Section 44-63-40. The State Registrar may disclose personal identifying information other than social security number on an uncertified vital record;

(5) on a recorded document in the official records of the county;

(6) on a document filed in the official records of the courts.

Section 30-2-330 (A) A person preparing or filing a document to be recorded or filed in the official records by the register of deeds or the clerk of court of a county may not include an individual's social security, driver's license, state identification, passport, checking account, savings account, credit card, or debit card number, or personal identification (PIN) code, or passwords in that document, unless otherwise expressly required by law or court order or rule adopted by the State Registrar on records of vital events. A loan closing instruction that requires the inclusion of an individual's social security number on a document to be recorded is void. A person who violates this subsection is guilty of a misdemeanor, punishable by a fine not to exceed five hundred dollars for each violation.

(B) Notwithstanding Section 30-1-30, or another provision of law, an individual or his attorney-in-fact or legal guardian may request that a register of deeds or clerk of court remove, from an image or copy of an official record placed on a publicly available Internet website or a publicly available Internet website used by a register of deeds or court to display public records by the register of deeds or clerk of court, the individual's social security, driver's license, state identification, passport, checking account, savings account, credit card, debit card number, or personal identification (PIN) code or passwords contained in that official record. The request must be made in writing, legibly signed by the requester, and delivered by mail, facsimile, or electronic transmission, or delivered in person to the register of deeds or clerk of court. The request must specify the identification page number that contains the social security, driver's license, state identification, passport, checking account, savings account, credit card, debit card numbers, or personal identification (PIN) code or passwords to be redacted. The register of deeds or clerk of court has no duty to inquire beyond the written request to verify the identity of an individual requesting redaction. A fee must not be charged for the redaction pursuant to the request.

(C) A register of deeds or clerk of court immediately and conspicuously shall post signs throughout his offices for public viewing and a notice on any Internet website or remote electronic site made available by the register of deeds or clerk of court and used for the ordering or display of official records or images or copies of official records a notice, stating, in substantially similar form, the following:

'A person preparing or filing a document for recordation or filing in the official records may not include a social security, driver's license, state identification, passport, checking account, savings account, credit card, debit card number, or personal identification (PIN) code, or passwords in the document, unless expressly required by law. An individual has a right to request a register of deeds or clerk of court to remove, from an image or copy of an official record placed on a publicly available Internet website or on a publicly available Internet website used by a register of deeds or clerk of court to display public records, any social security, driver's license, state identification, passport, checking account, savings account, credit card, debit card number, or personal identification (PIN) code, or passwords contained in an official record. The request must be made in writing and delivered by mail, facsimile, or electronic transmission or in person, to the register of deeds or clerk of court. The request must specify the identification page number that contains the social security, driver's license, state identification, passport, checking account, savings account, credit card, debit card number, or personal identification (PIN) code, or passwords to be redacted. There is no fee for the redaction pursuant to request.'

Section 30-2-340. Any affected individual may petition the court for an order directing compliance with this section. Liability may not accrue to a register of deeds or clerk of court or to his agents for claims or damages that arise from a social security number or other identifying information on the public record."

SECTION 4. A. Article 2, Chapter 13, Title 16 of the 1976 Code is amended by adding:

"Section 16-13-540. (A) If a person is named in a charge for an infraction or a crime, either a misdemeanor or a felony, as a result of another person using the identifying information of the named person the charge against the named person is dismissed, a finding of not guilty is entered, or the conviction is set aside, the named person may apply by petition or written motion to the court where the charge was last pending on a form approved by the Office of Court Administration and supplied by the clerk of court for an order to expunge from all official records entries relating to the person's apprehension, charge, or trial. The court, after notice to the county solicitor, shall hold a hearing on the motion or petition and, upon finding that the person's identity was used without permission and the charges were dismissed or the person was found not guilty, the court shall order the expunction.

Section 16-13-550. (A) A person who learns or reasonably suspects that he is the victim of financial identity fraud may contact the local law enforcement agency that has jurisdiction over the person's actual residence. If jurisdiction lies elsewhere for investigation and prosecution of a crime of financial identity fraud, the local law enforcement agency may take the complaint, issue an incident report, provide the complainant with a copy of the report, and refer the report to a law enforcement agency in that different jurisdiction.

(B) This section does not interfere with the discretion of a local law enforcement agency to allocate resources for investigations of crimes. A complaint filed or report issued pursuant to this section is not required to be counted as an open case for purposes of compiling open case statistics."

B. Sections 16-13-510 of the 1976 Code, as last amended by Act 350 of 2006, and 16-13-520 of the 1976 Code, as added by Act 305 of 2000, are amended to read:

"Section 16-13-510. (A) It is unlawful for a person to commit the offense of financial identity fraud.

(B) A person is guilty of financial identity fraud when he, without the authorization or permission of another person and with the intent of unlawfully appropriating the financial resources of that person to his own use or the use of a third party:

(1) obtains or records identifying information which would assist in accessing the financial records of the other person; ~~or~~

(2) accesses or attempts to access the financial resources of the other person through the use of identifying information as defined in subsection (C);

(3) knowingly obtains, possesses, or uses identifying information of another person, living or dead, with the intent to fraudulently represent that he is the other person for the purpose of:

(a) making financial or credit transactions in the other person's name;

(b) obtaining anything of value, benefit, or advantage;

(c) avoiding legal consequences; or

(d) obtaining employment.

(C) 'Identifying information' as used in this article includes the following:

(1) social security numbers;

(2) driver's license, state identification card, or passport numbers;

(3) checking account numbers;

(4) savings account numbers;

(5) credit card numbers;

(6) debit card numbers;

(7) personal identification numbers (PIN);

(8) electronic identification numbers, electronic mail, Internet accounts or Internet identification;

(9) digital signatures;

(10) other numbers or information which may be used to access a person's financial resources;

(11) identifying documentation that defines a person other than the person presenting the document. This includes, but is not limited to, passports, driver's licenses, birth certificates, immigration documents, and state-issued identification cards;

(12) biometric data;

(13) fingerprints;

(14) passwords;

(15) parent's legal surname before marriage.

(D) It is not a violation of this article for a person lawfully to:

(1) obtain credit information in the course of a bona fide consumer or commercial transaction;

(2) exercise, in good faith, a security interest or a right of offset by a creditor or financial institution;

(3) comply, in good faith, with any warrant, court order, levy, garnishment, attachment, or other judicial or administrative order, decree, or directive, when the person is required to do so.

(E) A person who violates the provisions of this ~~section~~ article is guilty of a felony and, upon conviction, must be fined in the discretion of the court or imprisoned not more than ten years, or both. The court may order restitution to the victim pursuant to the provisions of Section 17-25-322.

Section 16-13-520. In a criminal proceeding brought pursuant to this article, the crime is considered to have been committed in ~~a~~ the county where the victim resides, where the perpetrator resides, where any part of the financial identity fraud took place, or in any other county instrumental to the completion of the offense, regardless of whether the defendant was ever actually present in that county."

SECTION 5. Article 1, Chapter 11 of Title 1 of the 1976 Code is amended by adding:

"Section 1-11-490. (A) An agency of this State owning or licensing computerized data that includes personal identifying information shall disclose a breach of the security of the system following discovery or notification of the breach in the security of the data to a resident of this State whose unencrypted personal identifying information was, or is reasonably believed to have been, acquired by an unauthorized person. The disclosure must be made in the most expedient time possible and without unreasonable delay, consistent with the legitimate needs of law enforcement, as provided in subsection (C), or with measures necessary to determine the scope of the breach and restore the reasonable integrity of the data system.

(B) An agency maintaining computerized data that includes personal identifying information that the agency does not own shall notify the owner or licensee of the information of a breach of the security of the data immediately following discovery, if the personal identifying information was, or is reasonably believed to have been, acquired by an unauthorized person.

(C) The notification required by this section may be delayed if a law enforcement agency determines that the notification impedes a criminal investigation. The notification required by this section must be made after the law enforcement agency determines that it no longer compromises the investigation.

(D) For purposes of this section:

(1) 'Agency' means any agency, department, board, commission, committee, or institution of higher learning of the State or a political subdivision of it.

(2) 'Breach of the security of the system' means unauthorized access to, and acquisition of, computerized data that compromises the security, confidentiality, or integrity of personal identifying information maintained by the agency. Good faith acquisition of personal identifying information by an employee or agent of the agency for the purposes of the agency is not a breach of the security of the system if the personal identifying information is not used or subject to further unauthorized disclosure.

(3) 'Personal identifying information' has the same meaning as 'identifying information' in Section 16-13-510(C).

(E) The notice required by this section may be provided by:

(1) written notice;

(2) electronic notice, if the notice provided is consistent with the provisions regarding electronic records and signatures set forth in Section 7001 of Title 15 of the United States Code and Chapter 6 of Title 26 of the 1976 Code;

(3) substitute notice, if the agency demonstrates that the cost of providing notice exceeds two hundred fifty thousand dollars or that the affected class of subject residents to be notified exceeds five hundred thousand or the agency has insufficient contact information. Substitute notice consists of:

(a) e-mail notice when the agency has an e-mail address for the subject residents;

(b) conspicuous posting of the notice on the agency's website page, if the agency maintains one;

(c) notification to major statewide media.

(F) Notwithstanding subsection (E), an agency that maintains its own notification procedures as part of an information security policy for the treatment of personal identifying information and is otherwise consistent with the timing requirements of this section is considered to be in compliance with the notification requirements of this section if it notifies subject residents in accordance with its policies in the event of a breach of security of the system.
(G) A resident of this State who is injured by a violation of this section, in addition to and cumulative of all other rights and remedies available at law, may:

(1) institute a civil action to recover damages;

(2) seek an injunction to enforce compliance;

(3) recover attorney's fee and court costs, if successful."

SECTION 6. The repeal or amendment by this act of any law, whether temporary or permanent or civil or criminal, does not affect pending actions, rights, duties, or liabilities founded thereon, or alter, discharge, release or extinguish any penalty, forfeiture, or liability incurred under the repealed or amended law, unless the repealed or amended provision shall so expressly provide. After the effective date of this act, all laws repealed or amended by this act must be taken and treated as remaining in full force and effect for the purpose of sustaining any pending or vested right, civil action, special proceeding, criminal prosecution, or appeal existing as of the effective date of this act, and for the enforcement of rights, duties, penalties, forfeitures, and liabilities as they stood under the repealed or amended laws.

SECTION 7. If any section, subsection, paragraph, subparagraph, sentence, clause, phrase, or word of this act is for any reason held to be unconstitutional or invalid, such holding shall not affect the constitutionality or validity of the remaining portions of this act, the General Assembly hereby declaring that it would have passed this act, and each and every section, subsection, paragraph, subparagraph, sentence, clause, phrase, and word thereof, irrespective of the fact that any one or more other sections, subsections, paragraphs, subparagraphs, sentences, clauses, phrases, or words hereof may be declared to be unconstitutional, invalid, or otherwise ineffective.

SECTION 8. This act is effective July 1, 2007, except that Section 37-20-20(A)(2), (3), (4), and (5), as enacted in Section 2 of this act, becomes effective January 1, 2007. Section 30-2-300(B)(6), (7), (8), and (9), as enacted in Section 3.B. of this act, becomes effective July 1, 2008. Section 4 of this act applies to offenses committed, and to causes of action arising, on or after July 1, 2007.

House Bill 3198

This bill relates to the prohibition of knowingly obtaining or using personal information obtained from a public body for commercial solicitation directed to a person in this state. The bill substitutes the words "state agency" for "public body" and provides for an exclusion.

Senate Bill 417

This bill removes the requirement that an absentee ballot application contain the applicant's Social Security number.

Senate Bill 763

This bill relates to voter registration applications, deleting the requirement that an applicant's Social Security number be placed on the application form.

Chapter 41: South Dakota

South Dakota also does not have laws specific to any disclosure requirements in the event of a data breach. I was able to find two laws that spoke to the use and display of Social Security numbers.

Senate Bill 129

This bill prohibits the display of Social Security numbers on driver's licenses or non-driver identification cards.

Senate Bill 91

This bill eliminates the requirement of providing Social Security numbers in certain probate matters.

Chapter 42: Tennessee

Tennessee House Bill 931 revises the present authority for the disclosure of customer information by financial institutions in regard to suspected illegal activity to allow disclosure where a financial institution or its representatives believe information may be relevant, and includes as information that may be disclosed descriptive information and activities in addition to identifying information.

Chapter No. 98] PUBLIC ACTS, 2003 1

CHAPTER NO. 98

HOUSE BILL NO. 931

AN ACT to amend Tennessee Code Annotated, Title 45, Chapter 10, relative to disclosures by financial institutions. WHEREAS, a financial institution may disclose financial records relating to a customer only under certain limited circumstances as defined in the Financial Records Privacy Act; and WHEREAS, there is an interest to facilitate the sharing of information between financial institutions and appropriate law enforcement officials only on a voluntary basis without exposing any financial institution to liability for making such disclosures; now, therefore, BE IT ENACTED BY THE GENERAL ASSEMBLY OF THE STATE OF TENNESSEE:

SECTION 1. Tennessee Code Annotated, Section 45-10-104, is amended by deleting subsection (b) in its entirety and substituting the following language: (b) Nothing in this chapter shall preclude any financial institution, or any officer, employee, or agent of a financial institution, from notifying a government authority that such institution, or officer, employee, or agent has information which the financial institution or its representative believes may be relevant to a possible violation of any statute or regulation. Such information may include the name or other identifying or descriptive information concerning any individual, corporation, or account involved in any suspected illegal activity, and a description

of such activity. Such information may be disclosed notwithstanding any law or regulation of this state to the contrary. Nothing in this section shall create any duty to provide any information to a governmental authority except in accordance with subsection (a) of this section, nor relieve any duty to provide information to a governmental authority when otherwise required by law. Any financial institution, or officer, employee, or agent thereof making a disclosure of information pursuant to this subsection, shall not be liable to any person under any law or regulation of this state or political subdivision thereof, for disclosure or for any failure to disclose information required or permitted under this section. SECTION 2. This act shall take effect upon becoming a law, the public welfare requiring it.

House Bill 2170

This bill requires persons, businesses, or government agencies that discover a breach of information security resulting in disclosure of unencrypted personal information about persons to unauthorized third parties to provide notice of such disclosure.

Chapter No. 473]
PUBLIC ACTS, 2005
CHAPTER NO. 473
SENATE BILL NO. 2220
By Herron, Norris, Burks
Substituted for: House Bill No. 2170
By Maddox, Henri Brooks, Fitzhugh

AN ACT to amend Tennessee Code Annotated, Title 39; Title 47 and Title 48, relative to release of personal consumer information. BE IT ENACTED BY THE GENERAL ASSEMBLY OF THE STATE OF TENNESSEE: SECTION 1. Tennessee Code Annotated, Title 47, Chapter 18, Part 21, is amended by inserting the following as a new, appropriately designated section thereto:

(a) As used in this section, unless the context otherwise requires:

(1) "Breach of the security of the system" means unauthorized acquisition of unencrypted computerized data that materially compromises the security, confidentiality, or integrity of personal information maintained by the information holder. Good faith acquisition of personal information by an employee or agent of the information holder for the purposes of the information holder is not a breach of the security of the system, provided that the personal information is not used or subject to further unauthorized disclosure.

(2) "Information holder" means any person or business that conducts business in this state, or any agency of the State of Tennessee or any of its political subdivisions, that owns or licenses computerized data that includes personal information.

(3) "Personal information" means an individual's first name or first initial and last name in combination with any one (1) or more of the following data elements, when either the name or the data elements are not encrypted:

(i) Social Security number;

(ii) Driver license number; or

(iii) Account number, credit or debit card number, in combination with any required security code, access code, or password that would permit access to an individual's financial account.

"Personal information" does not include publicly available information that is lawfully made available to the general public from federal, state, or local government records.

(b) Any information holder shall disclose any breach of the security of the system following discovery or notification of the breach in the security of the data to any resident of Tennessee whose unencrypted personal information was, or is reasonably believed to have been, acquired by an unauthorized person. The disclosure shall be made in the most expedient time possible and without unreasonable delay, consistent with the legitimate needs of law enforcement, as provided in subdivision (d), or any measures necessary to determine the scope of the breach and restore the reasonable integrity of the data system. (c) Any information holder that maintains computerized data that includes personal information that the information holder does not own shall notify the owner or licensee of the information of any breach of the security of the data immediately following discovery, if the personal information was, or is reasonably believed to have been, acquired by an unauthorized person. (d) The notification required by this section may be delayed if a law enforcement agency determines that the notification will impede a criminal investigation. The notification required by this section shall be made after the law enforcement agency determines that it will not compromise the investigation. (e) For purposes of this section, notice may be provided by one (1) of the following methods:

(1) Written notice;

(2) Electronic notice, if the notice provided is consistent with the provisions regarding electronic records and signatures set forth in Section 7001 of Title 15 of the United States Code; or

(3) Substitute notice, if the information holder demonstrates that the cost of providing notice would exceed two hundred fifty thousand dollars ($250,000), or that the affected class of subject persons to be notified exceeds five hundred thousand (500,000), or the information holder does not have sufficient contact information. Substitute notice shall consist of all of the following:

(A) E-mail notice when the information holder has an e-mail address for the subject persons;

(B) Conspicuous posting of the notice on the information holder's internet website page, if the information holder maintains such website page; or

(C) Notification to major statewide media. (f) Notwithstanding subdivision (e), an information holder that maintains its own notification procedures as part of an information security policy for the treatment of personal information and is otherwise consistent with the timing requirements of this section shall be deemed to be in compliance with the notification requirements of this section if it notifies subject persons in accordance with its policies in the event of a breach of security of the system. (g) In the event that a person discovers circumstances requiring notification pursuant to this section of more than one thousand (1,000) persons at one time, the person shall also notify, without unreasonable delay, all consumer reporting agencies and credit bureaus that compile and maintain files on consumers on a nationwide basis, as defined by 15 U.S.C. §1681a, of the timing, distribution and content of the notices; (h) Any customer of an information holder who is a person or business entity, but who is not an agency of the state or any political subdivision of the state, and who is injured by a violation of this section may institute a civil action to recover damages and to enjoin the person or business entity from further action in violation of this section. The rights and remedies available under this section are cumulative to each other and to any other rights and remedies available under law. (i) The provisions of this section shall not apply to any person who is subject to the provisions of Title V of the Gramm-Leach-Bliley Act of 1999, Pub. L. No. 106-102.

SECTION 2. This act shall take effect July 1, 2005, the public welfare requiring it.

House Bill 3105

This bill creates the Anti-Phishing Act of 2006 and penalizes persons who, without authorization or permission of subject of identifying information, obtain, record, access, or distribute identifying information of another person through use of Internet, e-mail, or wireless communication.

House Bill 3886

This bill specifies that otherwise confidential information obtained by the commissioner of financial institutions or any bank examiner in making an examination into the affairs of the bank may be disclosed to certain state and federal officials for purposes of enforcing and complying with the federal Bank Secrecy Act.

House Bill 3599

This bill requires reported malpractice claims data to include certain damage and defense expenses. It also requires such data to include the Social Security number of claimants only if it is known to the reporting entity.

Senate Bill 2285

This bill concerns Consumer Protection; renames Tennessee Identity Theft Deterrence Act of 1999 to Tennessee Identification and Personal Information Protection Act of 2007; includes unauthorized transfer of personal information under such act.

Chapter 43: Texas

While Texas has had a data breach notification law several years, it has made an update to it in 2011 in the form of H.B. 300, which takes effect September 2012.

Perhaps the most interesting change in the law is the scope of who is covered. Rather than just applying to residents of the state of Texas, the law now applies to "any individual" whose personal sensitive information may have been acquired by unauthorized personnel. The text of H.B. 300 is below.

AN ACT relating to the privacy of protected health information; providing administrative, civil, and criminal penalties.

BE IT ENACTED BY THE LEGISLATURE OF THE STATE OF TEXAS:

SECTION 1. Section 181.001(b), Health and Safety Code, is amended by amending Subdivisions (1) and (3) and adding Subdivisions (2-a) and (2-b) to read as follows:

(1) "Commission" ["Commissioner"] means the Health and Human Services Commission [commissioner of health and human services].

(2-a) "Disclose" means to release, transfer, provide access to, or otherwise divulge information outside the entity holding the information.

(2-b) "Executive commissioner" means the executive commissioner of the Health and Human Services Commission.

(3) "Health Insurance Portability and Accountability Act and Privacy Standards" means the privacy requirements in existence on September 1, 2011 [August 14, 2002], of the Administrative Simplification subtitle of the Health Insurance Portability and Accountability Act of 1996 (Pub. L. No. 104-191) contained in 45 C.F.R. Part 160 and 45 C.F.R. Part 164, Subparts A and E.

SECTION 2. Subchapter A, Chapter 181, Health and Safety Code, is amended by adding Section 181.004 to read as follows:

Sec. 181.004. APPLICABILITY OF STATE AND FEDERAL LAW.

(a) A covered entity, as that term is defined by 45 C.F.R. Section 160.103, shall comply with the Health Insurance Portability and Accountability Act and Privacy Standards.

(b) Subject to Section 181.051, a covered entity, as that term is defined by Section 181.001, shall comply with this chapter.

SECTION 3. Section 181.005, Health and Safety Code, is amended to read as follows:

Sec. 181.005. DUTIES OF THE EXECUTIVE COMMISSIONER.

(a) The executive commissioner shall administer this chapter and may adopt rules consistent with the Health Insurance Portability and Accountability Act and Privacy Standards to administer this chapter.

(b) The executive commissioner shall review amendments to the definitions in 45 C.F.R. Parts 160 and 164 that occur after September 1, 2011 [August 14, 2002], and determine whether it is in the best interest of the state to adopt the amended federal regulations. If the executive commissioner determines that it is in the best interest of the state to adopt the amended federal regulations, the amended regulations shall apply as required by this chapter.

(c) In making a determination under this section, the executive commissioner must consider, in addition to other factors affecting the public interest, the beneficial and adverse effects the amendments would have on:

(1) the lives of individuals in this state and their expectations of privacy; and

(2) governmental entities, institutions of higher education, state-owned teaching hospitals, private businesses, and commerce in this state.

(d) The executive commissioner shall prepare a report of the executive commissioner's determination made under this section and shall file the report with the presiding officer of each house of the legislature before the 30th day after the date the determination is made. The report must include an explanation of the reasons for the determination.

SECTION 4. Section 181.006, Health and Safety Code, is amended to read as follows:

Sec. 181.006. PROTECTED HEALTH INFORMATION NOT PUBLIC.

Notwithstanding Sections 181.004 and 181.051, for [For] a covered entity that is a governmental unit, an individual's protected health information:

(1) includes any information that reflects that an individual received health care from the covered entity; and

(2) is not public information and is not subject to disclosure under Chapter 552, Government Code.

SECTION 5. Subchapter B, Chapter 181, Health and Safety Code, is amended by adding Section 181.059 to read as follows:

Sec. 181.059. CRIME VICTIM COMPENSATION. This chapter does not apply to any person or entity in connection with providing, administering, supporting, or coordinating any of the benefits regarding compensation to victims of crime as provided by Subchapter B, Chapter 56, Code of Criminal Procedure.

SECTION 6. Chapter 181, Health and Safety Code, is amended by adding Subchapter C to read as follows:

SUBCHAPTER C. ACCESS TO AND USE OF PROTECTED HEALTH INFORMATION

Sec. 181.101. TRAINING REQUIRED. (a) Each covered entity shall provide a training program to employees of the covered entity regarding the state and federal law concerning protected health information as it relates to:

(1) the covered entity's particular course of business; and

(2) each employee's scope of employment.

(b) An employee of a covered entity must complete training described by Subsection (a) not later than the 60th day after the date the employee is hired by the covered entity.

(c) An employee of a covered entity shall receive training described by Subsection (a) at least once every two years.

(d) A covered entity shall require an employee of the entity who attends a training program described by Subsection (a) to sign, electronically or in writing, a statement verifying the employee's attendance at the training program. The covered entity shall maintain the signed statement.

Sec. 181.102. CONSUMER ACCESS TO ELECTRONIC HEALTH RECORDS.

(a) Except as provided by Subsection (b), if a health care provider is using an electronic health records system that is capable of fulfilling the request, the health care provider, not later than the 15th business day after the date the health care provider receives a written request from a person for the person's electronic health record, shall provide the requested record to the person in electronic form unless the person agrees to accept the record in another form.

(b) A health care provider is not required to provide access to a person's protected health information that is excepted from access, or to which access may be denied, under 45 C.F.R. Section 164.524.

(c) For purposes of Subsection (a), the executive commissioner, in consultation with the Department of State Health Services, the Texas Medical Board, and the Texas Department of Insurance, by rule may recommend a standard electronic format for the release of requested health records. The standard electronic format recommended under this section must be consistent, if feasible, with federal law regarding the release of electronic health records.

Sec. 181.103. CONSUMER INFORMATION WEBSITE. The attorney general shall maintain an Internet website that provides:

(1) information concerning a consumer's privacy rights regarding protected health information under federal and state law;

(2) a list of the state agencies, including the Department of State Health Services, the Texas Medical Board, and the Texas Department of Insurance, that regulate covered entities in this state and the types of entities each agency regulates;

(3) detailed information regarding each agency's complaint enforcement process; and

(4) contact information, including the address of the agency's Internet website, for each agency listed under Subdivision (2) for reporting a violation of this chapter.

Sec. 181.104. CONSUMER COMPLAINT REPORT BY ATTORNEY GENERAL. (a) The attorney general annually shall submit to the legislature a report describing:

(1) the number and types of complaints received by the attorney general and by the state agencies receiving consumer complaints under Section 181.103; and

(2) the enforcement action taken in response to each complaint reported under Subdivision (1).

(b) Each state agency that receives consumer complaints under Section 181.103 shall submit to the attorney general, in the form required by the attorney general, the information the attorney general requires to compile the report required by Subsection (a).

(c) The attorney general shall de-identify protected health information from the individual to whom the information pertains before including the information in the report required by Subsection (a).

SECTION 7. Subchapter D, Chapter 181, Health and Safety Code, is amended by adding Sections 181.153 and 181.154 to read as follows:

Sec. 181.153. SALE OF PROTECTED HEALTH INFORMATION PROHIBITED; EXCEPTIONS. (a) A covered entity may not disclose an Individual's protected health information to any other person in exchange for direct or indirect remuneration, except that a covered entity may disclose an individual's protected health information:

(1) to another covered entity, as that term is defined by Section 181.001, or to a covered entity, as that term is defined by Section 602.001, Insurance Code, for the purpose of:

(A) treatment;

(B) payment;

(C) health care operations; or

(D) performing an insurance or health maintenance organization function described by Section 602.053, Insurance Code; or

(2) as otherwise authorized or required by state or federal law.

(b) The direct or indirect remuneration a covered entity receives for making a disclosure of protected health information authorized by Subsection (a)(1)(D) may not exceed the covered entity's reasonable costs of preparing or transmitting the protected health information.

Sec. 181.154. NOTICE AND AUTHORIZATION REQUIRED FOR ELECTRONIC DISCLOSURE OF PROTECTED HEALTH INFORMATION; EXCEPTIONS.

(a) A covered entity shall provide notice to an individual for whom the covered entity creates or receives protected health information if the individual's protected health information is subject to electronic disclosure. A covered entity may provide general notice by:

(1) posting a written notice in the covered entity's place of business;

(2) posting a notice on the covered entity's Internet website; or

(3) posting a notice in any other place where individuals whose protected health information is subject to electronic disclosure are likely to see the notice.

(b) Except as provided by Subsection (c), a covered entity may not electronically disclose an individual's protected health information to any person without a separate authorization from the individual or the individual's legally authorized representative for each disclosure. An authorization for disclosure under this subsection may be made in written or electronic form or in oral form if it is documented in writing by the covered entity.

(c) The authorization for electronic disclosure of protected health information described by Subsection (b) is not required if the disclosure is made:

(1) to another covered entity, as that term is defined by Section 181.001, or to a covered entity, as that term is defined by Section 602.001, Insurance Code, for the purpose of:

(A) treatment;
(B) payment;
(C) health care operations; or
(D) performing an insurance or health maintenance organization function described by Section 602.053, Insurance Code; or

(2) as otherwise authorized or required by state or federal law.

(d) The attorney general shall adopt a standard authorization form for use in complying with this section. The form must comply with the Health Insurance Portability and Accountability Act and Privacy Standards and this chapter.

(e) This section does not apply to a covered entity, as defined by Section 602.001, Insurance Code, if that entity is not a covered entity as defined by 45 C.F.R. Section 160.103.

SECTION 8. Section 181.201, Health and Safety Code, is amended by amending Subsections (b) and (c) and adding Subsections (b-1), (d), (e), and (f) to read as follows: (b) In addition to the injunctive relief provided by Subsection (a), the attorney general may institute an action for civil penalties against a covered entity for a violation of this chapter. A civil penalty assessed under this section may not exceed:

(1) $5,000 [$3,000] for each violation that occurs in one year, regardless of how long the violation continues during that year, committed negligently;

(2) $25,000 for each violation that occurs in one year, regardless of how long the violation continues during that year, committed knowingly or intentionally; or

(3) $250,000 for each violation in which the covered entity knowingly or intentionally used protected health information for financial gain.

(b-1) The total amount of a penalty assessed against a covered entity under Subsection (b) in relation to a violation or violations of Section 181.154 may not exceed $250,000 annually if the court finds that the disclosure was made only to another covered entity and only for a purpose described by Section 181.154(c) and the court finds that:

(1) the protected health information disclosed was encrypted or transmitted using encryption technology designed to protect against improper disclosure;

(2) the recipient of the protected health information did not use or release the protected health information; or

(3) at the time of the disclosure of the protected health information, the covered entity had developed, implemented, and maintained security policies, including the education and training of employees responsible for the security of protected health information.

(c) If the court in which an action under Subsection (b) is pending finds that the violations have occurred with a frequency as to constitute a pattern or practice, the court may assess a civil penalty not to exceed $1.5 million annually [$250,000].

(d) In determining the amount of a penalty imposed under Subsection (b), the court shall consider:

(1) the seriousness of the violation, including the nature, circumstances, extent, and gravity of the disclosure;

(2) the covered entity's compliance history;

(3) whether the violation poses a significant risk of financial, reputational, or other harm to an individual whose protected health information is involved in the violation;

(4) whether the covered entity was certified at the time of the violation as described by Section 182.108;

(5) the amount necessary to deter a future violation; and

(6) the covered entity's efforts to correct the violation.

(e) The attorney general may institute an action against a covered entity that is licensed by a licensing agency of this state for a civil penalty under this section only if the licensing agency refers the violation to the attorney general under Section 181.202(2).

(f) The office of the attorney general may retain a reasonable portion of a civil penalty recovered under this section, not to exceed amounts specified in the General Appropriations Act, for the enforcement of this subchapter.

SECTION 9. Section 181.202, Health and Safety Code, is amended to read as follows:

Sec. 181.202. DISCIPLINARY ACTION. In addition to the penalties prescribed by this chapter, a violation of this chapter by a covered entity [an individual or facility] that is licensed by an agency of this state is subject to investigation and disciplinary proceedings, including probation or suspension by the licensing agency. If there is evidence that the violations of this chapter are egregious and constitute a pattern or practice, the agency may:

(1) revoke the covered entity's [individual's or facility's] license; or

(2) refer the covered entity's case to the attorney general for the institution of an action for civil penalties under Section 181.201(b).

SECTION 10. Section 181.205, Health and Safety Code, is amended by amending Subsection (b) and adding Subsection (c) to read as follows:

(b) In determining the amount of a penalty imposed under other law in accordance with Section 181.202, a court or state agency shall consider the following factors:

(1) the seriousness of the violation, including the nature, circumstances, extent, and gravity of the disclosure;

(2) the covered entity's compliance history;

(3) whether the violation poses a significant risk of financial, reputational, or other harm to an individual whose protected health information is involved in the violation;

(4) whether the covered entity was certified at the time of the violation as described by Section 182.108;

(5) the amount necessary to deter a future violation; and

(6) the covered entity's efforts to correct the violation.

(c) On receipt of evidence under Subsections [Subsection] (a) and (b), a court or state agency shall consider the evidence and mitigate imposition of an administrative penalty or assessment of a civil penalty accordingly.

SECTION 11. Subchapter E, Chapter 181, Health and Safety Code, is amended by adding Sections 181.206 and 181.207 to read as follows:

Sec. 181.206. AUDITS OF COVERED ENTITIES. (a) The commission, in coordination with the attorney general, the Texas Health Services Authority, and the Texas Department of Insurance:

(1) may request that the United States secretary of health and human services conduct an audit of a covered entity, as that term is defined by 45 C.F.R. Section 160.103, in this state to determine compliance with the Health Insurance Portability and Accountability Act and Privacy Standards; and

(2) shall periodically monitor and review the results of audits of covered entities in this state conducted by the United States secretary of health and human services.

(b) If the commission has evidence that a covered entity has committed violations of this chapter that are egregious and constitute a pattern or practice, the commission may:

(1) require the covered entity to submit to the commission the results of a risk analysis conducted by the covered entity if required by 45 C.F.R. Section 164.308(a)(1)(ii)(A); or

(2) if the covered entity is licensed by a licensing agency of this state, request that the licensing agency conduct an audit of the covered entity's system to determine compliance with the provisions of this chapter.

(c) The commission annually shall submit to the appropriate standing committees of the senate and the house of representatives a report regarding the number of federal audits of covered entities in this state and the number of audits required under Subsection (b).

Sec. 181.207. FUNDING. The commission and the Texas Department of Insurance, in consultation with the Texas Health Services Authority, shall apply for and actively pursue available federal funding for enforcement of this chapter.

SECTION 12. Section 182.002, Health and Safety Code, is amended by adding Subdivisions (2-a), (3-a), and (3-b) to read as follows:

(2-a) "Covered entity" has the meaning assigned by Section 181.001.

(3-a) "Disclose" has the meaning assigned by Section 181.001.

(3-b) "Health Insurance Portability and Accountability Act and Privacy Standards" has the meaning assigned by Section 181.001.

SECTION 13. Subchapter C, Chapter 182, Health and Safety Code, is amended by adding Section 182.108 to read as follows:

Sec. 182.108. STANDARDS FOR ELECTRONIC SHARING OF PROTECTED HEALTH INFORMATION; COVERED ENTITY CERTIFICATION.

(a) The corporation shall develop and submit to the commission for ratification privacy and security standards for the electronic sharing of protected health information.

(b) The commission shall review and by rule adopt acceptable standards submitted for ratification under Subsection (a).

(c) Standards adopted under Subsection (b) must be designed to:

(1) comply with the Health Insurance Portability and Accountability Act and Privacy Standards and Chapter 181;

(2) comply with any other state and federal law relating to the security and confidentiality of information electronically maintained or disclosed by a covered entity;

(3) ensure the secure maintenance and disclosure of personally identifiable health information;

(4) include strategies and procedures for disclosing personally identifiable health information; and

(5) support a level of system interoperability with existing health record databases in this state that is consistent with emerging standards.

(d) The corporation shall establish a process by which a covered entity may apply for certification by the corporation of a covered entity's past compliance with standards adopted under Subsection (b).

(e) The corporation shall publish the standards adopted under Subsection (b) on the corporation's Internet website.

SECTION 14. Section 521.053, Business & Commerce Code, is amended by amending Subsection (b) and adding Subsection (b-1) to read as follows:

(b) A person who conducts business in this state and owns or licenses computerized data that includes sensitive personal information shall disclose any breach of system security, after discovering or receiving notification of the breach, to any individual [resident of this state] whose sensitive personal information was, or is reasonably believed to have been, acquired by an unauthorized person. The disclosure shall be made as quickly as possible, except as provided by Subsection (d) or as necessary to determine the scope of the breach and restore the reasonable integrity of the data system.

(b-1) Notwithstanding Subsection (b), the requirements of Subsection (b) apply only if the individual whose sensitive personal information was or is reasonably believed to have been acquired by an unauthorized person is a resident of this state or another state that does not require a person described by Subsection (b) to notify the individual of a breach of system security. If the individual is a resident of a state that requires a person described by Subsection (b) to provide notice of a breach of system security, the notice of the breach of system security provided under that state's law satisfies the requirements of Subsection (b).

SECTION 15. Section 521.151, Business & Commerce Code, is amended by adding Subsection (a-1) to read as follows:

(a-1) In addition to penalties assessed under Subsection

(a), a person who fails to take reasonable action to comply with Section 521.053(b) is liable to this state for a civil penalty of not more than $100 for each individual to whom notification is due under that subsection for each consecutive day that the person fails to take reasonable action to comply with that subsection. Civil penalties under this section may not exceed $250,000 for all individuals to whom notification is due after a single breach. The attorney general may bring an action to recover the civil penalties imposed under this subsection.

SECTION 16. Section 522.002(b), Business & Commerce Code, is amended to read as follows:

(b) An offense under this section is a Class B misdemeanor, except that the offense is a state jail felony if the information accessed, read, scanned, stored, or transferred was protected health information as defined by the Health Insurance Portability and Accountability Act and Privacy Standards, as defined by Section 181.001, Health and Safety Code.

SECTION 17. Subchapter B, Chapter 531, Government Code, is amended by adding Section 531.0994 to read as follows:

Sec. 531.0994. STUDY; ANNUAL REPORT. (a) The commission, in consultation with the Department of State Health Services, the Texas Medical Board, and the Texas Department of Insurance, shall explore and evaluate new developments in safeguarding protected health information.

(b) Not later than December 1 each year, the commission shall report to the legislature on new developments in safeguarding protected health information and recommendations for the implementation of safeguards within the commission.

SECTION 18. Subchapter B, Chapter 602, Insurance Code, is amended by adding Section 602.054 to read as follows:

Sec. 602.054. COMPLIANCE WITH OTHER LAW. A covered entity shall comply with:

(1) Subchapter D, Chapter 181, Health and Safety Code, except as otherwise provided by that subchapter; and

(2) the standards adopted under Section 182.108, Health and Safety Code.

SECTION 19. (a) In this section, "unsustainable covered entity" means a covered entity, as defined by Section 181.001, Health and Safety Code, that ceases to operate.

(b) The Health and Human Services Commission, in consultation with the Texas Health Services Authority and the Texas Medical Board, shall review issues regarding the security and accessibility of protected health information maintained by an unsustainable covered entity.

(c) Not later than December 1, 2012, the Health and Human Services Commission shall submit to the appropriate standing committees of the senate and the house of representatives recommendations for:

(1) the state agency to which the protected health information maintained by an unsustainable covered entity should be transferred for storage;

(2) ensuring the security of protected health information maintained by unsustainable covered entities in this state, including secure transfer methods from the covered entity to the state;

(3) the method and period of time for which protected health information should be maintained by the state after transfer from an unsustainable covered entity;

(4) methods and processes by which an individual should be able to access the individual's protected health information after transfer to the state; and

(5) funding for the storage of protected health information after transfer to the state.

(d) This section expires January 1, 2013.

SECTION 20. (a) A task force on health information technology is created.

(b) The task force is composed of:

(1) 11 members appointed by the attorney general with the advice of the chairs of the standing committees of the senate and house of representatives having primary jurisdiction over health information technology issues, including:

(A) at least two physicians;

(B) at least two individuals who represent hospitals;

(C) at least one private citizen who represents patient and parental rights; and

(D) at least one pharmacist; and

(2) the following ex officio members:

(A) the executive commissioner of the Health and Human Services Commission or an employee of the commission designated by the executive commissioner;

(B) the commissioner of the Department of State Health Services or an employee of the department designated by the commissioner; and

(C) the presiding officer of the Texas Health Services Authority or an employee of the authority designated by the presiding officer.

(c) Not later than December 1, 2012, the attorney general shall appoint the members of the task force and appoint a chair of the task force from among its membership. The chair of the task force must have expertise in:

(1) state and federal health information privacy law;

(2) patient rights; and

(3) electronic signatures and other consent tools.

(d) The task force shall develop recommendations regarding:

(1) the improvement of informed consent protocols for the electronic exchange of protected health information, as that term is defined by the Health Insurance Portability and Accountability Act and Privacy Standards, as defined by Section 181.001, Health and Safety Code, as amended by this Act;

(2) the improvement of patient access to and use of electronically maintained and disclosed protected health information for the purpose of personal health and coordination of health care services; and

(3) any other critical issues, as determined by the task force, related to the exchange of protected health information.

(e) Not later than January 1, 2014, the task force shall submit to the standing committees of the senate and house of representatives having primary jurisdiction over health information technology issues and the Texas Health Services Authority a report including the task force's recommendations under Subsection (d).

(f) The Texas Health Services Authority shall publish the report submitted under Subsection (e) on the authority's Internet website.

(g) This section expires February 1, 2014.

SECTION 21. Section 531.0315(b), Government Code, is repealed.

SECTION 22. Not later than January 1, 2013:

(1) the attorney general shall adopt the form required by Section 181.154, Health and Safety Code, as added by this Act; and

(2) the Health and Human Services Commission shall adopt the standards required by Section 182.108, Health and Safety Code, as added by this Act.

SECTION 23. (a) Not later than May 1, 2013, the attorney general shall establish the Internet website required by Section 181.103, Health and Safety Code, as added by this Act.

(b) Not later than December 1, 2013, the attorney general shall submit the initial report required by Section 181.104, Health and Safety Code, as added by this Act.

SECTION 24. Not later than December 1, 2013, the Health and Human Services Commission shall submit the initial report required by Section 531.0994, Government Code, as added by this Act.

SECTION 25. The changes in law made by Section 181.201, Health and Safety Code, as amended by this Act, Section 521.053, Business & Commerce Code, as amended by this Act, and Section 521.151(a-1), Business & Commerce Code, as added by this Act, apply only to conduct that occurs on or after the effective date of this Act. Conduct that occurs before the effective date of this Act is governed by the law in effect at the time the conduct occurred, and the former law is continued in effect for that purpose.

SECTION 26. The change in law made by Section 522.002(b), Business & Commerce Code, as amended by this Act, applies only to an offense committed on or after the effective date of this Act. An offense committed before the effective date of this Act is governed by the law in effect at the time the offense was committed, and the former law is continued in effect for that purpose. For purposes of this section, an offense was committed before the effective date of this Act if any element of the offense was committed before that date.

SECTION 27. This Act takes effect September 1, 2012.

The text of the State's 2009 data breach disclosure law is below.

BUSINESS AND COMMERCE CODE.

CHAPTER 48. UNAUTHORIZED USE OF IDENTIFYING INFORMATION

BUSINESS AND COMMERCE CODE

TITLE 4. MISCELLANEOUS COMMERCIAL PROVISIONS

CHAPTER 48. UNAUTHORIZED USE OF IDENTIFYING INFORMATION

Text of chapter as repealed by Acts 2007, 80th Leg., R.S., Ch. 885, Sec. 2.47 effective April 1, 2009

Chapter 48, consisting of Secs. 48.001 to 48.203, was added by Acts 2005, 79th Leg., Ch. 294, Sec. 2.

For another Chapter 48, consisting of Secs. 48.001 to 48.102, added by Acts 2005, 79th Leg., Ch. 298, Sec. 1, see Sec. 48.001 et seq., post.

For another Chapter 48, consisting of Secs. 48.001 to 48.006, added by Acts 2005, 79th Leg., Ch. 544, Sec. 1, see Sec. 48.001 et seq., post.

SUBCHAPTER A. GENERAL PROVISIONS

Text of section effective until April 01, 2009

Sec. 48.001. SHORT TITLE. This chapter may be cited as the Identity Theft Enforcement and Protection Act.

Added by Acts 2005, 79th Leg., Ch. 294, Sec. 2, eff. September 1, 2005.

Text of section effective until April 01, 2009

Sec. 48.002. DEFINITIONS. In this chapter:

(1) "Personal identifying information" means information that alone or in conjunction with other information identifies an individual, including an individual 's:

(A) name, social security number, date of birth, or government-issued identification number;

(B) mother's maiden name;

(C) unique biometric data, including the individual's fingerprint, voice print, and retina or iris image;

(D) unique electronic identification number, address, or routing code; and

(E) telecommunication access device.

(2) "“Sensitive personal information”:

(A) means an individual's first name or first initial and last name in combination with any one or more of the following items, if the name and the items are not encrypted:

(i) social security number;

(ii) driver's license number or government-issued identification number; or

(iii) account number or credit or debit card number in combination with any required security code, access code, or password that would permit access to an individual 's financial account; and

(B) does not include publicly available information that is lawfully made available to the general public from the federal government or a state or local government.

(3) "Telecommunication access device" has the meaning assigned by Section 32.51, Penal Code.

(4) "Victim" means a person whose identifying information is used by an unauthorized person.

Added by Acts 2005, 79th Leg., Ch. 294, Sec. 2, eff. September 1, 2005.

SUBCHAPTER B. IDENTITY THEFT

Text of section effective until April 01, 2009

Sec. 48.101. UNAUTHORIZED USE OR POSSESSION OF PERSONAL IDENTIFYING INFORMATION.

(a) A person may not obtain, possess, transfer, or use personal identifying information of another person without the other person's consent and with intent to obtain a good, a service, insurance, an extension of credit, or any other thing of value in the other person 's name.

(b) It is a defense to an action brought under this section that an act by a person:

(1) is covered by the Fair Credit Reporting Act (15 U.S.C. Section 1681 et seq.); and

(2) is in compliance with that Act and regulations adopted under that Act.

(c) This section does not apply to:

(1) a financial institution as defined by 15 U.S.C. Section 6809; or

(2) a covered entity as defined by Section 601.001 or 602.001, Insurance Code.

Added by Acts 2005, 79th Leg., Ch. 294, Sec. 2, eff. September 1, 2005.

Text of section effective until April 01, 2009

Sec. 48.102. BUSINESS DUTY TO PROTECT AND SAFEGUARD SENSITIVE PERSONAL INFORMATION.

(a) A business shall implement and maintain reasonable procedures, including taking any appropriate corrective action, to protect and safeguard from unlawful use or disclosure any sensitive personal information collected or maintained by the business in the regular course of business.

(b) A business shall destroy or arrange for the destruction of customer records containing sensitive personal information within the business 's custody or control that are not to be retained by the business by:

(1) shredding;

(2) erasing; or

(3) otherwise modifying the sensitive personal information in the records to make the information unreadable or undecipherable through any means.

(c) This section does not apply to a financial institution as defined by 15 U.S.C. Section 6809.

Added by Acts 2005, 79th Leg., Ch. 294, Sec. 2, eff. September 1, 2005.

Text of section effective until April 01, 2009

Sec. 48.103. NOTIFICATION REQUIRED FOLLOWING BREACH OF SECURITY OF COMPUTERIZED DATA.

(a) In this section, "breach of system security" means unauthorized acquisition of computerized data that compromises the security, confidentiality, or integrity of sensitive personal information maintained by a person. Good faith acquisition of sensitive personal information by an employee or agent of the person or business for the purposes of the person is not a breach of system security unless the sensitive personal information is used or disclosed by the person in an unauthorized manner.

(b) A person that conducts business in this state and owns or licenses computerized data that includes sensitive personal information shall disclose any breach of system security, after discovering or receiving notification of the breach, to any resident of this state whose sensitive personal information was, or is reasonably believed to have been, acquired by an unauthorized person. The disclosure shall be made as quickly as possible, except as provided by Subsection (d) or as necessary to determine the scope of the breach and restore the reasonable integrity of the data system.

(c) Any person that maintains computerized data that includes sensitive personal information that the person does not own shall notify the owner or license holder of the information of any breach of system security immediately after discovering the breach, if the sensitive personal information was, or is reasonably believed to have been, acquired by an unauthorized person. (d) A person may delay providing notice as required by Subsections (b) and (c) at the request of a law enforcement agency that determines that the notification will impede a criminal investigation. The notification shall be made as soon as the law enforcement agency determines that it will not compromise the investigation.

(e) A person may give notice as required by Subsections (b) and (c) by providing:

(1)written notice;

(2)electronic notice, if the notice is provided in accordance with 15 U.S.C. Section 7001; or

(3)notice as provided by Subsection (f).

(f)If the person or business demonstrates that the cost of providing notice would exceed $250,000, the number of affected persons exceeds 500,000, or the person does not have sufficient contact information, the notice may be given by:

(1)electronic mail, if the person has an electronic mail address for the affected persons;

(2)conspicuous posting of the notice on the person 's website; or

(3)notice published in or broadcast on major statewide media.

(g)Notwithstanding Subsection (e), a person that maintains its own notification procedures as part of an information security policy for the treatment of sensitive personal information that complies with the timing requirements for notice under this section complies with this section if the person notifies affected persons in accordance with that policy.

(h)If a person is required by this section to notify at one time more than 10,000 persons of a breach of system security, the person shall also notify, without unreasonable delay, all consumer reporting agencies, as defined by 15 U.S.C. Section 1681a, that maintain files on consumers on a nationwide basis, of the timing, distribution, and content of the notices.

Added by Acts 2005, 79th Leg., Ch..294, Sec. 2, eff. September 1, 2005.

SUBCHAPTER C. REMEDIES AND OFFENSES

Text of section effective until April 01, 2009

Sec. 48.201. CIVIL PENALTY; INJUNCTION.

(a) A person who violates this chapter is liable to the state for a civil penalty of at least $2,000 but not more than $50,000 for each violation. The attorney general may bring suit to recover the civil penalty imposed by this subsection.

(b)If it appears to the attorney general that a person is engaging in, has engaged in, or is about to engage in conduct that violates this chapter, the attorney general may bring an action in the name of this state against the person to restrain the violation by a temporary restraining order or a permanent or temporary injunction.

(c)An action brought under Subsection (b) shall be filed in a district court in Travis County or:

(1) in any county in which the violation occurred; or

(2)in the county in which the victim resides, regardless of whether the alleged violator has resided, worked, or done business in the county in which the victim resides.

(d)The plaintiff in an action under this section is not required to give a bond. The court may also grant any other equitable relief that the court considers appropriate to prevent any additional harm to a victim of identity theft or a further violation of this chapter or to satisfy any judgment entered against the defendant, including the issuance of an order to appoint a receiver, sequester assets, correct a public or private record, or prevent the dissipation of a victim 's assets.

(e)The attorney general is entitled to recover reasonable expenses incurred in obtaining injunctive relief, civil penalties, or both, under this section, including reasonable attorney 's fees, court costs, and investigatory costs. Amounts collected by the attorney general under this section shall be deposited in the general revenue fund and may be appropriated only for the investigation and prosecution of other cases under this chapter.

(f)The fees associated with an action under this section are the same as in a civil case, but the fees may be assessed only against the defendant.

Added by Acts 2005, 79th Leg., Ch. 294, Sec. 2, eff. September 1, 2005.

Text of section effective until April 01, 2009

Sec. 48.202. COURT ORDER TO DECLARE INDIVIDUAL A VICTIM OF IDENTITY THEFT.

(a) A person who is injured by a violation of Section 48.101 or who has filed a criminal complaint alleging commission of an offense under Section 32.51, Penal Code, may file an application with a district court for the issuance of a court order declaring that the person is a victim of identity theft. A person may file an application under this section regardless of whether the person is able to identify each person who allegedly transferred or used the person 's identifying information in an unlawful manner.

(b)A person is presumed to be a victim of identity theft under this section if the person charged with an offense under Section 32.51, Penal Code, is convicted of the offense.

(c)After notice and hearing, if the court is satisfied by a preponderance of the evidence that the applicant has been injured by a violation of Section 48.101 or is the victim of an offense under Section 32.51, Penal Code, the court shall enter an order containing:

(1)a declaration that the person filing the application is a victim of identity theft resulting from a violation of Section 48.101 or an offense under Section 32.51, Penal Code, as appropriate;

(2)any known information identifying the violator or person charged with the offense;

(3)the specific personal identifying information and any related document used to commit the alleged violation or offense; and

(4)information identifying any financial account or transaction affected by the alleged violation or offense, including:

(A)the name of the financial institution in which the account is established or of the merchant involved in the transaction, as appropriate;

(B)any relevant account numbers;

(C)the dollar amount of the account or transaction affected by the alleged violation or offense; and

(D)the date of the alleged violation or offense.

(d)An order rendered under this section must be sealed because of the confidential nature of the information required to be included in the order. The order may be opened and the order or a copy of the order may be released only:

(1)to the proper officials in a civil proceeding brought by or against the victim arising or resulting from a violation of this chapter, including a proceeding to set aside a judgment obtained against the victim;

(2)to the victim for the purpose of submitting the copy of the order to a governmental entity or private business to:

(A)prove that a financial transaction or account of the victim was directly affected by a violation of this chapter or the commission of an offense under Section 32.51, Penal Code; or

(B)correct any record of the entity or business that contains inaccurate or false information as a result of the violation or offense;

(3)on order of the judge; or

(4)as otherwise required or provided by law.

(e)A court at any time may vacate an order issued under this section if the court finds that the application or any information submitted to the court by the applicant contains a fraudulent misrepresentation or a material misrepresentation of fact.

(f) A copy of an order provided to a person under Subsection

(d)(1) must remain sealed throughout and after the civil proceeding. Information contained in a copy of an order provided to a governmental entity or business under Subsection (d)(2) is confidential and may not be released to another person except as otherwise required or provided by law.

Added by Acts 2005, 79th Leg., Ch. 294, Sec. 2, eff. September 1, 2005.

Text of section effective until April 01, 2009

Sec. 48.203. DECEPTIVE TRADE PRACTICE.

A violation of Section 48.101 is a deceptive trade practice actionable under Subchapter E, Chapter 17.

Added by Acts 2005, 79th Leg., Ch. 294, Sec. 2, eff. September 1, 2005.

Texas Senate Bill 122 is interesting as it relates to identity theft from more of a law enforcement perspective. It speaks to the requirement of law enforcement officers to remove certain information from a report before releasing it. Texas House Bill 698 speaks to the requirement to securely dispose of business records that contain non-public personal information.

Senate Bill 122

Relating to the prevention and punishment of identity theft and to assistance to certain victims of identity theft; providing penalties.

BE IT ENACTED BY THE LEGISLATURE OF THE STATE OF TEXAS:
SECTION 1.

(a) Chapter 2, Code of Criminal Procedure, is amended by adding Article 2.29 to read as follows:

Art. 2.29. REPORT REQUIRED IN CONNECTION WITH FRAUDULENT USE OR POSSESSION OF IDENTIFYING INFORMATION.

(a) A peace officer to whom an alleged violation of Section 32.51, Penal Code, is reported shall make a written report that includes the following information:

(1) the name of the victim;

(2) the name of the suspect, if known;

(3) the type of identifying information obtained, possessed, transferred, or used in violation of Section 32.51; and

(4) the results of the investigation.

(b) On the victim's request, the peace officer shall provide the report created under Subsection (a) to the victim. In providing the report, the peace officer shall redact any otherwise confidential information that is included in the report, other than the information described by Subsection (a).

(b) The change in law made by this section applies only to the investigation of an offense committed on or after September 1, 2005.

The investigation of an offense committed before September 1, 2005, is covered by the law in effect when the offense was committed, and the former law is continued in effect for that purpose. For purposes of this subsection, an offense is committed before September 1, 2005, if any element of the offense occurs before that date.

SECTION 2. Title 4, Business & Commerce Code, is amended by adding Chapter 48 to read as follows:

CHAPTER 48. IDENTITY THEFT AND PROTECTION
SUBCHAPTER A. GENERAL PROVISIONS

Sec. 48.001. SHORT TITLE. This chapter may be cited as the Identity Theft Enforcement and Protection Act.

Sec. 48.002. DEFINITIONS. In this chapter:

(1) "Peace officer" has the meaning assigned by Section 1.07, Penal Code.

(2) "Personal identifying information" means information that alone or in conjunction with other information identifies an individual, including an individual's:

(A) name, Social Security number, date of birth, or government-issued identification number;

(B) mother's maiden name;

(C) unique biometric data, including the individual's fingerprint, voice print, and retina or iris image;

(D) unique electronic identification number, address, or routing code; and

(E) telecommunication access device.

(3) "Required identifying information" means a copy of:

(A) a police report evidencing the filing of a criminal complaint alleging commission of an offense under Section 32.51, Penal Code, or a copy of a record created under Section 411.0421, Government Code; and

(B) personal identifying information used by the alleged perpetrator of an offense under Section 32.51, Penal Code.

(4) "Telecommunication access device" has the meaning assigned by Section 32.51, Penal Code.

[Sections 48.003-48.100 reserved for expansion]

SUBCHAPTER B. IDENTITY THEFT

Sec. 48.101. UNAUTHORIZED USE OR POSSESSION OF PERSONAL IDENTIFYING INFORMATION.

(a) A person may not obtain, possess, transfer, or use personal identifying information of another person without the other person's consent and with intent to obtain a good, service, insurance, an extension of credit, or any other thing of value in the other person's name.

Sec. 48.102. BUSINESS DUTY TO PROTECT AND SAFEGUARD PERSONAL IDENTIFYING INFORMATION.

(a) A business shall protect and safeguard any personal identifying information collected or maintained by the business in the regular course of business.

(b) A business shall implement and maintain reasonable procedures, including taking any appropriate corrective action, to prevent the unlawful use of any personal identifying information collected or maintained by the business.

(c) This section does not apply to a financial institution as defined by 15 U.S.C. Section 6809(3).

Sec. 48.103. DUTY TO PROVIDE INFORMATION TO CONSUMER.

(a) On a request and with required identifying information provided by a consumer, a person that engages in business with another person who allegedly used the consumer's personal identifying information shall disclose to the consumer or a peace officer without charge and not later than the 10th business day after the date on which the person receives the request:

(1) a copy of any application or transactional information related to an alleged violation of Section 32.51, Penal Code; and

(2) to the extent available, the personal identifying information of the consumer that the person who allegedly impersonated the consumer used to participate in the transaction or complete the application or information related to the use of that information.

(b) Before a person is required to disclose information under Subsection (a) to a peace officer, the person may require the consumer to submit a written statement dated and signed by the consumer. The statement must:
(1) state that the consumer may revoke authorization of the disclosure at any time before the disclosure is made;

(2) authorize the disclosure for a certain period of time;

(3) specify the name of the agency or department to which the disclosure is authorized; and

(4) identify the information that is requested to be disclosed.

(c) A person may not be held liable under this section if the person does not make a disclosure to a peace officer because a consumer fails to provide the authorization requested by the person as permitted by Subsection (b).

[Sections 48.104-48.200 reserved for expansion]

SUBCHAPTER C. REMEDIES AND OFFENSES
Sec. 48.201. A CIVIL PENALTY; INJUNCTION.

(a) A person who violates this chapter is liable to the state for a civil penalty of at least $2,000 but not more than $50,000 for each violation. The attorney general may bring suit to recover the civil penalty imposed by this subsection.

(b) If it appears to the attorney general that a person is engaging in, has engaged in, or is about to engage in conduct that violates this chapter, the attorney general may bring an action in the name of this state against the person to restrain the violations by a temporary restraining order or a permanent or temporary injunction.

(c) An action brought under Subsection (b) shall be filed in a district court in Travis County or:

(1) in any county in which the violation occurred; or

(2) in the county in which the victim resides, regardless of whether the alleged violator has resided, worked, or done business in the county in which the victim resides.

(d) The plaintiff in an action under this section is not required to give a bond. The court may also grant any other equitable relief that the court considers appropriate to prevent any additional harm to a victim of identity theft or a further violation of this chapter or to satisfy any judgment entered against the defendant, including the issuance of an order to appoint a receiver, sequester assets, correct a public or private record, or prevent the dissipation of a victim's assets.

(e) The attorney general is entitled to recover reasonable expenses incurred in obtaining injunctive relief, civil penalties, or both, under this section, including reasonable attorney's fees, court costs, and investigatory costs. Penalties collected by the attorney general under this section shall be deposited in the general revenue fund and may be appropriated only for the investigation and prosecution of other cases under this chapter.

Sec. 48.202. COURT ORDER TO DECLARE INDIVIDUAL A VICTIM OF IDENTIFY THEFT.

(a) A person who is injured by a violation of Section 48.101 or who has filed a criminal complaint alleging an offense under Section 32.51, Penal Code, may file an application with a district court for the issuance of a court order declaring that the person is a victim of identity theft. A person may file an application under this section regardless of whether the person is able to identify each person who allegedly transferred or used the person's identifying information in an unlawful manner.

(b) A person is presumed to be a victim of identity theft under this section if the person charged with an offense under Section 32.51, Penal Code, is convicted of the offense.

(c) After notice and hearing, if the court is satisfied by a preponderance of the evidence that the applicant has been injured by a violation of Section 48.101 or is the victim of an offense under Section 32.51, Penal Code, the court shall enter an order containing:

(1) a declaration that the person filing the application is a victim of identity theft resulting from a violation of Section 48.101 or an offense under Section 32.51, Penal Code, as appropriate;

(2) any known information identifying the violator or person charged with the offense;

(3) the specific personal identifying information and any related document used to commit the alleged violation or offense; and

(4) information identifying any financial account or transaction affected by the alleged violation or offense, including:

(A) the name of the financial institution in which the account is established or of the merchant involved in the transaction, as appropriate;

(B) any relevant account numbers;

(C) the dollar amount of the account or transaction affected by the alleged violation or offense; and

(D) the date of the alleged violation or offense.

(d) An order entered under this section must be sealed because of the confidential nature of the information required to be included in the order. The order may be opened and the order or a copy of the order may be released only:

(1) to the proper officials in a civil proceeding brought by or against the victim arising or resulting from a violation of this chapter, including a proceeding to set aside a judgment obtained against the victim;

(2) to the victim for the purpose of submitting the copy of the order to a governmental entity or private business to:

(A) prove that a financial transaction or account of the victim was directly affected by a violation of this chapter or the commission of an offense under Section 32.51, Penal Code; or

(B) correct any record of the entity or business that contains inaccurate or false information as a result of the violation or offense;

(3) on order of the judge; or

(4) as otherwise required or provided by law.

(e) A court at any time may vacate an order issued under this section if the court finds that the application or any information submitted to the court by the applicant contains a fraudulent misrepresentation or a material misrepresentation of fact.

(f) A copy of an order provided to a person under Subsection (d)(1) must remain sealed throughout and after the civil proceeding. Information contained in a copy of an order provided to a governmental entity or business under Subsection (d)(2) is confidential and may not be released to another person except as otherwise required or provided by law.

Sec. 48.203. DECEPTIVE TRADE PRACTICE.

A violation of this chapter, other than Section 48.103, is a deceptive trade practice actionable under Subchapter E, Chapter 17.

Sec. 48.204. AFFIRMATIVE DEFENSE.

Good faith reliance on a consumer report as defined by Section 20.01 by a financial institution as defined by 31 U.S.C. Section 5312 is an affirmative defense to an action brought against the financial institution under this chapter.

SECTION 3. This Act takes effect September 1, 2005.

House Bill 500

This bill amends Subchapter C, Chapter 11, of the Tax Code to make a driver's license number, personal identification certificate number, or Social Security account number provided in an application for exemption filed with a chief appraiser confidential and therefore not open to public inspection. The bill also prohibits the information from being disclosed to anyone other than an employee of the appraisal office who appraises property. The bill does, however, contain a list of exceptions that authorize such information to be disclosed.

Senate Bill 1559

This bill is related to the confidentiality of, as well as access to, certain personal information contained in instruments recorded with a county clerk.

Senate Bill 566

This bill requires that a local agency that attains identifying information of a person whose identity has been falsely used, once the true identity of the person has been determined, contact the person whose identity has been falsely used. The bill also requires notification to the identity theft victim that he or she is entitled to an expunction of that criminal record; establishes an application process for a person seeking expunction under this circumstance; and makes other provisions regarding the duties of law enforcement agencies regarding the misuse of a person's identity.

Senate Bill 611

This bill is related to the printing of a Social Security number on an identification card or other identification device, and providing a civil penalty.

House Bill 698

Pay close attention to the civil penalties associated with this bill, as they are on a per-record basis. Depending on the actual numbers of records involved, the financial penalties could be very severe. Consider that a CD or backup tape can contain millions of records. The bill provides for the disposal of business records that contain personal identifying information as defined by this section. A business that does not properly dispose of a business record that contains personal identifying information of a customer is liable for a civil penalty of up to $500 for each record. A business that modifies a record in good faith is not liable for a civil penalty. This bill grants the attorney general authority to bring suit against the business to recover a civil penalty, obtain any other remedy, including injunctive relief, as well as costs and attorneys' fees.

House Bill 853

This bill will be of particular interest to businesses that accept returns of product they sell, as it prohibits the collection of identifying information from a consumer for use in compiling or tracking their returns of merchandise. It grants the attorney general, or the county attorney, authority to bring suit to recover a civil penalty of up to $500 for each violation. The attorney general has authority to restrain or enjoin a person from violating this section. While this bill is aimed at protecting non-public personal information, it may also inadvertently aid those making excessive and at times fraudulent returns.

House Bill 1130

This bill requires that a person who requires the disclosure of an individual's Social Security number adopt a data privacy policy.

House Bill 1368

This bill relates to the confidentiality of and access to certain personal information, such as Social Security numbers, in instruments recorded with a county clerk.

House Bill 1430

This bill prohibits the unauthorized collection or transmission of personally identifiable information, including Social Security numbers and credit card numbers. It also prohibits the unauthorized transmission or modifications of computer settings, unauthorized interference with installation or disabling of computer software, damage, or any other deceptive act to obtain information from a consumer's computer. The bill also provides that the attorney general has authority to bring suit to seek injunctive relief and recover civil penalties of an amount not to exceed $100,000 for each violation of this statute as well as reasonable attorneys' fees and costs. In addition, the bill adds a definition for "cause computer software to be copied," provides clean-up language to incorporate this definition, and adds additional provisions to protect consumers.

House Bill 2191

This bill provides that the Social Security number of a living person is exempted from the requirements of Section 552.021 of the Government Code. It also allows a governmental body to redact the Social Security number of a living person from any information the governmental body discloses without the necessity of requesting a decision from the attorney general.

Senate Bill 450

This bill is specific to employees of a prosecutor's office and the confidentiality of certain personal information, including Social Security numbers.

House Bill 59

A BILL TO BE ENTITLED AN ACT relating to the management, security, and protection of personal information and governmental records; providing a criminal penalty.

BE IT ENACTED BY THE LEGISLATURE OF THE STATE OF TEXAS:

SECTION 1. Section 35.50, Business & Commerce Code, is amended by adding Subsection (b-1) and amending Subsection (c) to read as follows:

(b-1) A business that is not owned by a governmental entity may not require a biometric identifier of an individual for membership or to identify the individual.

(c) A person who possesses a biometric identifier of an individual:

(1) may not sell, lease, or otherwise disclose the biometric identifier to another person unless:

(A) the person is not a business or is owned by a governmental entity, and:

(i) the individual consents to the disclosure;

(ii) [(B)] the disclosure completes a financial transaction requested or authorized by the individual;

(iii) [(C)] the disclosure is required or permitted by a federal statute or by a state statute other than Chapter 552, Government Code; or

(iv) [(D)] the disclosure is made by or to a law enforcement agency for a law enforcement purpose; or

(B) the person is a business that is not owned by a governmental entity, and the disclosure is required by a warrant, subpoena, or other order issued after due process; and

(2) shall store, transmit, and protect from disclosure the biometric identifier using reasonable care and in a manner that is the same as or more protective than the manner in which the person stores, transmits, and protects the person's other confidential information.

SECTION 2. Title 6, Civil Practice and Remedies Code, is amended by adding Chapter 142 to read as follows:

CHAPTER 142. CONFIDENTIALITY OF SOCIAL SECURITY NUMBERS

Sec. 142.001. APPLICABILITY. This chapter does not apply to public records or court records.

Sec. 142.002. PROHIBITED USES.

(a) In this section, "publicly display" means to intentionally communicate or otherwise make available to the general public.

(b) A person, including a governmental body as defined by Section 552.003, Government Code, may not:

(1) publicly display in any manner an individual's social security number;

(2) require an individual to transmit a social security number over the Internet, unless the connection is secure or the social security number is encrypted;

(3) require an individual to use a social security number to access an Internet website;

(4) print an individual's social security number on any card required for the individual to have access to products or services provided by the person, unless required by state or federal law;

(5) except as provided by Subsection (c), print an individual's social security number on any materials that are mailed to the individual, unless state or federal law requires the social security number to be printed on the document to be mailed; or

(6) require an individual's social security number to allow the individual access to the products or services provided by the person, unless required by state or federal law.

(c) Subsection (b)(5) does not apply to an application or form sent by mail, including a document sent:

(1) as part of an application or enrollment process;

(2) to establish, amend, or terminate an account, contract, or policy; or

(3) to confirm the accuracy of a social security number.

Sec. 142.003. PERMITTED USES.

(a) A person may collect, use, or release a social security number for internal verification or administrative purposes.

(b) A person who, before January 1, 2007, has used an individual's social security number in a manner prohibited by Section 142.002 may continue using that individual's social security number in the same manner if:

(1) the use of the social security number is continuous; and

(2) the person provides the individual with an annual disclosure, beginning January 1, 2008, informing the individual of the right to stop the use of the social security number in the manner prohibited by Section 142.002.

(c) This chapter does not apply to:

(1) a person who collects, uses, or releases a social security number if the person is required to collect, use, or release the social security number by federal or state law, including Chapter 552, Government Code; or

(2) an institution of higher education if the use of the social security number by the institution is regulated under the Education Code.

Sec. 142.004. DISCONTINUANCE OF USE ON REQUEST.

(a) If a person receives a written request from an individual directing the person to stop using the individual's social security number in a manner prohibited by Section 142.002, the person shall comply with the request not later than the 30th day after the date the request is received.

(b) The person may not impose a fee or charge for complying with the request.

Sec. 142.005. DENIAL OF SERVICES PROHIBITED.

A person may not deny products or services to an individual because the individual makes a written request to discontinue use under Section 142.004.

SECTION 3. Section 560.002, Government Code, is amended to read as follows:

Sec. 560.002. DISCLOSURE OF BIOMETRIC IDENTIFIER.

A governmental body that possesses a biometric identifier of an individual:

(1) may not sell, lease, or otherwise disclose the biometric identifier to another person unless:

(A) the individual consents to the disclosure;

(B) the disclosure is required or permitted by a federal statute or by a state statute other than Chapter 552; or

(C) the disclosure is made by or to a law enforcement agency for a law enforcement purpose; [and]

(2) shall store, transmit, and protect from disclosure the biometric identifier using reasonable care and in a manner that is the same as or more protective than the manner in which the governmental body stores, transmits, and protects its other confidential information; and

(3) may not store a biometric identifier in a database.

SECTION 4. Subtitle A, Title 5, Government Code, is amended by adding Chapter 561 to read as follows:

CHAPTER 561. TEXAS PRIVACY AND SECURITY ACT
SUBCHAPTER A. GENERAL PROVISIONS

Sec. 561.001. SHORT TITLE. This chapter may be cited as the Texas Privacy and Security Act.

Sec. 561.002. LEGISLATIVE FINDINGS; GENERAL PRIVACY AND SECURITY PRINCIPLES.

(a) The legislature finds that:

(1) an increasing number of individuals in this state are concerned that:

(A) personal information held by government may be used inappropriately;

(B) unauthorized persons may have access to that information; and

(C) some of the information may be inaccurate, incomplete, or unnecessary for the effective functioning of government; and

(2) in response to the findings stated by Subdivision 1), each state and local governmental entity in this state must be committed to strengthening privacy protections for personal information held by government in a manner consistent with the public's right to complete information about the affairs of government and the official acts of public officials and employees.

(b) The legislature also finds that:

(1) because inadvertent release, careless storage, or improper disposal of information could result in embarrassment or other harm to individuals, each state and local governmental entity:

(A) has an obligation to protect personal information in the manner required by law; and

(B) must exercise particular care in protecting records containing sensitive and private personal information about health or financial matters and in protecting personal identifiers, such as a social security number;

(2) each state and local governmental entity must strive to balance the need to collect or protect information that relates to the security needs of this state with the need for open government and with the need to protect personal privacy; and

(3) each state and local governmental entity should take affirmative steps to make information about government activities fully and easily available to the public unless there is a demonstrated security risk in doing so.

(c) It is the policy of this state that:

(1) an individual has a right to know how personal information about the individual is handled by government and the extent to which the information may be disclosed or must be kept confidential under law; and

(2) state and local governmental entities should share information as necessary to ensure accountability in government programs or the security of this state while protecting personal information from inappropriate dissemination to the extent possible.

Sec. 561.003. DEFINITIONS. In this chapter:

(1) "Personal information" means information about an individual such as:

(A) the individual's home address, home telephone number, social security number, date of birth, physical characteristics, and similar information about the individual;

(B) information about an individual's marital status or history, whether the individual has family members, and information about the individual's family members; and

(C) personally identifiable information about the individual's health or health history, finances or financial history, and purchases made from government.

(2) "Governmental entity" does not include a court other than a commissioners court.

Sec. 561.004. APPLICABILITY.

This chapter does not apply to information held by or for a court other than a commissioners court.

Sec. 561.005. CONSTRUCTION WITH OTHER LAW.

This chapter does not affect:

(1) the ability of a state or local governmental entity to undertake a lawful investigation or to protect persons, property, or the environment in the manner authorized by law; or

(2) the duty of a state or local governmental entity to comply with applicable law.

[Sections 561.006-561.050 reserved for expansion]

SUBCHAPTER B. SPECIFIC PRIVACY PROTECTIONS

Sec. 561.051. DISCLOSURE OF CERTAIN PERSONAL INFORMATION; COMPELLING INTEREST OR INTENSE PUBLIC CONCERN REQUIREMENT.

(a) This section applies only to the disclosure by a governmental entity of information that reveals an individual's:

(1) social security number;

(2) bank account number, credit card account number, or other financial account number; or

(3) computer password or computer network location or identity.

(b) A state or local governmental entity may not disclose information described by Subsection (a) under Chapter 552 or other law unless the attorney general authorizes the disclosure after determining that:

(1) there is a compelling governmental interest in disclosing the information that cannot be effectively accomplished without the disclosure; or

(2) due to extraordinary circumstances, the information is especially relevant to a matter of intense public concern.

(c) The requestor of the information or the state or local governmental entity may request the attorney general to authorize the disclosure of information described by Subsection (a).

(d) A state or local governmental entity is not required to request a decision of the attorney general under Subchapter G, Chapter 552, before refusing to disclose a social security number, bank account number, credit card account number, other financial account number, computer password, or computer network location or identity in response to a request made under Chapter 552. The state or local governmental entity shall inform the requestor that the requested information is being withheld under this section and that the requestor is entitled to request the attorney general to authorize the disclosure.

(e) The attorney general may adopt rules to implement this section, including rules that describe appropriate and clearly defined circumstances under which a category of information described by Subsection (a) is presumed to satisfy a requirement of Subsection (b) and therefore may be disclosed without the necessity of obtaining specific authorization for the disclosure from the attorney general. A rule of the attorney general that describes circumstances under which information presumptively may be disclosed may limit disclosure to specific state, local, or federal authorities or may allow the information to be generally disclosed under Chapter 552, as appropriate.

(f) The attorney general shall develop procedures under which the office of the attorney general will expedite a decision whether to authorize disclosure of information described by Subsection (a) when expedited consideration is warranted under the circumstances.

(g) A decision of the attorney general under this section may be challenged in court in the same manner that a decision of the attorney general may be challenged under Subchapter H, Chapter 552.

(h) If information described by Subsection (a) is requested under Chapter 552, Section 552.325 applies in relation to the individual who is the subject of the information in the same manner as if the individual were a requestor of the information, except that the attorney general shall notify the individual under Section 552.325(c) if the attorney general proposes to agree to the release of all or part of the information.

Sec. 561.052. COLLECTION OF PERSONAL INFORMATION.

A state or local governmental entity shall establish procedures to ensure that the governmental entity collects personal information only to the extent reasonably necessary to:

(1) implement a program;

(2) authenticate an individual's identity when necessary;

(3) ensure security; or

(4) accomplish another legitimate governmental purpose.

Sec. 561.053. RECORDS RETENTION SCHEDULES.

(a) In adopting or amending its records retention schedule, a state or local governmental entity shall schedule the retention of personal information only for the period necessary to accomplish the purpose for which the information was collected or, if applicable, for the minimum period specifically prescribed by statute.

(b) Subsection (a) does not apply to the retention of personal information that has demonstrable historical or archival value.

Sec. 561.054. GENERAL PRIVACY POLICIES.

(a) A state or local governmental entity shall develop a privacy policy that completely describes in plainly written language:

(1) the reasons that the governmental entity requires or collects each category of personal information about individuals that the entity requires or collects;

(2) the procedures used to require or collect the information;

(3) the persons to whom the information may be disclosed;

(4) the manner in which the information may be disclosed; and

(5) any current arrangement under which the governmental entity sells personal information about individuals or discloses the information under a contract or agreement or in bulk.

(b) The state or local governmental entity shall promptly amend the privacy policy whenever information in the policy becomes incorrect or incomplete.

(c) The state or local governmental entity shall prominently post its current privacy policy:

(1) through a prominent link on the main Internet site maintained by or for the governmental entity; and

(2) next to the sign that the governmental entity posts under Section 552.205.

Sec. 561.055. GOVERNMENT INTERNET SITES; PRIVACY POLICY.

(a) The Department of Information Resources shall adopt rules prescribing minimum privacy standards with which an Internet site or portal maintained by or for a state or local governmental entity must comply. The rules must be designed to limit the collection of personal information about users of the government Internet site or portal to information:

(1) that the state or local governmental entity needs in order to accomplish a legitimate government purpose;

(2) that the user of the site or portal knowingly and intentionally transmits to the state or local governmental entity; or

(3) regarding the collection of which the user of the site or portal has actively given informed consent.

(b) In adopting its rules under this section, the Department of Information Resources shall consider policies adopted by other states and the federal government in this regard.

(c) A state or local governmental entity that maintains an Internet site or portal or for which an Internet site or portal is maintained shall adopt a privacy policy regarding information collected through the site or portal and provide a prominent link to the policy for users of the site or portal. The policy must be consistent with the rules adopted by the Department of Information Resources under this section and must be included as a prominent separate element of the general privacy policy that the entity is required to develop and to which it must provide an Internet link under Section 561.054.

Sec. 561.056. STATE AUDITOR.

(a) The state auditor shall establish auditing guidelines to ensure that state and local governmental entities that the state auditor has authority to audit under other law:

(1) do not routinely collect or retain more personal information than an entity needs to accomplish a legitimate governmental purpose of the entity; and

(2) have established an information management system that protects the privacy and security of information in accordance with applicable state and federal law.

(b) During an appropriate type of audit, the state auditor may audit a state or local governmental entity for compliance with the guidelines established under Subsection (a).

SUBCHAPTER C. GUIDELINES

Sec. 561.101. ATTORNEY GENERAL GUIDELINES FOR REVIEWING PRIVACY AND SECURITY ISSUES.

(a) The attorney general shall establish guidelines for state and local governmental entities to follow when considering privacy and security issues that arise in connection with requests for public information. The guidelines shall address procedural safeguards, legal issues, and other issues that in the opinion of the attorney general would help state and local governmental entities comply with applicable law and recommended information practices when handling personal information or information related to security. The guidelines shall balance the need for open government with respect for personal privacy and with the security needs of this state.

(b) The attorney general shall establish guidelines for sharing information for security purposes among state, local, and federal governmental entities and with the private sector. The guidelines must ensure the protection of personal privacy to the extent feasible and must clarify and explain the legal consequences of sharing the information.

(c) The guidelines do not create exceptions from required disclosure under Chapter 552.

Sec. 561.102. OPEN RECORDS STEERING COMMITTEE; RECORDS MANAGEMENT INTERAGENCY COORDINATING COUNCIL.

(a) The open records steering committee established under Section 552.009 shall periodically study and determine the implications for the personal privacy of individuals and for the security of this state of putting information held by government on the Internet and shall include its findings and recommendations in reports the committee makes under Section 552.009.

(b) The Records Management Interagency Coordinating Council established under Section 441.203 shall provide guidance and policy direction to state and local governmental entities in appropriately incorporating developments in electronic management of information into their information management systems in ways that protect personal privacy and the security of this state and promote appropriate public access to public information that is not excepted from required public disclosure.

SECTION 5. Section 118.0216, Local Government Code, is amended by amending Subsection (d) and adding Subsection (f) to read as follows:

(d) Except as provided by Subsection (f), the [The] fee may be used only to provide funds for specific records management and preservation, including for automation purposes.

(f) The commissioners court of a county may use the fees collected for "Records Management and Preservation" under Section 118.011 that are not needed for use as provided by Subsection (d) for any county purpose.

SECTION 6. Section 118.025(j), Local Government Code, is amended to read as follows:

(j) Any excess funds generated from the collection of a fee under this section remaining after completion of a county records archive preservation and restoration project may be expended only for any county purpose [the purposes described by Section 118.0216]. The commissioners court of a county may not order the collection of a fee authorized by this section after the county records archive preservation and restoration is complete.

SECTION 7. Section 32.51(c), Penal Code, is amended to read as follows:

(c) An offense under this section is a third degree [state jail] felony.

SECTION 8.

(a) An institution of higher education that is not exempt from Chapter 142, Civil Practice and Remedies Code, as added by this

Act, under Section 142.003(c)(2), Civil Practice and Remedies Code, as added by this Act, must comply with Chapter 142 on or before September 1, 2009.

(b) Each state and local governmental entity shall examine its records retention schedule and amend the schedule so that it complies with Section 561.053, Government Code, as added by this Act.

SECTION 9.

(a) The change in law made by this Act to Section 32.51, Penal Code, applies only to an offense committed on or after the effective date of this Act. For purposes of this section, an offense is committed before the effective date of this Act if any element of the offense occurs before the effective date.

(b) An offense committed before the effective date of this Act is covered by the law in effect when the offense was committed, and the former law is continued in effect for that purpose.

SECTION 10.

(a) Except as provided by Subsection (b) of this section, this Act takes effect September 1, 2007.

(b) Section 2 of this Act takes effect January 1, 2008.

House Bill 87

This bill relates to acquisition of personal information in a business record through fraudulent means. This practice is often referred to as pretexting.

House Bill 1262

AN ACT relating to civil liability for the breach of security of certain computerized data containing sensitive personal information.

BE IT ENACTED BY THE LEGISLATURE OF THE STATE OF TEXAS:

SECTION 1. Subchapter C, Chapter 48, Business & Commerce Code, as added by Chapter 294, Acts of the 79th Legislature, Regular Session, 2005, is amended by adding Section 48.204 to read as follows:

Sec. 48.204. STRICT LIABILITY FOLLOWING BREACH OF SECURITY OF CERTAIN COMPUTERIZED DATA.

(a) In this section, "breach of system security" has the meaning assigned by Section 48.103, including the exception provided by Section 48.103(a) for the good faith acquisition of sensitive personal information by an employee or agent of the person maintaining the information.

(b) A public or private entity that maintains computerized data that includes sensitive personal information is, following any breach of system security of that data, strictly liable to each individual whose sensitive personal information was acquired by an unauthorized person.

(c) The amount of liability to each individual described by Subsection (b) is:

(1)the amount of actual damages sustained by the individual as a result of the breach of system security;

(2)statutory damages in the amount of $1,000; and

(3)an amount necessary to cover the costs charged by a consumer reporting agency, as that term is defined by Section 20.01, for monitoring the individual 's consumer credit information for the two-year period following the date of the breach of system security.

(d) An individual described by Subsection (b) is also entitled to recover any court costs and reasonable attorney 's fees incurred in seeking damages and other amounts the individual may be entitled to recover for a claim under this section.

(e) Sovereign immunity to suit is waived and abolished to the extent of liability created by this section.

(f) An individual having a claim under this section may sue a governmental unit, as that term is defined by Section 101.001, Civil Practice and Remedies Code, for damages and other amounts the individual may be entitled to recover under this section.

SECTION 2. This Act takes effect September 1, 2007.

Senate Bill 223

AN ACT relating to a loss of computerized data or breach of computer security involving sensitive personal information.

BE IT ENACTED BY THE LEGISLATURE OF THE STATE OF TEXAS:

SECTION 1. The heading to Section 48.103, Business & Commerce Code, as added by Chapter 294, Acts of the 79th Legislature, Regular Session, 2005, is amended to read as follows:

Sec. 48.103. NOTIFICATION REQUIRED FOLLOWING BREACH OF SECURITY OR LOSS OF CERTAIN COMPUTERIZED DATA.

SECTION 2. Section 48.103, Business & Commerce Code, as added by Chapter 294, Acts of the 79th Legislature, Regular Session, 2005, is amended by amending Subsections (b), (c), (d), (g), and (h) and adding Subsection (i) to read as follows:

(b)A person that conducts business in this state, including any state or local governmental entity in this state, that [and] owns or licenses computerized data that includes sensitive personal information shall disclose any breach of system security or loss of the information, after discovering or receiving notification of the breach or after discovering the loss, to any resident of this state whose sensitive personal information was, or is reasonably believed to have been, acquired by an unauthorized person or was lost. A [The] disclosure required by this subsection shall be made as quickly as possible, except as provided by Subsection (d) or as necessary to determine the scope of the breach or loss and restore the reasonable integrity of the data or data system.

(c)Any person, including a state or local governmental entity, that maintains computerized data that includes sensitive personal information that the person does not own shall notify the owner or license holder of the information of any breach of system security or loss of the sensitive personal information immediately after discovering the breach or loss, if the sensitive personal information was, or is reasonably believed to have been, acquired by an unauthorized person or was lost.

(d)A person may delay providing notice as required by Subsections (b), [and] (c), and (i) at the request of a law enforcement agency that determines that the notification will impede a criminal investigation. The notification shall be made as soon as the law enforcement agency determines that it will not compromise the investigation.

(g)Notwithstanding Subsection (e), a person that maintains its own notification procedures as part of an information security policy for the treatment of sensitive personal information that complies with the timing requirements for notice under this section complies with the notice requirements of this section other than Subsection (i) if the person notifies affected persons in accordance with that policy.

(h)If a person is required by this section to notify at one time more than 10,000 persons of a breach of system security or loss of sensitive personal information, the person shall also notify, without unreasonable delay, all consumer reporting agencies, as defined by 15 U.S.C. Section 1681a, that maintain files on consumers on a nationwide basis, of the timing, distribution, and content of the notices.

(i)A person required to provide notice under Subsection (b) or (c) shall, without unreasonable delay, also notify the attorney general in writing of each incident involving a breach of system security or loss of computerized data containing sensitive personal information. The notice must contain:

(1)the person 's name and address;

(2)the date the breach or loss was discovered;

(3)a summary of the circumstances surrounding the breach or loss;

(4)the type of information that was lost, stolen, or compromised;

(5)the number of persons whose sensitive personal information was lost, stolen, or compromised as a result of the incident; and

(6)the name, mailing address, and telephone number of a contact person from whom a person affected by the incident may request additional information.

SECTION 3. Subchapter B, Chapter 48, Business & Commerce Code, as added by Chapter 294, Acts of the 79th Legislature, Regular Session, 2005, is amended by adding Section 48.104 to read as follows:

Sec. 48.104. REGISTRY OF PERSONS REPORTING BREACH OF SECURITY OR LOSS OF CERTAIN COMPUTERIZED DATA.

(a) The attorney general shall establish and maintain a central registry of persons required to provide notice under Section 48.103(b) or (c) of a breach of system security or a loss of computerized data containing sensitive personal information.

(b) The registry must include a record of each incident involving a breach of system security or loss of sensitive personal information reported under Section 48.103(i). The record must contain the required information listed under that section.

(c) The registry may include other information the attorney general considers necessary and appropriate to assist persons receiving notice under Section 48.103 that their sensitive personal information was lost, stolen, or compromised.

(d) The attorney general shall make the registry information available to the public on request and by publishing it on the attorney general 's website. The attorney general shall update the registry information on the website at least twice monthly.

(e) Any sensitive personal information received by or in connection with the operation of the registry by the attorney general is confidential and not subject to disclosure under Chapter 552, Government Code.

(f) The attorney general may adopt rules necessary to implement this section.

SECTION 4. The changes in law made by this Act apply only to a breach of system security or loss of data containing sensitive personal information that occurs on or after the effective date of this Act. A breach of system security or loss of data containing sensitive personal information that occurs before the effective date of this Act is governed by the law in effect on the date the breach or loss occurred, and the former law is continued in effect for that purpose.

SECTION 5. Not later than January 1, 2008, the attorney general shall establish the registry required by Section 48.104, Business & Commerce Code, as added by this Act.

SECTION 6. This Act takes effect September 1, 2007.

Chapter 44: Utah

Utah's Senate Bill 69 requires disclosure if the information on any of its state's residents is thought to have been disclosed. As with the disclosure laws of other states, the disclosure requirement applies only if the data was not encrypted. The law also states that if, upon an investigation, it is decided that the data that was compromised is not, and is unlikely to be misused, then disclosure is not required. As I have asked before, who performs these investigations? If it is the company that had the breach, there is a conflict of interest in having them decide whether the data that was lost may ultimately be misused.

This bill addresses the integrity of consumer credit databases. It defines terms and requires a person maintaining personal information in connection with a business to implement procedures to protect personal information. It also requires the destruction of certain records; requires disclosure of breaches of databases containing personal information; and provides for enforcement by the attorney general.

Protection of Information in Consumer Credit Databases–Senate Bill 69

LONG TITLE

General Description: This bill addresses the integrity of consumer credit databases.

This bill: defines terms; requires a person maintaining personal information in connection with a business to implement procedures to protect personal information; requires destruction of certain records; requires disclosure of breaches of databases containing personal information; and provides for enforcement by the attorney general. Monies Appropriated in this Bill: This bill appropriates from the General Fund to the attorney general: as an ongoing appropriation subject to future budget constraints, $89,400 for fiscal year 2006-07; and $23,000 for fiscal year 2006-07 only.

Other Special Clauses: This bill takes effect on January 1, 2007. Utah Code Sections Affected:

ENACTS: 13-42-101, Utah Code Annotated 1953 13-42-102, Utah Code Annotated 1953 13-42-201, Utah Code Annotated 1953 13-42-202, Utah Code Annotated 1953 13-42-301, Utah Code Annotated 1953 Be it enacted by the Legislature of the state of Utah: Section 1. Section 13-42-101 is enacted to read: CHAPTER 42. CONSUMER CREDIT PROTECTION ACT Part 1. General Provisions 13-42-101. Title. This chapter is known as the "Consumer Credit Protection Act." Section 2. Section 13-42-102 is enacted to read: 13-42-102. Definitions. As used in this chapter:

(1) (a) "Breach of system security" means an unauthorized acquisition of computerized data maintained by a person that compromises the security, confidentiality, or integrity of personal information.

(b) "Breach of system security" does not include the acquisition of personal information by an employee or agent of the person possessing unencrypted computerized data unless the personal information is used for an unlawful purpose or disclosed in an unauthorized manner.

(2) "Consumer" means a natural person.

(3) (a) "Personal information" means a person's first name or first initial and last name, combined with any one or more of the following data elements relating to that person when either the name or date element is unencrypted or not protected by another method that renders the data unreadable or unusable:

(i) Social Security number;

(ii) (A) financial account number, or credit or debit card number; and (B) any required security code, access code, or password that would permit access to the person's account; or

(iii) driver license number or state identification card number. (b) "Personal information" does not include information regardless of its source,

contained in federal, state, or local government records or in widely distributed media that are lawfully made available to the general public.

(4) "Record" includes materials maintained in any form, including paper and electronic. Section 3. Section 13-42-201 is enacted to read: Part 2. Protection of Personal Information 13-42-201. Protection of personal information.

(1) Any person who conducts business in the state and maintains personal information shall implement and maintain reasonable procedures to:

(a) prevent unlawful use or disclosure of personal information collected or maintained in the regular course of business; and

(b) destroy, or arrange for the destruction of, records containing personal information that are not to be retained by the person.

(2) The destruction of records under Subsection (1)(b) shall be by:

(a) shredding;

(b) erasing; or

(c) otherwise modifying the personal information to make the information indecipherable.

(3) This section does not apply to a financial institution as defined by 15 U.S.C. Section 6809.

Section 4. Section 13-42-202 is enacted to read: 13-42-202. Personal information -- Disclosure of system security breach.

(1) (a) A person who owns or licenses computerized data that includes personal information concerning a Utah resident shall, when the person becomes aware of a breach of system security, conduct in good faith a reasonable and prompt investigation to determine the likelihood that personal information has been or will be misused for identity theft or fraud purposes.

(b) If an investigation under Subsection (1)(a) reveals that the misuse of personal information for identity theft or fraud purposes has occurred, or is reasonably likely to occur, the person shall provide notification to each affected Utah resident. (2) A person required to provide notification under Subsection (1) shall provide the notification in the most expedient time possible without unreasonable delay:

(a) considering legitimate investigative needs of law enforcement, as provided in Subsection (4)(a);

(b) after determining the scope of the breach of system security; and

(c) after restoring the reasonable integrity of the system.

(3) (a) A person who maintains computerized data that includes personal information that the person does not own or license shall notify and cooperate with the owner or licensee of the information of any breach of system security immediately following the person's discovery of the breach if misuse of the personal information occurs or is reasonably likely to occur.

(b) Cooperation under Subsection (3)(a) includes sharing information relevant to the breach with the owner or licensee of the information.

(4) (a) Notwithstanding Subsection (2), a person may delay providing notification under Subsection (1) at the request of a law enforcement agency that determines that notification may impede a

criminal investigation. (b) A person who delays providing notification under Subsection (4)(a) shall provide notification in good faith without unreasonable delay in the most expedient time possible after the law enforcement agency informs the person that notification will no longer impede the criminal investigation.

(5) (a) A notification required by this section may be provided:

(i) in writing by first-class mail to the most recent address the person has for the resident;

(ii) electronically, if the person's primary method of communication with the resident is by electronic means, or if provided in accordance with the consumer disclosure provisions of 15 U.S.C. Section 7001;

(iii) by telephone, including through the use of automatic dialing technology not prohibited by other law; or

(iv) by publishing notice of the breach of system security in a newspaper of general circulation.

(b) If a person maintains the person's own notification procedures as part of an information security policy for the treatment of personal information the person is considered to be in compliance with this chapter's notification requirements if the procedures are otherwise consistent with this chapter's timing requirements and the person notifies each affected Utah resident in accordance with the person's information security policy in the event of a breach.

(c) A person who is regulated by state or federal law and maintains procedures for a breach of system security under applicable law established by the primary state or federal regulator is considered to be in compliance with this part if the person notifies each affected Utah resident in accordance with the other applicable law in the event of a breach.

(6) A waiver of this section is contrary to public policy and is void and unenforceable.

Section 5. Section 13-42-301 is enacted to read:

Part 3. Enforcement 13-42-301. Enforcement.

(1) The attorney general may enforce this chapter's provisions.

(2) (a) Nothing in this chapter creates a private right of action.

(b) Nothing in this chapter affects any private right of action existing under other law, including contract or tort.

(3) A person who violates this chapter's provisions is subject to a civil fine of:

(a) no greater than $2,500 for a violation or series of violations concerning a specific consumer; and

(b) no greater than $100,000 in the aggregate for related violations concerning more than one consumer.

(4) In addition to the penalties provided in Subsection (3), the attorney general may seek injunctive relief to prevent future violations of this chapter in:

(a) the district court located in Salt Lake City; or

(b) the district court for the district in which resides a consumer who is affected by the violation.

Section 6. Appropriation.

(1) There is appropriated from the General Fund to the attorney general:

(a) as an ongoing appropriation, subject to future budget constraints, $89,400 for fiscal year 2006-07; and

(b) $23,000 for fiscal year 2006-07 only.

(2) It is the intent of the Legislature that:

(a) the monies appropriated under Subsection (1)(a) be used to fund investigatory activities that may lead to an enforcement action by the attorney general under Section 13-42-301 ; and

(b) the monies appropriated under Subsection (1)(b) be used to purchase equipment required for investigatory activities that may lead to an enforcement action by the attorney general under Section 13-42-301 . Section 7. Effective date. This bill takes effect on January 1, 2007.

Senate Bill 202

This bill modifies the Government Records Access and Management Act regarding private information by providing that peace officers in specified classifications are "at-risk government employees" regarding specified personal information, including Social Security numbers.

Author's Note: As a former police officer myself, I appreciate the specific protection offered by this bill. I encourage my readers to try to imagine having to leave a restaurant because somebody you had either arrested in the past or issued a traffic ticket to recognizes you, and you are concerned what they might put on your or your family's food.

Senate Bill 195

This bill deletes the provisions that currently give the Utah Division of Consumer Protection authority to regulate the misuse of personal identifying information. It also modifies the provisions related to a deceptive act or practice by a supplier, and modifies certain administrative fines imposed for violations of the Utah Consumer Sales Practices Act.

The bill further modifies the definition of a credit services organization for purposes of the Credit Services Organizations Act; modifies the Charitable Solicitations Act to change certain requirements for an application for registration to enable electronic filing; and exempts certain corporations from the act. The bill also contains language that modifies the definitions of a telephone solicitation and a telephone solicitor for purposes of the Telephone Fraud Prevention Act to be consistent with other statutes, and makes technical corrections.

Senate Bill 52

The provisions of this bill carry the threat of jail time, as it provides that when an act of communications fraud involves obtaining sensitive personal identifying information, the offense is a second-degree felony. The bill further states that the penalty is not based on the value involved.

House Bill 245

This bill modifies the Insurance Code addressing the confidentiality and distribution of certain records or documents, and prohibits certain activities related to Social Security numbers.

House Bill 19

This bill relates to identification card expiration amendments and provides that an identification card may not bear a person's Social Security number or their place of birth.

Senate Bill 71

This bill allows a consumer to place a security freeze on their credit report; outlines the method for placing and removing a security freeze; provides exceptions; prohibits the release of a credit report that is subject to a security freeze, except in certain instances; allows certain fees to be charged in connection with a security freeze; governs changes to a credit report that is subject to a security freeze; prohibits some uses of a consumer's Social Security number; and provides for enforcement.

Chapter 45: Vermont

As with the laws of several other states, Vermont's Senate Bill 284 has an exemption from its disclosure requirement if, upon investigation, it is determined that the stolen data was not, and likely will not be, misused.

Senate Bill 284

This bill enacts a Security Breach Notice Act, a Social Security Number Protection Act, and a Document Safe Destruction Act.

CHAPTER 62. PROTECTION OF PERSONAL INFORMATION

Subchapter 1. General Provisions

§2430. DEFINITIONS

The following definitions shall apply throughout this chapter unless otherwise required:

(1) "Business" means a sole proprietorship, partnership, corporation, association, limited liability company, or other group, however organized and whether or not organized to operate at a profit, including a financial institution organized, chartered, or holding a license or authorization certificate under the laws of this state, any other state, the United States, or any other country, or the parent, affiliate, or subsidiary of a financial institution, but in no case shall it include the state, a state agency, or any political subdivision of the state.

(2) "Consumer" means an individual residing in this state.

(3) "Data collector" may include, but is not limited to, the state, state agencies, political subdivisions of the state, public and private universities, privately and publicly held corporations, limited liability companies, financial institutions, retail operators, and any other entity that, for any purpose, whether by automated collection

or otherwise, handles, collects, disseminates, or otherwise deals with nonpublic personal information.

(4) "Encryption" means use of an algorithmic process to transform data into a form in which the data is rendered unreadable or unusable without use of a confidential process or key.

(5)(A) "Personal information" means an individual's first name or first initial and last name in combination with any one or more of the following data elements, when either the name or the data elements are not encrypted or redacted or protected by another method that renders them unreadable or unusable by unauthorized persons:

(i) Social Security number;

(ii) Motor vehicle operator's license number or non-driver identification card number;

(iii) Financial account number or credit or debit card number, if circumstances exist in which the number could be used without additional identifying information, access codes, or passwords;

(iv) Account passwords or personal identification numbers or other access codes for a financial account.

(B) "Personal information" does not mean publicly available information that is lawfully made available to the general public from federal, state, or local government records.

(6) "Records" means any material on which written, drawn, spoken, visual, or electromagnetic information is recorded or preserved, regardless of physical form or characteristics.

(7) "Redaction" means the rendering of data so that it is unreadable or is truncated so that no more than the last four digits of the identification number are accessible as part of the data.

(8)(A) "Security breach" means unauthorized acquisition or access of computerized data that compromises the security, confidentiality, or integrity of personal information maintained by the data collector.

(B) "Security breach" does not include good faith but unauthorized acquisition or access of personal information by an employee or agent of the data collector for a legitimate purpose of the data collector, provided that the personal information is not used for a purpose unrelated to the data collector's business or subject to further unauthorized disclosure.

Subchapter 2. Security Breach Notice Act

§2435. NOTICE OF SECURITY BREACHES

(a) This section shall be known as the Security Breach Notice Act.

(b) Notice of breach.

(1) Except as set forth in subsection (d) of this section, any data collector that owns or licenses computerized personal information that includes personal information concerning a consumer shall notify the consumer that there has been a security breach following discovery or notification to the data collector of the breach. Notice of the breach shall be made in the most expedient time possible and without unreasonable delay, consistent with the legitimate needs of the law enforcement agency, as provided in subdivision (3) of this subsection, or with any measures necessary to determine the scope of the breach and restore the reasonable integrity, security, and confidentiality of the data system.

(2) Any data collector that maintains or possesses computerized data containing personal information of a consumer that the business does not own or license or any data collector that conducts business in Vermont that maintains or possesses records or data containing personal information that the data collector does not

own or license shall notify the owner or licensee of the information of any security breach immediately following discovery of the breach, consistent with the legitimate needs of law enforcement as provided in subdivision (3) of this subsection.

(3) The notice required by this subsection shall be delayed upon request of a law enforcement agency. A law enforcement agency may request the delay if it believes that notification may impede a law enforcement investigation, or a national or homeland security investigation or jeopardize public safety or national or homeland security interests. In the event law enforcement makes the request in a manner other than in writing, the data collector shall document such request contemporaneously in writing, including the name of the law enforcement officer making the request and the officer's law enforcement agency engaged in the investigation. A law enforcement agency shall promptly notify the data collector when the law enforcement agency no longer believes that notification may impede a law enforcement investigation, or a national or homeland security investigation or jeopardize public safety or national or homeland security interests. The data collector shall provide notice required by this section without unreasonable delay upon receipt of a written communication, which includes facsimile or electronic communication, from the law enforcement agency withdrawing its request for delay.

(4) The notice shall be clear and conspicuous. The notice shall include a description of the following:

(A) The incident in general terms.

(B) The type of personal information that was subject to the unauthorized access or acquisition.

(C) The general acts of the business to protect the personal information from further unauthorized access or acquisition.

(D) A toll-free telephone number that the consumer may call for further information and assistance.

(E) Advice that directs the consumer to remain vigilant by reviewing account statements and monitoring free credit reports.

(5) For purposes of this subsection, notice to consumers may be provided by one of the following methods:

(A) Direct notice to consumers, which may be by one of the following methods:

(i) Written notice mailed to the consumer's residence;

(ii) Electronic notice, for those consumers for whom the data collector has a valid e-mail address if:

(I) the data collector does not have contact information set forth in subdivisions (i) and (iii) of this subdivision (5)(A), the data collector's primary method of communication with the consumer is by electronic means, the electronic notice does not request or contain a hypertext link to a request that the consumer provide personal information, and the electronic notice conspicuously warns consumers not to provide personal information in response to electronic communications regarding security breaches; or

(II) the notice provided is consistent with the provisions regarding electronic records and signatures for notices as set forth in 15 U.S.C. §7001; or

(iii) Telephonic notice, provided that telephonic contact is made directly with each affected consumer, and the telephonic contact is not through a prerecorded message.

(B) Substitute notice, if the data collector demonstrates that the cost of providing written or telephonic notice, pursuant to subdivision (A)(i) or (iii) of this subdivision (5), to affected consumers would exceed $5,000.00 or that the affected class of affected consumers to be provided written or telephonic notice, pursuant to subdivision (A)(i) or (iii) of this subdivision (5), exceeds 5,000, or the data collector does not have sufficient contact information. Substitute notice shall consist of all of the following:

(i) conspicuous posting of the notice on the data collector's website page if the data collector maintains one; and

(ii) notification to major statewide and regional media.

(c) In the event a data collector provides notice to more than 1,000 consumers at one time pursuant to this section, the data collector shall notify, without unreasonable delay, all consumer reporting agencies that compile and maintain files on consumers on a nationwide basis, as defined in 15 U.S.C. §1681a(p), of the timing, distribution, and content of the notice. This subsection shall not apply to a person who is licensed or registered under Title 8 by the department of banking, insurance, securities, and health care administration.

(d)(1) Notice of a security breach pursuant to subsection (b) of this section is not required if the data collector establishes that misuse of personal information is not reasonably possible and the data collector provides notice of the determination that the misuse of the personal information is not reasonably possible pursuant to the requirements of this subsection. If the data collector establishes that misuse of the personal information is not reasonably possible, the data collector shall provide notice of its determination that misuse of the personal information is not reasonably possible and a detailed explanation for said determination to the Vermont attorney general or to the department of banking, insurance, securities, and health care administration in the event that the data collector is a person or entity licensed or registered with the department under Title 8 or this title. The data collector may designate its notice and detailed explanation to the Vermont attorney general or the department of banking, insurance, securities, and health care administration as "trade secret" if the notice and detailed explanation meet the definition of trade secret contained in subdivision 317(c)(9) of Title 1.

(2) If a data collector established that misuse of personal information was not reasonably possible under subdivision (1) of this subsection, and subsequently obtains facts indicating that misuse of the personal information has occurred or is occurring, the data collector shall provide notice of the security breach pursuant to subsection (b) of this section.

(e) Any waiver of the provisions of this subchapter is contrary to public policy and is void and unenforceable.

(f) A financial institution that is subject to the following guidances, and any revisions, additions, or substitutions relating to said interagency guidance shall be exempt from this section:

(1) The Federal Interagency Guidance Response Programs for Unauthorized Access to Consumer Information and Customer Notice, issued on March 7, 2005, by the Board of Governors of the Federal Reserve System, the Federal Deposit Insurance Corporation, the Office of the Comptroller of the Currency, and the Office of Thrift Supervision; or

(2) Final Guidance on Response Programs for Unauthorized Access to Member Information and Member Notice, issued on April 14, 2005, by the National Credit Union Administration.

(g) Enforcement.

(1) With respect to all data collectors and other entities subject to this subchapter, other than a person or entity licensed or registered with the department of banking, insurance, securities, and health care administration under Title 8 or this title, the attorney general and state's attorney shall have sole and full authority to investigate potential violations of this subchapter and to enforce, prosecute,

obtain and impose remedies for a violation of this subchapter or any rules or regulations made pursuant to this chapter as the attorney general and state's attorney have under chapter 63 of this title. The attorney general may refer the matter to the state's attorney in an appropriate case. The superior courts shall have jurisdiction over any enforcement matter brought by the attorney general or a state's attorney under this subsection.

(2) With respect to a data collector that is a person or entity licensed or registered with the department of banking, insurance, securities, and health care administration under Title 8 or this title, the department of banking, insurance, securities and health care administration shall have the full authority to investigate potential violations of this subchapter and to prosecute, obtain, and impose remedies for a violation of this subchapter or any rules or regulations adopted pursuant to this subchapter, as the department has under Title 8 or this title or any other applicable law or regulation.

(h) Vermont law enforcement agencies, including the department of public safety, shall not be considered a data collector. Except as provided in subdivisions (b)(2) and (b)(3) of this section, Vermont law enforcement agencies, including the department of public safety, shall be exempt from this subchapter.

Subchapter 3. Social Security Number Protection Act

§2440. SOCIAL SECURITY NUMBER PROTECTION

(a) This section shall be known as the Social Security Number Protection Act.

(b) Except as provided in subsection (c) of this section, a business may not do any of the following:

(1) Intentionally communicate or otherwise make available to the general public an individual's Social Security number.

(2) Intentionally print or imbed an individual's Social Security number on any card required for the individual to access products or services provided by the person or entity.

(3) Require an individual to transmit his or her Social Security number over the internet unless the connection is secure or the Social Security number is encrypted.

(4) Require an individual to use his or her Social Security number to access an internet website, unless a password or unique personal identification number or other authentication device is also required to access the internet website.

(5) Print an individual's Social Security number on any materials that are mailed to the individual, unless state or federal law requires the Social Security number to be on the document to be mailed.

(6) Sell, lease, lend, trade, rent, or otherwise intentionally disclose an individual's Social Security number to a third party without written consent to the disclosure from the individual, when the party making the disclosure knows or in the exercise of reasonable diligence would have reason to believe that the third party lacks a legitimate purpose for obtaining the individual's Social Security number.

(c) Subsection (b) of this section shall not apply:

(1) When a Social Security number is included in an application or in documents related to an enrollment process, or to establish, amend, or terminate an account, contract, or policy; or to confirm the accuracy of the Social Security number for the purpose of obtaining a credit report pursuant to 15 U.S.C. §1681(b)(2). A Social Security number that is permitted to be mailed under this section may not be printed, in whole or in part, on a postcard or other mailer not requiring an envelope, or visible on an envelope without the envelope having been opened.

(2) To the collection, use, or release of a Social Security number reasonably necessary for administrative purposes or internal verification.

(3) To the opening of an account or the provision of or payment for a product or service authorized by an individual.

(4) To the collection, use, or release of a Social Security number to investigate or prevent fraud; conduct background checks; conduct social or scientific research; collect a debt; obtain a credit report from or furnish data to a consumer reporting agency pursuant to the fair credit reporting act, 15 U.S.C. §1681, et seq.; undertake a permissible purpose enumerated under Gramm Leach Bliley, 12 C.F.R. §216.13-15; or locate an individual who is missing, is a lost relative, or is due a benefit, such as a pension, insurance, or unclaimed property benefit.

(5) To a business acting pursuant to a court order, warrant, subpoena, or when otherwise required by law, or in response to a facially valid discovery request pursuant to rules applicable to a court or administrative body that has jurisdiction over the disclosing entity.

(6) To a business providing the Social Security number to a federal, state, or local government entity, including a law enforcement agency, the department of public safety, and a court, or their agents or assigns.

(7) To a Social Security number that has been redacted.

(8)(A) To a business that has used, prior to January 1, 2007, an individual's Social Security number in a manner inconsistent with subsection (b) of this section, which may continue using that individual's Social Security number in that manner on or after January 1, 2007, if all of the following conditions are met:

(i) The use of the Social Security number is continuous. If the use is stopped for any reason, subsection (b) of this section shall apply.

(ii) The individual is provided an annual disclosure that informs the individual that he or she has the right to stop the use of his or her Social Security number in a manner prohibited by subsection (b) of this section.

(iii) A written request by an individual to stop the use of his or her Social Security number in a manner prohibited by subsection (b) of this section is implemented within 30 days of the receipt of the request. There shall not be a fee or charge for implementing the request.

(iv) The person or entity does not deny services to an individual because the individual makes a written request pursuant to this subsection.

(B) Nothing in this subdivision (8) is intended to apply to the collection, use or dissemination of Social Security numbers collected prior to January 1, 2007 and exempted from the provisions of subsection (b) of this section pursuant to subdivisions (1) through (7) or (9) and (10) of this subsection.

(9) To information obtained from a recorded document in the official records of the town clerk or municipality.

(10) To information obtained from a document filed in the official records of the courts.

(d) Except as provided in subsection (e) of this section, the state and any state agency, political subdivision of the state, and agent or employee of the state, a state agency, or a political subdivision of the state, may not do any of the following:

(1) Collect a Social Security number from an individual unless authorized or required by law, state or federal regulation, or grant agreement to do so or unless the collection of the Social Security number or records containing the Social Security number is related to

the performance of that agency's duties and responsibilities as prescribed by law.

(2) Fail, when collecting a Social Security number from an individual in a hard copy format, to segregate that number on a separate page from the rest of the record, or as otherwise appropriate, in order that the Social Security number can be more easily redacted pursuant to a valid public records request.

(3) Fail, when collecting a Social Security number from an individual, to provide, at the time of or prior to the actual collection of the Social Security number by that agency, that individual, upon request, with a statement of the purpose or purposes for which the Social Security number is being collected and used.

(4) Use the Social Security number for any purpose other than the purpose set forth in the statement required under subdivision (3) of this subsection.

(5) Intentionally communicate or otherwise make available to the general public a person's Social Security number.

(6) Intentionally print or imbed an individual's Social Security number on any card required for the individual to access government services.

(7) Require an individual to transmit the individual's Social Security number over the internet, unless the connection is secure or the Social Security number is encrypted.

(8) Require an individual to use the individual's Social Security number to access an internet website, unless a password or unique personal identification number or other authentication device is also required to access the internet website.

(9) Print an individual's Social Security number on any materials that are mailed to the individual, unless a state or federal law, regulation, or grant agreement requires that the Social Security number be on the document to be mailed. A Social Security number that is permitted to be mailed under this subdivision may not be printed, in whole or in part, on a postcard or other mailer not requiring an envelope, or visible on an envelope, without the envelope having been opened.

(e) Subsection (d) of this section does not apply to:

(1) Social Security numbers disclosed to another governmental entity or its agents, employees, contractors, grantees, or grantors of a governmental entity if disclosure is necessary for the receiving entity to perform its duties and responsibilities. The receiving governmental entity and its agents, employees, and contractors shall maintain the confidential and exempt status of such numbers. As used in this subsection, "necessary" means reasonably needed to promote the efficient, accurate, or economical conduct of an entity's duties and responsibilities.

(2) Social Security numbers disclosed pursuant to a court order, warrant, or subpoena, or in response to a facially valid discovery request pursuant to rules applicable to a court or administrative body that has jurisdiction over the disclosing entity.

(3) Social Security numbers disclosed for public health purposes pursuant to and in compliance with requirements of the department of health under Title 18.

(4) The collection, use, or release of a Social Security number reasonably necessary for administrative purposes or internal verification. Internal verification includes the sharing of information for internal verification between and among governmental entities and their agents, employees, contractors, grantees, and grantors.

(5) Social Security numbers that have been redacted.

(6)(A) A state agency or state political subdivision that has used, prior to January 1, 2007, an individual's Social Security number in a manner inconsistent with subsection (d) of this section, which may continue using that individual's Social Security number in that manner on or after January 1, 2007, if all of the following conditions are met:

(i) The use of the Social Security number is continuous. If the use is stopped for any reason, subsection (d) of this section shall apply.

(ii) The individual is provided an annual disclosure that informs the individual that he or she has the right to stop the use of his or her Social Security number in a manner prohibited by subsection (d) of this section.

(iii) A written request by an individual to stop the use of his or her Social Security number in a manner prohibited by subsection (d) of this section is implemented within 30 days of the receipt of the request. There shall not be a fee or charge for implementing the request.

(iv) The state agency or state political subdivision does not deny services to an individual because the individual makes a written request pursuant to this subdivision.

(B) Nothing in this subdivision (e)(6) is intended to apply to the collection, use or dissemination of Social Security numbers collected prior to January 1, 2007 and exempted from the provisions of subsection (d) of this section pursuant to subdivisions (1) through (5) or (7) through (11) of this subsection.

(7) Certified copies of vital records issued by the health department and other authorized officials pursuant to part 6 of Title 18.

(8) A recorded document in the official records of the town clerk or municipality.

(9) A document filed in the official records of the courts.

(10) The collection, use, or dissemination of Social Security numbers by law enforcement agencies and the department of public safety in the execution of their duties and responsibilities.

(11) The collection, use, or release of a Social Security number to investigate or prevent fraud; conduct background checks; conduct social or scientific research; collect a debt; obtain a credit report from or furnish data to a consumer reporting agency pursuant to the fair credit reporting act, 15 U.S.C. §1681 et seq.; undertake a permissible purpose enumerated under Gramm Leach Bliley, 12 C.F.R. §216.13-15; or locate an individual who is missing, is a lost relative, or is due a benefit, such as a pension, insurance, or unclaimed property benefit.

(f) Any person has the right to request that a town clerk or clerk of court remove from an image or copy of an official record placed on a town's or court's internet website available to the general public or an internet website available to the general public to display public records by the town clerk or clerk of court, the person's Social Security number, employer taxpayer identification number, driver's license number, state identification number, passport number, checking account number, savings account number, credit card or debit card number, or personal identification number (PIN) code or passwords contained in that official record. A town clerk or clerk of court is authorized to redact the personal information identified in a request submitted under this section. The request must be made in writing, legibly signed by the requester, and delivered by mail, facsimile, or electronic transmission, or delivered in person to the town clerk or clerk of court. The request must specify the personal information to be redacted, information that identifies the document that contains the personal information and unique information that identifies the location within the document that contains the Social Security number, employer taxpayer identification number, driver's license number, state identification number, passport number, checking account number, savings account number, credit card number, or debit card number, or personal identification number (PIN) code or passwords to be redacted. The request for redaction shall be considered a public record with access restricted to the town clerk, the clerk of court, their staff, or upon order of the court. The town clerk or clerk of court shall have no duty to inquire beyond the written request to verify the identity of a person requesting redaction and shall have no duty to remove redaction for any reason upon subsequent request by an individual or by order of the court, if impossible to do so. No fee will be charged for the redaction pursuant to such request. Any person who requests a redaction without proper authority to do so shall be guilty of an infraction, punishable by a fine not to exceed $500.00 for each violation.

(g) Enforcement.

(1) With respect to businesses, the state, state agencies, political subdivisions of the state, and agents or employees of the state, a state agency, or a political subdivision of the state, subject to this subchapter, other than a person or entity licensed or registered with the department of banking, insurance, securities, and health care administration under Title 8 or this title, the attorney general and state's attorney shall have sole and full authority to investigate potential violations of this subchapter, to enforce, prosecute, obtain, and impose remedies for a violation of this subchapter, or any rules made pursuant to this subchapter, and to promulgate rules under this subchapter, as the attorney general and state's attorney have under chapter 63 of this title. The attorney general may refer the matter to the state's attorney in an appropriate case. The superior courts shall have jurisdiction over any enforcement matter brought by the attorney general or a state's attorney under this subsection.

(2) With respect to a person or entity licensed or registered with the department of banking, insurance, securities, and health care administration under Title 8 or this title, the department shall have full authority to investigate potential violations of this subchapter, and to prosecute, obtain and impose remedies for a violation of this subchapter or any rules adopted pursuant to this subchapter as the department has under Title 8 or this title, or any other applicable law or regulation.

(3) With respect to the information provided by the Vermont department of public safety and law enforcement agencies, and any agent or employee thereof, to the Vermont attorney general or state's attorney pursuant to subdivision (1) of this subsection, the information provided or made available by the agency or department to the attorney general may be designated by the agency or department as confidential, and shall not be released under the provisions of 1 V.S.A. §317.

Subchapter 4. Document Safe Destruction Act

§2445. SAFE DESTRUCTION OF DOCUMENTS CONTAINING PERSONAL INFORMATION

(a) As used in this section:

(1) "Business" means sole proprietorship, partnership, corporation, association, limited liability company, or other group, however organized and whether or not organized to operate at a profit, including a financial institution organized, chartered, or holding a license or authorization certificate under the laws of this state, any other state, the United States, or any other country, or the parent, affiliate, or subsidiary of a financial institution, but in no case shall it include the state, a state agency, or any political subdivision of the state. The term includes an entity that destroys records.

(2) "Customer" means an individual who provides personal information to a business for the purpose of purchasing or leasing a product or obtaining a service from the business.

(3) "Personal information" means the following information that identifies, relates to, describes, or is capable of being associated with a particular individual: his or her signature, Social Security number, physical characteristics or description, passport number, driver's license or state identification card number, insurance policy number, bank account number, credit card number, debit card number, or any other financial information.

(4)(A) "Record" means any material, regardless of the physical form, on which information is recorded or preserved by any means, including in written or spoken words, graphically depicted, printed, or electromagnetically transmitted.

(B) "Record" does not include publicly available directories containing information an individual has voluntarily consented to have publicly disseminated or listed, such as name, address, or telephone number.

(b) A business shall take all reasonable steps to destroy or arrange for the destruction of a customer's records within its custody or control containing personal information which is no longer to be retained by the business by shredding, erasing, or otherwise modifying the personal information in those records to make it unreadable or indecipherable through any means for the purpose of:

(1) ensuring the security and confidentiality of customer personal information;

(2) protecting against any anticipated threats or hazards to the security or integrity of customer personal information; and

(3) protecting against unauthorized access to or use of customer personal information that could result in substantial harm or inconvenience to any customer.

(c) An entity that is in the business of disposing of personal financial information that conducts business in Vermont or disposes of personal information of residents of Vermont must take all reasonable measures to dispose of records containing personal information by implementing and monitoring compliance with policies and procedures that protect against unauthorized access to or use of personal information during or after the collection and transportation and disposing of such information.

(d) This section does not apply to any of the following:

(1) Any bank, credit union, or financial institution as defined under the federal Gramm Leach Bliley law that is subject to the regulation of the Office of the Comptroller of the Currency, the Federal Reserve, the National Credit Union Administration, the Securities and Exchange Commission, the federal deposit insurance corporation, the office of thrift supervision of the US department of the treasury, or the department of banking, insurance, securities, and health care administration and is subject to the privacy and security provisions of the Gramm Leach Bliley Act, 15 U.S.C. §6801 et seq.

(2) Any health insurer or health care facility that is subject to and in compliance with the standards for privacy of individually identifiable health information and the security standards for the protection of electronic health information of the Health Insurance Portability and Accountability Act of 1996.

(3) Any consumer reporting agency that is subject to and in compliance with the Federal Credit Reporting Act, 15 U.S.C. §1681 et seq., as amended.

(e) Enforcement.

(1) With respect to all businesses subject to this section, other than a person or entity licensed or registered with the department of banking, insurance, securities and health care administration under Title 8 or this title, the attorney general and state's attorney shall have sole and full authority to investigate potential violations of this section, and to prosecute, obtain and impose remedies for a violation of this section, or any rules adopted pursuant to this section, and to promulgate rules under this act, as the attorney general and state's attorney have under chapter 63 of this title. The superior courts shall have jurisdiction over any enforcement matter brought by the attorney general or a state's attorney under this subsection.

(2) With respect to a person or entity licensed or registered with the department of banking, insurance, securities, and health care administration under Title 8 or this title to do business in this state, the department of banking, insurance, securities, and health care administration shall have full authority to investigate potential violations of this act, and to prosecute, obtain, and impose remedies for a violation of this act, or any rules or regulations made pursuant to this act, as the department has under Title 8 and this title, or any other applicable law or regulation.

Sec. 2. 13 V.S.A. §5353(c) is amended to read:

(c) The application for compensation shall be signed by the applicant and shall contain at least the following information which shall be provided subject to the penalties of perjury:

* * *

(4) When reasonably available, copies of all law enforcement reports and reports from all health care providers who treated or examined the victim at the time of or after the crime or who treated or examined the dependent.

(5) The applicant's Social Security number for the purpose of making cash payment to the applicant in accordance with section 5356 of this title.

Sec. 3. REPEAL

13 V.S.A. §7043(d)(2)(B) (use of a criminal offender's Social Security number) is repealed.

Sec. 4. 13 V.S.A. §5362(c) is amended to read:

(c) The restitution unit shall have the authority to:

* * *

(3)(A) Share and access information, consistent with Vermont and federal law, from the court, the department of corrections, the department of motor vehicles, the department of taxes, and the department of labor in order to carry out its collection and enforcement functions.

(B) Provide information to the department of corrections concerning supervised offenders, including an offender's restitution payment history and balance, address and contact information, employment information, and information concerning the restitution unit's collection efforts.

(C) The restitution unit is specifically authorized to collect, record, use, and disseminate Social Security numbers as needed for the purpose of collecting restitution and enforcing restitution judgment orders issued by the court.

Sec. 4a. EXTENSION OF SUNSET; CONFIDENTIALITY AND NONCOMMERCIAL DISTRIBUTION OF CERTAIN TAX RECORDS AND DATA

Sec. 6 of Act No. 158 of the Acts of 2004 as amended by Sec. 54c of Act No. 71 of the Acts of 2006 (2005 Adj. Sess.) is further amended to read:

Sec. 6. SUNSET

This act shall expire on June 30, 2007, and sections of the Vermont Statutes Annotated which are amended by this act shall revert to the language in effect prior to the effective date of this act.

Sec. 5. SUNSET

9 V.S.A. §2435(h) (exemption for law enforcement agencies from security breach notice act) shall be repealed June 30, 2008.

Sec. 6. EFFECTIVE DATE

(a) This act, except for 9 V.S.A. §2440, shall take effect January 1, 2007.

(b) 9 V.S.A. §2440 shall take effect July 1, 2007.

Approved: May 18, 2006

House Bill 261

This bill amends the security breach law so that it applies to all acquisition of or access to personal information.

AN ACT RELATING TO NOTICE OF SECURITY BREACHES

It is hereby enacted by the General Assembly of the State of Vermont:

Sec. 1. 9 V.S.A. § 2430(8) is amended to read:

(8)(A) "Security breach" means acquisition of or access to computerized data that compromises the security, confidentiality, or integrity of personal information maintained by the data collector.

(B) "Security breach" does not include good faith acquisition of or access to personal information by an employee or agent of the data collector for a legitimate purpose of the data collector, provided that the personal information is not used for a purpose unrelated to the data collector's business or subject to unauthorized disclosure. "Security breach" does not include acquisition to access of personal information by a person authorized by the data collector when the personal information is accessible only through use of an access code, password, or other security measure issued by the data collector.

Chapter 46: Virginia

On July 1, 2008, Virginia joined the ever-growing number of states and passed its own data breach law. This new law, Va. Code § 18.2-186.6, states that companies are now required to disclose to affected individuals, and to the Virginia Attorney General as well, whenever there is any breach of their computerized data, if that information is unredacted and unencrypted if it contained personal information, if the breach will cause or is reasonably believed to cause identify theft or other fraud. Violators of this new law are subject to civil suit by affected individuals and penalties imposed by the State Attorney General of up to $150,000 per breach.

The state also has a couple of laws that speak to disclosure requirement upon the issuance of a subpoena *duces tecum*, and also makes it a felony offense for those that commit cybercrime.

V.A. Code § 18.2-186.6.

Breach of personal information notification.

A. As used in this section:

"Breach of the security of the system" means the unauthorized access and acquisition of unencrypted and unredacted computerized data that compromises the security or confidentiality of personal information maintained by an individual or entity as part of a database of personal information regarding multiple individuals and that causes, or the individual or entity reasonably believes has caused, or will cause, identity theft or other fraud to any resident of the Commonwealth. Good faith acquisition of personal information by an employee or agent of an individual or entity for the purposes of the individual or entity is not a breach of the security of the system, provided that the personal information is not used for a purpose other than a lawful purpose of the individual or entity or subject to further unauthorized disclosure.

"Encrypted" means the transformation of data through the use of an algorithmic process into a form in which there is a low probability of assigning meaning without the use of a confidential process or key, or the securing of the information by another method that renders the data elements unreadable or unusable.

"Entity" includes corporations, business trusts, estates, partnerships, limited partnerships, limited liability partnerships, limited liability companies, associations, organizations, joint ventures, governments, governmental subdivisions, agencies, or instrumentalities or any other legal entity, whether for profit or not for profit.

"Financial institution" has the meaning given that term in 15 U.S.C. § 6809(3).

"Individual" means a natural person.

"Notice" means:

1. Written notice to the last known postal address in the records of the individual or entity;

2. Telephone notice;

3. Electronic notice; or

4. Substitute notice, if the individual or the entity required to provide notice demonstrates that the cost of providing notice will exceed $50,000, the affected class of Virginia residents to be notified exceeds 100,000 residents, or the individual or the entity does not have sufficient contact information or consent to provide notice as described in subdivisions 1, 2, or 3 of this definition. Substitute notice consists of all of the following:

a. E-mail notice if the individual or the entity has e-mail addresses for the members of the affected class of residents;

b. Conspicuous posting of the notice on the website of the individual or the entity if the individual or the entity maintains a website; and

c. Notice to major statewide media.

Notice required by this section shall not be considered a debt communication as defined by the Fair Debt Collection Practices Act in 15 U.S.C. § 1692a.

Notice required by this section shall include a description of the following:

(1) The incident in general terms;

(2) The type of personal information that was subject to the unauthorized access and acquisition;

(3) The general acts of the individual or entity to protect the personal information from further unauthorized access;

(4) A telephone number that the person may call for further information and assistance, if one exists; and

(5) Advice that directs the person to remain vigilant by reviewing account statements and monitoring free credit reports.

"Personal information" means the first name or first initial and last name in combination with and linked to any one or more of the following data elements that relate to a resident of the Commonwealth, when the data elements are neither encrypted nor redacted:

1. Social security number;

2. Driver's license number or state identification card number issued in lieu of a driver's license number; or

3. Financial account number, or credit card or debit card number, in combination with any required security code, access code, or password that would permit access to a resident's financial accounts.

The term does not include information that is lawfully obtained from publicly available information, or from federal, state, or local government records lawfully made available to the general public.

"Redact" means alteration or truncation of data such that no more than the following are accessible as part of the personal information:

1. Five digits of a social security number; or

2. The last four digits of a driver's license number, state identification card number, or account number.

B. If unencrypted or unredacted personal information was or is reasonably believed to have been accessed and acquired by an unauthorized person and causes, or the individual or entity reasonably believes has caused or will cause, identity theft or another fraud to any resident of the Commonwealth, an individual or entity that owns or licenses computerized data that includes personal information shall disclose any breach of the security of the system following discovery or notification of the breach of the security of the system to the Office of the Attorney General and any affected resident of the Commonwealth without unreasonable delay. Notice required by this section may be reasonably delayed to allow the individual or entity to determine the scope of the breach of the security of the system and restore the reasonable integrity of the system. Notice required by this section may be delayed if, after the individual or entity notifies a law-enforcement agency, the law-enforcement agency determines and advises the individual or entity that the notice will impede a criminal or civil investigation, or homeland or national security. Notice shall be made without unreasonable delay after the law-enforcement agency determines that the notification will no longer impede the investigation or jeopardize national or homeland security.

C. An individual or entity shall disclose the breach of the security of the system if encrypted information is accessed and acquired in an unencrypted form, or if the security breach involves a person with access to the encryption key and the individual or entity reasonably believes that such a breach has caused or will cause identity theft or other fraud to any resident of the Commonwealth.

D. An individual or entity that maintains computerized data that includes personal information that the individual or entity does not own or license shall notify the owner or licensee of the information of any breach of the security of the system without unreasonable delay following discovery of the breach of the security of the system, if the personal information was accessed and acquired by an unauthorized person or the individual or entity reasonably believes the personal information was accessed and acquired by an unauthorized person.

E. In the event an individual or entity provides notice to more than 1,000 persons at one time pursuant to this section, the individual or entity shall notify, without unreasonable delay, the Office of the Attorney General and all consumer reporting agencies that compile and maintain files on consumers on a nationwide basis, as defined in 15 U.S.C. § 1681(a)(p), of the timing, distribution, and content of the notice.

F. An entity that maintains its own notification procedures as part of an information privacy or security policy for the treatment of personal information that are consistent with the timing requirements of this section shall be deemed to be in compliance with the notification requirements of this section if it notifies residents of the Commonwealth in accordance with its procedures in the event of a breach of the security of the system.

G. An entity that is subject to Title V of the Gramm-Leach-Bliley Act (15 U.S.C. § 6801 et seq.) and maintains procedures for notification of a breach of the security of the system in accordance with the provision of that Act and any rules, regulations, or guidelines promulgated thereto shall be deemed to be in compliance with this section.

H. An entity that complies with the notification requirements or procedures pursuant to the rules, regulations, procedures, or guidelines established by the entity's primary or functional state or federal regulator shall be in compliance with this section.

I. Except as provided by subsections J and K, pursuant to the enforcement duties and powers of the Office of the Attorney General, the Attorney General may bring an action to address violations of this section. The Office of the Attorney General may impose a civil penalty not to exceed $150,000 per breach of the security of the system or a series of breaches of a similar nature that are discovered in a single investigation. Nothing in this section shall limit an individual from recovering direct economic damages from a violation of this section.

J. A violation of this section by a state-chartered or licensed financial institution shall be enforceable exclusively by the financial institution's primary state regulator.

K. A violation of this section by an individual or entity regulated by the State Corporation Commission's Bureau of Insurance shall be enforced exclusively by the State Corporation Commission.

L. The provisions of this section shall not apply to criminal intelligence systems subject to the restrictions of 28 C.F.R. Part 23 that are maintained by law-enforcement agencies of the Commonwealth and the organized Criminal Gang File of the Virginia Criminal Information Network (VCIN), established pursuant to Chapter 2 (§ 52-12 et seq.) of Title 52.

Senate Bill 1135

This bill requires a financial institution or credit card issuer to disclose bank records or credit card information concerning a customer upon the issuance of a subpoena *duces tecum*. A subpoena *duces tecum* is one that requires the witness to produce documents pertinent to a proceeding. The bill does contain a provision for the financial institution or credit card issuer to move to quash or modify the subpoena *duces tecum* if compliance would cause an undue burden and for holding harmless the financial institution or credit card issuer or its employees for releasing such information or records pursuant to an order. The statement of facts documenting the reasons the records or information are sought will be sealed upon issuance of the subpoena *duces tecum*, and the use of such records or information is limited to the investigation and legitimate law enforcement purposes. At the end of the investigation, the records or information will be sealed. A provision is added allowing seizure of certain property used in money laundering and punishable as a felony under the laws of another state or territory of the United States, the District of Columbia, or the United States.

House Bill 2175

This bill limits the appearance of Social Security numbers on identification cards and parcels. It punishes the distribution or possession with intent to distribute another's personal identifying information or the distribution of the means by which personal information may be stolen, and creates a mechanism whereby a victim may expunge a criminal charge resulting from identity theft. The bill also punishes those obtaining goods and services, and identification documents and information of another. The bill requires that the Library Board develop regulations providing for the destruction of Social Security numbers in public records. It allows a clerk of court to refuse to record a document upon which there appears a grantor's or grantee's Social Security number, and sets up a procedure for blocking credit misinformation appearing in a credit report.

House Bill 2426

Provides that beginning January 1, 2004, no court clerk shall post on a website controlled by the court any document that contains the following information: (i) an actual signature; (ii) a Social Security number; (iii) a date of birth identified with a particular person; (iv) the maiden name of a person's parent so as to be identified with a particular person; (v) any financial account number or numbers; or (vi) the name and age of any minor child. It does provide an exception for court clerks providing remote access to their records if their network or system that is used to provide the access has been certified by the Department of Technology Planning. It also requires the Department to establish security standards that must be followed by court clerks providing remote access to records in consultation with circuit court clerks, the Supreme Court, the Compensation Board, users of land and other court records, and other interested citizens.

From a technology perspective, secure remote access would generally entail a VPN, or virtual private network type technology. While modems would also provide remote access, they also present numerous security concerns. I would also strongly advise against remote access type topologies that use an Internet-based service. You are in essence entrusting the security of your remote access to the company providing the Internet-based service. A VPN technology, where the VPN server is located, and maintained by court in this case, would offer the highest degree of control and security.

Senate Bill 815

This bill deletes the requirement that a beneficiary's Social Security number and birth date and the proposed dates of final and periodic disbursements be included in the court order and provides instead that the general receiver file a sealed affidavit with this information.

Senate Bill 878

This bill requires that insurance institutions, agents, and insurance support organizations implement a comprehensive information security program to safeguard the privacy of consumer information. The measure is required pursuant to the federal Gramm-Leach-Bliley Act and is based on model language adopted by the National Association of Insurance Commissioners.

Senate Bill 992

This bill requires a financial institution or credit card issuer to disclose bank records or credit card information concerning a customer upon the issuance of a subpoena *duces tecum*. It also contains a provision for the financial institution or credit card issuer to move to quash or modify the subpoena *duces tecum* if compliance would cause an undue burden and for holding harmless the financial institution or credit card issuer or its employees for releasing such information or records pursuant to an order. The statement of facts documenting the reasons the records or information are sought will be sealed upon issuance of the subpoena *duces tecum*, and the use of such records or information is limited to the investigation and legitimate law enforcement purposes. At the end of the investigation the records or information will be sealed.

House Bill 563

This bill removes the sunset provision prohibiting certain information from being posted on a website that is controlled by the court. The Compensation Board policies shall require court clerks to certify that proposed technology improvements of their land records will provide remote access to land records on or before July 1, 2007. If a court clerk provides remote access to land records on or before July 1, 2007, the clerk may then apply to the Compensation Board for an allocation from the Technology Trust Fund. The bill also requests that the Virginia Information Technologies Agency develop methods for the redaction of Social Security numbers from electronic land record documents and to submit a project budget to Compensation Board for approval.

House Bill 332

Provides that the Virginia circuit court clerks have the power to decline to accept any instrument submitted for recordation that includes a grantor's, grantee's or trustee's Social Security number. The bill also states that the attorney or party who submits the instrument has the responsibility for ensuring that the number is removed from the instrument before it is submitted for recordation.

House Bill 382

This bill allows a clerk of the court to withhold from public disclosure the Social Security number in a concealed handgun permit application in response to a request to inspect or copy such permit application. However, the Social Security number shall be disclosed to a law enforcement officer acting in the performance of his official duties.

House Bill 872

Authorizes the Virginia state attorney general, with the concurrence of the attorney for the Commonwealth, to assist in the prosecution of the crimes of identity theft (§18.2-186.3) and the use of a person's identity with the intent to intimidate, coerce, or harass (§18.2-186.4). Allows for a conviction under the identity theft statutes when the defendant uses a false or fictitious name. Requires the Virginia Department of Motor Vehicles (DVM), upon notification from the attorney general that an Identity Theft Passport has been issued to a driver, to note the same on the driver's abstract. The bill requires that child day programs that reproduce or retain documents of a child's proof of identity that are required upon the child's enrollment into the program to destroy them upon the conclusion of the requisite period of retention. The procedures for the disposal, physical destruction or other disposition of the proof of identity containing Social Security numbers shall include all reasonable steps to destroy such documents by (i) shredding, (ii) erasing, or (iii) otherwise modifying the Social Security numbers in those records to make them unreadable or indecipherable by any means.

House Bill 2482

Prohibits any person from (i) intentionally communicating an individual's Social Security number to the general public; (ii) printing an individual's Social Security number on any card required for the individual to access or receive products or services; (iii) requiring an individual to use his Social Security number to access an Internet website, unless an authentication device is also required; or (iv) mailing a package with the Social Security number visible from the outside. Exempts public bodies and public records. A violation is a prohibited practice under the Virginia Consumer Protection Act. The measure also requires the state employee's health insurance plan to use identification numbers that are not the employee's Social Security number.

Senate Bill 1019

This bill requires that the Social Security numbers, or any financial information, of any party or minor child not be contained in the record of any divorce. If such information must be provided to a Virginia government agency or recorded for the benefit of the parties, it shall be contained in a separate addendum. The addendum can be used to distribute the information as required by law but shall otherwise be made available only to the parties, their attorneys, and to such other persons as the court in its discretion may allow.

Senate Bill 1111

This bill requires marriage records and divorce and annulment reports to include the age and race of the parties. It also mandates that divorce and annulment reports also contain the number of minor children involved. Requires the State Registrar of Vital Records to compile, publish, and make available to the public aggregate data on the number of marriages, divorces, and annulments that occur each year in the Commonwealth from 2000 forward. The data shall be organized according to the locality in which the marriage license is issued or in which the divorce or annulment report is certified, and shall include but not be limited to information regarding age and race of the parties. The data on divorce and annulments shall also include information regarding the number of minor children involved. The Virginia State Registrar is required to post, update, and maintain this information on the Department of Health website. Names, addresses, Social Security numbers, and any other personal identification information shall not be included.

Senate Bill 1147

This bill actually carries the threat of jail time, as it makes it a Class 6 felony to fraudulently obtain, record, or access from a computer the following identifying information of another: (i) Social Security number; (ii) driver's license number; (iii) bank account numbers; (iv) credit or debit card numbers; (v) personal identification numbers (PIN); (vi) electronic identification codes; (vii) automated or electronic signatures; (viii) biometric data; (ix) fingerprints; (x) passwords; or (xi) any other numbers or information that can be used to access a person's financial resources, obtain identification, act as identification, or obtain goods or services. Any person who sells or distributes such information or uses it to commit another crime is guilty of a Class 5 felony.

House Bill 563

This bill removes the sunset provision prohibiting certain information from being posted on a website that is controlled by the court. The Compensation Board policies shall require court clerks to certify that proposed technology improvements of their land records will provide remote access to land records on or before July 1, 2007. If a court clerk provides remote access to land records on or before July 1, 2007, the clerk may then apply to the Compensation Board for an allocation from the Technology Trust Fund. It also requests the Virginia Information Technologies Agency to develop methods for the redaction of Social Security numbers from electronic land record documents and to submit a project budget to Compensation Board for approval.

House Bill 1583

The bill protects the identity of incapacitated individuals from identity theft by requiring the sealed filing of the Social Security number in any petition to a Circuit Court for the appointment of a guardian and conservator.

Senate Bill 369

Amends a Code section added in 2005 that provides that certain required information, including Social Security numbers and financial information, be contained in a separate addendum rather than in the petition, pleading, motion, order, or decree to add a requirement that the attorney or party who prepares the petition, etc. ensure that such an addendum be incorporated by reference into such petition, etc.

Chapter 47: Washington

Washington Senate Bill 6043 requires any person, business, or agency that owns and licenses computerized data that includes personal information to inform Washington consumers of any breach of their data security, following discovery or notification of the beach. The notification must be made without unreasonable delay, consistent with the needs of law enforcement. The bill also states that notification may not impede a criminal investigation. "Personal information" covered by the duty to notify includes: Social Security numbers, driver's license, or identification card numbers; and credit and debit card numbers in combination with access codes. Personal information does not include publicly available information from federal, state, and local government records. Notice of the security breach may be provided by written or electronic notice, or by a "substitute notice" by e-mail, conspicuous website posting, or major statewide media. As a matter of public policy, consumers cannot waive their right to notice. Remedies include a civil action to recover damages, or injunctive relief against a business that violates the notice requirements.

Senate Bill 6043

AN ACT Relating to breaches of security that compromise personal information; adding a new section to chapter 42.17 RCW; and adding a new chapter to Title 19 RCW. BE IT ENACTED BY THE LEGISLATURE OF THE STATE OF WASHINGTON: NEW SECTION. Sec. 1. A new section is added to chapter 42.17 RCW under the subchapter heading "public records" to read as follows: (1)(a) Any agency that owns or licenses computerized data that includes personal information shall disclose any breach of the security of the system following discovery or notification of the breach in the security of the data to any resident of this state whose unencrypted personal information was, or is reasonably believed to have been, acquired by an unauthorized person. The disclosure shall be made in the most expedient time possible and without unreasonable delay, consistent with the legitimate needs of law enforcement, as provided in subsection (3) of this section, or any measures necessary to determine the scope of the breach and

restore the reasonable integrity of the data system. (b) For purposes of this section, "agency" means the same as in RCW (2) Any agency that maintains computerized data that includes personal information that the agency does not own shall notify the owner or licensee of the information of any breach of the security of the data immediately following discovery, if the personal information was, or is reasonably believed to have been, acquired by an unauthorized person. (3) The notification required by this section may be delayed if a law enforcement agency determines that the notification will impede a criminal investigation. The notification required by this section shall be made after the law enforcement agency determines that it will not compromise the investigation. (4) For purposes of this section, "breach of the security of the system" means unauthorized acquisition of computerized data that compromises the security, confidentiality, or integrity of personal information maintained by the agency. Good faith acquisition of personal information by an employee or agent of the agency for the purposes of the agency is not a breach of the security of the system when the personal information is not used or subject to further unauthorized disclosure.

(5) For purposes of this section, "personal information" means an individual's first name or first initial and last name in combination with any one or more of the following data elements, when either the name or the data elements are not encrypted:

(a) Social Security number;

(b) Driver's license number or Washington identification card number; or

(c) Account number or credit or debit card number, in combination with any required security code, access code, or password that would permit access to an individual's financial account.

(6) For purposes of this section, "personal information" does not include publicly available information that is lawfully made

available to the general public from federal, state, or local government records. (7) For purposes of this section and except under subsection (8) of this section, notice may be provided by one of the following methods:

(a) Written notice;

(b) Electronic notice, if the notice provided is consistent with the provisions regarding electronic records and signatures set forth in

(c) Substitute notice, if the agency demonstrates that the cost of providing notice would exceed two hundred fifty thousand dollars, or that the affected class of subject persons to be notified exceeds five hundred thousand, or the agency does not have sufficient contact information. Substitute notice shall consist of all of the following:

(i) E-mail notice when the agency has an e-mail address for the subject persons;

(ii) Conspicuous posting of the notice on the agency's website page, if the agency maintains one; and

(iii) Notification to major statewide media. (8) An agency that maintains its own notification procedures as part of an information security policy for the treatment of personal information and is otherwise consistent with the timing requirements of this section is in compliance with the notification requirements of this section if it notifies subject persons in accordance with its policies in the event of a breach of security of the system. (9) Any waiver of the provisions of this section is contrary to public policy, and is void and unenforceable. (10)(a) Any customer injured by a violation of this section may institute a civil action to recover damages. (b) Any business that violates, proposes to violate, or has violated this section may be enjoined. (c) The rights and remedies available under this section are cumulative to each other and to any other rights and remedies available under law. NEW SECTION. Sec. 2.

(1) Any person or business that conducts business in this state and that owns or licenses computerized data that includes personal information shall disclose any breach of the security of the system following discovery or notification of the breach in the security of the data to any resident of this state whose unencrypted personal information was, or is reasonably believed to have been, acquired by an unauthorized person. The disclosure shall be made in the most expedient time possible and without unreasonable delay, consistent with the legitimate needs of law enforcement, as provided in subsection (3) of this section, or any measures necessary to determine the scope of the breach and restore the reasonable integrity of the data system. (2) Any person or business that maintains computerized data that includes personal information that the person or business does not own shall notify the owner or licensee of the information of any breach of the security of the data immediately following discovery, if the personal information was, or is reasonably believed to have been, acquired by an unauthorized person. (3) The notification required by this section may be delayed if a law enforcement agency determines that the notification will impede a criminal investigation.

The notification required by this section shall be made after the law enforcement agency determines that it will not compromise the investigation. (4) For purposes of this section, "breach of the security of the system" means unauthorized acquisition of computerized data that compromises the security, confidentiality, or integrity of personal information maintained by the person or business. Good faith acquisition of personal information by an employee or agent of the person or business for the purposes of the person or business is not a breach of the security of the system when the personal information is not used or subject to further unauthorized disclosure.

(5) For purposes of this section, "personal information" means an individual's first name or first initial and last name in combination with any one or more of the following data elements, when either the name or the data elements are not encrypted:

(a) Social Security number;

(b) Driver's license number or Washington identification card number; or

(c) Account number or credit or debit card number, in combination with any required security code, access code, or password that would permit access to an individual's financial account.

(6) For purposes of this section, "personal information" does not include publicly available information that is lawfully made available to the general public from federal, state, or local government records.

(7) For purposes of this section and except under subsection (8) of this section, "notice" may be provided by one of the following methods:

(a) Written notice;

(b) Electronic notice, if the notice provided is consistent with the provisions regarding electronic records and signatures set forth in 15 U.S.C. Sec. 7001; or

(c) Substitute notice, if the person or business demonstrates that the cost of providing notice would exceed two hundred fifty thousand dollars, or that the affected class of subject persons to be notified exceeds five hundred thousand, or the person or business does not have sufficient contact information. Substitute notice shall consist of all of the following: (i) E-mail notice when the person or business has an e-mail address for the subject persons; (ii) Conspicuous posting of the notice on the website page of the person or business, if the person or business maintains one; and (iii) Notification to major statewide media. (8) A person or business that maintains its own notification procedures as part of an information security policy for the treatment of personal information and is otherwise consistent with the timing requirements of this section is in

compliance with the notification requirements of this section if the person or business notifies subject persons in accordance with its policies in the event of a breach of security of the system.

(9) Any waiver of the provisions of this section is contrary to public policy, and is void and unenforceable. (10)(a) Any customer injured by a violation of this section may institute a civil action to recover damages. (b) Any business that violates, proposes to violate, or has violated this section may be enjoined. (c) The rights and remedies available under this section are cumulative to each other and to any other rights and remedies available under law. NEW SECTION. Sec. 3. Section 2 of this act constitutes a new chapter in Title 19 RCW.

Senate Bill 5718

This bill broadens the exemption from public disclosure under the Open Public Records Act for credit card numbers, debit card numbers, electronic check numbers, card expiration dates, or bank or other financial account numbers. It also removes the limitation that allowed the exemption only when the number or date was supplied to an agency for the purpose of electronic transfer of funds.

House Bill 1012

Makes it unlawful for a person who is not an owner or operator to transmit computer software to the owner or operator's computer to use such software to collect by deceptive means personally identifiable information (a) through the use of a keystroke-logging function that records all keystrokes made by an owner or operator and transfers that information from the computer to another person; (b) in a manner that correlates such information with data respecting all or substantially all of the websites visited by an owner or operator, other than websites operated by the person collecting such information; and (c) described in section 1(10) (d), (e), or (f)(i) or (ii) of this act by extracting the information from the owner or operator's hard drive.

Senate Bill 6494

This bill states that, after December 31, 2005, a health carrier that issues a card for their customers may display no more than four digits of the person's Social Security number.

Senate Bill 5459

Provides that when any instrument is presented to a county auditor or recording officer for recording, the document may not contain any of the following information: (1) a Social Security number, (2) a date of birth identified with a particular person, or (3) the maiden name of a person's parent so as to be identified with a particular person. The bill provides an exception for those instruments that are generated by governmental agencies.

Senate Bill 5132

This bill revises provisions for the protection of Washington state public employee information, including their Social Security numbers.

Senate Bill 5827

This bill is regarding consumer privacy and it prohibits the procurement of a consumer credit report for employment purposes where any information contained in the report includes a consumer's credit worthiness, their credit standing, or credit capacity, unless the information is substantially job-related and the employer's reasons for the use of such information are disclosed to the consumer in writing or required by law.

Chapter 48: West Virginia

CHAPTER 46A. WEST VIRGINIA CONSUMER CREDIT AND PROTECTION ACT.

ARTICLE 2A. BREACH OF SECURITY OF CONSUMER INFORMATION.

§46A-2A-101. Definitions.

As used in this article:

(1) "Breach of the security of a system" means the unauthorized access and acquisition of unencrypted and unredacted computerized data that compromises the security or confidentiality of personal information maintained by an individual or entity as part of a database of personal information regarding multiple individuals and that causes the individual or entity to reasonably believe that the breach of security has caused or will cause identity theft or other fraud to any resident of this state. Good faith acquisition of personal information by an employee or agent of an individual or entity for the purposes of the individual or the entity is not a breach of the security of the system, provided that the personal information is not used for a purpose other than a lawful purpose of the individual or entity or subject to further unauthorized disclosure.

(2) "Entity" includes corporations, business trusts, estates, partnerships, limited partnerships, limited liability partnerships, limited liability companies, associations, organizations, joint ventures, governments, governmental subdivisions, agencies or instrumentalities, or any other legal entity, whether for profit or not for profit.

(3) "Encrypted" means transformation of data through the use of an algorithmic process to into a form in which there is a low probability of assigning meaning without use of a confidential

process or key or securing the information by another method that renders the data elements unreadable or unusable.

(4) "Financial institution" has the meaning given that term in Section 6809(3), United States Code Title 15, as amended.

(5) "Individual" means a natural person.

(6) "Personal information" means the first name or first initial and last name linked to any one or more of the following data elements that relate to a resident of this state, when the data elements are neither encrypted nor redacted:

(A) Social security number;

(B) Driver's license number or state identification card number issued in lieu of a driver's license; or

(C) Financial account number, or credit card, or debit card number in combination with any required security code, access code or password that would permit access to a resident's financial accounts.

The term does not include information that is lawfully obtained from publicly available information, or from federal, state or local government records lawfully made available to the general public.

(7) "Notice" means:

(A) Written notice to the postal address in the records of the individual or entity;

(B) Telephonic notice;

(C) Electronic notice, if the notice provided is consistent with the provisions regarding electronic records and signatures, set forth in

Section 7001, United States Code Title 15, Electronic Signatures in Global and National Commerce Act.

(D) Substitute notice, if the individual or the entity required to provide notice demonstrates that the cost of providing notice will exceed fifty thousand dollars or that the affected class of residents to be notified exceeds one hundred thousand persons or that the individual or the entity does not have sufficient contact information or to provide notice as described in paragraph (A), (B) or (C). Substitute notice consists of any two of the following:

(i) E-mail notice if the individual or the entity has e-mail addresses for the members of the affected class of residents;

(ii) Conspicuous posting of the notice on the website of the individual or the entity if the individual or the entity maintains a website; or

(iii) Notice to major statewide media.

(8) "Redact" means alteration or truncation of data such that no more than the last four digits of a social security number, driver's license number, state identification card number or account number is accessible as part of the personal information.

§46A-2A-102. Notice of breach of security of computerized personal information.

(a) An individual or entity that owns or licenses computerized data that includes personal information shall give notice of any breach of the security of the system following discovery or notification of the breach of the security of the system to any resident of this state whose unencrypted and unredacted personal information was or is reasonably believed to have been accessed and acquired by an unauthorized person and that causes, or the individual or entity reasonably believes has caused or will cause, identity theft or other fraud to any resident of this state. Except as provided in subsection

(e) of this section or in order to take any measures necessary to determine the scope of the breach and to restore the reasonable integrity of the system, the notice shall be made without unreasonable delay.

(b) An individual or entity must give notice of the breach of the security of the system if encrypted information is accessed and acquired in an unencrypted form or if the security breach involves a person with access to the encryption key and the individual or entity reasonably believes that such breach has caused or will cause identity theft or other fraud to any resident of this state.

(c) An individual or entity that maintains computerized data that includes personal information that the individual or entity does not own or license shall give notice to the owner or licensee of the information of any breach of the security of the system as soon as practicable following discovery, if the personal information was or the entity reasonably believes was accessed and acquired by an unauthorized person.

(d) The notice shall include:

(1) To the extent possible, a description of the categories of information that were reasonably believed to have been accessed or acquired by an unauthorized person, including social security numbers, driver's licenses or state identification numbers and financial data;

(2) A telephone number or website address that the individual may use to contact the entity or the agent of the entity and from whom the individual may learn:

(A) What types of information the entity maintained about that individual or about individuals in general; and

(B) Whether or not the entity maintained information about that individual.

(3) The toll-free contact telephone numbers and addresses for the major credit reporting agencies and information on how to place a fraud alert or security freeze.

(e) Notice required by this section may be delayed if a law-enforcement agency determines and advises the individual or entity that the notice will impede a criminal or civil investigation or homeland or national security. Notice required by this section must be made without unreasonable delay after the law-enforcement agency determines that notification will no longer impede the investigation or jeopardize national or homeland security.

(f) If an entity is required to notify more than one thousand persons of a breach of security pursuant to this article, the entity shall also notify, without unreasonable delay, all consumer reporting agencies that compile and maintain files on a nationwide basis, as defined by 15 U.S.C. §1681a (p), of the timing, distribution and content of the notices. Nothing in this subsection shall be construed to require the entity to provide to the consumer reporting agency the names or other personal identifying information of breach notice recipients. This subsection shall not apply to an entity who is subject to Title V of the Gramm Leach Bliley Act, 15 U.S.C. 6801, et seq.

(g) The notice required by this section shall not be considered a debt communication as defined by the Fair Debt Collection Practice Act in 15 U.S.C. §1692a.

§46A-2A-103. Procedures deemed in compliance with security breach notice requirements.

(a) An entity that maintains its own notification procedures as part of an information privacy or security policy for the treatment of personal information and that are consistent with the timing requirements of this article shall be deemed to be in compliance with the notification requirements of this article if it notifies residents of this state in accordance with its procedures in the event of a breach of security of the system.

(b) A financial institution that responds in accordance with the notification guidelines prescribed by the Federal Interagency Guidance on Response Programs for Unauthorized Access to Customer Information and Customer Notice is deemed to be in compliance with this article.

(c) An entity that complies with the notification requirements or procedures pursuant to the rules, regulation, procedures or guidelines established by the entity's primary or functional regulator shall be in compliance with this article.

§46A-2A-104. Violations.

(a) Except as provided by subsection (c) of this section, failure to comply with the notice provisions of this article constitutes an unfair or deceptive act of practice in violation of section one hundred four, article six, chapter forty-six-a of this code, which may be enforced by the Attorney General pursuant to the enforcement provisions of this chapter.

(b) Except as provided by subsection (c) of this section, the Attorney General shall have exclusive authority to bring action. No civil penalty may be assessed in an action unless the court finds that the defendant has engaged in a course of repeated and willful violations of this article. No civil penalty shall exceed one hundred fifty thousand dollars per breach of security of the system or series of breaches of a similar nature that are discovered in a single investigation.

(c) A violation of this article by a licensed financial institution shall be enforceable exclusively by the financial institution's primary functional regulator.

§46A-2A-105. Applicability.

This article shall apply to the discovery or notification of a breach of the security of the system that occurs on or after the effective date of this article.

Senate Bill 400

Relates to authorizing limited disclosure of confidential information received by the West Virginia insurance commissioner, and makes amendments regarding the disclosure of confidential information by the insurance commissioner to federal banking agencies required by the federal Gramm-Leach-Bliley Act.

House Bill 4019

This bill prohibits the West Virginia Division of Motor Vehicles from selling personal information for bulk distribution of surveys, marketing, and solicitations.

House Bill 4020

This bill seeks to prevent identify theft by placing restrictions on the release of personal information contained in public records. The bill will exempt Social Security, credit card, or debit card numbers contained in a state agency's record from a Freedom of Information Act request. It would also protect the home address, maiden name, marital status, and driver's license number of West Virginia state employees.

House Bill 4565

This bill relates to the vital statistics maintained by the Bureau of Public Health, and limits the use of Social Security numbers.

Chapter 49: Wisconsin

Wisconsin's disclosure law requires most businesses operating in the state that maintain personal information about individuals who reside in Wisconsin to notify those individuals if an unauthorized person has acquired their personal information. This law also applies to a Wisconsin state government agency and to cities, towns, villages, and counties.

Wisconsin's Data Breach Notification Law: Act 138

The new law is set forth in Section 895.507 of the Wisconsin Statutes and became effective on March 31, 2006.

What Personal Information Is Covered

The law defines personal information to mean an individual's last name and the individual's first name or first initial in combination with any of the individual's following information:

- **Social Security number**
- **Driver's license number or state identification number**
- **Financial account number including a credit or debit card account number or any security code, access code or password that would permit access to the individual's financial account**
- **DNA profile**
- **Any unique biometric data including fingerprint, voiceprint, retina or iris image**

If any of the personal information described above is publicly available and is encrypted, redacted or altered in a manner that makes the information unreadable, it is not considered "personal information" for purposes of this law.

Who Is Required To Give Notice

Among those required to give notice are:

- Businesses that conduct business in the state and maintain personal information in the ordinary course of business
- Businesses that license personal information in the state
- Businesses that maintain a depository account for Wisconsin residents
- Businesses that lend money to Wisconsin residents
- The state and any office, department, independent agency, authority, institution, association, society or other body in state government created or authorized by Wisconsin law including the courts and the legislature
- A city, village, town or county

Certain financial institutions that are subject to and in compliance with the privacy and security requirements of federal law, as well as businesses that have contractual arrangements with such institutions and have a policy in effect regarding security breaches, are exempt from Wisconsin's law. Similarly, certain health plans and health care providers are not covered by Wisconsin's law.

When Is Notice Required

Generally, the law requires the business or governmental entity to notify an individual whenever personal information held by the business or governmental entity is acquired by an unauthorized person. However, no notice is required if the unauthorized acquisition does not create a material risk of identity theft or fraud, or if the information was acquired in good faith by an employee or agent and is used for a lawful purpose of the entity.

What Notice Is Required

In general, any entity that is required to give notice of the unauthorized acquisition of personal information must provide notice of that fact to persons whose information was acquired. The notice must be given within a reasonable time, not to exceed 45 days after the entity learns of the unauthorized acquisition. The notice must be given by mail or by a method that the entity has previously used to communicate with the subject of the information. For example, if a business has communicated with a customer by email, notice may be given by email. Upon written request of the person whose information was acquired, the entity must also identify the nature of the personal information acquired. If an entity cannot determine the mailing address of the person whose information was acquired, and if the entity has not previously communicated with that person, the entity must give notice in a manner that is reasonably calculated to provide notice. Such methods might include notice in the newspaper or on television or radio.

In cases where the personal information of more than 1,000 individuals was acquired at one time, the entity from which the information was required must also give notice to all consumer reporting agencies that compile and maintain files on consumers on a nationwide basis. This would include the major credit reporting agencies. A law enforcement agency may request that an entity not provide notice in order to protect an investigation or homeland security. In such cases, the entity may not provide notice until permitted by the law enforcement agency.

Chapter 50: Wyoming

S.F. 53

AN ACT relating to consumer protection; providing for notice to consumers affected by breaches of consumer information databases as specified; authorizing consumers to prohibit release of information maintained by credit rating agencies as specified; providing definitions; providing exceptions; and providing for an effective date.

Be It Enacted by the Legislature of the State of Wyoming:

Section 1. W.S. 40-12-501 through 40-12-509 are created to read:

ARTICLE 5 CREDIT FREEZE REPORTS

40-12-501. Definitions.

(a) As used in this act:

(i) "Breach of the security of the data system" means unauthorized acquisition of computerized data that materially compromises the security, confidentiality or integrity of personal identifying information maintained by a person or business and causes or is reasonably believed to cause loss or injury to a resident of this state. Good faith acquisition of personal identifying information by an employee or agent of a person or business for the purposes of the person or business is not a breach of the security of the data system, provided that the personal identifying information is not used or subject to further unauthorized disclosure;

(ii) "Consumer" means any person who is utilizing or seeking credit for personal, family or household purposes;

(iii) "Consumer reporting agency" means any person whose business is the assembling and evaluating of information as to the credit standing and credit worthiness of a consumer, for the purposes of furnishing credit reports, for monetary fees and dues to third parties;

(iv) "Credit report" means any written or oral report, recommendation or representation of a consumer reporting agency as to the credit worthiness, credit standing or credit capacity of any consumer and includes any information which is sought or given for the purpose of serving as the basis for determining eligibility for credit to be used primarily for personal, family or household purposes;

(v) "Creditor" means the lender of money or vendor of goods, services or property, including a lessor under a lease intended as a security, rights or privileges, for which payment is arranged through a credit transaction, or any successor to the right, title or interest of any such lender or vendor, and an affiliate, associate or subsidiary of any of them or any director, officer or employee of any of them or any other person in any way associated with any of them;

(vi) "Financial institution" means any person licensed or chartered under the laws of any state or the United States as a bank holding company, bank, savings and loan association, credit union, trust company or subsidiary thereof doing business in this state;

(vii) "Personal identifying information" means the first name or first initial and last name of a person in combination with one (1) or more of the following data elements when either the name or the data elements are not redacted:

(A) Social security number;

(B) Driver's license number or Wyoming identification card number;

(C) Account number, credit card number or debit card number in combination with any security code, access code or password that would allow access to a financial account of the person;

(D) Tribal identification card; or

(E) Federal or state government issued identification card.

(viii) "Redact" means alteration or truncation of data such that no more than five (5) digits of the data elements provided in subparagraphs (vii)(A) through (D) of this subsection are accessible as part of the personal information;

(ix) "Security freeze" means a notice placed in a consumer's credit report, at the request of the consumer, that prohibits the credit rating agency from releasing the consumer's credit report or any information from it relating to an extension of credit or the opening of a new account, without the express authorization of the consumer;

(x) "Substitute notice" means:

(A) An electronic mail notice when the person or business has an electronic mail address for the subject persons;

(B) Conspicuous posting of the notice on the website page of the person or business if the person or business maintains one; and
(C) Publication in applicable local or statewide media.

(xi) "This act" means W.S. 40-12-501 through 40-12-511.

(b) "Personal identifying information" as defined in paragraph (a)(vii) of this section does not include information, regardless of its source, contained in any federal, state or local government records or in widely distributed media that are lawfully made available to the general public.

40-12-502. Computer security breach; notice to affected persons.

(a) An individual or commercial entity that conducts business in Wyoming and that owns or licenses computerized data that includes personal identifying information about a resident of Wyoming shall, when it becomes aware of a breach of the security of the system, conduct in good faith a reasonable and prompt investigation to determine the likelihood that personal identifying information has been or will be misused. If the investigation determines that the misuse of personal identifying information about a Wyoming resident has occurred or is reasonably likely to occur, the individual or the commercial entity shall give notice as soon as possible to the affected Wyoming resident. Notice shall be made in the most expedient time possible and without unreasonable delay, consistent with the legitimate needs of law enforcement and consistent with any measures necessary to determine the scope of the breach and to restore the reasonable integrity of the computerized data system.

(b) The notification required by this section may be delayed if a law enforcement agency determines in writing that the notification may seriously impede a criminal investigation.

(c) Any financial institution as defined in 15 U.S.C. 6809 or federal credit union as defined by 12 U.S.C. 1752 that maintains notification procedures subject to the requirements of 15 U.S.C. 6801(b)(3) and 12 C.F.R. Part 364 Appendix B or Part 748 Appendix B, is deemed to be in compliance with this section if the financial institution notifies affected Wyoming customers in compliance with the requirements of 15 U.S.C. 6801 through 6809 and 12 C.F.R. Part 364 Appendix B or Part 748 Appendix B.

(d) For purposes of this section, notice to consumers may be provided by one (1) of the following methods:

(i) Written notice;

(ii) Electronic mail notice;

(iii) Substitute notice, if the person demonstrates:

(A) That the cost of providing notice would exceed ten thousand dollars ($10,000.00) for Wyoming-based persons or businesses, and two hundred fifty thousand dollars ($250,000.00) for all other businesses operating but not based in Wyoming;

(B) That the affected class of subject persons to be notified exceeds ten thousand (10,000) for Wyoming-based persons or businesses and five hundred thousand (500,000) for all other businesses operating but not based in Wyoming; or

(C) The person does not have sufficient contact information.

(iv) Substitute notice shall consist of all of the following:

(A) Conspicuous posting of the notice on the Internet, the World Wide Web or a similar proprietary or common carrier electronic system site of the person collecting the data, if the person maintains a public Internet, the World Wide Web or a similar proprietary or common carrier electronic system site; and

(B) Notification to major statewide media.

The notice to media shall include a toll-free phone number where an individual can learn whether or not that individual's personal data is included in the security breach.

(e) Notice required under subsection (a) of this section shall include:

(i) A toll-free number:

(A) That the individual may use to contact the person collecting the data, or his agent; and

(B) From which the individual may learn the toll-free contact telephone numbers and addresses for the major credit reporting agencies.

(f) The attorney general may bring an action in law or equity to address any violation of this section and for other relief that may be appropriate to ensure proper compliance with this section, to recover damages, or both.

The provisions of this section are not exclusive and do not relieve an individual or a commercial entity subject to this section from compliance with all other applicable provisions of law.

(g) Any person who maintains computerized data that includes personal identifying information on behalf of another business entity shall disclose to the business entity for which the information is maintained any breach of the security of the system as soon as practicable following the determination that personal identifying information was, or is reasonably believed to have been, acquired by an unauthorized person. The person who maintains the data on behalf of another business entity and the business entity on whose behalf the data is maintained may agree which person or entity will provide any required notice as provided in subsection (a) of this section, provided only a single notice for each breach of the security of the system shall be required. If agreement regarding notification cannot be reached, the person who has the direct business relationship with the resident of this state shall provide notice subject to the provisions of subsection (a) of this section.

40-12-503. Security freeze.

(a) Except as provided in W.S. 40-12-505, a consumer may place a security freeze on the consumer's credit report by:

(i) Making a request to a consumer reporting agency in writing by certified mail; and

(ii) Providing proper identification.

(b) If a security freeze is in place, a consumer reporting agency may not release a consumer's credit report or information derived from the credit report to a third party that intends to use the information to determine a consumer's eligibility for credit or the opening of a new account without prior authorization from the consumer.

(c) Notwithstanding subsection (b) of this section, a consumer reporting agency may communicate to a third party requesting a consumer's credit report that a security freeze is in effect on the consumer's credit report. If a third party requesting a consumer's credit report in connection with the consumer's application for credit is notified of the existence of a security freeze under this subsection, the third party may treat the consumer's application as incomplete.

(d) Upon receiving a request from a consumer under subsection (a) of this section, the consumer reporting agency shall:

(i) Place a security freeze on the consumer's credit report within five (5) business days after receiving the consumer's request;

(ii) Send a written confirmation of the security freeze to the consumer within ten (10) business days after placing the security freeze; and

(iii) Provide the consumer with a unique personal identification number or password to be used by the consumer when providing authorizations for removal or temporary lift of the security freeze.

(e) A consumer reporting agency shall require proper identification of the consumer requesting to place, remove, or temporarily lift a security freeze.

(f) A consumer reporting agency shall develop a contact method to receive and process a consumer's request to place, remove or temporarily lift a security freeze.

The contact method shall include:

(i) A postal address;

(ii) An electronic contact method chosen by the consumer reporting agency, which may include the use of fax, Internet or other electronic means; and

(iii) The use of telephone in a manner that is consistent with any federal requirements placed on the consumer reporting agency.

(g) A security freeze placed under this section may be removed or temporarily lifted only in accordance with W.S. 40-12-504.

40-12-504. Permanent removal or temporary lift of security freeze; requirements and timing.

(a) A consumer reporting agency may remove a security freeze from a consumer's credit report only if:

(i) The consumer makes a material misrepresentation of fact in connection with the placement of the security freeze and the consumer reporting agency notifies the consumer in writing before removing the security freeze; or

(ii) The consumer reporting agency receives the consumer's request through a contact method established and required in accordance with W.S. 40-12-503(f) and the consumer reporting agency receives the consumer's proper identification and other information sufficient to identify the consumer including the consumer's personal identification number or password.

(b) A consumer reporting agency shall temporarily lift a security freeze upon receipt of:

(i) The consumer's request through the contact method established by the consumer reporting agency;

(ii) The consumer's proper identification and other information sufficient to identify the consumer including the consumer's personal identification number or password;

(iii) A specific designation of the period of time for which the security freeze is to be lifted; and

(iv) The consumer reporting agency receives the payment of any fee required under W.S. 40-12-506.

(c) A consumer reporting agency shall temporarily lift a security freeze from a consumer's credit report within:

(i) Three (3) business days after the business day on which the consumer's request to temporarily lift the security freeze is received by the consumer reporting agency through the contact method developed by the consumer reporting agency as required under W.S. 40-15-503(f); or

(ii) On or after September 1, 2008, within fifteen (15) minutes after the consumer's request is received by the consumer reporting agency through the electronic contact method developed by the consumer reporting agency as required under W.S. 40-12-503(f) or the use of telephone, during normal business hours and includes the consumer's proper identification and correct personal identification number or password.

(d) A consumer reporting agency shall permanently remove a security freeze from a consumer's credit report within three (3) business days after the business day on which the consumer's request is received by the consumer reporting agency through the contact method developed by the agency to receive such requests as required under W.S. 40-12-503(f).

(e) A consumer reporting agency need not temporarily lift a security freeze within the time provided in subsection (c) of this section if:

(i) The consumer fails to meet the requirements of subsection (b) of this section; or

(ii) The consumer reporting agency's ability to temporarily lift the security freeze within fifteen (15) minutes is prevented by:

(A) An act of God, including fire, earthquakes, hurricanes, storms or similar natural disaster or phenomena;

(B) Unauthorized or illegal acts by a third party, including terrorism, sabotage, riot, vandalism, labor strikes or disputes disrupting operations or similar occurrence;

(C) Operational interruption, including electrical failure, unanticipated delay in equipment or replacement part delivery, computer hardware or software failures inhibiting response time or similar disruption;

(D) Governmental action, including emergency orders or regulations, judicial or law enforcement action or similar directives;

(E) Regularly scheduled maintenance, during other than normal business hours, of, or updates to, the consumer reporting agency's systems;

(F) Commercially reasonable maintenance of, or repair to, the consumer reporting agency's systems that is unexpected or unscheduled; or

(G) Receipt of a removal request outside of normal business hours.

40-12-505. Exceptions.

(a) Notwithstanding W.S. 40-12-503, a consumer reporting agency may furnish a consumer's credit report to a third party if:

(i) The purpose of the credit report is to:

(A) Use the credit report for purposes permitted under 15 U.S.C. § 1681b(c);

(B) Review the consumer's account with the third party, including for account maintenance or monitoring, credit line increases or other upgrades or enhancements;

(C) Collect on a financial obligation owed by the consumer to the third party requesting the credit report;

(D) Collect on a financial obligation owed by the consumer to another person; or

(E) The third party requesting the credit report is a subsidiary, affiliate, agent, assignee or prospective assignee of the person holding the consumer's account or to whom the consumer owes a financial obligation.

(b) The consumer's request for a security freeze does not prohibit the consumer reporting agency from disclosing the consumer's credit report for other than credit related purposes consistent with the definition of credit report in W.S. 40-12-501(a).

(c) The following types of credit report disclosures by consumer reporting agencies to third parties are not prohibited by a security freeze:

(i) The third party does not use the credit report for the purpose of serving as a factor in establishing a consumer's eligibility for credit;

(ii) The release is pursuant to a court order, warrant or subpoena requiring release of the credit report by the consumer reporting agency;

(iii) The third party is a child support agency, or its agent or assignee, acting under Part D, Title IV of the Social Security Act or a similar state law;

(iv) The third party is the federal department of health and human services or a similar state agency, or its agent or assignee, investigating Medicare or Medicaid fraud;

(v) The purpose of the credit report is to investigate or collect delinquent taxes, assessments or unpaid court orders and the third party is:

(A) The federal internal revenue service;

(B) A state taxing authority;

(C) The department of transportation, division of motor vehicles;

(D) A county, municipality, or other entity with taxing authority;

(E) A federal, state or local law enforcement agency; or
(F) The agent or assignee of any entity listed in this paragraph.

(vi) The third party is administering a credit file monitoring subscription to which the consumer has subscribed; or

(vii) The third party requests the credit report for the sole purpose of providing the consumer with a copy of the consumer's credit report or credit score upon the consumer's request.

(d) The security freeze provisions of W.S. 40-12-503 do not apply to:

(i) A consumer reporting agency, the sole purpose of which is to resell credit information by assembling and merging information contained in the database of another consumer reporting agency and that does not maintain a permanent database of credit information from which a consumer's credit report is produced;

(ii) A deposit account information service company that issues reports concerning account closures based on fraud, substantial overdrafts, automated teller machine abuse or similar information concerning a consumer to a requesting financial institution for the purpose of evaluating a consumer's request to create a deposit account;

(iii) A check services or fraud prevention services company that issues:

(A) Reports on incidents of fraud; or

(B) Authorizations for the purpose of approving or processing negotiable instruments, electronic funds transfers or similar methods of payment.

(iv) A consumer reporting agency, with respect to its database of files that consist entirely of public records and is used solely for one (1) or more of the following:

(A) Criminal record information;

(B) Tenant screening;

(C) Employment screening; or

(D) Fraud prevention or detection.

(v) A database or file which consists solely of information adverse to the interests of the consumer including, but not limited to, criminal record information which is used for fraud prevention or detection, tenant screening, employment screening or any purpose permitted by the Fair Credit Reporting Act, 15 U.S.C. 1681b;

(vi) A person to the extent the person offers fraud prevention services which provide reports on incidents of fraud or reports used primarily in the detection or prevention of fraud; or

(vii) Setting or adjusting of a rate, adjusting a claim or underwriting for insurance purposes.

(e) Nothing in this article prohibits a person from obtaining, aggregating or using information lawfully obtained from public records in a manner that does not otherwise violate this article.

40-12-506. Fees for security freeze.

(a) Except as provided in subsection (b) of this section, a consumer reporting agency may charge a reasonable fee not to exceed ten dollars ($10.00) to a consumer for each placing, temporary lifting or removing of a security freeze.

(b) A consumer reporting agency may not charge a fee for placing, temporarily lifting or removing a security freeze if:

(i) The consumer is a victim of identity theft as defined by W.S. 6-3-901; and
(ii) The consumer provides the consumer reporting agency with a valid copy of a police report or police case number documenting the identity fraud.

40-12-507. Changes to information in a credit report subject to a security freeze.

(a) If a credit report is subject to a security freeze, a consumer reporting agency shall notify the consumer who is the subject of the credit report within thirty (30) days if the consumer reporting agency changes their information concerning the consumer's:

(i) Name;

(ii) Date of birth;

(iii) Social security number; or

(iv) Address.

(b) Notwithstanding subsection (a) of this section, a consumer reporting agency may make technical modifications to information in a credit report that is subject to a security freeze without providing notification to the consumer. Technical modifications under this subsection include:

(i) The addition or subtraction of abbreviations to names and addresses; and

(ii) Transpositions or corrections of incorrect numbering or spelling.

(c) When providing notice of a change of address under subsection (a) of this section, the consumer reporting agency shall provide notice to the consumer at both the new address and the former address.

40-12-508. Violations; penalties.

(a) If a consumer reporting agency intentionally or negligently violates a valid security freeze by releasing credit information that has been placed under a security freeze, the affected consumer is entitled to:

(i) Notification within five (5) business days following the agency's discovery, or notification from another source, of the release of the information. The notification under this paragraph shall include specificity as to the information released and the third party recipient of the information;

(ii) Notification that the consumer may file a complaint with the federal trade commission and the state attorney general.

(b) If a consumer reporting agency intentionally or negligently violates a valid security freeze by releasing credit information that has been placed under a security freeze and fails to take steps to correct the release and fails to give the notification required under subsection (a) of this section, the affected consumer is entitled to, in a civil action against the consumer reporting agency, recover:

(i) Injunctive relief to prevent or restrain further violation of the security freeze;

(ii) A civil penalty in an amount not to exceed one thousand dollars ($1,000.00) plus any damages available under other civil laws; and

(iii) Reasonable expenses, court costs, investigative costs and attorney's fees.

(c) Each violation of the security freeze shall be counted as a separate incident for purposes of imposing penalties under this section.

40-12-509. Factual declaration of innocence after identity theft.

(a) A person who reasonably believes that he or she is the victim of identity theft as defined by W.S. 6-3-901 may petition a court, or the court, on its own motion or upon application of the prosecuting attorney, may move for an expedited judicial determination of his or her factual innocence, where the perpetrator of the identity theft was arrested for, cited for or convicted of a crime under the victim's identity, or where a criminal complaint has been filed against the perpetrator in the victim's name, or where the victim's identity has been mistakenly associated with a record of criminal conviction. Any judicial determination of factual innocence made pursuant to this section may be heard and determined upon declarations, affidavits, police reports or other material, relevant and reliable information submitted by the parties or ordered to be part of the record by the court. Where the court determines that the petition or motion is meritorious and that there is no reasonable cause to believe that the victim committed the offense for which the perpetrator of the identity theft was arrested, cited, convicted or subject to a criminal complaint in the victim's name, or that the victim's identity has been mistakenly associated with a record of criminal conviction, the court shall find the victim factually innocent of that offense. If the victim is found factually innocent, the court shall issue an order certifying this determination.

(b) After a court has issued a determination of factual innocence pursuant to subsection (a) of this section, the court may order the name and associated personal identifying information contained in court records, files and indexes accessible by the public deleted, sealed or labeled to show that the data is impersonated and does not reflect the defendant's identity.

(c) Upon making a determination of factual innocence, the court shall provide the consumer written documentation of the order.

(d) A court that has issued a determination of factual innocence pursuant to this section may at any time vacate that determination if the petition, or any information submitted in support of the petition, is found to contain any material misrepresentation or fraud.
(e) The supreme court shall develop a form for use in issuing an order pursuant to this section.

(f) The attorney general shall establish and maintain a data base of individuals who have been victims of identity theft and that have received determinations of factual innocence. The attorney general shall provide a victim of identity theft or his authorized representative access to the database in order to establish that the individual has been a victim of identity theft. Access to the database shall be limited to criminal justice agencies, victims of identity theft and individuals and agencies authorized by the victims.

(g) The attorney general shall establish and maintain a toll free number to provide access to information under subsection (f) of this section.

(h) In order for a victim of identity theft to be included in the database established pursuant to subsection (f) of this section, he shall submit to the attorney general a court order obtained pursuant to this section, a full set of fingerprints and any other information prescribed by the attorney general.

(j) Upon receiving information pursuant to subsection (h) of this section, the attorney general shall verify the identity of the victim against any driver's license or other identification record maintained by the department of transportation, division of motor vehicles.

Section 2. This act is effective July 1, 2007.

S.F. 108

This is related to the dissolution of marriage, and it makes financial information provided by parties for child support confidential, and removes parties' Social Security numbers from divorce decrees.

Chapter 51: District of Columbia

The language in the District of Columbia's data breach notification law is quite interesting. It does not specifically name either encryption or redaction as appropriate means to protect data to render it unusable in the event of a breach, so as to not mandate notification. Instead, the laws says "Acquisition of data that has been rendered secure, so as to be unusable by an unauthorized third party, shall not be deemed to be a breach of the security of the system."

DC ST § 28-3852

District of Columbia Official Code 2001 Edition Currentness

Division V. Local Business Affairs

Title 28. Commercial Instruments and Transactions. (Refs & Annos)

Subtitle II. Other Commercial Transactions.

Chapter 38. Consumer Protections. (Refs & Annos)

Subchapter II. Consumer Security Search Term Begin Breach Search Term End Notification.

§ 28-3852. Notification of security Search Term Begin breach Search Term End.

Best Section Begin

(a) Any person or entity who conducts business in the District of Columbia, and who, in the course of such business, owns or licenses computerized or other electronic Search Term Begin data Search Term End that includes personal information, and who discovers a Search Term Begin breach Search Term End of the security of the system, shall promptly notify any District of

Columbia resident whose personal information was included in the Search Term Begin breach Search Term End . The notification shall be made in the most expedient time possible and without unreasonable delay, consistent with the legitimate needs of law enforcement, as provided in subsection (d) of this section, and with any measures necessary to determine the scope of the Search Term Begin breach Search Term End and restore the reasonable integrity of the Search Term Begin data Search Term End system.

Best Section End

Best Section Begin

(b) Any person or entity who maintains, handles, or otherwise possesses computerized or other electronic Search Term Begin data Search Term End that includes personal information that the person or entity does not own shall notify the owner or licensee of the information of any Search Term Begin breach Search Term End of the security of the system in the most expedient time possible following discovery.

Best Section End

(c) If any person or entity is required by subsection (a) or (b) of this section to notify more than 1,000 persons of a Search Term Begin breach Search Term End of security pursuant to this subsection, the person shall also notify, without unreasonable delay, all consumer reporting agencies that compile and maintain files on consumers on a nationwide basis, as defined by section 603(p) of the Fair Credit Reporting Act, approved October 26, 1970 (84 Stat. 1128; 15 U.S.C. § 1681a(p)), of the timing, distribution and content of the notices. Nothing in this subsection shall be construed to require the person to provide to the consumer reporting agency the names or other personal identifying information of Search Term Begin breach Search Term End notice recipients. This subsection shall not apply to a person or entity who is required to notify consumer reporting agencies of a Search Term Begin breach Search Term End pursuant to Title V of the Gramm-Leach-Bliley Act, approved November 12, 1999 (113 Stat. 1436; 15 U.S.C § 6801 et seq).

(d) The notification required by this section may be delayed if a law enforcement agency determines that the notification will impede a criminal investigation but shall be made as soon as possible after the law enforcement agency determines that the notification will not compromise the investigation.

(e) Notwithstanding subsection (a) of this section, a person or business that maintains its own notification procedures as part of an information security policy for the treatment of personal information and is otherwise consistent with the timing requirements of this subchapter shall be deemed to be in compliance with the notification requirements of this section if the person or business provides notice, in accordance with its policies, reasonably calculated to give actual notice to persons to whom notice is otherwise required to be given under this subchapter. Notice under this section may be given by electronic mail if the person or entity's primary method of communication with the resident is by electronic means.

(f) A waiver of any provision of this subchapter shall be void and unenforceable.

(g) A person or entity who maintains procedures for a breach notification system under Title V of the Gramm-Leach -Bliley Act, approved November 12, 1999 (113 Stat. 1436; 15 U.S.C § 6801 et seq.) ("Act"), and provides notice in accordance with the Act, and any rules, regulations, guidance and guidelines thereto, to each affected resident in the event of a breach, shall be deemed to be in compliance with this section.

Chapter 52: Puerto Rico

§ 4051. Definitions.

For the purposes of this chapter:

(a) Personal information file Refers to a file containing at least the name or first initial and the surname of a person, together with any of the following data so that an association may be established between certain information with another and in which the information is legible enough so that in order to access it there is no need to use a special cryptographic code.

(1) Social security number.

(2) Driver's license number, voter's identification or other official identification.

(3) Bank or financial account numbers of any type with or without passwords or access code that may have been assigned.

(4) Names of users and passwords or access codes to public or private information systems.

(5) Medical information protected by the HIPAA.

(6) Tax information.

(7) Work-related evaluations.

Neither the mailing nor the residential address is included in the protected information or information that is a public document and that is available to the citizens in general.

(b) Department Refers to the Department of Consumer Affairs.

(c) Violation of the security system Means any situation in which it is detected that access has been permitted to unauthorized persons or entities to the data files so that the security, confidentiality or integrity of the information in the data bank has been compromised; or when normally authorized persons or entities have had access and it is known or there is reasonable suspicion that they have violated the professional confidentiality or obtained authorization under false representation with the intention of making illegal use of the information. This includes both access to the data banks through the system and physical access to the recording media that contain the same and any removal or undue retrieval of said recordings.

(d) Entity Means every agency, board, body, examining board, corporation, public corporation, committee, independent office, division, administration, bureau, department, authority, official, instrumentality or administrative organism of the three branches of the Government; every corporation, partnership, association, private company or organization authorized to do business or operate in the Commonwealth of Puerto Rico; as well as every public or private educational institution, regardless of the level of education offered by it.

(e) Citizen's advocate Refers to the "Citizen's Advocate Office."

(Sept. 7, 2005, No. 111, § 2; June 19, 2008, No. 97, § 1.)

§ 4052. Notification.

Any entity that is the owner or custodian of a database that includes personal information of citizens residents of Puerto Rico must notify said citizens of any breach of the security of the system when the database whose security has been breached contains, in whole or in part, personal information files and the same are not protected by an encrypted code but only by a password.

Any entity that as part of their operations resells or provides access to digital data banks that at the same time contain personal information files of citizens must notify the proprietor, custodian or holder of said information of any violation of the system's security that has allowed access to those files to unauthorized persons.

Clients must be notified as expeditiously as possible, taking into consideration the need of law enforcement agencies to secure possible crime scenes and evidence as well as the application of measures needed to restore the system's security. Within a non-extendable term of ten (10) days after the violation of the system's security has been detected, the parties responsible shall inform the Department, which shall make a public announcement of the fact within twenty-four (24) hours after having received the information.

(Sept. 7, 2005, No. 111, § 3; June 19, 2008, No. 97, § 2

§ 4053. Notification - Character and method.

The notice of breach of the security of the system shall be submitted in a clear and conspicuous manner and should describe the breach of the security of the system in general terms and the type of sensitive information compromised. The notification shall also include a toll free number and an Internet site for people to use in order to obtain information or assistance.

To notify the citizens the entity shall have the following options:

(1) Written direct notice to those affected by mail or by authenticated electronic means according to the Digital Signatures Act.

(2) When the cost of notifying all those potentially affected according to subsection (1) of this section or of identifying them is excessively onerous due to the number of persons affected, to the difficulty in locating all persons or to the economic situation of the enterprise or entity; or whenever the cost exceeds one hundred thousand dollars ($100,000) or the number of persons exceeds one

hundred thousand [(100,000)], the entity shall issue the notice through the following two (2) steps:

(a) Prominent display of an announcement to that respect at the entities premises, on the web page of the entity, if any, and in any informative flier published and sent through mailing lists both postal and electronic, and

(b) a communication to that respect to the media informing of the situation and providing information as to how to contact the entity to allow for better follow-up. When the information is of relevance to a specific professional or commercial sector, the announcement may be made through publications or programming of greater circulation oriented towards that sector.

§ 4054. No conflict with institutional information and security policies.

No provision of this chapter shall be interpreted as being prejudicial to those institutional information and security policies that an enterprise or entity may have in force prior to its effectiveness and whose purpose is to provide protection equal or better to the information on security herein established.

(Sept. 7, 2005, No. 111, § 5, eff. 120 days after Sept. 7, 2005.)

§ 4054a. Notification regarding breach or irregularity in security systems.

In those cases in which the breach or irregularity in the security systems of the database occurs in a government agency or public corporation, it shall be notified to the Citizen's Advocate Office, which shall assume jurisdiction. For this purpose, the Citizen's Advocate shall designate a Specialized Advocate who shall address these types of cases.

§ 4054b. Specialized Advocate; regulations.

The Citizen's Advocate shall create within its Office the position of Databases Security Systems Specialized Advocate of the

Government of Puerto Rico and shall draft and establish bylaws for compliance with the provisions of this act within one hundred and twenty (120) days after its approval.

(Sept. 7, 2005, No. 111, added as § 8 on June 19, 2008, No. 97, § 5.)

§ 4055. Fines.

The Secretary may impose fines of five hundred dollars ($500) up to a maximum of five thousand dollars ($5,000) for each violation of the provisions of this chapter or its regulations. The fines provided in this section do not affect the rights of the consumers to initiate actions or claims for damages before a competent court.

(Sept. 7, 2005, No. 111, § 8, renumbered as § 10 on June 19, 2008, No. 97, § 6.)

Chapter 53: Virgin Islands

Finally, we are at the Virgin Islands, which is the last chapter of the book. I hope you found the collection of data privacy laws, along with my commentary, useful. As I stated at the beginning of the book, data privacy and the associated legal and compliance issues require the input of experts in their respective fields. The best and brightest are out there, and I have had the privilege to talk with many of them. Seek them out, as they can save your company a lot of money and embarrassment. I also believe good data security is not only smart business, but it is the right thing to do for those who entrust their personal information to us.

VIRGIN ISLANDS CODE ANNOTATED

***** Statutes current through Act 7278 of the 2011 Regular Session *****
***** Excludes Acts 7264 *****

TITLE FOURTEEN **Crimes**
Chapter 110. Theft
Subchapter I. Identity Theft

14 V.I.C. § 2208 (2011)

§ 2208. Notices of security breach

(a) Any agency that owns or licenses computerized data that includes personal information shall disclose any breach of the security of the system following discovery or notification of the breach in the security of the data to any resident of the Virgin Islands whose unencrypted personal information was, or is reasonably believed to have been, acquired by an unauthorized person. The disclosure must be made in the most expedient time possible and without unreasonable delay, consistent with the legitimate needs of law enforcement, as provided in subsection (c),

or any measures necessary to determine the scope of the breach and restore the reasonable integrity of the data system.

(b) Any agency that maintains computerized data that includes personal information that the agency does not own shall notify the owner or licensee of the information of any breach of the security of the data immediately following discovery, if the personal information was, or is reasonably believed to have been, acquired by an unauthorized person.

(c) The notification required by this section may be delayed, if a law enforcement agency determines that the notification will impede a criminal investigation. The notification required by this section must be made after the law enforcement agency determines that it will not compromise the investigation.

(d) For purposes of this section, “breach of the security of the system” means unauthorized acquisition of computerized data that compromises the security, confidentiality, or integrity of personal information maintained by the agency. Good faith acquisition of personal information by an employee or agent of the agency for the purposes of the agency is not a breach of the security of the system, provided that the personal information is not used or subject to further unauthorized disclosure.

(e) For purposes of this section, “personal information” means an individual's first name or first initial and last name in combination with any one or more of the following data elements, when either the name or the data elements are not encrypted:

(1) Social Security number.

(2) Driver's license number.

(3) Account number, credit or debit card number, in combination with any required security code, access code, or password that would permit access to an individual’s financial account.

(f) For purposes of this section, "personal information" does not include publicly available information that is lawfully made available to the general public from federal, state, or territorial government records.

(g) For purposes of this section, "notice" may be provided by one of the following methods:

(1) Written notice.

(2) Electronic notice, if the notice provided is consistent with the provisions regarding electronic records and signatures set forth in section 7001 of Title 15 of the United States Code.

(3) Substitute notice, if the agency demonstrates that the cost of providing notice would exceed $100,000, or that the affected class of subject persons to be notified exceeds 50,000, or the agency does not have sufficient contact information. Substitute notice shall consist of all of the following:

(A) E-mail notice when the agency has an e-mail address for the subject persons.

(B) Conspicuous posting of the notice on the agency's Website page, if the agency maintains one.

(C) Notification to major territory-wide media.

(h) Notwithstanding subsection (g), an agency that maintains its own notification procedures as part of an information security policy for the treatment of personal information and is otherwise consistent with the timing requirements of this part shall be deemed to be in compliance with the notification requirements of this section if it notifies subject persons in accordance with its policies in the event of a breach of security of the system.

State Summary Table

State	Statute	Covered Entities	Covered Media	Exceptions to Disclosure
		B=Business G=Govern-ment	E=Electronic P=Physical	E=Encrypted R=Redacted M=Misuse unlikely
AK	HB 31	B,G	E,P	E,R
AZ	SB 1338	B,G	E	E,R
AR	SB 1167	B,G	E,P	E, R
CA	SB 1386	B,G	E	E
CO	HB 1119	B	E	E,M
CT	SB 650	B,G	E	E, M
DE	HB 116	B,G	E	E,M
FL	HB 481	B,G	E	E
GA	SB 230	B	E	E, R
HI	SB 2290	B,G	E	E,M,R
ID	SB 1374	B,G	E	E,M
IL	HB 1633	B,G	E,P	E
IN	SB 503	B,G	E	E,R
IA	HF 655	B	E	E
KS	SB 196	B,G	E	E,R,M
LA	SB 205	B,G	E	E,M
ME	LD 1671	B	E	E
MD	HB 90	B	E	E,R
MA	HB 328	B,G	E,P	E,R
MI	§ 445.72	B,G	E	E,R,M
MN	SF 2118	B	E	E
MS	HB 583	B	E	E,
MO	§407.1500	B,G	E,P	E,R
MT	HB 732	B	E,P	E
NE	LB 876	B,G	E	E,M
NV	NRS 603A.220	B,G	E	E,M

NH	HB 1660	B,G	E	E,M
NJ	AB 4001	B,G	E	E,M
NY	AB 4254	B,G	E	E
NC	HB 1048 & 1248	B,G	E,P	E,R
ND	SB 2251	B	E	E (R?)
OH	HB 104	B,G	E	E,R,M
OK	HB 2357	G	E	E
OR	SB 583	B	E	E,R
PA	SB 712	B,G	E	E,R
RI	H6191	B,G	E	E,M
SC	HB 3035		E,P	E,R
TN	HB 2170	B,G	E	E,M
TX	HB 300	B	E, P	E
UT	HB 69	B	E,P	E,M
VT	SB 284	B,G	E,P	E,R,M
VA	§ 18.2-186.6	B	E	E,R
WA	SB 6043	B,G	E	E
WV	§ 46A-2A-101	B,G	E	E,R
WI	Act 138	B,G	E	E, R, M
WY	SF 53	B	E	E,R,M
DC	§28-3852 et seq.	B	E	E
Puerto Rico	§ 4051 et. seq.	B,G	E	E
Virgin Islands	§ 2208	G	E	E

States with no security breach law: Alabama, Kentucky, New Mexico, and South Dakota

About the Author

Philip Alexander began his career in computers back in the late 1980s while serving in the US military. Since then, he has worked in both the public and private sectors in positions including engineer, project manager, principal security consultant, security architect, and information technology director. He currently works for a major US financial institution as an information security officer. He has also taught computer courses at the University of Phoenix, and has presented at several computer conferences across the United States. Philip has written a number of books on computer security, including *Information Security: A Manager's Guide to Thwarting Data Thieves and Hackers* and *Home and Small Business Guide to Protecting Your Computer Network, Electronic Assets, and Privacy.*

ASPATORE